PHILOSOPHICAL DICTIONARY

PHILOSOPHICAL
DICTIONARY

Walter Brugger

Editor of the Original German Edition

Kenneth Baker

Translator and Editor of the American Edition

Gonzaga University Press
Spokane, Washington 99202

1972
GONZAGA UNIVERSITY PRESS
Gonzaga University
Spokane, Washington 99202
USA

1st Printing—1972
2nd Printing—1974

Library of Congress Catalog Card Number: 72-82135

Original edition:
Philosophisches Wörterbuch
© Verlag Herder KG Freiburg in Breisgau 1967

American edition:
© Kenneth Baker 1972

TABLE OF CONTENTS

PREFACE TO THE THIRTEENTH EDITION

The present *Philosophical Dictionary* attempts to examine the major questions of human existence — the problems of modern philosophy and of today from the point of view of that Western tradition which culminates in the work of a Plato, Aristotle, Augustine and Thomas Aquinas. It is intended to help the reader achieve a true view of himself and his attitude to reality — a reality which is understood according to all its dimensions.

The fresh ordering of life on the basis of healthy principles is a task that constantly presses in on all of us. The *Philosophical Dictionary* should make its own contribution to this. What it hopes to offer is not lengthy treatises, but intellectual insight. Our intention is not to explain each expression which perhaps is rarely employed. Our intention is not to replace a popular lexicon or a dictionary of foreign words. Our concern is to present in their true context the philosophical concepts which have become a part of Western culture and which have remained active in contemporary philosophy. Therefore it seemed imperative not to devote a separate article to every expression in some atomizing way. Rather, we decided to take into consideration the fact that in philosophy it is above all a matter of the interrelationship of ideas.

A certain intellectual openness on the part of the reader is presupposed here. Thus the dictionary tries as best it can to lead the reader to the experience of what is called "philosophizing," since it not only treats philosophical material, but also tries to present this material in a philosophical way. Therefore it does not attempt merely to compile texts from the history of philosophy, but it does try, by means of active thinking, to clarify philosophical ideas in their full sense, taking into account also their historical conditioning.

When foreign words in parenthesis follow English expressions it is not because the English word cannot express the meaning of the concept itself, but in order to explain the foreign word in accordance with the purpose of the dictionary.

The *Philosophical Dictionary*, formerly a supplementary volume to the collection *Mensch, Welt, Gott*, has now been incorporated into the series

PREFACE TO THE THIRTEENTH EDITION

Philosophie in Einzeldarstellung. However, it can be used as an independent work. Its relationship to the latter series can perhaps be expressed thus: On the one hand it makes the most important themes available in a handy, one-volume dictionary; on the other hand, given its limitations, it obviously cannot repeat the more profound development and the penetrating demonstrations which were presented in the fuller systematic treatment. Yet it does include the goal of a true dictionary, namely, that many questions are discussed which were not handled in the larger volumes of the series, since they were limited to the principal areas of philosophy.

For the publication of the dictionary the editor is grateful to his many collaborators. This holds particularly for the professors of the Berchmanskolleg in Munich, and especially for Fathers J. B. Lotz and Josef de Vries. Both of these men steadfastly assisted the editor both in the original planning of the book and in the final editing, and they had no small part in bringing it to completion.

Of the first collaborators six have already been summoned into eternity. But others came forth to take their places. Since 1947 the *Philosophical Dictionary* has seen thirteen German and seven foreign editions (Spanish, Italian, Portugese). In 1953 and 1960 it was partially rewritten and new articles were also added. This thirteenth edition has also been updated. In addition to various minor changes, the following articles were completely rewritten: Dialectical Materialism; Middle, Principle of the Excluded; Knowledge; Marriage; Mathematics, Philosophy of; Number.

For the thirteenth edition new articles were added: Analytic Philosophy, Democracy, Historicity, Historical Materialism, Cybernetics, Pluralism, Quantum Mechanics, Tolerance.

May the book continue to render its good services.

WALTER BRUGGER, S. J.

March 7, 1966
Pullach, Germany

PREFACE

This *Philosophical Dictionary* is a translation and adaptation of Walter Brugger's very successful *Philosophisches Wörterbuch* which, since 1947, has seen thirteen editions. But the present American version is both less and more than a translation; for, many articles in the original that are not suitable for an American readership have been dropped; the bibliographies after each article have been omitted; the outline of the history of philosophy (at the end of the German volume) has likewise been left out; and a number of new articles dealing with contemporary Anglo-American concerns (e. g., Behaviorism, Lonerganism, Process Philosophy, etc.) have been added. Thus I have tried, wherever necessary and possible, to omit those matters in the original volume that are of particular concern to Germans and then to supplement it with articles dealing with the present American problematic. For the freedom to adapt the dictionary in this way I am most grateful to P. Walter Brugger, the editor of the original German volume.

Each article speaks for itself and stands by itself. Although there is quite a bit of diversity between the philosophical positions of some of the contributors, the basic thrust of the book is that of moderate realism; this of course allows of many shades of opinion and most of them are represented in this dictionary. Moreover, the articles offer more than just a historical summary of a position; the attempt has been made in most of the basic articles to evaluate and to take a position. Recognition, in the form of the authors' initials, is given at the end of each article. When particular words are preceded by a star (*), this means that the reader is referred to another article in the book under that heading.

To translate and edit a volume such as this, which deals with topics and terminologies from many specialized fields, would be impossible for one man without the assistance of many qualified experts. I have had such assistance and wish to thank all those who have helped so generously. I wish to thank in particular the administrators of Gonzaga University who have made time available for me to do this work; my thanks go also to the new contributors to this American version of the dictionary; thanks also to my fellow faculty members at Gonzaga who have read and approved the translation of the articles in their own specialized areas —

PREFACE

esp. to Rev. Louis St. Marie, Dr. Zane Motteler, Mrs. Marilyn Stanton and Rev. Theodore Wolf. I wish finally to thank Sr. M. Josephina Daly for her painstaking scrutiny and correction of the final manuscript and Mr. Stephen V. Sundborg for his careful proofreading.

I hope that this book, which should be used in conjunction with the Rahner-Vorgrimler *Theological Dictionary*, will be of real service to those seeking a ready reference to the great philosophical ideas of past and present.

KENNETH BAKER, S. J.

x

COLLABORATORS

KB	Kenneth Baker (Spokane)	JJM	John J. McNeill (New York)
PB	Paul Bolkovac (Hamburg)	PM	Philip McShane (Dublin)
WB	Walter Brugger (Pullach/ Munich)	ZM	Zane Motteler (Spokane)
WoB	Wolfgang Büchel (Pullach/ Munich)	VN	Viktor Naumann (Innsbruck)
VFC	Van F. Christoph (Spokane)	OvNB	Oswald von Nell-Breuning (Frankfurt)
LDD	Leo Don Davis (Spokane)	MR	Maximilian Rast (Sitten, Switzerland)
JJE	John J. Evoy (Spokane)		
HF	Heinrich Falk (Pullach/Munich)	VR	Vladimir Richter (Innsbruck)
RLF	Robert L. Faricy (Rome)	KR	Klaus Riesenhuber (Pullach /Munich)
KF	Karl Frank (†)		
JF	Josef Fröbes (†)	JS	Josef Santeler (Innsbruck)
TRG	Thomas R. Garvin (Seattle)	JSch	Josef Schröteler (†)
		JoS	Johannes Schuster (†)
AH	Adolf Haas (Pullach/Munich)	JES	Jerome E. Schwegman (Spokane)
NJ	Nikolaus Junk (Frankfurt)	FTS	Frank T. Severin (St. Louis)
WaK	Walter Kerber (Pullach/ Munich)	MS	Marilyn Stanton (Spokane)
WK	Walter Kern (Pullach/Munich)	JHT	John Hammond Taylor (Spokane)
JK	Johannes Kleinhappl (Vienna)	GT	George Trapp (†)
JBL	Johannes B. Lotz (Rome - Pullach/Munich)	JdV	Josef de Vries (Pullach/Munich)
EM	Edward MacKinnon (Cambridge, Mass)	AW	Alexander Willwoll (†)

INTRODUCTION

THE FUTURE OF CHRISTIAN PHILOSOPHY

Philosophy is a science that is little understood today. There is also a growing amount of evidence pointing to the fact that other sciences, especially the social sciences, have taken over areas of human concern which traditionally have been a part of philosophy. It seems to me that philosophy has fallen on hard times; many of its followers seem to be playing around in sand-boxes where they can construct their own worlds that have precious little to do with the world most people must live in, struggle in and die in.

For Catholic Christians who are at pains to preserve and reconcile the due claims both of reason and revelation the present decline of philosophy is a matter of real concern. For, if either reason or revelation is neglected (or, for that matter, exaggerated) there is an ever-present danger of serious distortions creeping in, as the history of the Church since the time of the apostles clearly shows. Now as far as I can see, since about the end of World War II, at least on the Catholic scene, most of the action of an intellectual character has been taking place in the field of theology. There has been a great improvement in theological thinking over what was current before the war; this is especially true in the fields of scripture, morality and doctrine. But, unfortunately, there has not been a corresponding advance in the philosophical thinking of Catholic Chistians; and what advance there has been seems to be in the area of adaptation of insights from other philosophies, such as Marxism, existentialism, analytic philosophy, personalism, pragmatism, positivism, etc. It seems to me that, while theology is making bold attempts on almost every front, philosophy is standing on the sidelines watching the show and having little influence on the outcome of it all. But in order to make solid advances in the study of hermeneutics, doctrine and morality theology is in desperate need of a vitally aware philosophy.

The history of philosophy is the history of the human spirit; it is the history of man's attempts to understand his experiences of himself and the world he lives in; it is the history of man's effort to find order and unity in the multiplicity and diversity that surround him; it is the history

INTRODUCTION

of man's most serious quest for an answer to the riddle of a precarious human existence which also shows signs of a desire for a more permanent form of life, for something absolute, for . . . God.

Man is spirit in the world; he is reflective consciousness; he is self-awareness; he is transcendence beyond the limits of the here and now. This is true of every man with the use of reason — it is not the preserve of the intellectual, the scientist, the literateur. The philosopher attempts to put order in the whole of reality or to come up with some kind of a world-picture; he does not restrict his reflection to just one aspect of reality — he explicitly considers the totality. Now we know that every man, be he learned or unlearned, has his own ideas about himself, the world and God. Thus, in a very true sense, every man is a philosopher, but not every man is a chemist or a sociologist or an engineer. However, the greater part of such common-sense philosophy is pre-reflective, disorganized and generally only implicit. The professional philosopher tries to proceed in his analysis of reality in an orderly way; he tries to make whatever is implicit in his experience of himself, the world and God as explicit as possible. Thus, philosophy (or metaphysics) is most adequately defined as that special kind of reflective thinking whereby a man becomes explicitly aware of what he has always already known implicitly. No tools are required; no laboratories; no computers — just a man and his experience of the world.

Just as the science of physics is not the product of one man, but is the result of the combined efforts of thousands of men over a long period of time, so also philosophy is a science that has grown out of the concern of many individuals during the past thousands of years. There are many different philosophies but most (if not all) philosophers have striven for the same end: to give some kind of meaning to man and his universe. True, they have arrived at many different conclusions (often contradictory) but they have studied the same object (reality) and have employed the same basic method (reflection on human experience).

Philosophy represents the noblest effort of the human spirit, in spite of the fact that the results of its effort do not make the same impression on the public as the feats of technology do. In this regard Thomas Aquinas says in his commentary on the *Metaphysics* of Aristotle that: "The little that is won here [in metaphysics] weighs more than all that is won in all the other sciences." Will this statement be judged as fantastic by our scientists and technocrats? Perhaps, but it is true nevertheless because of the dignity of the object studied and the dignity of the end in view. The vastness of the object and the end, however, seem to exceed the capacities of human intelligence. The philosopher

INTRODUCTION

by definition strives for wisdom, for ultimate truth in the midst of a changing world, but no one yet has been able adequately to grasp the whole.

What are the possibilities and the limits of philosophy? With regard to the possibilities, the history of philosophy shows that some men at least can arrive at a limited amount of truth about man, world and God. Some philosophers have achieved a high degree of certainty in these areas, while others have tended to be skeptical about the whole or about some parts (e. g., those who claim that man can know nothing for certain about God but can attain certain knowledge about material things). Through self-reflection man can arrive at a knowledge of his own spirituality, his own power of thinking and willing; through reflective thinking and through study of the cosmos man can also come to some (though analogical) knowledge of Absolute Being (God). He can reach reflective awareness of his own power of understanding; moreover he can come to see that God is intelligent and so could speak to man if he chose to do so. However, if God speaks to man in past, present or future it must be in a way that is adapted to man's mode of understanding, which means that it must be in history (in time and place) and it must be by means of a human word — since that is the only word that man can understand. Thus, the philosopher is led inexorably by his own study of the human condition to the practical question: Has God ever spoken to man? Has God ever manifested his mind and his will to man? In order to answer this question he is necessarily turned to history and to the various claims that have been made by individuals and groups that God has actually spoken to them. At this point we find the limit of all philosophical speculation, since reflection on man and the cosmos cannot of itself tell me what the personal will of God is for man in general and for me in particular. If God wants to reveal that he must take the initiative and he must speak. Only history or the testimony of others can adduce evidence for such a claim and can appeal for my assent.

Now it is precisely at this point that Christianity generally, and the Catholic Church in particular, makes a claim that it proclaims to all men without exception: God has spoken to man in Jesus of Nazareth; he is the way, the truth and the life; he is now present in his Church which is the Kingdom of God on earth; and he has the audacity to say that he is the answer to man's quest for life, so much so that the man who accepts him will live whereas the man who rejects him will die forever. Here, as you will immediately notice, there is a certain overlapping of philosophy (human reason) and Christian revelation, since both offer an answer to the riddle of human existence. The goals of human living that philosophy rightly establishes are human, limited goals that are necessarily terminated by death; Christian revelation infinitely surpasses philosophy by clearly making known to man that God personally loves him and offers him a share in his own eternal, divine life as the end result of faith and obedience. One could say that philosophy gives a limited, incomplete answer to man's question about the meaning of his human existence, while Christian faith (and theology which is the systematic study of that faith) gives the complete answer to why man exists at all and what his final destiny is.

Given the truth and validity of the Christian claim, it might seem to some that the Christian believer has no need of philosophy because it cannot supply the whole truth about man. This was indeed the position of Tertullian and every age has had its own "Tertullians." This view, though narrow, has something in its favor, but it does tend in the direction of a fideism that is very distrustful of the power of man's intelligence. It was rejected by most of the Fathers of the Church, by the distinguished scholastics of the Middle Ages, and by the best theologians of the Catholic Church since the time of the Reformation. In more recent times the question of the possibility of a "Christian Philosophy" has been raised by a number of serious Catholic thinkers (e. g., E. Gilson, M. Blondel, H. de Lubac, K. Rahner). The problem is to state clearly what you mean by philosophy: what is its object, principles and methodology. Then, however, you must explain how the adjective "Christian" modifies the substantive "philosophy." (Since it is not my intention to explain the views of the men involved, the reader is referred to their writings on this subject; see also the article "Christian Philosophy" by L. B. Geiger in the *New Catholic Encyclopedia*, vol. 3, 640-644).

Distrust of human reason has been a characteristic of much Protestant thought since the time of Luther (who spoke of "the beast reason"); such distrust, though found among Catholic thinkers (e. g., in the 19th century: de Bonald, Bautain, Bonnetty), is not characteristic of Catholic thought. If anything, since the time of the reformers, Catholic thinking has tended in the direction of rationalism in an effort to speak to and answer the rationalists of the 18th and 19th centuries. In any event, trust in the value of human reason, and consequently trust in philosophy, is a common characteristic of most Catholic thinking. A fundamental problem arises, however, once we begin to probe into the precise relationship that exists between philosophy and Christian theology of faith.

Among Catholic thinkers, there are those who repudiate philosophy completely; there are also those who say that philosophy is wholly autonomous and so absolutely independent of theology; there are those who say that philosophy is the servant or "handmaid" of theology; there are those, finally, who maintain that real philosophy is already Christian and is influenced more or less by Christian faith depending upon the level of knowledge of Christianity on the part of the philosopher in question.

INTRODUCTION

I think that the last position is the most correct one. Let me explain. Theology is first of all a hearing of the word of God; it is reflecting on that word and then living by it. But in order to hear the word of God a man must first know something. He must have reflective consciousness; he must have an idea of who he is, what the world is; he must have experienced concretely the problem of human existence; and he must have some idea of a transcendent being. Ideas along these lines, and along others, are absolutely essential pre-requisites for a man to hear the word of God. Now a concern with these ideas is what we mean by a philosophy. Since every man has them in one form or another, then every man has a philosophy and so faith and theology depend upon philosophy, but philosophy does not depend on or demand Christian faith.

Just because philosophy and theology overlap in the consideration of the final end of man, and just because theology has a higher source of its knowledge (the word of God), it does not follow that philosophy is not an autonomous science. In the natural order it is the highest science since it treats of reality as such; philosophy also has its own method and its own principles — which are not derived from theology. But since we know from Christian faith that the free will of God has set an end for man that goes beyond the realm of nature, the goal that philosophy sets for itself cannot be attained by merely human means. Thus it is more proper to say that philosophy is an autonomous science, but one that nevertheless cannot give the final answer to the mystery of man; to this extent it is an incomplete or inadequate science and therefore one that must be complemented by a higher science, namely, the science of faith, or theology.

The relationship between philosophy and theology has vexed Christian thinkers since the second century of our era. This problem, however, cannot be solved without reference to another, larger question, that is, the question of the relationship between nature and grace. Christian doctrine, based on Scripture, teaches us that man has never been in a state of pure nature — he has never been without the grace of God. This means that man as he has existed concretely in history has always been influenced, in mind and in will, by the loving grace of God. It is most important to recall that grace is to be thought of in personal categories that affect the whole man; it should not be reduced to the category of quantity so that a person is led to compare grace in man to something like milk in a bottle. Thus, grace affects the whole man; this includes necessarily, therefore, man's reason and intelligence. If this is so, then it must be asserted that man's view of the world since the dawn of intelligence has been affected to some extent by the influence of God. It also follows that a state of "pure nature" (which is spoken about by theologians) does not in fact exist and has never existed; it is rather an abstract idea of what man would be like if he did not exist in a supernatural state. Thus in a very real sense it is a "remainder concept," that is, one that is left over when we mentally remove from man the historical situation of being called to a personal knowledge and love of God. In this connection it is most important to remember that nature is necessary so that grace can be grace; for grace is the free gift that God makes of himself to the creature who is created in a way that makes him capable of receiving God. If nature demanded grace, then grace would no longer be grace.

I stated at the beginning of this essay that philosophy, in my opinion, has fallen on hard times. What is the future of philosophy in the Catholic community? The numbers of graduate students now doing philosophy is not impressive; there is also a noticeable lack of enthusiasm among them; some seem to be casting a longing eye in the direction of theology; in the recent past many have gone over to theology. At present there is definitely a pluralism of thought in the Catholic Church. This pluralism centers around theological questions to a great extent. In the world at large there are many conflicting ideologies; nominalism is rampant, so much so that it is becoming increasingly difficult to communicate with those who do not share your immediate intellectual concerns. There is the knowledge explosion that we are all aware of: Will it be a boon to man in the long run? or will mankind be smothered by mountains of facts, data, position papers, magazines, books, computer tapes and IBM cards? Because of this knowledge explosion and the wonders of instant communication that are the result of electronics, the world and everything in it seems to be getting more fragmented at a time when it should be tending towards greater unity. Thus, there is a pressing need that the parts should be related to the whole, that some order be put in the growing mass of information. Now what applies to the world in general with regard to diversity also applies to the Church; because of the present multiplicity of views on almost every subject in theology, there is much confusion in the Catholic Church. In the midst of this present general confusion there is, in my view, a great need for a renaissance of philosophical thought among Christian thinkers. The need is now; and when there is a need for something, given the almost infinite talents of man, someone always comes forward. Consequently, if I may be permitted to gaze into my crystal ball, I expect to see a revival of interest in philosophy among Catholic thinkers during the latter part of this decade. It is in this belief that I have undertaken the task of translating and editing this dictionary; it is my earnest hope that this volume may contribute in some small way to the needed revival of Christian philosophy in the years ahead.

A great deal has been written about the problem of "Christian Philosophy" since Etienne Gilson opened the debate in the early 1930s. Question:

INTRODUCTION

What is the difference between a "Christian" philosophy and a "non-Christian" philosophy? A philosophy worthy of the name deals with the basic problems of the meaning of human existence, the nature of the world and the existence of God; it questions all reality and is open to all being. Further, a real philosophy looks into the problems of the freedom and spirituality of man, his survival after death and his relationship to the Absolute. Now Christianity, through divine revelation, possesses God's own answers to these perplexing questions; and the Christian answers do not negate either the question or the answers of a valid philosophy; rather, they build on them and complete them. But the best that philosophy can do is to refer man to history to see if God has ever spoken to man and communicated his will to him. Thus, in the light of Christian revelation, it seems to me that any philosophy that is truly philosophy is in some sense a Christian philosophy; or, conversely, it seems that there is no such thing as a non-Christian philosophy. For, if philosophy is true to man, true to the world and true to God, it has already been influenced by the grace of God and is certainly open to the fulfilling effect of the word of God found in the revelation of Jesus Christ.

If the above is true, then it would follow that there are two kinds of Christian philosophy: explicit Christian philosophy and implicit Christian philosophy. For, the explicitly Christian philosopher has formal access to the truths of revelation; he did not discover them by the use of his own mind, but once in possession of them, he is at liberty to reflect on them and draw out further conclusions (e. g., the idea of "person" that came into philosophy by way of Trinitarian speculation in the 4th century). And the possession of these truths will necessarily color his whole philosophy. The implicitly Christian philosopher, on the other hand, is the philosopher who, true to his science, fearlessly reflects on the questions of man, world and God and remains open to the whole truth; he has not yet discovered the full will of God but he is moving towards it since God "wants everyone to be saved and reach full knowledge of the truth" (I Tim 2, 4).

In the past perhaps Christians and explicitly Christian philosophers have been too narrow in their views of the value of philosophies from other traditions; they have perhaps been too ready to condemn them as "pagan" and not ready enough to look for their good elements — those elements that contain an openness to Christian revelation and just might be there due to the influence of God's grace.

Now that the Second Vatican Council has advised Catholic Christians (and, indeed, all men) to look for the good in non-Christian traditions and has opened the Church up to be positively influenced by them,

INTRODUCTION

there is hope that in the future we will be better prepared to see the finger of God wherever it is present in the midst of all mankind. And it is my hope that this *Philosophical Dictionary* will be of some help thereto.

March 25, 1972
Gonzaga University
Spokane, Washington

KENNETH BAKER, S. J.

ALPHABETICAL LIST OF ARTICLES

Absolute
Abstract
Abstraction
Accident
Act
Activity
Actuality
Aesthetics
Affirmation
Agnosticism
Analogy
Analysis
Analytic Philosophy
Anthropology
Antinomies
A Posteriori
Appearance
Appetite
A Priori
Aristotelianism
Art
Atheism
Atomism
Augustinianism
Authority
Autonomy

Beauty
Becoming
Behaviorism
Biologism
Blondelianism
Body
Body, Living
Body-Soul Relation
Buddhism

Capital Punishment
Cardinal Virtues
Cartesianism
Categorical Arguments
Categorical Imperative
Categories

Causality
Causality, Law of
Causality, Principle of
Cause
Certitude
Chance
Change
Characteristic
Christian Philosophy
Collectivism
Common Good
Community
Complexity-Conscious-
    ness
Concept
Conceptualism
Concrete
Concurrence
Confucianism
Conscience
Consciousness
Contingency
Contradiction, Principle
    of
Creation
Critical Philosophy
Culture
Culture, Philosophy of
Cybernetics

Dasein
Death
Deduction
Definition
Deism
Democracy
Demonstration
Denial
Determinism
Development
Dialectic
Dialectical Materialism
Dialectical Theology

Disjunction
Disposition
Disputation
Distinction
Divisibility
Division
Dogmatism
Doubt
Dualism
Duty
Dynamic
Dynamism

Eclecticism
Economics
Ego
Emotion
Empiricism
End
Enlightenment
Ens Rationis
Epicureanism
Epikeia
Error
Essence
Essential Knowledge
Eternity
Ethics
Euthanasia
Evidence
Evil
Evolutionism
Existence
Existence, Levels of
Existence, Principles of
Existential, -ell
Existential Philosophy
Experience
Explanation

Fact
Faith
Fallacy

ALPHABETICAL LIST OF ARTICLES

ALPHABETICAL LIST OF ARTICLES

A

ABSOLUTE

Absolute (unrelated, unconditioned, in itself) is that which is totally or in all respects free from any relation whatsoever to anything else. From the conceptual point of view, "absolute" is that which can be defined without reference to another. — From the point of view of·existence, "absolute" is: 1) whatever possesses existence in itself (as a substance or as a so-called absolute *accident) and not just because it stands in *relation to another; 2) whatever is not just a determination of something else *substance; 3) that form of existence that excludes every real relation to others (= the Absolute). Since everything finite is caused and therefore related to a cause, the Absolute can only be uncaused and infinite. However, it is not contrary to the nature of the Absolute that it be the terminal point of relations. The concept of the Absolute does not coincide without qualifications with the theistic or with the pantheistic idea of God. For, in the pantheistic view the totality of all mutually related things is itself unrelated (the All). But in the theistic view even the totality of all mutually related things is itself still related to another that is itself unrelated (God). (*Immanence, *Transcendence). — From the point of view of validity, "absolute" is that which has worth independently of any condition. — Since the contents of concepts, when considered without reference to their bearers or subjects, are not subject to the limiting conditions of the latter, the word "absolute" often means: in the fullest meaning of the idea, unlimited, unconditioned (e. g., wisdom as such). — See also God, Pantheism, Relative.

WB

ABSTRACT

Those representations are abstract to which no sensible *intuition corresponds or which represent their object without the traits of individuation. Abstract representations serve either the process of division that

1

produces a summary view, since the intellect by disregarding the particular characteristics moves forward to more universal concepts such as man, sensible being, living being, etc. (= *total abstraction*), or it helps in the knowledge of the logical structure of concepts and the metaphysical structure of reality, since the intellect by disregarding the carrier separates out the form-giving essential parts such as wisdom from the wise man (= *formal abstraction*). Accordingly, abstract representations are either universal concepts which are still concrete insofar as they are composed of a carrier (*Subject) and a *form (e. g., man), or they are *formal concepts* which present the form without the carrier (e. g., humanity, personhood). — Abstraction from the carrier, however, is not always the same. In a *physical formal concept* at least the relation to an indefinite carrier is still preserved, because the physical form is an essential part of a physically concrete reality (as for example "roundness" in a baseball). On the other hand, in the *metaphysical formal concept* the mind abstracts even from every relation to a carrier. Therefore, this metaphysical consideration is directed to the form as such and it is applicable only to the so-called pure perfections (*God); such perfections can exist without a carrier, but then they must be identical with subsisting existence (*Subsistence). Thus, the metaphysically abstract is the most real of all, but it is known by us only through the use of logical deduction. — Complete human knowledge leads back over the abstract to a more profound grasp of the concrete that is given in experience. — See also *Abstraction, Concrete*.

WB

ABSTRACTION

Abstraction (Lat: *ab*, from + *trahere*, to draw) literally means to separate a part out from a whole. In philosophical terminology "abstraction" does not mean the detachment of a concrete, really separable part from a whole (e. g., a branch from a tree), but only the separation of a non-autonomous characteristic (e. g., color, form), which cannot exist all by itself (*Abstract), from a *concrete, intuitively given whole. Therefore, the separation is not a physical one, but an intentional or mental one; the result is called a *concept.

In modern psychology abstraction (1) usually refers to this mental separation of a non-autonomous characteristic from an intuitively given image. Such an operation presupposes a special attention to the characteristic in question. But if abstraction did no more than isolate definite characteristics out of the sensibly given, then it would certainly be only a diminution and so *empiricism would be fundamentally correct. However, the scholastic *theory of abstraction* holds that in abstraction (2) the undeniable lessening of the content is more than counterbalanced by the greater profundity of the knowledge achieved: by means of abstraction, somehow or other, the "essence", or better, something essential in the object is grasped by the mind. This presupposes that abstraction is not a simple separation of a sensible characteristic from a sensible whole, but that it is an operation on at least two levels in which the essential element is first of all made visible and then is detached out of the concrete composite existent. Therefore, the *intellect as the *power of abstraction* is not merely a power of dividing and composing sensible impressions (not just "reason"), but it is a kind of creative power that allows the essential to shine forth in the sensible (intellect in the narrower sense). Thus, the creative "illumination" of the sensible impression, by means of which the essential content (which can only be grasped spiritually) is made visible, is attributed to the "agent intellect" (intellectus agens) and the apprehension of the essence itself is attributed to the "possible intellect" (intellectus possibilis) (*Concepts, Formation of). Even this apprehension of the essential in the sensible impression is often called "abstraction"; but abstraction is complete only when the apprehended essence has been drawn out of the concrete whole and represented in a definite concept. (On the more precise meaning of "essence": *Essential Knowledge).

A distinction is made between the abstraction of the universal from the particular (e. g., of the universal concept "man" from a particular man) and the abstraction of the "form", that is, a perfection of being, from the subject (e. g., of humanity from concrete men or motion from moved bodies). While the latter is called *formal abstraction*, the former is termed *total* abstraction, because its result is always a whole, namely, a composite made up of a subject and a "form" (e. g., man = a subject that has a human nature). Insofar as the "form" is grasped essentially, for the abstraction of the universal there is no need of any inductive *generalization*. However, the formation of empirical *universal concepts, to the extent that they do not present merely one particular characteristic but a totality of traits that are always connected with each other, does depend upon a type of *induction.

JdV

ACCIDENT

Accident in the broadest sense is everything added to a *substance as a further determination. In logic an accident is every determination that can either be added to a subject or removed from it (e. g., the state of having black hair for a man) (*Predicables). In the order of existence an accident is something that further determines a *substance which already possesses a definite level of being from itself (e. g., the activity of thinking in the spiritual soul). An accident determines a substance either in itself, as quantity and quality (absolute accidents), or in relation to others, as determinations of space and time (relative accidents). Accidental form is distinguished from substantial form in that the latter simply constitutes the essence of a thing (e. g., the soul makes the body into a living body), while the former presupposes the essence of a thing as already existing and merely adds a further determination to the substance. An accident can never exist independently in itself as a substance does; by its very nature it needs a substance in which to inhere. However, through God's almighty power an accident can continue to exist separate from substance (as Catholic theology assumes in the case of the substantial change involved in the Eucharist), but even here the accident's exigency for a substance in which to inhere is not removed.

An accident is also an existent, but it exists in a way that is essentially different from the mode of substantial existence (*Analogy). The inherence of the dependent accident in the substance, in spite of the real difference between the two, should not be thought of in an external way as, for example, in terms of the relationship between a man and his clothes; rather, this inherence should be thought of as an inner existential unity. This unity is similar to the unity between body and soul, but since we always experience only the concrete unity of substance with its accidents, we can never completely penetrate the mysterious character of this inherence.

The affirmation of real accidents distinct from their substance is a conclusion the mind must arrive at when it considers the fact of change in the things of experience; for, many of these things, while remaining essentially the same, undergo changes in other respects. This conception occupies a middle position between the opinion of those who, like Hume and other empiricists, admit the reality only of unsubstantial and flowing appearances (and thereby eliminate all essential perdurance of things) and the view of Descartes and Spinoza who raise accidents themselves (like quanity and thinking) to the level of substantial existence. The accidental determinations of a substance always indicate its finiteness; for, accidental existence is incompatible with the simplicity of the infinite. Conversely, accidental determinations belong necessarily to every created existent. For, *activity which is the result of all existence cannot constitute the substantial existence itself of any finite being.

JS

ACT

Act (Gr.: *enérgeia*) and *potency are the structural factors of the finite existent by means of which first Aristotle and then the Scholastics explained change or becoming. In contrast to potency, act signifies a

4

developed reality. The word takes on different shades of meaning depending on whether it refers to this or that kind of becoming or to a reality that transcends change.

It is essential to act that it be a certain fullness, that is, a certain fulfillment of possibilities which can be realized to a greater or lesser extent of knowledge. If all the possibilities of an act have been completely realized, then we have an *unlimited act*, e. g., the fullness of all knowledge which is not limited by any ignorance. A *limited act*, however, embraces only a part of the possibilities, for example, the knowledge of a man which is accompanied with ignorance. Thus a distinction should be made between a *mixed act* which already in its essence says limitation and therefore is incapable of an unlimited realization, and a *simple act* which in its essence contains no limitation and therefore is capable of an unlimited realization. Thus, sense knowing as such is essentially a mixed knowing that contains ignorance, since it cannot grasp supra-sensible being; but spiritual knowing is essentially a pure, simple knowing (not involving ignorance), even though, when actually realized, it may be affected by ignorance. Limited act is always a *received act*, because it is always limited by the receptive capability of its bearer (e. g., knowledge in a man). However, if pure act (in the order of reality) remains free of every limiting subject, then by that very fact it exists as a subsisting and *non-received act*. Thus it is the full realization of itself and therefore unlimited: this is the case with God.

While in the case of God, because of his simplicity, the one act of his subsisting existence means the highest and absolute reality, the reality of the finite existent is composed of different partial acts. *Entitative act* means the *existence (*Dasein*); in addition to this there is the *formal act* or the essential form which determines the "what" of a thing and which along with the accompanying principle of matter constitutes the essence of corporeal things. The substantial core of a thing is called *first act* as over against the accidental determinations which are called *second act*. In a more restricted use of the terms, the *substance along with its active powers is usually called *first act*; and the activity itself is then called the *second act* (e. g., an act of the will). If a change is brought about in gradual stages, then the imperfect middle stages are termed *imperfect acts*, while the final term is called the perfect or the *last act* (e. g., the growth of a child into a man).

JBL

ACTIVITY

Activity or "doing" is something that we encounter in one form or another in every existent that we observe. It might at first appear that the essence of activity is to produce something or bring something into existence. But when it is looked at more closely, two types of activity begin to be apparent. The first type is external or *transient activity* (Lat: *actio*) in which the agent works upon another existent (e. g., a sculptor hews a piece of marble into a statue). The second type is inner or *immanent* activity (Lat: *operatio*) in which the agent develops itself (e. g., the growth of a plant). Both kinds of activity are often intertwined, especially when transient activity is rooted in immanent (e. g., the thinking and willing of the sculptor which permeate every blow of the chisel). Since activity proceeds from an existent being, the perfection of the activity corresponds to the level of existence of the existent; this fact is expressed neatly in the principle: *agere sequitur esse* (activity depends upon the level of existence). Also, a universally valid principle is: The more perfect a being is, the more immanent is its characteristic activity. Inorganic or lifeless things are totally lost in external activity and for this reason they can work only on other things. With the plant there is a beginning of the existent that manifests immanent activity; such inner activity is the same thing as *life. Nevertheless, the plant is still totally enclosed within its body. This form of externality can only be overcome by sense-consciousness (which is also completely tied to the body) and especially by spiritual life which is intrinsically independent of the body. While the lower kinds of activity do not extend beyond a limited circle of corporeal things, spiritual activity embraces the whole world of existence and even reaches all the way up to God.

The above description of activity could only be provisional. For, causation or the reduction of something from *potency to *act applies only to created activity and does not constitute the real essence of activity as such. The reason for this is that the finite existent in its activity perfects or "fulfills" itself and thus achieves its full reality. It is only in his thinking and willing that a man possesses the fully developed reality of himself, while without this activity he is still in a kind of slumber. Such causal activity belongs to the fulfillment of a thing only to the extent that this fulfillment is not given with the substance of an existent, but must first be produced as a further accidental determination. In sharp contrast to every creature, God's thinking and willing self-possession is pure inner fulfillment; in this activity no production of any kind is involved and so it is referred to as "pure act" (*actus purus*); nor does God's activity outside of himself (i. e., creation) mean or imply the production of something within him. It is precisely the meaning of activity that it brings the existent to the full possession of its own existence and ultimately (for spiritual existents) to the possession of absolute existence. Therefore activity can be identified only with the substance of that being that is absolute existence itself; in the case of finite existents, however, activity must be an accidental determination by means of which they strive for the full possession of themselves and for an approximation to absolute existence. This situation is expressed in the formula: Everything strives for God (*omnia appetunt Deum*).

According to its innermost structure activity belongs with the *transcendentals. Certainly everything cannot be dissolved simply into a free-floating, fluctuating activity, as the advocates of *dynamism would have it. And yet, the very essence, as it were, of existence fulfills itself in activity so that existence is really only completely itself in achieving this fulfillment. Activity, however, is not a special transcendental; rather, it is contained in the true and the good (*truth and *value) which show forth the essential connection of existence with thinking and willing and so with activity.

JBL

ACTUALITY

Actuality designates the existent thing on the basis of its *activity and thereby gives an indication that existence both manifests and perfects itself in activity. In contemporary philosophical terminology, "actual" is applied for the most part to the existent being; and it has this meaning both in contrast to mere appearance and in contrast to mere possibility. Primarily, therefore, the "actual" (1) is not what is imagined or thought, is not purely "ideal existence," but it is that which exists by itself independently of our imagination and thinking. In this sense the word "real" (from the Lat. *res* = thing) is also used; this word can also designate something that is merely possible, whereas "actual" is almost always used for an existing thing, which is often emphasized by saying that it is something "actually existing." The opposition to the merely possible, which is contained in the second meaning of "actual" (2), has therefore an influence, at least in terminology, on the first meaning of "actual" (1).

Accordingly, "actuality" signifies the state of actual existence in both of the given meanings, that is, opposition on the one hand to *appearance and on the other hand to *possibility. In the first sense, the word "reality" is also used for "actuality" (1). Thus, for example, one speaks of the actuality (or reality) of the external world. Actuality (2) in contrast to possibility means the same thing as *existence. According to its linguistic form, the word "actuality" characterizes actual existence as the state of an existent thing; but sometimes it is also used as a concrete expression for an actually existing thing; less often it is applied to a particular existent (e. g., an actuality), more often to the totality of all actually existing things (e. g., actuality); the same thing can be said for the word "reality." — Epistemological *idealism, maintaining that the thing in itself is unknowable, must give a new meaning to actuality if it wants to retain a knowable reality which is still not just appearance; for this view "actual" is something like a formally shaped *appearance as such: Kant attributes to it "empirical reality" in spite of its "transcendental ideality."

In scholastic philosophy the word-pair, actuality and possibility, are frequently used for *act and *potency. Actuality (3) in this sense is not to be equated with actuality (2) in contrast to pure possibility; for it does not simply signify the subsistence of the existent thing, but is' only one of the intrinsic principles of existence over against which in the existent itself stands potency as the other principle of existence. To be sure, the act is the determining principle — the existential perfection, while the potency is only the undeveloped, determinable principle.

JdV

AESTHETICS

Aesthetics as a word was first coined by Alexander Baumgarten (1750). It is derived from the Greek *aisthesis*, which means "sense perception," and primarily designates the science of sense perception in contrast to the science of spiritual knowing. Kant had this general meaning of the word in mind when in his *Critique of Pure Reason* he entitled the first part of the elementary teaching "Transcendental Aesthetics." Baumgarten adduced as the purpose of aesthetics: the perfection of sense knowledge as such, for it is in this that beauty consists. Right here we find the special meaning of aesthetics which has been generally accepted, especially through the influence of Schiller. According to this view, aesthetics is the science of the beautiful whose central point is in turn the philosophical teaching on the beautiful (philosophical aesthetics). This is what we are concerned with here, for it is based on that part of metaphysics which considers the *transcendentals; and the beautiful belongs here. Aesthetics in this sense cannot simply be identified with the philosophy of art; for, beginning from the beautiful in general it moves on to include the consideration of natural beauty along with artistic beauty. However, artistic beauty is the principal object of aesthetics.

It is possible to object to a philosophical aesthetics by claiming that the beautiful (*Beauty) is experienced by an aesthetic *taste* or feeling and is therefore inaccessible to philosophical inquiry. Several things can be said in answer to this objection. The fact that feeling is involved in the perception of beauty does not necessarily imply that the beautiful is just a matter of feeling or something purely subjective about which there can be no argument; rather, the beautiful stands there as something real. It is not encountered by personal taste as a completely irrational experience. For, just as existential structures make up the beautiful, so also do rational factors permeate one's aesthetic taste. It follows, then, that philosophical abstraction is able to encompass both of these aspects without doing them violence. However, since the beautiful is not exhausted by the concepts which we form within the horizon of existence, but rather adds a new transcendental, it finds only in the full breadth of the aesthetic experience its own true answer — something it cannot find in mere concepts. In this experience the whole man is involved, just as in the beautiful all aspects of the existent harmoniously resound. In a very special way the form of the beautiful, which for us is primarily related to the sensible, necessarily requires the employment of sense perception; the name "aesthetics" therefore has a certain justification. Because of the necessary cooperation of many different elements in the perception of the beautiful, that which is perfectly beautiful is an exception as is likewise the perfect aesthetic taste.

On the basis of the above it is possible to give a more precise description of philosophical aesthetics. Its first task is to expound the essence of the beautiful in general and in particular (*Nature and *Art) from its foundation in existence; this is its ontological task. Then it must shed light on the nature of the aesthetic experience in its two typical forms (creative artist and understanding admirer) from the point of view of man himself; this is its anthropological-existential task, which of course also has its ontological roots. This double consideration naturally includes the problems of aesthetic value and aesthetic evaluation.

Among the ancients, Plato, Aristotle and Plotinus offer the beginnings of an aesthetics, as also do Augustine in the age of the Fathers and Thomas Aquinas in the Middle Ages. In Germany Baumgarten founded systematic aesthetics; Schiller then gave this science a great push with his aesthetic writings. Kant gave it his own peculiar stamp in his *Critique of Judgment* which is bogged down in subjectivism. Among the German idealists, Schelling gave art the highest place and Hegel gave it a great deal of attention, but their presentations are pantheistic in direction because they see the beautiful as the sensible appearance of the Absolute. Schopenhauer also thought of the beatutiful as an idea rendered sensible which brings salvation from the pain of this world. In the past hundred years there has been a constant succession of works on aesthetics.

JBL

AFFIRMATION

Affirmation is the name given to that aspect by which the *judgment distinguishes itself from the other knowing functions. The concept exhausts itself in the representation of contents without taking a position with regard to them: e. g., man, immortal. Since everything is still undecided, the concept offers knowledge only in a beginning way. Knowledge is not fully realized until it becomes a judgment, which takes a position and decides — which, in fact, adds affirmation to the content: e. g., Man is not immortal. As the example shows, "affirmation" expresses itself in the copulative verb "is" and can appear either as an assertion or a *denial. Affirmation is not performed blindly, but it proceeds from an insight into the relationship between the two contents (subject and predicate). Although it manifests a certain similarity to an act of the will, it is the work of the intellect — a work in which the intellect achieves its highest perfection. When it says "is" of that which is and "is not" of that which is not (the formula of Aristotle), then it names things according to what they are and penetrates down to the existence of the existent, while the concept represents only the essence as an appearance that is not yet related to existence. The existence that is achieved in the affirmation also makes the judgment to be true. — The affirmation of the judgment is rooted ultimately (at least mediately) in the real, objective affirmation, that is, in the actual or possible positing of the existent itself; this is usually called *existence.

JBL

AGNOSTICISM

Agnosticism (Gr.: *ágnostos* = unknown; first used by T. H. Huxley) literally means the theory of unknowability; as actually used, it means the philosophical position which holds that the supra-sensible is unknowable; thus, it is a denial of the possibility of *metaphysics as a science and it is especially a denial of the knowability of God. The possibility or even the thinkability of an existent beyond the realm of man's possible experience is of course not contested, but the ability to know with certainty the existence and especially the essence of a "transcendent" existent is rejected as impossible for the human mind. Human knowledge, therefore, is restricted to this-worldly material things, while knowledge of the transcendent (*Transcendence) — through a failure to appreciate the possibility of *analogous* knowledge — at best is left to an *irrational presentiment, feeling or "belief." Agnosticism is an essential part of all positivism; further, it is present in Kant's *critical philosophy, in the philosophy of religion (which has been decisively influenced by Kantianism), of Catholic Modernism and of modern Protestantism, and also in *dialectical theology. On the other hand, a logically worked-out *idealism professes that fundamentally everything is knowable, since it reduces all reality to consciousness; it is therefore able to escape the pitfall of agnosticism only by denying the existence of anything transcendent.

JdV

ANALOGY

Analogy comes from the Greek *aná-logon* which means the proportion or likeness that exists between two or more things. By this is meant primarily an analogy of knowledge which grasps one existent according to its relationship to some other. Thus the existence of an existent is manifested by comparison with some other existent or at least made clear (e. g., "that idea hit me like a bolt of lightning"). This analogy can be described as "knowledge through comparison." It presupposes that the existent with which something is compared (at least under the aspect of the comparison) is more known than the latter and that there is both similarity and difference between them. Without similarity there is absolutely no possibility of a comparison; without difference the comparison presents merely a repetition of the same thing with no new information. Therefore analogous knowledge is rooted in the analogy of existence by reason of which two or more existents are at the same time similar and different in their existence. This type of analogy is discussed here. It is mirrored in our concepts and words.

Because of the lack of any similarity, the *equivocal* word (there is no question here of an equivocal concept) falls short of analogy; for it unites two completely different ideas or things under the same name (e. g., "rod" as a mechanical part and as a pistol). Because of the lack of any difference, *synonymous* and *univocal* words likewise are not analogous; for, the former signify the exact same thing (e. g., rational animal and man), while the latter take two concepts, which as a whole are different, and isolate out one aspect in which they both agree without any difference (e. g., sensation in reference to animal and man). For analogous knowledge only those concepts can be considered which contain within themselves inseparably (*metaphysical analogy*) or at least in an unseparated state (*physical analogy*) both similarity and difference; in the first case the concept is analogous right down to its metaphysical structure and therefore it is not univocal in any sense, while in the second case the concept is analogous only in its concrete reality but is univocal in its metaphysical structure. The second case is found realized in the genus "animal"; the first case, which is the only one that is essentially an analogous concept, is found realized in the concept of the existent.

In order to arrive at a more precise determination of the analogous concept it is necessary to consider the two basic types of analogy: the analogy of attribution and the analogy of proportionality. In this matter a clear distinction must be made between the common analogous content of the concept or name (e. g., the existent) and the carriers of the analogous relationship (e. g., of the *analogates* God and Creature). In the *analogy of attribution* the analogous common element is assigned to the second analogate in dependence on the first one. Since, because of this dependence, either the analogous name alone or the reality intended by it can be applied to the second analogate, there is both an *extrinsic* and an *intrinsic* analogy of attribution. A good example of the first kind is the predicate "healthy"; the primary analogate is the human body which realizes in itself the quality of being healthy; the secondary analogates are something like the color in one's face or food which are called "healthy" because of their relationship to the health of the body (as signs or as contributors to health), but which do not carry within themselves the quality of being healthy. A good example of the second kind is the existent; God is said to be "existing" as the primary analogate; the creature is said to be "existing" as the secondary analogate because in itself it really does exist, but only in absolute dependence on God. Between both God and the creature there is agreement in existence, but an agreement which is colored by an essential difference because God is independent and perfect existence, while the creature possesses a dependent and therefore imperfect existence.

The *analogy of proportionality* is based on the affirmation that each of the analogates possesses a relation in which all at the same time agree and disagree. This is an analogous relation of two relationships, which is what the word "proportionality" means. It is called *proper* when the relation in both analogates is ordered to the same reality present in both of them, and *improper* when the secondary analogate is not ordered to the same reality present in both of them, but only to an effect which in some way resembles the reality in the primary analogate. Thus, both God and creatures are related to existence in its essential reality, but in essentially different ways: God necessarily, the creature contingently. If we speak of a "smiling" meadow, this is not because it really smiles, but only because it cheers us up in the same way that a smiling human face does. This is called a *metaphysical* way of speaking.

The importance of analogy stands out especially with regard to the problem of God. Insofar as it says agreement and similarity, it overcomes a complete separation of God and world; in this respect it makes some knowledge of God possible in contrast to all forms of *agnosticism. Insofar as it also says difference, it excludes the pantheistic identification of God and world; in this respect it prevents man from acquiring an exhaustive understanding of God.

JBL

ANALYSIS

Analysis literally means the "breaking down" of a whole into its parts. In philosophical terminology analysis signifies the *method of the mental *division* of a whole — either an actual whole or some mental construct

— into its components; in this way the parts, which at first are known only *implicitly* in their undivided unity, are singled out and known *explicitly*. The opposite mental operation is called *synthesis. — In particular, the analysis of a concept signifies the division of a conceptual whole into the individual parts which at first are grasped only implicitly; they are then called "notes". Then if one of these notes is affirmed in a judgment as a predicate of the subject designated by the whole concept, then one speaks of an *analytic judgment* (e. g., a square has four angles); at least this is the way Kant understands the expression. Less appropriately, others also speak of an analytic judgment if the predicate from the beginning is not thought of as belonging to the concept of the subject, but is necessarily deduced from the content and so represents an "essential characteristic" (a "property") of the subject (*Predicables). — A somewhat different meaning of analysis is present when the reduction of conclusions to basic principles (*Knowledge, Principles of) is called "analysis." — The word "analytic" designates something that uses analysis as a method or that which is acquired or to be acquired through analysis.

JdV

ANALYTIC PHILOSOPHY

Analytic philosophy is a catch-all expression for twentieth century philosophical works, chiefly English and American, which rely heavily on techniques of linguistic and logical analysis. One of the central and abiding contentions is that a clarification of the meaning and use of words is indispensible in treating philosophical problems, and that such explications often dissolve traditional problems, particularly metaphysical ones, by showing that they rest on a misuse of language. Apart from such trends and shared methodological principles there is no body of doctrine that can be referred to as "analytic philosophy." The movement is best understood historically.

The analytic movement began with G. E. Moore's reaction against late nineteenth and early twentieth century idealistic metaphysical systems, particularly Bradley's neohegelianism. Moore defended a common sense realism by analyzing the language used to express philosophical claims and arguing that they could not support the extended significance metaphysicians attempted to give them. Bertrand Russell argued that ordinary language is hopelessly ambiguous on issues of philosophical concern and that analysis should follow the norms established by formal logic. This doctrine of *logical atomism* was developed in a more consistent and profound manner by the early Wittgenstein. What he did, in effect, was to argue from the logical structure of an ideal language to the nature of the world that grounds the meaningfulness of this language. The logical positivists attempted to fuse this interpretation of logic with the empiricist tradition. In his later years Wittgenstein thought this approach misleading and concentrated on the way in which the meaning of terms in ordinary language is a function of their use. Some of his followers have frequently attempted to dissolve traditional philosophical problems by applying his techniques, though usually without his finesse.

The Oxford school took over the later Wittgensteinian ideas and focused on the analysis of ordinary language. Here one may roughly distinguish two phases. The earlier phase either focused on logical behaviorism (G. Ryle) by explaining the meaning of terms apparently referring to mental acts and states as really referring to overt behavior and dispositions to such behavior, or (J. Austin) concentrated on precise analysis of selected terms and their varied usages, while generally prescinding from traditional philosophical problems. The recent phase (Strawson, Hampshire, Kenny) involves a return to metaphysics through conceptual analysis. Ordinary language implicitly involves a conceptualization of reality which when made explicit, is labelled "descriptive metaphysics." The basic contention is that this rather Aristotelian descriptive metaphysics is more fundamental in our understanding of reality than any revisionary metaphysics that seeks to replace it. This, in turn, has stimulated a renewed interest in the Kantian problem of the relation between a conceptual framework and the reality it seeks to represent. This school also manifests an abiding concern with the distinctive role and significance of ethical language.

Though this Oxford type analysis has strong support in the United States and other English speaking countries, a distinctive type of American analysis is emerging which represents a fusion of elements drawn from the analytic, positivistic, and pragmatic movements (W. Quine, W. Sellars). An underlying idea is that knowledge, or at least its expression, can be represented as a collection of systems, e.g., ordinary language, scientific systems, etc. Each system implicitly entails a minimal metaphysics or a functional ontic commitment to the entities spoken about within the system and to the basic properties which the system attributes to these entities. Such commitments are made explicit by linguistic analysis for ordinary language and by formal logical analysis for technically developed systems. The pragmatic contribution enters with a stress on a theory of acceptance, or a doctrine of judgment applied more to systems than to individual propositions, and with a careful distinction between explication, or meaning analysis, and *explanation. Though ordinary language has a methodological priority in questions concerning explication, scientific systems are used to give explanations which are accepted as more basic.

The ideal goal is a consistent synthesis of knowledge. In practice this goal is developed, or anticipated, more by concentrating on the formal structures of systems and strategy arguments concerning the replaceability of some systems by more basic ones than by an analysis of the actual content of presently operative scientific systems. The conflict between the competing ontic commitments of differing systems (e.g., to man as an irreducible unit in ordinary language and as a collection of fundamental particles in physical language) should ultimately be settled by the criterion of which systems are fundamental and irreducible in giving explanations. This emphasis on the acceptance of systems effectively transforms the critical question, concerning the relation between a conceptual system and the reality it seeks to represent, into a pragmatic question concerning which systems should be accepted as most fundamental and most useful in describing and explaining reality. However, a certain degree of dissatisfaction with this has generated a renewed interest in Kantianism.

Any *appraisal* of this movement should respect it complexity and increasing sophistication. Early analytic works tented to be epistemologically naive and biased against metaphysics, though they rarely relied on the dogmatic dismissal of metaphysics as meaningless characteristic of positivism. Formal analysis often reveals an *a priori* bias in favor of materialism. Yet, from the beginning this movement had the advantage of concentrating on presuppositions concerning the meaning and use of language which were often uncritically accepted in other philosophical traditions. A long and varied development gradually led to the general abandonment of sense-data theories of knowledge, to a clarification of the relation between language and concepts, and to the elaboration of finely-grained techniques of conceptual and linguistic analysis. As a methodology, analysis is philosophically neutral in that it can be used to clarify and often support quite varied philosophical positions. Though the early analysts tended to be ahistorical, if not antihistorical, more recent writers have employed analytic techniques, with very uneven results, to clarify the meaning and significance of earlier philosophical positions.

Analysis becomes something of a doctrine when the position is held that all that the philosopher can properly do is clarify the meaning and usage of terms in ordinary and scientific languages. The underlying idea, stemming from the later writings of Wittgenstein, is that philosophy is essentially a second order discipline with no proper content of its own. Its proper role is to study first order disciplines and clarify their significance by removing ambiguities and inconsistencies. On the other hand, many philosophers who rely on analytic techniques insist that the philosopher must go beyond mere analysis and aim at a synthesis which is properly, though often in a rather minimal sense, called "metaphysical." Through such developments analytic philosophy is rejoining the main-stream of philosophy and reconsidering perennial questions posed by Plato, Aristotle, Aquinas, and Kant.

EM

ANTHROPOLOGY

Anthropology as a word comes from the Greek and means: the science of man. At first the word was used for the physical scientific version of anthropology, which investigates man in his bodily characteristics with scientific methods (in contrast to the methods of the *human sciences). But in recent decades *philosophical anthropology* has asserted itself decisively, particularly through the influence of Max Scheler.

A few observations here will have to suffice for a historical evaluation of this change. To be sure, the question of man is in some way *the* theme of philosophy; yet in the early stages it did not constitute the dominant point of interest. Ancient culture revolved around the "cosmos" or nature and saw man in relationship to that. In the thinking of the Middle Ages man was a part of the "order" established by God. The modern mind separated man from such supports and set him out on his own, but predominantly as "subject" or reason, with the result that this reason as transcendental subject or as a pantheistically conceived absolute reason did violence to man; and as a passing moment in the developmental process of the Absolute it reduced him to insignificance. Finally, modern man grew aware of the nihilism of these constructions, and he noted that he had lost himself and everything else, that he had sacrificed life for an abstract concept and now stood before nothingness. The new birth began when he saw that he was thrown back upon himself, and (in contrast to idealism) thrown back upon the personal and historical concreteness of his own life that precedes all concepts and breaks through them. Thus man himself becomes *the* theme of all philosophizing; and it is worthwhile to study man and all other things only in him. Therefore, philosophy changes more or less into anthropology and is often absorbed by it. The first move in this direction was taken by the later Schelling and by Kierkegaard. Then the development moves through Nietzsche, *life philosophy and *phenomenology to Max Scheler who explicitly formulated the anthropological theme as such. Finally, *existential philosophy accomplished the most recent philosophical synthesis and a certain definite conclusion.

The different directions of anthropology bring out at the same time the dangers hidden in it. If the primary emphasis is placed on life (especially the life of the body), then the very special nature of man is again missed; this tendency is noticeable in Nietzsche, in *life philosophy, and especially in Max Scheler's later work. This usually leads to a biological, relativistic, psychological disappearance of the other values in life. Others try to work out the special nature of man who, as existence, by reason of his spiritual self-actualization is superior to everything that is simply "at hand"; this is what Kierkegaard did and the existentialists generally. Still, in this regard one frequently notes the tendency to reduce everything simply to the modes of existence of man; this attitude will turn anthropology into a one-sided

16

anthropologism. An important source of the above-mentioned dangers is always to be found in irrationalism (*Irrational) which does not go beyond the immediate experience of life and man, but only allows its exposition or *hermeneutic* (Dilthey) or phenomenological analysis (Husserl).

For an evaluation of anthropology it is necessary to say that all philosophy can never be reduced to it (anthropologism). Looked at metaphysically, it is rather that part of philosophy that studies man's essential make-up. Nevertheless, man does stand at the hub of all philosophizing insofar as everything else in the cosmos is revealed to us through man, and insofar as, being related in the modes of his existence to realities that lie beyond him, he makes them accessible. Therefore, the way into the particular areas of ontology is opened up only by going through a fundamental-ontological explanation of man. In this sense, a preliminary anthropology is the door that opens into philosophy with the result that it remains anthropologically determined in the mode of its expression.

JBL

ANTINOMIES

Antinomies are either the apparent contradiction between demonstrated propositions or the real contradiction between apparently demonstrated propositions. The semblance of a contradiction can have an objective basis if it is a question of objects that can be known by us only analogically. Then the resolution of an antinomy lets us know that it is not a matter of a formal contradiction, but it still does not tell us how the objects are in fact related to each other. Thus, for example, the concepts of the immutability and *freedom of God, if understood properly, do not necessarily exclude each other even though we cannot positively see the possibility of their standing together.

According to Kant, human reason falls unavoidably into contradictions as soon as it applies its principle of absolute unity to the world of appearances. The study of these necessary contradictions and their causes is called *antithetics;* the contradiction itself is called an antinomy.

The first antinomy (of quantity) concerns the finiteness or infinity of the world according to space and time: With regard to time the world has a (no) beginning and with regard to space a (no) limit. The second antinomy (of quality) concerns the dividing up of a whole given in sensible appearance: Every (no) composed substance is made up of simple parts. The third antinomy (of relation) concerns the nature of the causality by means of which appearances come to be: Causality according to the laws of nature (in contrast to the type of causality involved in the exercise of personal freedom) is (not) the only one from which appearances as a whole can be deduced. The fourth antinomy (of modality) concerns the existence of a necessary being: An absolutely necessary being does (not) belong to the world as a part or cause of it.

According to Kant, the proofs for the first two (the so-called *mathematical*) antinomies presuppose that the *world* (the totality of all appearances) is a self-existing whole. But since this presupposition is false, the conclusions drawn from it are also false. The opposite of this antinomy is not contradictory, but contrary. — Kant's solution of the first antinomy: The world as appearance (which is given merely in an empirical regress to empirical conditions) is neither infinite nor finite; that is, the empirical regress can be pushed back further from any point arrived at (*in indefinitum*). — The solution of the second antinomy: All parts of a whole are indeed given in intuition, but never the whole division which (with regard to the mere appearance in space) can go on indefinitely.

While in regard to the mathematical antinomies the regression necessarily led to similar, sensible conditions, in the case of the *dynamic* antinomies (the third and fourth) there can be a regression to a dissimilar, purely intelligible condition (attainable by the intellect), so that both the thesis and the antithesis can be true. — The solution of the third antinomy: All appearances do indeed hang together according to some rule (the casuality of nature), but possibly they still have bases which themselves are not an appearance and accordingly are not determined in their causality by any appearances (the causality of personal freedom). — The solution of the fourth antinomy: In the totality of all sensible appearances no such thing as a necessary being can be found. Nevertheless, there would be no contradiction if the whole order of the sensible world depends on a necessary being that is wholly outside of it. Of course, one cannot conclude from sensible appearances to the existence of such a necessary being, since appearances are only sensible representations.

Critical evaluation of the above: It must be conceded that the antinomies are rooted in the double character of human reason. For, on the one hand, as reason it is directed to the unconditioned element of existence as such, and on the other hand as human reason it is limited primarily to sensible things. The result is that, even when the human mind rises above the things of sense, in its entire conceptual framework it still uses corporeal objects as its model and frame of reference. The solution of the antinomies by distinguishing between things in themselves and mere appearances also contains a grain of truth. For, what is true of things as appearances (objects of the senses) is not necessarily true of them as things in themselves (objects of the mind). Thus, it is certainly correct that the visible world as a whole can never be the object of an experience and the complete division of an extended thing cannot be accomplished in any experience. Yet Kant goes too far when he reduces appearances to mere sensible representations, instead of seeing them as reflections of things in themselves. Because of this presupposition a causality based on freedom and an absolutely necessary being would not only be possible — they would also be a requirement of reason. — The solution, moreover, of the third antinomy is not adequate (*Freedom). — See also *Critical Philosophy*.

WB

A POSTERIORI

In general, by the expression "a posteriori" is meant that one proceeds in an orderly fashion from a more recent (*posterius*) element to something earlier; whether the sequence is temporal or not is inconsequential. "A posteriori" stands in contrast to *a priori and, depending on the difference in the point of comparison, it can mean different things. In comparison to another, something can be taken as "more recent" according to time (tomorrow—today), according to nature (effect—cause), or according to logical dependence (conclusion—premise). — In scholastic logic demonstrations are termed "a posteriori" if they conclude from the effect or the attribute (therefore, from that which comes after nature) to the cause or the essence. Since Kant, that knowledge is called "a posteriori" whose validity logically depends on experience (= perception). That which comes after either logically or in nature, does not also have to be later in time.

WB

APPEARANCE

Appearance in general means that which is intuitively given (*Object). In particular cases the intended sense is different according to a difference in the object. Most common is the opposition between the appearance (1) and the *thing-in-itself; this comes from Kant. In this case, appearance means the sense image produced in the knowing subject by the thing known; in this image the thing appears to us according to the peculiarity of our senses. A true appearance is distinguished from a false appearance by the fact that it is essentially related to a thing-in-itself that causes the appearance according to recognized norms. According to Kant, experience, considered as a spatio-temporally formed sense impression, is still wholly "subjective"; it can only become an objective appearance, which he calls a *phenomenon*, when it is grasped under one of the categories (*Critical Philosophy). Insofar as Kant says that we know only the appearance of a thing and not the thing in its own proper existence, his view is a type of *phenomenalism. According to scholastic *realism the sense image is not just a mere appearance, but — within certain limits — a true representation of the thing that corresponds with reality. — A second pair of opposites is that of appearance (2) and *essence. Here "appearance" signifies the object, not in its essence but only according to its way of sensibly manifesting itself; in this sense it is just an empirical object (*Experience). This opposition is not the same as the first one mentioned above, since appearance in this sense does not exclude actual existence and conversely the essence can be something that is only imagined. — The word "appearance" (3) or phenomenon also has another meaning in the terminology developed by *phenomenology. Here "phenomenon" means every directly perceived or experienced thing, in contrast to everything that is only thought or indirectly known; notice that in this sense even the really existent (e.g., one's own interior acts) or the object grasped in its essence (e.g., triangle) can be a phenomenon. The word "phenomenon" is taken in this third sense to mean that all speculation must begin with phenomena.

Outward appearance means that the sensible or even the conceptual data are so constituted that they can suggest a false judgment; then the objective reality expressed in the judgment "seems" to exist, although in actuality it does not exist. Mere sensible appearance consists in this, that one's perception presents the object differently than it really is; conceptual (logical) appearance usually rests on a similarity between ideas which, if one is not careful, can easily be equated in a false way. Mere sense appearance (e.g., a bent oar in water) in many situations occurs regularly because of the external stimulus, so that for an experienced person there is no danger of being deceived. In such cases one does not speak of *sense deception* (mere outward appearance in the narrow sense), for this takes place only when sense experiences are in some way falsely interpreted by the influence of the imagination. Sense deception becomes *false perception* when, because of the addition of elements from the imagination, objects appear differently than they are in reality (illusion), or when mere products of the imagination assume the concreteness of a perception and thus simulate things that are not there at all (*hallucination*). There is no deception in the true sense until a man is led to make a false judgment on the basis of mere outward appearance.

Illusionism is the view that everything or almost everything that a person normally considers to be real, is nothing but mere outward appearance; this is the same as *skepticism. Similarly, the *As-If-Philosophy* of Hans Vaihinger (*fictionalism*) assumed that all human knowledge is composed of fictions, however, it is blindly asserted that many of these fictions contribute to a full life (*Pragmatism).

JdV

APPETITE

Appetite as an active tendency towards an *end is proper, in the broadest possible sense, to all finite existence. We designate as a "natural appetite" (*appetitus naturae*) the tense reaching out of a being for the full realization of its real possibilities — this "reaching out" is at the root of every (even conscious) act of striving. For example, the plant strives unconsciously for its own full development. — Appetite in the narrower sense of the word is the conscious striving (*appetitus elicitus*) for goals known either spiritually or sensibly. Since the conscious appetite is based on a natural striving, it can only tend to ends that in some way correspond to this natural striving and so contribute to the existential perfection of the striver. There is no such thing as a desire of evil for the sake of evil. — According to the level of the end, the act and the knowledge of the end, a distinction is made between the *intellectual appetite* (*Will) for spiritually known goals and *animal-sensible appetite* (drive in the narrow sense). In man both types of appetite are found. However, they are there in such a way that they are closely tied to each other in spite of their differences. Thus, blind indulgence of the sensible appetite tends to destroy the being and value of man, while the mere repression (instead of a proper subordination) of sensible appetites can lead to serious mental disturbances. See also *Passion, Will*.

AW

A PRIORI

In general, by the expression "a priori" is meant that one proceeds in an orderly fashion from an earlier (*prius*) element to a later one; whether the sequence is temporal or not is inconsequential. In order for the expression "a priori" to be clear, the nature of the sequence must always be established and the element in reference to which something is said to be "earlier" must be indicated. An element can be a priori or earlier (in contrast to *A Posteriori), according to time (yesterday—today), according to nature (cause—effect), or according to logical sequence (premise—conclusion). — In scholastic logic demonstrations are termed "a priori" if they begin with that which is actually prior, if they therefore conclude from the cause to the effect or from the essence to the attribute. Since Kant, that knowledge is called "a priori" whose validity is logically independent of *experience (= perception). By this Kant does not mean to deny a certain dependence of such knowledge on experience with regard to time and origin. For this expanded concept of the a priori Kant uses the word "transcendental." — According to Kant, the validity of a priori knowledge rests on this, that because of it experience (as an objective and universally valid field of knowledge) is established and made possible. Therefore, the value of a priori knowledge is limited to the realm of possible experience (*Critical Philosophy), that is, it is viewed by Kant as the condition of the possibility of experience. According to the scholastic view, however, the validity of a priori knowledge is based on the insight into the essential relations of the objects known. The absolute value of such insights for the order of reality is ultimately rooted in the fact that both the subjective and the objective realms are based on the same pure identity of knowing and existing—an identity that is characteristic of pure spirit. Consequently, the objective validity of a priori principles, in spite of their fundamental dependence on experience, goes way beyond this experience and is wholly unlimited. — "A priori" is sometimes used in a derogatory way to mean: prior to critical evalution = uncritical; a better word for this meaning is "aprioristic."

WB-KB

ARISTOTELIANISM

Aristotelianism is the philosophical teaching of Aristotle (384-322 B.C.) and his school (*Lyceum* or *Peripatetics*) which later achieved a dominant influence in the Middle Ages among the Arabs (Averroes), Jews (Moses Maimonides) and since the thirteenth century, chiefly through the work of Albert the Great and Thomas Aquinas, among most Christian thinkers of the West where, however, it underwent some fundamental changes as the result of its contact with Christian faith (*Scholasticism). Aristotle bases the truth of human knowledge not on a transcendent world of ideas distinct and separate from the things of daily experience (*Platonism), but on the forms which are contained in things and which are the objective, real counterparts of human concepts.

Sense experience and intellectual abstraction cooperate in the formation and development of human knowledge. First philosophy or metaphysics, which is the science of being and its highest forms, is the queen of all the sciences. The contingent, changing existent which is subject to becoming and corruption is composed of a potential and an actual principle which Aristotle called "matter" and "form". Becoming is not the beginning of something totally new that was not there before, but an essential change whereby matter, which is thought of as the eternal, uncreated, determinable part, loses its former essential form and under the influence of an efficient cause obtains another, new formal determination (*Hylemorphism). There are a number of conflicting explanations of the precise nature of these essential components, especially of the form and how it differs from the Platonic idea. Forms are the inner principle of determination and purpose (*telos*; thus *en-tel-echy*). This holds especially for the formal principles in living things: the plant soul, the animal soul and the human soul. The one human soul also exercises the functions of vegetative and animal life. Man achieves spiritual knowledge not by producing it purely out of himself, but as the result of determinations that come to him through his senses; in this process, however, he is not completely passive but operates through the spontaneous power of the "agent intellect" which determines the "passive intellect" from which it is really distinct. Only the agent intellect is immortal; it is not produced by generation but comes "from the outside." The Arabs interpreted the unclear texts of Aristotle on this point in the sense of a *Monopsychism*, i.e., they said that there is just one agent intellect that functions in all men.

With regard to the will, Aristotle taught that man has freedom of choice, but he did not make a clear distinction between the free and the voluntary. God is conceived as pure thought (*noēsis noēseos* = thought of thought) and the first mover of the heavenly bodies. It is doubtful whether or not he thought of God as personal; and God is not the creator of the world. In his ethics the goal of human life is described as happiness which consists in the practice of virtue; and the highest type of happiness consists in the contemplation of truth. He also taught in his politics that the family and the state, as social communities, are natural in origin. Likewise he rejected Plato's utopian ideas of common wives and possessions for the ideal state. Thus Aristotle's teaching is usually developed in a prudent, critical but thorough confrontation between his own ideas and those of his predecessors, especially Plato.

JoS

ART

Art (Lat.: *ars*) is the power to perform certain actions guided by special knowledge and executed with skill; it is the outstanding ability to do or produce something according to aesthetic principles. Art and handicraft agree in that both produce a work that can be perceived by the senses. Still, handicraft is ordered to something useful, while art is dedicated to the production of beauty. A thing is *naturally beautiful* if it permits the idea residing in it to shine forth with splendor. Something *artistically beautiful* is not just a repetition or carbon copy of the things of nature; rather, it is the task of art to allow ideas to shine forth with a wholly new profundity and power and to reflect the ultimate secrets of reality in her creative works. For this reason the primary purpose of art is the presentation of ideas, not the production of things. The artist is a seer who penetrates to the innermost depths of every existent, even to God's creative ideas; and he is a maker who is able to express his vision in his work; in him seeing and making are one. Thus in spite of all temporal and personal limitations the artist moves beyond himself and stands out among his fellow men as a prophet, as one who glorifies existence; there is even something priestly about the true artist.

Art of necessity demands sensible clarity and its very language embraces sensible forms; *beauty itself, however, does not necessarily require a sensible expression. In contrast to art, the basic element of science is the concept which has its irreplaceable meaning alongside of the artist's vision. Yet art can speak more effectively with beauty than science can with concepts. To be sure, neither the artist nor his public should concentrate solely on sensible beauty; if they do, the soul of art withers away. Moreover, it is precisely the increasing de-sensualization that makes possible the inner sequence of the arts: architecture, sculpture, painting, literature (the emphasis here is on the spoken word), mimicry (esp. dancing), music. A distinction is also made between the spatial and the temporal arts insofar as the first three create something permanent in space, while the last three produce something ephemeral, something that must always be realized anew in time.

JBL

ATHEISM

Atheism (godlessness) is the denial of the existence of God. The *practical atheist* is convinced of the existence of God, but in fact denies it by the way he lives; the *theoretical atheist* makes the judgment that God does not exist. A grosser form of atheism is involved in *materialism and *positivism which reject all spiritual, transcendent existence. *Pantheism in its different forms rejects a personal, transcendent God, but by recognizing something *absolute (moral law, beauty, etc.) that is not identical with the world of experience it still possesses the seed of faith in God. *Polytheism* and *deism should not be ranked with atheism.

The theoretical *negative atheist* knows nothing at all about God or else he has only a distorted notion of him. Such an attitude of mind is not possible for a long period of time for an adult, normal man, since man's whole natural tendency is ordered to God (*God, Idea of). Apparent cases of such ignorance can be explained by a totally positivistic, skeptical upbringing. — The theoretical *positive atheist* doubts either the existence of God as not sufficiently proved (particular *skepticism), or he considers every clear statement about God to be impossible because it exceeds our knowledge which is limited to experience (*Agnosticism), or he is subjectively convinced about the non-existence of God. This latter position can be explained from the nature of the evidence used in the proof for the existence of God, because the evidence is only mediate, because the constructed argument is usually very complex, because of the many epistemological presuppositions; it can also be explained by the force of philosophical "objections" and by the influence of personal passions. However, such a person has permitted his innermost inclinations to atrophy and can hardly be excused from all guilt. The *postulatory atheism* of F. Nietzsche and N. Hartmann denies the existence of God because of the supposed danger coming from God to human or ethical values.

MR

ATOMISM

Atomism is the philosophical position which seeks to explain the essence of material bodies in terms of the combination of atoms. Since the time of Leucippus and Democritus (5th cent. B. C.) atomism has appeared again and again in the history of philosophy under a number of different forms. According to this view, atoms are infinitely small particles which are separated from each other by empty space. Extension is usually ascribed to these particles and they are all said to have the same nature; they differ only according to their shape, size and position in space. According to atomism all bodies are composed of these primordial particles. *Mechanistic atomism* attributes to the atoms only motive power; a more *dynamistic atomism* claims that the atoms have other and different powers. In any event, *change consists only in the joining and separating of the smallest particles, while there is no such thing as real *becoming and corruption. — Hence, the explanation of the essence of bodies through atomism is not sufficient. The combination of ultimate particles is only one aspect of macroscopic bodies; their many other characteristics and powers cannot satisfactorily be explained on the basis of a mere joining together of atoms; but that should be possible if the essence of material bodies is to be found in their atomic structure. — The *atomic theory* of physical science should be clearly distinguished from philosophical atomism. For, according to this theory, without detriment to their specific essences, bodies are divisible into ultimate particles, which are called atoms and molecules, out of which they are composed. This theory does not attempt to give an explanation of the essence of corporality; the ultimate particles themselves, however, are still bodies and it is the task of the *philosophy of *nature* to explain their nature—this is not the task of physical science.

NJ

AUGUSTINIANISM

Augustinianism is a conservative, philosophical-theological school, primarily of the 13th century, which leaned heavily on Augustine (354-430). It counted among its adherents very influential men not only among the Franciscans and secular clergy, but also among the early Dominicans, and later among the Augustinian Hermits. Its dominant position was threatened by Albert the Great and Thomas Aquinas, but after having brought about a temporary condemnation of certain Aristotelian-Thomistic theses at Paris and Oxford in 1277, it was eventually reduced by the impact of the *via moderna* to a state of secondary importance. Augustinianism is marked by a strong preference for Plato and the Platonic tradition over Aristotle. It tends to view wisdom as the philosophy of the Good rather than the philosophy of the True and to reject any rigid distinction between philosophy and theology, between rational truth and revealed truth. The School follows Augustine (*Solil.* 1.2.7) in looking upon *God and the *soul as the two matters of supreme importance in the quest of wisdom. The soul with its three powers, memory, understanding, and will, is an image of the Blessed Trinity. It is viewed as being basically independent in its relation to the body, rather than as being its substantial *form. In his early writings Augustine had spoken of man as if he were a soul using a body, but he later admitted under the influence of revelation that there is a mysterious union between them so that the two somehow form one man. The Augustinian School, however, teaches that the soul is a substance having its own principle of individuation (thus rejecting the theory of *materia signata* of Aquinas). The faculties of the soul, in both Augustine and his followers, are not really distinct from the soul but are merely functions of it. In the formation of ideas, there is no such thing as an active intellect abstracting the essences of things from the data of sense knowledge, but rather the mind sees within itself the images of eternal truths produced within it by a light given to it by God (*Illumination). The Augustinian School accepts Augustine's active theory of sensation, according to which soul can act on body but not body on soul. The soul, therefore, is on the alert to perceive through the sense organs what goes on in the sensible world, and thus these changes in the body "do not escape" its notice. After Scotus the School taught that the mind has a direct intuitive knowledge of individual sensible beings. Matter, according to the School, is not pure potency in the Aristotelian sense. Following Plotinus, Augustine had held that it was the absence of all form and the basis of change in the world of mutable beings, and yet it was thought of as something, *nihil aliquid* (*Conf.* 12.6.6); and his followers continued to teach that prime matter had some positive actuality however slight and rudimentary. They also follow their master in teaching that there is matter in all created beings, even in the angels and in the soul, since they are mutable. Traditionally the Augustinian School teaches the possibility of more than one substantial form in a created composite, and specifically that there is in man a plurality of forms corresponding to his vegetative, sensitive, and rational functions. But following Giles of Rome in the late 13th century, the Augustinian Hermits rejected this doctrine. The theory of the *rationes seminales* of Augustine was also embraced by the School. These "seminal reasons," proposed by Augustine in his *De Genesi ad Litteram*, are invisible seeds or causes, postulated to explain how God "created all things together" (according to the Latin text of Ecclesiasticus 18.1), even though Genesis 2.4-5 says: "When the Lord God made the earth and the heavens, there was not yet any field shrub on the earth, etc." The seminal reasons are hidden in the bosom of nature so that by them the proper measures and numbers and weights of things may be unfolded in due time. Following Augustine, who maintained (*De Civ. Dei* 12.16) that creatures coeternal with the Creator are impossible, the Augustinian School rejects the possibility of creation from eternity (*creatio ab aeterno*). Finally, in explaining the beatific vision, Augustinianism maintains that the union of the soul with God is primarily through the will.

LDD-JHT

AUTHORITY

Authority is the sum total of those attributes of physical or moral persons (and in a broader sense of traditions and customs) which can and do motivate personal consent to the directions of the one who possesses authority. Accordingly, authority is to be distinguished both from physical or moral coercion and from assent which results from an intellectual insight into a given situation or proposition. Assent of the intellect based upon authority is called *faith; consent of the will and execution is called obedience. If assent is based only on the personal superiority of the one in authority (because of his experience, knowledge, ability, character), then this is a case of personal authority. Such authority is not binding in conscience—it remains on the level of a counsel. If a given authority derives from legitimate juridical power which is essentially independent of the personal talents of the one possessing it (public authority), then its categorical ordinations within the limits of its own designated competency (commands, precepts, prohibitions) bind in conscience under pain of sin or punishment.

The ultimate foundation of all authority depends upon one's basic philosophy of life; thus authority has an essentially different meaning in individualistic, materialistic, scientific and theistic outlooks on human existence. The theist finds the ultimate reason for authority in the finiteness of human existence which, in all of its dimensions, ultimately points beyond its own limited self to a personal God, Creator and Lord. In this view, then, human authority is man's representative exercise of God's own authority and so it is fundamentally protected against human caprice and the egoistic drive for power. — Authority can be communicated by an express commission of God (e.g., the mission of the Church founded by Christ) or by the fact that man is naturally the member of certain societies and so is subject to the directing power flowing from the natures of these societies (family, state) or finally by the fact that a man freely places himself under some authority (by entering into any free organization). — Authority in the area of education is of a special kind. This authority arises out of the parent-child relationship and it is supplemented by the educational authority of state and church. It has the task of taking the place of the deficient intelligence and will-power of the child and adolescent until he reaches maturity. Therefore it is essentially a supplement to the child's developing reasoning powers until such time as the child can stand on his or her own; when that occurs, then this authority ceases. Thus the formal purpose of such authority is true adult independence and responsibility. Objectively the educational authority is ordered to help growing young men and women to fulfill in a balanced way all of their personal and social obligations with a sense of true responsibility to their fellow men and to God.

JSch-KB

AUTONOMY

Autonomy (Gr.: *autós* = self, and *nómos* =law). The will derives its motives for action from the whole of reality. Moral, religious and profane motives all have some influence on the particular act. *Autonomous* (independent) *morality* (Kant and others) tends to dissolve this connection and advocates a personal law in the field of ethics which in many ways leads not only to conceptual clarification but also to a real separation. The good alone or even one's *duty are supposed to be the only motives for moral action, since all other motives—transcendent as well as immanent: interest and inclination, advantage and disadvantage, reward and punishment, subjective happiness and objective common good, human and divine authority, in fact any relation to God including that of love—corrupt the "pure will."

In contrast to the many changing forms of ethical pragmatism which at their best preserve external propriety, autonomy rightly places the heart of *morality in the inner attitude. The limitations of this theory, however, become apparent even on the level of this-wordly considerations when it rejects all other earthly motives which might assist the principal moral motive (order, law, virtue); the reasoning seems to be that even though such auxiliary motives might render the practice of morality easier, still they do not contribute to the moral foundation of this activity. Since morality grows in accordance with its connection with ethical values, but does not always require the exclusion of all other motives, these motives cannot destroy the moral quality of an act as long as they are subordinate to the highest moral value.

The contrast between autonomy as a self-imposed law and heteronomy as a law imposed from without reaches a climax in the question regarding the other-worldly foundation and motivation of morality. Autonomous morality generally rejects the necessity of any transcendence, and in some cases even its possibility. The demand that morality be separated from religion is based on a completely secularistic outlook which has no understanding of the analogy of being with its similarity and difference between

God and man which is the result of creation. The existential distinction between creator and creature justifies and demands heteronomy: Man's freedom is inescapably tied to the order of being established by God. An autonomy which sees in morality not only a value independent of human caprice but also the ultimate, absolute value, forgets man's creaturehood and God's claim to lordship over this world. Religion actually relativizes morality by elevating it to a higher level. However, such heteronomy does not exclude a relative self-imposed law, since on the basis of analogy as a being-relationship the divine law objectively coincides with the laws of human nature; the moral will must accept that law in its own *conscience and, if it is to be binding on the person, the will must impose it on itself. — See also *Categorical Imperative*.

PB

B

BEAUTY

The Middle Ages offer us two significant attempts at capturing the nature of beauty. Thomas Aquinas defined beauty as that which gives pleasure when it is seen (*quae visa placent*); thus he approaches beauty from the experience of it. Albert the Great placed the foundation of beauty in the beautiful thing itself which is the source of the aesthetic experience; this he termed the splendor of the form (*splendor formae*). We will begin our discussion with the second formulation.

Form refers to the essence and thereby to the existential basis of things. The *transcendentals, however, express the content of existence: unity, truth, goodness. Now since beauty is the splendor of form, in the beautiful thing these qualities must shine forth with luster. This means: they must be perfect in themselves (not distorted), they must resound together harmoniously (not be disorganized or conflict with each other) and finally they must shine forth brilliantly in their perfection (not remain hidden and be accessible only through toilsome labor). Therefore, beauty is that form of perfection in which an existent perfectly expresses existence in accordance with its own proper form or idea and so arrives at its own ideal structure (of course there are many degrees of approximation).

The experience of seeing is man's primary response to the beautiful. Since the beautiful existent brilliantly shines forth in its perfectly expressed existence, nothing remains for the intellect to seek and the peace and tranquility of its perfect act of vision will continue throughout and beyond the anxiety and difficulty of discursive thinking. But out of the perfection of seeing and of the beautiful grows *pleasure* as an enchanting repose in the achieved perfection. In this repose the most intense desire experiences the satisfaction of an unspeakably beatifying possession as its supreme act; when caught up by the beautiful, a man gives himself in self-forgetfulness to that which is most perfect. Corresponding to the perfect self-revelation of existence in the beautiful existent is the perfect performance and cooperation of the powers of the soul; this is one of the highest states that a man can achieve.

From this point of view a number of things stand out, especially the demonism or magical spell of beauty. Its fascination can so bewitch a man that he will offer everything for it. He can forget that he sees and experiences in the beautiful perfection as contained in a representation, but that he does not yet live a perfect life and personally possess perfection. Often also a person fails to see the different levels at which beauty becomes constantly more luminous and profound. Since, as a being tied to the senses, man is beguiled by the full blossoming of his bodily powers, he pays scant attention to the blossoming of his spirit, even though it is only in the latter that the beauty of the body achieves its perfection. — If a man does not allow himself to be seduced by this demonism, then he will discover that beauty is a reflection of the transcendent world, of the absolute perfection of God and of his creative ideas. For this reason, the heart intoxicated with beauty rises from the tainted beauty of this earth to primordial beauty plain and simple. Here we touch on Plato's *eros* whose ascent he penetratingly develops in his *Symposium*. — Finally, it gradually becomes clear that perfect beauty in this earthly life can be a very risky thing, for it persists only for a fleeting moment. Whoever tries to cling to beauty alone must discover again and again that he cannot hold onto it. Therefore we note the profound sadness of certain kinds of art, for example the ancient Greek sculpture.

Is beauty a *transcendental? Its close relationship to unity, truth and goodness seems to say that it is. But then every existent would have to be beautiful. In actual fact every existent is beautiful to the extent that it is perfect in its existence. Since the existent, as long as it exists in any way at all, never lacks at least a certain trace of its own perfection and therefore a certain resplendence, it also always possesses at least an inchoative beauty. — If every existent is beautiful in the sense described, then beauty belongs above all to the spiritual existent because it possesses existence in the most perfect way. But is sensible clarity not an essential aspect of beauty? Sensible resplendence is indeed demanded by the beauty of bodily things; and it also offers us our first most thrilling experience of beauty. However, there is also a spiritual resplendence that makes us happy when we successfully arrive at an intuitive grasp of spiritual realities; this is especially true of someone gifted with spiritual insight.

A very important special kind of beauty is the *sublime*. That which shines forth possesses greatness, is essentially raised above the usual, has the imprint of the extraordinary, the transcendent; when it is related to us it appears to be super-human, astonishing, and often also as immeasureable, infinite. In addition to this there must also be a certain resplendence that is worthy of the sublime reality. Mixed with one's pleasure at this encounter is amazement, awe and frequently a certain fear.

The opposite of beautiful is *ugly*. Without detriment to that inchoative beauty that necessarily belongs to every existent, a given existent in its concrete realization can be in such basic conflict with the fundamental laws of existence and in particular with its own idea that everything in it is distorted and the distortion is clearly evident. We tend to respond to such ugliness with *abhorrence*. Nevertheless, something like an ugly human face can be so radiant with spiritual beauty that this spiritual dimension outweighs everything else. See also *Aesthetics*.

JBL

BECOMING

Becoming characterizes fundamentally all of us and everything around us in the world. It is for this reason that, from its infancy, philosophy has striven to understand becoming; in this quest the decisive question has been the relationship of becoming to *existence. At first, there seemed to be only two possible solutions: either existence absorbs becoming or becoming absorbs existence; and so either becoming or existence was declared to be appearance only. Both views confront each other in Parmenides and Heraclitus, although not in such an extreme form as has been thought for some time. In the course of history, becoming has time and again tried to get the upper hand. And to the extent that God has been acknowledged in this view, he has been the becoming God of Pantheism or the evolving God of contemporary thinking which has a strong historical orientation.

A true solution of the problem demands that both becoming and existence retain their full value. Nietzsche agrees with scholasticism on this basic principle. However, both views then immediately separate because Nietzsche identifies existence with becoming and so establishes an absolute contradiction at the center of everything, while scholasticism overcomes this contradiction which, if true, would tear everything to pieces. Nietzsche was not able to find any other answer; for, like the pre-Socratics, he saw becoming as something ultimate and inexplicable. But following Plato and Aristotle, scholasticism penetrated to the inner structure of becoming and saw that it is essentially reduced to ultimate principles that transcend the realm of change. Aristotle's great intellectual discovery was the insight that becoming is necessarily caused; on the basis of this insight he developed his doctrine of the four *causes and this doctrine was further refined later by the scholastics.

Philosophical analysis of this problem begins with becoming in the fullest sense, with the gradually progressing transition (e. g., the growth of a tree).

BECOMING

If we concentrate on a definite level of the process, then we find that a certain degree of perfection has already been achieved, while the further levels or stages are only striving for realization. From this perspective, becoming appears as something composed of already realized *act and a *potency still awaiting its realization. These are the intrinsic *causes or principles of the *existence of all becoming. These principles, however, enter into the process of becoming only through the influence of an extrinsic efficient cause; it is called "extrinsic," because it is not itself a constitutive part of the becoming process, but it must not lie outside of the thing changing or becoming. The tree is the most proximate efficient cause of its own growth. The efficient cause, in turn, depends for its activity on a further extrinsic cause, namely on the *end of the "wherefore" which attracts the efficient cause and in this way releases and directs its activity; thus the whole becoming process strives for this end (*Finality). The "end" is also called an extrinsic cause, because it is not itself a constitutive part of the becoming process but is superior to it as a perfection to be achieved; still it does not necessarily come from the outside, but it can be set before the becoming process by the changing thing itself, as the tree by reason of its en-tele-chy (i. e., by reason of the essential law impressed on it: *Form) unconsciously establishes for itself its own full development as its end.

As long as we consider only the changing thing itself as the agent and the goal-setter, then we have still not reached the ultimate reason for becoming; for, the changing thing itself as such is still a caused reality, and consequently its efficient causality ultimately depends on an uncangeable cause and its finality depends on an unchangeable final cause. So there must be something absolutely unchangeable over and above all becoming as its ultimate foundation; Aristotle called it the "unmoved mover" and scholasticism pushed it further and arrived at the notion of subsisting existence (God). This is both the first beginning and the last end of all becoming. The tension between the existential principles of act and potency leads to this subsisting existence insofar as the act, which has been received by the potency and limited by it, presupposes unlimited, subsisting act which is ultimately subsisting existence itself. Therefore, becoming as a transition from non-existence to existence is finally grounded in absolute existence.

Let us take a brief look at the different forms of becoming. Becoming as a change of qualities or of accidental acts while the substance remains the same, happens every day; in this case the substance supports the accidents as a passive, and often also as an active potency (*accidental change*). *Substantial change* (as that of an animal or of a tree) reaches still deeper into reality; here the change touches the substantial center itself, inasmuch as the material substratum (e. g., of food) is informed by the act of the soul. The most profound meaning of becoming is to be found in creation, where a being is produced out of nothing with no previous substratum. Creation — the most mysterious form of becoming — can only be brought about by divine omnipotence (*Creation) and the very concept remained hidden from Aristotle.

JBL

BEHAVIORISM

Behaviorism refers to a set of attitudes and assumptions which some psychologists consider essential to the scientific study of behavior. Since its introduction by John B. Watson in 1913, three phases of development have been identified by Sigmund Koch.

Classical behaviorism (1913-1930) defined psychology as a purely objective experimental branch of natural science which aims at the prediction and control of behavior. No dividing line between man and brute was recognized. The following guiding principles, although not uniformly interpreted, were generally emphasized:

1) The psychologist can dispense with consciousness and all experiential terms such as sensation, perception, image, and even thinking and emotion as they are traditionally defined. Introspection is of as little use in psychology as in physics or chemistry. Nonetheless "verbal reports" of experimental subjects may be admitted since speech reactions are observable.

2) The task of psychology is to explain all behavior in terms of stimulus and response. A stimulus is anything that causes behavior. It may range from a loud noise or muscle twitch to a complex social situation. Responses are observable reactions to effective stimuli. In any case they can be reduced to muscular or glandular activities.

3) All "mental" phenomena must be explained objectively in terms of conditioned responses. To a large extent the brain was bypassed in favor of peripheral receptors, connectors, and effectors. An emotion is not an inner experience but a bodily reaction to some specific stimulus. Thinking consists of implicit movements of the muscles of articulation. A child at play says everything he does. As he grows older these conversations with himself become less and less audible until he comes to believe that thinking is somehow different than other sensorimotor responses.

4) Human inheritance consists exclusively of physical traits. Such terms as instinct and temperament are meaningless. Watson went so far as to boast: "Give me a dozen healthy infants, well-formed, and my own specified world to bring them up in and I'll guarantee to take any one

at random and train him to become any type of specialist I might select...
regardless of his talents, penchants, tendencies, abilities, vocations, and
race of his ancestors."

5) Learning is the central process in psychology and all learning consists
of conditioned responses.

Neobehaviorism. In spite of its insistence upon objective methodology
in the gathering of data, classical behaviorism found itself increasingly
involved in speculation and debate. It possessed no set of guiding
principles equivalent to Newton's laws of motion to stitch together and
direct its research. In the period roughly bounded by the 1930's and the
1950's serious but unsuccessful attempts were made to construct broad
empirically based theories modeled upon physics. Logical positivism,
pragmatism, and operationalism were the guiding philosophies. While
the notions of stimulus and response were retained, "intervening variables" of the same general type were introduced between S and R in
an attempt to explain what goes on inside the organism.

Neo-neobehaviorism. In spite of B. F. Skinner's restatement of radical
behaviorism in modern dress, there is a growing trend for the movement
to lose its distinctive character. Under the impact of other theoretical
viewpoints and renewed interest in such areas as perception, thinking,
creativity, and value judgments, the original attitudes of behaviorism
have been modified to such an extent that they are scarcely recognizable.

FTS

BIOLOGISM

Biologism is the name for a type of thinking that looks at reality exclusively from the biological point of view. According to biologism, organic
life (*Organism) is either identical with all reality or it is at least the only
form of *life. While *mechanism sees only the material side of the
living thing and *vitalism tries to make up for this deficiency by adding
a directing principle of *life, biologism looks upon the living thing as an
unbroken unity. Biologism is distinguished from *life philosophy in
that the latter, generally speaking, emphasizes the value of life in contrast
to a purely mechanistic or conceptual view of reality, while the former
restricts life to plasmic life. Biologism should also be distinguished
from that organic view of the world which considers all reality to be
some kind of an organism, but at the same time attempts to explain
the world as the revelation or unfolding of spirit (or mind).

According to biologism, individual organisms are not the first bearers
of life, but only particularizations of an all-embracing life (*bios*), a life
that either can only exist as divided up among its individuals or is

understood as the primordial basis of everything living. In this second view inorganic matter is that which has separated itself from the life-process only for a time and death is the return of the individual into the living primordial basis. Supra-individual organic units (sexual differentiation, races, societies and so forth) do not arise from the purposeful cooperation of individuals, but they are the higher particularizations of the one all-embracing life. Man's *ego is only a transitory appearance of life or a way in which living plasma adapts itself to a certain level of differentiation. *Spirit is not a different, independent kind of thing. All consciousness necessarily depends on organic conditions and disappears when they disappear. — Epistemologically biologism is in the camp of *relativism and it is also close to *pragmatism. For, thinking and knowing do not open up an insight into the nature of reality — they only help to achieve biological adaptation. What a person thinks to be true is dependent on the hereditary and racially conditioned qualities of his brain. — The first principle of *biologistic ethics* is the self-assertion of plasmic life, not only in the individual but especially in the higher individuations: family, people and race. There is a place for some kind of *religion in biologism only where the various forms of life are seen in conjunction with the primordial basis of life.

Biologism is blind with regard to the special characteristics of vast areas of reality. It cannot stand up under either scientific or philosophical criticism. As a form of *relativism it abandons all claim to be true knowledge. It is materialistic, not just because it admits the validity only of what is measureable but also because it denies the existence of all spiritual reality. Moreover, it does not hesitate to interpret the external dependence of the human *spirit on sense knowledge in the sense of an intrinsic dependence of his existence itself on matter. See *Body-Soul Relation*.

WB

BLONDELIANISM

Blondelianism refers to the philosophical synthesis attemped by Maurice Blondel (1861-1949) in his principle work *L'Action* (1893). Blondel placed his philosophy of action within the framework of an historical development of moral philosophy beginning with Spinoza and carried on by Kant, Fichte, Schelling and Hegel. Blondel understood that development as a continual movement toward greater subjectivity. He felt there is only one legitimate philosophical method to deal with the subject: one must renounce the effort to make the subject only a content of consciousness and be content to seize it in its activities as subject. Consequently, Blondel proposed his counter-copernican revolution toward an even greater degree of subjectivity: instead of assuming that it is thought that determines action, let us assume that it is action that determines thought. The center of perspective of philosophy should be transposed from the analytical element of thought into the synthetic element of action.

Action, Blondel claimed, has its own a priori structure from which the whole of thought derives its meaning. What Blondel proposed was a study of *ideogenesis*, the derivation of thought from action, resulting in an understanding of the a priori structure implicit in the will, which in turn explains and founds the a priori structures in thought. This new center of perspective demands the acceptance of the methodological principle of immanence: nothing can impose itself on man as truth or value unless in some way it finds its source within man himself.

The central problem Blondel felt was left unanswered by his predecessors was the problem of the disjunction between abstract reflection and existential commitment. He hoped to overcome that disjunction by clarifying the reciprocal inclusion of reflection by commitment and commitment by reflection. By means of an original dialectical methodology Blondel sought to preserve the undeniable exigencies of freedom, subjectivity and existence within the context of a philosophy which recognizes objective and universal truths and values.

The basic distinction underlying Blondel's method is the distinction within thought itself between the plane of action or existence and the plane of thought or reflection. As act, thought participates in the spontaneity of the subject; it is commitment and freedom. As knowledge, thought reflects the given and ascertains its necessary relations. In the first step of his dialectic Blondel sought the pre-reflective unity of thought with existence in human action. He speaks of a direct, practical method of experimentation. At this stage the will element takes precedence over the intellectual element of thought. The criterion of certitude is to be found in the effect of action on the individual's self-consciousness, the feeling of congruity or incongruity which the object of choice has with his fundamental experience of himself. This feeling cannot be conscious until the will responds to a call from within self. In this manner freedom becomes interior to the very operation of thought itself.

This initial pre-reflective unity in man must pass through the disjunction of thought and existence in order to achieve the post-reflective unity of rational free commitment. Thus, in the second stage of the dialectic on the plane of reflection intellect takes precedence over will. The method here is one of total doubt; no moral postulate or intellectual given can be accepted a priori. One starts with the problem of human action: What must a man think or do in order to achieve self-fulfillment? A type of phenomenological reduction is employed, which consists in eliminating provisionally from the field of reflection the synthetic activity of the subject. Blondel searches out all possible escapes from structure in freedom with the methodological assumption that the only means of proving necessity is to prove impossibility. The criterion of judgment here is the rational consistency between the objective essence of the action proposed and an objective concept of human nature. At this stage Blondel attempts to show how human action cannot reach its goal of self-fulfillment without the entire rational order appearing step by step as its immanent law. Reflective thought's organic role in the dialectic of life is to lead man to place the ideal goals of his action not in what 'is' but in what 'ought-to-be', by projecting out the law immanent in his will as a conscious goal to be freely pursued.

At this stage Blondel makes use of a form of transcendental reflection, beginning with the given in consciousness and searching out its conditions of possibility. The analysis moves from objective positional will (volonté voulue) to the necessary subjective conditions of will-act (volonté voulante). This phenomenology of will follows approximately the same steps as did Hegel in *Phenomenology of the Spirit*, starting from the *syn-ergie* of the human will with the forces of nature, passing through its *co-ergie* in social life to its final expansion in the *thé-ergie* of religious life.

Option or rational commitment is the final synthetic stage of Blondel's method. At this point free affirmation appears legitimately within the field of reflection. Option represents the necessary juncture in thought between the two planes of affirmation and reflection. The free assent, which until now supported the dialectic from without is reflected from within; reflective thought returns on the reality of its own synthetic activity. The two previous criteria of certitude are fused here. Experiential criteria, however, take precedence over the rational, using them as directives but finding ultimate certitude in the immediate experience of fulfillment or privation consequent on commitment.

An option or self-transcendence reveals itself in Blondel's philosophy as the final necessary condition for man's self-fulfillment. The necessity for this option is established when man becomes aware of those commitments which remain simultaneously necessary and impossible. As necessary they represent a potential immanent aspect of man's existential reality. Insofar as they remain impossible for man to realize by his own unaided freedom they indicate a potentiality within man which transcends man himself. The projecting out of these "unused and unusable potentialities" of the human will is, Blondel contends, the genetic source of our idea of God as the immanent-transcendent.

Blondel maintained that the dialectic of action does not come to an end with the rational justification of option for self-transcendence on the level of reflection. Philosophy is capable of showing the necessity of a final option and clarifying its terms, but it cannot supply for option itself.

BODY

Philosophy is necessarily false precisely when it tries to enclose life within reflective thought. Only a philosophy of action permits one to reflect the totality of existence without refusing to acknowledge the reciprocal transcendence of existence over thought. Free commitment, then, has the last word, and philosophy must give way to a new dialectic of religious commitment and theological reflection based in the immediate certitude of the experience of religious faith as a response to revelation.

Despite an onset of blindness Blondel dictated ten major volumes between 1924-49 including his famous trilogy, *L'Action, La Pensée, L'Etre et les êtres*. This final synthesis of his thought remains largely unexplored to date. Blondel had an important influence on the members of the French École d'Esprit such as La Senne and Nedoncelle. Through his disciple Valensin and others he provided the philosopical background for Teilhard de Chardin's thought. But his major influence was on Catholic theologians such as Dumery, Daniélou and DeLubac who used Blondel's philosophy as a tool for a reform of apologetics, moral and dogmatic theology. Through these men Blondel's thought became one of the primary sources for the reforms proposed by the second Vatican Council.

JJM

BODY

The sensibly perceptible things that surround us are called "bodies." The common traits of all bodies are extension (*Quantity) and the filling of a definite *space. While extension concerns the disposition of the parts of a body in reference to each other, *impenetrability* has to do with the exclusion of other bodies from the space occupied by the first body. It is based on powers of repulsion. A *compenetration* of bodies would mean that several bodies occupy the same space. Naturally speaking, this is impossible, although it does not imply any inner contradiction. There is no compenetration (in the philosophical sense) in a chemical *solution* or in the mixture of different gases.

The problem about the existence of a world of bodies that are independent of human consciousness is treated in epistemology or the *theory of *knowledge*. The objective existence of such a world is affirmed by *realism and denied by *idealism and *phenomenalism. The question about the essence of bodies is one of the principal concerns of the *philosophy of *nature*. Its chief task is to clarify whether or not sensible appearance or, more precisely, extension and impenetrability belong to the essence of a body. According to Descartes, the essence of a body consists in extension itself. According to the scholastic view, it is just the necessary orientation of a body to extension and actual impenetrability that belongs to the essence of a body, not actual extension and impenetrability themselves.

Further questions about the essence of body concern the relationship of its parts to each other and to the whole (*Divisibility): Does the whole arise out of the combination of the parts that are not further divisible (thus *Atomism)? or is the whole before the parts which are themselves always further divisible? Are the parts already separate in space by reason of their essence or only as the result of mutual influence (*Dynamism)? — Both the question of unity-in-duality that arises from the divisibility of bodies as well as the problem of *change lead to a more profound question: Does the essence of a body proceed from one or several fundamental principles? In answer, *hylemorphism teaches that bodies are composed of *prime matter and the essential *form.

Very special questions about the essence of bodies arise out of what modern physical science has to say about bodies. For, modern science says that the whole corporeal world is built up out of 92 *elements*. From the philosophical point of view, an element is a basic unit of matter that cannot be further divided into qualitatively different units of matter. But by saying this we still do not know whether or not we have arrived at the elements of a body. For, in their particular characteristics the chemical elements manifest a multiplicity of relationships that make possible a systematic ordering of them in the so-called Periodic Table. The ultimate parts into which an element can be divided without destroying its essence are called atoms (*Atomism). By combining several elements together there arise *chemical compounds*. The basic building-block of such a compound is the *molecule* to which several atoms are joined through their chemical properties. In contrast to the compound there is also the *aggregate* which is a loose combination of several bodies that does not result in some new thing. — It is in this context that the question about the difference between bodies must be posed. The difference is both *numerical* and *specific*. Numerical difference means that there is a multiplicity of bodies; thus, the cosmos is not just one massive body, as *monism teaches. A specific difference (in the sense of physical science) is to be assumed to exist between different chemical substances, whether they are elements or compounds. To be sure, elements and compounds are ultimately composed of the same basic parts: protons, neutrons, electrons, etc. They are brought together in different ways (which are only accidentally different) to form a whole, but they still produce material substances that can rightly be called specifically different. However, the difference between living and non-living bodies is essential, so that the gap cannot be bridged by any accidental *change (*Vitalism). A further question which has been posed by the physical sciences concerns the relationship (identity or difference) between mass and energy.

While physical science and the philosophy of nature are concerned with bodies which occur in nature as real things, mathematics deals with bodies as abstract images. Thus, the *geometric* body abstracts from all corporeal properties with the exception of three- (or more-) dimensional extension. By an *algebraic* body is understood a set whose elements constitute a closed whole in such a way that every combination of several elements by way of mental computations produces an element that belongs to the same set (e. g., the set of rational numbers).

NJ

BODY, LIVING

A living body is the body of men and animals. Simply as a *body it is a part of the material cosmos, but as a "living" body it manifests the subordination of the laws of inorganic, chemical processes to the laws of organic life. — The human body in relation to the *soul of a *man in many ways is the foundation, field of expression and the special object of a man's experience. "Foundation": The entire activity of the sensible soul is interiorly so tied to corporeal events that together with these it constitutes the "one" animal activity and the soul cannot exist without it. Indirectly, through its relationship to sense life, even man's spiritual life is in many ways dependent on the body. In particular, one should remember the importance of the brain and nerves, blood structure and inner secretion (hormones), as well as heredity, for spiritual experience and activity. — "Field of expression": Many spiritual experiences do not achieve full development even interiorly, if they cannot express themselves in some kind of corporeal activity. A person's appearance, physiognomy, posture, gait and coordination often make known the individuality and rhythm of his mental activity. Social contact from soul to soul occurs through some kind of corporeal action (*Language). — United with the soul, the body forms the first and most important material "object of experience" for the soul; as such it can either further or restrict spiritual life.

Through its union with the spiritual soul and because of its great importance to the soul, the human body merits a special dignity. Most men are spontaneously aware of this dignity and they show it in their natural abhorrence of the degradation of the body (*modesty*). Each person has a moral responsibility towards his own body; this imposes upon him the obligation to care for his body by nourishing and protecting it. In a very special way he has the obligation to strive for a proper ordering and subordination of his bodily powers. This includes, among other things, temperance (*Cardinal Virtues) and *chastity* (that is, a reasonable ordering of one's sexual life; its misuse = *unchastity, lewdness*). Man

41

does not have the right of disposal over the substance of his body (*Suicide). Guidance in the proper evaluation of the body is one of the most important tasks in the formation of true humanity.

AW

BODY-SOUL RELATION

The body-soul relation has confronted philosophers from time immemorial with a series of difficult questions. This relationship is partially open to empirical experience and it is partially known as the result of a philosophical inquiry into the connection between the animated body and the spiritual soul that animates and directs the body. — The living body reveals itself to empirical observation as the special object, as the foundation, and as the field of expression of spiritual experience (*Body, Living). — Metaphysical theories about the body and the soul tend to stress one-sidedly either the unity of human existence (*Monism), or the duality and opposition between the two (pure *Dualism), or they attempt to do justice both to the experienced unity and duality in man (Duo-Monism).

Materialistic monism recognizes only the reality of the material and denies the existence of the immaterial soul (*Materialism, *Soul). Spiritual monism sees the body as only an external appearance of the one, spiritual reality (*Spiritualism). Modern *psycho-physical parallelism* or the *theory of identity* looks upon soul and body as two aspects or appearance-modes of a unique reality that is unknowable in itself. It logically asserts and must presuppose that bodily and spiritual events (experiences) are coordinated with each other in a strictly parallel fashion (G. Th. Fechner and the monism popular towards the end of the 19th century). In all of its forms monism runs contrary to the evident reality and the essential opposition between the material world and the world of spirit (i. e., the *life principle, all conscious life and especially spiritual existence). It does not explain how it is that matter "appears" as spirit and spirit as matter. But the presupposition of an absolute parallelism between spiritual experiences and material events is contradicted by the two facts that mental life proceeds without the inner cooperation of matter and the unconscious world is operative without conscious awareness of it.

Pure dualism in its most extreme form (Malebranche, Leibnitz), which was prepared for by Descartes' too absolute separation of the soul (*res cogitans*) from the body (*res extensa*), denies all mutual influence between the soul and the body; and then it interprets the facts which obviously point to some kind of a mutual relationship in the sense that from the very beginning the creator so coordinated bodily and spiritual events that they are ordered to each other in a *preestablished harmony* (*harmonia* *prestabilita*) without any reciprocal influence. This opinion, which today has only historical interest, too obviously contradicted man's entire experience of himself. It especially contradicted man's awareness of his own responsibility for his bodily actions and it explained in a very unscientific way by turning immediately to God, the first cause, that which first of all demands a natural explanation. The dualism of the *theory of mutual causality* (Plato and many modern neo-vitalists such as Becher) is closer to nature. They look upon the body and the soul as two complete substances which influence each other through accidental causality. (Think, for example, of the old image of the soul as the captain of the ship, or even as a prisoner in the prison of the body). The modern proponents of this view were able to answer the objections which, through an appeal to the law of the conservation of energy, were raised against all forms of dualism. However, this theory of mutual causality has too little correspondence to the real unity of the organic, living thing (it is not the entelechy alone nor the matter alone that "lives," but life is the mode of existence of an indivisible one—the living being) (*Life Principle).

Duo-monism, which is the theory of *hylemorphism that comes from Aristotle, considers the body and the soul as two "incomplete substances" from the viewpoint of their substantial existence. These two do not work upon each other in accidental, particular acts, but are joined together in their substantial existence to form the totality of the one, living, complete substance. This latter substance is the bearer of the life activity. Thus, the soul is the determining, forming principle (the *form of life*) which elevates the other partial substance, the material principle, to participation in the living existence of the whole. According to a later, more moderate view of hylemorphism, this material principle preserves its own material existence with its physical-chemical determinations, and the informing soul gives only the specific living existence. However, perhaps according to Aristotle himself, and certainly according to Thomas Aquinas and other representatives of a stricter hylemorphism, in addition to the form (the soul) there is only a purely passive principle (prime matter), which lacks all determination and all existence, and which is raised only through the form to participation in existence and in being alive. Both of these scholastic views appeal to metaphysical and empirical considerations, but here we will not go into the differences within the school. At least in its milder form hylemorphism, by excluding the extreme forms of dualism and monism, is the only explanation that does justice both to the unity and the duality in human existence, even though it also labors under certain obscurities (not contradictions!).

A special problem that Aristotle gave no clear answer to and for which Thomas Aquinas first clearly worked out a satisfying formula is this: How can the spiritual soul be so closely united to the body in a substantial unity? There are not two souls in man — a vital soul and a spiritual soul separate from the body (today frequently designated as *Pneuma* by a theologically false use of St. Paul); nor is the situation such that the spiritual soul has subordinate parts by means of which it animates the body (so J. P. Olivi). Rather, the one, simple, spiritual soul is at the same time the vital soul, while it performs its spiritual activities wholly on its own. — From the *substantial unity* of soul and body (in spite of their essential difference) we can arrive at a metaphysical understanding of empirically known facts, namely, that on the one hand even man's spiritual activity is co-conditioned by material existence (cosmic influences, heredity, sickness) and on the other hand spiritual experience instinctively seeks to express itself in the body (*Body, Living). The wholeness of human existence, which has recently been again emphasized by modern, empirical *anthropology, thus finds in duo-monism its metaphysical foundation.

AW

BUDDHISM

Buddhism, which took its origin from the preaching of Gautama Buddha (died ca. 480 B. C.), was originally an Indian sect of Brahmanism. Since the teaching of Buddha himself cannot be fixed certainly in all of its detail, we will first of all describe Buddhism in the oldest form known to us. Buddhism is a doctrine of salvation. A presupposition of this doctrine is the theory of the *transmigration of souls. Fundamental to the whole system are the *"four noble truths"*: 1. Man's entire life is *suffering* because all things are transitory. Within the horizon of our knowledge there is no solid foundation, no substance — everything is becoming: there is no soul and no personal self beyond the constant change of internal attitudes. Reincarnation does not consist in the return of the same earthly personality, but in a strictly causal connection that is no less operative from one form of existence to another than it is from one state to another in the life of some existent. — Although the Buddha wished to make no statement about the subject of salvation, still he does make it clear that the basis of reality is to be found in the unchangeable, supra-individual and therefore incomprehensible Self. — 2. The source of suffering is craving or sensible desire. This doctrine of suffering is minutely built up on the theory of causal nexus which has twelve divisions. Age and death presuppose birth. But there is birth only if there is becoming. Becoming, in turn, is conditioned by the apprehension of something. For, without the apprehension of the sensible world a life leading to a rebirth would have been impossible. But apprehension occurs on the basis of craving or sensible desire which feeds itself by means of perception. Perception is caused by the contact of the senses with things. The senses presuppose the soul and the body ("name and form"). Body and soul are constituted when the consciousness of the coming man enters into the mother. The new consciousness is the continuation of the mental states of a former consciousness. But these states are caused by the ignorance of that which the Buddha characterized as the saving truth (the fourfold truth). Therefore, one must remove this ignorance. If that occurs, then the mediate cause and the final effect (i. e., suffering) are also removed. 3. The cessation of suffering results from the complete eradication of sensible desire. A merely partial eradication leads either to a heavenly existence or only to a particular earthly existence from which the ultimate goal, *nirvana*, can be reached. Yet this state can take over even before death if the flame of sensible desire is completely extinguished. Nirvana is not nothingness, but a state of being completely freed from everything transitory and painful. One cannot say what it is beyond this negative description, because it surpasses all experience and all concepts which are themselves transitory. Imaginary descriptions, which have attempted to make the doctrine suitable to a larger audience, have often given the impression that nirvana is a state resembling paradise. 4. The way to this end is the *noble eightfold path*. In general, this path contains the same requirements as *yoga. At the head of the ethical demands, which are not sought for themselves but are the means of eliminating obstacles from the way of spiritual ascent, stands the concern for every living thing which is shown in deeds, words and thoughts.

In the course of history Buddhism was further developed and embellished. While in *southern Buddhism* (Hīnayāna = Lesser Vehicle) this development consisted more in a systematic rounding off of the old Buddhistic image of the world, in *Northern Buddhism* (Mahāyāna = Greater Vehicle) it took a direction that in some respects greatly differed from the old Buddhism. Out of the respect for the historical Buddha grew a loving respect for the divina Buddha or for a multiplicity of divine Buddhas which are now, purely spiritual; finally, these Buddhas, going back to a primordial Buddha, resulted in a form of panentheism. While in the old Buddhism only the monk could attain nirvana through his training, the new form, through love and generosity, also gives to the laity the possibility of attaining perfection. But in the Mahāyāna this no longer consists in a state of holiness, but in expectation of Buddhahood in order to contribute, in the course of innumerable rebirths, to the salvation of all mankind. — The theory of knowing of the Hīnayāna is realistic, while that of the Mahāyāna is idealistic. Another variation of the Mahāyāna Buddhism is the *magical Buddhism* of the so-called *Diamond Vehicle*. — See also *Suffering*.

WB

C

CAPITAL PUNISHMENT

The problem of capital punishment is whether or not the state's punitive power over lawbreakers and violators of the common good includes the right to take their lives. There were a few opponents of capital punishment in Christian antiquity and also in the Middle Ages. But it was not until the 18th century that it was seriously challenged theoretically by Beccaria as the result of the killing of an innocent person; later, under the influence of humanitarian movements and the reform of brutal penal laws, as well as for philosophical reasons, it was not only opposed but also abolished in many European countries or at least not carried out. However, there is no doubt about the liceity of capital punishment in itself. It is justified when in common estimation it is the only means of securing public order effectively and without too great expense, and when at the same time the criminal justly merits total exclusion from the goods of society. Just retribution and atonement, therefore, are not the only foundation of capital punishment — a foundation independent of securing the common good. Capital punishment does not contradict the precept of the moral law: Thou shalt not kill. For, the meaning of the precept is that unjustified killing is forbidden. The creator and lord of life can and must confer on state authority the right to exact capital punishment under the above-mentioned conditions, but only insofar as, without it, the necessary ends of the state cannot be adequately attained. A man does not possess an unlimited right to improve himself and his own personal lot at the expense of the common good. However, as a rule capital punishment should not be applied in a case of circumstantial evidence, and it should be carried out only when very serious crimes have been committed or in a situation of general disorder (e. g., a state of siege; impending revolution). Pardons in particular cases are allowable; however, a universal pardon for all as a matter of principle, especially in dangerous times, could not be reconciled with the necessary protection and fostering of the common good.

JS

CARDINAL VIRTUES

Cardinal Virtues or "hinge" virtues (*cardo* = hinge) are called such because the whole moral life revolves and hangs on them just as a door swings on its hinges. They are also called the *fundamental virtues*, since they are the necessary presupposition for all the other virtues. Since they are ordered to that which is morally the most important and the most difficult, they are also designated the *primary virtues*; the other virtues are related to them as *subordinate virtues* that are in some way dependent on them. — From antiquity the number of the cardinal virtues has been four: prudence, justice, fortitude, temperance.

[*Justice* as a virtue is the firm and constant will to render to each person that which belongs to him by *right. Related to justice are *religiosity* or the will to worship God (*Religion), *piety* (*Family) or the will to respect one's parents and one's country, *obedience* (*Authority) or the will to show respect for legitimate superiors and to follow their directions in the proper things, and *gratitude* or the will to recognize good things done for us by others and to return good when the opportunity presents itself.]

WB

Prudence is the virtue that enables the reason to consider the means to the end (God), to judge and to decide what is the reasonable thing to do, both in general and for each particular case. The virtue of prudence is to be distinguished from a sharp business sense, for the latter can also function immorally. Prudence is a virtue of the intellect (*Virtue) and as such it does not itself posit the moral action. However, since it demands right order in willing and acting, it is a moral virtue. Prudence directs the will, but in a sense it is still dependent on the will for its full influence. For, if the will is not generally well affected towards the morally good, then in accordance with its own inclination it will reject the judgment of the intellect. There are two kinds of prudence: prudence in the direction of oneself and prudence in the direction of others. The following are closely connected with prudence: deliberation or skill in finding the proper means to the end; insight or dexterity in deciding clearly and definitely in normal situations; a higher sense of judgment, that is, the ability to find the right thing to do in difficult circumstances.

Fortitude consists in the readiness to expose oneself to dangers in a way that is reasonable, that is, for the sake of some higher good, to suffer evil, and even not to shrink from death (*heroism*). It overcomes *fear* which pulls back from a threatening evil, and curbs *boldness* which courts danger and death. It controls grief and prefers virtue to biological life. It is active in aggressiveness and perseverance. The auxiliary virtues

47

of courage are: *patience*, which is constancy in the midst of suffering; *bravery*, which is action and determination when one is on the offensive. Related to these are: *confidence*, which is a justified trust in oneself in the midst of danger; *generosity*, which is the willingness to sacrifice one's own possessions for a noble cause; *steadfastness*, which is constancy in the face of external difficulties; *persistence*, which is steadiness in the face of inner resistance.

Temperance perfects sense desire by keeping the search for sense pleasure within the bounds of reason. Sensible pleasure, which is connected with a number of activities, is not in itself objectionable; rather, it serves to move men to perform actions that are necessary for the preservation of the individual and of the species. Therefore, it should be sought in reasonable moderation. The different forms of temperance are: *moderation* in the use of food, *sobriety* in the matter of drink, *chastity* with regard to sex. The auxiliary virtues are: propriety and a sense of honor. Related to these are: *self-denial* or *self-control* which is the will not to allow oneself to be drawn away from the good even in the midst of the strongest temptations; *gentleness*, which is the will to control anger; *modesty*, which regulates external behavior.

Temperance and fortitude agree in this, that both avoid the opposite faults and hold to a middle course, as prudence prescribes it for them. See also *Virtue, Justice*.

JS-WB

CARTESIANISM

Cartesianism is the philosophy of the French thinker, René Descartes (Cartesius), 1596-1650. He was a pioneer in the area of epistemology, since by means of his "methodical doubt" he placed every fact and truth in doubt except the one proposition, *"Cogito ergo sum"* (I think, therefore I am). Proceeding on the basis of this one principle (whose precise meaning is still debated), Descartes then attempts to build up again the whole world by means of a criterion that flows from his principle: namely, that clear and distinct ideas cannot be false. Thus, he says, we know our soul as an immaterial substance whose essence it is to think; further, we know the existence of God from a consideration of the concept of God which clearly and distinctly includes existence (he gives two other proofs for the existence of God that are less characteristic of his philosophy); finally, we know the existence of the external world which is guaranteed for us by the truthfulness of God who cannot allow that our natural drive to affirm the existence of the material world is a mere deception. — In his anthropology Descartes does not take into consideration the mutual relationship between the soul and the body; for, he maintains that thinking is the essence of the soul, whereas mere extension is the essence of body, so that local motion is its only activity. Consequently, there is no more inner unity between the soul and the body; the soul dwells in the body as in a machine or automaton. The body is kept alive by the "bodily heat" which is situated in the heart, while the soul is localized in the pineal gland. Since there is no mutual influence between the soul and the body, the soul does not receive its concepts from the world of sense; however, the soul does have "innate" ideas in the sense that she produces them out of herself and in this process the external experience constitutes only an occasion.

As a result of his theory of knowledge Descartes became the father of modern subjectivistic criticism of knowledge; his *occasionalism found a more radical expression in the thought of Malebranche (*Ontologism); his rationalistic method was further developed by Spinoza and Leibniz, and above all his mechanistic view of nature strongly influenced the modern concept of the world; the modern world view, however, in recent years has added to Descartes' "motion" the idea of *energy*, which resides in or even constitutes things, as a second dynamic element. — Criticism: Descartes' criterion of truth is insufficient; moreover, the existence of God can in no way be established by means of it. His natural philosophy is too simple and it does not correspond to reality that reveals different natures and powers in bodies in addition to their extension. It is even more difficult for this dualism to explain the mutual relationship between soul and body (*Body-soul Relation); for, the living being as such and the problems peculiar to it are not accounted for.

MR

CATEGORICAL ARGUMENTS

Categorical arguments are *inferences which consist only of *categorical* judgments, that is, of judgments which directly express something about an object, not just about the connections between statements. The most simple form of the categorical argument is the syllogism, consisting of two premises and a conclusion. That the subject and predicate of the conclusion belong together is deduced from this, that both the subject (S) and the predicate (P) are identical in one common *middle term* (M). This identity is expressed in the major and minor premises, as is shown in the figure:

$$M - P$$
$$S - M$$
$$\overline{S - P}$$

If one of the two *outer concepts* (S or P) is identical with M but the other is not, then one concludes: S is not P; if none is identical with M, then nothing follows. The rules for the logical consistency of categorical arguments follow from the nature of the argument. The most important of them are: 1. The middle term must be used at least once in a universal sense (*Concept). 2. The extension of the subject and predicate in the conclusion must not be greater than it was in the premises; in this case it is also to be noted that a denied concept has infinite extension. — Depending on the different position of the middle term there results the different *figures* of the syllogism; depending on the different arrangement of the quantity and quality of the propositions (signified by the letters A = universal affirmative, E = universal negative, I = particular affirmative, O = particular negative) there results the different *modes* or ways of concluding. — See also *Logic*.

WB

CATEGORICAL IMPERATIVE

In contrast to all relative values of life, according to Kant the only absolute value for man is the morally *good will* which binds itself to the moral law without any reservations. This law establishes no "hypothetical imperatives" (demands) in the conscience as is the case with means and ends (If you want to be a scholar you must study), but it recognizes only the categorical (unconditioned) imperative: "You ought." What is always and everywhere morally good cannot be deduced a posteriori from experience but must be determined a priori by a universally valid principle. Kant formulates his principle thus: "Always act in such a way that the maxims of your will could function as the basis of a universal law of action" (*Critique of Practical Reason*, no. 7). Therefore, the moral quality of an act is known by this formality, viz., that it fundamentally can and should be posited by all men. Morality does not exceed *legality* when the act is in accordance with the categorical imperative, but its motivation is heteronomous instead of autonomous. When the heteronomy of worldly and transcendental motives is removed from the self-imposed law in the area of morals, then in this transition from heteronomy to *autonomy legality becomes true *morality*. The good will is always the *pure will* which as the norm and motive of its actions heeds neither its own advantage nor its inclinations, but only the moral law.

It is to Kant's credit that he pointed out once again most emphatically the special nature of moral phenomena. Thus he stressed that *duty has an absolute character: that the advantage or disadvantage of a particular act does not determine its moral quality, that the interior motive has a certain priority over the external act, that the development of a strong moral character is closely tied to struggle and sacrifice. — However, the limitations of his theory appear as soon as he introduces the ideas of formalism and autonomy into his explanation. His categorical imperative separates the "ought" of morality from the objective order of being. And the universally valid norms of human action can only be determined by an objective evaluation of the goals and needs of human existence. The absolute character of morality excludes the validity neither of this-worldly relative goals nor the ultimate other-worldly goal of man; rather, it supplies the ordering of all perspectives that leads to a unified whole and relates them to the final end. Thus, when morality is based on the order of being, the radical separation between autonomy and heteronomy as the basis of human motivation cannot be maintained, but what morality does need is a criterion for the priority of various motives.

PB

CATEGORIES

The word itself is derived from the Gr. "*kategorein*" which has the meaning of "predicate." Thus, the categories signify the different ways of predicating something and so, since existence is always expressed in some way, the different modes of existence. The exact same meaning is found in the Lat. "*praedicamenta*" which comes from the verb "*prae-dicare*" (assert). Even this verbal explanation shows that the categories are closely connected with judgment, for it is in judgment that predication takes place; that was firmly established by Kant, following in the footsteps of Aristotle and the scholastics.

In judgment we encounter a bewildering complexity of predicates and modes of existence (e. g., man, mortal, green, large, running, etc.). If we try to put some order into all of these, then many of them can be reduced to others. Thus we find *subgeneric concepts* which have less extension but more comprehension, which are the lower divisions of *generic concepts* that have greater extension but less comprehension. For example, "man" is a subgenus of "sentient being" which includes not only rational animals but also all beings with sense powers, including those without reason. This process leads to the primary genera which are not subordinate to any higher unity and therefore are called *primary* or *fundamental concepts*. They constitute the basic multiplicity of the categories or the supreme genera. Above the categories there stands only *existence, which is not itself a genus; the categories participate in existence as the primordial *modes* of *existence*. In addition to the categories, the *transcendentals are also primary determinations (modes) of existence; the categories are also called particular determinations because they are the bases of the different classifications and affirm that which is peculiar to each classification, while the transcendentals are called common determinations because they apply to all the classifications. Existence and the transcendentals are called "supra-categorical" because they apply to all the categories. The categories themselves, however, with all of their subordinate genera and species constitute the realm of *categorical* (predicamental) concepts. The various levels within this realm are also called the *metaphysical grades*, since they are grasped by an insight into things that goes beyond the physical appearances. For the category of substance the so-called *Porphyrian tree* (*arbor Porphyriana*), which was first worked out by the Neo-Platonist, Porphyry, presents the hierarchy of these grades in a schematic form.

The establishment of a complete table of categories has always been a concern of philosophers. Aristotle enumerated ten of them; for him, *substance stands over against the nine classifications of *accident. He also added various characteristics which are common to all or several of the categories; later they were called *postpredicamenta* (e.g., opposition, earlier, later, simultaneously, motion, having). This catalogue of the categories was accepted by the scholastics and is still exercising its influence. Thomas Aquinas tried to establish the inner necessity of these categories. Kant made a new attempt in this area; he took from a table of judgments twelve categories and tried to show in his transcendental analysis that they are necessary and complete. Fichte thought that this was insufficient and so he worked out a new deduction from the activities of spirit. Hegel's *Logik* is the most complete attempt at such a deduction although he did great violence to the evidence. After Hegel a number of important contributions to the understanding of this question were made. Nevertheless, the final solution has still not been found. In recent decades *existential philosophy has emphasized the difference between the category of the merely given (*das Vorhandensein*) and the existentials of human existence (*Existenzialien*).

With regard to the value of the categories, each philosopher's position is determined primarily by what he holds concerning the *universal concepts. Conceptualism is opposed to the ultra-realism of the Platonists. Kant's transcendental idealism is related to the Platonic view, for he sees the category as having value only for the things as an appearance but not for the thing as it is in itself. Moderate realism is the view of the Aristotelian-scholastic tradition.

JBL

CAUSALITY

Causality means the influx of a *cause on its effect and also the relation that comes into existence as the result of this activity. Usually what is meant is the relationship established through the operation of an efficient cause; this is particularly brought out when one contrasts the causality of a final cause as compared with an efficient cause. Causality can also mean the formulated regularity with which an effect depends upon its cause (*Principle of *Causality*) or the cause brings forth its effect (*Law of *Causality*).

*Natural causality is the special kind of active relationships that exist in visible nature. By *psychic* causality is understood the causal influx of mental powers and mental occurrences. A very different kind of causal connection exists between the following pairs, each having its own peculiar difficulties: between knowing and willing, between sensible and spiritual activities, between single acts and acquired habits, between images produced by the laws of association and those produced by logical connection, between the conscious and the unconscious levels, between the unconscious processes in relation to each other, between the soul and the body. The image of mechanical efficient causality as it is described in physical science cannot do justice to psychic causality. For, in a unique way the spiritual soul possesses an original, inherent active power which cannot be explained on the basis of material causes alone. See also *Mutual Causality*.

VN

CAUSALITY, LAW OF

This is the name given to the application of the *principle of *causality* to events in the irrational world and especially in inanimate nature. It is the most fundamental principle of the exact physical sciences and is formulated as follows: "If all the elements involved in a natural event are determined at one definite moment, then thereby its future course is also determined," or more succinctly: "Similar causes have similar effects." The law of causality means that an occurrence in the irrational world takes place with necessary conformity to the law (*Natural Causality). This signifies the *regularity of nature* (uniformity, constancy). From a philosophical viewpoint, the law of causality expresses a real relationship between the cause and the effect. In contrast, the purely physical grasp of causality is limited, by reason of the scientific method used to arrive at it, to a temporal sequence of events which is regular and observable by the senses. If this diluted concept of causality, based on temporal succession, is accepted in place of the real dependence of the event on its cause, then because of the basically imperfect observability of events in the microphysical world the door is open for the positivistic denial of the law of causality in the atomic and sub-atomic world. (*Quantum Mechanics, *Induction, *Natural Law).

NJ

CAUSALITY, PRINCIPLE OF

The metaphysical principle of causality is one of the most important of the principles of *knowledge; and it is absolutely necessary for a valid proof of the existence of *God. — With regard to the formulation of the principle: the formula "no effect without a cause" is unsuitable because it is tautological. Also, the expression, "Everything that begins to exist must have a cause," is useless because the temporal beginning of many things — the cosmos, for example — is hardly demonstrable with any degree of certainty according to the methods of the experimental sciences. Therefore, a preferable formula for this reality is: "Every contingent existent has a cause" (*Contingency). Here "existent" is understood as something actually existing; "has a cause" means more exactly: produced or brought into existence by the operation of an efficient cause (*Cause). The formula also means that an existent that is essentially indifferent to existence and non-existence is a dependent existent; that it owes its existence to the activity of another—namely, of a cause; that, therefore, it is "made." A cause can only be considered a *sufficient* cause if it is at least of equal perfection of existence as the effect it is supposed to explain.

The validity of the principle of causality follows a priori from the essential concept of the contingent and the caused. A contingent essence of itself says only the possibility (*Potency) of existence, but not the reality (the *Act) of existence; thus, *of itself* it is completely incapable of contributing anything whatever to its own actualization and therefore is referred to the help of another which, for its own part, actually exists independently of this contingent existent and which, by its activity, is the cause of the existence of the contingent. — With regard to the logical character of the principle of causality, the question has been much discussed whether or not it is an "analytic" or a "synthetic" principle (*Knowledge, Principles of). The proponents of its analytic nature are often only saying that it rests on an a priori insight which follows from a comparison of the concepts and therefore that it affirms an unconditioned essential necessity; actually, both views are correct. However, if only those judgements are to be called analytic in which the predicate represents an aspect that is already included in the concepts of the subject, then the principle of causality cannot properly be called analytic, since "to be actually caused" is not necessarily included in the concept of the contingent existent; in this sense, therefore, the principle of causality is a "synthetic a priori" principle. Thus, also, it cannot be reduced to the principle of contradiction by means of an indirect demonstration, if the demand is made that the reduction must proceed solely with the help of the *analysis of concepts. On the relation between the principle of causality and the principle of *sufficient reason, see the latter article.

A special instance of the principle of causality is found in the so-called law of motion which was first formulated by Aristotle: whatever is moved (= changed) is moved (= changed) by another (*Quidquid movetur, ab alio movetur*). According to this principle, every change requires a cause — he means a change to a greater fullness of existence, to perfection (= the transition from potency to act); the principle also means that this cause, partially at least, must be located in another existent that is distinct from the one that is changing, and that, therefore, the being that changes is not enough to explain the development of its own tendencies. The reason for this is that the lack of perfection found before the change in the existent that is to be perfected, is not a sufficient cause of the increase of existential perfection that is to be produced. — The physical law of *causality is to be distinguished from the metaphysical principle of causality; for, the former law is restricted to the happenings within the world of bodies and in order to explain them naturally it requires a cause that produces the particular event with physical necessity. From the exclusive consideration of this *natural causality it should be understood that the expression, "causal occurrence," is frequently taken to mean about the same thing as "necessary occurrence." The metaphysical principle of causality, however, leaves the possibility open for a freely operating cause.

JdV

CAUSE

Aristotle and many scholastic philosophers call a cause every principle of *existence upon which the existence of a contingent existent really depends in any way whatever; the influx of the cause (*Causality) therefore is the existential *ground of the caused reality; the converse, however, is not true, that every existential ground is a kind of causality. The reason for this is that the ground-result relationship can be present in a case of real identity (therefore, without real existential dependence of the one upon the other), while the cause and the caused, precisely because a real relationship of dependence exists between them, can never really be totally identified. Because of its real influx on the caused reality a cause is also to be clearly distinguished from a *necessary condition* which is required for the coming into existence of the existent (e.g., because the cause cannot operate without it), but does not itself exercise any influence on the caused reality (e.g., light as the necessary condition but not the cause of writing). Similarly, unnecessary occasions and circumstances surrounding certain actions are not properly causes.

Depending upon whether or not a cause enters into the construction of a caused reality as an intrinsic principle, a distinction is made between an *intrinsic* and an *extrinsic* cause. According to the theory of *hylemorphism, the intrinsic causes of all bodies are *matter* and *form* which constitute the whole reality of a body by each communicating itself to the other; matter, because it receives within itself and carries the form, and form, because it determines the matter and so gives to the whole its own specific stamp. The principal extrinsic cause is the *efficient cause* (cause in a narrower sense) which produces an existent reality as the result of its *activity; the product of such activity is called an *effect*. According to the principle of *finality every activity is ultimately determined by an *end* or *purpose*; the known and willed *value of this end attracts the efficient cause or else it is placed before blind natural activities by the Creator himself as their end. Therefore, the end or purpose, as that for the sake of which the existent exists, is the extrinsic cause of the existent itself. In addition to the four principal kinds of causes just enumerated, there is also the *model* or *prototype* (= exemplary cause) which, as the extrinsic form according to which the existent is patterned, can be reduced to the causality of the form.

A complete philosophical explanation of the spatio-temporal existent must consider the question of causes from all possible directions. The narrow, scientific orientation of much philosophy (often feebly trying to imitate the physical sciences) is directly responsible for the fact that the consideration of causes has been restricted to the area of the efficient cause. Closely connected with this impoverishment of philosophical investigation is the result that even the words "cause and causality" have been limited to the efficient cause. And finally, even this concept of cause was replaced in physics by the concept of the (mathematical) *function which only says that two physical occurrences are so related to each other that the change of one corresponds to the change of the other in a definite proportion that can be measured numerically. A "causality" understood in this way, which consciously abstracts from the existential connection between the cause and the effect, is totally unsatisfactory from a philosophical point of view (*Natural Causality, *Causality, Law of).

Inner-worldly causes are *second causes* in comparison with God, the *first cause*. The limited existence of these second causes is proportioned to the level of existence of their effects; for this reason they are actually real principal causes and not just *instrumental causes or mere occasions (*occasionalism). They are not, however, proportioned to existence simply (in opposition to non-being), since, because of their *contingency, neither second causes nor their effects are originally identified with existence. Therefore, the totality of inner-worldly causes, effects and causal relationships is dependent in its very existence upon the *creation, conservation and *concurrence of the first cause.

The objective validity of the concept of the efficient cause is clearly established from our own consciousness in which we experience ourselves as the cause or producer of our own acts (e.g., we make our own choices and think our own thoughts). Therefore, the image of causality does not rest, as Hume assumed, just in interpreting a regular sequence of events as having an intrinsic connection with each other; nor is the concept of cause, as Kant asserted, merely a category of the mind (*Critical Philosophy).

CERTITUDE

The insight into the *principle of *causality* gives us the possibility of establishing true causal relationships even in the external world. — On the other kinds of causes see *Matter, Prime Matter, Form, End, Purpose, Instrumental Cause.*

VN

CERTITUDE

Certitude is a type of perfect knowledge both in the psychological order of fulfillment as well as in the realm of logical validity. It can be defined as a firm assent founded on the *evidence of the object. (For the sake of simplicity in terminology, certitude is defined here not as a characteristic of the judgment, but concretely as the certain judgment itself). — On the psychological side, certitude is a judgment that is perfected in the assent — and this assent is "firm," i.e., it excludes all *doubt as a conclusively posited judgment; thus it stands in contrast to *opinion* which is a provisional assent that does not exclude all doubt. Normally certitude is accompanied by a calming of emotion; still, even a more or less lasting feeling of disquiet does not destroy the essence of certitude. Certitude in the psychological sense is also called *conviction,* i.e., insofar as it is considered not only as a transitory act but as a permanent mental attitude. — Perfect certitude is only present when the subjective conviction finds its logical foundation in the evidence of objective reality (*objective certitude*); only in this way is the truth of a given proposition guaranteed. If a proposition expresses an immediately intuited object, then we speak of *immediate certitude;* if it rests on evidence that has been supplied by proof, then it is *mediate certitude.* If the required objective foundation is lacking to the conviction, then we are speaking of a purely *subjective certitude.*

Different modes of certitude can be distinguished — in addition to the differences found in the objects — according to the special nature of the foundation and according to the degree of consciousness with which it is grasped; they can also be distinguished according to the level of dependence or independence on the will. If we distinguish *theoretical* from *practical* certitude, then this can be understood of the object in view; thus, theoretical certitude means the certitude of an existential statement, while practical certitude means the certitude of a law that expresses an "ought." More frequently theoretical certitude means the same thing as logically valid certitude, while practical certitude signifies a high degree of probability sufficient for daily life or it might mean a conviction that has only the value of a *postulate. According to the difference in the *evidence on which logically valid certitude rests, a distinction is made between *absolute* and *conditional certitude.* Absolute certitude is also called *metaphysical.*

CHANCE

Conditional certitude is either *physical* or *moral*, depending upon whether it rests on physical or moral evidence. Moral certitude in the broader sense is a practical certitude which is sufficient to exclude the probability of the opposite. Sometimes a conviction is said to be *relatively* certain if it is based on reasons that suffice for an undeveloped, uncritical mind, but would not suffice for a fully developed, independent thinker; an example of such certitude is the authority of parents as a motive of certitude for their children. — According to the degree of consciousness a distinction can be made between *natural* and *scientific* (reflex) certitude; in natural or spontaneous certitude the reasons for it are not methodically examined and therefore they are usually hardly adverted to; scientific certitude, however, includes a greater awareness of its foundation. — With regard to the relationship of certitude to the will we can say: The grasp of the object (corresponding to the evidence) does not depend immediately on free will, but at most mediately because of the willed direction of attention. On the other hand, the assent and its firmness frequently depend on the will, not only in their realization or non-realization but often also in their Yes or No to the same object (*free certitude*); this is particularly true of *faith.

JdV

CHANCE

Chance can mean: 1. that which is neither necessary by reason of its essence or determined by reason of an efficient or final cause (*absolute chance* (*Causality, Principle of); 2. that which has an efficient cause but no final cause (*Finality, Principle of). — "Accidental" can be understood either in the sense of *contingency or of chance (2). — Absolute chance (1) signifies the complete meaninglessness of the real; it is opposed to the unity of *existence. There cannot be even relative *chance* (2) in reference to the first *cause (God); relative chance is found only in the case of secondary causes as the unintended side-effect of something directly willed. It is also found as the effect that is brought about through the meeting of two or more efficient causes that are ordered to this meeting neither naturally nor through the direction of some outside cause. Chance in this sense is neither natural nor regularly intended. — The *theory of chance* (*casualism*) is the attempt to explain that what appears in nature to be finalized is actually without any final cause at all, for example, the order of one group of things to another group and the origin of the higher levels of existence out of the lower (*Finality). Casualism is unscientific, because it demands no cause for the transition of things from a confused situation to the presently-given orderly and regular world. — It is also arbitrary because it restricts the influence of chance to the very first beginning of all things.

KF

CHANGE

Change (*mutatio*) means to become something else; it is a transition from one form of existence to another. Change in the improper sense is *extrinsic change* in which a thing receives a new designation because of a change which has actually occurred in some other thing with which it is related in some way; thus, the sun "changes" from a rising to a setting sun when the earth revolves in the course of a day, while the sun itself does not undergo any real change. Change in the proper sense is only *intrinsic change* in which some determination of a thing becomes another determination. Every change presupposes a subject which undergoes the change, a beginning state in which the subject finds itself before the change, a substratum, which is the foundation of all change and which is common to both the beginning and the terminal states, remains intact, for the basic reason that change does not mean the annihilation of one thing and a completely new beginning of something else. A change demands as cause a *power which effects the change. — In a *substantial change* the substance, the essence itself, becomes something else. The changes back and forth between the basic chemical elements were formerly thought to be substantial changes; according to the present position of science, however, these changes are not substantial. An *accidental change* occurs when an accidental determination becomes something else. Accidental change can be quantitative, qualitative and local. If a qualitative change is only a change in the external form, then this is called a change of shape. A change in place means the same thing as *motion in the narrower sense. Change is an imperfect reality insofar as it signifies a transition from the possibility (*potency) to the actuality of a thing or state.

NJ

CHARACTERISTIC

A characteristic is a species of determination. A determination is that which makes something that is in any way undetermined into something more particular. A distinction is made between real determinations (like the essential form, the accidents) and conceptual determinations (like the specific differences of the genera), depending upon whether or not the thing in question is determined in the extra-mental order or in the mind. One can only speak of characteristics (or attributes) when a real or conceptual determination presupposes something that is already in some sense determined. The first determinations of a being that is still wholly undetermined are not its characteristics, for the first determinations constitute its very essence. Characteristics in the strict sense (property, *proprium*) are those that necessarily belong to a subject. They can be related to existence as such, like the *transcendentals, or to the *genus, the *species, the *individual. The characteristics of one individual, one species, one genus and so forth, are considered their *distinguishing* characteristics. In the wider sense, characteristics are also the occasional determinations. — See also *Predicables*.

JS

CHRISTIAN PHILOSOPHY

The problem of Christian philosophy arises from the fact that *philosophy, in contrast to *theology, according to its very nature is knowledge gained by the use of reason alone and not from divine *revelation, while on the other hand certain historical forms of thought which one is accustomed to call "philosophy", such as *patristic philosophy, the *scholasticism of the Middle Ages and the modern transcendental forms of scholasticism, cannot be understood without recognizing the profound influence on them of Christian faith. Some Catholic thinkers (e.g., Mandonnet) try to avoid this difficulty by denying that the "philosophy" of the Church Fathers and of the early scholastics is true philosophy; then they say that the scholastic version of *Aristotelianism is based on pure reason without dependence on divine revelation; and according to them the concept of "Christian philosophy" actually involves an inner contradiction. However, this view is not exactly in accord with the historical reality. Other thinkers would prefer to abandon the usual idea of philosophy as being too rationalistic and institute a "philosophy based on faith" as the only possible form of philosophy for a Christian; but this view seems to incline in the direction of *traditionalism. Jacques Maritain claims, at least as far as moral philosophy is concerned, that Christian philosophy should begin with principles derived from revelation.

To resolve this question a distinction has to be made between the general concept of philosophy and the concrete historical ways in which it has been actualized; the concept of philosophy as such affirms nothing about "Christianity"; therefore the question touches only on certain historical forms of philosophy, such as patristic and scholastic philosophy. Further, with regard to the latter a distinction should be made between the logical basis of their positive teachings and all the psychological influences that are at work on the mind of the particular philosopher in question. In order to speak of philosophy at all (and not of theology) it is necessary that the logical foundation flow from principles and insights accessible to natural reason; a process that began with the principles of Christian faith would no longer be philosophy. However, that does not exclude the fact that Christian faith from a psychological point of view can be very helpful, at least in the sense that it suggests new problems and facilitates the grasp of transcendent truths by encouraging the formation of "analogous" concepts. There is no doubt but that Christian faith has had this kind of influence on scholastic philosophy. In this sense, the expression "Christian philosophy" is certainly justified. Moreover, it does not follow from this situation that one can simply deny that a certain proposition is a philosophical insight just because it is affirmed only by Christian thinkers, while it remains hidden from the greatest non-Christian philosophers. Perhaps a good example of this would be the whole complexus of questions surrounding the problem of *creation.

JdV

COLLECTIVISM

Every group-idea is said to be a *collective* idea; the word "collective" is also given to every gathering-together of many individual things, often with the derogatory meaning of the "mass"; in the mass the special nature and value of the individual parts (men or things) is lost. Therefore, a man as a member of a collective is usually thought of as robbed of his own personal worth and reduced to the level of a mere thing-object.

Accordingly, collectivism is that kind of social order that so emphasizes the social whole (the collective), of whatever kind it may be, that the above-mentioned degradation of the individual necessarily takes place. This collectivism (*Social Philosophy, no. 2) stands in contrary opposition (not contradictory!) to individualism (*ibid.*, no. 1). But since collectivism makes just as much of an absolute out of the collective as *individualism does out of the individual, it also removes it from all connections with higher and more universal societies. Thus, it actually reveals itself as essentially related to individualism — but as individualism on a higher level. — It is always a *primary concern* — one that is proper to the collective and to which it frequently appeals — to establish and defend the absolutizing of itself. Any conceivable value can be elevated to the first place; it is for this that the members of the collective are supposed to live and die. In *Marxism it is an economic value; in National Socialism it was a biological value (race); in Mussolini's Fascism it was a national and cultural value (Latinita, Romanita). Since collectivism magnifies any such value to be man's first concern and thereby actually deifies it, it is idolatrous and overturns the whole order of values. Whether or not the deified value stands high or low in the total scale of values, is of minor importance. However, the vitality of this value is decisive for the virulence of the collective that is obsessed by it.

Everyday speech tends to characterize as collectivism any over-emphasis on the collective; this is especially so with regard to the tendency to place one's trust in the help of large organized bodies (unions, state) instead of helping oneself or promoting mutual help on a smaller scale (family, business, etc.).

OvNB

COMMON GOOD

Common Good (*bonum commune*). Every common body, whether it be a *society or a *community, has its own proper task for the sake of which it exists, which gives it its character and formal principle — almost like the soul in the body. Clearly this task must consist in some *good that is to be accomplished by the activity of the common body; and this must be done in such a way that this good is useful not only for the common body as such, but ultimately for the members themselves. This good is called the "common good." Thus we discover a mutual relationship here: every perfection of the whole means an increase for all the members; and conversely, the improvement of the members strengthens the whole and increases its effectiveness.

(1) Many philosophers understand by "common good" primarily the perfection of the *members*; however, the common body exists in the first place in order to assist its members in the acquisition of this perfection: The common good of the *family — taken in this sense — would consist, therefore, in that all the members of the family are really able to become perfect family-members, enriched with all the human values that make for a full family life. The common good of the *state as a natural, perfect and all-embracing common-body — taken again in the same sense — would consist in leading the citizens to an all-inclusive perfection of their humanity. The main proponents of the common good in this sense are a number of authors of the Thomist school.

(2) The majority of authors by the phrase "the common good" understand a *state of the common body* itself. In this sense they characterize the common good as an "organizing value." In the first place, the common body must be correctly structured in such a way that it is capable of achieving its own proper goal (an army is not organized like a business). To this proper construction of the common body belongs not only what we narrowly designate as its structure or organization, but also the endowment with the means necessary for the attainment of its goal and the influence of the common body on its members; by means of this influence it leads them to effective cooperation.

If one thinks not so much about a particular common body as about human communitarian life as such, then in the sense of the second formulation above we have the usual definition: the common good is the sum total of all the presuppositions and arrangements of a general, public kind which a common body needs so that the individuals as members of a body can fulfill their earthly task and can themselves realize their earthly happiness by means of their own activity. According to this view the common good is a social state which in the first place guarantees to each person that place in the community which belongs to him and in which he can freely develop his God-given talents, so that he can attain his own bodily, spiritual and moral perfection and so that, through his service to the community, he himself can become richer in external and internal goods. — What belongs to the common good of a particular common body is determined by its special tasks and goals.

According to the terminology in use in the *political* sphere, the well-being of the public or national body politic is characterized as the common good; there it is made equal to the "public interest." But from the point of view of social philosophy one should remember that every community (even a private one) has its own common good and should be evaluated on the basis of its success in realizing it.

Whatever is really demanded of the members of a community for the sake of the common good is owed to the community by them by reason of social *justice.

OvNB

COMMUNITY

While *society in the broader sense means every social structure, that is, every permanent association of men for the achievement of a common goal, we usually give the name "community" only to natural groupings (family, people) or to those associations which grow out of a common, unifying idea or purpose. In contrast, a society in the narrower sense is a club with one definite purpose which rests chiefly on some reasonable calculation; in this case the members do not have to know each other (e.g., an athletic club). Related to this is the fact that a community is based more on a unity of love and mutual concern, while a society is primarily a legal structure — the "organization." Formerly the word society was used for associations based on love, but today these are usually called "communities." As a result of individualism, which had a deep understanding of the intrinsic value of community life, the meaning of the word "society" became somewhat distorted, so the newly awakened desire for true community led to the use of the word "community" to express its innermost desires. Along with this was often found a strongly emotional aversion for all legal structures, as if the inner union of the community were in some way endangered by them. In actual fact, however, legal ties are unavoidably necessary whenever a large number of men are to be held together for some lasting common work on a major project. It is not law as such that endangers true community, but only an unbending and unloving application of the law. Accordingly, the simple opposition between community, which is said to rest exclusively on "necessary will," and society which is said to rest just as exclusively on "arbitrary will," is to be rejected; this is especially so if it is proposed in the sense that community grows out of purely irrational forces and so is removed from reason and will.

The existential foundation of every community is a communion; it is the common participation in some good that it strives to preserve or increase; or it is a common necessity, a common fate. A group of men who are bound together by such communion is sometimes called a community (in the broader sense), especially if the common fate is consciously recognized by the majority and thus awakens a sense of togetherness. This feeling of togetherness is only the first spiritual presupposition for a community in the full sense. If there is to be not just a mass of men but a true community, then a purely emotional attitude is not sufficient; for, there must also be spiritual values, mutual respect and love, or at least some regard for the personal worth of the others. The common resolve of many individuals, which is based on this foundation, to strive for the common goal with a united effort makes up community in the full sense of the word. A legal structure with true authority is a requirement that flows from the essence of community, since otherwise the effective pursuit of the goal cannot be guaranteed. The moral bonds which preserve a community and assure the beneficial cooperation of its members, therefore, are not only bonds of love but also of *justice.

A distinction is made between natural communities which are given with human nature itself (marriage, family, people, nation), the supernatural community of the Church which is based on the activity of divine grace, and free communities which are the result of free human choices (e. g., a ski club). — A community has its own proper worth and beauty ultimately because it represents in a new way certain traits of the divine essence. But insofar as this representation takes place by means of an impersonal arrangement it is not ultimately directed to its own good, but to the well-being and perfection of the persons who are its members.

JdV

COMPLEXITY-CONSCIOUSNESS

Complexity-Consciousness is the unifying concept of Pierre Teilhard de Chardin's theory of evolution. By "complexity" is meant that quality by which something is composed of a larger number of elements which are more tightly organized among themselves. Complexity is a matter not merely of a thing having a large number of elements, but of the organization of those elements; complexity if not simply *multiplicity, it is organized multiplicity. An atom is more complex than an electron; a molecule is more complex than an atom, a cell is more complex than a molecule. Material bodies, then, besides being small or large, light or heavy, are also simple or complex. Complexity, like length and weight, is a dimension of the material world.

"Consciousness" is taken in a broad sense to mean any kind of psychic interiority, no matter how minimal. *Life is a high form of *consciousness; intelligence is a still higher form of consciousness. Relying on ordinary observation and on scientific data, one can see that there is a correlation between complexity and consciousness. At least among living beings, the more complex a being is, the more conscious it seems to be. For example, animals are apparently more conscious than plants, and the more complex animals give evidence of greater consciousness than less complex animals. For experimental science, life is seen as a function or an effect of complexity, and the level of life depends, to all appearances, on the degree of the *organism's complexity.

Using scientific *induction, Teilhard de Chardin postulates that the structural relationship observed between complexity and consciousness is a universal law. This is the "law of complexity-consciousness," that complexity and consciousness are correlative, directly proportional to one another at every level of being. "Spiritual perfection (or conscious 'centreity') and material synthesis (or complexity) are but the two aspects or connected parts of one and the same phenomenon" (*The Phenomenon of Man*, Harper & Row, 1965, 60-61). Teilhard, in *The Phenomenon of Man*, refers to the "without" and the "within" of things. Every material being has some structure, a "without;" and, commensurate with that structure's complexity, every material being has some psychic interiority, some form of consciousness, a "within." That is, everything, even the most simple being that exists, has not only some structure but also an at least rudimentary form of consciousness. At levels of very low complexity, in megamolecules and below, the simplicity of the structure is such that the consciousness is so rudimentary as to be imperceptible. However, it is logical to assume that such consciousness does exist in a diffuse way and at a low level even in those cases where it cannot be observed. And as we mount in the order of complexity, we discover, at the level of the virus, that consciousness begins to be perceptible increasing as we go beyond the virus to more complex forms of existence. Besides postulating the *universality* of the structural relationship between complexity and consciousness, Teilhard de Chardin makes another *postulate concerning complexity-consciousness, a postulate again based on scientific induction from several observable cases. The postulate is this: matter presents itself to us as having the property of arranging itself, in time, in more and more complex groupings that have commensurately higher degrees of consciousness.

Science habitually views material reality as structured on one axis in space, on a line that stretches from the infinitesimally small to the cosmically large. The dimension of size has been the general criterion for science in arranging in categories the material confronting it. There is, however, another axis, another line along which material reality is structured, the axis of complexity. Material beings can be arranged on a size scale from the very small particles to the galaxies; but they can also be arranged on a complexity scale from the extremely simple (for example, the hydrogen atom) to the extremely complex (the higher animals). When we place things on a scale of ascending complexity, we can observe two things. First, as complexity increases, so does consciousness; they are correlative, and this is the law of complexity-consciousness. And, secondly, the scale of increasing complexity shows things to be in the order of their appearance in time, in the order of their coming into existence in the process of evolution. In other words, it seems true to say, looking at the history of evolution, that the evolutionary process has produced, successively, beings of ever higher complexity and, thus, of ever higher consciousness. Teilhard de Chardin makes this a postulate of his theory of evolution: that, over long periods of time and through the various chance combinations that occur in very large populations, matter becomes arranged in more highly complex forms that have a higher degree of consciousness. This is not at all a teleological postulate; there is here no assumption of some inner *force vitale*, *telos*, or metaphysical finality. It is simply a statement of what has apparently happened in evolutionary history.

In this perspective, evolution is seen to have a direction; it moves in the direction of producing entities of always higher complexity and consciousness. The appearance in the evolutionary process of life can now be seen to be the outcome of ages of progress along the axis of complexity-consciousness. Evolution, proceeding by billion-fold trial and error, advancing in the direction of more complex arrangements of matter, resulted in life. This grouping process, together with the mechanisms of heredity and reproduction, has produced in time the various species of living things.

The appearance of life marks a "critical point" on the evolutionary axis of complexity-consciousness, a critical point somewhat analogous to the vaporization of water when it boils and to the liquefaction of ice when it melts. The appearance of life marks a change of state, a marked change in quality of existence. It is as though the degree of complexity had reached a point where a breakthrough had to take place, a move to a qualitatively new kind of being. With the appearance of life, evolution shows an increase in speed, and now evolution takes place almost entirely in the zone life.

The appearance of properly human consciousness marks a second critical point on the axis of complexity-consciousness. Man is not only aware;

he knows that he knows, and he knows himself as knower. He has reflexive consciousness, "consciousness squared." This is a qualitatively new kind of life. Just as when life appeared evolution speeded up and took place almost exclusively among living things, so now — with the appearance of man and the passing of a second critical point — evolution accelerates greatly and takes place now chiefly in *society. Human progress is evolution in the *thinking zone of the *world, and it continues to follow the axis of complexity-consciousness, producing higher levels of civilization and *culture. Human evolution takes place mainly through the process of *socialization. — See also *Becoming, Development, Evolutionism, Life Philosophy, Vitalism.*

RLF

CONCEPT

The concept is the simplest form of thought in contrast to *judgment and *inference which are thought patterns composed of a number of concepts. While a judgment expresses a certain reality as existing, the concept is a thoughtful or abstract-spiritual expression of a "whatness"; for it grasps an object, re-presents "what" it is without making a statement about it. The verbal expression of a concept is a word (e. g., number) or a combination of words which still does not make a statement (e. g., even number). In opposition to *nominalism (and all forms of sensism) it must be said that the concept as a spiritual-intellectual representation of the thing is essentially superior to imagination in the narrow sense, that is, imagination as a sense representation. However, by reason of its abstractive character it is also essentially different from the intellectual intuition of pure spirits. — *Rationalism has not always given enough attention to this distinction (for example, in the identification of concept and *idea and in the doctrine of "innate ideas").

In every concept a distinction should be made between the concept as a "thought-act," the concept as a "thought-content" and the "object" of the concept. The concept as a thought-act is a spiritual (immaterial) act, even though in its origination (*Concept, Formation of, *Abstraction) it is dependent on the body and the senses. It is not according to these characteristics that the concept is a representation of the object, but only insofar as the thought-act carries within itself a determined content in an ideal way (insofar as it is, for example, the concept of number and not of something like space); the concept "means" the object and refers to it in an *intentional way. The *object of the concept is not the inner "content" of the concept but the object which exists independently of thought and which is meant or intended by the concept; thus, for example, the concept "man" does not refer to itself (man as conceptually represented) but to the essence of a real man. With regard to the object a distinction is made between the *material object*, that is, the existent in its concrete totality to which the concept refers, and the *formal object*, that is, the partial content, the "side," the characteristic or characteristics of the object which are grasped in the concept. As an abstractive representation the concept does not present things in their concrete, intuitively evident fullness; it only gives individual characteristics. (The word "characteristic" signifies first of all the partial contents which can be distinguished in the object itself, then the partial contents of the concept itself; the word "determination" indicates that the so designated characteristic is either removed from or added to a conceptually undetermined subject; *Concrete, *Abstract.

A further distinction is made for every concept regarding its *comprehension* and *extension*. The comprehension of a concept is the totality of its characteristics, while the extension is the totality of the things to which it can be applied. The general principle is: the greater the comprehension of a concept is the more limited its extension and vice versa. The only addition to the comprehension of a concept that does not limit its extension is that which occurs in the realm of the essential notes of the object (*Predicables). — A distinction is made between *simple* and *complex* concepts depending on whether the concept contains one or several characteristics. A concept is *clear* when it adequately distinguishes the intended object from every other object. The complex concept is *distinct* when it indicates the various characteristics included in the object: the *definition strives for a perfectly distinct concept. On the basis of the extension of a concept a distinction is made between a singular concept (*individual) and a *universal concept. — There is an essential difference between a *proper* and an *analogous* concept, based on the kind of its conformity to the object. The proper concept is derived from the intuition of its object and therefore contains the positive characteristics of the object as positive thought-contents. The analogous concept, on the other hand, designates a supra-sensible object on the basis of an imperfect similarity it has with another object grasped by sensible intuition. The analogous concept retains in itself as a positive content the perfection of existence common to both objects involved; however, the mode of existence *proper* to the supra-sensible object, which in itself is purely positive, can only be thought of by denying the mode of existence of the sensible object; such concepts are not positive distortions but they do contain essentially less conformity to the object. The distinction between a *univocal* and an *analogous* concept is not the same as that between proper and analogous given immediately above, for the proper-analogous concepts concern the relationship of a concept to its own object to which it is suited (thus in this sense our concept of God is analogous), while univocal-analogous concepts concern the relationship of a concept to different objects, logically subordinated, in which the concept is realized either in the exact same way or in a partially different way (thus in this sense the concept of an existent being is analogous with reference to a creature or to God) (*Analogy).

Certainly conceptual thought, even in the case of the proper concept, because of its abstractness does not equal *intuition in regard to fullness of content; nevertheless it does surpass sensible intuition because of its spirituality in regard to the way it attains the object (*Essential Knowledge). And even though the concept cannot exhaust the fullness of reality, still its content is basically realized in the existent object as *realism justly emphasizes in opposition to *conceptualism and the *critical philosophy of Kant. Therefore, the disdain of conceptual thinking, which is characteristic of *intuitionism, *life philosophy and to some extent of *existential philosophy, lacks all objective foundation. For without conceptual thought our human knowledge cannot achieve perfection; nor can it transcend the realm of sensible experience and so advance towards *metaphysics. On the other hand the value of the concept is overestimated when a Hegel makes it the totality of all reality and the driving force of the development of reality.

JdV

CONCEPTUALISM

Conceptualism is the philosophical view according to which the universal has existence only in the concept. Conceptualism differs from the older *nominalism in that it accepts not just common names, but also *universal concepts. In contrast to *realism, however, it denies that there is something in reality that corresponds to universal concepts. If this were meant in the sense that in the world of things there are only individuals there would be no objection to it. Conceptualism goes even further in asserting that absolutely nothing in the objective order corresponds to universal concepts, or what does correspond to them has no significance for our knowledge of things. — Conceptualism arose in the 14th century as a reaction against a form of realism that overstressed the presence of the universal in things. According to William of Ockham the universal concept is a natural *sign as, for example, smoke is a sign of fire. The reality of smoke is not realized identically in the thing, but it is only like it. But in thought it does take the place of the thing, and it does this for each individual in the totality. Later thinkers even dissolved the natural connection of the sign with the thing. For them universal concepts are only an instrument in the logical division and ordering of things. — While *empirical conceptualism*, to which *life philosophy also belongs, places little value on "fixed" concepts for a knowledge of constantly-changing reality, *rationalistic conceptualism* (*Critical Philosophy) stresses the necessity and universality of conceptual knowledge. This latter view, however, does not find the foundation of this necessity in things and their essences; rather, it finds it only in the a priori functions of the subject so that actually the things-in-themselves are not known. As a result of the philosophical position of conceptualism a certain encouragement is given to *individualism; moreover, it is a flight from metaphysics. — The opposition or contrast between abstract concepts and concrete reality is overcome in the scholastic theory of abstraction in this sense that the content of the concept is actualized in the given object, but in a different way, namely, in a real unity with other determinations that do not enter into the concept; and the theory also affirms that the abstract mode of existence proper to the concept can never be attributed to things. See also *Abstraction.*

JS

CONCRETE

Mental images that represent their object just as they are given in sense intuition are called "concrete." In a wider sense, those universal concepts can also be termed "concrete" which include not only the determining form (e. g., human nature) but also the undetermined carrier of the form (e. g., man = the subject or carrier of human nature). Concrete thinking is that which presents its objects not only by means of concepts, but also by means of the institutions and perceptions that correspond to them. Both pre-scientific and fully human thinking are predominantly concrete. Therefore, the style of anyone who hopes not only to convince the minds of his hearers but also to move men to action must be concrete wherever possible. According to Hegel, the concrete is the concept that is full of the developing moments of the system, and so it is synonymous with that which is metaphysically first; it stands in contrast to the *abstract* concept which is stripped of the fullness of the developing moments. — See also *Abstract, Individual.*

WB

CONCURRENCE

Concurrence (*concursus divinus*) means the immediate influence of God on the activity of creatures and the results of their activity; it does not mean simply, as Darandus thought, a mediate influence by maintaining the creature and its powers in existence. The immediate divine concurrence with all created things is deduced from their intrinsic dependence on the being of God which is alone independent. But this does not exclude the possibility that God can also influence free creatures in a moral way through promises, commandments and warnings.

There are different viewpoints among scholastic philosophers about the nature of the divine concurrence and especially about how it can be reconciled with human freedom. Bánez as well as some modern Dominicans and neo-Thomists teach that there is not only an immediate impetus coming from God (*praemotio physica*) to lead the creature from the proximate disposition to act to real activity, but in addition to this there is also a predetermination of his will (*praedeterminatio physica*). Without this divine impetus man cannot act and with it he cannot avoid acting. Thus the infallible connection between the divine impulse and human activity guarantees the fulfillment of the divine will and the validity of God's foreknowledge. Nevertheless, according to Bánez neither the divine impulse nor the predetermination adversely affect the freedom of the created will, because God moves each creature according to its nature; therefore, he moves the free creature in such a way that its freedom is preserved even when it is subject to the divine influence. — Other scholastics have taught that there is just an indifferent impulse from God without a predetermination of the will.

*Molinism, which was strongly advocated by the Jesuit theologians of the 16th century, sees in the "Thomistic" doctrine of Bánez, a serious threat to human freedom and so also to the holiness of God who, if this theory were correct, would seem to bear the responsibility for men's sins. According to Molinism, the free creature does not need any divine impulse or predetermination in order to act; rather, as an active nature it produces its act out of its own activity and in a free decision it also gives the direction to its act. Thus dependence on God (absolute existence) that is essential to everything created is always preserved because God and the creature produce one and the same act at the same time — God under the aspect of existence, the creature under the aspect of particularity. So human freedom remains unimpaired. — According to the "Thomists" the weakness of the Molinist theory lies in its "violation" of the principle of causality, in the "dependence" of God on man who determines his own way for himself and so determines the divine concurrence, and especially in the difficulty of satisfactorily explaining God's foreknowledge. — The weaknesses in both of these attempted explanations have led to other different suggestions, but they all seem to end up in one of the two camps. Although the fact of the divine concurrence is certain, the "how" of it seems to have escaped adequate human comprehension up to the present.

MR

CONFUCIANISM

Confucianism is mainly (1) the teaching of Confucius (551-479 B. C.), the most revered person in Chinese history. Confucianism is less a philosophy than a moral teaching based on the old traditions. The command to love children is a central point. The ideal is the "nobleman" who possesses moral perfection along with the education of a gentleman. Metaphysical and religious problems are foreign to Confucius. After further elaboration and struggle, ancient Confucianism achieved a dominant position in China about the time of Christ. It was not until the 12th century that Confucianism (2) received a metaphysical foundation in the *neo-Confucianism* of the Hsing-li School. The most important representative of this school and China's greatest philosopher was Chu Hsi (1130-1200). He traces all reality back to two principles: reason and matter which flows from reason. An idealistic monism, however, opposed this realistic dualism. Later Confucianism (3) which was established as a state religion should be distinguished from neo-Confucianism as a philosophy. The ethics of ancient Confucianism made use of the permanent elements of Taoism, *Buddhism and the cult of ancestors in which Confucius was eventually included as a divine being.

WB

CONSCIENCE

Conscience in the broad sense means the capacity of the human spirit to know moral values, commands and laws (*synderesis*); in a more limited sense it means the application of these norms to the immediate task to hand. It is that inner voice which in a very personal way informs man what he should or should not do; it manifests itself as a warning or encouraging voice before the deed is done and as a praising or blaming voice after the fact (pangs of conscience). An impressive witness to the power of conscience is the fact of *repentance*; for, by repenting a man as it were frees himself from his past evil deeds; and this feeling of regret will sometimes move him to make a public confession of guilt. The source of conscience is to be found in the tendency of man as a person and as the image of God to seek moral values; it also resides in his capacity to know these values and to apply them in his own particular case. Just as in the development of the other aspects of man's spiritual life so also in the ethical realm instruction, education and direction by competent authority is of the utmost importance. A distinction can be made between an *antecedent* and a *consequent* conscience as also between a true and an erroneous conscience. The erroneous conscience can be invincibly so and guiltless or vincible and therefore responsible for its acts. A well-balanced, tender conscience stands midway between the lax conscience and the scrupulous conscience.

Since conscience applies the universal principles of the moral law to the present, particular case, the following obligations are always operative: In a state of real, unresolved doubt about the morality of some action a man may not act. Thus a practical (not strictly scientific) *certitude is required first. (On the problem of achieving a certain conscience, see *Probablism). But a person must always follow the indications of a certain conscience. This holds even in the case of the invincibly ignorant conscience. The moral agent has no other reasonable alternative. He conforms himself to the will of God inasfar as it is possible at the given moment. However, a person should not be hasty in appealing to his own certain conscience, especially if more knowledgeable authorities view the situation differently; for then the case of a guiltlessly erroneous conscience would not occur. Thus there is a strict obligation to form one's conscience properly by reflection, instruction, advice of others, and so forth.

The obligation to follow one's conscience, even if erroneous, is the basis of *freedom of conscience* and *tolerance*, that is, the need to respect others' dictates of conscience even when I consider them to be erroneous and to refrain from forcing others to act in a way that is contrary to their consciences. However, granted the above, it is still not forbidden to protect oneself against persons who are acting out of an erroneous conscience and who violate the rights of individuals or of society. The state can also effectively counter an objectively unjustified refusal to respect the rights of others by restricting the freedom of the persons concerned.

A special difficulty in the formation of one's conscience occurs when there is a *conflict of duties*. This is not a case of an evil that can be clearly or easily recognized, but of two obligations which cannot be fulfilled at the same time, which seem to be equally important and both of which require attention at the same time. In actual fact, there cannot be a true conflict of duties which is based on the objective moral order. Such a conflict would be contrary to the holiness and wisdom of God who cannot force a man to sin. The conflict lies only in man's defective knowledge; and it must be resolved by investigating which duty takes the priority at a given moment. If this priority cannot be established in a particular case then the freedom required to posit morally good or evil acts is just not present.

Casuistry, which attempts to solve such conscience problems, is an aspect of ethics which is very misunderstood today but still extremely important — at least for an ethics that hopes to have any influence on man's daily activities. Analogously, no reasonable jurist doubts the necessity of dealing with concrete, detailed cases in civil or penal law in order to make clear the extent and the precise application of the laws; he also handles such cases in order to aid the learning student of the law and other jurists who are more concerned with the practical side of the law. This necessity is also operative for the moralist who has the very difficult and responsible task of aiding men to make correct moral judgments. To be sure, the positive exposition of the moral law must precede all casuistry. Also, the solutions to problems of conscience must avoid all abstruse and unreal possibilities.

JoS-WB

CONSCIOUSNESS

Consciousness in the proper and narrow sense of the word (1) is a type of companion-knowledge (*con-scientia*) concerning one's own spiritual existence and its momentary condition. While the plant indeed "lives," yet does not know about its own vital activities, man can "experience" his activities through his accompanying knowledge of them and he can possess them as "his own experiences." Perfect reflex consciousness is ordered to mental processes and situations (*act-consciousness*) to the object orientation of acts (*object-consciousness*), and also to one's own Ego as the carrier of the experiences (*subject-, ego-, self-consciousness*). This reflex consciousness makes it possible for us to distinguish between the Ego, the act and the object, to take a step, as it were, away from them, to question their mutual relations as well as the logical, ontological and ethical value of the acts and so to arrive at real human culture. In the imperfect, reflex consciousness of everyday life attention is centered directly and for the most part on the objects known, but always in such a way that the personal self as such that is experiencing the objects is touched and co-known by that attention. (Otherwise, later we could not remember our former experiences as being our own). These forms of reflex consciousness are proper only to the spiritual being and the capacity for it belongs to the essence of the *spirit that "possesses itself" and "is present to itself." But we must ascribe at least an *indirect consciousness* also to the mere animal existent; for, by means of this indirect consciousness the animal somehow "experiences" its own orientation to objects, even though it is not able to reflect on its own self and on the subjective side of its acts. Consciousness is not just an attendant circumstance (*epiphenomenon*) of matter; rather, it essentially implies a relation to a substantial *soul.

In its transferred meanings, the word "consciousness" (2) often refers to a knowledge of experiences which no longer belong to the psychic present (recollection); further, it can mean (3) the knowledge of the value or non-value of one's own action (a person is "conscious" of having done a good deed) or of the value of one's own personal existence ("self-awareness" as pride); finally, it can signify (4) the capacity for conscious experiences (i. e., a person "loses" consciousness).

In order to clarify how spiritual acts become conscious some scholastic philosophers assumed the existence of separate acts of a proper sensible power (a *sensus intimus*) to explain sense-consciousness and a separate act of knowing of the spirit to explain reflex spiritual consciousness. Insofar as it is a question of consciousness in the narrower sense and of the experience of present acts and situations, it does not seem necessary to postulate a separate act for this. Rather, it is the special nature of spirit that it also possesses itself through its own acts; it is the special nature of the spiritual act to be "conscious" through itself. With regard to this last point, a similar situation also holds for the sensibly conscious act. For, the human spirit, if it were free of the limits put on it by the body, would immediately behold its own spiritual essence as such, while our body-laden spirit must first conclude to this essence.

The individual experiences of consciousness do not remain isolated from one another, but they are normally united in a double way: through their being attached to one and the same *ego which always remains the same in the flux of different experiences and through their intelligible connection with each other. Therefore, one speaks also in metaphorical language of consciousness as if it were a type of spatial container in which the particular experiences are located as the "*contents of consciousness*," yet with regard to the clarity of this awareness one also speaks of the "different levels of consciousness." While at any given time only one object can be in the center of consciousness ("*narrowness of consciousness*"), many things, more or less weakly attended to, can shimmer at the same time on the "*edge of consciousness*." As a result of some disease, a series of experiences that still hang together can be mentally split off from an understandable connection from the other contemporaneous or previous experiences to such an extent that one can speak of a real "split" in the (psychological) *personality (but in the strict sense not of a "double ego"). Likewise, particular experiences or the remembrance of them can be suppressed into the subconscious level in a way that severely restricts good mental health.

For the theory of knowledge the witness of immediate consciousness shows itself as the first and most certain source of objectively certain knowledge, so that the realistic *theory of *knowledge* at present usually begins with the testimony of consciousness and its evaluation.

AW

CONTINGENCY

In logic contingency designates one of the *modalities of judgment (*logical contingency*). In a wider sense, contingency means the modality that is contradictorily opposed to *necessity, that is, the possibility of non-existence; in this sense the contingent also includes the impossible: for, it is above all true of that which cannot be, that it is not. But the idea of contingency is normally used in a more restricted meaning; thus, the contingent excludes not only the necessary but also the impossible. Therefore, it designates the middle ground between the two, that is, every existent that can both exist or not exist; for example, the fact that the door is closed, is contingent. In English we sometimes say that the contingent in this sense is "accidental"; but this meaning is not to be confused with the unintentional or the irregular (*Chance).

Accordingly, the logical contingency of judgments is the expression of the *ontic contingency* of the objective reality itself; this, in turn, rests ultimately on the *metaphysical contingency* of the *existence of every-thing within the cosmos. In this sense, every existent that does not necessarily have existence because of its very essence, is contingent. Therefore, even physically necessary events (on the basis of *Natural Laws) are still not essentially necessary, but remain metaphysically contingent. Of course, this contingency is not an immediately perceptible fact — it must be proved. Since, according to the metaphysical principle of *causality, every contingent existent is caused, the proof of the contingency of the world is the decisive step in every "causal" demonstration of *God's existence, that is, in every proof for God that concludes to God as the source or creator of the empirically given. However, the contingency of all this-worldly existents does not mean just dependence on God at the beginning of the world; rather, as soon as one has thought through the problem of contingency to the end, it becomes clear that every contingent existent can exist only so long as it is supported by God's conserving activity.

JdV

CONTRADICTION, PRINCIPLE OF

The principle of contradiction, or, more precisely, the principle of non-contradiction, was rightly considered in classical scholasticism as the first principle (*Knowledge, Principles of), that is, as the universal basic principle whose grasp is of the utmost importance for all human thinking. Unfortunately many recent philosophers have attempted to replace this principle with the so-called *principle of identity*; if this principle is not supposed to be just a tautology (whatever is, is; A = A) or another form of the principle of contradiction, its meaning remains indefinite and it is not explained by all in the same way. Aristotle expressed the principle of contradiction in the following terms. "It is impossible that the same thing (the same determination) belong and not belong to an existent at the same time and under the same respect" (*Metaphysics* 4, 3; 1005b 19f). The principle is based on the concept of *existence and on the absolute irreconcilability of existence with non-existence; it says of the existent (i. e., the "something" that has existence) that, insofar as it is

(= at the same time and under the same respect), it cannot not be. — From the above it is clear that the principle of contradiction first of all says something about the existent itself; therefore, it belongs primarily not in logic but in ontology. The logical principle of contradiction is first based on the ontological order. It affirms that two contradictorily opposed propositions cannot both be true, that therefore the same thing can never be affirmed and denied at the same time and in the same sense. The observance of this first principle is the primary condition of all organized, orderly thinking. — Se also *Opposition*.

JdV

CREATION

Creation (1) refers first of all to the created *world, and then (2) to the act of creation, that is, the free production of a thing according to its whole existence. Creation (2) in this (theistic) sense is creation from nothingness. This does not mean that nothingness temporally preceded the created reality, nor that nothingness is a kind of material out of which the created thing was produced, nor that an efficient cause is not necessary for the production; rather, it simply means that the created thing is produced without the help of any pre-existent material. Every production different from creation is an action performed on something already existing that is changed in some way. Creation, however, occurs without a true *change. Therefore it is not a temporal happening, even though time can begin with it. As an activity of God it is his inner act of will which is identified with his essence and whose external efficacy results in the world as his effect — but this external effect can only take place in such a way that there is no internal change in God.

Creation (3) in a neutral sense (neither theistic nor pantheistic) refers to an origin of the world dependent on the *absolute, without indicating more precisely the nature of this dependence. In *pantheism, creation (4) means a certain directed unfolding of the absolute in finite forms (while maintaining a substantial identity with the absolute), or it can mean a real but necessary (5) production of the world. Because of this necessity, God and the world become polar, mutually demanding opposites. Both of these positions in effect destroy the real *infinity and *transcendence of God. That God produced the world by creation (2) is shown by the *contingency of the world. The power of creating belongs to God alone, the first *cause, since it proceeds from the power over existence as such and not from the power just over this or that existent. That which is itself created cannot be a principal or *instrumental cause in the creation of something. It cannot be a principal cause because creation is essentially related to the whole existence of that which is to be created; it cannot be an instrumental cause since creation is a production out of nothingness, while the instrumental cause either prepares something already existing for the activity of the principal cause or directs that activity to the already existing thing. — It follows from this that a *demiurge* (= a world-shaper dependent on God) is possible only as a world-orderer, not as a world-creator. However, there is no reason to assume the existence of such a world-orderer.

The Conservation of the world: From the essential dependence of the creature on the omnipotent efficacy of God right from the first moment of its existence there necessarily results an immediate dependence with regard to continuance in existence, since this continuance does not in any way alter the essence of things. Therefore, the *annihilation* of the world would occur if God's conserving activity ceased; some activity could not annihilate the world because nothingness cannot be the goal of some action. That God cannot have a reason to completely annihilate the world is related to the necessary ordination of the *world to spiritual beings and their *immortality.

The purpose of creation can be looked at from the side of creatures or from the side of God. The world or creation (1) finds its end in God insofar as his infinite perfection manifests itself in the world in a finite fashion (= the glory of God). Since this manifestation would be meaningless without the existence of a finite spirit to perceive it, creation without the presence of created intelligences is impossible. Irrational creatures, therefore, in their totality are ordered to God only through rational creatures, while rational creatures are directly ordered to him. — Because of his infinite perfection it is impossible that God wants to attain some good for himself by means of creation (2). Thus, the purpose of creation must be God's already-existing infinite perfection insofar as he wishes to communicate it through finite participation. This goal helps us to understand something about God's creative will and at the same time it does not make it necessary. God cannot have a "motive" in the full sense in which we understand the term, since God creates the world without himself undergoing any change (*Immutability).

In a transferred sense, ceation (6) is every production in which something new appears — something that is more than just a sum of what went into it. In this sense the activity that is proper to intellectual life must be designated as creative.

VN

CRITICAL PHILOSOPHY

Critical philosophy in general (1) is that intellectual attitude which makes speculative philosophy or metaphysics dependent upon a previous investigation of the capabilities and limitations of human knowledge; in this regard it is to be distinguished from *dogmatism which presupposes the validity of our knowledge without examining it, and from skepticism which puts everything in a state of universal doubt. Usually "critical philosophy" has a pejorative connotation and indicates an attitude of excessive criticism. In a more limited sense (2) "critical philosophy" designates the philosophy of Immanuel Kant. Since many of Kant's basic concepts now have a permanent place in the common philosophical vocabulary but can hardly be understood properly except in the context of his whole position, in the following paragraphs we will give a short summary of his most important doctrines and an explanation of his basic ideas insofar as these are not treated in other articles.

Because of the continual confusion that Kant saw in the realm of metaphysics it seemed absolutely necessary to him to begin with the investigation into whether or not human reason is capable of any metaphysical knowledge. When he calls this investigation the *Critique of Pure Reason* he is giving us a clue to an important presupposition which he makes from the beginning and practically passes over in silence: All metaphysical and absolutely all universally valid knowledge must be based on a *pure knowledge*, a *pure reason*, i. e., on a knowledge or a reason independent of sense experience. Thus all aspects of consciousness which are produced by an *affection* or a determination of the senses, that is, by an impression which the senses receive from things in themselves, are and remain merely sensible, merely "empirical" and contingent; the idea that the intellect could derive a spiritual content from them by means of a creative abstraction was completely foreign to Kant. Therefore where do the absolutely necessary ideas or principles come from which are found in the synthetic a priori judgments (*Synthesis) of mathematics and, as Kant assumed, also in the "pure" natural sciences? They cannot come from a purely spiritual "intellectual intuition," because our intellect is not an *intuitive intellect;* for Kant only the divine intellect is intuitive — that is, to the extent that it is the source of finite existent realities. Only a certain *spontaneity* of thinking is proper to our intellect; by this Kant means the active uniting (synthesis) of the multiplicity given to us by the senses into the unity of one *object by a process that brings the many under one concept. Therefore there must be "pure concepts" in the intellect which are independent of all experience (*A Priori) and which are the ultimate foundation of the absolute necessity and universality of scientific principles: Kant calls these ideas the *Categories. There must also be forms of "pure intuition" at the root of all *sensible intuition* which, in contrast to intellectual intuition and to thinking is characterized, by its *receptivity* (the ability to receive impression), because (e. g., in Geometry) intuitive spatial conditions are known as absolutely necessary. So Kant attempts to find and fully describe the a priori *forms of intuition and thinking* by means of a transcendental investigation of our knowing powers.

CRITICAL PHILOSOPHY

The *Transcendental Aesthetic* does this for sense knowing which is characterized by the a priori forms of *space* and *time*. The *Transcendental Analytic* investigates the judging "intellect" and derives the *pure ideas of the mind* or the *categories* from the different kinds of judgments. Since these concepts are not abstracted from a given object their validity cannot be established on the basis of experience; rather, their justification ("deduction") can only be a transcendental one, i. e., they are shown to be the *constitutive principles of knowledge*: Without them there can be no "object" of knowledge, that is, no universally valid unity of a sensible multiplicity, no universally valid judgment.

The first condition of all objective knowledge is the *transcendental apperception*, the self-awareness, to which the whole content of consciousness is referred and which therefore is the first condition of all objective unity. The result of this transcendental deduction is that our knowledge is restricted to the world of the senses which as such does not exist in itself but is only a world of appearances, produced by our intuitive principles of space-time. For without sensible matter the categories remain *empty concepts* by means of which we can think of the thing in itself in an indefinite way, but we cannot "know" it or grasp it according to its particular, concrete existence. The concept of the "thing in itself" and of the *intelligible world*, i. e., the real world which is knowable only through spiritual intuition, remains a necessary "limiting concept" (*Grenzbegriff*) "in order to contain the arrogance of sensibility" in the words of Kant himself; for if there was nothing behind appearances then they themselves would be the ultimate, unconditioned reality. Therefore, according to Kant, that which exists in itself is not subject to the conditions of sensibility (space and time).

Therefore, as the result of Kant's transcendental analysis every scientific metaphysic is really rendered impossible. His *Transcendental Dialectic*, by investigating the ideas which control logical thinking, undertakes an explicit confrontation with the contemporary, rationalistic metaphysics and attempts to show that its rational conclusions are only a *transcendental appearance*. These ideas are deduced, somewhat artificially, from the kinds of logical conclusions; they are the *cosmological idea* or the idea of the world as the epitome of all appearances, the *psychological idea* or the idea of the ego as the unconditioned unity of the thinking subject, and the *theological idea* or the idea of God as the unconditioned condition of absolutely every object of thought. It cannot be proved theoretically that existence in itself belongs to these ideas; and the attempt to prove that it does leads necessarily to *Antinomies, i. e., to false conclusions (especially in speculative psychology which confuses the undetermined transcendental subject with the simple substance of the soul) and to proofs for the existence of God which, according to Kant, are equally deceptive. The positive meaning of these ideas is that they are to be *regulating principles of knowl-*

edge; i. e., they are supposed to urge us on, in a kind of constant progress of thought, to come ever closer to the unconditioned unity of a system even though we can never attain this goal. To be sure, the theoretical intellect cannot find a contradiction in the ideas, so the idea of God remains the *ideal of pure reason.* Thus the door is open for an irrational metaphysics which tries to prove that the freedom of will, the immortality of the soul and the existence of God are postulates of the practical reason.

On the historical influence of critical philosophy: *Idealism, *German Idealism, *Neo-Kantianism. The critique of critical philosophy must begin with its bases and presuppositions: *Consciousness, *Abstraction, *Essential Knowledge, *Knowledge, Principles of.

JdV

CULTURE

Culture (Lat.: *colere* = cultivate) originally meant (1) the cultivation and development of human powers beyond their mere natural state (culture as spiritual formation). The ancient world and the Middle Ages called this *humanitas, civilitas.* In the 17th and 18th centuries the concept of culture was expanded. At this time it was taken to mean (2) that which man adds to nature, either in himself or in other objects (culture as the sum total of cultural goods). Accordingly, while *nature designates that which man is born with and that which is given outside of him without his cooperation, culture includes everything that is the result of man's conscious and free activity. For, man's ability to produce culture can always be further developed, but it is still ultimately rooted in nature — it is innate. Even so, culture finds its proper end in the completion and perfection of man's nature. Nature is the essential determinant of the direction and extent of cultural activity. A cultural development which is contrary to the nature of man is not true, but merely apparent and *false culture.*

Depending upon whether or not a particular cultural activity is directed immediately to the human person and his perfection or to objects which exist independently of him, a distinction is made between *personal culture* (such as language, community life, science, morality, religion) and *material culture* (such as technology, art). Most cultural activities, however, actually include both areas. While culture in the wider sense embraces both morality and religion, in the more restricted sense (3) it stands over against both of them. And then it means the cultural development that is ordered to this-worldly goals. Mere external, material culture is called (at least in German) *civilization.* Its task is to serve as a foundation and presupposition for inner, spiritual culture. Insofar as it is advanced at the expense of inner culture, it is only *half-culture* and actually hostile to true culture. It should also be noted that only the external goods of culture can be inherited. Ideal and personal cultural goods must be newly acquired by each generation (*Education, Philosophy of). The possession of culture can be retained only as the result of effort. However, *leisure is also necessary for the general development of human powers. Leisure is much more than mere *free time* (i. e ., time left over from necessary work); moreover, it presupposes that man's basic, material needs are cared for or, insofar as this is possible, that he freely decides not to satisfy some of them. — Culture results only from the cooperation of many individuals in the human *community. From the contributions of the different national cultures there arises a common *human culture* which is conditioned in its possibility by the faculty of speech common to all races. A minimum of culture is necessary for man to continue to live. See also *Culture, Philosophy of.*

WB

CULTURE, PHILOSOPHY OF

While the *human sciences and especially the *history of culture* attempt to provide us with a comprehensive picture of the phenomenon of culture — its forms, values and creations, it is the task of the philosophy of culture to investigate the nature of *culture, to understand it from its essential causes and conditions, to reduce it to its ultimate goals and thereby also to determine the direction and extent of cultural development. — Since culture concerns the essential development and perfection of man, the basic outlines of a philosophy of culture are necessarily laid out by philosophical *anthropology which tells us what man is, by *ethics which tells us what man should do, and by natural *theology which tells us what man's natural goal is. The ultimate foundation of this anthropology and so also of the philosophy of culture is *metaphysics. The different views of these disciplines are reflected in the many different directions of the philosophy of culture. And this latter study has been pursued as a special science only since the 18th century. Special branches of the philosophy of culture are sometimes allied with the different areas of human culture (*Science, *Society, *Art, *Religion, *History, *Language, *Technology, *Right, *State).

The conditions of culture should be distinguished from its causes; for, the conditions do not actually produce culture, but they are only the reason why culture develops easily or in a particular way. In this category should be included the geographical surroundings of a people, its place in history, the time and manner of its contacts with other peoples and cultures, the cultural institutions and directions inherited from the past. These factors condition the ebb and flow of the cultural movement. There is no such thing as constant *cultural progress* or even *cultural permanence*. The real causes of culture are man's abilities and needs. Thus, science springs from the desire to know of the theoretical intellect, social organization and technology from the desire rooted in the practical intellect to order things, art from the desire to create, morality and religion from man's moral inclinations. The difference in men's talents and inclinations, along with their careful development, leads naturally to a variety of professions which complement each other and which contribute to the cultural advancement of all. Man himself is the bearer and creator of culture, not in isolation, but as a member of different communities and in the context of a historical tradition, that is, as a spiritual link and continuer on the basis of what has been received from others. — Certainly, the goal of culture is primarily the satisfaction of human needs; but it is also the development of the riches contained in human nature and thereby the representation of man as the image of the creating God. The regulation and extent of culture depend upon whether or not the individual and the community correctly evaluate man's true needs, subordinate the lower to the higher and the higher to man's ultimate end. An essential consideration here is whether man's ultimate perfection (*Happiness) is sought wholly in this life or in the next life. Man's ordination to eternal life does not negate the requirements for an earthly culture, but rather subordinates them to the total good of the human person who is not limited just to this life. — By bringing out the true goal of all culture and the defects in present-day culture, the philosophy of culture should exercise some influence on the reform and advancement of culture for all men.

WB

CYBERNETICS

Cybernetics is the science of directing and regulating technical, biological, economic, social and other types of activity. In the most simple case the regulation proceeds according to the principle of a set sequence, as in the case of a thermostat: A sensitive "feeler" compares the actual temperature with the desired temperature and then turns on either a heating or a cooling element. In more complicated cases, as in the direction of a complex chemical fabrication process, a computer is used. For example, a program in the computer might read in data describing how single tools react to separate adjustments, and use this data to calculate what happens when a number of tools interact in various quite complicated ways. The settings which the computer determines in this manner to be optimal are then used in carrying out the actual process. All deliberations and decisions which can be reduced to a purely logical evaluation of *information* — information that can be given to an automaton or derived from it — can be taken over by computers. Indeed, the information (or the content of a communication) consists of "bits," i. e., of the number of (equally probable) yes-no decisions contained in a communication. The range of these purely logical decisions is extremely great; two examples are "learning" in the sense of the accommodation of future conduct to the success or failure of past conduct and "conditioned" reactions, as we find in the ability to sort out letters on the basis of differences in handwriting. The superiority of a man (e. g., a translator) over a machine made to do his work consists partly in that the man in the course of his life has absorbed more relevant information than the machine has.

Biological, neurophysiological and sociological events can be imitated by cybernetic machines (called "simulators") because of the formal correspondence between their operations (which on other counts are very different); this is possible because of the principle of *analogy. Here also belongs the possibility that one machine can make another machine just like itself or that an aggregate of such machines can imitate the evolution, regeneration and so forth of an organism. Such imitation is possible to the extent that the processes are clearly definable by means of mathematical-logical formulation. But this is not necessary for every individual event; it is sufficient, if the situation demands it, that the probability of the average can be statistically established or that in one system a definite output follows a definite input, even though the intermediate processes are not known (the "black-box" method). Since man's free activity is not the result of mere whim (*Free Will) but proceeds from motives, it is possible to apply statistics and cybernetics to various types of free behavior if that behavior can be established in a large number of cases.

Formal objectifiability which is the basis of cybernetics' success, also sets certain limitations. The existential foundation of spiritual operations is not definable nor can it be formalized. The self-reflection of the spirit, its inner intelligibility for itself (in which all knowledge of truth is rooted) and its self-direction in making free decisions cannot be imitated by registering one event in terms of another; for, this results only in a regressus in infinitum. An intuitively creative self-progamming of a machine is impossible; all the machine can do is find new combinations of the material put into it by man. The inner reality of the world of consciousness, which includes moods, feelings, etc. (even in those living beings that are not on the level of self-consciousness), is qualitatively different from the yes-no impulses of an electric circuit. Insofar as the total dynamism of vegetative-organic life can be reduced to cybernetic systems, it should be noted that, as a result of the intake and digestion of the information fed into them, these systems represent a higher type of organization than the "classical" machines. If vegetative life is to be thought of as an evolutionary step between inorganic matter and the higher levels of sensitive and intellectual life, so also here cybernetics seems only to undertake the imitation of a specific vital activity on another, analogous, functional level. Of course, cybernetic investigation is in a state of flux all along the line, and therefore there is also a certain degree of hesitation in the philosophical evaluation of it.

WoB-WB-WK-ZM

D

DASEIN

Dasein (existence) is the basic principle which, along with the *essence, constitutes and therefore characterizes every finite reality. While the essence says "what" something is, existence affirms "that" something is. If something exists, then it is not just thought or the product of the imagination, but independently of thought in and of itself it is simply there or present (*vorhanden*). Therefore, we discover it before us, we are impressed by it, we experience its resistance; we must reckon with its pre-given peculiarities and we cannot do whatever we like with it as we can with our own thought and imaginations. Although our ordinary consciousness is always tempted to think that only visible-tangible things are real, still this characteristic is not of the essence of existence; for, we experience in our own acts and egos an existent that is not at all something visible-tangible, but is nevertheless a reality — in fact, a spiritual reality. Yet our interior life manifests itself as an existent that is located in time and thus is capable of being experienced. However, spatio-temporal being that is capable of being experienced is likewise not of the essence of existence, since the absolutely supra-temporal and supra-spatial God exists more intensively than any finite existent.

From a metaphysical point of view, there are two fundamentally different kinds of existence; this is implied in what has been said so far. Our existence and that of all earthly things is limited — in fact it is only a "being there"; in other words, it is an existence limited to a definite spatio-temporal "there." The limitation comes directly from our finite essence, since only according to the power of our intellects are we able to grasp *existence or to participate in existence. A finite essence, therefore, does not attain the fullness of existence and so is not identical with existence. Accordingly, there is a distinction between the essence and the existence in a finite being. Thus a finite thing is a non-necessary (contingent) being; since its essence of itself does not necessarily include existence, it can either be or not be, it can be either actually present or only possible. Over against the finite

existent is infinite existence which exhausts the absolute fullness of existence, whose essense is identified with its existence. It is an absolutely
independent existence that exists in and of itself (subsisting) and so is
wholly necessary.

Within the limits of finite existents *existential philosophy also claims that
there are two fundamentally different kinds of existence. Everything sub-
human is merely the *given* which, without the knowledge of being as such,
achieves its full realization simply by "being there" and by operating according to the blind laws of nature. Man, on the other hand, "understands"
existence and is therefore placed in a position to decide about existence;
and he will only achieve his full reality, which he can certainly fail to attain,
by freely accepting and fulfilling existence. Thus man is an existent who
is also "there" or existing in order to have his own experience. Therefore,
existential philosophy reserves for him alone the term "existence" (*Dasein*).
Thus, Martin Heidegger calls man *Da-sein* insofar as he is that existent in
the world in whom alone the "being there" of existence occurs. — *Mathematical existence* is attributed to a mathematical concept (1) in relation
to a definite theory when it must necessarily be thought in accordance
with the axioms and logical principles of that theory and (2) in general
when it can be thought in a way that does not involve a contradiction.

JBL

DEATH

In general, death is a biological and physiological happening and so it
affects all living corporeal things. It consists in the cessation of life. This
end is expressed in the stopping of all life activities, i. e., growth, nutrition
and propagation in the vegetative world; for animals death means the
cessation of sensible awareness, desire and all types of motion. After death,
the more or less rapid decomposition of the organism sets in so that it
dissolves into the inorganic matter that originally constituted it. These
visible processes indicate that what constitutes the essence of death has
actually taken place, namely, the separation of the life principle (the soul)
from the body, because the body is no longer able to be a supporter of
life as the result of age or sickness or injury. With this separation, plant
and animal souls cease to exist, since they cannot exist at all without a
body; the spiritual soul of man, however, begins its immortal existence and
for this reason its thoughts and desires no longer appear corporeally (*Immortality).

Death rounds off life in the sense that it brings it to conclusion and so
manifests the final meaning of life. In death, sub-human living beings
show themselves as passing moments in the total context of this spatio-
temporal world. In sharp contrast to animals and plants, for man death

means a return from the alienated multiplicity of the spatio-temporal world to the interiorized unity of the spirit.

A profound insight into the personal meaning of human death was achieved in the 19th century by Kierkegaard; Rilke and Heidegger have turned this insight into a determining factor of the present intellectual climate. These philosophers see man as enclosed in a world in whose nothingness he is in danger of losing himself, because the totality of his existence is in disarray. Not until he experiences and decisively takes hold of his "*existence towards death*" does he raise himself up to the fullness of his human existence; once this has been accomplished, they say, man is able to take possession of his own inner self. This view of life has a good deal of truth to it, if "existence towards death" means man's innermost dependence on God and if death itself means man's going home to God, as Kierkegaard (in his own special way) intends it. Yet this "existential" view is most questionable if death is only a tumble into nothingness, as Sartre and perhaps also Rilke say. Even according to Heidegger the only thing that remains in death is nothingness — but a nothingness that is the veil of existence; thus in Heidegger it should be understood not in a nihilistic way.

JBL

DEDUCTION

Deduction is an *inference or argumentation from a universal to a less universal or particular, and in some cases also to another universal; its opposite is *induction. Since Francis Bacon the following objection has been raised against deduction: One either knows or does not know that the major premise contains the particular. If the former, then the result is already known through the major premise alone; if the latter, then the conclusion does not follow with certainty since, in such a case, one does not know whether the major premise is universally valid. The objection, however, fails to recognize that the *universal concept used in the major premise contains only the nature that is common to all the objects that fall under it; but it does not at all indicate which objects fall under this concept. For example, in the major premise "What is simple is indestructible," only the relationship of simplicity to indestructibility is affirmed; but nothing is said about which objects are simple. Such information must come from the minor premise, for example, "The human soul is simple." We can conclude then from both propositions: "The human soul is indestructible." — Kant calls "deduction" a proof that establishes a legal claim (in contrast to a factual proof). Also according to Kant, deduction is *transcendental* (or *objective*) if it explains how a pure concept is related a priori to objects, and it is *empirical* (or *subjective*) if it shows how a concept is acquired through experience and reflection (*Critical Philosophy).

JS

DEFINITION

The definition of a term is the linguistic expression that briefly but completely sets forth what is to be understood by a word or by some thing. The purpose of a *nominal definition* is to circumscribe the precise meaning of a given word, while the purpose of the *real definition* is to indicate the specific *essence of something. A definition should be brief, that is, it should avoid all superfluous determinations; and it should be complete, that is, it should mention all the characteristics that are necessary not only to distinguish the word or thing from all other things, but also to allow the inner differences and the essential structure of the sense to shine forth. Simple contents or realities can be manifested with one word, but they cannot really be defined through one word. — A genuine *essential determination* is realized by indicating the proximate genus and the specific difference (e. g., man = rational animal; *Species) or by naming the essential parts of the thing in question (e. g., man = a being that is composed of a body and a rational soul). Often the only definition possible is a *descriptive* one; in this case so many characteristics are added to the general determination of the genus that the object is thereby sufficiently distinguished from all other things. A *genetic definition* determines and explains an object by furnishing the mode of its origin. With regard to the *implicit definition*, that which is to be defined is made known by being used in a relationship to something that is already known both as a whole and in its parts; thus there is a movement from the known to the unknown. A very special difficulty is presented by the definition of objects that are given neither in internal nor external experience and are not constructed out of simpler elements merely by thinking about them; we are referring here to realities that can be grasped only as the (external or internal) conditions of the possibility of objects given in concrete experience. However, the meaning of such objects can be exactly described by unfolding the systematic inter-relations of these conditions. — The rules of a definition: The parts of a definition must be more known than the reality being defined. The definition and the defined must be mutually interchangeable. — There are two ways of arriving at a good definition: one either divides and subdivides a higher genus until one arrives at the desired species, or else one looks for some common element in the objects to be defined that belongs to all objects thus designated and only to them.

WB

DEISM

Deism, which appeared in England about the middle of the 16th century, recognizes a personal Creator-God, but it denies that he has any further interest in or influence on the world. Accordingly, it also denies the sustaining power and *concurrence of God with his creatures, *miracles and all supernatural *revelation. Thus the advocates of this point of view say that there cannot be a revealed religion, but only a rational or natural religion. — This English deism led finally in France to a materialistic and atheistic *enlightenment. Since the middle of the 18th century this position has had some champions also in Germany.

MR

DEMOCRACY

Democracy (= government by the people) originally meant in Greek thought the political form in which the people themselves possess and exercise all political authority; this they proposed in opposition to the rule of one man (monarchy) or a privileged group (aristocracy) and the corrupted forms of these (tyranny and oligarchy). In the course of history the meaning of the word has changed considerably; in Aristotle it signifies a decadent form of the *politeia* or city-state (in which there is a balance between democracy and oligarchy); today the word is often used simply as a political slogan (e. g., "The People's Democracy").

The foundation of modern thinking about democracy is the philosophical-political idea of the sovereignty of the people; this means that all political power is traced back to the people themselves as the primordial subject of this authority. Added to this is the requirement that all citizens capable of using their reason and having a developed conscience, as free and basically equal men, should themselves take part in arriving at decisions about political matters that concern them. The people as a whole, however, can exercise the supreme power of the state jointly only to a very restricted degree (*immediate or pure democracy*). Therefore legal processes must be laid down in a constitution; such processes enable the people to take part indirectly in the formation of political policy by means of secret, free elections of representatives who remain in office for a definite length of time. These representatives are elected according to a defined principle of a definite majority and they are given rights and duties that are precisely outlined (*representative democracy*). A plurality of political parties should offer the people well-thought out political alternatives by means of public discussion and the exposure of well qualified persons. Democracy in this sense is not bound to the political form of a *republic* (in which the representative head of state is elected by the people or their representatives).

A viable democracy presupposes on the part of its citizens political maturity, good judgment and the readiness to subordinate their own private interests to the demands of the common good. When these pre-conditions are fulfilled, then a people should not be denied the opportunity to take part in government when they request it. Democratic decisions arrived at in a just fashion must be recognized as binding on all citizens, for in a democracy legitimate authority, given to the people by God, is truly exercised; however, the formal rules of democratic decision-making of themselves do not provide an absolute guarantee against injustice. — Democratic forms of participation in responsibility are beginning to operate more and more outside of the strictly political arena (e. g., democratic processes in businesses, in schools and universities, etc.).

WaK

DEMONSTRATION

Demonstration (1) in the strict sense is an *inference from true and certain premises; as the result of such argumentation, a previously questionable reality is known not only as logically connected with the premises, but also as true and certain. Demonstration (2) in a wider sense is every type of thinking that reveals a questionable reality as either certain or probable through the use of some process other than the inference. This is found either in an immediate transition from one proposition to another (*Opposition, *Modality) or in the exhibition of the immediate evidence of the proposition through analysis and comparison of the concepts. Every demonstration is a *grounding* insofar as through it the reason for the knowledge is indicated and this reason is the basis for the assent of the mind to the questionable reality. The *argumentum ad hominem* is valid only for a definite opponent. — While the *demonstratio quia* indicates only the reason for the knowledge, the *demonstratio propter quid* also gives an insight into the objective reality. With regard to the other types of demonstration: *Deduction, *Induction, *A Priori, *A Posteriori. — Whoever in the course of a demonstration slips from one logically closed area into another (e. g., from the order of possibility into the order of reality) falls into the fallacy of a *metábasis eis állo génos*.

JS

DENIAL

Denial (negation) is located in man's judgment. Normally it denies the existence of an *objective reality or affirms its non-existence: for example, "Today it is not raining." Such a denial is true if the reality in question is actually not given. Yet often a positive state of affairs is expressed through a denial: for example, "This man is not blind." Denials of this kind are true if the respective state of affairs (here: the power of sight) is really present. A second kind of denial is of decisive importance for metaphysics; for, it is only because of denial or negation that the finite spirit is able to press forward towards the infinite. Since infinity is not immediately accessible to the finite spirit, he forms his concept by affirming the positive content of a (pure) perfection of God and at the same time denying all limitations in it. Thus, one can attribute life to God in its infinite (= without limits) fullness by denying all limits in his life. Basically this gives us a denial of a denial, since "limit" says nothing else but a denial of further perfection beyond the limits. Such a judgment is true to the extent that God is actually infinite. Here we are touching upon the heart of the "power of the negative" which played such an important role in the thought of Hegel. — The way of knowing described here is called in technical philosophical language "the way of negation"; *negative theology, which is named for this way of knowing, adheres to it too one-sidedly. Often the mystics, including a religious thinker like Meister Eckhart, also move in this direction.

JBL

DETERMINISM

Determinism is the doctrine opposed to *indeterminism* which says that all of our will-acts are unequivocally determined by a constellation of operative motives and by the momentary, conscious or unconscious, state of the mind. Frequently this position rests on a false understanding of the meaning of *free will, as if it means a power of causeless and motiveless willing (*excessive indeterminism*). Generally, determinism bases itself primarily on the principle of causality, but understands it not only in such a way that every effect must have an adequate cause (which is the only way in which it can be proved as a universally valid and necessary principle), but also in such a way that every effect must be clearly predetermined in its total cause (a point that has not been proved with regard to the totality of reality; *Causality, Law of).

Proceeding according to the empirical method, determinism interprets man's awareness of personal freedom as a false judgment that arises out of ignorance of unconscious drives (*determining tendencies*). In this it fails to see that we consider experiences based on unconscious complexes (e. g., scientific and artistic inspirations, tricks of the imagination and so forth), because of our ignorance of their causes, not as "freely willed" by us but rather as somehow "mysterious." Another alleged empirical basis for determinism is the fact that, when we are familiar with the character, habits, inclinations and circumstances of other men, we can predict fairly accurately what they will do; and we can also point to the regularity of many "free" actions which shows that some law is operating, as *moral statistics claims. However, these empirical indications prove only that there is no motiveless willing, that people generally follow their own inclinations and character, that they readily avoid conflicts with their own desires, but they do not resolve the question as to whether or not this avoidance is a free act. When free will is abandoned, then the ideas of responsibility, reward, punishment and so forth lose all meaning; determinism tries to save these notions by declaring that the "character" of a guilty person is responsible and punishable (in which case, however, the guilty individual can no longer be distinguished from the psychopath); further, it interprets punishment as a means of deterrence or as a means to protect the community against asocial persons (but in this case the value of the ethical person is destroyed and man is made into a spiritual marionette). — As a result of their fundamental principles, the following systems are basically deterministic: all forms of materialism and monism, pantheism, positivism, empiricism, extreme rationalism as well as extreme biologism. — From the point of view of the philosophy of nature, determinism is thought of as the theory about the simple determination of every natural event (*Causality, Law of, *Quantum Mechanics). — On economic determinism, see also *Marxism*.

AW

DEVELOPMENT

Development has many meanings: (1) it can mean a process by which an inner principle, which is at first hidden, comes to light (e. g., the development of an idea by a speaker); (2) it may be a slow, step by step transformation (which is not necessarily directed to one definite goal: e. g., many historical developments); (3) or it may be a transformation that is guided in a definite direction; (4) it can be a transformation that leads from the unformed and less determined to the formed and fully determined (= differentiation); (5) finally, it can be a transformation from one form or species to another, and this either slowly or by leaps. — These abstract meanings of the word "development" are not necessarily mutually exclusive. Several of them can be realized together in the concrete processes that we call "development." Everything changeable can, in some sense, be subject to development.

Development in the realm of organic life is called *ontogenesis*, i. e., the development of the germ of life or the embryo into a mature being capable of independent life. This is development (1), not in the sense of the out-dated theory of preformation which claimed that the *organism with all its parts is already present in the fertilized egg and is only unfolded and enlarged by means of its development; rather, it is development in the sense that only through ontogenesis does the hidden purpose and planning of nature become manifest. Since something really new is brought forth in ontogenesis, it is also called *epigenesis* or a *new develop-*

ment. It is development in sense (3). It is also development in sense (4) not only in reference to the structure, which is better differentiated, but also in reference to function: while in the earliest stages any part can assume any function, very soon a moment comes after which the parts are more and more determined for their own special functions so that they can no longer substitute for each other. The completion of ontogenesis is the full development of the sexual functions or puberty. Growth, however, is clearly distinguished from ontogenesis, because it brings no new formation. It is development in the sense of (5), not of (1) and (4). The aging and decline of an organism is only development in sense (2). The other important form of development in the organic world is called *phylogenesis* or the appearance of new species. This is development in sense (5) (*Evolutionism). The fact of directed development (3), as is apparent in ontogenesis, cannot be explained without some kind of anticipation of the end *before* its realization. The possibility that at the beginning of the process every part can assume every function leads to the problem of *vitalism.

The intellectual life of man also manifests a development above that of the organic world and not necessarily parallel to it. This is partially tied to the subject as a personal development and it partially transcends the individual as a supra-personal development. Even the personal development of man embraces meanings (1) to (4). And it finds the limits of its possibility in its innate tendencies; profoundly influenced by the surrounding world, it maintains its course by means of the free decisions of the will (*Free Will). — Supra-personal developments include all historical development (1, 2 and in some degree 3) (history of ideas, cultures, peoples, nations, etc.). It is a prejudice unsupported by the facts that the supra-personal development of mankind takes place only in the sense of progress to a higher and better form of life.

According to evolutionism, development becomes the schema of the entire world process with a greater (Spencer, Alexander) or lesser (Bergson) dependence on natural science. The underlying absolute expresses itself in this process and assumes different forms. In this case the processes either replace each other or else one arises out of the other (emergent evolution). Aristotle observed long ago that an absolute becoming, operating without a first, transcendent efficient principle, cannot solve the problems that are presented by becoming and wasting away. — See also *Becoming, Evolutionism, Process Philosophy.*

WB

DIALECTIC

Dialectic (Gk.: *dialégesthai*) literally is the art of conversation. Even though it was in use before Socrates, he gave it its classic form. By means of dialectic Socrates wanted to bring men to the true essence of things by a gradual clarification of concepts. Plato's *Dialogues* carry on this effort, for they attempt to dig out the essence of things through a process of statement and contradiction and so to prepare for the ascent to the primordial reality, that is, the Ideas. Thus, for Plato dialectic is the method of metaphysics. The scholastic method used in medieval metaphysics was somewhat similar. The *disputations were conducted as colloquies or dialogues; the same character determined the structure of the scholastic "*Quaestio*" (Question). In each case the dynamism of the "*Sic et Non*" (Yes and No) propel thought forward.

The extent to which dialogue characterizes man in that which is proper to him is expressed by these words of Hölderlin: "We have existed since the first conversation." In reality we are always conversing, if not with others then at least with ourselves. Even the spiritual progress of mankind is an on-going conversation between the different epochs. In this way the complete truth is only gradually revealed in the encounter of statement and contradiction. Thus, human history is caught up in the dialectic of the spirit. From this perspective it is not difficult to elevate dialectic to a basic principle of existence. Heraclitus already saw in "war," i. e., in the conflict of opposites, the "father of all things" or the innermost essence of reality. *German idealism, and especially Hegel, developed this idea further. According to Hegel, the real is essentially becoming, which moves on from stage to stage in the triple pace of thesis — antithesis — synthesis; therefore, our thinking too must proceed in the same way. There is something very true about this insight, but it becomes mixed up with pantheism to the extent that God is also subjected to the dialectic or to becoming; moreover, the fact is usually overlooked that the dialectic proceeds not according to a contradictory but according to a contrary *opposition. When Nicolas of Cusa, at the beginning of the modern age, characterized God as the "*coincidentia oppositorum*" (coincidence of opposites) he did not mean that in a pantheistic sense. — Under the influence of Hegel *dialectical materialism has applied dialectic to the world of matter and to economics.

In a wider sense, dialectic is identical with formal *logic, with the study of the forms and laws of human thinking as such. This meaning of the word is explained by the fact that it was prepared for by the science of rhetoric and by scientific debates. In periods of intellectual decline dialectic has been misused to foster useless sophistries so that at present dialectic sometimes also signifies sophistry.

The above-enumerated meanings are found all together in Kant's "*transcendental dialectic.*" Under this title metaphysics along with the whole philosophical tradition is handled. The contradiction also comes into play in the form of the *antinomies in order to bring to light the uncritical combination of physical-scientific and philosophical thinking. Finally, however, Kant's dialectic attempts to unmask all knowledge of transcendental reality as a kind of deceptive appearance of something that is not there.

JBL

DIALECTICAL MATERIALISM

Dialectical materialism is the attempted philosophical justification of the economic and political theses of Karl Marx; the theory was worked out and formulated mainly by Friedrich Engels. If *historical materialism attempted to demonstrate the materiality and thereby also the necessary development of human history down to communism, dialectical materialism does not hesitate to affirm the materiality of absolutely all existence; also, in this way every doubt about a materialistic explanation of history is supposed to be removed on ontological grounds. Among the proponents of dialectical materialism there is a lack of unity with regard to its object; usually, following Engels, it is said to be "the most universal laws of nature, society and thinking"; but more recently it is said to be "the relationship of thinking to existence, of mind to nature" — something Engels had characterized as "the basic question of philosophy." Dialectical materialism is divided into a theory of existence and a theory of knowing; the former deals with *matter and the objective dialectic operating in it, while the latter deals with the subjective dialectic of human thinking. The other philosophical disciplines are replaced by the positive science most closely related to them through the introduction of the dialectical method.

On the level of ontology, dialectical materialism simply presupposes the objective reality of a purely material world as self-evident. Lenin's definitions of matter are considered binding in spite of their inner contradictions: "Matter is a philosophical category used to designate objective reality; it is given to man in his perceptions; it is copied, photographed, represented by our perceptions and it exists independently of them" (Werke 14, p. 124); also, "The only 'characteristic' of matter that philosophical *materialism is bound to recognize is: to be objective reality, to exist outside of our consciousness" (ibid., p. 260). *Consciousness is designated the "characteristic," "product," "function" of the most highly organized (= brain) matter (or also as the movement of brain-matter); nevertheless, it is explicitly spoken of as "immaterial," as the "ideal reflection of objective reality by means of the central nervous system"; and in recent years, surprisingly, it is called "mind" with increasing frequency. The essential characteristics of matter are said to be motion and infinite extension in space, in time and in "depth." Materialistic *monism is especially emphasized.

DIALECTICAL MATERIALISM

The self-motion of matter is brought about according to the laws of *dialectic. According to this theory, everything that is (thesis) conceals contradictions within itself — contradictions that lead to conflict and thereby to *development or evolution. This involves movement from the lower to the higher, from inanimate matter to life, perception, consciousness. The sudden change of the thesis is prepared for by quantitative changes which can be continued up to a critical point that is peculiar to each thing (e. g., heating water to the boiling point). However, if this limit is exceeded, a qualitatively new thing (e. g., steam) arises in a *dialectical leap* as the negation of the former thing (antithesis). Then the *negation of the negation* leads to the third step (synthesis). At the same time the synthesis offers another new beginning: the dialectical process keeps rising endlessly like a climbing spiral.

The epistemology of dialectical materialism affirms two things: (1) human consciousness arose by means of a dialectical leap from less organized matter and (2) it faithfully represents its surroundings. According to Lenin, our perceptions (and in a wider sense even our concepts) are faithful "reflections" of "objective reality." The *subjective dialectic* of thinking corresponds to the *objective dialectic* according to which matter unfolds. Because existence, which is supposed to abound in intrinsic contradictions, cannot be adequately grasped by formal logic and its priniple of contradiction, but also because no meaningful statement can totally reject formal logic, dialectical materialism attempts to construct a new "dialectical" logic in order to present existence (allegedly full of contradictions) in a way that is not contradictory. The ultimate criterion for the validity of knowledge is practical life, that is, "the total economic process of the transformation of objective reality by man," or in other words: the production of consumer goods and the struggle for communism. Since the elementary evolution of the world, which is independent of man's will, supposedly runs also in this same direction, so also a conscious self-insertion into this process corresponds to reality and so is true and correct (*Pravda* = reality, truth and justice). Practical life is directed by the communist party which knows best the way to the goal and therefore makes the final decisions in every area of knowledge and life. From this structure proceed the two basic methodological postulates of dialectical materialism: unity of theory and practice and a philosophy supporting the communist party.

The heart of dialectical materialism is the impossible absolutizing of a matter that is moving in time and space or the affirmation of a *becoming that is without a cause. The "contradictions" or opposites in nature which are affirmed by this theory can only be the conditions of the possibility of further development, but they cannot be the adequate foundation of it. The human *spirit, therefore, cannot be the product of a purely natural development that rises from the lower to the higher, for it presupposes an adequate cause that operates through inorganic and organic nature.

Moreover, the ontology of dialectical materialism can at best establish some kind of *realism, but not a materialistic monism. Also, a reality that contradicts itself, and this is what is demanded by the materialistic dialectic, is simply non-existent. See *Contradiction, Principle of*.

HF

DIALECTICAL THEOLOGY

Dialectical theology is a branch of Protestant theology, represented chiefly by K. Barth, E. Brunner and F. Gogarten, which attempts to renew the original theology of the reformers. Following Luther, it asserts the total incapacity of fallen man to know God and to do anything naturally good. Reason cannot affirm anything about God even in an analogous sense. There is such a gap between God and the world that it is not possible to know anything about God from earthly things. This gap can be bridged only by God himself when he speaks to man in revelation. And this revelation must be its own self-justification. It is not possible to bring forth a rational proof of its facticity. The object of revelation can be determined only by dialectical statements which can neither be raised to a higher third level (as in Hegel), nor harmonized with each other (as in scholasticism). Responding in his later development to many criticisms, K. Barth modified the rigidity of his teaching in that he recognized a certain analogy, based upon God himself, in affirmations of faith.

Dialectical theology, which is presented here only from the philosophical point of view and in the rigid way it was first proposed, sees nothing but opposition between God and the world. In the *analogy of being, which it calls the "original sin" of human reason, it claims to detect a doctrine which puts God and the world on the same plane; but in this it misunderstands the classical teaching according to which God is the foundation of the whole order of existence by reason of his very essence without in any way being subordinate to finite existence. No predicate, not even existence, is attributed to God and creature in the same way; and we know only by negation what the divine mode of existence is. — For dialectical theology, created existence is the same thing as sin and rejection of God, while according to the scholastic view the existent as such is existentially good (*Value) and also recognized by God as having value. In Catholic theology original sin involves the loss of *supernatural grace, but it is not a destruction or essential perversion of human nature; moreover, man's nature retains the basic capacity, even though it is greatly limited by concupiscence, to arrive at some natural knowledge of God and to posit moral acts in accord with nature. — *Faith and revealed truth must be reasonable. Therefore, man must acquire practical *certitude about the fact of *revelation. He must also be able to form some idea of the content of revelation that is at least free of all formal contradictions;

this holds even in those areas where the intrinsic possibility of the matter affirmed (e. g., Trinity) cannot be seen by the human mind.

WB

DISJUNCTION

Disjunction is the name given to the relationship that exists between the member statements of a *disjunctive* judgment. The disjunctive judgment belongs to the family of *hypothetical judgments (in the broad sense). A disjunction is made up of several member statements; in a *complete disjunction* it is affirmed that one of them is necessarily true, while all the others are false ("either-or"). The member statements cannot all be true nor can they all be false; one of them and only one is necessarily true. In the *incomplete disjunction* it is only affirmed that at least one of the members is true, without indicating which one ("or"). The member statements in a disjunction can all be true, but all of them together cannot be false. On the disjunctive inference: *Hypothetical Syllogisms.

WB

DISPOSITION

Disposition in the broadest sense means the ability to effect or to suffer something. Understood in this way, a disposition is the same thing as a subjective *potency. Usually, however, it is used in a narrower sense and means the innate readiness of a living being for certain kinds of activity, passivity, reaction, development, etc. In biology the inherited dispositions associated with particular characteristics of an organism are called *genes*. In psychology and philosophical anthropology the notion of a "disposition" is taken less in relation to particular characteristics; rather, it tends to signify the innate and wholly unified nature of a fundamental operation (like knowing, willing, feeling) or of the soul as such.

A disposition certainly gives the fundamental possibility for particular kinds of activity and experience, but it does not by itself confer completeness and the full readiness to act. This must be acquired by practice and by the growth of habits which are the goal of the motive power residing in every disposition or tendency. Just as dispositions bestow on each living thing a certain direction of its possible activities, so also they impose certain limitations. Given these restrictions, however, the development of dispositions depends on the environment, the necessities of life and, for men, on the free decisions of his will. — "Disposition" is the English equivalent of the Latin *dispositio*, first of all in the sense of arrangement (e. g., of a written text). In another sense, however, it signifies not just innate and permanent, but also acquired and temporary qualities and habits, like attitudes, frames of mind, etc.

WB

DISPUTATION

A disputation is a scientifically ordered debate. Often in disputations arguments and counter-arguments are set forth in a rather free style; this easily leads to the danger that the debaters do not really collide "head on." The *scholastic* type of disputation proceeds in strict form according to set rules. After the "exposition" of a "thesis" and the presentation of the proof by the defender (*defendens*), the objector (*obiciens*) counters with an objection presented in strict syllogistic form; the defender repeats the objection word for word and passes judgment on each one of its propositions. If he denies one of the premises, then it is incumbent upon the objector to offer a proof for the proposition that has been denied. The principal means available to destroy fallacious counter-arguments is the *distinction (*distinctio*) which is applied to the ambiguous terms or propositions which may be contained in those counter-arguments. In the Middle Ages the disputation was considered an important help for the clarification of difficult questions; today it is rarely used, but when it is used it serves primarily as an educational tool and thus is a help for students to think through difficult problems.

JdV

DISTINCTION

Distinction (1) is the act whereby the different is recognized as different, or it is the *difference* itself (2). Difference in the broad sense is non-*identity or the relation of one to another insofar as it is another. It is based on *multiplicity or the *denial of *unity; therefore it has as many kinds as unity itself. Fundamentally different (= *disparate*) are those realities that belong to different genera or orders, such as "blue" and $\sqrt{2}$. Difference in the narrow sense is that in which several things, which have something in common, are different; therefore what one has the other does not have, for example, the whole and the part or the species concept and the genus concept. — A *real distinction* is given where a denial of identity in the mind is also a denial of identity in the thing referred to; this can occur either because the distinction is given in experience (= *physical distinction*, as between concrete things), or because the distinction is knowable only by means of thinking, as the necessary condition of the possibility of an object (= *metaphysical distinction* between non-intuitable partial principles of a material existent; it would be, for example, in the Thomistic synthesis the distinction between essence and existence in the finite existent). — A *conceptual* or *logical* distinction is found to be present in something grasped by means of different concepts, but this does not mean that the distinction corresponds to a similar real multiplicity in the thing. For, the logical distinction is based on the fact that in our human condition we must separate objective contents from each other by means of *abstraction, although they are really one in the thing and belong to it because of the same principle. Thus, for example, the whole man is sense-endowed and rational, and both characteristics pertain to him by reason of the same soul. If one idea-content (as is the case here) is not reduceable to another but is conceptually self-contained, so that the other can be added only on the basis of experience, then one speaks of a logical distinction that is *perfectly grounded objectively.* However, a logical distinction is said to be *imperfectly grounded objectively,* if the complete thinking through of one idea-content necessarily leads into another; such is the case with the *transcendentals, with the attributes of God and with the first differences of *existence. — See also *Opposition.*

WB

DIVISIBILITY

Divisibility is the possibility of a whole being cut up into parts. Every divisibility presupposes a composition of parts which together constitute a whole; in this whole a natural unity dominates the multiplicity. Indivisibility presupposes *simplicity. If several things are connected in such a way that a natural unity does not result, then the solubility of those things from each other is called "separability." — Divisibility is purely mental or it is real, depending upon whether it is a question of mental parts or real parts. — Divisibility is the chief characteristic of *quantity and extension. Quantitative parts are also termed *integrating parts*, which have the same nature as the whole. If an extended reality is divided according to a definite measure, the resulting parts are said to be *numerical parts.* We have *proportional parts* if we continually divide according to the same relationship, for example, if we halve something and go on halving the resultings parts. So long as there is just a question of extension, a constantly extended thing can be further divided without end. However, this conceptually infinite divisibility can be limited by the physical nature of the thing to be divided; such a limit may prevent any further division. *Bodies are divisible by physical and chemical methods into molecules and atoms which, in turn, can be further divided into protons, neutrons and electrons as the ultimate, physically indivisible, structural elements of the material world. — In contrast to the integrating parts, the non-homogeneous parts are called the *constitutive or essential parts*; such parts, when they are united, constitute an essence, such as body and soul in man or body and life principle in animals and plants. A separation of the constitutive parts simply means the destruction of the essence of a thing.

NJ

DIVISION

Division in the broader sense is the separation of a whole into its parts; it includes a whole that is separated, parts that are established and a basis of division according to which the whole is dismembered. Division in the narrower sense concerns the extension of a *universal concept or of a class. A *class* is the totality of objects that are actualizations of a concept. Thus, sense-endowed living things are the class of objects that realize the concept "sense-endowed living things." Through further conceptual-determinations, such as rational and irrational, further incomplete classes (corresponding to the subordinate concepts) can be specified; if the totality of these objects is equal to the objects of the *complete class*, then the division of the complete class is perfect. — A distinction should be made between division in the narrower sense and *partition*, whether it is the partition of a concept into its special notes or of a real whole into its real parts. In the case of division, the full concept of the whole or of the class belongs to all the subordinate members; in the case of partition, this is not always so. — A true division must be: (1) exhaustive, i. e., the objects numbered in the sub-classes may not be more nor less than the objects of the major class; (2) it must consist of mutually exclusive members, i. e., no object can belong to several sub-classes; (3) it should be arranged in an orderly fashion, i. e., the basis of the division should not be changed before the division of the class is completed. — Depending upon whether the basis of division rests upon an essential or an accidental characteristic, one can distinguish between essential and accidental divisions. If one member of a division is then divided again, the result is a major division and a sub-division. An orderly series of major and sub-divisions is called a *classification*. See also *distinction*.

JS

DOGMATISM

Dogmatism as a philosophical position means (1) primarily the opposite of *skepticism. By dogmatism Kant understands (2) *rationalism and also every philosophy that attempts to construct a metaphysics without first developing an epistemology. In general, every philosophy that consciously removes its affirmations and presuppositions from the field of reasonable criticism can be characterized as a dogmatism (3). Dogmatism (4) as a personal attitude is the inclination to have the last word in everything and not to tolerate any opposition. — *Dogmatic* can mean either: (1) uncritically; or (2) apodictic, conclusive, necessary on the basis of rational principles; or (3) pertaining to the theological dogma of the Church.

JS

DOUBT

Doubt is a hesitation between yes and no, between contradictory opinions, without assenting to one or the other. Doubt presupposes awareness of a judgment that one must take a position on; it also presupposes that there are reasons or at least apparent reasons for both of the contradictory opinions. Particularly when it is a matter of serious questions concerning one's personal life, doubt is often accompanied by a tormenting feeling of unrest. Doubt is justified as long as the reasons either for or against a given opinion do not add up to real *evidence; when there is a noticeable preponderance of reasons for one side, then a well-founded opinion (i. e., a provisional decision) is justified. However, as long as no real evidence is adduced a firm assent, excluding all doubt, should not be given (*Certitude); if one persists in doubt, in spite of sufficient evidence to the contrary, then such doubt has no foundation.

Doubt as we have described it is a *real* and *positive* doubt. To be distinguished from positive doubt is a real but *negative doubt* which is brought about by the absence of any reasons either for or against a given statement; this is perhaps better described simply as ignorance. There is also the apparent or *fictitious doubt* which means only a non-consideration of one's own natural certitude in many things in order to arrive at scientific certitude by means of an orderly examination of the evidence and the reasons for it. The fictitious doubt is often equated with the *methodical doubt*. Yet the "methodical doubt" in itself does not necessarily refer only to an apparent doubt; rather, it signifies every doubt that is intentionally embraced for the purpose of scientifically searching out the truth, whether it is only an apparent doubt or a real doubt. The latter is fully justified if the object to be studied is truly doubtful.

JdV

DUALISM

Dualism in general, in contrast to *monism, preserves the basic differences that exist in reality between contingent and absolute existence (world and God), between knowing and existing in the contingent realm, between matter and spirit (or between matter and life that is bound to matter), between substance and accident, etc. — Of course, all multiplicity is ultimately reducible to unity, but it cannot be cancelled out in its own sphere. — On the other hand, dualism often signifies the opposite extreme of monism; a totally unrelated duality. Thus, extreme *metaphysical dualism* explains limitation and evil in the world by affirming that there are two basic principles at work. One is God; the other is an eternal, "potential" principle (Plato's eternal matter) that impedes and limits God's acts in the world; sometimes it is also thought of as an independent evil power that operates in opposition to the good principle (*Manicheanism). Also anthropological dualism as it was proposed by Descartes misconceives the unity of soul and body in man (*Body-Soul Relation). Concerning *physical dualism*, see *Quantum Mechanics*.

AW

DUTY

The heart of *morality is made up of the commands and prohibitions which a man is bound to by reason of his duty or obligation. The "ought" included in man's sense of duty has an absolute character so that the carrying out of this "ought" is demanded of all men everywhere and at all times. Biological constitution and spiritual make-up, surroundings and tradition, advantage and damage, pleasure and pain do not of themselves explain the origin of *obligation*; for they merely help or hinder its fulfillment. The source of all moral obligation is primarily the order of existence. Since man as a spiritual and free being is not subject to an inner compulsion and therefore has the right to be free from all external coercion, there can only be direction in his life to the extent that the image of what he should be is presented to his free choice by the "you ought to do this or avoid that" which resides in his own conscience. The totality of human existence with all of its ramifications is the source of the norms of human activity. Man's freedom is bound by his duty not only hypothetically (conditionally) but also categorically (unconditionally) to the tasks imposed upon him by his own human existence, since the integral parts of his essence are constant and his very existence is given to him by God.

More can be said on this question. The historical connection between morality and religion is founded in the reference of each order to the other. An attitude which begins with the fact of *religion and thus relates the totality of human life to God, also finds the ultimate justification of all real moral obligation in God. On the basis of this transcendental foundation the tasks and challenges which flow out of human nature become God's commandments and prohibitions — commands which are rooted in the essence and will of God. On the other hand, man's "ethical" tendency points beyond moral phenomena and demands a religious explanation.

This necessity appears as soon as the problem of life's purpose leads a person to consider the question of "motivation." An autonomous moral philosophy, lacking any sort of transcendental foundation, can only base itself on this-worldly motives. To desire and to do the right thing only because it is in itself good, presupposes external and internal conditions which for the most part are valid only for small groups of people. All men will only then both externally and internally be able to fulfill the whole moral law for a long time and especially in borderline cases, which frequently demand great sacrifices, if their relationship to God and the knowledge of a just recompense in the next life give them the necessary spiritual power to do it. The history both of moral consciousness and of autonomous moral philosophy shows that, when religion and morality are separated, slowly but surely in the course of generations a breakdown in the level of human living and an eroding of moral standards go hand in hand. This is the psychological and historical consequence of an isolation which separates a man from contact with the real world and which allows only a part of the world of objective values to function as the source of his motivation. Therefore, for its own sake morality demands, as long as the question of the motives for moral action is raised, that it be connected with religion as the normal thing.

However, the transcendental foundation of duty becomes a universal and absolute requirement which allows of no exceptions when one considers the "experience of contingency" which is inherent in all moral phenomena. Experienced and known *contingency leads a man out of this world to God. In fact, it is the only way to God outside of divine revelation. The proofs for the existence of God are distinguished only according to the different objects which manifest their own form of contingency. The distinction between existence and ought as well as the gap between the ideal and the real are merely forms of contingency; when these contrasts are recognized and thought through they lead man out of the finiteness and limitations of his moral existence and bring him to the higher level of religion. — See also *Autonomy, Categorical Imperative.*

PB

DYNAMIC

Anything related to *motion, *activity and *power can be called "dynamic." A dynamic way of looking at things stresses the activity and creative process of things in contrast to their static qualities. A dynamic view of order = *finality. See also *Dynamism.*

WB

DYNAMISM

Dynamism can be the name given to any philosophical theory that (1) either explains what the non-philosopher considers as immobile existence by means of *power and *activity, or (2) in contrast to other philosophers, extends this explanation to broader areas, or (3) actually extends it to the whole of reality = integral dynamism. — Scholastic philosophy recognizes a dynamism of *form insofar as it brings to its bearer not only a tranquil existence, but also gives it power and orientation towards an attainable end and so also endows it with striving and activity (*Finality). This is true both of the substantial form and also of the accidental forms that follow it. In applying this theory to the act of knowing, Joseph Maréchal taught that the relationship of our mental images to objects is possible only by reason of the dynamic character of the knowing power as it reveals itself in the judgement; this is *epistemological dynamism*. Scholastic dynamism is to be distinguished from integral dynamism first of all in that, according to it, form is not a mere concept (as Bergson affirms) that is necessarily put in the service of flowing existence — a concept that unnaturally chops up reality into little pieces; form is an essential component that determines the existence of the object in every way and orientates it towards its fulfillment. Secondly, scholasticism (with a Thomistic bent) sees in every corporeal existent a *prime matter that is wholly undetermined in itself, purely determinable and therefore essentially lacking all activity. However, the more existence frees itself from matter, the more it possesses the character of activity; in absolute *existence it is absolute activity. — According to integral dynamism (Bergson: *Life Philosophy) reality is a unique, steady flow of free involvement and *creative development* (with no distinction between the process and the subjects of it); this process is carried along and directed by the drive for life or the *elan vital* which permeates everything and takes the place of efficient and final causes. — *Cosmological dynamism* claims that there is a dynamic filling of space brought about by unextended units of power; this can be conceived in such a way that each of these units limits a sphere of empty space for itself alone through its activity (Leibnitz: *Monad; Boscovich, E. von Hartmann) or in such a way that all of them together fill space by means of mutual attraction and repulsion. — See also *Dynamic, Becoming, Voluntarism*.

WB

E

ECLECTICISM

Electicism is the name given to the position of those philosophers whose thinking is limited to examining the results of the intellectual labor of others. They then pick out what seems true and valuable without making a serious philosophical effort to combine these truths into a unified whole. If this borrowing of ideas from different systems occurs without a careful examination of their validity and without seeing them in the total context, then this is referred to as *syncretism*. The following are eclectics: most Greek and Roman philosophers after the first century B. C., many thinkers during the time of the Fathers of the Church, the popular philosophers of the Enlightenment, Victor Cousin (1792-1867). A great part of American philosophy tends to be eclectic.

WB

ECONOMICS

Economics is a social science concerned with scarce resources and unlimited desires. It is divided into positive economics (economic theory) and normative economics (or the application of this theory in a given society). Normative or applied economics is concerned with the structuring of human social living; it attempts to bring harmony between supply (scarce goods and services) and demand (unlimited desires) so that the greatest welfare is attained and as such it is an aspect of culture and an integral part of human social living.

Applied economics must be based on economic theory just as social living is based on *social philosophy. Since man is a being composed of body and soul, human culture must be concerned with both the material and the spiritual needs of man. Economics is all pervasive and even affects the highest cultural activities (e. g., art, science and religion) which are not just frills but an integral part of human culture.

Economics is concerned with the production, consumption and distribution of goods and services which are also affected by *technology. Technology should be guided by the structure of *society and so, although economics has its own immediate end, it is subservient to politics.

In the capitalistic era the economic practices of various groups worked against given political structures and had the effect of dismembering the social order itself. Though the immediate end of economics is production, consumption and distribution of goods and services, the final end is the general well-being of society. The science of economics has means to attain its immediate end, but in order to produce a desired future society the necessary means must be employed; such means must be freely and responsibly determined by man himself. — See also *Ethics*.

OvNB-JES

EGO

In all of man's spiritual acts the ego is co-given as their unifying point of reference, ultimate supporter and active source. It manifests itself first of all in the undeveloped *ego-consciousness* (self-consciousness) that accompanies the acts directed to other objects or dwells in the direct attention of our spirit that goes for things outside of us (*accompanying* or *direct ego-consciousness*. For, the spirit never loses itself entirely in the other; rather, it internalizes the other by bringing it into the depths of its ego; spiritual knowledge occurs only through this "*reditio completa*" (Thomas Aquinas), this perfect return of the spirit to itself. Developed or explicit ego-consciousness is built up on this return; it follows the direct awareness of the other; it bends back on the ego which was only co-affirmed before and makes it into its own unique object (*subsequent* or *reflex ego-consciousness*). This makes possible a type of *self-knowledge* that is both more extensive and more profound. — Those who restrict ego-consciousness to the flow of acts give a false interpretation. For, in actual fact we do not grasp a freely flowing thinking and willing, but a thinker and a willer, that is, a subject determined by such acts. But this subject remains the same throughout the whole change of acts (I, who am now writing, clearly experience myself as exactly the same person who has had innumerable past experiences as my own and perhaps I must give an account of them — something I might just as soon avoid). Thus we know the *substantiality of the ego*; as a permanent substratum it supports and causes the acts as its own accidental determination, without itself being the determination of another. See also *Pantheism*.

Historically it was St. Augustine who penetratingly reflected on the ego and ego-consciousness. Therein he found the indubitable starting point of the guarantee of truth; for, no one can doubt without at the same time making a certain affirmation of his own existence. This problematic was again taken up in the Middle Ages. And Descartes returned to it with his, "I think, therefore I am," and so set the course for the whole modern period. Kant traced all knowledge back to the *transcendental ego, i. e., to the ground that makes knowing possible; but he does not identify this with the ego as a thing-in-itself, for this is closed to our knowing; only the moral ego reaches into the "in-itself" (*das An-sich*). Starting from here the German idealists made explicit what was only implicit in much of the modern thinking: they make the human ego an absolute and even identify it with the divine ego and thereby they make it simply creative. *Existential philosophy throws the Ego back into the limitations of its own finiteness. As far as the evaluation of the ego is concerned, it has usually merited a very high place in Western thought. Pessimism, especially as found in Schopenhauer, took the opposite view; he held, along with Indian thought, that the extinction of the ego is the highest value. With regard to terminology, it is important to note that modern psychotherapy (Jung) distinguishes between the conscious "ego" and the "self," which also includes the unconscious (and even the divine).

JBL

EMOTION

We do not give the name emotion to inner spiritual life as such, as was commonly done at the beginning of the 19th century; nor do we attribute it only to the totality of sensual feelings, but rather to the close unity of the spiritual and the sensual in our human experience. In colloquial language the "emotional man" is usually contrasted with the rationalist or the voluntarist. Emotion influences the entire personal, social, ethical and religious experience of values. While an inauthentic (= artificial, sentimental, exaggerated) emotional life is not good and while an abnormal lack of emotions has a crippling effect on one's mental life, an authentic, strong emotional life is a powerful force for mental growth and a valuable goal of character formation.

AW

EMPIRICISM

Empiricism or the philosophy of experience is the view that recognizes *experience as the only source of knowledge. Empiricism fails to see that experience is possible only on the presupposition of non-experienceable conditions. A special concern of empiricism is the explanation of universal conpects and of universal judgments through experience alone. — There is no doubt that "all of our knowledge begins with experience" and is conditioned by it in some way. The limitation of our knowledge to the mere realm of experience cannot be maintained by itself alone. Not even the proposition, "All experiential knowledge is true," can be deduced from experience; and the fundamental principle of empiricism that experience alone guarantees true knowledge is even harder to establish on the basis of experience alone. — Empiricism is doomed to failure when it attempts to explain *universal concepts. The common sensible representations or *schemata* are not sufficient to explain them, since they cannot be affirmed in identically the same way about several real objects. The logical concept of "man" is strictly one, while its sensible schema can assume different forms. Consequently, such schemata cannot serve as a subject or predicate in a universal judgment. They themselves need a norm in order to be produced and to be recognized as schemata, namely, the logical concept. The appeal to unconscious, sensible or accompanying imaginations is likewise insufficient. For, the universal concept is a fully conscious and clear representation. That the concept is clothed, where possible, with a sensible schema and is accompanied with sensible representations, is not to be denied; but this process presupposes the logical concept. — Further, empiricism confuses the intuitively-grasped subject-predicate relationship in the judgment with non-intuitive association. It tries to establish the validity of universal judgment on the basis of induction. But *induction has certain presuppositions (such as the principle of *sufficient reason) which cannot themselves be established from experience alone. — The rejection of metaphysics as a knowledge that exceeds experience fails to see that experience itself is conditioned by foundations that exceed experience; thus, in all true knowledge experience is always already surpassed.

The *nominalism of the late Middle Ages was a precursor of modern empiricism. Francis Bacon († 1626) in his *Novum Organum* expressed clearly and unambiguously the principles of empiricism and he praised induction as the only proper method of science. This idea was spread far and wide by the sensualism of John Locke († 1709) and the *positivism of Condillac († 1780). Neo-positivism is also a branch of empiricism. Kant recognized early that experience is possible only because of the non-experienceable functions of the mind; however, since he lacked an adequate analysis of these functions, he also limited their objective validity (in the sense of empiricism) to the field of experience. — See also *Rationalism*.

JS

END

Just as the *will in all of its activities directs itself to some known *value (i. e., the goodness of its object), so also with regard to its willing in the narrower sense there is always a value for the sake of which the will strives for the realization of some existent. Thus, a value, as that to which some existing reality is ordered, becomes a *cause of the existent. Formerly the Latin word *"finis"* was usually translated into English as *"purpose"; in more recent terminology a distinction is made between end and purpose. Thus, the "end" is related to striving, while "purpose" is especially concerned with the means. Therefore, the end is a good to be produced or attained through the striving of an appetite. This is primarily the self-appointed end, as in the case of man's free choice. But also the natural inclination that is implanted in things through God's creative will, is directed towards an end; thus, we see that growth and reproduction are ends of animals and plants that they naturally and necessarily strive for. Finally there is the end that stands as a goal for the free will; in this sense moral perfection is the end of man, even when it is not actually striven for. — The end is normally not achieved by the mere fact of desiring it; it is attained by using external actions or things as *means* in the service of achieving the end. Thus a direction to the desired end is communicated even to the means. The means then have the "purpose" of helping the person in the prosecution of his end. But their purpose is not their "end" (keeping time is not the "end" of the clock, but its "purpose"), unless they possess an inner impetus that of itself is striving for the purpose. On the other hand, the person, precisely because he cannot be used as a means, is not determined for any "purpose," but his determination is his "end"! — Sometimes "purpose" is also ordered to striving, as in the expression "to pursue one's own purposes"; then "purpose" does not mean the inner end corresponding to the full reality of the one striving; rather, it refers to an external end which in turn again as a means is subordinate to one's own proper advantage. Closely associated with this is the fact that "purposeful activity" often appears to be nothing but cold calculation. However, if a person simply rejects all conscious striving for ends and recognizes only a drive for life that is not even conscious of its own ends, then we have a one-sided over-evaluation of the *irrational that blinds a person to the incomparably more profound and formative power of spiritual love and spiritual value-striving. — See also *Purpose*.

JdV

ENLIGHTENMENT

Enlightenment is the name given to a cultural and intellectual movement that attempted to dominate man's whole world through the use of human reason. — There have been several movements of this kind. The period of the 17th and 18th centuries is especially referred to by this term. — The cause of the Enlightenment was the exuberant drive for intellectual freedom which was associated with the coming of age of the Western peoples and the growing self-confidence which resulted from the successes of the natural sciences. Man began to believe that human reason is capable of perfectly comprehending all reality; he began to re-shape all dimensions of life according to his new insights without respect for historical development. Therefore, we find that there was a proselytizing character to the philosophy of the Enlightenment and that it had a strong influence on most intellectuals. From the point of view of religion, the Enlightenment was caused by a certain weariness with the long religious divisions; in the face of these, there grew a hope of finding a principle of unity and reconciliation in the one common human reason. An attempt was made to find the common denominator in all the religious confessions, but it ended up in a kind of natural or rational religion that excluded all revelation and supernatural ties, as well as all natural authority that comes from God. Men of the time looked upon this religion, usually advocated in the form of *deism, as the most original and pure religion.

The Enlightenment began in England and France. In England it joined up with the empiricism of Locke and Hume, in France and Holland with Descartes and Spinoza. The foundation of the French and German Enlightenment (Leibnitz, Wolff, Reimarus, Lessing, Kant) is *rationalism. The moral philosophy of the Enlightenment, developed particularly in England (Hobbes, Shaftesbury, Bentham), depended partially on deism and to some extent it freed itself of all religious and metaphysical presuppositions (Bayle). The Enlightenment reached its conclusion and its real dissolution in the radicalism of Voltaire and the encyclopedists and finally in the crass materialism of Holbach and Lamettrie. Alongside the rationalism of the Enlightenment and contrary to it, arose another current which stressed the right of feeling (which is also a gift of nature) as the deepest source of human activity (Rousseau and others). Likewise, Herder's philosophy of history was directed against the lack of historical sense found in the thinkers of the Enlightenment and he pointed out the role of history in all human development.

WB

ENS RATIONIS

Ens rationis (being of the mind) is the Latin expression for something that can exist only as an object of thought, but does not exist "in itself," i. e., as a real existent independent of the mind (e. g., a triangular circle). An *ens rationis*, therefore, is a "thing" only in a very improper sense, because we think of it as a thing. But the *ens rationis* is not necessarily just an illusion; instead, as a rule it has a definite foundation in reality (*fundamentum in re*) to which is added, in accordance with the special mode of operating of the human mind, a purely mental determination. This addition does not occur haphazardly, but has a real function in the knowledge process. Thus, for example, in the concept of *space the real extension of bodies is the foundation in reality; however, to think of this extension as an independent existent that can hold different bodies is a purely mental addition — an addition, however, that makes possible objective statements about the state of bodies. The chief categories of beings of the mind are those that arise from negation (e. g., nothingness, blindness) and those that assert purely mental relationships (e. g., the "left" side of a tree; the *identity of subject and predicate).

WB

EPICUREANISM

Epicureanism is the school and doctrine founded by Epicurus (342/1 - 271/70 B. C.). The teaching of Epicurus, based mainly on the atomism of Democritus, was divided into Canonic (logic), Physics (including psychology and theology), and Ethics. The Canonic is concerned with the criteria and tests of truth. Sense knowledge is the one infallible criterion, and all knowledge is explained in terms of the action of material things (composed of atoms) on the material soul (also composed of atoms). The whole of reality is made up of atoms, infinite in number, perpetually falling in an infinitely extended void. There is no place for a guiding intelligence in the world, for the atoms come together by chance to form worlds and individual things in worlds. The motion of the atoms is downwards, but an unpredictable "swerve" (*parenclisis*) causes them to collide and form visible objects. The swerve also explains the possibility of free will in an otherwise deterministic world. The gods, composed of the finest atoms, dwell in the spaces between the worlds, living a life of perfect serenity completely unconcerned about man. Man's life is made miserable by two fears: fear of the gods and fear of death. Both of these fears are groundless because (1) the gods care nothing about man, and (2) the soul ceases to exist at death. Pleasure is the greatest good of man, according to Epicurus and his followers, and it is based principally on a peace and tranquility of mind (*ataraxia*) brought about by the removal of all perturbation and anxiety caused either by fear of death and of the gods or by ignorance of the natural limits of pleasure and pain. Bodily pleasures are to be sought, but in moderation. The followers of Epicurus prided themselves on fidelity to the teaching of their master. The doctrine was propounded at Rome by Lucretius (c. 98-55 B. C.) in *De Rerum Natura*, a Latin hexameter poem in six books, which was admired by Virgil but otherwise had little influence until the Renaissance. In popular usage the term "Epicureanism" has been employed to mean a crass and sensual hedonism.

JHT

EPIKEIA

Epikeia (Gr.: *epieikeia* = equity) according to Aristotie is the equity or reasonableness that stands above positive law; it is a higher law of *justice in virtue of which a man may act against the explicit requirement of some law because, as a general norm, it does not apply in this particular case; also, he must act according to the intention of the lawgiver. Since a universal, positive norm (*Law) can never cover exactly every possible particular case, the higher law of epikeia requires at times a reasonable departure from the letter of the law. Consider, for example, this general norm: Goods kept for another should be returned when they are asked for. This norm, however, is not binding when someone asks for the return of his gun so that, in a fit of passion, he can kill a person. The conditions for the use of epikeia are: a real, certain necessity which renders the general norm unreasonable in this particular case and the impossibility of readily approaching the lawgiver for information. Epikeia cannot be applied to the negative precepts of the natural *moral law. With regard to its positive precepts, in a real case of necessity this higher principle enters into the picture in the sense that they do not obligate if there is a disproportionately heavy burden involved. There is disagreement as to the application of epikeia to the so-called *invalidating laws* which render some legal transactions invalid.

JoS

ERROR

Error is an explicit judgment in which the one judging, without knowing it, misrepresents the objective reality. Error is distinguished from logical *falsity in that falsity concerns only the objective relationship of a judgment to the matter in question, while error also includes the subjective disposition. The content of a judgment that does not correspond to the objective reality is false; in addition to this, it belongs to the notion of "error" that a false judgment, which is not recognized as false, is affirmed as true. — The possibility of error is familiar to all, but it is still a problem: for, how can the intellect err, when by its very nature it is ordered to the truth? As a result of its finiteness it can succumb to the mere appearance of truth and to the non-theoretical concerns of the will that move it to make hasty judgments. — With regard to error, we can distinguish between its logical and psychological *sources*. Both are always present and operative, but in different degrees. The most important logical sources of error are the following: universalizing, without sufficient justification, from one case or a few cases to all cases; the use of slogans or catch-words, i. e., popular phrases that imply an emotional attitude that has no objective foundation; the conclusion from the incomprehensible to the impossible: for, it does not simply follow that something is impossible just because our limited intellect is not able to understand it; the conclusion, "*post hoc, ergo propter hoc*": just because one event temporally follows another it does not necessarily follow that the former is the cause of the latter; finally, all forms of *fallacies. — The psychological sources of error are to be found in our limited thinking and willing which are often obscured by passion. On the side of the intellect, errors can be occasions: through the dependence of our thinking on language which is often ambiguous; through dependence on the senses and on memory which sometimes are deceiving; through prejudice and a distorted education; through a lack of experience and knowledge, together with the necessity on occasion to make a quick decision; further, through stupidity and intellectual laziness; through a too-high regard for human authority. More on the side of the will, the following sources of error can be found: impetuosity of character, a twisted inclination of the heart towards the wrong thing, an obstinate spirit, a failing desire for the truth, hastiness in judging. — The particularly human way of knowing has the inevitable result that error, although fundamentally avoidable through a close examination of the bases of judgment, in actual fact cannot be avoided because of the great difficulties involved and because of the time that is required of individuals and of whole generations. Sometimes, in order to discover the truth, one must expose oneself to the risk of error, even though error in itself is an evil for man. Error that cannot be overcome because of insurmountably great difficulties, is called *morally invincible*. A man is responsible for an error that is *morally vincible*.

JS-WB

ESSENCE

Essence signifies first of all "to be such" as opposed to "to be" and is then called "whatness." Just as existence answers the question "whether" something is, so also "to be such" answers the question "what" (Lat.: *quidditas*) something is. In this connection the individual, determined essence or the substantial core of the existent in its concrete individualization is meant (e. g., "this" man Peter), since the universal as such cannot exist. — The essence of a finite existent, because it is finite, lacks the fullness of existence; it includes only a small part of the possibilities of existence while the essence of God embraces the

114

infinite fullness of existence — in fact, it is existence itself (*ipsum esse*). Thus God's essence excludes any distinction whatsoever from existence; the finite existent, however, is characterized precisely by such distinction and so the essence as subjective potency and existence as *act (both as principles of being) constitute the finite existent.

According to a second meaning, essence signifies the intrinsic essential foundation of things in contrast to their external appearance. In this case essence is the real or true existence of things which their external appearance manifests, supports and makes intelligible. Because of their contrary attributes these two aspects of finite existents remain distinct. While the external appearance is subject to individuation, change and contingency, the essence itself is necessary, unchanging and above individuation. Plato's doctrine of *ideas was based on the discovery of this duality; and ever since Plato philosophical systems have been divided as a result of their positions on this question. Conceptualism tends to see essence absorbed into the external appearance of a thing and therefore ultimately says that all metaphysics is impossible. Pantheism, on the other hand, reduces the external appearance to the essence when it affirms that absolute existence is the immanent essential foundation of all finite things. Our view of this matter represents a middle position according to which a separate, immanent essential foundation belongs to each finite existent; this foundation is a participation in transcendent, absolute existence and therefore it is able to reflect the attributes of the absolute in an analogous manner. By our knowledge we grasp the immanent, essential foundation of finite existents through *abstraction in the universal concept and we grasp the ultimate transcendent foundation through reasoning in the proof for the existence of God. — The immanent essential foundation can be considered either metaphysically or physically. *Metaphysical essence* means the innermost center of a thing without which this essence would cease to exist; *physical essence* includes in addition to the above the essential properties which necessarily flow from the metaphysical essence and without which this particular essence cannot be physically (*Physical) actualized.

JBL

ESSENTIAL KNOWLEDGE

Essential knowledge, in contrast to a purely empirical knowledge that grasps only sensible *appearance (how a thing appears, etc.), means that knowledge through which the essence (i. e., what the object is) of a thing is uncovered. An immediate and direct grasp (i. e., given not only in reflection on one's own acts) of the essence of a concrete existent can be called an *essential intuition*. Certain forms of *intuitionism assume the existence of an essential intuition in man that is independent of *experience.

115

On the other side, *empiricism denies all essential intuition because, the empiricists say, we have no intuition except experience. Both of these positions share a common notion, namely, that human experience is purely sensible. In contrast to these views, the perennial philosophy holds that there is an immediate grasp of the essential in our given experience; that is the meaning of the expression "*intelligibile in sensibili*", i. e., an intellectually comprehensible content in a sensible object. If this essential content is abstracted from the concretely given object and thought of by itself, then we have an *essential concept* (*Abstraction). Essential concepts are the necessary presupposition of a priori insights into essential relations (*Knowledge, Principles of).

Immediate essential knowledge in man is severely limited; the scholastic theory of abstraction by no means says as many seem to assume, that we can easily grasp immediately the specific essence of all things (e. g., man, horse, etc.) and that from this essence we can deduce a priori all further determinations. Rather at first only certain — not all — sensibly given characteristics are grasped essentially; the minimum of essential knowledge consists in this, that the given thing is grasped as an existent. Therefore, it is perhaps better to speak of an immediate grasp of the "essential" than of an intuition of the "essence" without qualification. The substantial essences of things are known only mediately, proceeding from the immediately grasped essential characteristics. And even so our essential knowledge remains extremely limited. The species of the natural sciences (animals, plants, inanimate bodies) are for the most part known only by empirical universal concepts which do not present the inner essence of things but only the typical kinds of appearances.

JdV

ETERNITY

Eternity is the duration of something that excludes both a beginning and an end as well as all change or succession. According to Boethius eternity is "the full and perfect possession of endless life always present in its entirety." Such life belongs to God alone. — Eternity does not allow for the temporal co-ordination of temporal events; it neither precedes nor accompanies nor follows them. God is present to all times and things insofar as he keeps them in existence. The temporal difference that we affirm of his activities concerning things outside of himself are only valid, strictly speaking, of the changing things that are effected by him. "God will judge the world" means: "The world will be judged by God." — The scholastics gave the name of "*aevum*" to the duration proper to pure spirits. *Aevum* can have a beginning, but it excludes all substantial change which is always rooted in matter; it does not, however, exclude all accidental *change. It is disputed whether or not the thinking and willing of a pure spirit is characterized by real succession. Abstract truths as well as the possibility of finite things are not eternal, but rather *timeless*, that is, they hold true independently of any definite time and in their actualization they are not bound to any definite time.

MR

ETHICS

Ethics or *Moral Philosophy* is the philosophical investigation and explanation of the so-called moral facts; these facts include such things as moral evaluations, commandments, norms, virtuous acts, the manifestations of conscience, etc. — *Moral theology* or *theological ethics* explains and establishes moral norms on the basis of supernatural revelation. Prescinding from revelation, from a practical point of view moral regulations can be presented as a kind of catechism with a pedagogical end in view. According to one view, ethics can restrict itself to a mere description of the moral life and customs of individual men, tribes, peoples, etc. (cultural history and ethnology). Such an attitude implicitly states that what is is what ought to be. A truly penetrating ethics goes beyond mere descriptive morality and seeks to give the reasons for lived values and attitudes; and it tries to explain them through the history of their development or by using psychological methods it looks for their source in mental abilities, tendencies and functions (*Moral Psychology*). As that part of metaphysics which questions the ultimate bases of moral action, philosophical ethics seeks to investigate moral norms more precisely with regard to their existence and their meaning and so arrive at a *metaphysics of morality*. This purpose cannot be achieved by a strictly empirical method. Nor will the appeal to mere feeling which defies analysis be sufficient. Thus the chief purpose of philosophical ethics is to explain the morally *good and that which is proper to it, for example, the sense of obligation. The many different ethical systems try to work out answers to this problem.

Utilitarianism or the ethics of enlightened self-interest (Bentham) is too external; this system is a kind of amorality which denies the real existence of ethical values and elevates the profit of the individual to the supreme norm of morality; the same must be said about *hedonism (Aristippus, Epicurus) which considers a shrewdly calculated pleasure and satisfaction as the basis of all ethical evaluation. The "Universal Benevolence" theory of R. Cumberland gives a better explanation of social obligations than the above systems, but it neglects the obligations a man has to himself (temperance, purity, patience). Moreover, it presupposes the moral nature of society without giving it any real basis. A similar judgment can be made regarding W. Wundt's theory of cultural progress; this system places cultural activities and works above the individual person and his dignity, subordinating the person as a mere means to an impersonal progress. This becomes at the same time a purely external ethics of success at the expense of the moral convictions of the person. An *aesthetic morality*, which advocates a certain harmony in the personal style of living, does not really come to grips with the seriousness of moral demands and with the sacrifices which these frequently require. Actually, the morally good act can only be explained on the basis of the peculiarity of the human person (teleological ethics). Still the way in which this goal is to be achieved must be sketched out more clearly. *Perfectionism* (C. Wolff) is too indefinite because not just any realization of human inclinations leads to the morally good. For morality touches something central in man that proceeds from the freedom of the spiritual person, and it also involves a certain totality in him which emphasizes the value of his spirit in his own body, in the community, in the realm of material things and in subordination to God, his creator and ultimate, transcendent end. This *ethical personalism* does not lead to a godless *autonomy which denies religious duties and values (Kant); it does not lead to a purely immanent, subjective ethics lacking all influence of objective values based on the real world; it does not lead to an extreme *moralism* which attempts to make morality or will the absolute foundation of metaphysics (Kant); it avoids the extreme narcissism, pride and self-love of the Stoics. Since the spiritual person as the image of God is present in every human being, there is a universal, moral order which binds all men, at least with regard to its fundamental requirements. Individual and social differences specify these obligations. Thus there cannot be a *double morality*: one for the private citizen and one for the politician, one for husband and one for wife, one valid before marriage and another after marriage, one for the rich and another for the poor; at least this cannot be so in the sense that certain persons or groups would be excepted from the universal moral law (honesty, justice, purity), but only in the sense that in certain situations the moral law is susceptible of a special application. Thus one person is not allowed to kill another except as a matter of self-defense, but the state is allowed to impose the death penalty in certain cases.

JoS

EUTHANASIA

Euthanasia or *mercy killing* is the direct induction of a painless *death in the incurably ill out of a motive of compassion. It can also mean the use of death-bringing expedients in the case of those persons who cannot lead a full human life (cripples, deformed children, mental defectives, the aged, etc.). Some advocates of this policy say that it should be carried out only with the consent of the sick person, while others advocate it even without their consent. The motives adduced in support of this idea are the relief of suffering, the improvement of the *race and the saving of the cost of upkeep. The moral evaluation of this procedure does not depend primarily on the external motive of the act, but rather on the intrinsic nature of it. Euthanasia is a usurpation of the right over human life that is reserved to the Creator alone and therefore absolutely forbidden by the natural *moral law which binds all men without exception, just as murder and *suicide are forbidden. Moreover, in the important matter of the preservation of human life there is always a great danger that this practice would be criminally extended to many other cases; it would likewise lead to a feeling of mistrust with regard to one's doctor and one's relatives in a time of sickness.

JoS

EVIDENCE

Evidence sometimes means the clear self-manifestation, revelation and clarity of an objective reality (*objective evidence*) and sometimes the corresponding spiritual "seeing," insight and perception of the objective reality (*subjective evidence*). Since both points of view are only two aspects of the same knowledge relationship, it scarcely makes a difference whether one prefers the former or the latter mode of expression; if we distinguish "objective" and "subjective" evidence in the way described here, then misunderstanding is avoided. However, it should be noted that the expression "subjective evidence" is used by some philosophers in the sense of only apparent evidence, of a purely subjective conviction of evidence or certitude. True evidence is either *immediate or mediate,* depending upon whether or not the objective reality manifests itself by itself or through the mediation of another existent; in the latter instance, a necessary connection must exist and be knowable as such between the existent, which is the medium of knowing, and the objective reality to be known. If the *necessity involved in this connection is absolute, then the evidence is likewise absolute and excludes error unconditionally, just as immediate evidence does; however, if the necessity of the connection is only hypothetical (physical or moral), then the evidence is also only *hypothetical* (physical or moral) and so normally excludes error, but not absolutely. An example of mediate evidence that is still absolute would be a mathematical proof in which the conclusion is seen to be true on the basis of its absolutely necessary sequence from directly grasped axioms. Our sense perception offers physical evidence for the reality of perceived things which cause those perceptions according to the laws of physical necessity; we have moral evidence on the basis of a trustworthy witness who relates what really happened. — Evidence is the norm of *truth, that is, it is the epistemological sign of truth (cognitional truth). Since evidence means the self-manifestation of the existent to the knower, this principle ultimately means nothing else but that truth is measured by the existence of things. Evidence is the necessary, logical, *foundation* of *certitude. But it is not the psychological *motive* of assent in every case; and this distinction between foundation and motive should be particularly noted with regard to the matter of *faith.

JdV

EVIL

An evil (1) is first of all a state as the result of which something is bad or morally wrong (evil in the formal sense); less often the thing afflicted with an evil (1) is itself called an "evil" (2). Since every existent as such is good (*Transcendentals, *Value), evil (1) is not a positive determination of a being; rather, it consists in the lack of some goodness (perfection) which corresponds to the existent thing and belongs to it (*Privation). It is misleading, however, when Leibniz speaks of the lack of any perfection as a "*metaphysical evil*": for, the lack of further possible perfections is essential to every finite existent, even if it is perfect in its own species.

A distinction is made between moral and physical evil. Moral evil is primarily a free, faulty decision of the will that goes contrary to that which is morally *good; then it is the external act flowing from that decision, an inner attitude and a firm bad habit. A physical evil, on the other hand, is the morally indifferent lack of some perfection demanded by the nature of the thing in question (*Pain, *Suffering, *Purposelessness). — Since every lack, every deficiency, presupposes a subject which, as an existent, possesses at least a minimum of goodness, there is no such thing as subsisting evil; that is, there is no being that is absolute badness or evil. This insight reveals the falseness of the dualistic doctrines which assume the existence of an original principle of evil alongside the good principles of the world (*Manicheanism, Parsism).

Concerning the question about the source of evil, it should be noted carefully that activity in itself always produces something positive, not a mere absence of being; therefore, evil never has a cause immediately directed to its production, but always results somehow or other as a side effect. Thus, for example, a cause that is itself defective also produces its proper activity defectively. Physical evil can occur through the meeting of two causes, when both of them are striving for a good, but this chance encounter results in an evil (e. g., a traffic accident). Moreover, an evil can arise from the fact that a good is desired and effected — a good which necessarily excludes another good (thus, in a surgical operation the health of the whole organism demands the removal of a part). Moral evil has its basis always in a faulty decision of the created free will. The possibility of evil is given ultimately with the finitude of creatures. — For more on the meaning of evil see also *Theodicy, Providence.*

VN

EVOLUTIONISM

Evolution — cosmic, biological, and human — is a dominant category of contemporary thinking. The term is sometimes restricted to «organic» or "biological" evolution, but the other two categories actually preceded Darwinism in history.

Christopher Dawson and some other historians hold that the idea of progress (evolution of human societies) came to fruition only in Western culture because Christianity is, among the great religions of the world, most explicitly history-conscious — and in this sense, evolutionistic. Eastern cultures were either dominated by the idea of the "eternal return" or by myths combining evolutionist and non-evolutionist views. The cosmology of the Vishnu Purana is an example of the latter. Here the universe is presumed to exactly repeat itself in cycles of 311,040 billion years.

It is therefore probably not an accident that the idea of human progress grew and developed in the Judaeo-Christian cultural background, although largely in secular rather than in religious contexts. The Encyclopedists generally believed in the total mass of the human race moving always slowly forward. Voltaire thought that man advances "from the barbarous rusticity to the politeness of our era." The Age of Enlightenment closes with the first full-fledged theory of progressive evolution of mankind, that of Condorcet. On a different philosophical basis the evolutionary ideas of Herder, Kant and Fichte led to Hegel's system, in which history is understood as progressive manifestation of the Spirit. Marx put Production and Economics in the place of the Spirit, and substituted Socialism and Communism for the Kingdom of God. Marx discovered his "evolution of society" at about the same time as Darwin published his account of biological evolution. Marx recognized in Darwin a fellow evolutionist, but Darwin was reluctant to accept such an affiliation. Soon thereafter Spencer, Tylor, Morgan and others founded evolutionary social anthropology, expressly built on Darwinian theoretical premises.

Theories of cosmic and terrestrial inorganic evolution also appeared well ahead of biological evolution. Kant (1775) advanced the primal nebula theory in which Newtonian gravitational forces were to have gradually assembled the originally scattered matter of the cosmos into sun and planets. The doctrine of uniformitarianism, put forward by Buffon and Hutton in the 17th century was developed by Lyell in the 19th century as the basis for the study of the geological changes of the earth. Skeptical at first of biological evolution, Lyell later inspired and supported Darwin and Darwin's theory.

Modern cosmological theories fall into two major groups. The steady-state theories (as per Bondi, Gold or Hoyle) assume that new matter continuously arises in the universe. The "big bang" theory (Gamow) assumes that the universe began some five to ten billion years ago from a state of extreme compression which gave rise to a stupendous explosion, causing the expanding universe. Astronomers generally hold that stars undergo evolutionary changes which follow a fairly predictable path (Hoyle's "Main-Sequence," 1955).

Charles Darwin and Alfred R. Wallace are credited with the "discovery" of biological evolution (1859), although there were several important predecessors, of whom Lamarck was the most prominent. Modern biological theory is far from identical with Darwin's of more than a century ago, and yet there is an unbroken intellectual continuity between them. The modern theory (Neo-Darwinian) is called "synthetic" because it represents a convergence and synthesis of findings and interpretations of all the biological disciplines. This is in itself an evolutionary development, since until about thirty years ago geneticists, systematists, paleontologists, embryologists, etc., were expounding theories which seemed to them to fit only their particular fields.

The modern theory is also called "synthetic" because it resolved the conflict which existed in the early part of this century between the Darwinian naturalists, the Mendelian geneticists, and the neo-Lamarckians. Population genetics has now furnished mathematical evidence that Darwin was correct in holding that the fabric of evolution is « the full effects of many slight variations, accumulated during an almost infinite number of generations." The "struggle for survival" as Darwin saw, but some of his followers overlooked, includes not only differential survival but also relative reproductive capacity. Also, natural selection is comparable, not to a sieve sorting out "good" or "bad" gene mutations, but a regulatory mechanism in a cybernetic system. In this sense, evolutionary changes are "creative" responses to the challenges of the environment. They are not alterations imposed by the environment as Lamarckists mistakenly thought.

Modern evolutionists presume a chemicial evolution took place on our planet a billion or so years after it was formed. The Haldane-Oparin theory envisions a reducing atmosphere that permitted large amounts of ultra-violet and other penetrating radiations from space to reach the surface of the earth, supplying energy for the polymerization of various organic molecules in the newly formed seas. This pre-biotic phase presumably

EVOLUTIONISM

lasted up to two billion years and led to the formation of one or several primordial populations of pro-karyote cells.

In the past, various philosophers of evolution (e. g., Lecomte du Noüy) have argued that cosmogenesis and biogenesis would have to be the result of very improbable chance events because of entropy. In fact, some considered organic evolution to be contrary to the second law of thermodynamics, which requires that any process taking place in nature must go toward a more random state. However, when one is discussing entropy, using classical thermodynamics, he is talking about a closed system, for example, the universe itself as a finite system. On the other hand, living cells are open systems by their interaction with the environment through mass and energy exchange. On the basis of the ideas of Onsager, Prigogine and others, scientists now hold that whereas closed systems strive to reach a state of maximum entropy, open systems try to reach a state in which minimum changes of entropy occur at some particular level. This means that cells and their chemical constituents show an inherent tendency towards organization, i. e., the preferred state is one of low entropy. Moreover, current biochemical experimentation suggests that with any one of a variety of conditions which could have occurred on the primitive earth, the appearance and evolution of living systems would have been a very likely occurrence, in fact, one which may have been rather difficult to prevent.

Once primitive cells were formed, the neo-Darwinian theory envisions a progressive formation of higher organisms due to the responses of biological species to the challenges of the changing earth environment. Organic evolution involves these stages: 1. production of genetic raw materials through mutation of nucleic acids; 2. formation, through natural selection and Mendelian recombination of genetic endowments, of some variants adapted to survive and reproduce in certain environments; and 3. establishment of species barriers by reproductive isolation. Some examples of evolutionary changes resulting from rapidly changing man-made environments of today are the changing color of the peppered moth (*Biston betularia*) to adapt to industrialized surroundings, the evolution of bacteria resistant to drugs, and of insects resistant to insecticides.

The two types of evolutionary change are (1) phylogenetic or anagenesis, which is the gradual change in a population and (2) speciation or cladogenesis, which is the breaking up of a single population into separate, non-interbreeding groups. Essential to the origin of a new species is sexual isolation, and this generally requires that a population be isolated by actual physical barriers (as in the case of Darwin's finches on the Galapagos Islands). Two principal components of genetic differentiation in populations are (a) a small founding population and (b) a change in environmental conditions.

Speciation can also occur as a result of abrupt chromosomal changes. Polyploidy, a condition in which a cell has more than two sets of chromosomes, is one of the few known means for producing a new species in a single step without genetic isolation. This condition rarely occurs in animals, but it is frequently found in plants. Auto-polyploids, in which each set of chromosomes present is the same, arise from a single parent; in allo-polyploids the chromosomes of two or more diploid species are combined. Translocations and inversions may also lead to rapid speciation.

Darwin believed that evolutionary changes took place at a steady rate. More recent studies of the paleontological record indicate that the great evolutionary steps probably took place fairly rapidly. At least four factors are required for these rapid advances. First, there must be an ample store of genetic variation in the gene pool of a population. Second, a genetic upheaval must occur — most likely in a small population under environmental stress. The third necessary condition is the existence of previous structures that can be modified to other uses. For example, the lungs and lobes of lungfish, which made it possible for them to survive in pools during drought seasons, made it possible for descendents of these ancestral types to begin the invasion of land once plant life had become established there. In the case of the insects, the rapid development of a great multitude of species depended upon the existence of appendages in their arthropod ancestors that could be modified into a large number of specialized structures.

The fourth condition is that a new adaptive zone must be available. The land was once such an adaptive zone, and the air another. Once an adaptive zone (new environmental area or "ecological niche") becomes available, divergent lines of ancestral stock try to cross the barrier. The shift either is rapid or fails completely. But once the shift is made, radiation takes place until the zone is filled. A striking example of such "adaptive radiation" is found in Australia. Because of geographic isolation there was no competition from placental mammals. Marsupials therefore took over the areas which on other continents were occupied by placentals — giving rise to a marsupial "rat," "woodchuck" (Wombat), "bear" (Koala), "dog" (Tasmanian wolf), etc.

Current data indicates that there has been a general acceleration of evolution in that cosmic evolution took more time than biological, and human evolution is of the shortest duration. Also there seems to have been a gradual relaxation of "rigid determinism" as evolution progressed. While biochemists see the formation of cells in the primitive seas as "biochemical predistination," geneticists point out that in higher organisms only a minuscule fraction of the possible gene combinations can ever be actualized. Consequently, every individual in a sexually reproducing species, such as man, has a genetic endowment which is unique, un-precedented, and non-recurrent. Moreover, evolutionary changes seem to be unique events; for example, the evolution of man from his prehuman ancestors is infinitely unlikely to be either repeated or reversed. If life exists on other planets, it is highly improbable that the evolutionary process there went exactly as it did here.

The history of life is therefore comparable to human history in that both involve novelty. Both seem to proceed by gropings, trial and error, many false starts, failures ending in extinction. Both had, however, also their successes, and both have achieved an overall progress in the sense of more efficient utilization of available energy. Man is obviously the present climax of the evolutionary process since he now has the capabilities of controlling his environment, of transmitting cultural information via education, and of manipulating his genetic material via directed changes in the DNA content of cells involved in embryogenesis.

From a philosophical point of view, the scandal of evolution is the appear-ance of getting something out of nothing — of having more at the end of the process than there was at the beginning. This apparent violation of the principle of causality is the chief difficulty with which any serious philosophy of evolution must come to terms. Proposed solutions to the problem have included: 1. reducing the "higher" to the "lower" (= various forms of materialism); 2. claiming the presence of the "higher" in the "low-er" from the outset (= various forms of panpsychism); 3. claiming there really is no continuous development from the lower to the higher (= various forms of porphyrian conception of the hierarchy of beings). Since the universe cannot lift itself by its own bootstraps, the higher perfections must be successively inserted by God, and the universe does not really advance — it is just added to; 4. claiming that both the distinction and continuity of the different grades of perfection are real and analogous; that there is immanent action by creatures, and also immanent action of a Transcendent Being. The tendencies of creatures are seen as not primari-ly and *per se* directed to the perfection of the individual or the species but rather toward the production of something more perfect than them-selves.

MS

The theory of evolution elaborated by Pierre Teilhard de Chardin is an ordered series of hypotheses that make up an evolutionary view of the world in progress. Teilhard de Chardin finds that the process of evolution has a direction: toward higher degrees of material complexity or organiza-tion, and toward correlatively higher levels of *consciousness or *spirit. Evolution, having passed through the critical point marked by the appear-ance of life, continued at an accelerating rate in the zone of living things. Once evolution passed a second critical point, the origin of mankind, it again sharply accelerated and now takes place in human society. Evolution, conscious of itself in man, continues to follow an axis of increasing *complexity-consciousness through the process of human *socialization, or progressively greater unification of man. Evolution, since it is in the direction of greater organization of mankind, is convergent. Teilhard de Chardin, by extrapolating along the axis of the cone of evolution, posits an apex or future focal point of evolutionary convergence. This future maximum limit of the evolutionary process he calls the Omega point. In Teilhard's theology, Omega is identified with the risen Christ who will come again at the end and final transformation of the world.

RLF

EXISTENCE

Existence (*esse*) is that *perfection by means of which something is an existent (*ens*). This is not identified with what can be perceived with the senses as the positivists maintain; long ago Plato labeled those who assert that the only thing that exists is what they can touch with their hands as the "uninitiated." Also, existents do not constitute some kind of a special territory alongside other blocks that are more or less the same; such is the position of pluralism and sometimes also of modern *value philosophy. For, each thing distinguishes itself from *nothing only in this that is possesses existence or is an existent; something which was totally unrelated to existence and therefore did not appear in any way to be an existent, would not be "something" but simply nothing. Consequently, since the perfection of existence resides in "everything" the concept of the existent as the most comprehensive or most universal has an objective foundation; it is not just an empty word or a fiction of our understanding. Insofar as this concept, by reason of its widest extension, surpasses all special areas, it is called "transcendent" or *transcendental (logical *Transcendence). According to its content it affirms only this one determination: that existence belongs to a something (*Essence); therefore, since is disregards all particular content-determinations of the existent, it is the most undetermined concept; yet it does not on this account coincide with nothingness, as Hegel claims. This description shows that the existent is the first or proper primordial concept; it cannot be reduced to anything prior to itself, but everything else is reduced to it and must be understood from it. Existence is the first, fundamental perfection of every existent whose other perfections appear as reflections or participations of existence, as this or that kind of existence. Accordingly, neither time (apparently in Heidegger) nor becoming (Hegel) precede existence, but rather both are rooted in existence which expresses itself in and through them in this particular way.

EXISTENCE

According to its basic intention existence means: actually or really exist; so the existent (1) primarily is something which actually has existence. Now since the finite existent only "has" existence and therefore does not necessarily exist, a capacity for existence or pure *possibility lies at the bottom of its real existence; in a broader sense, the existent (2) therefore also includes possible being and then means something which either has or can have existence. All other meanings of existence can be traced back to this basic intention; therefore outside of and in addition to existence there simply are no fully independent ways of being. In particular, *ideal existence* contains nothing but the essential structures of the actual or possible existent. Emphasized for their own sakes by means of abstraction, they possess a necessity and timelessness which are ultimately based on infinite existence. Even *logical existence* which is expressed in the copulative verb of the *judgment is rooted in existence, since it asserts a real or ideal continuance. Finally, the same must also be said of the *intentional existence* of conceptual knowing, since according to its content it only reproduces the existent in the mind. Even a mere *ens rationis (Gedankending)* by reason of a certain foundation in existence is at least indirectly related to existence.

The question about existence touches on the innermost core which is the support of every existent. The ability to grasp this depth constitutes the very essence of *spirit and it has been "the" preoccupation of Western philosophy since the time of the Greeks. In this process it is ultimately a matter of moving from the finite existent, which only "has" existence or participates in it, to infinite existence, which essentially "is" existence (in its complete fullness) and therefore is called "existence itself" (*Ipsum Esse*) (*Subsistence). This presentation of the problem has given rise to two partial problems since Aristotle: the "existent as such" with its bare, abstract form (act) of existence, and the "divine existence" as simple, subsisting form (act). Both are most intimately related to one another; for, existence is that ultimate in the finite existent by reason of which it is rooted in infinite existence. Because of this intertwining the Stagirite assigns both problems to one, bipolar science; he calls this science "first philosophy" because it concerns itself with the first things; later on it is called "meta-physics" because it investigates that which transcends the physical and finite. Today the two poles are emphasized as *ontology and natural *theology, the former considering the existent as such and the latter the divine existence. The type of ontology which has been revived in recent times often is aware only of the existent as such and so becomes a philosophy of limitation, while pantheism lets the existent as such be absorbed into the divine existence.

The task of *ontology is to bring out the kinds of questions put to us by the existent as such and existence as such. The first problem is to work out the *essence of the existent as such and of existence as such. And the first thing we derive from the finite existent is the idea of the existence as such which leads us directly to subsisting existence as its primordial source. Having received its peculiar stamp from subsisting existence, the existent as such appears as the metaphysical and the precisive immaterial (i. e., disregarding matter and somehow transcending it) heart of all that is physical and corporeal. Since the existent includes such essentially different ways of existing as infinite existence and the finite existent, *analogy is closely connected with its transcendence. The question about how the finite existent is even possible leads to the distinction between essence and existence which constitute the finite existent as potency and act or as its principles of *existence. Secondly, it is necessary to investigate the essential characteristics of existence which belong to every existent and therefore are called *transcendentals. Specifically, they are: *unity, *truth, goodness (*value) and *beauty. Closely related to these are the absolutely valid principles of existence (*Contradiction, *Sufficient Reason, *Causality, *Finality). — Thirdly, the differentiation of the existent into the special areas of the *categories must be taken into account; for only in this way does it fully manifest its essence as a finite existent. In this analysis the duality of *substance and *accident must be given very close attention. Among the accidents that of *relation plays a very special role, especially in the matter of *causality. For, the category of relation links together the multiplicity of the finite existent with unity and further unites both of these with infinite existence.

JBL

EXISTENCE, LEVELS OF

Existence, levels of (= *Grades of Perfection*). The levels of existence in their difference and in their similarity constitute the order of the universe. They are all open to us in man himself, for in man as the center they all converge. As a *microcosm* (universe in miniature) he reflects the *macrocosm* (universe in its magnitude). It is primarily in man that the two realms of spirit and matter meet each other and become "one" nature or "one" essence. In this union, however, the spirit is the reality that is the richer in the fullness of existence. According to Thomas Aquinas, it represents the highest mode of existence, the highest degree of life, for it somehow says infinity. — From man as the center, the levels of *spirit open up into the trans-human and the levels of the *body open up to the sub-human.

Infinity belongs to the human spirit in its proper activities insofar as its knowing and willing can encompass absolutely everything and in this sense it can become all things in some way, as Aristotle and Aquinas have expressed it. Nevertheless, man is still finite in his existence and by reason of his body subject to space-time, so that he must first master everything with his conceptual thinking which starts with sensible intuition. Long ago Aristotle saw that a spirit, free of a body and on a higher level of existence than the human spirit, is possible; for, even the human spirit needs the body only as a pre-condition for its act, not as an equal principle. God is a pure spirit; he is the absolute fullness of existence, infinite without qualification. Therefore, he sees everything in himself and is dependent on nothing else. According to Christian revelation, there seem to be pure spirits below God and above man who are finite beings. Each one according to the level of his existence, participates in God's creative knowledge, for from the moment of their creation God infuses into them a finite reflection of his own ideas.

By considering the different levels in man we come to some understanding of sub-human reality. Take spiritual life away from man and what remains is animal life. The animal has only sensible consciousness which as such is limited to the present moment and to the pressing needs of biological life. If we remove all levels of consciousness, then we have the plant which still possesses immanent activity. Finally, if we wish to abstract completely from *life, then we have the inorganic body which depends on external forces for its activity.

The various levels that compose the inner-worldly existent are real levels of existence, because the existent exists only through *participation in *existence. — See also *Existence, Ontology, Metaphysics.*

JBL

EXISTENCE, PRINCIPLES OF

The principles of existence can be grasped only from an understanding of the nature of a principle in general. A *principle is that from which something else proceeds. In the logical order it is knowledge from which other knowledge flows, but in the ontological order it is something existing from which another proceeds in some way. With regard to these latter existential principles, a distinction is to be made between external and internal principles. The *external principles*, for which currently the designation "cause" is usually reserved, exercise their influence in such a way that they remain outside of the thing they influence; they are above all the efficient and the final cause. The *internal principles*, however, enter into the composition of the thing proceeding from them as partial elements or *co-principles*; they are called in a pregnant sense of the word: "principles of existence." Such a principle by itself is not an existent (subsistent independent reality); rather, it is a real part which goes in to make up the whole reality. As essential parts which constitute the existent in its essential structure they are to be distinguished from the extended parts (e. g., in man the soul and the body in contrast to head, arms and legs).

The metaphysical importance of the principles of existence is seen in this, that God alone is absolutely simple, while everything finite is composed of partial principles. For this reason, a truly philosophical understanding of the finite existent demands an advance from the con-crete given (the "grown-together") that first confronts us to the principles of existence that go to make it up. It is only in this way that the road is open to the ultimate ground of all composed, finite existents — to that which is simply infinite.

In particular, there are three levels of existential principles, of which two touch the very substance. Every finite being is composed of *essence and *existence; this "twoness" constitutes finiteness as such (creaturehood, contingency) and is the foundation of all the other principles of existence. The essence of body includes *matter and *form as its principles of existence (also called incomplete substances); according to the classical Aristotelian-scholastic position, these two principles constitute corporality as such. In every finite existent the accidental determinations, which as further principles of existence complete the full reality of the finite, flow from the substance. In each of the three cases the relationship of *potency and *act is operative between the poles of tension. — In a transferred sense the principles of *knowledge, which give expression to the universal principles of existence, are also called principles of existence; an example of this would be the principle of *contradiction.

JBL

EXISTENTIAL, -ELL

The terms "existential" and "existentiell" derive from the usage of *existential philosophy, esp. from the German wing of it. The *existential(s)* (used both as an adjective and as a noun) is that which determines man's self-understanding independently of his own free choice. Thus, some of my existentials are that I am in the world, I am doomed to die, I live in the 20th century, I speak the English language, etc. These are pre-given to man's exercise of freedom — but he must face them and come to terms with them.

The *existentiell* is that which affects my concrete human existence here and now, and it is usually thought of as the result of my free choice. Thus, what I am today as a person is the result of my own previous decisions for good or for evil. These two ideas are more or less equivalent to the contemporary use in philosophy and theology of the expressions "nature" (= existential) and "person" (= existentiell).

KB

EXISTENTIAL PHILOSOPHY

Existential philosophy today is a vibrant current of thought with far-reaching influence. Although it was not worked out systematically until the 20th century, its beginnings can be traced back to the first half of the 19th century. More specifically, it is a counterattack against the one-sided results of *German idealism. Hegel was generally understood in such a way that the individual person was reduced to a mere phase in the growth of the absolute Idea and so the fullness of personal existence was made over into a necessary expression of a concept. But the independence and uniqueness of the individual person began to prevail over this tyranny of the universal. At first, both positivism and the shallow establishment kept this movement from achieving any significant results, because it rejected the absolute idea without offering anything to take its place. It is right here that existentialism enters the picture, for it confers meaning and dignity to the individual by calling him to true "existence."

Romanticism prepared the way for existentialism because it allowed a man to be proud of his own concrete existence and saw the fullness of existence in him; it also aroused a sense for the uniqueness of history. In his later period Schelling clearly saw the problem: the problem of human existence goes beyond the logical necessity of the universal to the whole question of freedom and demands will as its ultimate source — a source that precedes mere reason; or, as he says, "Primordial existence is willing."

The existential theology of Soren Kierkegaard was the decisive breakthrough towards the philosophy of existence. He wants to lead the individual person to the fullness of his own human existence (*dasein*).

This is accomplished by means of a *free decision* in which a man posits himself or takes his destiny in his own hands, and by means of faith through which he establishes himself in God; this is preceded by *Angst* or anxiety as the shaking of everything finite and the experience of nothingness. Faith is understood in the Christian sense and is thought of as a leap; its unexplainable uniqueness grows into a *paradox* insofar as the Christian appears as a contradiction to mankind.

Related movements continued what Kierkegaard had started. Thus, *life philosophy tried to save life in its concrete fullness and depth from the destructive force of the universal concept; accordingly, it was open only to a pre- or supra-rational form of understanding, such as instinct (Nietzsche) or intuition (Bergson). To this was added the *hermeneutic* (explanation) of historical events (Dilthey) which cannot be explained in their uniqueness by means of universal concepts and laws, but can be understood only through the exposition of their meaning (*Understanding, Act of). The *phenomenology of Husserl with its view of essences is closely related to this method insofar as it strives for an exposition of their inner structures; in the later work of Max Scheler this method approaches that of life philosophy, in which the drive for life — an idea that was central for Nietzsche and also (but in a different sense) for Bergson — occupies the first place.

We now turn to the leading representatives of existentialism in Germany. Karl Jaspers (1883-) is closest to Kierkegaard, but he has also come under the influence of Kant. The individual person as existence is not to be understood from general principles, but is to be clarified from himself as this particular one in his own unique historical situation. Existence asserts itself against the nothingness experienced in anxiety by means of a decision for one's own personal reality. And this latter is founded on the *transcendence that is revealed in our passage through extreme situations (Grenzsituation). Corresponding to this transcendence is a supra-conceptual "philosophical faith" which is able to direct itself only to the absent or hidden God and which is opposed to "religious faith" which embraces God as present.

In one way or another, all of these ideas have left their mark of Martin Heidegger (1889-). His thinking, however, is not existential (*existentiell*) in a personalist sense, that is, seeing everything in its importance for the individual; rather, it is existential (*existenzial*) in a metaphysical sense, that is, through the individual it is striving for human existence, and ultimately absolute existence. Therefore, his thought moves from the *ontic* to the *ontological*, from the factually existent to the existence that supports it. Thus, the existential (existenzial) analysis of man is only *fundamental ontology* which is followed by *ontology* as the exposition of existence itself; more recently, however, Heidegger means by the word "ontology" the investigation of the existent that is identical with metaphysics, while by "fundamental ontology" he characterizes the illumination of existence which (according to him) completes the victory over metaphysics. Existence manifests itself first of all as the design of man caught up in contingency; this is the fundamental state of determination in which he always finds himself as human existence in the world. Existence is then clarified in its various modes or *Existenzialien*. By caring about worldly things man loses himself in inauthenticity. But he is raised above that by anxiety or *angst* which uncovers nothingness as the ground of all existents. This is revealed in the present as the nothingness of daily cares; in the past, insofar as the origin remains hidden, as being cast into the world (*geworfen*); and in the future as death, because with regard to the future only one thing is certain and that is the fact that it issues in death. Therefore, the experience of nothingness embraces all levels of human existence and so places a man squarely before the totality of his human reality. To the extent that he takes hold of himself with fixity of purpose he achieves authenticity. His existence would mean unintelligibility and so

EXISTENTIAL PHILOSOPHY

hopeless *tragedy*, if nothingness meant absolute emptiness. But actually existence manifests itself in the veil of nothingness (the "not" of the existent); this existence is in no way just a projection of man; rather, it precedes it as the ground of every existent. Although existence opens up a place for the holy, for divinity and for God, the problem of God still has received no clear answer from Heidegger.

In conjunction with German existential philosophy, French existentialism should be mentioned; it is here that the spiritual heritage from men like Pascal and Maine de Biran continues to live. It has developed in two distinct ways: on the one hand there is the atheistic-nihilistic version whose chief representatixe is Jean Paul Sartre (1905-), and then there is the metaphysical-theistic version developed by Gabriel Marcel (1889-).

The chief influences on Sartre have been Heidegger, Husserl and Hegel. According to Sartre, man's existence precedes his essence; by this he means that man, as absolute and unlimited *freedom*, is the one who first determines his own nature and the guiding values of human existence. Since man as total freedom must seek his own way by himself alone, without God and without any norms, he seems to be condemned to freedom as the burden he must carry. Freedom includes consciousness which is essentially present to itself and therefore is not wholly itself; being prevented by this nothingness from being completely itself, it is a kind of existence that is divided by nothingness. Over against consciousness stands the unconscious corporeal existent as the undivided fullness of existence. Because consciousness strives necessarily, but in vain, to be completely itself as consciousness, it reveals itself as a useless passion or as absurdity; proof of this is found in *nausea* as man's basic experience of his own human existence. — Maurice Merleau-Ponty (1908-61) also has an atheistic orientation. His phenomenological analysis strives for the original source or the pre-reflective element not only in human conduct but also in the incarnate meaning of the world and of history. Man cannot go beyond the free realization of inner-worldly and inter-personal solidarity. Because of the radical contingency of everything, no road leads to the Absolute; moreover, an Absolute would destroy man's freedom and it would leave him with nothing more to do.

Gabriel Marcel occupies a position somewhat contrary to the above. He came to his basic conclusions about human existence before Sartre did, and he arrived there independently of Kierkegaard and of German existentialism. Like the others, he also was investigating the mystery of the human person and of human freedom. When his concrete situation is illuminated, man at first appears to be broken and cut off from his own true life. Yet he finds his true life and therefore himself when he goes beyond himself towards *transcendence by exercising composure and trust; in this way he roots himself in the divine "Thou." Consequently, for

EXPERIENCE

Marcel human existence is less characterized by anxiety and grief than it is by hope and adoration.

Existentialism is correct in affirming that man is not just another thing, but is human existence; that is, he fulfills himself only in decisions by means of which he embraces and realizes the fullness of his own being. Thus, will and freedom — and so primarily action — occupy the central position; personal involvement and existential seriousness are demanded. Here we also find the profound insight that this corruptibility of ours is rooted in transcendence, in a dependence on something or someone other-worldly. Nevertheless, it is precisely the veil surrounding the transcendent that shows up the limitations of existential philosophy. For it is suspicious (and rightly so) not only of the idealistic universals, but also (not rightly so) of all universal concepts whatsoever and of reason itself. But since the *irrational discloses all things only in their existential relationships, it harbors the danger that the objective aspect of things will evaporate into the mere *Existenzialien* of man; it also contains the danger that objective reality only "is" to the extent that man projects it as a manifestation of his own "human existence." But it is not necessary that existentialism succumb to this danger, for, in the journey through the *Existenzialien* a newer, more vibrant approach to *existence itself can be uncovered.

JBL

EXPERIENCE

Experience (from Lat.: *experiri* = to test, to try) signifies (1) a state of subjectivity or awareness with an emphasis on the spatio-temporal dimensions involved. Connected with this is the idea of the reception of an impression from the things that "happen" to a person. So it follows that not every possible *intuition is an experience, since God knows all things in himself without being determined by them. Moreover, experience is to be distinguished from *thinking which is a more active type of knowing — a knowing that reaches beyond received impressions. — In everyday language (2) "experience" usually means the knowledge derived from much association with people and things, as opposed to the knowledge gained from books. The philosophical use of the term is much broader. There "experience" (3) frequently signifies every simple perception that is produced by an impression from without: since this is possible only through the influence of external bodies on the sense organs, experience in the true sense is proper to a soul bound to a body; this does not mean, however, that it is necessarily just sensible (see below). (If someone speaks of a "mystical experience" produced in the soul by the direct activity of God, then this is an extension of the common use of the world). In a narrower sense, Aristotle does not characterize the particular perception as experience; rather, an experience (4) (*empeiria*) for him is the concentra-

134

tion of many perceptions and memories of the same kind and in this concentration the common element is grasped in a schematic image. Other philosophers give the name "experience" (5) to a judgment made on the basis of perception. Kant has an even narrower view (6) of this concept: according to him, not every judgment based on perception is an experience, but only one that includes an a priori form of understanding and which, therefore, has universal validity (*Critical Philosophy).

A distinction is made between *external* and *internal* experience. "External experience" means the perception of corporeal objects and agents by means of the external senses (*Sense Knowledge); "internal experience" means being aware of one's own internal (mental) states and activities (*Consciousness). Even this latter type is experience in the sense described above; it is not a purely spiritual vision of the essence of the soul and its activities because it is essentially conditioned by influences on the soul that come from the outside. — From another point of view, a distinction is made between ordinary, *pre-scientific* and *scientific* experience; this latter is either a planned *observation* of natural occurrences usually with the help of special instruments, or it is an *experiment* in which certain conditions are artificially produced and the results carefully recorded.

The content of experience (the "given" in all experience) is sometimes said to be purely sensible. If this is meant in the sense that every spiritually grasped aspect of the given (*intelligibile in sensibili*) is to be denied, then it is to be rejected. For, in actual fact we grasp immediately not only our own spiritual acts and in them our own "ego" in the internal experience, but we also gain — admittedly within very narrow limits — essential knowledge of sensible objects; and this is something that is knowable only by a spiritual power (*Essential Knowledge). Therefore, our human experience is characterized by both sense and spirit. To be sure, the purely sensible aspect of our experience is usually referred to as the "empirical" quality. In any event, experience always offers only particular facts, not universal and necessary essences or principles. — It is nót easy to overestimate the importance of experience. All of our basic concepts arise out of it and to this extent all of our thinking must be related to experience in some way. Specifically, all knowledge of existence is based on immediate experience or on a conclusion drawn from it. Still, experience is not the only original source of knowledge, as *empiricism maintains; for, the absolutely universal and necessary principles of *knowledge cannot be explained on the basis of experience alone. Moreover, even *induction, which is a most valuable method of discovering new knowledge, cannot be explained and justified from experience alone.

JdV

EXPLANATION

To explain something means, in general, to reduce or trace back an unknown to something known. One explains a concept by pointing out the particular/characteristics out of which it is composed and which are previously known. In this sense, since the 18th century philosophers have spoken of the explanation of a concept as being equivalent to a *definition. An idea is explained when it is reduced to its necessary causes or, if it is a particular case, when it is traced back to a universal law. — While human life and its creations are characterized by the freedom of the human spirit (which freedom is removed from all purely legal control), sub-human nature is ruled by very definite laws (re apparent exceptions: *Indetermination, Principle of). Rightly, therefore, since the work of Wilhelm Dilthey († 1911) "explanation" has been considered the characteristic method of the physical sciences as opposed to the method of understanding which is proper to the human sciences (psychology, religion, literary criticism, etc.). For, here it is a matter of tracing appearances back to their basic components, of grasping them in the context of their causal relationships, of knowing the particular, which in this case (otherwise than in the case of human things) has no proper value in and of itself, as an individual realization of a universal principle. (The intention of physical science is not to understand "this" rainbow, but rainbow as such; however, a human science like the history of art does not consider paintings in general but particular masters). Along with the object and goal of physical science is connected the fact that its method or its mode of explanation is both rational and conceptual. But even though the tracing of appearances back to their efficient causes is the principal thing, it would still be one-sided to overlook *finality (which of course is unconscious outside of man) there and in the biological realm; moreover, there is a certain wholeness operative also in inanimate nature. The two ways of looking at things are not mutually exclusive; rather, they complement each other. When physical science attempts to "explain" the principles of its own explanation, then it has reached the limits of its own competence and becomes the *philosophy of *nature*. Such a philosophy of nature must trace back the known to the unknown which, as the condition of the possibility of the known, is also a necessary.

WB

F

FACT

A fact is a perceptible, concrete, *objective reality; it is also a thing and its relationships in the concrete world of activity. All facts belong to the order of reality. They do not, however, completely exhaust the totality of objective reality. Purely essential relationships are also real. Factual sciences (in contrast to essential sciences) are those which have for their objects experienceable facts. Therefore, not all science is based on facts, but is based on objective reality. See also *Experience, Positivism, Reality*.

WB

FAITH

The words "faith" and "believe" have long been used in English for the biblical notions *fides* and *credere* (Gr.: *pistis* and *pisteuein*); they have, therefore, a religious and especially a Christian coloring. Thus faith (1) often signifies in the writings of St. Paul that new way of salvation which was opened up to us by the grace of Christ as opposed to the "law" of the Old Testament. More specifically, faith (2) is the free act of man by which he responds to the call of God's grace, that is, a free affirmative response to the self-manifestation (*Revelation) of God: this is revelation-faith. To be reasonable, this faith presupposes a certain *evidence as a logical foundation insofar as the fact of revelation and the authority (i. e., truth and veracity) of God as the revealer must be known; but it is not the same thing as a logical conclusion which flows from known principles. Rather, it is a firm assent of the intellect, excluding all prudent doubt, to revealed truth which is given on the basis of the authority of God himself. This assent as free *certitude depends upon the will and therefore upon the values which determine the will as its motive. But the motive of the assent of faith is not, as in the science of theology, a purely theoretical, limited knowledge of an article of faith which is established through logical argument; the motive is the authority of God alone which man trusts and completely subjects himself to. The expression "faith in Christ" emphasizes, beyond the submission of one's own viewpoint, the trusting dedication and adherence of the whole man who expects from Christ alone his complete salvation. Luther understood this dedication in a very narrow sense when he required faith (3) alone for justification, that is, confidence that my sins are forgiven because of the merits of Christ (*fiducial faith*). — The name "faith" is often transferred from the act and the *virtue of faith to the object or content of faith; this use occurs when one says that he knows his faith. When the Church declares in a formal definition that a truth of faith is revealed by God, then this teaching is called a "dogma." On the relationship between faith and knowing see *theology.

On a broader scale faith (4) means belief in God, that is, every religious conviction, even if it is not founded on divine revelation. In this situation also faith remains a free and therefore a morally significant commitment of the whole person. The so-called philosophical faith (Jaspers; *Existential Philosophy) belongs here. As the rational foundation was removed from faith (2 and 4) by modern *agnosticism there has been a greater tendency to substitute an irrational faith (5) for a faith that was shown to be in some sense reasonable. Thus Kant wanted "to remove knowledge in order to make room for faith." For him moral faith is the acceptance of the *postulates of practical reason, especially that of the existence of God, not because there are objectively sufficient reasons for doing so, but because they are subjectively necessary as the presupposition of a meaningful observance of the moral law. Sentiment or feeling (*Fideism) as advocated by the irrationalistic philosophy of religion (especially since Schleiermacher) has taken the place of the Kantian voluntaristic foundation of faith. According to this view, faith is a conviction which is the result of a certain religious feeling; and sometimes it is identified with this feeling itself.

Theologically, *unbelief* is the lack of revelation-faith; sometimes it means the lack of any faith (4 and 5) in God whatsoever and therefore is practically equivalent to *atheism. Unbelief involves personal guilt before God if one refuses to believe, even though he knows with sufficient certitude about the fact of revelation or the basic reasons for the existence of God; guilt is also present if a person deliberately and antecedently refuses to inform himself properly. *Superstition* is a type of false faith, especially faith in the efficacy of certain formulas or rites which do not naturally have the power to produce the desired effect and which — more or less consciously — are supposed to force preternatural, mysterious powers into the service of man.

In a non-religious sense, faith (6) means affirming something as true as a practical *certitude or accepting the statement of another on his word alone. This natural faith is similar to faith (2) and includes trust in the truthfulness of the other. In this way it is distinguished from a type of knowledge which accords only marginal credence to the statements of others because, for example, the particular circumstances do not offer any reason for suspecting a lie; in this case one could perhaps speak of "evidential knowledge." — In a much wider sense, "to believe" can mean in ordinary everyday language "to think" or even "to suppose."

In recent times a completely secular meaning has been developed out of the religious content of "belief in Christ" or "belief in God"; according to this sense, faith (7) means a firm conviction and trust, strongly influenced by feelings and perfectly resistant to any troubling doubts. With this kind of faith an individual will cling to the person or thing in which he believes with almost religious fervor.

JdV

FALLACY

An *inference that lacks logical consistency is a *false inference* (*paralogism*). False inferences that appear to be logically correct are called fallacies (*sophisms*). — Since the *categorical inference is based on the comparison of the extremes (= subject and predicate) with one and the same middle concept, it must contain only three concepts. If it contains four terms by reason of some *equivocation* (= *quaternio terminorum*), then the ability to conclude is lacking. — Begging the question (*petitio principii*) means that what is to be proved is itself presupposed as the starting point of the argument. — In the *vicious circle* the former is proved by the latter and again the latter by the former. — The *ignoratio elenchi* (ignorance of the question) is given if, in a discussion, the precise question at issue is not recognized and some proposition is proved which is neither identical with the point that is to be proved nor necessarily implies it.

WB

FALSITY

Falsity is the opposite of truth. Corresponding to the different meanings of *truth one usually distinguishes logical, ontological and ethical falsity. — (1) Logical falsity is present when a judgment does not correctly represent the matter in question. Characteristic of logical falsity is that something is affirmed that really should be denied, or that something is denied that really should be affirmed. Concepts of themselves are neither true nor false. One can only speak of false concepts to the extent that they are applied to objects as the result of incorrect judgments. — (2) Ontological falsity consists in the departure of a thing from its *idea. One cannot speak of ontological falsity when the intended object has a richer content than the idea expresses, but only when it contains something that contradicts its idea. There is no such thing as ontological falsity as such in the realm of nature, since all things — at least essentially — correspond with their divine ideas. In the world of art, however, something is ontologically false if it contradicts the idea and intention of the artist or the principles of art itself. Sometimes a thing is said to be false with respect to casual, imprecise human ideas that are generated because of a certain similarity with something else (e.g., false diamonds). — (3) Ethical falsity consists in this that a person deliberately conducts himself or speaks in a way different from what he thinks (*Lie). The mere hiding of one's inner thoughts is not ethical falsity. — See also *Error.*

JS

FIDEISM

Fideism (Lat: *fides* = faith, therefore = faith philosophy) designates the doctrine that metaphysical, moral and religious truths are inaccessible to human reason and can be grasped only by *faith. Then, if this faith is understood as coming from some authority, it is the same thing as *traditionalism. Fideism usually refers to those theories that claim that the supra-sensible is grasped by a sense of feeling or faith. The Scottish School (Thomas Reid: 1710-1796) appealed to *common sense* as the philosophical basis of truth; F. H. Jacobi (1743-1819) postulated a special *sense of reality* on the basis of which we assent in faith to religious and moral truths; F. D. E. Schleiermacher (1768-1834) based all religion on "feeling of absolute dependence." This reduction of religion to an *irrational faith, a type of thinking that was quite extensive in Protestant philosophy of religion (A. Ritschl, A. Sabatier), made some inroads into Catholic thinking through the Modernist movement at the beginning of this century. — Very close to fideism are those thinkers who say that the first principles of thinking are accepted by the mind only as the result of an act of trust. — The following points should be made against all forms of fideism: (1) the assumption that human reason cannot know the supra-sensible is false (*Metaphysics, *God's Existence, Demonstration of); (2) fideism offers an inadequate *norm of *truth*, since in reality only the *evidence can give the ultimate guarantee of the truth.

JS

FINALITY

Finality (teleology) means the attainment of an *end (*finis*) by an existent, in which the existent achieves a fulfillment and perfection in accordance with its essential structure. Finality is rooted in the fact that every existent finds meaning in its existence and in its activity — a meaning that finds expression in the general *principle of *finality*. Metaphysical richness of meaning finds an expression that is empirically detectable in ordered structures (*Order) of the most different complexity. Since the meaning and *unity that permeate these structures are intelligible only from the end intended, they are said to be *finalized* in the double sense of *purposeful* (i. e., corresponding to the end and *purpose) and end-striving (i. e., attaining an end). — The operation of finality is most clearly visible in the man who, after consciously knowing and setting definite ends, is guided by them and freely strives for them (*complete* and *intentional, autonomous finality*). Here one can see how the end precedes the striving activity and how, in truly causal influence (but not efficient causality) on the efficient cause (*Cause), it is a principle of its own proper realization. The constituent elements of finality in sub-human nature are only partially detectable; for this reason it is also called *imperfect* or *natural finality* (1). The remaining basic elements must be deduced from the full intelligibility of the existent and from the particular orderly structures in which this intelligibility appears to us. Thus natural finality manifests itself as *heteronomous*. *External* or *accidental* finality is present when the end-to-be-achieved is imposed on an agent from the outside, for example, on a bullet by the marksman, on a clock by the mechanical connection of the parts; *internal* or *immanent* essential finality is that which belongs to a thing naturally so that it strives for and attains the end by means of its own natural activity. Moreover, according to the particular point of view a distinction is made between *static* or *structural* finality and *dynamic* or *natural finality* (2) as also between *self-serving* and *altruistic finality*. Immanent finality, which is proper to all living things, always presupposes in a thing its own proper substantial basis of finality (*Form, *Life Principle). The form of the whole cosmos should be looked upon as a finality of order.

The acceptance of a constitutive, essential finality is unavoidable in those cases where a true natural striving and its constant realization in orderly structures can be proven on the basis of certain norms of finality, such as are clearly evident to the impartial viewer in such processes as ontogenesis, regeneration and so forth, in organisms. And even the inorganic systems (star systems, crystal systems, the periodic table of elements), according to many authors, border upon some kind of finality. The complexity of the whole cosmos (the inorganic world and the world of living things) without doubt manifests final relationships. For, the partial orders do not, as efficient causes, summon each other into existence (e.g., plants are not the necessary effect of the inorganic world); the temporally later and constitutively higher orders have their own proper laws as contrasted with the earlier and lower orders. Therefore, the mutual dependence of these orders (governed according to certain laws), a fact that is easily observable, is not possible without the ordering influx of a supra-cosmic, intelligent efficient cause. — The final cause, through whose influence all activity is striving for some end, is not an ersatz for the efficient cause. For, the end is realized or attained only through the activity of efficient causes. Therefore, it is false to look upon efficient causes as the only causes that give us any knowledge of reality — a mistake that is sometimes made by researchers in the natural sciences. The investigation of efficient causes (causal analysis) helps toward the *explanation of natural events, while the investigation of finality leads to the deeper meaning of nature and provides us with a broader understanding of it in its totality.

On the basis of certain epistemological prejudices Kant and his followers understood finality not as a constitutive principle of reality, but as merely a regulating principle of the power of *judgment (*Urteilskraft*) that is searching for unity (*Critical Philosophy). The so-called hypothesis of chance is no foundation of finality: according to its basic concept *chance can explain no event that occurs regularly according to set laws. — Pantheism, pan-vitalism and pan-psychism have looked for an autonomous foundation of finality. The pantheistic arguments fall with the whole system of *pantheism. According to pan-vitalism (hypothesis of a cosmic organism) the whole cosmos is a living substance with a complete entelechy or world-soul; the partial orders then receive their immanent finality from this world-soul. However, the substantial unity of the cosmos is contradicted by the essential differences between the partial orders which cannot be simply reduced to each other so that there is no basic difference between them (*Vitalism). — Pan-psychism traces every purposeful happening — even those in elements, plants and animals — back to a subjective, intelligent thinking and willing of the particular efficient causes, because (as they say) a communicated or objective intelligent activity is a contradiction. Experience, however, shows the exact opposite of this. For example, a clock executes the intelligent planning of man without itself being rational. Analogously, the sub-human things of nature carry out the plan and will of the supra-cosmic originator of nature; their finality is natural, but communicated (*Vitalism, *Life Principle). — Heteronomous but not completely worked out is the foundation of finality by means of a "supra-individual spiritual something" that remains undetermined (the universal idea in the sense of Plato). But nothing definite is said about the way in which these ideas are individualized in the concrete particular existent. They also demand an explanation through an absolute, all-embracing, intelligent and supra-cosmic cause which we call God.

KF-AH

FINALITY, PRINCIPLE OF

In scholastic philosophy by the "principle of finality" is usually meant that every agent acts for an end (*omne agens agit propter finem*); sometimes it also means, in a sense that is close to that of the first principle, that a natural tendency cannot be meaningless (*impossibile est desiderium naturale esse in vanum*). For the sake of distinction we call the former principle the *principle of steadily pursuing one's goal* and the other the *principle of certainty as to one's goal*. As principles of *knowledge with metaphysical value both principles find their justification not through the experience of *finality, but only through the a priori essential insight. The principle of steadily pursuing one's goal is very clear with regard to all activity that immediately proceeds from intelligent planning (of course it is to be noted that the motive of God's activity is not in any sense an end to be achieved, but the divine goodness as communicable: *Creation). But even an activity that does not proceed directly from a rational planner is ordered to some definite end, because it proceeds from a natural tendency (*Appetite) that resides in all natural things as a power moving them towards some definite activity and, ultimately, because it can be explained only in terms of the divine mind of the creator who knows and established the ends to be striven for.

The principle of certainty as to the goal says in addition that the end of a natural tendency is also attainable; for, a natural tendency would be "meaningless" if it tended towards a wholly impossible goal or if the inclinations necessary for the attainment of the goal were lacking in the nature of those things. However, this does not exclude a frustration of a tendency in particular cases because of opposing powers that are also working towards their own ends; in fact, this is often necessary in order to achieve higher ends. With regard to subordinate natural tendencies, the number of beings that fail to attain their direct end can be much larger than the number of those that do (e.g., think of the relatively small number of seeds that reach full development). It is disputed whether or not the principle of certainty as to the goal is a "first principle" in the sense of a directly or almost directly self-evident principle. In any event it is ultimately rooted in the wisdom of the creator.

JdV

FINITE

Finite (*limited*) in the usual sense is primarily a thing that is extended, that could be larger, that has a *limit*. A "limit" is the cessation of a perfection of a reality; thus, before all else it says cessation, but it also includes the presence of the limited characteristic plus the possibility of a "more." In the qualitative sense, finiteness signifies a material or spiritual characteristic insofar as it allows for an intensive increase. Finite *existence as such is an existence in comparison to which a greater fullness of existence is possible. Thus, we arrive at the empirical concept of finiteness by merely comparing things with each other. — In the deeper, metaphysical sense we call that existent finite that belongs to a definite *category. Every created existent must be included here. According to *Cartesianism and *ontologism the idea of metaphysical finiteness already presupposes the idea of the *infinite, just as the negative concept presupposes the positive one. Perhaps it would be more accurate to say that we grasp both of them at the same time.

Within the scholastic tradition there are two principle views about the inner constitution of the finite existent and both appeal to the authority of Thomas Aquinas. According to the neo-Thomistic view, existence (which of itself alone is infinite) is limited by its relation to a real principle of limitation which is distinct from itself; this principle is the potential essence. Accordingly, the less potency finite creatures have, the higher they stand on the ladder of existence. — Suarez, however, says that such a really distinct principle of limitation is superfluous. In his view, existence can be limited of itself (because *act of itself does not signify positive infinity but only disregards all limitation. According to him, therefore, finite things are metaphysically composed only of an existence that naturally disregards limits and of a limiting potency or essence. In other words a particular finite existent is not, as it were, a slice of divine existence; it is rather a very special imitation of it. Therefore, *Suarezianism sees the fundamental characteristic of all finite things in their *contingency, whereas *Thomism sees it in the real composition of essence and existence. Corresponding to this difference is a different approach to the proofs for the existence of God.

MR

FORCE

Force in the proper sense (*physical force*) is the necessity of positing an external act which is brought about by the application of physical power and so is wholly subject to *external necessity*; therefore it is neither a free nor a responsible act. *Moral force* is caused by threats and unjustly aroused fear in order to extort or to prevent a particular action. Although the freedom of decision is thereby diminished, as long as not all power of deliberation is excluded, it still remains intact and so not all responsibility for evil done under the influence of fear is removed. A contract that has been entered into under the influence of an unjust fear can be annulled, since a moderate level of freedom is necessary for the preservation of normal social life. Psychological freedom (*Free Will) becomes impossible through the operation of all *inner necessity*, that is, through all those situations (such as hallucinations, phobias, compulsions) which, independently of all conscious choice, set loose their corresponding actions (*psychological force*).

Some of the causes of psychological force are states of exhaustion (e.g., in puberty), a false education, and especially mental illnesses. Moral force is often the result of social prejudices and not infrequently it makes heroic demands on a person's moral integrity and honesty. Outside of situations of a justified self-defense, the use of physical force on other people is immoral. However, for the preservation of the common good civil authority has the right to use physical force (*legal compulsion*) against criminals, fugitives and violators of the law.

JoS

FORM

Form (Lat.: = *forma*; Gr.: = *morphē*) has the primary meaning (1) of the external shape, the outline, the figure, the visible structure of a body; since form within the world of bodies in this sense offers an important basis for determination and distinction, "morphology" gives it very special attention. A second sense of the word is closely connected with this primary meaning, and this is that form (2) is the external expression, established by universally valid norms, of a thought or of a decision of the will; in particular, it is the established way of stating some legal matter (e.g., the form of a last will and testament). In this sense, a demonstration is "in form" if its individual steps and their logical connection clearly stand out in the verbal expression.

Since the shape or form (1) is much more useful than, say, color in characterizing the specific differences of things, philosophy, especially since Aristotle, has transferred the name "form" to the intrinsic essential reason for the specific difference of things. Form in this sense, the *substantial form* (3) exists in bodies as the opposite of matter (*Hylemorphism). It is the substantial principle of a specific kind of existence and of all purposeful activity (*Dynamism). In living things the *soul (or *Life Principle) is the form; therefore, it is only an essential part of the whole existent and in plants and animals it is an essential part that is incapable of separate, independent existence. The spiritual human soul, however, is a form that subsists in itself, i. e., it is capable of a separate independent existence. A pure spirit is a "pure form," i.e., a form which exists as a complete whole for itself and is essentially independent of all matter.

From the substantial combination of bodies out of matter and form the word "form" is carried over and applied to every combination made up of a determinable basis (not necessarily corporeal) called "matter," and a determining principle called "form" (4). Thus the conceptual pair "matter-form" is similar to the other pair: *potency—*act. In this sense, every accident in reference to the substance in which it inheres can be called an *accidental form*. Thomas Aquinas also characterizes existence itself in

145

contrast to the essence as "form," in fact he says that it is form in the highest sense (*maxime formale*). In logic the concepts of subject and predicate are called the matter of the *judgment, while the "is," which determines the concepts to be a judgment, is called the form of the judgment. In this case the matter of the judgment is at the same time the changing "content" with regard to the form which remains the same. A similar situation holds for the logical *inference. In ethics the "ought," the binding character of the good, is called the form of the moral law in contrast to the various moral values which are called the matter or content of the moral law. — In all of these cases the form stands in contrast to a matter which is already in some sense determined. In other cases a wholly undetermined *subject is set over against the form (5); this subject is the ultimate carrier which "has" all the forms or existential determinations. An example of form in this sense would be human nature about which it is said that this or that particular being (e.g., Peter) has it. Form in this sense does not coincide with form (3) as an essential component of an existent. The soul alone is form in this latter meaning, but there is no doubt at all that the body or matter in general belongs to human nature. Many distinguish form in this sense as the "*metaphysical form*" from the "*physical form*" which is the form as an essential principle. This distinction has important applications in the realm of knowledge. For, the metaphysical form is the basis of the knowability of any finite existent as opposed to the individual subject which is always shrouded with a certain darkness as far as we are concerned.

All of the forms mentioned so far (1-5) are existential forms or *forms of existence*; the *form of knowledge* (6) (the *species* or the representation in the knowing power) stands over against them and can be either a sensible or a spiritual form. In this form the known object acquires a new type of existence in the knowing power of the knower which is called *intentional existence*. If the form of the object is characterized as the content of the intentional representation, this should not be taken to mean primarily the essential form but the totality of the formal aspects of an existent in the sense mentioned (form 4 and 5) which, as was said, is the basis of knowability. Also, the matter or subject is not completely excluded from the intentional representation, since it is simultaneously grasped in the sensible perception and in the *concrete concept. — See also *Hylemorphism*.

JdV

FREEDOM

Freedom in general is the state of not being forced or determined by something external, insofar as it is joined to a definite internal faculty of self-determination. Different kinds of freedom are distinguished according to the kinds of pressures which are excluded. Consciously striving beings

FREEDOM

(men and animals) and even, though to a lesser degree, plants enjoy *physical* freedom to the extent that external, material obstacles do not impede them. *Moral* freedom (1) in the broad sense consists in the ability to determine oneself to something without being hindered by external causes (e.g., threats) which work interiorly on the mind (by way of the imagination); *moral* freedom (2) in the narrow sense consists in the ability to determine oneself to something without running up against an opposing obligation (e.g., going to the theatre). *Psychological* freedom, which does not exclude but is actually the presupposition of physical limitations and moral obligations, consists in the ability to determine oneself to something without any psychic pressures, preceding the act of decision, which would clearly force the will in one determined direction; in other words, it consists in the ability "to choose as one wishes" (*Free Will). Without a certain superiority of the interior over the exterior, which is absent in the inorganic world, one cannot properly speak of "freedom."

According to Kant *intelligible* freedom consists in the fact that the will, independent from the influence of all sensual drives, is determined by pure reason alone. As such the will obeys the *categorical imperative and therefore is necessarily a moral will. In the world of appearances it is able to be effective (this is only a postulate of the practical reason), because its intelligible causality stands as it were in a diagonal relationship to the necessary causal series of appearances. — Kant fails to see that the well-balanced reason, although always tending in the direction of moral values, does not necessarily prescribe that these are to be realized in one way only. He fails to see that the objective evaluation of sensual desires does not necessitate reason. The compatibility of intelligible and empirical causality is only possible when the latter is not absolutely necessary.

It flows from the very nature of man as a finite, bodily-spiritual, reasonable and social being that his freedom cannot be unlimited, as *liberalism, anarchism* and *antinomianism* (the rejection of all law) would have it. Reason itself demands that man submit himself to the moral law on the basis of his own insights and not merely from external force, that he recognize the personal God who is the source of all spiritual, moral and physical order, that he become an active member of the natural social orders in a way that is not prejudicial to his personal dignity (*Person, *Society). That opinion of Marxism and National-Socialism, which was prepared for by the philosophy of Hegel, is false which asserts that that action is free which is posited with an insight into its necessity. — According to the object in relation to which a person is free, the following distinctions can be made: *freedom of *conscience,* i. e., the right to follow one's own conscience without hindrance (which does not exclude the obligation to form one's conscience according to objective norms and to respect the basic rights of others); *freedom of religion* (which is a part of the freedom of conscience); *academic freedom* (which is the possibility in the areas of research and teaching to abide only by known truth and certainty); *freedom to express one's opinion publicly* (freedom of speech, freedom of the press). It is self-evident that all these freedoms have some limitations so that they cannot be extended so far that they present a real danger to society and to the values that society is supposed to protect.

WB

FREEDOM OF GOD

God is free with regard to that which is outside of himself, i.e., he can create or not create, he can create this or that. His freedom is also a freedom of choice, for it is not merely an acting from the necessity of his nature (Spinoza) or an absolute independence from the object to be produced (Hegel). God created the world neither from an inner unconscious drive (*Pantheism) nor from psychological necessity, as if he must always choose the most perfect object (Leibniz: *Optimism), nor from a kind of moral necessity, as if he necessarily loves himself in his creatures. — Divine freedom agrees with human freedom to the extent that it means a freedom of choice with regard to different objects. Man, however, can choose between good and evil, whereas God can only choose from among different goods. Man chooses not only between different objects, but also between different acts of the will by which he directs himself to the objects. God can only choose between different objects, since his willing is one unchangeable act which is actually identified with his essence (*Will of God).

The antinomy between God's eternal act of will and his freedom, since freedom seems to imply deliberation and succession, can be resolved by an appeal to the infinite knowledge of God which embraces everything knowable in one act. At best, we can distinguish different logical moments which condition one another. Thus, for example, from all eternity God sees the prayer of petition and determines from eternity to hear it. — The antinomy between God's freedom and his immutability is solved by the classical scholastic authors in the following way: By one infinite act of his will God can accomplish that which would only be possible to finite creatures by a number of different acts, just as he possesses in himself in his infinite perfection all the limited perfections found in the diversity of creatures, but he possesses them in an eminent way; or in other words, in the very same necessary act of his will by which he loves himself necessarily he can at the same time freely will contingent objects. The freedom of God presupposes the possibility of contingent things; for this reason *pantheism always denies both the freedom of God and the existence of contingent things.

MR

FREE WILL

Free will is the power of a spiritual being to determine itself with regard to known, limited values (i.e., without having been previously determined to one rather than another), to choose or not to choose any limited good which is known as such. Therefore there is only a question of free will when a value is perceived as real, but limited and so not possessing all possible perfection. If something appears as an absolute value and so is not bound up with any imperfection, then the will must necessarily affirm and strive for this good; this is not a matter of force, but of the natural reaction of the finite spirit in the face of the good (*Appetite). Further, free will does not mean a capacity for uncaused or motiveless willing, as many opponents of free will (determinists) repeatedly assert without really understanding the teaching on freedom. There is no such thing as motiveless willing. Nor does free will mean that the will cannot be strongly influenced and attracted by motives or that it is completely indifferent to them. Also, free will does not mean that men in concrete situations always will freely, since many daily activities are performed without any consideration of the motives involved. Moreover, since the intellectual consideration required for a free choice can be limited by passion or pathological circumstances like compulsions and so forth, in such cases it is legitimate to speak of diminished freedom and imputability; and freedom is usually not totally blotted out except perhaps in the case of acute mental illness.

The fact of free will becomes clearer when it is considered in relation to the ethical activities of persons. Without free will, and therefore without the possibility to will this or that, clearly a man cannot be held any more responsible for his willed actions, he is no more worthy of praise or blame than a sick man is for his sickness. Consequently, without free will the moral goodness or wickedness of an act of the will could not meaningfully be separated from sheer utility. And the categorical imperative of conscience would be just as meaningless as the experience of a good or bad conscience, of a sense of guilt, of remorse, etc. If free will is abandoned then the moral dignity of the person must also be renounced; this would be equivalent to saying that there is no sense whatsoever to human existence. — Furthermore, the awareness of one's own freedom before, during and after particular choices is such a universal, undeniable fact (which is even admitted by many who deny free will) that it cannot be explained away in every case as the result of mere self-deception or ignorance of unknown forces: it can only be explained by the reality of free will. The possibility of predicting with a high degree of accuracy the future choices of individuals placed in certain circumstances, given the necessary information about their character, likes and dislikes, can be explained by the fact that men usually choose that which is in accordance with their habits, their preferences and their circumstances; this is especially true when the particular situation offers no weighty reason why they should choose something out of the ordinary. Thus such prediction is no argument against the fact of free will. — Likewise, one cannot say that basic moral principles retain their meaning for man even if he does not enjoy free will, since, for example, a man should have given a better formation to his character which now determines him to evil. For if this man is not free to begin with, then he did not have the possibility of forming his character differently from what it now is and so he is not really responsible for his present evil actions.

The ultimate foundation of free will is to be found in the essence of the spiritual being whose horizon is being as such. This spiritual knower must necessarily come to a knowledge of the relative value of all limited goods; that is, it must come to the realization that a given earthly goal is partly good and partly non-good, that it can be an object of choice and still not totally satisfy the will, that it therefore cannot exhaust the possibility of willing. If this were not so, then by the perception of any particular good the will would necessarily be determined to choose it and so the whole meaning of free will would be destroyed. — Free will in no way contradicts the universally valid principle of sufficient reason or the equally universally valid *principle of *causality*; a particular form of the latter principle, the *law of *causality*, is limited in its application to bodily activities. The perceived goodness of the end always remains the sufficient basis for any act of willing, but since it is always a limited good it cannot necessitate the will. The will itself, when given the proper motives, is the sufficient efficient cause for the act of the will, insofar as it possesses within itself the generative power to produce choices not just in one direction but in many different directions. However, it has not been established as a universally valid and necessary principle of thought that an adequate cause in every case, even when it manifests itself as the decisive influence in the light of a knowledge embracing several possibilities, should necessarily be a determining cause which is applicable only to the particular end in view.

Advocates of free will (indeterminists) in penetrating, speculative discussions over the years have attempted to explain more precisely the "how" involved in the possibility and the actuality of free acts of the will and how they can be reconciled with divine power and knowledge. Important thinkers who attempted this in the 16th and 17th centuries were Banez, Molina, Bellarmine (*Concurrence, *Molinism), Leibniz (see his doctrine on the choice of the end which seems better — a doctrine which logically implies the denial of freedom), etc. Final agreement on this thorny problem has not yet been reached; and perhaps such agreement is not psychologically possible because of the impossibility of man's being able to grasp with his limited intelligence the nature of God's activity both in itself and in relation to creatures. In the evaluation of all such attempts it is absolutely essential to safeguard and reconcile the following facts: man's freedom, responsibility and ethical worth; God's justice and truthfulness as well as the total dependence of the creature on the creator. — According to Kant free will cannot be demonstrated theoretically. However, he says, it must be practically accepted as the presupposition of all moral demands made on man. It consists in the possibility, independent of all selfish interest, to subject oneself to the moral law in such a way that the will establishes that law for itself.

AW

FUNCTION

(1) In Mathematics "function" means a relationship between variable quantities which stand in a definite state of dependence on each other, so that the value of the one corresponds directly to the value of the other: $y = f(x)$, i.e., y is a function of x. In this way the states of dependence found in nature, which manifest themselves in natural laws, are formulated mathematically (quantitatively); however, these relationships are not just functional, but are also causal (*Causality, Principle of). In *Symbolic Logic the logical relations are represented in the form of mathematical functions. — (2) Physiologically and psychologically a function is the mode of operation and the performance of organs, of an *organism, of the *soul and her power (brain and liver functions; the function of thinking). Elementary feelings are explained as an inclination or disinclination to function, i. e., through the corresponding mode of the "functioning" of the physiological process. — (3) By the term "function" Kant means "the unity of acting or the ordering of different representations under a common one." The result of such functions are the concepts by means of which judgments are formed. Thus, Kant also says, "All judgments are the functions of the unity of our representations."

NJ

G

GERMAN IDEALISM

German idealism is the name given to one of the most important philosophical breakthroughs in the history of man. In the short space of about forty years (1790-1830) an intellectual movement began that is without parallel in depth and riches. It is referred to as "idealism" because for it existence and idea are identical and so in its own way it is a renewal of Platonism. It is called "German" because it began with Immanuel Kant and was further developed by German successors. The chief representatives are Fichte, Schelling and Hegel. In spite of profound differences on particular points, these men all agree on two basic ideas: the primacy of mind or spirit and the dialectical movement. Reason is the idea of ideas and the absolutely primordial basis: reason posits itself and everything else in itself as its own developing moments or appearances. Therefore it is essentially at the root of becoming. The path this becoming must follow is laid out for it by the dialectical movement; even our own thinking must fulfill itself in terms of this movement if it hopes to attain absolute truth in a philosophical way. Three stages are involved in this process. The *thesis* is the undeveloped, quiet beginning; the *antithesis*, which is already embedded in the thesis, sets the latter in motion: the negation separates itself from the affirmation; the *synthesis* leads the two contradictories to a deeper unity. This movement embraces endless stages because every synthesis on a higher level again appears as a thesis. In order to clarify these three steps we offer the following example: because of its onesidedness, a partial truth forces its equally onesided opposite out into the light; only the comparison and completion of both untruths bring out the real or full truth, which itself from a broader point of view becomes once again a partial truth.

This basic principle shows up in the work of Fichte (1762-1814) as a *theory of knowledge*. First developed in his principal work, *The Foundation of a Complete Theory of Knowledge* (1794-5) this basic position is subsequently developed further, refined and applied to different areas. Fichte begins

152

with Kant and tries to overcome his splits or divisions between the theoretical and the practical, between consciousness and the thing in itself. Therefore he established the practical ego with its freedom as the central point. Naturally, he here means the *pure ego* which is related to the empirical ego as the all-embracing primordial source is related to its particular manifestations. As pure activity this ego posits itself in intellectual intuition and posits everything else in the dialectical process. This process arises from the need of the ego, in order to achieve its own development, to find a limit; for this reason it sets the non-ego in opposition to itself. The theoretical ego is subordinated to the practical ego, because the world of objects alone is projected as the material of moral obligation. Later Fichte reduced the ego, now seen more clearly from the point of view of man, to absolute reason which appears explicitly as the pantheistic source of all.

Beginning as an expositor of the theory of knowledge and having been formed chiefly in the romantic tradition, Schelling (1775-1854) created his own system; however, as time went by he introduced significant changes in it. These are usually divided into five main periods. First of all he developed his philosophy of nature which had been neglected because of Fichte's emphasis on the primacy of the ethical. *Nature* is unconscious intelligence which strives for self-consciousness through the abundance of its forms. Transcendental idealism then presents the spirit in its conscious life; and so with the introduction of history and art it leads way beyond Fichte. If one is able to see these two phases of his philosophy as thesis and antithesis, then his *philosophy of identity* is the appropriate synthesis; for all differences (even those of nature and spirit) are overcome in the absolute or in absolute reason as total indifference. Methodically Schelling advocates intellectual intuition which unfolds itself according to the principle of polarity or of the dialectical movement and includes the primacy of aesthetic values. From about 1809 on, Schelling tried to overcome the pantheism of previous German philosophy by his doctrine of freedom and his philosophy of religion. He does concede a certain degree of independence to the world because only in this way are freedom and religion possible. The last phase of his *positive philosophy* is very closely related with these views; this phase of his philosophy he opposes to Hegel's *negative philosophy*. Positive philosophy adds a consideration of the "that" of things to the consideration of their "what"; in this way it completes reason and universal essence by the addition of will and concrete existence. Thus it profits from the experiences of religious consciousness in myth and revelation and strives for harmony between knowledge and faith. — In spite of everything, Schelling's last two periods suffer under the weight of his former pantheism; their ingenious starting points influenced the course of philosophical thinking only very slowly. (*Existential philosophy).

According to the richness of the material and the rigidity of the method, Hegel (1770-1831) brought German idealism to its completion. This is shown in his principal works: *Phenomenology of Mind* (1807), *Science of Logic* (1812-16), *Encyclopedia of the Philosophical Sciences in Outline* (1817). They all champion the primacy of thinking. The innermost foundation is the idea which, in absolute knowing, elevates itself to absolute idea; it unfolds all realities in a necessary process as its own appearances. Hegel presents this process in two ways: (1) phenomenology leads to absolute knowing through appearances; (2) within absolute knowing the real system moves from undetermined existence to the fullness of its forms. With regard to these forms, logic is directed to pre-worldly existence, the philosophy of nature to "outside-itself-ness" (*Aussersichsein*) and the philosophy of mind to the "self-presence" (*Beisichsein*) of the idea. The latter embraces three steps: *subjective mind* in individual human subjects, *objective mind* in the real existential forms of the community (law, morality, history) and *absolute mind* which reaches its full stature in art, religion and philosophy. — Methodically Hegel directs the dialectical movement to its completion. He overcomes the *philosophy of reflection*, which makes its arbitrary "reflections" on all onesided opposites, by the "cancellation" of the opposites (*Aufheben*); such cancellation does not annihilate the opposites, but it preserves them in its higher unity. The expression "in-itself" (*an-sich*) corresponds to the thesis which is already everything "in-itself," i.e., in an undeveloped way; "for-itself" (*für-sich*) corresponds to the antithesis where the opposites are "for-themselves" or in a state of alienation from their own Self, that is, they assert themselves separately and therefore appear only in what they are "for-themselves"; "in-and-for-itself" (*an-und-für-sich*) corresponds to the synthesis which presents its truth in the unity of the opposites and thus in the "for-itself" unfolds the hidden fullness of the "in-itself." Fichte and Schelling did not build up a school of followers, but a *Hegelianism* developed which broke up into two camps — one idealistic and the other materialistic; the latter school did not last long but its ideas now live on in *dialectical materialism. Hegel's political theory had a profound influence, but not until years after his death. After World War I there was renewed interest in Hegel's thought; although a neo-Hegelianism as an independent movement was not so successful, Hegel's influence on modern thinking is very extensive.

German Idealism has great constructive power by which it is able to derive the multiplicity of the real from one primordial source according to strict logical principles. It has also been able to grasp the essence of spirit and its metaphysical significance as perhaps no other thought-movement has been able to do; for according to its view, the body itself must be understood from the side of spirit. But right here we also find the limitations of German idealism. We see its basic error in the primacy of becoming over existence, as it especially stands out in the beginning of Hegel's *Logic*; here existence is seen simply as one partial moment alongside of nothingness within the whole context of true reality — which is becoming. Therefore, since the absolute primordial source is subject to becoming, it is immanent to the world of becoming and it achieves the development of its fullness only through becoming: this is pure pantheism. Also, in this view the divine primordial spirit arrives at the consciousness of itself only in the human spirit; the highest realization of human knowing, therefore, coincides with divine knowing, and so man thinks he can exhaustively comprehend the world process in absolute knowing. In actual fact, however, man gets lost in a mental construct which is not able to do justice to the independence of either the infinite ground of things or of finite beings; moreover, this view destroys all true freedom. — Schelling, in his later period, had already begun to overcome German idealism by striving for reality whole and entire. For, the true nature of spirit demands the transcendence of infinite spirit that brings forth, in a free creative act, independent finite beings; but these latter for this reason do not participate any less in the dignity of spirit.

JBL

GOD

Since the question about *existence necessarily opens up into the question about God, the quest for existence is ultimately a quest for God. Consequently, along with its answer to the question about existence every philosophy in some way or other takes a position with regard to God. Its image of God is the best evidence of its spiritual parentage and the clearest indication of its greatness or its failure. According to this norm the perennial philosophy (*Philosophy) vastly exceeds all other philosophies in its grasp of truth.

God is the primordial source of the multiplicity of existents that compose the *world. Everything is founded on him, insofar as everything proceeds from his as the first efficient cause (*Cause, *Creation) and is attracted by him as the last *end, insofar as everything participates in his fullness (*Participation) and so presents an image or at least a trace of his glory. The primordial source himself is not dependent on any other but only on himself; the first and last cause of all things must itself be uncaused, for it exists by reason of the absolute necessity of its own essence (aseitas = to be from oneself). Therefore, in God *essence and *existence are perfectly identified; he does not just have existence like an existent thing, but he is existence itself in person — he is subsisting existence (*Subsistence). This is God's *metaphysical essence*; it constitutes his innermost nature and by reason of it he must be distinguished from absolutely everything else that exists.

God's *physical essence* includes all of his perfections together with his subsisting existence which is the innermost source of these perfections. Insofar as they offer a further determination of subsisting existence we call them *God's attributes*. In himself they do not constitute a multiplicity, but rather they are a simple (*Simplicity) though infinite fullness. Since we do not immediately perceive these perfections, we find it necessary to form a partial picture of them from their reflections in creatures and by means of our concepts which are derived from earthly things (*God, Idea of). To be more precise, only the *pure perfections* can be ascribed to God because they signify essentially pure existence (wisdom, goodness, power); the *mixed perfections*, however, cannot be attributed to God because in their essence they include non-being or imperfection (e.g., emotions which can be attributed to God only in a transferred sense: *Analogy).

It is first necessary to consider each of the divine attributes in particular before we can come to a full realization of who God is in all his majesty. As existence itself God is the complete fullness of all existence and therefore *infinite. Here existence is not limited by any non-being and therefore it is pure existence, pure actuality (*actus purus*: *Act, *Potency) which, because becoming presupposes something not yet in existence, rests perfectly in itself from the very beginning. For this reason God ineffably surpasses the finite, changing existent (*Transcendence), but in order at the same time to be present in it as its primordial source (*Immanence). Since corporeal existence essentially involves non-being, God is a pure *spirit and therefore also a personal being (*Person) who possesses himself in knowledge and love and guides all other things with his providence. Man enters into a personal relationship with this deity through *relation which prepares him for the happiness God will grant him in the next life (*Immortality).

Every deviation from this refined image of God means failure of some kind. This goes for polytheism (*Theism) and also for *pantheism, which pulls God down into the changing process of the world, does not adequately distinguish him from the world and often reduces him to a blind, impersonal foundation of things (Schopenhauer). Closely related to this is the idea that God causes himself (causa sui: Spinoza), brings himself forth or posits himself by thinking (Fichte, Schelling). Even further from the truth are those who see in God only an abstract world-law (Renan, Taine) or the epitome of all laws (nomotheism) or the world of values.

JBL

GOD, IDEA OF

Man's representation of God can be found in a number of different stages. It can be quite undetermined for many pantheists who, even though they deny a personal God, still recognize something absolute and above the visible world as, for example, an absolute moral order, an absolute law, etc. Among primitive peoples we find an idea of God that is often clearly outlined but little developed; they recognize a supreme lawgiver, a judge of good and evil, a loving father. Through intellectual effort the idea of God which is heavily colored with phantasy and emotion is gradually formed into a scientific concept of God, i.e., into a conceptually refined idea with special emphasis on God's metaphysical attributes: God as infinite, subsisting existence. The end result of man's natural knowledge of God is a developed concept of God containing the explicit knowledge of his most important attributes. The essential elements of the theistic concept of God are his transcendence and personality.

Our representations and concepts can never adequately grasp God; for they are never free of human traits and in addition they are strongly influenced by character, upbringing and cultural milieu. These factors play a large role in the formation of the different ideas of God in different religions. In this sense man creates for himself his own God, or rather, his own image of God. Still, we can arrive at an analogous knowledge of God that is essentially correct (*God's Existence, Proofs for). For whatever is good and beautiful in this world and especially in man, as existence, life, knowledge and love, must also be attributed to God as the primordial source of all existence, although in an essentially different and incomparably higher way; but we can grasp this divine mode of existence only by denying of it the creaturely mode of existence which is the only kind we know from experience. Any idea of God becomes *anthropomorphic* if this essential difference in the mode of existence is overlooked and thus human limitations are attributed to God. *Analogy permits us to maintain a middle position between *gnosticism which considers God to be only an unknown X, and *pantheism which denies the essential difference between God and man. — From our analogous knowledge of God it follows that the "contradictions" in the concept of God (immutability and life, necessity and freedom, creative activity and perfect rest) dissolve into *mysteries which we can never completely unravel, but which likewise cannot be shown to be true contradictions. Therefore God is the *union of opposites* (*coincidentia oppositorum*) only in the sense that he stands above all opposites conditioned by finiteness, but not in the sense that for him the principle of contradiction would not hold. It is even less true to say that our knowledge about God is "only" a *learned ignorance* (*docta ignorantia*). Mystically inclined men and times as well as others who are perplexed by human knowing tend to prefer a *negative theology (*Neo-Platonism, medieval mysticism, modern agnosticism). Intellectuals and times with confidence in human knowing talk about God in positive concepts and images (high scholasticism, German idealism).

The psychological origin of the idea of God resides, on the one hand, in the totality of man's tendencies, i.e., in his need to seek the causes of things, in his need to conceptualize, in his hunger for the infinite and in his phantasy and feeling which strengthen the former tendencies; on the other hand, it also resides in the contingency of the world, in its wonderful harmony, in its rays of the beautiful and the good and the true. All of these things together testify to the objectivity of the idea of God or to the reality that in some way corresponds to our idea.

MR

GOD'S EXISTENCE, DEMONSTRATION OF

Its purpose is to present the scientific proof for the existence of God, to show that God is not just some idea in the mind (Kant), a product of the will (Feuerbach) or a "useful fiction" (Vaihinger) to which no object in reality corresponds. In contrast to the experience of God which gives us a psychologically unmediated conviction about the existence of God through personal intuition, the demonstration of God's existence distills the logical structure from that experience. By the conscious removal of all purely subjective factors it achieves its logical necessity and universal validity, but thereby it also loses a great deal of its personal persuasiveness. The presuppositions of the demonstration of God's existence are partially philosophical, partially moral in character. Within the framework of *realism, certain presuppositions are made: the existence of the external world, the inner experience of knowledge, the objective validity of *universal concepts, the transcendental quality of the principle of *causality; this amounts to an acceptance of the fundamental theses of the perennial philosophy. Because of these presuppositions which must be explicitly established one by one, because of the complicated argumentation and because of the practical consequences, the evidence or suasiveness of the demonstration can be quite obscure. In any event it does not force the intellect into an assent; conviction about the existence of God cannot be demonstrated "to" someone in such a way that he is forced to assent, for this conviction always remains dependent on a free decision of the whole man (free *Certitude). Therefore, without prejudice to its logical validity, the acceptance of a demonstration of God's existence presupposes a definite outlook: an honest search for the truth and the desire not to allow oneself to be hindered by any prejudices or passions from following the known truth (*Atheism). — Therefore, the practical goal of such a demonstration is not primarily to convert pagans, but to give an intellectually sound foundation and justification for the faith which for many is at first based on authority or a religious experience.

The logical structure of a demonstration of God's existence is in all cases the same. The starting point is never a mere idea; it is always an experiential fact whose contingency or finiteness must be clearly established. The supporting principle that allows us to conclude to God's existence is always the principle of *causality (as efficient, final or exemplary causality). Therefore, from the point of view of the basic structure of the process, there is only one demonstration of God's existence and that is the deduction from the relative to the absolute; within this framework, some consider *contingency to be a better expression of relativity, while others prefer finiteness or the composition of *act and *potency. However, we still have the right to speak of different proofs because of the different starting points which in turn highlight the different attributes of God (*God, Idea of).

Criticism of the demonstration of God's existence is principally directed at its foundations and presuppositions. Thus, the *agnosticism of Kant, which has had considerable influence right up to the present, denies the validity of *universal concepts and of the principle of *causality outside of the realm of sense experience; with this one blow the foundation of any demonstration of God's existence is destroyed (*Transcendence). For most Protestant theology and especially for *dialectical theology with its denial of the *analogy between God and creature every demonstration of God's existence is arrogant because it would make God dependent on our thinking. Henri Bergson and his followers consider the scholastic demonstration of God's existence to be a "dismemberment," a distorsion of flowing existence (*Life Philosophy). Because of a certain anti-intellectualism many thinkers doubt the practical value of such a demonstration and want to see it supplanted by more intuitive ways (Scheler, Hessen, Laros).

MR

GOD'S EXISTENCE, PROOFS FOR

Viewed historically, it was first of all the consideration of the order of nature which, since the very beginnings of Western philosophy, suggested the conclusion that there is a spiritual source of the world (*nous*). The beginnings of this *teleological* argument are already present in the thought of Anaxagoras, then in Plato and in Cicero, the Stoic; the Christian apologetes of the second and third centuries explicitly adduce it as proof of a personal, transcendent God. — Plato's doctrine of ideas contains the basis of a proof for the existence of God from the degrees of perfections: the varying degrees of beauty and goodness in things show that they are beautiful and good "by participation" and presuppose perfect beauty and goodness themselves as their ultimate foundation and exemplar. These ideas had a definite influence on Augustine and Anselm and through them on Thomas Aquinas and scholasticism generally. — In his proof from motion Aristotle begins with the local motion of bodies, especially from the rotations of the heavenly bodies, and argues from them to God as the *first mover* who is himself unmoved because he moves only as the desired end.

In contrast, Thomas Aquinas shows that God can also be considered the efficient cause of motion without destroying his immutability: and most importantly, he raises the proof to the metaphysical level by showing that "motion" is a transition from *potency to *act. Nevertheless, this proof has been sharply criticized by other scholastic philosophers. — Cicero and the Christian apologetes of antiquity found the basic ideas for a proof for the existence of God in the almost universal conviction of various peoples about the existence of God (historical or ethnological proof). — Augustine's proof which he derived from the changelessness of truth, which in turn presupposes a first, subsisting truth, has received a number of different interpretations. This argument probably should not be thought of as an "ideological proof" proceeding from pure values to their necessary existential foundations; rather, the inference goes to God as the Light that enlightens our spirit and to subsisting truth which is the foundation and exemplar of everything (ontologically) true. — Anselm of Canterbury was the first to attempt to prove the existence of God from the idea of God in the mind. This proof, which was named the "ontological proof" in the 18th century, was adopted by Descartes, Scotus and Leibniz; however, it was rejected not only by Kant, but also by Aquinas and most of the scholastics. — The proofs for the existence of God, which Thomas Aquinas proposed in his famous "five ways," in the course of time became classical. With the help of the principle of *causality they all conclude to God as the first cause of the world. — The proofs for the existence of God were further developed by the Christian apologetes at the end of the 18th century in their fight against the atheism of the time. They were the first to speak of metaphysical, physical and moral proofs. They tended to neglect the metaphysical proofs and to prefer the physical and moral ones. Among the latter we find the moral proof in the narrower sense, i.e., the proof derived from moral obligation which presupposes a divine law-giver; here should also be placed the proof from man's desire for happiness, which concludes to God as the highest good and end of man. More recently, other proofs have been thought up, for example, from the necessity of a first temporal beginning of the world which some tried to establish by a priori consideration or with the help of the physical law of entropy, i.e., the increasing transformation of all energy into heat energy. Similarly, the most recent attempts have been in the direction of trying to establish the first beginning of the development of the world from the growing extension of the universe and from the breakdown of radioactive compounds. In contrast to the accumulation of proofs so common about 1900, in the systematic treatment of the proofs at present the chief emphasis is rightly placed on the presuppositions and the soundness of the arguments. From this point of view the "classical" proofs of St. Thomas merit a certain preference. For, they begin from the characteristics of all earthly existents that are known from experience of the external world; then, from these characteristics they show the metaphysical *contingency of the things involved and finally with the help of the principle of *causality conclude to a transcendent God as the first cause of the world. In this way the teleological proof concludes from the special character of the experienced order of nature that there is a true, spirit-produced *finality in things, especially in living beings; but since the directing spirit can be found neither in the individual natural existents nor in the world as a whole (as world-soul), there must be a transcendent orderer. The argument from motion, understood metaphysically, shows that every act, which involves an existential increase in an existent in potency, is dependent on some other existent which already externally possesses this particular perfection; and when the argument is pushed as far as it will go it leads to a pure act as the primordial source of all higher development in this temporal world. The cosmological proof concludes from the generation and corruption of things to their contingency, from the mutability even of the basic particles, which cannot be shown experientially to have had a beginning, to their contingency also; in this way it shows that the world in every respect whatsoever has been caused by a transcendent creator. The most profound but also the most difficult proof is that from the degrees of perfection; this argument shows from the finiteness of all earthly things that the unmixed perfections of existence belong to them only "through participation" and not necessarily; thus it leads to a first cause which, as subsisting existence, is the fullness of all existence.

The remaining proofs for the existence of God deviate more or less from the classical ones. The proof from the temporal beginning of the world (e.g., entropy-argument) do indeed conclude with the help of the principle of causality, but the crux of the argument depends on the proof of those traits which indicate contingency (i.e., the temporal beginning). Moreover, weighty objections have been raised precisely against this proof. Other arguments, while circumventing the idea of efficient causality, attempt to reach God immediately as the model or end of the world. Closely related to these is the argument from the desire for happiness; this argument is based on the principle of *finality and thereby on the intelligibility of all existence; however, there is a question here as to whether or not this way already presupposes the wisdom of the creator. It is common to both the *moral* and the *historical* proofs that they do not trace the real existence of an inner-wordly existent back to God as its cause (efficient, final or exemplary); rather, they proceed from a kind of intentional obligation on our spiritual powers in order to explain them, each in its own way, as receiving some influence from God. According to this view, then, the moral binding of our will can come about only by a divine law and the natural necessity that moves the intellect finds its explanation only in the evidence of the existence of God. With regard to the ideological proof, the point to bring out is that the transition from the mere validity of truth to the eternal existence of a subsisting truth is not unjustified. But it is certain that the ontological argument, which deviates more than any other from the classical arguments because of its a priori approach, contains an illegitimate leap from the order of thought to the order of extramental existence.

JdV

GOOD

Good is that which can perfect an existent and therefore, for it, is worth striving for. A distinction is to be made between the concrete good, i.e., an existent being that is good, and goodness or value which is the intrinsic reason why a thing is good. According to their significant characteristics goods or values are distinguished into those which are purely material, biological (e.g., health), psychic (e.g., pleasure), and spiritual (e.g., intellectual, aesthetic, moral, religious) (*Goods). In modern *value philosophy the holy (*Holiness) is considered to be the highest value. The formal division of intrinsic good and extrinsic or instrumental good (*bonum utile*) should not be confused with the distinction given immediately above. An instrumental good is one that leads to something else, for example, medicine leads to health. An intrinsic good is either a perfection (*bonum honestum, bonum per se*) or a satisfaction (*bonum delectabile,* something pleasant); this latter good is a reaction to something else acquired or achieved, which is naturally connected with the attainment of one's own intrinsic good and therefore is subordinate to it (e. g., joy in knowing the truth, the peace that comes from a good conscience). It follows then that the intrinsic good is not necessarily the same as a moral good; for it can also be a physical good (e. g., physical strength).

More often the intrinsic good (*bonum honestum*) has the more particular meaning of the morally good (*bonum morale*) (*Morality), which is also called "the" good without any qualifications. For, the morally good perfects the human personality completely, in contrast to the purely intellectual or aesthetic values which perfect primarily only certain powers of the person and do not become morally meaningful until they have been properly incorporated into the totality of the person. Moral goodness requires the active cooperation of man; this must be a free activity (*Freedom) by which a man moves himself to objective values and goals. Therefore the truly moral act is the act of the free will, not just in the sense of a desire to act, but also and especially in the sense of personal *love.

Since such acts are essentially related to an object (*Intentional), a distinction must be made between the morally good *act* (*bonum morale subiectivum*) and the morally good *object* (*bonum moral obiectivum*) — a distinction which is not admitted by *value ethics. When one wishes to act, the moral object is the action which is willed (e.g., to speak the truth);

in the case of personal love it is the value of the *person. Since man as a spirit in matter (*Spirit) is ordered, beyond all finite limits, to absolute being and absolute goodness, he can only achieve his full perfection by directing his whole life to this absolute goal. The object, therefore, which ultimately determines the moral quality of actions is absolute goodness. This object, when clearly grasped, is the personal God to whom man turns in love. However, a rather indefinite perception of the absolute value is possible in which its personal character remains more or less hidden. The human person as the image of God participates in the dignity of the absolute good (*Man). Further moral values can be deduced from this fact, for example, justice, truthfulness (*Virtue).

JdV

GOODS

Goods (possessions, perfections, property) are those "things" which are striven for because they offer or promise to a man the support, completion or fulfillment of his whole being. — The presupposition of any striving after things is the judgment that they have supporting, completing or fulfilling characteristics. Things are goods and are striven for because they are good; they are not goods because they happen in fact to be the object of desire. An individual's judgment about the suitability of some object may be erroneous; the goals men set for themselves are often the result of mere caprice; but to conclude from that that things become goods because they are actually the object of desire is not correct. Things are goods because of their perfections; only insofar as they are real can they supply maintenance, completion and fulfillment. Each thing, insofar as it exists, has already by reason of its existence a beginning of goodness or *value. To this extent the existent and the good are objectively the same. However, in the full sense "good" is only that which is perfect with regard to its goal or purpose.

Goods can be distinguished variously. On the distinction between intrinsic good and instrumental good see *good. — Further, goods can be divided into *interior* and *exterior*, depending upon whether they are of essential concern to man or merely affect him exteriorly. The interior goods are those of man's spirit, like knowledge and virtue, and those that affect his body and his life, like bodily strength, etc. Exterior goods include honor, freedom and the whole gamut of material goods. Thus the exterior goods are either economic or non-economic (i.e., free) goods. *Economic goods —* which include possessions and services — are those which can be obtained and managed only by some kind of expenditure.

Ethics and law deal with the various kinds of goods. Ethics points out which goods man should and can strive for and which things he should avoid. The role of law is to protect man in the possession of his property and create the atmosphere in which he can obtain the necessities of life. — Since ethics points out man's way to his final goal, it also establishes a priority of goods. The highest good is God himself; next comes that which makes man like God and binds him to God: holiness and virtue. The interior goods of man's spirit belong in this category: knowledge and strength of will. Then come the exterior goods of honor and freedom; after these belong the interior goods of the body like health and strength. Exterior material goods belong in the last place. — *Body, *Culture, *Economic Theory, *Good, *Happiness, *Value Ethics.

JK

GROUND

Ground (foundation, reason). Just as "ground" in its original meaning signifies something basic that gives permanence to everything that rests on it, so also in its transferred meaning, which is all we are concerned with here, it signifies that through which a thing has permanence or that because of which a thing exists. That which is "established" by the ground insofar as it is necessarily given along with the existence of the ground, is called the *result*. The *Why*-question can have a double meaning: We can ask why or for what reason an objective reality exists; or we can ask whence we know or with what right we can at least surmise that the objective reality exists and that our judgment about it is true. The first question is directed to the real or existential foundation; the second question is directed to the foundation of the knowledge, the logical foundation. If the real foundation resides in an existent distinct from that which is "founded" (e.g., in the activity of another existent) then the other existent is the *cause. The ultimate existential ground that is itself rooted in no other is called the *first foundation (Urgrund). The foundation of knowledge, which gives a knowledge of the truth, must always be accompanied by the *evidence of the reality in question. If a particular foundation of knowledge offers only an indication of some reality so that between it and this reality there is only a possible or probable, but no necessary, connection, then it can indeed support a conjecture or an opinion, but not real knowledge; also, it is usually not sufficient to justify a firm assent. — According to the scholastic view, in *a priori knowledge the existential foundation and the foundation of the knowledge actually coincide, but in *a posteriori knowledge they are different.

JdV

GUILT

Guilt is the free and therefore imputable decision that goes contrary to the moral law and moral value. Because moral obligation has its ultimate foundation in God's will to establish the law, the guilty deed is not the disruption of an impersonal world-order, nor is it merely opposition to some moral value, to the dignity of one's own person and to the just rights of other persons; rather, in addition to this, it is also a *sin*, that is, an offense against the will, order and purpose of God—yes, against God's majesty and goodness itself. Thus, *moral evil takes on the character of a personal affront. This view alone does justice to the seriousness of a developed moral consciousness, to the overwhelming tradition of all peoples, to the testimony of conscience and to the actual position of man in the world where he is preparing himself for his eternal destiny. Great poets and thinkers of all ages have found in man's sense of personal guilt the echo of a profound conviction that sin is the greatest of all *evils; the reason is that because of evil God's holy will and plan have been violated. The religious expiation-rites of most peoples show the same thing. A *sense of guilt*, therefore, is not a degradation of man (Nietzsche), but an expression of the inviolable dignity of one's own person and of a highly developed conscience. Of course, there can also be a pathological sense of guilt based on error. — Since all guilt is an offense against the will of God, there is no such thing as the so-called "philosophical sin" (*peccatum philosophicum*), which a man allegedly commits who is innocently ignorant of God but nevertheless does something morally wrong; thus, it is said, he has not violated the divine will and is not subject to punishment because he does not know anything about the will of God. Whoever does something he knows is morally wrong, Geels in some way, at least obscurely, that he has acted against a higher law and so he becomes responsible for all the consequences of his act. *Collective guilt*, in the sense that the guilt of the responsible leaders of a community, without taking into consideration the personal approval of the members involved, also includes or indicates the guilt of all the members of that community, cannot be reconciled with the nature of guilt as a free and therefore imputable decision. The community as a whole becomes guilty only through the guilt of the individuals and according to the degree of their approval or cooperation with the decisions of the responsible leaders, or through their negligence in doing their duty.

JoS

H

HABIT

Habit (Lat.: *habitus*) is an inclination to act in a certain way; it is formed by the conscious repetition of the same act and once acquired facilitates the performance of subsequent acts. A good habit is called a *virtue and an evil habit is called a vice. The formation of a habit depends upon a pre-given *disposition and acquired habits make the operations of the various powers of the soul easier and more perfect; this state is produced by the interaction between one's surroundings and one's reaction to them with the result that certain associations and complexes are formed. When acquired habits diminish through lack of use (e.g., speaking a foreign language), in virtue of the after-effect of the previously developed habit it can be re-acquired more quickly and with fewer exercises. An acquired habit can be held in check by positing acts contrary to it, even though the original inclination may remain. In order to acquire good habits it is especially important that in the initial stages the precise and proper acts be performed carefully and with determination (e.g., correct enunciation as soon as a child begins to speak) and that the formation of the corresponding complexes occur within the context of intense experience.

The importance of habits for the whole of man's life is hard to exaggerate: it stretches all the way from learning how to walk, to speak, to eat, etc., to various exacting technical skills; it plays an important role in the experience of values, in patterns of thought, in the control of one's passions and, in fact, in the whole field of character formation. Getting used to that which is right must begin in early childhood, since otherwise complexes are acquired through spontaneous self-direction which are directly opposed to later mature education and self-development. Nevertheless, a habit only achieves its full stature when it becomes more than just external training; it must be actively taken over and exercised by the one who is being trained. Moreover, this goal is to be achieved through a complex of motives which enable him to act on his own without external pressures, not just now but also in the future. Thus, habits contribute to what is

166

called "strengthening of the will"; or better, they make it easier for the will to embrace the good within the corresponding total structure of the mind — a structure which is itself built up by habits. For externally imposed habits alone can lose their effectiveness very rapidly.

AW

HAPPINESS

Happiness (*eudaemonia*) in Greek philosophy is the final goal and the highest good of man—a good that gives true meaning to his life. Of course, in the most important matter only the imperfect, earthly realization of the highest good was seen. There were different views with regard to the content of this happiness, whether it consists in pleasure, in material possessions, in virtue or in knowledge; there is the further problem of whether or not it is a gift of the gods or the result of personal effort. In this regard Aristotle made the most important observations in his *Nicomachean Ethics;* according to him, happiness consists in the natural activity of the mind by which it knows the truth. Joy and pleasure are only the echoes of the acquired perfection. Moreover, the moral virtues make up an essential part of this happiness which is understood as something purely earthly. Augustine and Thomas Aquinas applied the concept of eudaemonia to the beatific vision which is known only through Christian *revelation. Pure *eudaemonism*, which proclaims the end of human life to be a kind of satisfaction that is not thought of in teleological terms, is overcome by the idea of the inner perfection of the personality; but this perfection is achieved only through the possession of God in knowledge, love, perfect holiness and joy. More precisely, Christian teaching distinguishes between *natural happiness* which corresponds to the faculties and tendencies of man's spiritual nature, and *supernatural happiness* which in the present order is the only goal of man and consists in the immediate vision of the triune God. This also satisfies the natural desire for happiness which is rooted in man's spirit and enhances the value of his moral striving. On the contrary, moral striving and its unconditioned value are rendered meaningless by the denial of immortality and of eternal happiness; for, these belong essentially to the spiritual personality and to the core of an adequate conception of human life.

JoS

HEDONISM

Hedonism is the theory that *pleasure (sensual or spiritual satisfaction of a drive) determines the ethical value of any action. At the same time this theory presupposes that men act only out of a desire for pleasure. Some of the chief advocates of hedonism are Democritus, Aristippus of Cyrene, Eudoxus, Epicurus and *materialism. According to hedonism all ethical requirements are only cleverly worked out practical norms which, if followed, will greatly diminish the amount of pain in a person's life and enable him to enjoy life to the maximum. — The silent presupposition behind this theory that man acts only from the desire for pleasure is unproved and self-contradictory. Ethical value or the *good is more than a mere sublimation of pleasure. Pleasure and joy are either the stimulus or the echo of true personal self-fulfillment which flow naturally from right action. The most noble and the most difficult duties frequently involve the renunciation of pleasure. Moreover, ethical value and the satisfaction of a desire are often diametrically opposed.

JoS

HISTORICAL CERTITUDE

Historical certitude is *certitude about historical facts of the past. It is based primarily on *witnesses*, i.e., on human statements that are usually preserved in a written form. Alongside of these written "sources" archeological ruins as "factual sources" are also very important; in fact, we are completely dependent on them for the so-called prehistoric times (e.g., ancient cities, graves, pottery, tools, etc.). If historical certitude is to be gained from the sources, then their *authenticity* must be established; i.e., there must be certitude that the written sources were actually written by the authors whose names they carry or at the very least that the (written or) factual sources really belong to the time or period attributed to them. If historical certitude is to be gained from one particular witness, then the credibility of the witness must be established; i.e., it must be proved that he was able to know the reported facts and that he wanted to transmit this information truthfully. The grounds that prove that we really have a witness and that he is credible are sometimes called the reason or motives of credibility. The distinction of these motives from the credibility of the witness himself are important for a correct understanding of the act of *faith. Further, in order to arrive at historical certitude a right interpretation of the statements and remains of the past is necessary, for it is through interpretation that their true meaning is mediated.

JdV

HISTORICAL MATERIALISM

Historical materialism or also *materialistic views of history*. In the midst of real concern for the socially oppressed and exploited laborers of the 19th century Karl Marx saw the total communization of all means of production as the only solution to the problem, since only in this way could the "alienation" be done away with. Following Hegel and Feuerbach he thought of this as the whole historical, social situation in which the products of man's material and psychic activity — especially material goods, the state, God — were actually working against him just like hostile powers. In his economics (*Marxism) he tried to establish an "absolutely necessary" transition from an economic order of private capital to a communistic order. Therefore he explains *history as a material process according to "bronze" laws (*Das Kapital*, Preface). But since economic activity is human activity, the question was soon posed about the role of *free will and so of the human *spirit in this apparently wholly necessary process. Historical materialism attempts to overcome this contradiction by following Hegel in identifying *free will* with a "knowledge of necessity" — which is actually a denial of free will. The objects of historical materialism are "the most universal laws of movement and development of human society" or the primacy of social existence over social consciousness. The foundations of all social development are said to be production, exchange and consumption or, in short, *social existence;* this then produces *social consciousness* (all social ideas and theories). The elements of social existence are *productive powers* (men and machines) and the *conditions of production*, the latter of which are also called the economic *basis* (the mutual relations of men in the process of production), while the superstructure built upon this basis (political, juridical, scientific, philosophical, artistic and religious ideas along with the institutions that correspond to them) belongs to the *social consciousness*. Ideas, which are said to be only a "reflection" of production, are not given any history-making power and are thought of only as a "reaction." This reaction is partly progressive, partly non-progressive. *Religion, the "opium of the people," is the embodiment of reaction; its purpose is to feed the masses with the hope of a future life and so to discourage them from revolutionary agitation for a better (i.e., communist) world in this life.

Through a change of the productive powers that is at first quantitative and then also qualitative a conflict arises with the unchanged conditions of production. This conflict is expressed in societies which permit the private possession of the means of production in *class warfare* and by means of *revolution* it leads to a re-structuring of society. In this way an allegedly primitive communistic society is supposed to have changed into ancient slavery, then into feudalism, capitalism and finally *socialism (USSR); in this socialist state, which apparently resembles the primitive society except that it is on a much higher technical and cultural level, all the means of production are owned in common and consequently all exploitation of man by man is eliminated. The future stage of socialism is called *communism*: this is an earthly paradise in which each person works freely and enthusiastically according to his ability for the collective; then he will not be paid, as happens in socialism, according to what he does, but he will receive everything he needs. Class warfare is already stilled in socialism, since the social form of modern production already agrees with the social form of property and consequently there are no more antagonistic contradictions. Now the dialectic inherent in all existence no longer manifests itself in social revolution, but in criticism and self-criticism, industrial competition, etc. A more profound philosophical justification of historical materialism is supposed to be offered by "dialectical materialism."

The humanistic goal of the founders and best representatives of *Marxism, for whom the state was only a means to the end, was for the most part lost sight of by Lenin and his followers in their desire for political power. To this desire the freedom, happiness and dignity of whole peoples and generations were sacrificed. The theoretical foundation is materialism (*Dialectical Materialism). A true *ethics is necessarily lost here, for it is wholly subordinated to the good of the state. The individual person has value only insofar as he is useful to the state (*Collectivism). — However, not everything in *history is simply material, since spiritual consciousness is necessary even for economic life, especially if economics does not constitute the most decisive factor in social living. One must attribute more than simple "reaction" to human ideas. The communistic view of history and society has not been able to base itself on fact; moreover, most of Marx's predictions have not come true and those that have had different causes. Marx wrote in his eleventh thesis on Feuerbach: "Philosophers have merely interpreted the world in different ways; but the important thing is to change it" (Werke 3, 535). The concern of historical materialism, as of every *ideology, is not primarily to explain the world but to change it. Its recent success is to be attributed not only to élan and to the unscrupulous use of power on the part of its leaders, but especially to the resonance and hope of the exploited, impoverished masses; these people have sought and still seek liberation and social betterment in the half-truths of the communist gospel.

HF

HISTORICISM

A real understanding for *history — one that learned how to measure the past according to its own proper norms — did not come on the scene until late in the history of man's spirit. It developed out of the opposition to the rationalism of the 18th century; then it was strengthened by similar endeavors in the natural sciences (evolution) and for the first time given a philosophical foundation by the speculative work of Hegel. He gives every historical form its necessary place in the evolutionary process of the absolute idea and therefore also a supra-temporal value, but at the same time he robs the historical event of its own proper character because he removes its freedom and unpredictability (*speculative historicism*). In direct contrast to this view, Wilhelm Dilthey emphasizes precisely this peculiar characteristic of the historical event, but in his pan-historical consideration he does away with all supra-temporal norms and values. Thus he arrives at a *relativistic historicism* which permits only an immanent criticism of the past. One consequence of historicism is that the science of history is also relativized; thus even history is wholly conditioned by time and culture, not just with regard to the choice and presentation of events but also with regard to their very validity. Consequently historicism ends up in some form of *life philosophy or *pragmatism which consider knowledge as a means to be used by the will for life.

WB

HISTORICITY

Historicity should first be distinguished from *history. History in the proper sense is an event insofar as it is determined by historicity; therefore historicity means the foundation that makes an event into history and so constitutes history as such. But since history in the full sense of the word belongs only to the human dimension, *man also appears as the only carrier of historicity; he is *the* historical existent. With this we are saying that man not only is ontically, but that he exists ontologically, for, by reason of his historicity he manifests himself as the existent (*on*) who is always open to the ground (*logos*) of the existent and therefore is able to realize (*vollziehen*) it as such. The ground of the existent is *existence — that to which man arrives by means of a perfect return to himself (*reditio completa*); in this return he brings the world, into which he has first gone out, back to his innermost self; and there he encounters its relationship to existence and thereby also existence itself. This briefly sketched return to existence actually constitutes the transcendental condition of the possibility of historicity, for only on this basis can the historical be distinguished from the *unhistorical*. Thus, while the unhistorical is unconsciously overpowered by the event, the historical is characterized by conscious planning and by a free structuring of the event. But conscious planning presupposes the comprehension of the existent out of its existence as the true; and free structuring includes the choice of the existent out of its existence as the good. That in this limits are imposed on man is something that belongs essentially to his historicity; thus in this inseparable interaction he always remains an actively determining subject and a passively receptive object of the event. The great historical moment and the great historical personality reveal themselves in a remarkable way as subject; they are often the source of a unique idea which shapes events for a long time. Moreover, the historical as the unique also is clearly distinguished from the sameness of the unhistorical.

Historicity permeates everything that man is and does; his search for truth, his moral striving and his development of culture. Thus he often falls a prey to relativity; however, this is not of the essence of historicity—something which should be stressed in response to a number of views on the subject. In particular, historicity does not exclude the essence of man which remains in the midst of all change; rather, the permanent core of the person — that which is described by perfect return — must remain, because historicity itself disappears without the foundation that makes it possible. Moreover, essence is of such a kind that it is not opposed to historical change, but actually gives it its foundation. Insofar as change brings out different permanent characteristics of man, one can speak of many historical forms in which the one basic essence expresses itself. Concerning truth and moral values, it is clear that they apply in their essential content to all historical times and places. Yet man's grasp of truth grows in the course of history; even ancient truths come to be understood more fully and viewed in a newer light. Moreover, the moral value is again and again concretized differently according to changing historical situations; in this process the legitimate variations agree with the basic essence while the illegitimate ones contradict it.

Historicity directs man to the *community because history develops only through the cooperation of many individuals together and of many successive generations. Only in this process do the powers that lie hidden in man's nature make their appearance. Therefore, every individual, every people, every epoch present just one part of the fullness of human existence; at the same time, however, by reason of his perfect reflection the individual always has the totality of his essence and existence in view. As a result of this, the individual person both stands as a member in the service of the historical process and at the same time surpasses it as he strives for his own unique goal. Since the individual, who is so characterized in his historicity, is essentially a *person, historicity is necessarily both borne and transcended by the person. Moreover, since the existence in which the person with his historicity is rooted ultimately means eternity, the person already participates in a most intimate way in that eternity into which his historical existence will enter through the portal of death.

After Wilhelm Dilthey and the neo-Kantians of the Baden School had distinguished the *human sciences from the natural sciences and so had brought out the special nature of historicity, philosophy, which was questioning man as existence (*Existential Philosophy), turned to the problems of historicity; the important men to mention here are Martin Heidegger and Karl Jaspers.

JBL

HISTORY

History in the widest sense (1) is every event (happening). Thus we speak of a history of the earth or of natural history. History in the proper sense (2) must be distinguished from every event of nature that is explicable on the basis of its efficient causes and so is only one instance of a law; for, in this sense history is a human event which has its roots in the free self-realization and decision of the spirit. It fulfills itself in space and time, in the contacts and successions of races and peoples, in the manifold limitations of sub-personal nature both inside of man and outside of him. These limitations of human activity are not just accidental to man — they flow out of his very *nature. Thus, history (2) reveals itself as the specifically human mode of operation (history as the place and direction of human life). It belongs to man's nature that he stand in history and that he make history; everything that man does he does as a historical being. Even the immediacy of the human spirit to God is *transcendence, which never completely leaves behind itself the world and history. Therefore man can only fulfill his transcendent task by actively taking up his task in history (history as man's time of testing).

For an event to be historical it must be related to men, and not just to individuals as such but to the human family. For, the individual is not immediately a member of humanity but only as the member of a tribe, a race or a people. In actual fact an historical event always takes its rise from individual persons, but it is still essentially related to the community. One cannot speak of *historical necessity* in a way that would destroy the free, responsible decision, but only in the sense of a limitation of freedom and its possibilities by the sub-personal part of man's nature, by the limits of man's perspective, by historically produced hard facts with their inner logic and their given direction. Only that event is historically fruitful that is nourished on the maternal powers of the past (*tradition*) and does justice to those impulses that are pointing towards the future. And ethical failures carry their own punishment right in themselves, maybe not immediately but certainly in the long run. — For philosophical anthropology history is important both in its general nature (as the dynamic development of human nature and so as the way to understand that nature) and in its concrete form, since the essence of history makes its appearance only in the concrete.

Further, the investigation of history (2) (= the science of history) and its execution (e. g., the history of the civil war) is also called history (3). According to the mode of presentation a distinction is made between narrative, interpretative and genetic or developing history.

WB

HISTORY OF PHILOSOPHY

Philosophy, just like every science, has its own *history in the double meaning of the word: as a temporal succession of events and as their scientific presentation. The principal object of the history of philosophy (as a science) is not external events, but the results of thinking reason, the philosophical ideas as well as their content and their subsequent influence. (*Myths and the *mysteries of Christian *revelation do not belong in *philosophy and therefore also not to the history of philosophy). But the results of thinking reason externalize themselves in a multiplicity of finite subjects; concretely, they are human thoughts with all of the conditionality and contingency of the course of history that is characteristic of everything human. The question is whether and to what extent these also are a part of the object of a history of philosophy. A treatment of philosophy from the point of view of the history of civilization will consider philosophical ideas with all of their implications as aspects of other cultural areas. However, as expressions of a human person, philosophical ideas have a synthetic point of unity because of which they stand out from the flow of all other events and from which they receive a very personal, unique coloring. This offers the basis for a biographical treatment of the history of philosophy. Connected with this is the method which traces the history and common traits of peoples and races.

Nevertheless, the goal of a true history of philosophy will always be the treatment of problems and ideas in their origin and development. This in turn presupposes a faithful and accurate evaluation of the philosophical past, without at the same time taking everything indiscriminately into consideration, which would be impossible. Textbook philosophy and the simple application of inherited principles to new areas are of minor concern to this science. Its real object is the principles themselves and their continuing development, and the ideas of the philosophers, not insofar as these ideas arose as the result of certain accidental "influences," but insofar as they were even thought in the first place; therefore, it is interested in the dynamism that resides in these ideas as such. The norm of what belongs to a history of philosophy in this sense is not the abstract relationship of formal truth or falsity, but the contribution that a philosophy makes in any area beyond the already-achieved position to a further grasp of existence or to reason's understanding of itself. This manner of dealing with the history of philosophy stretches beyond the "scandal" of the philosophers who contradict one another, and it also avoids the temptation to skepticism which is never very far removed from the consideration based merely on the history of civilization.

Philosophy and its history find themselves in a state of mutual relationship. Philosophy as a product of the human spirit comes into being only in the form of *history. Therefore it cannot "abstract" from its own history if it desires to be a creative philosophy that knows itself and what it is striving for. However, a genuine history of philosophy (at least according to the method of the history of ideas) is only possible for someone who has a profound and all-inclusive systematic philosophy.

WB

HISTORY, PHILOSOPHY OF

From the science of history, which strives to lift the historical event out of its sources and to clarify it for others, is to be distinguished the philosophy of history (or metahistory) which attempts to subject *history itself as well as the science of history to a thorough investigation and to understand it from the ultimate principles of existence and of knowledge. The philosophy of history embraces as major disciplines the *logic of history* and the *metaphysics of history*. The former investigates the foundations, presuppositions and methods of the science of history (*Historical Certitude); the latter searches for the essence, causes (*History) and meaning of history. It is valuable both to grasp history in its essential relationship to man and to fit it into its proper place in the basic structures of existence. Hence it is evident that philosophical *anthropology and *metaphysics are of decisive importance for the philosophy of history. Moreover, the *theology of history* actually builds upon the philosophy of history, because Christian *revelation enables one to recognize world history as salvation history. Therefore, if the philosophy of history still has the task of understanding history from the grasp of existence and from an understanding of man's essence, then it must allow itself to be complemented by the theology of history so that it can achieve a new, more profound insight into human history that it cannot of itself produce.

The *meaning of history* can be gathered from the parade of fact only with regard to definite, relatively closed periods. For the totality of world history one can say only in general that the meaning of history is no other than that of the world event and of the *world as such: the announcement and representation of the infinite existential fullness of God in a finite, human way. Every time and every man in it has his own contribution to make to this announcement. It includes both the full realization in time of all human potentialities (the immanent meaning of history) and the attainment of the eternal goal set for man (the transcendent meaning of history). But what this goal concretely consists in depends entirely on the free determination of God.

A concern about the philosophy of history is noticeable even in the beginnings of philosophy (e. g., cultural myths). The statements of the Greek philosophers point in different directions (theories of decline, progress, permanence, eternal return). Although the concept of history in the Old Testament has a theological orientation, nevertheless through its emphasis on the unity of the human race and through its view of history as a unique process with a meaningful conclusion it greatly influenced the shaping of the philosophy of history. The same can be said for Augustine's *City of God* which, though primarily a theology of history, still contains many ideas pertaining to the philosophy of history. After him philosophical and theological ideas about the nature of history were also combined by men like Otto von Freising, Dante, Mousset, Schlegel and Görres. As a separate discipline the philosophy of history has existed since the Enlightenment when man began to occupy the central place in philosophical thought. The phrase "the philosophy of history" comes from Voltaire; the founder of German philosophy of history was Herder. The idealistic version of the philosophy of history thought of history as the realization of a divine idea, while the naturalistic version thought of it as the necessary result of natural laws. The former view appeared in theistic and pantheistic forms. According to Hegel, who, in spite of a number of distortions, contributed profound insights to the philosophy of history, history is the evolution of objective spirit (*Spiritual Existence, *German Idealism). The *positivism of Comte and *historical materialism belong to the naturalistic tendency. Nietzsche's position on the eternal return is a combination of the idealistic and naturalistic viewpoints.

WB

HOLINESS

In modern value philosophy and philosophy of religion "the holy" is considered as the supreme *value, specifically different from all other values, which is proper to the divine; *religion is directed to the holy. According to Rudolf Otto "the Holy" is above all the "numinous" and as such something *irrational which can be described only as the result of its influence on the feelings as *mysterium tremendum* and at the same time *fascinosum*; by this he means that it is a mysterious, tremendous power before which the creature cringes and trembles and which at the same time charms and delights the creature. On the other hand, some theologians seem to consider holiness as the apex of moral goodness, clearly grasped in conceptual terms. — Both views are onesided. In the first place, true holiness is the infinite fullness of the divine being, of the divine goodness, power and majesty which we are able to grasp in some degree in analogous concepts (in opposition to the irrationalistic view), but which still always remain an ineffable mystery and before which we tremble in awe. Secondly, holiness signifies the "moral" holiness of God, i. e., the holiness of his will which essentially consists in his love; with his holy will he necessarily embraces his own infinite goodness which is the archetype of all created perfection. The holiness of God, even when it is understood in this way, always remains an unfathomable mystery for us; before it man trembles with the perception of his own sinfulness (Isaiah 6, 5) but nevertheless feels himself irresistibly attracted by its radiant purity. — On the basis of a special relationship to God holiness is attributed to some creatures: Thus persons and things are holy (*sacer*) insofar as they are totally dedicated to the service of God; persons are holy (*sanctus*) insofar as they are united to God and like him by reason of their morally perfect lives.

JdV

HORIZON

Horizon in a philosophical sense is a term that occurs in Husserl's phenomenology, in certain existential writings and in the metaphysics of Karl Rahner and Emerich Coreth. When used in reference to human knowing, the word "horizon" is employed in a way that is analogous to its use in the field of vision. Thus, a horizon is a background against which other things are seen; and, unless reflection is directed to the horizon itself, it is normally adverted to only implicitly or unthematically. In the realm of knowledge a horizon can be either limited or unlimited.

Now a metaphysical analysis of human acts of knowing or inquiring shows that every real or possible object of knowledge, that every act of knowing itself is something that exists, is something that "is." Man cannot know nothing since "nothing" is merely a denial of being. Thus, a transcendental reflection on human knowing reveals that something must exist (either actually or potentially — we are not speaking here of mental constructs or projections) or else it cannot be known. Therefore the aspect under which (formal object) we know anything is being. This, in turn, implies a certain openness to being or pre-knowledge of being in the knower that precedes (not temporally but metaphysically) every particular act of knowledge. This means that the human mind itself provides a background or horizon of being that precedes and accompanies all knowledge or inquiry about particular beings. Moreover, such a horizon of being is not just accidental to the human act of knowing, willing and inquiring; it is in fact the condition of the possibility of knowing particular beings and of every human act.

So an analysis of human knowing and inquiring reveals that it presupposes as a condition of its possibility a pre-knowledge of being which can be called a "horizon of being" that is the background of all knowing and willing. — See also *Question, Thematic, Transcendental Method.*

KB

HUMAN SCIENCES

Human sciences (*Geistewissenschaften*). Since the time of Wilhelm Dilthey (1833-1911) the studies that concern man have been set over against the *physical sciences; both groups together constitute the total area of scientific investigation. As the names themselves suggest, these studies are distinguished according to the areas they research and also according to the methods which are, to a great degree, determined by the material itself.

Physical science is not concerned with the particular individual but with the universal, i. e., with propositions and laws that apply in the same way to many individual things or events. Its procedure is rooted in the conviction that the particular natural thing does not possess any significant individual traits, but simply presents its species in a constant repetition of the same thing. Since it lacks uniqueness and is indefinitely repeatable, it is an object of research only as the carrier of its species (not as *this* individual). Because the individuals very closely resemble each other their succession does not really constitute a historical becoming, but merely a historical, undifferentiated multiplication in the proximity of space and the sequence of time. Behind this lies the natural necessity that fixes everything clearly and unalterably according to the principle: similar causes always have similar effects; physical science, accordingly, aims at the causal *explanation.

In contrast, the human studies can be sketched in their basic outlines. They are concerned with the different aspects of the spiritual life of man and their objectifications; therefore they appear as literature, art, philosophy and religion. These studies are also called *cultural sciences* because man with his mental-creative powers necessarily develops the naturally given; human activity is already in itself "culture" and it produces cultural goods. However, this means that the limits of pure nature are surpassed so that man comes to a real historical event; thus intellectual life or culture develops necessarily in a historical way. Human studies, then, develop within the context of history; it is possible to say that they are concerned about the understanding of history and the results of history. Yet in history it is not a question of the nature of war or leadership in general, but of this particular World War II and General Eisenhower. Therefore, attention is directed to this concrete individual in its unique, unrepeatable particularity. This is where we find the principle of choice according to which only those men, groups, events and structures are adduced that really offer something new and unique, that represent an essential contribution to the development of the whole human race and so have a profound influence on history. Such a choice is possible because here, in spite of human nature which is common to all, the individuals do not completely resemble each other. For, by reason of the creative power and freedom of the spirit the individuals are always capable of coming up with new forms and structures. Since no specific causes of this process can be established, the causal explanation of the physical sciences is not sufficient here and so the power of *understanding appears as the only adequate method.

The distinction between human studies and the physical sciences offers weighty testimony for the special nature of spirit as over against everything else in the world of nature. However, the orientation towards the concrete individual led to a certain relativism in the position of Dilthey and those influenced by him.

JBL

HYLEMORPHISM

Hylemorphism is the theory, first worked out by Aristotle and then later refined by the scholastic philosophers, about the combination of all material beings (which constitute a natural whole) out of matter (*Matter: hylē) and *form as the two essential principles that are combined in order to produce a natural unity. We usually think of the elements, real compounds, plants, animals and men as unified bodies composed in this fashion. Theories opposed to hylemorphism are, on the one hand, *atomism and scientific *dynamism which hold for only one essential principle in bodies and, on the other hand, a one-sided *dualism which, in living things or at least in man, holds that there are two wholly independent existents that are bound together only by some kind of accidental mutual causality. Hylemorphism is also called *peripatetic philosophy* and Aristotle's followers "peripatetics"; the name comes from the peripatos or corridor where Aristotle taught as he walked to and fro. The postulation of this oneness-from-two occurred to Aristotle as a solution to the cosmological problem of change in the material world. Ordinary, daily observation shows that in nature there are changes and transformations that at least apparently result in something completely different. Aristotle interprets such occurrences (usually too hastily), like the change of water into steam, as *substantial* change or becoming; i.e., it is not just a question of a change in position or motion, but new, essentially different material substances result (e. g., "air" is produced from water). Therefore Aristotle uses the expression "generation" for these new results, even in the inorganic world; thus it means the origin of a new substance from the previous one. Conversely, the passing away of the substance that is changed into another is called *corruption* (*phthora*).

However, if substantial change is to be a real change and not annihilation or a new creation, then there must be a permanent substratum common to both the corrupting and the originating body: this is formable *prime matter. On the other hand, if the substance itself is to be different in both bodies, then there must be a changing, substantial principle in them as the source of the specific difference: this is the *substantial* form. But since, according to the view of Aristotle, all bodies are mutually interchangeable, there must ultimately be a *prime matter or a "first matter" common to all bodies as the basic substratum of all substantial becoming. The origin of a new form is explained by the activity of an external efficient cause that produces the form out of the matter (*eductio formae e materia*); obviously that does not mean that the form was already contained actually in the matter, but only that the matter has now been made into that which it could become or that for which it was in *potency.

In the scholasticism of the Middle Ages logical and metaphysical considerations gradually became more important than cosmological ones. Substantial becoming is distinguished from essential change (*transsubstantiation*) in accordance with the Catholic teaching about the change of bread and wine into the body and blood of Christ at Mass; while in a normal substantial change one essential principle (namely, prime matter) perdures as the carrier of the changing forms, in an essential change the whole substance — matter and form — is changed, and only the sensibly perceptible accidents remain. — The attempt is also made to establish the essential composition of all bodies, in addition to the evidence from change, on the opposition between unity and multiplicity in continually extended substances; further, on the basis of the limitation of essentially spiritual existence to unspiritual, unconscious existence; finally, on the multiplication of individuals in the same species, which seems to be only possible by means of a *subject (namely, matter: *Individual, The) that is both different from the species-conferring form and indefinitely repeatable. In the mind of Bonaventure and others this last idea leads to an extension of hylemorphism to all created existents, even to the created pure spirits which, in an analogous way, are thought to be composed of a spiritual "matter" and an essential form.

There is a dispute about the more precise nature of the essential constitution of things, especially of living beings. The Thomistic school holds that a strictly unified natural being (*unum per se*) demands the *unicity of the essential form*, i.e., composition out of a wholly undetermined prime matter (which is pure potency) and the soul as the only essential form; all bodily powers, therefore, are the result of the activity of the soul. If one were to postulate a composition out of the soul and a real body existing independently of that soul, then the whole would only be an arrangement of two or more independent substances (*unum per accidens*). The main objection against this latter view is the difficulty it finds itself in in explaining, for example in the death of a living body, the origin of apparently new essential forms; in the medieval view of the world the imagination of a mysterious influence from the heavenly bodies (a control of generation and corruption "by the moon") tended to obscure the importance of this difficulty. Nevertheless, outside of the Thomist School the usual view has been that a living thing is composed of a soul and a real body existing by itself; therefore it has thought of the body as composed of prime matter and one or more essential forms, i. e., one assumed a *multiplicity of essential forms* at least in living things (and often also in compounds).

When passing judgment on hylemorphism one must distinguish between the physical composition of living beings which can certainly be proved from vital processes (*Vitalism) and from the cooperation of body and soul in sense perception (*Body-Soul Relation), and a corresponding physical composition of inorganic bodies whose proof depends upon the occurrence of substantial changes in the inorganic world; such changes are at least suggested by the results of modern physics as, for example, the production of a pair of electrons from a quantum of light (a negatively charged electron and a positively charged "positron"). In addition to this physical composition, the possibility of a more profound "metaphysical" composition of bodies — one based on the speculative considerations mentioned above — should be given some thought; the latter avenues of thought are independent of the constant changes in the scientific view of the universe.

JdV

HYPOTHESIS

Hypothesis is the term given in the natural sciences to an assumption or presupposition which is made in order to explain certain observed facts; at this stage the observed reality is not open to direct verification. Thus, in order to explain the chemical laws of combining, the assumption was made that bodies are composed of minute particles called "atoms." An hypothesis has *heuristic value* if it also leads to the discovery of previously unknown facts and laws. If the hypothesis leads to no explanations that are free of contradictions and so is certainly false, it can still be used temporarily as a *working hypothesis* in the hope that it might lead to some true discovery. As long as we are dealing with an hypothesis, then we have only a greater or lesser degree of *probability but no *certitude, since the same set of facts is open to more than one explanation. By means of *verification*, i. e., through direct and indirect confirmation, the present probability can grow and finally lead to certitude after the other explanations have been excluded; in this way the hypothesis becomes a *theory. Thus the atom-hypothesis became the atom-theory through many different and mutually independent confirmations, so that the existence of atoms is no longer a conjecture but a fact. — The opposition of positivistic thinkers against the building of hypotheses is only a logical consequence of their view of natural sciences; for, according to them, the task of science is simply to describe the results of observation and not to explain them.

NJ

HYPOTHETICAL JUDGMENTS

While in the *categorical judgment* something is affirmed directly of an object, the hypothetical judgment in the broad sense is an affirmation of the necessary connection between several statements. In this case the member-statements themselves are not affirmed, but only the nature and validity of their connection. Thus, a hypothetical judgment can be true even if the member-statements are not true or are even impossible. The most important connection between statements — the one from which the whole class usually gets its name — is the *conditional proposition*. This is a connection between statements according to which, if A (the antecedent) is true, then B (the consequent), is also necessarily true. — *Material implication* is not identical with the hypothetical judgment. It is defined in *symbolic logic as the connection between two propositions, p and q, which is false only when p is true and q is false; it is then said that "p *implicates* q." But this implication is not a valid hypothetical judgment, because it does not affirm a necessary sequence of q from p. And therefore the use of the "if — then" for material implication is at least ambiguous. — Other hypothetical judgments in the broad sense are: the *conjunction*, according to which it is impossible for all of the member statements together to be true, and the *disjunction.

WB

HYPOTHETICAL SYLLOGISMS

Hypothetical syllogisms are those in which the premises contain at least one *hypothetical judgment (in the broad sense). In a *conditional syllogism* one can conclude from several conditional propositions to another proposition in the form: If A, then B; if B, then C; therefore if A, then C. — However, with the help of a categorical proposition one can conclude from a conditional proposition to another categorical proposition. Thus, there are two possible forms: the inference from the condition to the conditioned (= *modus ponens*: If A is, B also is; but B is not; therefore A also is not). The following is to be observed: If A or B are used in the major premise as negatives, then the negative must also be retained in the conclusion. In the case of the *modus tollens*, a double negative in the conclusion results in an affirmation (e. g.: If not-A, then B; but B is not; therefore not-A is not = therefore A is). — The inference from the truth of the conditioned to the truth of the condition is inadmissible as is also the inference from the falsity of the condition to the falsity of the conditioned. The inference from the conditioned to its necessary condition is an inference by the *modus tollens* (e. g.: If not-A, then not-B; B is = not not-B; therefore A is = not not-A). — In the *disjunctive syllogism* the major premise consists of a *disjunction. If it is complete, then by denying one member (or all except one) one can conclude to the affirmation of the other and by affirming one member (or all except one, one can conclude to the denial of the other. (Either A or B; A is not, therefore B; or: A is; therefore B is not). However, if the disjunction is not complete, then merely by denying one (or all except one) one concludes to the affirmation of the other member. Even here in the case of denied members, in some cirumstances, one must allow for a double negation in the conclusion. — In a *conjunctive syllogism* the major premise consists of a conjunctive judgment (in the form: A and B cannot both be true). The falsity of one member is deduced from the truth of the other. However, from the falsity of one member nothing follows for the other, since both together can be false, but they need not be. — The *dilemma* is related to conditional and disjunctive syllogisms. Its major premise consists of a conditional proposition whose apodasis is a complete disjunctive judgment (If the disjunction is composed of more than two members, then the conclusion is called a *polylemma*); the minor premise denies all the members of the disjunctive judgment; then it follows that the protasis of the conditional proposition must also be denied (If A, then either B or C; but neither B nor C; therefore also not A).

WB

I

IDEA

Idea (Gr.: *idein* = to see) means first of all the easily perceptible appearance of a thing according to its characteristic traits, and then especially the inner nature or essence which is revealed through these traits. While the *concept follows the existence of things and copies their essences, the idea precedes the existence of things as their eternally perfect *exemplar* after which they are fashioned. So the idea is essentially in the order of an exemplary cause (*causa exemplaris*). Once grasped by the intellect the idea becomes the *norm* (*rule, canon*) by which the intellect judges contingent things or by which it is led in the realization of the idea (*Ideal).

Plato looks upon the ideas as non-sensible, other-wordly realities which make up a separate world under the primacy of the highest idea of the Good. *Augustine* (following Plotinus) looks upon them as the creative, primordial thoughts of God. God himself is the absolute idea or the idea of all ideas, insofar as his infinite fullness includes all essences most perfectly (i. e., according to their positive content with the exclusion of all negative limitations). *Thomas Aquinas* fits this doctrine into his Aristotelianism. This same understanding is adopted by *Hegel* when he names his first principle the "absolute idea"; still, in his system everything ends in pantheism because the absolute idea is not perfect in itself, but only becomes perfect through the development of the finite.

Since earthly things are patterned after the ideas, the ideas must be in things in some way. Plato and Augustine did not find any satisfactory formulation for this. It was Thomas Aquinas who first saw the possibility of a solution in the Aristotelian doctrine of the inner essential forms of things (*Form). Thus he sees the essential forms as a participation in the divine ideas and as their copies; each thing is stamped with a divine thought which determines it from the very beginning to be what it is.

Our concepts are able to grasp the ideas. Plato tried to explain this through a vision of the ideas (*Intuitionism) and Augustine tried to explain it

184

through the illumination of a light proceeding from the divine ideas (*Illumination). Thomas Aquinas, by applying Aristotle's principles, was the first to speak of the *abstraction of ideas from things. Insofar as our concepts reflect the ideas they can themselves be called ideas in a very true sense. It is only since *conceptualism separated the connection between concept and idea — a relationship mediated by essential knowledge — that every concept and even (in empiricism) sense impressions have been called "ideas." — Insofar as it gives a true view of the existent every concept can be called an "idea" provided that in addition to this superficial sense the deeper meaning behind it is not forgotten or excluded. — In a very special sense human thoughts are called "ideas" when they represent creative archetypes (artistic ideas) or are the stimulus to much thought.

Kant's transcendental ideas (World, Soul, God) are colored by conceptualism because they are only the thoughts of men and so do not have any objective validity. However, there is still something deeply metaphysical about them because they are sketched out by us as the ultimate totalities which absolutely direct our striving for knowledge.

JBL

IDEAL

Ideal is the term we apply to the perfect realization of an *idea. Therefore, the ideal is attained if an idea is developed according to all of its possibilities (at least to some degree). It is imagined as either existing in a definite being or as a distant goal not yet realized . In the first sense the Platonic idea is simultaneously the ideal; for, it exists as a supra-sensible reality which expresses completely in itself all the possibilities of the idea in question. The most sublime idea of the good appears as the ideal of all ideals, insofar as it embraces all other ideas as their source. This notion reappears explicitly in our image of God: God is the absolute ideal, because he unites in himself all (pure) perfections most perfectly or according to all their possibilities. From this point we can understand that God appears in Kant's philosophy as the "transcendental ideal." Just like the Platonic idea, so also is God the primordial exemplar according to which everything earthly and finite is formed because everything participated in him (*exemplarism*). It is out of this connection that we should understand the ideals of our moral life as well as those of education. But they do not attain their full efficacy until they meet us in a concrete model, namely in a man who perfectly realizes them, just as Christ shines before us as the absolute ideal of holiness. — The adjective "ideal" can be related to the noun, ideal, which has just been explained, and then it means: in conformity with the ideal; or it can be related to *idea and then it means:

to exist according to the mode of (or only in) the idea; often it simply signifies the opposite of "real" and then means: unreal, merely imagined. See also *Reality*.

JBL

IDEALISM

Idealism etymologically is that point of view which, in the total realm of being, gives the first place to *ideas, to the *ideal and so to *spirit: Being is ultimately determined by ideas, by spirit. In this sense idealism is not opposed to genuine *realism, but only to *materialism. The first existence is the purely spiritual existence of God in which existence and spiritual knowing are completely one and according to whose ideas every non-divine being is formed; therefore every existent from its very origin is penetrated by spirit and so "true" and knowable (*Truth). This valid type of idealism actually belongs to the inalienable heritage of scholastic philosophy.

But idealism comes immediately into a sharp opposition to the realism of scholasticism when spirit or thought, on which all objective being depends, in one way or another is identified with human thinking. In this vein an epistemological idealism is proposed which gives a completely new meaning not only to the essence of human knowing but also to existence as such. According to this theory human knowledge is not an act of being conformed to an existent which is a pre-given object, but a production of the object; but since thinking itself cannot posit things in themselves, being, which is the object of knowing, appears as a mere content of thought, as a purely ideal position. Thus if a reality which is independent of thinking is accepted in certain, not completely logical forms of idealism, then this is taken as irrational either completely or at least with regard to us.

The question which receives a different answer from the different forms of idealism is the question about the nature of "thinking," or "consciousness," or the "subject" which posits all objectivity. According to *empirical (psychological) Idealism* the consciousness of the individual as such establishes the object; thus existence is nothing but the consciousness-content of the individual (*esse est percipi*). This view leads logically to *solipsism, i. e., to the position that only the personal self (*solus ipse*) is knowable. Berkeley tries to escape this conclusion by limiting the thesis of empirical idealism to the material world; he denies absolutely that it has any existence independent of thought (*acosmic idealism*). However, most idealists do not recognize empirical idealism as genuine idealism because it leads to complete subjectivism and relativism and also cannot explain the universal validity of science which is independent of the contingent experiences of individual men. Therefore Kant assumes that it is not the individual contingent subject, but a "*transcendental subject" that determines the object whose universal, a priori forms of intuition and thought, as opposed to the changeableness of sensation, are the absolutely valid law for all thinking subjects like man (*transcendental* or *critical* idealism; *Critical Philosophy). The transcendental subject, whose characteristics Kant never clearly defined, was given different interpretations by Kant's successors. If it is thought of as the spiritual nature of man, as for example J. F. Fries did, then it develops into a kind of *psychologism and leads to the disappearance of the unconditioned validity of knowledge. If, however, that validity together with the starting point of idealism is retained, then the transcendental subject must be thought of as an absolute, divine consciousness. This results in *metaphysical idealism* which includes *pantheism. (However the name "metaphysical idealism" can also designate a valid type of idealism mentioned at the beginning of this article). We find this pantheistic, metaphysical idealism in *German idealism where it is developed in different ways by *Fichte*, *Schelling* and *Hegel*.

Logical idealism, especially as it was developed by the neo-Kantians, no longer considered the forms of thought as the consciousness-contents of an actually thinking subject, but as the self-sufficient ground of all value. They usually ignore the question of the ultimate supporter of these forms of thought and direct their attention only to the logical structures of the contents of thought. When they completely deny a real subject then they descend (according to N. Hartmann) to the nonsense of a "subjectivism without a subject." — The expressions "subjective" and "objective" idealism are not always understôod in the same way. Sometimes subjective idealism is considered to be psychological idealism which makes the empirical consciousness of the individual the norm of reality or it is thought to be any idealism according to which the object proceeds from the subject (as in *Fichte*); and objective idealism is that which absolutely identifies subject and object (as in *Schelling* and *Hegel*). In the strictest sense objective idealism is a purely logical idealism in which the question about the thinking subject recedes completely into the background.

As an all-embracing world-view idealism naturally has its applications in the areas of ethics and sociology. In contrast to the shallow waters of positivism it emphasizes with intense sincerity that the norms which govern the life of the individual and of society are independent of contingent circumstances and opinions; but when, in accordance with idealistic presuppositions, it separates these norms from the essential nature of the concrete existent and tries to base them on the empty, merely "formal" attitudes of a "pure" subject then it lapses into lifeless abstractions.

JdV

IDENTITY

That two realities are identical means that they are not two but only one. Nevertheless, identity as a *relation necessarily implies two relative terms. The apparent contradiction is resolved in that the identical realities are both two and one, but from different points of view. Thus, in *logical identity* we find that several existents are said to be identical insofar as they agree in the same concept; this is better spoken of as *likeness* — and indeed *essential likeness* if the concept in question designates a common essence (as men, Peter and Paul are essentially alike), as likeness in a narrower sense in a case of agreement in *quantity, as *resemblance* when there is partial essential likeness or when there is agreement in *quality. According to the (disputed) principle of the *identity of the indistinguishables* (*principium identitatis indiscernibilium*: Leibniz and others) complete similarity in all particular determinations brings real identity along with it. *Real identity* — also called "objective" identity — is first of all the coincidence of several ideas or thought-contents in one and the same existent. Such is the basic meaning of *judgment. Because of the absence of really different relational terms it is not a real relation, but only a relation of reason.

Real identity is either formal or only material. Concepts that designate the same existent according to the same *form are *formally identical*; thus, the identity expressed in the proposition "Every existent is true" is formal, because "being true" is given with the form of being. This example likewise shows that formal identity does not necessarily mean a purely analytical relationship of similar concepts that are distinguished from one another only through the varying degrees of clarity with which the attributes are expressed; when such a relationship occurs one can speak of *conceptual identity*. (The expression "inner identity," which is often used in this sense, could be applied to every formal identity). Only *material identity* is had if the concepts designate different forms or principles which come together in the same *subject (e. g., "This man is just"). And finally, one can also speak of *real* identity when the same existent continues to exist in time (i. e., a *substance) in spite of the accidental changes it undergoes. This identity can be understood either more or less strictly; thus, the human body, in spite of the gradual change and replacement of all its parts, even after many years is still considered to be the "same" body; the same thing also holds good for societies. — The principle of identity ("Whatever is, is"), if it is not just a simple tautology, has been the object of different interpretations. Many look upon it as another form of the principle of *contradiction. Others claim that it means that every existent as such has a definite form, a definite essence; or also that it is spiritually graspable (intelligible) because of its form.

If the principle of identity is understood in this way, then it is certain that it cannot stand as the absolutely first principle.

JdV

IDEOLOGY

Ideology (in older writings) sometimes means the "science of ideas or concepts" (in the different meanings of these words); at other times it is more or less equivalent to: an abstract system of ideas that is not in accordance with reality. The word "ideology" gets a more precise meaning in *historical materialism. The latter calls every system that claims to have some spiritual values (ideas) an "ideology," for example, philosophy, religion, ethics, political science; for, it claims that these are merely functions of a purely material (especially economic) process or situation. — This explanation of ideology is merely an escape mechanism of *materialism from the obvious reality of spiritual existence. Materialists find an apparent justification for their position in the circumstance that man in his activities is very much tied to material (also economic) presuppositions and that he is especially prone to consider true what he wants to be true.

WB

IGNORANCE

Ignorance (moral) is the lack of the necessary knowledge of the moral value of some action; this can be ignorance of the law (*ignorantia legis*) or of a fact covered by the law (*ignorantia facti*). Whoever enters into marriage without knowing that bigamy is forbidden is ignorant of the law; whoever does not know that his marriage partner is already validly married is ignorant of the fact. Moral ignorance can be either vincible or invincible. *Vincible ignorance,* insofar as it involves negligence in acquiring the requisite knowledge, brings with it moral guilt. The person who does something morally wrong out of *invincible ignorance,* is not responsible for this in conscience. However, in the external legal forum there are a number of consequences in spite of this ignorance: liability for an injury inflicted on another, invalidity of a marriage because of a secret impediment, etc. Inexcusable ignorance does not eliminate responsibility for moral evil and its consequences, nor does it remove guilt and its deserved punishment from God. The guilt is already present before the deed in the hesitation to acquire the necessary information, and in the thoughtlessness with which the anticipated evil effects (somehow, though obscurely seen) are accepted. — The most universal principles of morality (e. g., "Good is to be done") cannot remain unknown without guilt by anyone who possesses the full use of reason. The same holds true for the proximate conclusions and applications derived from such principles (e. g., "One should respect one's parents"), unless a contrary education has distorted one's natural judgment in these matters. In more difficult applications, however, (e. g., the immorality of suicide even in exceptional cases) a guiltless ignorance is rather common.

JoS

ILLUMINATION

Illumination according to Augustine and the Franciscan epistemology of the 13th century (e. g., Bonaventure) is a special divine influence that takes place in the production of certain, necessary and universal knowledge in man. Just as, in the production of sense knowledge, along with the sense power and the influence of the present body there must still be a light, so also for the perfection of spiritual knowing (which is characterized by absolute certainty, necessity and universality), along with the knowing power of the intellect and the presentation of the object through sense perception, there must be a special (not just the general) cooperation of God; there must be an *illumination* or *irradiation* of a spiritual *light* in which man, through a kind of vision of the *rationes aeternae* (eternal principles), comes into contact with God himself, the eternal, immutable truth. Yet this is not meant in the sense of a vision of God, such as takes place in heaven, nor is it to be taken in the sense of *ontologism. However, the power of the agent intellect (*Aristotelianism) is not sufficient for this kind of knowledge, whereas for Thomas Aquinas it is. According to more recent views, the illumination spoken of in *Augustinianism is only the supernatural light of faith. One should always remember that the Augustinian theologians philosophize out of the Christian faith-experience in accordance with Anselm's words: *Credo, ut intelligam*: I believe in order to arrive at insight.

JoS

IMAGINATION

Imagination, as distinguished from *memory, is the power of freely combining images and ideas. It uses the material in the memory and moulds it into new forms; still, it remains bound by the laws of association. It is often put at the service of spiritual creativity by a free or passive direction of attention. Special attention should be called to the importance of imagination in dreams, play, fairy tales and myths, in all truly creative thinking.

The function of imagination in dreams presents the consciousness with an apparently irregular and senseless sequence of pictures which is to a

190

great extent not controlled by logical thinking and free choice and in which the basic laws of association and desire work themselves out. The result is that the general organization and purposefulness of conscious activity is lacking in dreams; nevertheless, dreams can lead to valuable effects such as poems, inspirations, the solution of some vexing problem. Moreover, *depth psychology* looks for a deeper meaning in the apparently senseless play of the imagination in dreams. Thus, dream-phantasies are taken as symbols that permit the expert interpreter to discover the unconscious center of personality and the hidden spiritual drives that have not yet become conscious. Even though the basic insights behind these attempts contain much good, they are also often distorted by aprioristic onesidedness and fancy. However, they should not be wholly rejected because of these aberrations. — The free use of imagination in play joins together in its own way both caprice and order. It manifests not only the natural drive "to exercise one's powers," but also the need of the human spirit for some kind of creative illusion alongside of his daily work that is so tiring, the need for an illusion that relaxes the mind and at the same time pleases and fulfills it. — The use of imagination in the making of fairy tales and myths reveals not only certain relationships of the motives behind them to the ages of the persons involved, but it also shows striking similarities in different peoples and cultures. Thus, it has been surmised that a "collective unconscious" is at work in man's play, not in the sense of some supra-individual reality, but rather as an unconscious basic tendency to produce certain forms of imagination — a tendency present in all men of all times.

The power of imagination exercises its most important function as *creative imagination* in the service of productive thought, in scientific, artistic, technical, and religious "inspiration." In the case of men, all new thinking naturally requires the help of imagination with its freedom to play around with ideas. Of course, new inspirations must be carefully examined and tested, since the irrational element in the play of the imagination can bring forth both nonsense and works of genius. — Just as an uncontrolled imagination is injurious to the full growth of the personality, so the careful development of a rich, psychologically and ethically healthy imagination is both valuable and important for all spiritual progress.

AW

IMMANENCE

Immanence (Lat.: *immanere*) literally means: to remain in something. In the sense of "not-going-beyond" it means the opposite of *transcendence and can be taken in a number of different ways. — In epistemology immanence means (1) dependence upon consciousness. Therefore, the object is not something independent that transcends the act of knowing and so possesses its own proper existence; rather, it is posited by the act of knowing and remains in it in such a way that its only existence is a thought-existence. This view is defended by the philosophy of immanence or epistemological *idealism (existence coincides with the idea or with being-thought). Of course, the proponents of this philosophy do not usually claim that the object proceeds from the empirical consciousness of the individual man, but only from the all-embracing absolute or transcendental *consciousness. Thus, even though the object at first appears to be transcendent, still it is ultimately only immanent. In all of this there is an element of truth: absolute, divine knowledge (together with the divine omnipotence) posits finite objects; this does not destroy their real existence — it supplies the true foundation for it.

With regard to human experience, immanence (2) means the limitation to the field of possible experience. Since he is not able to surpass this field man is closed off from the supra-sensible world. Such, at any rate, is the teaching of Hume's empirical *phenomenalism and Kant's *Critique of Pure Reason*. As both men show, this position reduces even the experienceable object to a mere appearance produced by us. In a similar vein, *Modernism* teaches that religion is limited exclusively to purely subjective experience. Thus the second meaning of immanence usually ends up in the first meaning. — Somewhat differently from the Modernists, Maurice Blondel with his "method of immanence" attempts to highlight the transcendence of religious truth through the insufficiency of the human consciousness left totally to itself (*Blondelianism).

In the metaphysical view, immanence (3) means the "indwelling" of the absolute in the world or in the finite existence. Such *divine immanence* is claimed by *pantheism in opposition to any transcendence, insofar as this system sees only one world-soul or source of the world in relation to which all other beings are only developmental moments. Hence, the true infinity and freedom of God are denied as well as any real creation. The true immanence of the world in God and of God in the world does not destroy God's transcendence — rather, it necessarily includes it; God dwells in his creation precisely because of his infinity, so that he would not even be infinite if he could establish it completely on its own.

We use "immanence" (4) in a wholly different sense when we designate life as immanent *activity in contrast to transient activity. With this expression we want to say that the activity occurs and remains within the agent.

JBL

IMMORTALITY

Since antiquity the problem of immortality has been one of the most important human problems, since a mere "heroic" Yes to one's own human existence as an "absurd existence towards *death" would not be heroism, but a dulling of the human spirit in search for the meaning of life. Rejected by materialism, positivism, critical philosophy, pantheism and biologism, the immortality of the human soul has been defended by the world religions, by a certain spontaneous conviction of men everywhere, by the great thinkers of the ancient world (Pythagoras, Plato, Plotinus; there is no agreement about the meaning of immortality in the work of Aristotle) and of the Middle Ages (Augustine, Thomas Aquinas), by the rationalists Descartes and Leibniż, even by some empiricists and by Kant as at least a postulate of practical reason.

Immortality as the capacity to perdure in *life without end belongs only to living beings, and belongs naturally only to *spirit. With an absolutely essential necessity, which renders the opposite simply impossible, immortality is proper to the divine being, since here essence and existence are identified. It belongs to the created, contingent spirit as a continuance (demanded by its nature) in existence once its reality is given. — The fact of the immortality of the human soul is existentially grounded in the simple (therefore not divisible into parts) and spiritual (therefore ordered to eternal life) essence of the soul. Its transcendental consciousness, which is reaching out for the unlimited (*Intellect, *Will) and whose meaningful activity demands an unrestricted continuance in existence, would be intrinsically meaningless if it did not include the guarantee of a fulfillment that is at least fundamentally possible. Likewise, the moral dignity of man requires an eternal life to resolve the tensions between moral and immoral commitments with rewards and punishments. Therefore, the acceptance of eternal life is justly a conviction found among all peoples; were this conviction false, then this would be an indication of the essential distortion and absurdity of human existence.

The form of eternal life is not an absorption into an impersonal Absolute, but a personal existence of full-spiritual fulfillment through the possession of infinite truth and infinite value; for, this is what constitutes eternal happiness. If the soul makes itself unworthy of eternal life, then sound thinking demands a sanction which in effect means the loss of God in the next life. The ever-recurring phantasy of the *transmigration of souls has not been established empirically, nor can it be proved a priori; moreover, it contradicts the personal dignity of man.

AW

IMMUTABILITY

The immutability of an existent excludes every kind of real *change from it, but not that which is attributed to it merely externally (according to our mode of speaking) because of a change in another. Material beings and beings tied to matter manifest only a relative immutability, since all life, growth and activity in this visible world depend on motion, i. e., change. However, the more *activity is removed from dependence on matter, the less change it has in itself. Even in man change or motion stands in an inverse relationship to the level of his spiritual activity, as is shown by spiritual intuition, by a moving contemplation of a work of art, and especially by mystical experiences. Therefore, activity and immutability do not mutually exclude each other from a conceptual point of view. — The *physical* immutability of God which is rooted in his simplicity and infinity does not negate all activity in him, but it does exclude all change in his existence, all increase or decrease of his perfection; therefore, it rules out all development in God and even the possibility of "growth." For this reason, *pantheism in all its forms is entangled in an inner contradiction. — The *moral* immutability of God makes it impossible that he could change an eternal decree of his will. God neither conceives new plans nor does he change the "old" ones. He knows the changing event in his own unchanging act. In God a single eternal act corresponds to the different, changeable moods of men (e. g., sin and repentance); this act, because of its infinite nature, is equivalent to the attitude of hate and love in its simplicity (*coincidentia oppositorum*: *God, Idea of). At the temporal creation of the world, that which is new and changeable is present strictly on the side of the world (*Freedom of God).

MR

IMPOSSIBILITY

Impossibility is the contradictory opposite of *possibility and therefore it is opposed both to chance and to necessity. Just as in the case of possibility, here also a distinction is made between *intrinsic* and *extrinsic* impossibility. The intrinsically impossible or absolute *nothing is that which is contradictory in itself (= *metaphysically impossible*). That which is intrinsically impossible is also absolutely or in every respect impossible. On the other hand, that which is not intrinsically impossible, is not yet therefore absolutely or in every respect possible. — Extrinsic impossibility refers to the inability of a cause to produce something. Thus, it is impossible for an infant to carry a hundred-pound load (active inability) or for wet wood to burn under normal conditions (passive inability). Since the non-philosophical sciences consider primarily extrinsic impossibility and judge it only according to the active or passive inability of the proximate causes, in the sense of the physical sciences that is impossible which is contrary to the laws of nature (= *physical impossibility*). With regard to God's *omnipotence there is no (extrinsic) impossibility. The *morally impossible* is that which the free will can affect only with difficulty and with extraordinary effort, so that it rarely happens. See also *Possibility*.

WB

INDIVIDUAL, THE

The individual or the individual thing is the concrete bearer of an essence in its non-communicable particularity, as this pine tree or this man Peter. The individual stands in contrast to the universal or the essence which abstracts from every definite bearer and as such can be communicated to different subjects or carriers. Only the individual really exists outside of the mind, while the universal as such exists only in conceptual thinking. "Individual" is a Latin word which means literally: the undivided. The reason for this is that is represents an essentially undivided and indivisible unity, because this one thing as such can never be multiplied and so exist more than this once; this particular pine tree or this particular man can, of necessity, exist only once. "Individuation" is derived from "individual"; the word signifies the *individual determination*, i. e., the determination by reason of which this individual is precisely this one in contrast to all others (e. g., this particular existent Peter). Duns Scotus and his school call individuation *haecceitas* (thisness), insofar as Peter is this particular individual, by reason of his individual existence, to whom one can refer as "this." In the realm of knowledge the *particular concept* represents the individual as such. — The non-communicable particularity of the individual and its separation from everything else increases with the greater perfection of the higher levels of existence. In the inorganic world individual beings are least in evidence; they continually enter into larger (atomic and molecular) combinations and still have not been clearly identified. In the plant and animal worlds each individual clearly distinguishes itself (usually) from all others. Man possesses an essentially higher type of particularity, inasmuch as his spiritual soul elevates him to the level of a *person. A pure spirit is higher still. And finally, God possesses absolute particularity or individuality, because he infinitely surpasses everything else.

Opinions are divided on the question of the *principle of individuation* or the intrinsic existential reason for individuation. It is certain that the whole reality of every existent is determined by individuation. In the world of bodies there is a mere *numerical difference* between individuals, i. e., they agree in all their essential characteristics and are distinguished from one another only according to number. Thomas Aquinas reduces this difference to matter, the principle of space-time. According to him, the individual is "this one," because it occupies this spatio-temporal location or (in the case of men) this place in history, because it belongs precisely in this context of the visible cosmos. And he logically concludes that, in the case of the pure spirit where matter is not involved, every individual difference necessarily signifies a difference in species (with generic homogeneity): so each angel is a species by itself. Thus the angel is this individual not by reason of a spatio-temporal determination, but by reason of his specific degree of existence. However, it should be noted that even here we have one individual alongside of another; but in the case of God we find an individual above all others because of his infinite fullness of existence. — Leibniz formulated the *principle of indiscernibles* according to which two things, which agree with each other in every respect, would necessarily be identified; therefore, there could not be two completely similar things distinguished from each other only by reason of their spatial location. In order not to be identified they would have to differ from each other in some other way. This is also supposed to hold good for the smallest particles of matter (like electrons). As a metaphysically necessary principle, however, this position can hardly be proved.

JBL

INDIVIDUALISM

Individualism (1) means the value, care and development of the human *personality in contrast to treating men as a herd of animals; in a broader sense it can also be applied not only to the individual person, but also to families and other groups in which the consciousness of one's own personal worth — even "in" the larger whole and "for" it — is cultivated and leads to positive results. Individualism (2) can also refer to the over-emphasis of the individual or of a particular group with the result that the relationship to the higher community is slighted (e. g., by striving for a super race [Nietzsche]. Individualism (3) is also the name given to the view of society (*Social Philosophy) that so stresses the value of the individual that *society turns out to be only the sum of the individuals, but not a real whole or unity. The rights and freedom of the individual in this view are supposed to be limited only by the very same rights of the other person and not by an inner relationship to the community. Thus, "order" can be established only when (as they hope) the reasonable personal interest of each individual leads to a kind of cooperation or harmony ("*harmonia praestabilita*"). In actual fact, however, the stronger devour the weaker and in place of a "free" society appears a tyrannical, irresponsible use of power under the guise of freedom and equality. — In the 19th century this form of individualism (in politics it was called "liberalism") was dominant in both social and economic thinking, and then it fell into disrepute; but it still lives on as individualism on a higher level in the form of *collectivism where it has been magnified to gigantic proportions.

OvNB

INDUCTION

While *deduction concludes from the universal to the particular or from the essence of an object to its necessary attributes, induction (*epagogē*) attempts to derive from observed individual cases a general law that also holds good for the unobserved cases. In the field of induction belong such things as the laws of physical science and experimental psychology. — The so-called *complete induction*, which consists in the observation of all the individual cases, is not a conclusion but a summation. On the other hand, *mathematical induction*, i. e., the conclusion that a certain formula which is valid for n is also valid for $n + 1$, is proven in a strictly deductive way from the nature of the formula; and this is done in such a way that this formula holds for a definite number. In reality, therefore, it is a deduction. — Real induction is what is known as *incomplete induction*: this argumentation concludes from the observation of relatively few cases to all similar cases. The conclusion is justified by the principle of *sufficient reason which excludes a chance similarity in the regularly observed cases and therefore demands a certain *necessity in the pertinent event under the observed conditions; thus, if the event is necessary under the given conditions, then it will always occur under the same conditions. Of course, induction does not lead to absolute *certitude, but it still provides a genuine ("hypothetical") certitude.

The methods of induction that lead to a clear knowledge of causal connections were gradually worked out, especially by men like Francis Bacon and John Stuart Mill. Bacon wanted to determine the essence of the different characteristics of physical objects. In the sense of modern physical science Mill attempted to discover causal laws and he proceeded with the help of experiments. His methods reflected the work of Bacon, but they offered more precise norms of procedure. An *experiment* (the importance of which has rightly been stressed in connection with induction) is a controlled observation of some event under deliberately chosen, simplified conditions. The experiment has produced results that are vastly superior to those of simple observation. — Subsequently, careful criticism provided essential improvements of Mill's methods — a fact that was recognized by Mill himself. To be more specific, the critics furthered the connection of the real inductive method with the method of *hypothesis; for, from time immemorial this has been the principal method of the great searchers into the secrets of nature.

JF-JdV

INFERENCE

Inference is that kind of mental activity in which one moves from the affirmation of one or several propositions to the affirmation of another on the basis of an insight into their necessary connection. In an *immediate inference* (*simple deduction, illation*) the transition takes place without the mediation of a third proposition (e. g., *Opposition, *Modality); in a *mediate inference* (*ratiocination*) or syllogism one concludes from several (and in a simple syllogism from two) *premises* to a *conclusion*. Such argumentation includes two steps: the insight into the content and necessary connection between the propositions and the extension of the affirmation from the premises to the conclusion. The *logical consequence* (or consistency) of the inference is based only on the necessary connection of the contents of the propositions, regardless of their truth or falsity. The validity of the logical connection is guaranteed by the particular form of the inference. The form of the argumentation is different in the *categorical and in the *hypothetical inference.

There are different kinds of inference. A syllogism with more than two premises is called a *polysyllogism*. If two simple syllogisms are joined in such a way that the conclusion of one immediately becomes the major premise of the other, then the first part is called a *prosyllogism* and the second an *episyllogism*. If several propositions are so joined together that in every following proposition the predicate of the former becomes the subject, but in the conclusion the subject of the first proposition is united with the predicate of the last, then we have a *chain argument* or *sorites*. In the Goklenic sorites the subject of the previous proposition becomes the predicate of the following one and in the conclusion the subject of the last proposition is joined with the predicate of the first. — If the reason is added to one of the premises, then we have an *epicheirema*; if we omit one of the premises and allow it to be supplied mentally, then we have an *enthymeme*. In the *argument from analogy* one concludes from the similarity of two relationships that also the characteristics of the related terms of the first relationship are similar to those of the other. The presupposition for this is that those characteristics are either the basis of the relationship or grow out of it precisely insofar as it is similar to the other one. In the *argument from convergence* one concludes to some fact from several different reasons among which no one of itself is sufficient. This argument leads to certitude only when the common direction of the reasons can have its cause only in this fact. — In the *refutation* of an argument the impossibility of a proposition is demonstrated by showing that contradictory conclusions flow from it. — See also *Modality*.

WB

INFINITE

The concept "infinite" denies all limits (*Finite). The relatively infinite is that which has no limit with regard to certain attributes and perfections; the absolutely infinite is that which has no limits with regard to absolute *existence. — In Greek philosophy, where the formed and therefore limited thing was thought of as perfect, "infinite" (*apeiron*) is the expression of the unfinished, undetermined and so imperfect thing. Thus, for Aristotle and many scholastics, *prime matter is infinite insofar as it is not determined by a *form but is merely *determinable* by an indefinite number of forms (successively). Opposed to material infinity is the infinity of form with regard to the individual carriers of it; from among these no one can exhaust the form. Moreover, scholastic philosophers distinguish between the potentially *infinite* or the *indefinite*, which of course in itself is finite but is infinite according to its *potency because it can be increased or diminished without ceasing (the divisibility or augmentablity of a number is infinite in this sense), and the *actually infinite*, which excludes every positive limit beyond which there cannot be any more (under the given conditions). According to the Thomistic position, pure *form and pure *act possess this infinity. — Mathematics calls a quantity infinitely great that is larger than every numerable multitude of quantities included in the unity; and it calls that quantity infinitely small that is so small that every multiple of the same is smaller than the unity. To compute with *mathematical infinities* is called "infinitesmal calculation." It is a disputed point whether or not there is at least an abstract possibility of an actually infinite multitude. However that may be, a *number cannot be termed infinite, if "number" is understood in such a way that it means a multitude that is completely numerable in a finite series of steps. — Infinity as applied to *space and *time means for the most part the basic, endless augmentability of extended bodies or of successive events; therefore it is a potential infinity.

The infinity of God is infinity in the actual sense and it affirms the limitless fullness of the divine being; therefore, it is absolute infinity, i. e., the highest perfection of God which does not fit in any finite category and which stands essentially above all the existence-levels of finite existents. It also includes absolute simplicity in itself. It is not the totality of existence, as the pantheists maintain, nor does it contain in itself the particular existence of creatures as such; rather, it possesses their particular perfections in another, higher way (more or less as a learned mathematician possesses the same knowledge his students have).

MR

INSTRUMENTAL CAUSE

Instrumental cause is the name given to every *cause whose make-up and power are not proportioned to the desired effect; therefore, it needs a superior cause — one equal to the job — that can move and direct it. The instrumental cause, however, influences or prepares for the effect as a real cause. The principal cause as well as the instrumental cause are sub-divisions of the efficient cause. Artistic and useful tools of all kinds are good examples of instrumental causes; another example is the direction and control of the powers of nature. However, there is a difference here: the principal cause must take up and put fabricated tools to work, while the powers of nature, since they are already active of themselves, need only to receive intelligent direction from the principal cause.

WB

INTELLECT

The human intellect is the power of *thinking, i. e., the power of non-intuitive insight into existence and relationships. As such it is essentially different from animal *intelligence* (somewhat ambiguously named), even in its most perfect instinctual operations. — The intellect is grounded in the nature of the human soul as a spiritual being (*Spirit, *Soul), but in its special nature as a human intellect it is at the same time restricted to the particular conditions of the human spirit which is the essential form of a body. Although intellect is primarily known to us as human intellect, *absolute intellect* according to its essence is not the same as *human intellect*. Absolute intellect is ordered to spiritual knowledge as such, independent of whether it is realized in an unlimited way, as in the infinity of God, or in a limited way, as in the created or even body-related spirit. The characteristic object for spiritual knowing and for absolute intellect is the existent as such (*Existence). But since man is a finite spirit in matter who is wholly dependent on sense knowledge, existence is presented to his human intellect only in and through the essential that shines forth in the sensible thing (*intelligibile in sensibili*).

Therefore, the special nature of the human intellect is characterized by the following pairs of opposites: It is spiritual and it is ordered to the spiritual, yet it is tied to sense functions and so to material existents. It is spiritual: for, only a power whose acts are not immediately produced by a material principle (one therefore that is immaterial in the strict sense) can direct itself to spiritual objects and find in them the fulfillment of its own meaning and existence. Only a spiritual faculty can represent the non-sensible and the simple in their special mode of existence. Also, the distinction between the ego, the non-ego and the act, and the further question (occasioned by this distinction) about the logical, ethical and aesthetical value of these acts and one's own existence, as well as the perfect self-presence involved in self-consciousness — all presuppose a spiritual principle of knowledge. On the other hand, the dependence on sense knowledge is evident: the human intellect must derive all of its concepts from sense experience, for it does not possess a direct intuition of spiritual essences (*Concepts, Formation of; *Ontologism). In all areas of thought the intellect is dependent ultimately on the original sense impressions (the scholastic "conversion to the phantasm"). The intellect rises to the level of spiritual and supra-sensible things only by way of *analogy (*Denial). The discursive and abstracting character of human intellectual activity is connected with its dependence on sense knowledge, so that *intellect in the narrow sense* refers to the power of discursive and abstracting thinking (*Reason).

The special character of the human intellect also reveals itself in the opposition of receptivity and spontaneity. The distinction between the *active* and the *passive* intellect in the theory of abstraction has been a classical one since Aristotle and it has been proposed under many different forms (*Concepts, Formation of). In addition, the spontaneity of the spirit reveals itself in the direction of one's attention to this rather than to that, in attitudinal acts of judgment and in creative thinking. Creative thinking, however, always presupposes the prior reception of thought-contents from the other.

The spiritual knowledge-image, the *verbum mentis* (*Knowledge), bridges over the opposition between the immanence and transcendence of intellectual activity . This "mental word" really remains completely in the knower, but by reason of its image-character it leads the knower beyond himself to the object. — Essentially surpassing the sense power, the intellect still remains naturally tied, even in its most perfect manifestations of creative thinking, to the totality of the sense-spiritual mode of knowing and at the same time to the totality of the psychological personality along with its *irrational aspects. On the other hand, the cultivation of the so-called supra-intellectual intuition of "purely spiritual" realities, by reducing or even excluding the role of the intellect, is even more misdirected than a one-sided exaltation of intellect alone.

AW

INTELLECTUALISM

Intellectualism is a term that can be applied to every philosophical position that gives preference to spirit, ideas and intellect. This can occur in different areas either properly or improperly. *Metaphysical intellectualism* in grossly exaggerated in transcendental or *German Idealism which teaches that existence in every respect is a product of reason. With a healthy sense of balance Thomas Aquinas defends a metaphysical intellectualism according to which existence in its divine source is one with reason; it follows, then, that every existent, even though it is not exclusively reason and spirit, is in some sense reasonable and spiritual. *Epistemological intellectualism* (*Intelligibility) is a variation of metaphysical and should not be confused with *rationalism. As opposed to *voluntarism, intellectualism does not necessarily designate the exclusion of will from existence (for, where reason is, there is also will), but only the conceptual precedence of reason before *will; for, will cannot even be thought of without reference to reason. That which distinguishes will from every other type of striving is precisely reason which permeates will and forms it. *Psychological intellectualism* refers either to the above-mentioned precedence of the intellect before the will, or it can go further and mean the erroneous view that the psychic functions of will and feeling can be reduced to different aspects of the intellect.

In more practical areas (education, culture) we speak of intellectualism when too much stress is laid on intellectual development with the result that the other powers of man are neglected. Among the Greeks Socrates propounded an *ethical intellectualism* according to which virtue is nothing other than knowledge of the good and therefore learnable. — The word "intellectualism" is often used in the same sense as *rationalism. However, in contrast to rationalism, intellectualism signifies a certain pre-eminence of spirit and reason, without at the same time restricting it just to concepts and discursive thinking which are proper to man's intellect; therefore, it also includes the infinite, divine spirit.

WB

INTELLIGIBILITY

"To understand" something means first of all to see through it, to penetrate it to its roots. What is perfectly understood is seen as it is, i. e., in the very ground out of which it grows. But since a contingent being never has the adequate source of its existence in itself but always in another — its cause, to understand a contingent reality means to know it through its causes. An *explanation or the reduction to necessary natural causes and natural laws is a great help in understanding natural events, as is also the perspective of *finality; spiritual *understanding and the reduction to ends are a help in understanding *spiritual existence. If a contingent being is to be understood completely, that is, not only in this or that characteristic but in its contingency itself, then the inquiry must go back to the ultimate, necessary causes. For the intellectual grasp of essentially necessary connections one usually employs the words "*comprehend*" or "*understand*"; the essential relations themselves are *intelligible*.

INTELLIGIBILITY

The intelligibility of objects corresponds to the power of comprehension on the part of the intellect. There is some question as to whether objects in their totality or the existent as such are intelligible. In any event, the intelligibility that is essential to the existent as such should not be referred simply to the human intellect. For, it refers to *intellect as such and therefore in the first place concerns the absolute, infinite intellect of God. For God alone there is an absolute intelligibility of everything that is, since, because of the complete identity of being and knowing, he is perfectly intelligible to himself and likewise sees through all other things insofar as they flow forth from him (and from the free act of his will). The principle of the complete intelligibility of every existent characterizes all metaphysical *idealism. It excludes the possibility of anything above the realm of the intelligible, anything wholly unknowable (N. Hartmann); but it does not rule out the possibility that the intelligibility of existents has various levels that correspond to the levels of more or less existence (*Existence, Levels of). Whatever *is* only in an improper and diminished sense (as, for example, *evil), is likewise intelligible only in a diminished sense.

Since the human intellect is truly and in the full sense an intellect, it is in some way open to everything that is, i. e., everything can be the object of its knowing even though it may not know all things perfectly. For, certain limits are set on human knowing that prevent it from being comprehensive. We cannot grasp all reality by means of proper *concepts, as *rationalism (and *dialectical materialism in its principle of the *knowability of the world*) claimed; rather, we are only able to determine a middle area by means of concepts — and even this we can do only imperfectly (*System). Far removed from every complete and positively conceptual determination are both the indeterminateness of the material (non-conceptual) remainder involved in every abstraction and of the materially conditioned individuality (*Individual, The), as well as the infinity of pure *act that transcends all form and limitation. But in that middle area mentioned just above, there is the matter of human feelings and the fact of free decision which are not capable of being entirely comprehended by means of concepts. Our thinking is able to approach all of these objects only through analogous concepts (*Analogy, *Concept) and reflection. Thus, the non-conceptual remainder of an object can be mediately and analogously known through its relation to the conceptual essence, and the infinity of pure act as the source of finite existence can be known in the same way. But the possibility of understanding (at least imperfectly) one's own feelings and will acts is basically given by the fact that man's intellect permeates the other powers of the *soul and that it is not the individual powers which act, but rather the whole man through his powers. Man not only sees, feels and desires, but he also knows that he is doing those things; with his intellect he is able to reflect on what he does and so arrive at an indirect insight into these activities and their objects.

WB

INTENSITY

Intensity is the magnitude of *quality or the level of participation that a subject has in a particular attribute. The magnitude of the subject should be distinguished from the magnitude of the quality itself: e. g., a larger or smaller illuminated surface; a stronger or weaker light on the same illuminated surface. While the intensity of spiritual qualities can be measured only in an improper sense, corporeal and changeable qualities are subject to real *measurement*, i. e., to a knowledge of size measured in numbers. The number that indicates the magnitude of the quality is called a *degree* or a *degree of intensity*. Intensity is measured either on the basis of the effects which can be known by their size (e. g., expansion produced by heat) or through the causes which can be counted (e. g., candle power). The magnitude of the effect permits us to conclude to the magnitude of the *power that produced it (intensity = *strength*). The numbers with which intensity is measured are primarily only the ordinal numbers. However, proportional numbers can also be used. The idea that the scholastic position on qualities rules out the use of mathematics to gain knowledge about nature, though widely accepted, is false.

WB

INTENTIONAL

Everything that can perform something is intentional (1) (such as the existent with regard to existence, the doer with regard to his activity and its object). In a narrower sense, everything is "intentional" (2) that has a conscious orientation to an object. Imaginations, concepts, knowing and willing acts of all kinds belong in this category. They all "mean" or intend something. Further, the signified objects themselves as signified are intentional (3). Thus, they possess (besides their possible or real existence in themselves), as imagined, thought or willed objects, an "intentional" existence in the mind.

WB

INTUITION

Intuition in the strict sense is the direct look at an existing particular thing that shows itself immediately in its concrete fullness (i. e., without

INTUITION

the mediation of other knowledge contents). Therefore, in the strict sense only that knowledge can be called *intuitive* that grasps its object in its present reality; in contrast, all knowledge that abstracts from the corporeal presence of the thing known is *abstractive*. — Intuition is found in two forms — as sensible and as intellectual intuition; the latter is also termed "spiritual vision."

Sensible intuition is found in animals and (more perfectly) in men. Being tied to bodily organs, it is limited to the appearance of the world of bodies. The name "intuition" comes from man's sense of sight (Lat.: *intueor* = I look at); still, the other senses also possess (a more or less elevated) "intuition" in their own way. In the full sense, only immediate perception can be characterized as intuition, because it alone co-represents the existence of the individual in the sensible appearances. In a wider sense even *imagination is called intuitive insofar as it is composed of purely sensible, intuitive elements, while at the same time abstracting from the existence of the represented particulars. — Sensible intuition as perception and imagination is of the utmost importance for human thought, because our thinking wins many of its basic concepts from this intuition and even in its further development it remains constantly rooted in it (the *conversio ad phantasma* of scholastic philosophy) (*Concepts, Formation of, *Intellect).

Strictly speaking, only a pure spirit has perfect *intellectual intuition*; its exemplar is the vision in which God grasps himself and in which he "sees" all finite existents (*Omniscience). It is ordered to existence (in contrast to appearance) and thus in bodily things it is directed to their essential core from which point it views the appearances. Therefore, it is not just an opaque grasp of the actually given (like sensible intuition), but it is at the same time necessarily the mental grasp of it from its ground in being. Intellectual intuition of this kind is denied to man, even though "ontologism" and (very often) *idealism attribute it to him. Nevertheless, in man's spiritual knowing there is an intuition in the broader sense, insofar as it participates in some of the essential traits of intellectual intuition.

The closest thing to this intuition is the grasp of the spiritual acts of thinking and willing. Because they present themselves immediately as particular existents one can speak here of intuition but not in the full sense; for, such acts do not reveal themselves in a direct view but only through *reflection. — Our conceptual knowledge at first appears as the opposite of all intuition, since it is directed to the universal, abstracts from existence and highlights only particular traits of the concrete whole. Moreover, it is never an immediate grasp, but it is always mediated by sensible intuition or by reflection. However, since the universal is known chiefly as wholly embedded in these intuitive modes of understanding, even the concept attains a certain intuitiveness so that one can speak of an "essential view." In addition, conceptual knowing is called intuitive insofar as it grasps its objects immediately, i. e., without the mediation of a thought process or a conclusion, whether it is a matter of particular essential characteristics or relationships. In this sense Thomas Aquinas speaks of *intellectus principiorum* (understanding of principles) and distinguishes between *intellectus* and *ratio* as intuitive and discursive knowing; he says further that the former is a minimal participation in the intellectual vision of the pure spirit. — One speaks of intuition in a special way if one encompasses larger perspectives in *one* glance (without discursive mediations); this is especially true of the artistic mind, because here what is seen is concretized also in sensibly intuitive forms. If such a view suddenly opens up undreamed of possibilities and if it arises spontaneously, a gift of grace as it were, then one experiences it as an *inspiration*. — That such intuitive knowing is not radically different from discursive thought is evident in the analysis by Aquinas of the fact that *intellectus* and *ratio* constitute only two functions of the one spiritual knowing power.

Modern philosophy in many ways greatly restricts the range of theoretical (taken mainly as discursive), knowledge; in particular, it has removed from its influence all life-guiding insights and all metaphysical realities. The latter are then referred to non-intellectual, irrational or emotional modes of apprehension which often seem to be intuitions. In addition to *life philosophy, "emotional presentation" and the "intentional feeling" of modern *value philosophy, the irrational apprehension of God proposed by some contemporary philosophy of religion also belongs in this category. If such directions suffer from an underestimation of the rational, they have nevertheless brought out strongly the insufficiency of recent shallow, mathematical and technical reason. They also teach us that it is first of all the incorporation in the totality of the powers of the soul that gives knowing its full power and vitality; in such situations very often a total intuitive grasp precedes all rational analysis.

JBL

INTUITIONISM

Intuitionism designates the tendencies that give the first place in human knowing to "intuition"; the advocates of this view usually overrate the knowledge-value of intuition or even attribute to man ways of knowing that exceed the possibilities of his nature. By "intuition" here is not meant *intuition in the normal sense, but higher acts of knowledge that really or supposedly approach the immediacy and fullness of a spiritual intuition. Such an approach more or less occurs in the creative grasp of the relations between things, especially as this sometimes occurs in highly gifted individuals; nevertheless, for the most part this "intuition" presupposes a long, thought-filled familiarity with the object, and subsequently it must be justified by means of methodical thinking. — *Ontologism is a special form of intuitionism; this system falsely supposes that man possesses an innate vision of God. Other thinkers, such as Plato, speak of a spiritual vision that man is supposed to be able to attain through innate ideas. More recently intuitionism has often been associated with irrationalism in that it has assumed in man an immediate *irrational or emotional grasp of suprasensible reality (e. g., Henri Bergson and Max Scheler).

JdV

IRRATIONAL

Irrational in general means that which is opposed to or at least foreign to spirit, especially to conceptual thinking (reason or *ratio*). That which is simply foreign to spirit and to thinking is sometimes said to be *alogical* (*Logos). The adjective "irrational" can be applied psychologically (subjectively) to mental acts, or objectively to the objects to which the acts are directed. In the psychological sense the irrational (1) is the non-spiritual, conscious life that is more or less removed from the control of reason (e. g., drives, feelings, emotions). But even spiritual willing includes an element that is not wholly and rationally intelligible, namely when the lesser good is freely chosen. In the objective sense, "irrational" (2) means that which is unknowable because of its obscurity, that which is inaccessible to reason, that which is perceptible only through irrational acts.

Irrationalism usually signifies an over-emphasis on the irrational element. Psychological irrationalism gives the first place to the irrational (1) element in human life (*Life Philosophy, Psychoanalysis). Metaphysical irrationalism affirms that all existence and every existent is essentially irrational; thus, the existent is thought to be ultimately only blind will or a drive for life (Schopenhauer, Nietzsche, Eduard von Hartmann), or else man despairs of attaining any positive determination of the irrational nature of existence (Nicolai von Hartmann). Metaphysical irrationalism is irreconcilable with a clear concept of God (*Truth). Epistemological irrationalism claims that reality or at least definite areas of reality, which are normally thought to be accessible to our reason, are irrational (2) as far as we and our mode of thinking are concerned. Thus, according to Max Scheler and N. von Hartmann we grasp existence only in irrational (emotional) acts; according to value-irrationalism all *values are irrational; according to the philosophy of religion of Rudolf Otto God is irrational; since he can be perceived only by an emotional experience of the "numinous." — It must be admitted that some things are irrational (2) as far as we are concerned. Thus, the individual as such can never be fully grasped by our conceptual mode of thinking. Still, it is not correct to consider existence and values as irrational. God is indeed incomprehensible to us, but he is not wholly unknowable. The divine *mysteries which are beyond our reasoning power are better termed *"supra-rational," since they are unintelligible to us not because of their intrinsic obscurity, but rather because of their blinding fulness of being and light.

JdV

J

JUDGMENT

Judgment is the central act of human knowing which philosophy studies for its logical and metaphysical value. The logical study investigates the judgment as a thought-form according to its essential structure and its necessary characteristics. Thus it distinguishes itself from the simple concept and the inference. The *concept offers knowledge only in a beginning way, because it merely grasps idea-contents without relating them to existence and without expressing them in their existence through an *affirmation. The judgment, however, brings knowledge to its full actualization, because it relates idea-contents to existence and expresses them in their existence through an affirmation. On the other hand, the *inference does not signify a further perfection of the being-affirmation as such, but rather the advance from one affirmation to another.

The more precise structure of the judgment can be clarified in the case of the proposition; for, the task of the proposition is to be the linguistic expression or the sensible sign of the judgment. The proposition attributes a predicate to a subject by means of the *copula* "is". In contrast to a composite concept (e. g., a mortal man) the essence of the proposition and therefore also of the judgment resides in the copula. The copula is not completely effective if it simply establishes the connection of the predicate with the subject; it is completely effective as soon as it expresses the relation of the connected predicate to *existence and so gives it *affirmation (e. g., "Man is mortal"). In order to guarantee the truth of the proposition and the judgment, some philosophers assumed the operation of *propositions as such*, which do not exist outside of reality but do stand in some way (cf. the unreal symbols of Heinrich Rickert). This view, which reflects the Platonic theory of ideas, is not necessary because the truth of the judgment is fully guaranteed by the fact that expressed idea-content is given in reality. Also, the form of the statement simply represents the way (grounded in the given reality) in which we men must shape that reality in order to grasp it in thought.

JUDGMENT

Let us clarify some of the attributes and divisions of the judgment. The *quality* of the judgment resides in the copula insofar as it attributes the predicate to the subject or removes it from the subject, either as an affirmation in "is" or as a *denial in "is not." Thus we have affirming and denying judgments. Likewise, the *modality* of the judgment belongs to the copula, whereby it also expresses the mode of the "is" and the "is not." Accordingly, there are *apodictic* judgments which state something as absolutely necessary or as absolutely impossible, *assertatory* judgments which simply say "is" or "is not" without determing the mode, and *problematic* judgments which express a possibility or even a possibility of non-existence. According to the extension of the subject there is a different *quantity* of the judgment. Thus a distinction is made between *universal, particular, singular* and *indefinite* judgments; in the latter the extension of the subject remains undetermined. Concerning the relationship of the predicate to the subject, the affirming judgment always posits the identity of both — at least the material identity, because of which the predicate actually belongs to the subject (e. g., Peter is at home). Yet a formal identity can also be pesent so that the predicate is essentially included in the subject; such judgments are called *judgments of identity.* But they are in no sense to be identified with *tautological judgments* in which the predicate merely repeats what the subject has already stated, nor are they essentially analytical (*Analysis); rather, they can also be synthetic essential judgments (e. g., "Every contingent existent demands a cause": *Synthesis). The composite judgments stand alongside the simple ones. While simple *categorical judgments* state something absolutely (Dick will study), *conditional judgments* add a condition in a more developed proposition (Dick will study, if he has the time). *Disjunctive judgments* establish an either/or situation (Dick will either study or play). On the other hand, *conjunctive judgments* deny that two statements can be true at the same time (Dick cannot study and play at the same time). *Copulative judgments* connect in the same proposition several subjects or (and) several predicates (Dick and Tom are studying; Dick is studying and earning money at the same time). Between several judgments there is an equivalence, if their truth (or falsity) is mutually implied.

The metaphysical consideration places the human thought-form of the judgment in the total context of a metaphysics of knowledge. Thus one must begin with the primordial instance in which the essence of the sensible particular thing is expressed. Our knowledge begins first of all with the sensible appearance of a thing; if it did not go beyond that, then it would be mere sense knowledge. Actually, as spiritual knowledge it presses forward to the innermost core of the appearing thing, namely to *existence. However, existence never belongs to a finite thing in its complete fullness or according to all its possibilities, but only according to the power of the *essence which always presents a limited mode of existence. The three levels — particular thing, essence, existence, are all possessed by the thing in a compact, opaque *synthesis. The judgment conjoins the same three levels, after they have been separated out by means of abstraction, in an organized and luminous synthesis — i. e., in a judgment. While the real synthesis fixes the two other factors within the limits of the particular thing, the judgment-synthesis elevates the two other factors into the horizon of existence. Thus, in its own way it imitates the divine view which is already given in absolute existence and therefore grasps everything from the inner ground of existence. This copy of the divine vision is also expressed in the natural striving of the human spirit for absolute being; according to Joseph Marechal, it is only this infinite striving that roots objective truth in the judgment.   JBL

JUSTICE

If rights and law establish the order of the *community, the task of justice is to preserve that order or even to produce it when the existing circumstances do not form a true and meaningful social order which promotes the common good. — Within an established order, primarily for the sake of the community (*Common Good), those norms or *laws should be observed which build up order: *general* and *legal* (or "social") justice. — The distribution of burdens and duties, of honors and privileges, to the members of the community is to be based upon their kind of membership and according to their strengths and capacities: this is called *distributive* justice. The members of a community must guarantee to each other that which rightly belongs to each; a principal application of this principle is the preservation of equivalence between output and return, i. e., the preservation therefore of equivalence in economic activity; thus this type of justice is called *commutative* justice. In contradistinction to the first-mentioned general justice, distributive and commutative justice are spoken of as *particular* justice.

In actual fact the existing order is never exactly what it should be; in order to be a purer and more perfect expression of man's basic rights and thereby "order" in the full sense of the word, it needs to be constantly improved and adapted to the changing historical situation; for, laws which at one time were the expression of justice can become, with a change in circumstances, meaningless, harmful to the community and even unjust. The one who profits from such laws will normally try to preserve them as his established right; the one who suffers under them is inclined to violate them, with force if necessary, as being unjust. Thus only organic growth is of lasting benefit to a society: the desire and readiness to accomplish this growth is what is meant by *social justice*; it is so named because it is constantly creating anew the true order of society and thereby continually protecting and furthering the *common good.   OvNB

K

KNOWLEDGE

Knowledge is that life process that is known to man directly from his own consciousness; in this event the knower (the *Subject) possesses the known (the *Object) in himself in such an active way that he at the same time sets it over against himself in the active unity. "Knowledge" refers to the amazing fact that an existent, the knower, is not only present in the midst of other existents, but also is, as it were, transparent to himself, conscious of his own self and so "present to himself"; but he also goes out beyond himself when he reflects the other in himself and so "in a certain sense becomses all things," as Aristotle says. Knowledge is one of the *intentional acts, i. e., those that posit a tension between subject and object. It is to be distinguished from other intentional acts, such as acts of the will, because — although it is measured by the reality of the object — it is not related to this reality as a good end to be striven for, but as the existence of the known in the knower. A unification that is achieved in the knower, in which the "to be such" of the known object becomes the "to be such" of the knowledge and so also of the knower as such, is only possible if the nature or form of the object involves a certain difference and neutrality with regard to the materiality both of the subject and of the object and if, in this difference, it becomes the form of that activity in which the subject is related to the object of the knowledge. Thus, Thomas Aquinas speaks of a certain immateriality of knowledge, even of sense knowledge.

Knowledge takes place in man on the levels of sense knowledge and intellectual knowledge. In *sense knowledge, the impressions received into the sense organs from the surrounding world are further assimilated; they are received (*species impressa*) by the sense power in a biologically favorable simplification and then brought to consciousness in an active way. In this consciousness certain definite aspects stand out which are in a definite correlation to the objective realities of the surrounding world. Yet all of this remains on the level of sense knowledge. It is only on the

212

level of intellectual knowledge that the subject completely returns to himself and possesses himself along with his total experience of the world in its relationship to existence as such. These relationships are expressed in *thinking in accordance with the particular moments (the a priori *categories), which are intrinsic to the existent as such and on the basis of the received material they lead to the different empirical *concepts. For, human knowledge rests on assimilation (*representation theory*) in contrast to the projecting knowledge of the creator which sets the limits for things. Not until the knowing power is assimilated to the object in an immaterial way (through the so-called *intelligible species*) is it able to set itself over against the object (in the *verbum mentis* = mental word).

From this fully human knowledge, which includes both sense and intellectual knowledge as its two necessary aspects, a reductive concept of pure sense knowledge can be formed; such a concept serves as a guide for the interpretation of the analogous utterances of animals which indicate some kind of knowledge. Further, an analysis of intellectual knowledge shows that it is not necessarily restricted just to man's way of thinking about a sensibly given object, i.e., insofar as, in a purely spiritual act of knowing, the existence of the knower can be presented to him as being "for itself" in pure *intuition. Whether such purely spiritual acts exist, either in some bodiless afterlife of the *soul or in another way (in *God, for example), is a point that must be established by special arguments. While sense knowledge supplies primarily an orientation in the world and serves biological ends, it offers man in his *intellect a view of the *world and in his *reason a view of *existence as such; thus, it creates the presupposition for a free decision that is to be guided by the norms of *morality.

In a wide sense, knowledge means every intentional presence of an object in a subject; but in a narrow sense and in contrast to mere imagination or thinking, it means only the true and certain *judgment (*Truth, *Certitude) in which the subject is aware of his own relationship to the object and of the object's relationship to existence. — In general, it is correct to speak of knowledge only as a "conscious" experience; for, exactly how a person can be "aware" of an existent without the presence of that existent in him, is very difficult to see. But this does not at all exclude an abundance of unconscious happenings that prepare for and support conscious knowing and which can lead to "intelligent reactions" without recollectable consciousness. (Concerning the problems of Extra-Sensory Perception and Extra-Rational knowledge: *Occultism, *Mysticism; *Irrational, *Intuition).

AW

KNOWLEDGE, PRINCIPLES OF

The Latin word *"principium"* (*Principle) means the beginning or source from which something issues forth. In contradistinction to the principles of *existence, the expression "principles of knowledge" signifies what is first and most fundamental in our knowledge. (According to Aristotle, what is first in the order of existence is often only deduced in the realm of human knowledge.) Thus, the first, unmediated knowledge contents, the fundamental axioms, from which inductive and deductive reasoning take their start, are called "principles." In a more common, narrow sense the word is restricted to immediate or almost immediate universal propositions. A fundamental axiom in this sense affirms something of all the individuals contained in a totality that is expressed by the subject, and it affirms it of them with absolute *necessity: e. g.: Two things equal to a third are also (necessarily) equal to each other. Such propositions are known and used in mathematics (usually termed "axioms"), in *metaphysics and in *logic.

The critical study of human knowledge investigates the validity of the fundamental principles; the questions it asks in this area are closely related to the psychological question of the origin of knowledge. *Empiricism tries to understand all universal propositions as inductively acquired generalizations of particular experiences (*Induction). In reply we must say: In this way the unconditional necessity and universality of these propositions cannot be established with certainty. There is even less validity for that view according to which fundamental principles are based on some kind of an agreement (as *conventionalism* says) or, without the help of an insight, are merely accepted *postulates only on the basis of practical necessity. Even if, going along with Kant, one finds the fundamental principles only in the categories of the transcendental subject (*Critical Philosophy), their validity in the order of reality will not be guaranteed. Rather, we grasp these fundamental principles in an a priori knowledge (*A Priori) which in a special sense is called "insight." This insight takes place in one glance directed at both conceptual contents that are given in the subject and the predicate of the pertinent propositioh — a glance that relates both of them to each other. In such a case one discovers either that the predicate represents a part of the subject-concept, or that the content of the predicate, although not yet seen to be contained in the subject, still follows with necessity from the content of the subject. In the first case one speaks of an *explanatory* or strictly *analytical judgment* (*Analysis; e. g.: A triangle has three sides); in the latter case one speaks of an *a priori amplifying judgment* that can simply be called *synthetic a priori* (*Synthesis; e. g.: The adjacent angles of a parallelogram are equal). At least in the case of the synthetic a priori judgment it is required for the possibility of an insight that the contents

214

KNOWLEDGE, THEORY OF

of the subject and the predicate be grasped not merely in a purely empirical way (*Experience), but they must be apprehended essentially (*Essential knowledge). Therefore, a priori intuited fundamental principles are neither *falsifiable* by means of experience nor are they *verifiable* in their necessity and universality.

JdV

KNOWLEDGE, SOURCE OF

The source of knowledge is that from which true and certain *knowledge, such as is found in the *judgment, can be drawn. The source should be distinguished from the mere condition of knowledge, e. g.: the circumstance of being awake. With regard to *truth, in a primary sense (1) the sources of knowledge are the objects themselves (objective sources of knowledge) and with regard to *certitude they are also the corresponding knowing powers (subjective sources of knowledge), since the knowledge of truth is possible only through reflection on the act of knowing itself (*Knowledge, Theory of). In a derived sense (2), a source of knowledge is also everything in which the objects and the knowing subject, before he makes a definitive judgment, are given. Accordingly, a distinction is made between the external sources of knowledge (such as the testimony of another) and the internal. To these also pertain internal and external *experience and *thinking in its threefold activity of forming concepts (*Analysis, *Synthesis), *judgment (immediate insight), and *inferences (*Deduction, *Induction). — The sources of knowledge are also called the *means of knowledge* (in order to reach the goal of knowledge) and the *criteria of knowledge* (in order to distinguish true from false knowledge).

JS

KNOWLEDGE, THEORY OF

In a wide sense the theory of knowledge (1) includes both the psychological investigations into the becoming and essence of human *knowledge and the critical study of its validity; one can also add to it the *metaphysics of knowledge* which considers human knowing in the total context of everything existing. In a narrower sense the theory of knowledge (2) is the same as the critical study of knowledge. As such, in general, it is the philosophical investigation of the objective *validity of our knowledge. In contrast to *logic, it considers not only the conditions of validity which are based on the relations of the thought-contents to each other, but it also poses the decisive question about the "objective" validity of the thought-contents, i. e., about their validity in reference to the *object or, if only valid thinking is to be termed "knowledge," the question about the possibility of knowledge as such. Since the drive to know of the uneducated man is naturally ordered to the existent, at least as the principal object of knowledge, and since, on the other hand, the validity of the knowledge of things is *truth and the knowledge of the truth is *certitude, from the very beginning the question can be posed in a more definite form as the question about the truth and certitude of our knowledge. Thus, the theory of knowledge is the philosophical investigation of our mind's *capacity for truth* and at the same time it is a study of the *limits of knowledge*: Can we in any way be certain of the truth of our knowledge and, if we can, what is the extent of this possibility?

In the historical development of philosophy these questions were not asked at the beginning, but at first with an original trust in the power of reason questions were directed to things. It was only after the confusing contrariness of opinions that the great difficulty of the task became clear, so that there followed the reflection on the conditions of truth and certitude in the knowing subject. Special studies of this kind are not lacking even in ancient times and in the Middle Ages; thus, we can mention Aristotle's theory of abstraction, Augustine's refutation of *skepticism by appealing to self-consciousness, the dispute over universals in the Middle Ages. But it is only since Descartes that there have been orderly whole treatises on the question. In the 17th and 18th centuries these investigations were dominated by the opposition between *rationalism and *empiricism. Kant's *critical philosophy tries to combine these opposites into an inner unity but only by partially abandoning a realistic view of knowledge. Since that time the opposition between *realism and *idealism has above all determined the discussions centering around the theory of knowledge.

The *epistemological method* one employs often already implies a prior choice for a definite direction. For example, if one chooses a purely psychological method, then that usually means that the validity of knowledge is made ultimately dependent on the normal working of the processes of knowledge, i. e., *psychologism and thus *relativism. Conversely, a purely logical (or "transcendental") method, which attempts to arrive at a solution by merely separating the necessary from the contingent in the contents of consciousness, is intrinsically connected with an idealistic view of knowledge. If truth in a realistic sense is going to be grasped at all, then the theory of knowledge must look for a case where the agreement between thinking and existence is immediately experienced and where therefore the existent itself immediately manifests itself. Long before Descartes, Augustine saw that our knowledge of our own existence, thinking and loving (*Consciousness) is precisely this privileged case. On this fact rests the absolute necessity of the "introspective method" or the method of self-reflection for the validity of the theory of knowledge.

KNOWLEDGE, THEORY OF

The theory of knowledge has a fundamental importance for all sciences, even for the other branches of philosophy, because it investigates the conditions of validity of all the sciences. And it has no dispute with *metaphysics about its claim to be a basic science, since, at least in its fundamental aspects, it is nothing else but *fundamental metaphysics* which has been brought to reflex consciousness. — The following are synonymous terms for the "theory of knowledge": *gnoseology* (= the theory of knowledge), *noetics* (= the theory of thinking), *epistemology* (= the theory of knowing), *criteriology* (= the theory of the criteria or norms of truth).

JdV

L

LANGUAGE

Language means: (1) the universal human activity of shaping a system of *signs according to definite, generally accepted rules of association; and (2) the historically and socially conditioned forms of human speech — the particular languages. In every language the following distinctions must be made: (a) the sum total of all the signs and forms which the one speaking can make use of; (b) the mental-bodily activity of speaking; (c) the uttered and heard word. Language in its original sense is the phonetic representation of thoughts. The bearer of language is man, who alone among all visible beings has thoughts which he can communicate to others, and who alone among all spiritual beings is capable of expressing them through sensible sounds. Therefore, language reflects the bodily-spiritual essence of man and follows its laws. As sound, language exists only while it is being produced. Although speaking, even abstracting from the ideas communicated, is always a certain expression of the soul of the one speaking, still the principal purpose of speech (as distinguished from other forms of expression) is not to be just an expression of the soul; rather, its prime purpose is the representation and communication of ideas. While a figurative representation imitates the intended object according to its sensible form and thus is immediately understood by every viewer, language does not make the object itself present, but just its idea and it renders this idea present not by a picture but by a sign that stands for it. Therefore, it will be understood only by the person who knows the *sense and thereby the meaning of the sign. Originally, of course, language also worked with immediately intelligible, pictorial modes of representation. The connection of a sensible (basically indifferent) sound with a definite sense, i. e., with a reference to its *meaning* (its realm of objects), is possible because in man there is no separation between sense intuition and spiritual thoughts; for, ideas are derived from sense intuition by means of *abstraction and they always retain a certain relationship to the sensible schema. Moreover, the pointing gesture permits man to establish connections, communicable to others, between the articulated sound and

218

the sensed object; through repeated use these connections can be fixed and agreed upon. The presupposition for the mutual understanding of the ones speaking is their common bodily-spiritual nature and especially the identity of the object thought.

The question about the origin of language is related to man's basic capacity for speech or to his developed language skill. Language capacity is given with man's nature. Language skill includes the discovery and first use of sensible signs as substitutes for concepts; it also includes the further construction of a system of signs. How man originally acquired his language skill is something we can only surmise from the way in which man now develops his language skill. — We can speak of *animal languages* only in a very limited sense, since animals cannot express ideas nor can they communicate their feelings and desires through concepts. (On pre-logical language: *Social Psychology).

The phonetic symbols of language can be replaced by other signs, for example, by writing which substitutes the more permanent marks of writing for fleeting phonetic symbols. However, the representation of ideas by writing can take place without going through the medium of sound as, for example, in the Chinese symbols for ideas. — The basic form of sound is the *syllable*; the basic form of the language symbol that carries a meaning is the *word*; the basic form of language itself is the *sentence*. It takes a sentence to express a complete idea. It is only from the language situation and from the context of the sentence that the words get their definite meaning. To a certain extent this also holds true of the sentence insofar as it is a part of a larger whole.

We find language (1) in a rich variety of particular languages = language (2), which differ from each other consideraby both in vocabulary and in grammar. The possibility of translating what is expressed in one language into another language, is basically always open, but in many ways it is still limited, especially with regard to the always-present emotional overtones. — For precisely defined materials, *universal* or *formalized* languages of great exactness can be constructed; this has been done in mathematics and *symbolic logic, which serve only for the transmission of concepts and abstract almost entirely from the human dimension. Since statements can also be made about the natural or formalized languages, the *meta-languages* (which are possible on several levels) are distinguished from the object-language; with the help of such meta-languages semantic antinomies can be avoided. — Although language is not the indispensable condition of spiritual knowledge, still it is a great help towards the preciseness and clarity of conceptual thinking. — Since language arose out of the need of the individual as a member of the community, it is neither the discovery of one person nor could it possibly be preserved or developed outside of community. A whole people is the creative, organic and natural language community; and conversely, language plays an important role in the growth of a people. Without language, neither human society nor any higher level of culture would be possible. From the importance of language for the whole community there is a resulting obligation on each individual with regard to language; in particular, each person is obligated not to use language in a way that goes against its nature — which is to express ideas truthfully.

WB

LANGUAGE, PHILOSOPHY OF

Philosophy's concern with *language is as old as philosophy itself. Even among the ancients there was an opinion that language is based on an arbitrary agreement among men (Sophists); this view was opposed to that of the Stoics who held that language is something naturally given. Plato and Aristotle took a middle position. The philosophy of language as a special discipline has been known only since the work of W. von Humboldt (1767-1835). It was especially furthered by comparative philology (the exposition of language function in general and of the essential structure of language) and by empirical psychology (investigation of the elements of language and their psycho-physical conditions). — The most important tasks of the philosophy of language are the clarification of the relationships between thinking and speaking (priority and influence), between the expressive and representative functions of language; the explanation of the psycho-physical conditions of speech, the role of the individual and the community in the growth of a language, the relationship between common language-types and the structure of the particular language; the investigation of the temporally first sources of a language and the present new production of it in the child and the constant elaboration of it. — Views on the philosophy of language diverge chiefly over the question of the relationship between thought and speech. While the older philosophy of language agreed in the recognition of the independence and priority of thought over speech, but disagreed in explaining it (e. g., language as caused by thought for the purpose of communication: empirical direction; language as the fully adequate appearance of thought: idealistic direction), some modern thinkers see thought as absorbed by speech (G. Ipsen) or as arising from it (J. Stenzel).

WB

LAXISM

Laxism in the doctrine according to which a trifling doubt concerning the existence of some law does away with the obligation to obey it; this view is opposed to *rigorism. Laxism has not been defended directly as a theory, but indirectly a certain danger was occasioned in dispute concerning doubts of conscience (*Conscience).   Laxism is objectionable because a slight doubt cannot remove the obligation that adheres to a law certainly known as such.   In the past, *probabilism has been unjustly accused of being a form of laxism.   As an essential presupposition for the validity of its principle, probabilism demands that the reasons which permit a person to act contrary to a known law must be sound and serious.

JoS

LEISURE

Leisure has to do with man's use of time when he is neither working nor sleeping.   It is a concept whose meaning ultimately depends on one's philosophy of life, esp. one's philosophy of man or anthropology.   For the materialist, the positivist and the pragmatist, leisure is "free time" that is a break from the routine of work or that is used to improve the quality of human life (e. g., hobbies, art, music, sport, etc.).   Karl Marx says that, in Capitalism, leisure is a period of recuperation from the alienating effect of work, but it is *for* work, so that man can work better. In antiquity and in the Christian tradition (also in some aspects of the oriental religions) leisure has been related to the dignity of the human person, to the transcendence of man over matter and beasts, and to the affirmation of the wholeness of the world and God as the source of the world.

Leisure is usually opposed to work.   Work is primarily human activity that is necessary for man's biological sustenance; it is *useful*, planned and in some sense economically profitable.   Because of man's unchanging, constant physical needs, work is always necessary (at least for most men). Leisure, however, is human activity that celebrates the goodness and beauty of the world in some way; it affirms reality and man's solidarity with it, and it proclaims man's spirituality and freedom; it is activity engaged in for its own sake — not for any other, gainful purpose (though economic profit may accidentally result from it or be a subordinate purpose).   Thus Leisure is not for the sake of work.   Either receptivity or activity may predominate in leisure depending upon the level of contemplation involved.   In a very true sense, therefore, leisure is *useless* activity that affirms man's basic superiority over matter and strives in some sense to imitate and grasp God — the Absolute in whose image man is formed; for, like God, man is self-directive, autonomous and capable of fully gratuitous actions (love).   Accordingly, as Josef Pieper has shown, the foundation of true leisure is religion (= affirmation of a personal God, divine worship, sacrifice, etc.).   For, if man is not ordered to the absolute mystery of a transcendent God, he is then unalterably tied to the here and now in such a way that all "useless" activity such as leisure is meaningless and everything man does must necessarily be utilitarian — his activity must be either work or for the sake of work or in the service of some type of atheistic "humanism."

Since man is a finite spirit in matter and since, therefore, as a unity all of his activities share (more or less) in the characteristics of both mind and matter, it follows, as Karl Rahner has pointed out, that all human activity is a combination of both leisure and work, in varying degrees. Different activities, therefore, are thought of as "leisure" or "work" depending upon which characteristic is paramount. Thus, gardening for a professor can be true leisure, while a gardner may find his leisure in reading one of the professor's books. In both cases it is the subjective attitude of free choice and self-determination that makes the given activity "leisurely" and not the amount of physical effort involved; for, both are (or at least can be) affirming their transcendence and spiritual dignity — they are "above" work, at least for a time.

For the men of the second half of the 20th century, play and sport are important ingredients of their "leisure time." Play is the exercise of human powers for the sheer joy of using these powers; play can be either an individual activity or a group activity. Though it may be very strenuous, play is not work since it does not aim at producing goods and services to sustain life. An important part of play is sport which involves performance, competition (frequently), social growth and the advance of the brotherhood of man (e. g., the Olympic Games).

KB

LIE

A lie is a consciously untrue affirmation which usually results in the deception of one's neighbor. All forms of lying are intrinsically not allowed because they militate against honesty and faithfulness in the community and because reasonable exceptions with definite limitations cannot be determined. Hypocrisy or pretending to be something one is not is equivalent to a lie. Also to be rejected is the *strict mental reservation* (*reservatio stricte mentalis*), which means that a literally false statement is restricted to some true sense but this true sense is not manifested in any external way. Equivocation, however, is not a lie because it contains both a true and a false sense according to general verbal usage. The same holds for the *broad mental reservation* (*reservatio late mentalis*) in which the true meaning is not evident from the linguistic usage, but can be grasped from the particular circumstances. In both forms the truth is uttered even though it is obscure. The immediate result is that the listener is left in the dark. Both of these forms of speech may be employed, not whenever one feels like it (for this would have consequences similar to the consequences of lying) but in order to protect legitimate *secrets*; this holds true especially when there would be a danger of revealing the secrets if one attemped to remain silent or to avoid the question entirely. Therefore, the lie is not a natural means that may be used to protect necessary secrets. Thus the distinction proposed by Grotius and others between a lie (= unjustified deception) and *falsiloquium* (= justified deception) is untenable and contrary to the virtue of *truthfulness*.

JoS

LIFE

Life means immanent activity (*actio immanens*) in contrast to the kind of activity that is directed outwards to the transformation of other things (*actio transiens*); this latter type of activity is characteristic of lifeless things. Life is evident to us in the world of nature in the sprouting, growing, blossoming and fruit-producing of plants; in the growing, reproducing and self-motion of animals; and it also appears over and above the individual organisms in the development of various species — a process that has been producing ever new forms in the course of millions of years. As it were from the inside, life appears to us in our own *experience, in conscious seeing, thinking, feeling, striving; of course, the relative intensity of these activities depends upon the freshness and power of the bodily organs. In both cases life reveals itself as a constant becoming and an inexhaustible, many-faceted self-development that proceeds from the inside; this stands in sharp contrast to the rigidity and opaqueness of lifeless bodies, especially machines (*Cybernetics).

Therefore, it is somewhat understandable that life appears to the advocates of *life philosophy as a mysterious, creative power that has been coursing through the world since primeval times; they look upon life as an essentially irrational power that escapes all conceptual definition; but as constant becoming it is opposed to the immutability of existence. *Spirit, then, is thought of either as the last stage in the development of corporeal life or as the adversary of life; for, they say, it only oppresses life with its rigid concepts and results in sheer mechanical order.

However, there are some serious misunderstandings involved in this position. It is certain that even the vegetative life of plants, because it is an immanent activity, essentially surpasses the mechanical activity of inorganic bodies; but this inner activity is still dependent on the assimilation of outside matter (nutrition) and in reproducing it strives to bring forth other living beings like itself. The full richness of this life is restricted in every species to narrowly limited possibilities of change and it exhausts

223

itself in withering and death. Sensible life labors under similar limitations, even though in the realm of interiority it essentially surpasses simple vegetative life through its dull, primitive *consciousness. But all forms of vegetative and sensible life, as organic life tied to corporeal organs, in comparison with spirit (which is free of matter) is an alienated form of life, since it runs its course in the spatio-temporal dimension. In contrast to the wealth of this life as it manifests itself in the many shapes of man's internal and external *culture, organic life is shabby indeed, not only in the individual living thing but also in the whole of nature, in spite of its abundance. The opposite view could only arise on the supposition that one looks at spirit in the sense of a dry *rationalism only as a calculating, schematizing intellect, and at the same time ignores its essential profundity: its power that embraces all existence, its search for value that is open to all goodness, its free self-determination in the face of all limited values, and especially its immortality. All of our spiritual life, however, (just like all created life) remains *self-motion*, i.e., an interior activity leading to a change and perfection of one's own existence; so it seems to us that immutability cannot easily be coupled with true life. Nevertheless, we must think of *God's life* as somehow immutable, precisely because it is life itself and therefore the infinite fullness of life. Obviously, though, his life should not be thought of in terms of the inertness of a stone, but as a living activity that is eternally fresh, eternally self-sufficient. The necessity of progress and so of change in our lives is based on the fact that we are always lacking something of the fullness of life; and at the same time change always means a dependence on the external sources of life and therefore a diminution of the pure interiority of life.

Since plant life is essentially superior to the activity of inorganic bodies that is directed outward, it cannot be explained simply on the basis of the powers of material bodies; thus, it presupposes a *life principle that is in some sense immaterial. Therefore, the *origin of life* cannot be made intelligible through the powers of matter, but only through the immediate intervention of the creator of nature. Similarly, the essentially higher levels of life cannot be derived in a causal sequence from the lower levels; in particular, spiritual life is not the product of organic life. — On the meaning of human life see *Man*.

JdV

LIFE PHILOSOPHY

Life philosophy in everyday speech means (1) the way or view of life which tends towards a practical ordering of things. Ethics as a science of the goal and norms of ethical life can also be called a life philosophy (2). Therefore, those philosophical systems are usually called "life philosophy"

(3) which give a dominant place to practical ethics and views of life, as for example *stoicism and *epicureanism.

A distinction should be made between these practical forms of life philosophy and the life philosophy that appeared about 1900 (4); this latter view attempted to establish the priority of the life-concept even in the realm of theory. It was prepared for by the life-concept of Goethe and the romantics and set loose by the predominance of physical science and the advancing technology of the 19th century. But what is known as "life philosophy" is not a unified movement. In general, its advocates see the real basis and content of reality in "life" as something dynamic, changing and developing; and it is seen in contrast to everything static, mechanical and conceptually closed. But what they understand by "life" in more precise detail, is often very difficult to determine. Heinrich Rickert distinguishes two chief direction which, however, often overlap. One conceives of life more in biological terms and expands those categories to the whole of reality. One then speaks of *biologism. The other direction thinks of life in terms of inner experience; this is never just knowledge — much less is it abstract, scientific knowledge; rather it is the full use of all the emotions, a constant stream that can never be perfectly represented by "rigid" concepts. All culture is then interpreted or "understood" on the basis of this inner experience (*Human Sciences, *Understanding).

We find the expression "philosophy of life" already in Fr. Schlegel (1827) as a flight from Hegel and a turning towards inner life-experience. The work of Soren Kierkegaard is in the same direction; his work influenced both *dialectical theology and *existential philosophy. The cultural criticism of Nietzsche had perhaps the greatest after-effect, for he bluntly set life and experience over against existence and knowledge. For him the greatest good is the fullness and power of life; it finds its perfect expression in his "superman." Knowledge is supposed to serve life. One cannot raise the question about truth or falsehood; the decisive thing is whether or not something furthers life (*Pragmatism). Related to these thoughts, but transformed from the individual to the race or nation, are the views of the proponents of *race philosophy* (Joseph Arthur de Gobineau, Houston S. Chamberlain, Alfred Rosenberg): race is not only a complex of external characteristics that can be transmitted, but it is also the expression of the soul (of a race) which is the inner side of the race. Race is the ultimate reality and the highest value that our thinking and questioning can arrive at. All culture, art, science, religion and history must be understood and evaluated from the point of view of race (Rosenberg). Thus, there are no criteria above race (*Relativism).

Henri Bergson was influential in France and beyond her borders in the sense of "life philosophy" through his doctrine of the *élan vital* (or the centrifugal force of life) and the *évolution créatrice* or the creative drive

225

of development; this drive in its first stage moves up to the instinct of animals, in a second stage to human intelligence. It creates human communities and social morality. Beyond that, in the great prophetic figures of dynamic religion it rises to religious mysticism and produces a morality binding on all mankind. Abstract, conceptual thought contributes to the external, technical control of nature; but a more profound grasp of reality is possible only through "intuition" which must make use of flexible, overlapping, metaphorical "concepts" in order to represent it.

It cannot be denied that life philosophy stood up strongly against many abuses of a rationalistic, mechanistic culture. But it is also certain that it went much too far in its criticism. For, it is not a question of *existence or *becoming; rather, it is necessary to have a depth of comprehension that does justice to both realities. Certainly, everything is rooted in the reality of God who is absolute *life. But it does not follow from this that there is just one thing that includes both living and non-living. Certainly, the richness of the concrete and constant change are beyond the grasp of mere concepts. But concepts do reach into a depth which supports concrete reality and change, and they join themselves to concrete experience in order to give meaning to it. See also *Rationalism, Intellectualism, Intuitionism*.

WB

LIFE PRINCIPLE

The life principle is the substantial source of the immanent activity of *organisms — something that stands in sharp contrast to everything inorganc. Following Aristotle, the vitalistic philosophers of nature call this immaterial principle, which brings about organic wholeness through final causality, "entelechy." Entelechy can be understood from different points of view: (1) as the principle of a species or as the idea that incorporates or manifests itself in matter; (2) as the essential *form (*morphē*) which, together with prime matter, constitutes a living thing in existence (*Hylemorphism); (3) as the heart and foundation (first *Act) of all animation and so given the name of *soul (which is not necessarily conscious). — Depending upon how a person thinks of the union of the life principle with matter, this life prnciple is conceived either as a complete substance in itself (an *assisting form*), which joins itself to matter only in the area of activity and therefore does not form a substantial unity. Or the life principle is something substantially incomplete which only becomes a natural, living whole by informing matter which is also substantially incomplete.

Vitalism has worked out the proof for the existence of a life principle in organisms. A valid philosophical interpretation of many observations and experiments (Driesch, Spemann, etc.) has shown that "a machine theory of life" (i. e., the automatism of any kind of physico-chemical system) cannot explain the primary wholeness of the organism. This wholeness expresses itself (1) in the development to a full organism even from a part of the bud or embryo in an early ontogenetic stage or in the combination of several embryos or in the artificial mutation of the genes. The immaterial nature of the life principle also flows from this. At the moment of separation there was only one whole and therefore also just one real principle of the wholeness; by means of simple separation the organism, even as a whole, is multiplied. If a mere bodily structure after the fashion of a machine, i. e., a material system extended and differentiated in space, were the basis of the wholeness, then this structure would have to be just as completely present in each part as it is in the whole. But that contradicts the spatial nature of a machine. Therefore, there is an immaterial principle of wholeness present in every organism; in every organism this principle is actually one, but potentially many, i. e., potentially it is capable of being multiplied insofar as it can be multiplied through a simple process of division. Such an immaterial principle of organic wholeness is called a "life principle." Embryo-development also cannot be directed just by some mechanical system; for, on the one hand, this system would have to remain the exact same individual, since in the course of development the individuality remains fully constant, and at the same time it would have to become another, since the successively different stages of development (e. g., stages of metamorphosis in insects) demand different machines as causes; such a machine is impossble. The same thing follows (2) from the facts of propagation and heredity, regulation and restitution and (3) from the finalized behavior of organisms not only on a basis of stimulation-response, but on the basis of the fundamental meaning of biological activity.

AH

LOGIC

The object of logic is *thinking, not considered as the attribute or activity of an existing *subject (in this sense thinking is the object of *psychology), but looked at from the point of view of the relationships existing between ideas themselves which can be attributed in the same sense to many individuals. Therefore, it is erroneous to see in logic a part of psychology, as *psychologism does. Thought-contents can be studied in themselves, according to their inner structure, according to their form (as *Concepts, *Judgments, *Inferences) and according to their mutually necessary relationships (logical laws) — this is the task of pure or formal logic; or they can be studied according to their relationship to the objects they represent — a task which is at times assigned to "real" or "material" logic. The latter science is better known as epistemology or the *theory of *knowledge*. Formal logic or logic in the stricter sense looks only to the *correctness* or logical consistency of thinking (*laws of thinking*); the theory of knowledge considers correspondence with reality or *truth; and methodology concentrates on the ways of finding the truth. The heart of formal logic is the doctrine on inference. Concepts and judgments are important in logic primarily as the elements of an inference. Moreover, logic is basically a theoretical science, even though it also includes some practical directions, as for example the rules of a good definition. Man is naturally ordered to correct thinking (*natural logic*); but he has special need of *scientific logic* in order to examine his thought processes in difficult or controversial cases.

Logic has been frequently divided into three parts: analysis of the concept (word), the judgment (proposition), and the inference. Even Aristotle, the originator of scentific logic, in his treatment of inference goes into the more general questions of *science and *method as such. Modern logicians often add a fourth main divison of logic in which they treat the whole question of the nature of *inducton, the formation of concepts in the physical sciences and in the *human sciences. Much of this material belongs also in material logic. — Kant's *transcendental logic* is a special form of the theory of knowledge (*Critical Philosophy). Since for Hegel the content of thought and the object of thought are the same thing, then for him logic must consequently be also ontology (*German Idealism). — Many make a distinction between *classical logic* and *modern* logic (= *Symbolic Logic*).

WB

LOGICISM

The word "logicism" refers to *logos or *logic. Logicism (1) means that all things are moments of the self-development of the logos or stages of development towards the logos = *Panlogicism*. In reference to logic, logicism means in the theory of knowledge either (2) the doctrine that the logical constitutes an independent sphere alongside the real and the psychic = *Logical Transcendentalism* (*Objective Reality), or (3) the doctrine that deduces the whole content of knowledge from the formal thinking of logic (e. g., Herman Cohen). In psychology, logicism (4) is the view which attempts to reduce independent psychic functions (e. g., feelings, acts of the will) to acts of thought. — Hegel's philosophy, which is often characterized as a form of logicism, is so only as logicism (1), not as logicism (3).

WB

LOGOS

Logos means (1) speech, the *word*, the meaningful word. The name is then transferred (2) to the *meaning itself, the concept, the thought content, the inner "word" which finds expression in the external word. In particular, the content that supplies the *ground or reason for something is called the "logos" (3). Sometimes even the whole realm of thoughts, ideas and spirit is called "logos" (4), in contrast to the realm of material existents or in contrast to the realm of organic, corporeal life (*bios*), or in distinction to the realm of moral behavior (*ethos*); the word is meant in this sense, when, for example, one speaks of the "superiority of the logos." — Everything that belongs to this area of thought can, in a wider sense, be called "logical." Usually, however, the word is used in a narrower sense for those purely conceptual relationships of the thought-contents among themselves; these arise because of the abstract mode of human thinking, are not found as such in the actual existent things and therefore are beings of the mind, as for example the *identity between the subject and the predicate; the logical in this narrower sense is the object of *logic. Thinking itself is said to be logical when it abides by the laws which are based on the above-mentioned relationships between thought-contents; otherwise it is *illogical*. On the other hand, the word "alogical" is used in the sense of something that is foreign to thinking or spirit; thus, feelings and desires are said to be alogical insofar as they are removed from the direction of thought (*Irrational).

Then the *idea which has entered, as it were, into reality and even into the world of bodies, is called the logos (5); this is conceived of as the shape and form of things determined by ideas, the structure that gives them inner meaning. Through this meaningful structure and order the physical world becomes the *cosmos*; in contrast to a meaningless *chaos*. The philosopher understands logos in this sense when he speaks of the "logical structure of reality" (*Truth). — The world of ideas does not exist in itself, but only in a real, thinking spirit; likewise, the intelligent structure of the physical world presupposes a real, spiritual origin. This spiritual foundation of the world (bearing all ideas in itself) also received in ancient philosophy the name of "logos." Heraclitus and similarly the Stoics understood this logos (6) as the Reason of the World that permeates everything (*World Soul). For others, such as Philo, the logos (7) was an intermediary being between God and the world which was used by God in the creation of the world. John the Evangelist confronts both of these views in the beginning of his gospel with the Christian teaching of the consubstantial, incarnate Son of God. With unheard of daring he takes up the old watchword of Greek philosophy — Logos — and calls the Son of God the only true logos (8). Since Augustine Catholic theology has interpreted the logos-name in the sense of the generation of the Son through the knowledge of the Father: the Father speaks his whole being and the fullness of his ideas in the Son as his word.

JdV

LONERGANISM

Lonerganism is the philosophical approach developed by Bernard J. F. Lonergan (1904 -   ); it can be described as a philosophic stance which requires of the philosopher a self-attention of scientific dimensions. In order to convey briefly some notion of Lonerganism it seems best to express here directly the orientation or viewpoint given by that stance.

The scientific dimensions of the enterprise of self-attention can be indicated best by adverting to the fact that the procedure required may be accurately specified as generalized empirical *method. In empirical method the attention of the subject, the scientist, is on data of some particular kind, data on plants for instance. The scientist moves through experiment and insight to a formulated *understanding of the data, which he seeks to verify. The procedure of empirical method is a spiral process from data through insight to ever more adequate verified theory. In generalized empirical method the subject takes as data his or her own conscious activities, centrally the activity of understanding, and proceeds through experiments in insight and through insight into insight to an ever more adequate formulation of what it is to understand. The experiments in attention to insight or understanding must range over all areas in which understanding is operative if the enterprise is to result in adequate viewpoint. So, self-attention is called for, not only in such elementary procedures as solving geometry problems, but also in the complex area of interpersonal understanding, in which area the basic norm for dialogue may be summed up in the phrase "be understanding."

But one may question the possibility of generalized empirical method: for, is not empirical enquiry limited by the orientation of intellect to phantasm? Still, insight is into phantasm, and, insofar as it is, it too can become data for empirical investigation.

Further, one may admit the possibility of generalized empirical method, but fail to acknowledge the dimensions of the enterprise. To return to an analogue already suggested, adverting to insight and describing various types of insight is no more the fruit of generalized empirical method than adverting to and describing various types of plants is adequate biology. In either case one is only at the beginning. But there is an evident difference in the two beginnings. The beginner in biology is to himself manifestly such, for there is a well-developed science of biology available in the culture and stretching before him as a projected habitual understanding. The beginner in generalized empirical method, however, lacks the evidence of the fruits of scientific self-appropriation in the culture and so can scarcely appreciate the dimensions of the personal project. So, for example, the beginner who is also a physicist is opening up through the methodological stance of self-attention the possibility of transforming the meaning of his or her physics, of reorientating it in a wider context of a personal horizon of cognitive self-possession. Contemporary talk of the meaning of physics regularly lies outside that horizon at best being descriptive of the insights and methods of physics — where the word descriptive is used for the stages of scientific procedure prior to explanation or theory. That talk only serves to expose a complex of fundamental methodological problems in relativity, in quantum theory, in statistical physics. Only talk mediated by cognitive self-possession can adequately resolve such issues.

Here a difference should be noted between sciences such as physics or biology and the *human sciences. Unlike physics, a human science involves intrinsically the contribution of generalized empirical method: for, the object of human science understands, and to omit an understanding of understanding from the science is to relegate a central section of the data to the area of mere description. Indeed, to be adequate, the human sciences require that the context of self-appropriation be enlarged to include the horizon of *theology and *Faith: we can only hint at this in the conclusion.

Scientific self-possession mediates a transformation not only of science but also of human living, not only of the talk of physicists but also of the talk of sociability which is a form of human play. But such mediation is possible only insofar as generalized empirical method becomes a communal undertaking. Historically it would seem that Aristotle, Augustine and Aquinas all made use of introspective understanding, but none of them raised it to the level of a culturally available scientific technique. For the past century in philosophy the *subject, the self, has become increasingly the focus of attention of the thinker, but again such attention has not blossomed into a scientific technique. It tends to remain aesthetic, dramatic. In contrast, the technique of generalized empirical method, precisely by being radically intellectualist, shifts the philosopher's discourse to a new horizon and mediates a liberation of the aesthetic and the dramatic within a more precisely differentiated consciousness.

While that shift of discourse and liberation of psyche and differentiation of consciousness lie largely in the future, the generic structure of the shift may be identified and basic invariant elements of the shift can be formulated. The generic structure of the shift is from cognitive and affective possession of the object by the subject to a self-possession of the subject. So it is that what is primary in the Eternal Subjects — self-understanding — is secondary in the human subject. From another point of view one way note that the shift is related to the two different types of intelligibility; there is the intelligibility which is merely intelligible, and there is the intelligibilty which is not only intelligible but is also intelligent. It is the merely intelligible that initially falls scientifically under human wonder. Only later does the subject's wonder center on the intelligible which is also intelligent — the subject's own intelligence. The procession of the planets is a less elusive object of investigation than the procession of the inner word.

Fundamentally the human self-possession involved in the shift is possession on the level of the *Question. Not the pure question directly: it is only insofar as answers are found in common sense, physics, sociology, etc. that self-possession can be adequately pursued. Through the mediation of such answers with concomitant self-attentive effort the meaning of the Question is thematically revealed to the questioner. The Question is limitless in intention and it is structured in operation. The threefold operative cognitional structure is manifested elementarily through a self-appropriation of the generic structure of the procedure of empirical science from instances to theory to verification. On the side of the subject there is correspondingly data-orientated wonder in its two complementary modes of quest for concept and quest for judgment. Obviously of central importance to the appropriation of the structure is the appreciation of the manner in which direct insight mediates conception and reflective insight mediates judgment and commitment — commitment however constituting a fourth level of consciousness which we cannot elaborate on here. Much of contemporary philosophic discourse overlooks this mediation so that the intelligibility of the intelligible emanation of concept and judgment is excluded as an object of investigation. Yet implicit in all such discourse is an assumption of the structure of questioning intelligence, and that implicit performative assumption grounds the dialectic of content and performance which can enable any thinker to move to a horizon of cognitive self-possession and can force the subject within that horizon to more adequate authentic nescience. This dialectic can be illustrated in the case of the basic Lonerganist position on objectivity and the real: the real is what is to be reached by correct understanding. Insofar as this position is denied the content of the denial is in conflict with the denier's intelligent argument: the dialogue of denial presupposes that correct understanding is what in fact is relevant. Central to the Lonerganist's viewpoint is the fact that the critical problem is not whether I know but what goes on when I know, nor is it a matter of moving out from the subject, but a matter of correctly conceiving the movement from the pure question to objective knowledge of either subject or object. The Lonerganist's position is, then, an invulnerable assumption that the structured known corresponds isomorphically to structured knowing.

Moreover, that structure has the complexity of a world view. Generalized empirical method grounds isomorphically the subject's metaphysics, an appropriated integral heuristic structure of being, proportionate and transcendent. That metaphysics involves the affirmation of six basic elements in proportionate being which constitutes a revivification, through the cognitive approach, of Aquinas' matter, form and esse: six, because of the triple structure of knowing and the two types of what-insight, the insight yielding correlations and the insight related to the notion of *thing*. But the metaphysics has a complexity which accounts for coincidental aggregates of events, statistical science, levels of genera and species, development and dialectic. The subject is thus enabled to envisage a world whose heuristic form is that of emergent probability, the realization of a conditioned series of recurrence-schemes and things in accord with successive schedules of probability. But the subject with such a view in the present world, if he is psychologically integral, is radically open to further questions regarding the concrete facts of history: the limitless question takes in the meaning of the world as religious.

Concretely, Lonerganism emerged in a theological context. One may trace it in part to the influence of Newman and Aquinas on Lonergan, in part to the need for methodological revival of theology in the context of the Faith of Lonergan. In that wider context the self-appropriation becomes the appropriation of the Faith-ful subject, continual intellectual conversion through dialectic becomes continual religious conversion, theology becomes a reflection on personal conversion which is permanently incomplete and authentic nescience becomes repentant quest in the slow dialectic symbiosis of grace and nature through which God makes man both self-possessively and self-transcendently understanding.

PM

LOVE

Love is the value-affirming and the value-creating primordial power of the willing spirit. Considered essentially and experientially, love is an attitude of the will; it is the affirming (recognizing, creative, union-seeking), all-embracing deportment of the spiritual soul with regard to *persons as real or potential subjects of spiritual values and also with regard to these values themselves. Thus love leads the individual person out of his isolation to a sense of "togetherness" in the different basic forms of human *community. Rooted in the perception of values, it can grow in intensity beyond the clarity of pure knowing and assist in the fashioning of knowledge itself. Frequently but not necessarily love overflows into the realm of feelings and is reenforced by them, but it is not just a feeling of pleasure or some other kind of "higher feeling." Thus, for example, there can be a will-act affirming the supreme value of another person (e. g., God) and this act of the will can persist even while one's feelings follow another scale of values. It is especially important that love can, indeed, be fused with the animal instincts and lead to unified experience; and it can also elevate these instincts to a higher level of expression for the whole person as occurs in marriage; however, when considered in themselves, the animal drives as such strive for the satisfaction of their desires and use the partner as a means to this end, whereas love looks to the good of the partner and affirms his value. Obviously, as an attitude of the whole person human love will assume different forms. Thus the typical man loves somewhat differently than the woman.

Love and respect do not exclude each other. Rather, they are two aspects of the basic attitude of the spiritual-personal existent in the face of other persons possessing intrinsic personal value. For, just as in every search for truth the existential movement of the spirit is an unconscious one in the direction of absolute truth, so also in every truly spiritual love the movement is towards the absolute value of the other which demands respect.

The opposite of love is hate which is a denial of the proper worth of the hated person. Just as love is value-affirming and society-building, so also hate is destructive both of values and society.

Since every human being possesses unique worth because of his personal ordination to infinite value (God) and since no man, as long as he is still living, can be thought to have failed irrevocably in attaining the final goal of his life, the duty to love one's neighbor is universal and allowing of no exceptions. However, instead of excluding, this really includes order and gradation of love according to the different human relationships and societies and according to the basic values which are the foundation of these relationships. The infinitely personal worth of God, which in itself is subsistent love, is the basis of the obligation to love God. On the one hand, the obligation to love is tied not only to external works but also to the inner attitude; on the other hand, this obligation does not touch the inner attitude insofar as the inner attitude is not under the mediate or immediate influence of the free will (as for example in emotional reactions like *sympathy* and *antipathy*). For, such an obligation depends upon the free affirmation of the will which is itself rooted in knowing and which tends to recognize personal worth.

*Self-love is not contrary to the love of God and love of neighbor; in fact it is presupposed by these. Selflessness, which is a breaking out of oneself to others, is not at all opposed to an ordered self-love, but only to a disordered selfishness which tends to lock a person up within his own desires. — The personal love of one's neighbor, which is founded on the objective order of existence and personal value, is as far away from sentimental *philanthropy* (a frequent front for a refined egoism) as it is from that extravagant altruism which maintains that only those actions are moral which are performed for the good of someone else. — *Compassion* (feeling one's way into another's suffering) should further mutual love and effective assistance, but it is by no means the only measure of human activity, since suffering is frequently the necessary avenue to the realization of higher values.

Since love aims immediately at value as such and since it urges the spiritual soul in its highest faculties to union with objective values, it is at the same time a mighty force for the formation of a dignified human existence and for the full realization of the moral order.

AW

M

MAN

Man comes from the Anglo-Saxon word "mann." What the root meaning of this word is is not clear, but it may be related ultimately to the Latin "*mens*" with the meaning of "a thinking being." Nor is the basic meaning of the Greek "*anthropos*" perfectly clear; it is now taken to mean "the face of a man," but formerly it was explained in the sense of "one who looks upwards." And finally, the Latin "*homo*" means "one born of the earth" (cf. *humus*). Even this short etymological consideration gives an indication of the essence of man. On the one hand a creature of the earth like all earthly things, on the other hand he rises above the earth and strives for a higher world. In any event, he will always remain the most questionable existent in the world — the source and object of the greatest questions, but at the same time the one most worthy and rewarding to question. Serious research reveals over and over again his incomparable greatness according to that immortal verse from Sophocles' *Antigone*: "Many mighty things exist but nothing is mightier than man."

Human nature, i.e., man in his existence and activity, is characterized by a number of levels. First of all, man is a corporeal being composed of the material stuff of the inorganic world. If one attempted to explain man entirely on the basis of this matter, he would be advocating a kind of *anthropological materialism* which is a basic misunderstanding of the essence of man. Further, we know man as a living body or organism who unites within himself all the appearances and activities of bodily life. His *body is similar to the bodies of the higher animals; therefore the essential plant-like functions (assimilation, growth and reproduction) that are proper to all animals are found also in him. Also, with the animals he shares in sense awareness. In fact, man is so much a part of organic life that even in the case of man the question can be raised concerning the origin of his body or the development of his body from sub-human forms (*Evolution). Still, man cannot be completely explained in terms

236

of his corporeal life alone just as it is not true to say that his development comes after everything else; such a primacy of life would be *biological materialism.*

So far we have considered man as a part of nature; but from the point of view of that which is proper to man as such he is more than *nature. For he possesses spiritual-intellectual life which is intrinsically independent of everything material. Therefore, his spiritual knowing penetrates to the innermost heart of things, to existence as such and to the ultimate foundation of all finite existence: absolute existence (God). It is for this reason that the will remains internally free in the face of all finite goods and is able to encompass all good, even the highest good (God). Since in this way man's spiritual-intellectual life moves beyond all finite limits towards the infinite, it shares in the highest degree of *life itself. Although man possesses this type of life in a finite way only, and God possesses it infinitely, still in his knowing and loving man mirrors God and therefore is the *image of God.* It follows from this that what is primary in man is his *spirit to which everything else is subordinate. This supreme quality permeates and puts its stamp on the other levels of man's existence, for example his sense experiences and even his outward appearance (physical movements, style of walking, etc.), so that he exists as a unified whole in spite of his complexity. This unity is particularly furthered by the fact that the spiritual *soul is also the principle of the existence of man's vegetative and sensible activities and together with the body forms *one* existent.

Man's spiritual nature endows him with the unique worth and inviolability of being a *person. His uniqueness is especially apparent in his personal *immortality which gives him the power in the midst of this transitory world, to strive for his personal, transcendent goal: the possession of God. Therefore, he can never be used by another as the means to an end and his inalienable rights must be protected (social *Freedom, inviolability, freedom of conscience, freedom of religion, private property, etc.). It is not his external accomplishments but his moral dignity that determines the true worth of man. Nevertheless, it is in the material world of time and space that man must work for full moral maturity. And in this enterprise man's spiritual nature gradually reveals itself in the creative shaping and transformation of historical *culture.

The spiritual in man permeates his sexual polarity just as much as it does the other areas of his existence. Sex is primarily something biological: *man* and *woman* belong together as the impregnating and the impregnated. This event, however, is elevated in the case of a man to the dignity of fatherhood and in the case of a woman to motherhood; in this relationship the whole personality both of parents and children gets into the act. Conversely, the whole personality of a man or a woman often undergoes a kind of transformation by becoming a father or a mother. In addition to its influence within the context of marriage and the family, the special nature of parenthood has great significance with regard to the fulfillment of the different tasks of humanity; this is particularly true for the development of human *community. Since the community is built up on the spirit of man, it surpasses all sub-human associations; it is the place of man's social living and without it he could not achieve his full development. From this it follows that each individual must make his own contribution to the common well-being.

The universal development of the inclinations and powers of human nature will ultimately lead to that noble humanity which *humanism* proclaims as the goal of mankind. The ideals of humanism can also be affirmed by Christians as long as humanity is not closed off from God and the supernatural order of revelation.

JBL

MANICHEANISM

Manicheanism is the doctrine named after Manes who was executed in Persia in 276 A.D. The teaching involves a combination of the Persian dualism of Zarathustra (Zoroaster) with gnostic and Christian elements. According to this theory, the world is composed of two principles: a good principle of light and an evil principe of darkness (matter). Good and evil emanations spring forth from these principles and ultimately there are combinations of the two. There dwells in man a light-soul and a body-soul which comes from the principle of evil: these two are in a constant state of conflict. The Manicheans deny that sin and guilt are the free, responsible causes of evil. Since matter and evil were thought to be the same thing, the three levels of the "chosen ones" promised to abstain from eating meat, from owning property, from bodily labor and from marriage. While Manes was still living his ideas had already spread into India and China. They were influential in the Christian West well into the Middle Ages (Catharists). Before his conversion to Christ Augustine was a Manichean for a number of years.

WB

MARRIAGE

Man finds himself in the world as man and woman; and he discovers a difference that is not limited just to the composition of the body, but also forms and permeates his entire spiritual experience. The fullness of what it means to be human stands out in the polarity of the sexes that have equal worth. In a special form of *love, as it grows between a man and

238

a woman, the two discover themselves as called to a free decision, to belong to each other and to enter into a full life-association; this community of life is also expressed in the sexual gift of the one to the other. Such a life together is more basic and profound than all other forms of human *community. Thus, the essence of marriage can be determined from a teleological consideration of sexual differentiation with the possibilities and necessities it reveals for finding true human values. From this point of view, marriage is the proper form of sexual relationship which is prescribed for man prior to his free choices; an such it has its own ends and characteristics which are independent of man's caprice.

With regard to the various ends of marriage, one of the first things to be experienced is a special kind of completion and assistance, as is possible only in a loving community of life between a man and a woman and in which the sexual drive also finds its fulfillment and rest. By its very nature, however, married love pushes beyond itself to the generation and education of children. Children are involved in the primary purpose of marriage, if one understands by purpose in the strict sense not the inner meaningfulness of an action but a goal to be attained by the use of means and a goal that surpasses the means used to reach it. In this sense, the intimate loving community of spouses of its very nature makes sense and even gives adequate meaning to a marriage in which, because of special circumstances, there is no hope of children. It is an offense against the moral order arbitrarily to limit the number of children (without serious reasons: e. g., only because of selfishness) and to use means to achieve this that are not in accordance with human dignity. However, this must be qualified by saying that the undisturbed course of biological necessity as such does not necessarily indicate a *natural law in the sense of the natural *moral law.

The matrimonial community of life and bond is constituted by the *marriage contract*. Because of the social importance of marriage, this contract should be entered into publicly before certain witnesses authorized by the competent civil society (sacramental marriage is authorized by the Church). In this contract the spouses promise mutual love and fidelity that would be seriously violated by adultery. The characteristics of marriage — unity (monogamy, the opposite of polygamy) and indissolubility (which is opposed to divorce with the possibility of remarriage) — flow from the full meaning of the loving gift of self which can seize a person with such intensity that, as the personal affirmation of another "thou", it can only be completely realized with regard to one person. These characteristics also flow from the responsibility of spouses to the children that may proceed from this union. For, children have a claim to a healthy family environment and to the love of *both parents*. Even though the moral awareness of the absolute demand for the unity and indissolubility of marriage is lacking in many cultures, still marriage did not develop slowly from an original state of universal promiscuity.

In spite of the great importance of marriage for the personal development of a man and a woman, it is not absolutely necessary for each individual. For, the free renunciation of marriage by those who are of marriageable age (virginity, celibacy) assumed because of religious motives, can open up for the one who is called to it almost unlimited possibilities of growing in the love of God and of one's fellow men.

WaK

MARXISM

Marxism in the broadest sense (1) is the teaching of Karl Marx. It embraces both *dialectical as well as *historical materialism and their application to social living. In a somewhat narrower sense (2) some understand Marxism only as historical materialism. In the most restricted sense (3) Marxism is a very incisive (though often erroneous) criticism of capitalism which proceeds on the philosophical foundation of dialectical and historical materialism. According to this view, human history is only a history of class warfare and the state is only the tool of the ruling class which is used to suppress all opposition. Proceeding from the opposition between the "capitalists" who possess the means of production and the "proletatriat" which does not, Marx interprets *capitalism* by means of his theory of work surplus-value as a system of exploitation of workers by capitalists; for, the capitalists keep for themselves the surplus-value that is created by the workers. The accumulation and concentration of wealth in the hands of a smaller and smaller group of capitalists, along with the law of the declining rate of profit, leads to the self-destruction of the system of exploitation: ultimately the "expropriation of the expropriators" takes place, i. e., the worker class (Proletariat) takes control of the means of production and establishes temporarily the "dictatorship of the proletariat" as the preliminary stage in the transition to the "classless society."

In contrast to the older forms of *socialism, which were rejected by it as "utopian," Marxism claims to be "scientific socialism." But it also loses itself in the utopian dream of a classless society. For the establishment of a final goal, no matter what it is, stands in direct contradiction to the dialectical principle. The revolutionary élan of Marxism likewise contradicts strict economic determinism = historical materialism.

In older Marxism, which has been called "the natural child of bourgeois liberalism and *individualism," the sacrifice of freedom which results in a society that is highly organized in order to produce more material goods is supposed to enable man finally to shape his life in freedom when he has an abundance of consumer goods. Modern Marxism (Leninism, Stalinism) has developed into a strict *collectivism: The production of material goods is no longer directed towards the improvement of personal existence, but to the growth in power of the collective.

OvNB

MASS

Mass in ordinary speech means the matter of a body. In *physics* the idea of mass appears in the basic principle of mechanics as a proportionality factor: the acceleration communicated to a body by some pre-given force is inversely proportional to the mass. Thus, mass itself is also a measure of the matter contained in the body. It is the cause of the inertia (*Motion) and the weight of bodies; therefore, physicists speak of *inertial* and *gravitational* mass; in the general theory of *relativity both of these are brought together in a higher point of view. Mass is an additive property of bodies, that is, several masses which are in any way combined constitute a total mass according to the laws of normal addition. The theory of relativity shows that the mass of a body is dependent upon its velocity. — From a *sociological* point of view, a mass is a group of men large in number, brought together by special circumstances, by similar feelings, desires and ideas; it often happens that these special circumstances of a mass curb to a great extent the personal feelings, desires and ideas of the individual man — and can even blot them out (depersonalization). In contrast to a *community, social organization is lacking in a mass either completely, or else it is not at all effective in it. A mass as a whole is subject to very diverse influences which are studied by *mass psychology*.

NJ

MASTER MORALITY

F. W. Nietzsche criticized the morality of his time not primarily because of its specific requirements, but because of its ultimate foundation. According to him, the truth and goodness of a morality depend upon whether or not its evaluations proceed from a strong, powerful life (from a master-race) or from a weak, incompetent spirit. Good and evil originally meant excellent and bad. Christian morality is a typical slave-morality which grew out of a feeling of weakness. In order to repress the spirit of resentment against the strong and creative — a spirit resulting from the feeling of weakness, the slavish persons developed a new evaluation of persons and things in which the weak and the sick are marked as having the greatest value. Corresponding to this falsification of values are the ideals of Christian humility and the universal love of mankind which spring from a sickly compassion; both of these latter attitudes seek with every means possible to preserve the weak and the unsuccessful.

Nietzsche's ideal is the superman, the genius; the world only achieves any meaning whatsoever through the production of such individuals. The morality of the superior individual full of noble pride must necessarily bring about a revaluation of all traditional values and a rejection of the Christian slave-morality of humility and brotherly love; it must discover the harmful distortion of values which has grown out of this resentment and the false values which have been operative in society, especially the contempt of the body; and it must generate a new attitude beyond good and evil, i. e., principally beyond the traditional norms of judging good and evil. Even the expression "immoralism" in Nietzsche means only the rejection of customary morality. — Criticism: In a one-sided fashion Nietzsche glorifies biological values and, not without a great deal of resentment of his own, under the influence of Schopenhauer completely falsifies the true meaning of Christian morality. For in Christian morality, humility as the desire to order all things properly under God is joined with a sense of one's own true worth. And love is based primarily in the recognition of the personal worth of each spiritual person.

JoS

MATERIALISM

Materialism as a philosophical position teaches that all reality can be reduced to *matter and to certain powers that are wholly subject to the conditions of matter. According to *rationalistic materialism* (*Mechanism), all reality is fully intelligible on the basis of measure and number, while *mythical* or *biological* materialism claims to perceive in material events a mystery that surpasses us (*Life) — but a mystery that is not related to an immaterial principle. — A partial materialism is advocated by those who in any area reduce the immaterial or formal element to something material and thereby in effect deny its special character; an example of this view is the machine theory of life (*Vitalism). — *Anthropological* materialism appears in two forms: either as a denial of the *soul, which is identified with matter and its physical-chemical changes, or as a denial of the existential independence of the soul from matter (*Spirit). — *Dialectical* materialism combines the view of the real as simply matter with the "dialectics" of Hegel. Its application to social living results in *historical* materialism according to which the essence of history consists in economic processes; they claim that the events of man's spiritual history and development are simply the results and the reflections of his economic activity (*Marxism, *Ideology). — Materialism is completely blind to a large segment of reality, since it fails to see the special nature of the immaterial and the laws proper to it.

MATHEMATICS, PHILOSOPHY OF

While *materialism as a theory* denies the reality of spirit, as a *method* it abstracts provisionally from the immaterial in order to try to explain it from its material conditions. By "matter" here we mean not only spatio-temporal matter, but also that which is lower in contrast to that which is higher. Since many things that appear to us as original and imma-terial can be traced back to their material parts or at least can be shown to depend on material conditions, so a limited validity cannot be denied to the material method of explanation. But the unrestricted principle that the higher must be explained from the lower is false, because it incorrectly turns a partial method into a comprehensive method. The reduction to matter must be complemented by a consideration of the formal element, for only such a consideration is able to grasp the special nature of the object. — The mistaken identification of perceptibility with reality has shown that it is the road to materialism, since as a result of this confusion material reality is confused with *reality as such. See also *Spiritualism, Biologism, Anthropology.*

WB

MATHEMATICS, PHILOSOPHY OF

Mathematics is a science of *number (arithmetic) and *space (geometry). Ever since the days of Greek antiquity mathematics has been closely associated with philosophy. Shortly after the concepts of the *infinite (*ápeiron*) and the continuous (*synechès*) appeared in Greek mathematics, they gave rise to some profound philosophical reflection (e. g., Zeno's antimonies). — The Pythagoreans held that numbers are *principles of things. And they discovered the *incommensurable quantities*, i. e., quanti-ties that cannot be described as a relationship of two whole numbers (*Number). The discovery of these quantities established, among the Greeks, the priority of geometry over arithmetic. This incommensurability was also the reason why Plato held that the objects of geometry are not "sensibly perceptible" figures, but rather "spiritually perceptible" ones (*Republic*, 510 D). According to Aristotle's account (*Metaphysics* I, 6: 987b 14ff.), Plato assumed for mathematical entities their own intermediate mode of existence between sensible things and the ideas. In the dialogue, Euthydemus (290 B), Plato defends the thesis that geometricians and arithmeticians find their object already there (as the hunter his prey) — they do not produce it (against the sophists). Aristotle argued against the separation of mathematical entities from sensible things (*Metaphysics* III, 2: 297 a 34 ff.; XIII, 2: 1076 b 11 ff.). And in his *Physics* he proposed a solution to the problem of mathematical infinity (III, 4-8) and the continu-um (VI, 1 ff.). He defines this infinite as the *potentially infinite* (*dynámei* ápeiron), and he explains it thus: "For generally the infinite has this mode of existence: one thing is always being taken after another, and each thing that is taken is always finite, but always different." (206 a 27 ff.). In other words, it is a question of the "and-so-forth-structure" of mathematical activity (counting or dividing). Aristotle defines the *continuum* by saying that "everything continuous is divisible into divisibles that are infinitely divisible," (231 b 15 f.) or "the continuous is divisible *ad infinitum*" (185 b 10). This view rules out, for example, that time is composed of "nows" and that a line is composed of points; and it completely excludes the possibility of dividing motion into elementary parts which are not themselves motion.

The Aristotelian notion of the continuum and the infinite was the (unchallenged) common property of all mathematicians up till the time of Georg Cantor (1845-1918). Cantor opposed this traditional conception with his set theory in which he assumed the existence of actually infinite aggregates (or sets). At the root of Cantor's theory lies a conception of mathematics according to which mathematics deals with "objects of an ideal kind" and these objects are considered to be pre-given to human knowledge. This view is related to the teachings of Plato and even more to historical Platonism. Recently it was even characterized as *Platonism* (or the ontological conception of mathematics). A great number of mathematicians still hold this view. However, L.E.J. Brouwer (since 1907) has been sharply critical of Cantor's set theory and his idea of mathematics. Brouwer found the essence of mathematics in doing (counting; "intuition of the natural series of numbers"), not in a theory of objects of some kind or other ("mathematics is more doing than theorizing"). Since his program was directed primarily towards the destruction of a large part of modern mathematics, the result was a crisis over the foundations of mathematics. Today the different constructive movements (continuing Brouwer's *intuitionism*) regarding the foundations of mathematics offer the most satisfying way out of the crisis: A. Heyting, H. Weh. P. Lorenzen's operative mathematics, the constructive formalism of R. L. Goodstein (inspired by L. Wittgenstein), the constructive mathematics of A. A. Markov's school, etc. Basically these movements signal a return to Aristotle's view of the continuum and the infinite. — The different *axiomatic* movements (the *logicism* of Frege and Russell; the *formalistic* school of Hilbert) contributed essentially to the clarification of the logical problematic of mathematics and so to the development of mathematical logic (*Symbolic Logic).

In the area of geometry, the 19th century saw the construction of non-Euclidian geometries (Lobatschewski [1829], Bolyai, Riemann, Gauss). The logical connection of these systems among themselves and with Euclidian geometry was greatly clarified by *projective geometry* (F. Klein). These geometries have many applications in modern physics (*Relativity, Theory of). The works on the foundations of geometry which are written from the axiomatic standpoint are of less importance for the philosophy of mathematics. See also *Number*.

VR

MATTER

Matter (Gr.: *hýlē*) in almost all of its meanings is the relative opposition to *form. Originally matter (1) meant the basic material out of which man created works of art (e. g., wood, marble, gold), in contrast to the form or shape which the material received as the result of human effort. Then the opposition between form and matter was conceptually transferred to the things of nature. Thus matter (2) is "that out of which" a body is made; and while the concept "body" signifies and individual thing with a determinate size and shape (e. g., this block of marble), the concept of matter itself (e. g., any marble) disregards these definite characteristics. Therefore, matter is that which primarily appears as the substance of a body, in contrast to its accidental shape, size, etc. Chemistry, which has directed its attention to the investigation of matter, has been able to reduce the incalculable multiplicity of material things down to 92 basic elements; these in turn are also composed of atoms, i. e., small particles having a determined *mass and a determined weight. The phenomenon of radioactivity and other manifestations suggested the idea that the heavier atoms are composed of lighter ones and that perhaps ultimately all atoms are composed of a certain number of the lightest atoms — hydrogen. For a long time the atom was thought to be a continuously extended very small body; the recent developments in physics, however, have made it necessary to assume that even in the atom there is a delicate structure composed of different particles (protons, neutrons electrons, etc.). The question of the physical sciences concerning the nature of matter is directed primarily at these particles. At the present time the whole situation is in a state of flux; the primary reason for the great difficulty here is that the same matter gives evidence at one time of being a particle and at another time of being a wave. — The matter (2) which is the object of study of the physical sciences is called *second matter* (*materia secunda*) in scholastic philosophy in contrast to *first matter* (3) or *prime matter. Prime matter is not, like second matter, a definite corporeal substance and therefore it cannot be detected or studied by the methods of physics; for, it is an essential principle of a body which can be grasped only by the intellect and it does not enter into the composition of a corporeal substance until it is united with the essential form (*Hylemorphism).

In philosophical language the word "matter" (4) is used to designate realities beyond the realm of bodies and so it has come to signify in its

245

broadest meaning whatever is determinable in contrast to the determining form. Thus, the concepts of subject and predicate are called the matter of a judgment in contrast to the "is" or copula which is the form; likewise, the premises, from which the conclusion of an argument is drawn, are called the matter of the conclusion in contrast to the connecting sequence which is the form. In these and similar cases the matter (4) is also the changing "content" in contrast to the form which remains more or less the same. — Concerning the special application of the concepts of matter and form in the epistemology of Kant see *critical philosophy.

That is above all called *material* which is composed of matter (2) or is characteristic of a body; therefore, it means the same thing as "corporeal." In scholastic terminology the word "material" often also designates that which is bound to matter, i. e., that which is itself neither a body nor an attribute of a body, but is intrinsically dependent upon matter so that without it it can neither exist nor act (e. g., the animal soul as opposed to the immaterial [spiritual] soul of man).

JdV

MECHANISM

Mechanism is the attempt to give a *mechanical* explanation (i. e., through the local motion of intrinsically immutable parts) for the inner structure of natural bodies and for the whole of nature. The oldest form of mechanism is found in the *atomism of the Greek philosophers (Leucippus, Democritus); according to them bodies are composed of unchangeable, minute parts (atoms) which are distinguished from each other only according to size, shape and position. *Change occurs only as the result of local motion in which the atoms work on each other and by reason of their shape can combine to form larger or smaller bodies. In this process everything occurs according to blind necessity, so that all *finality is excluded. Among the later forms of mechanism, Descartes and .*Cartesianism retained the main points of general mechanism: There is only quantity and number and local motion; there are no powers other than the mechanical, i. e., those that produce motion; there is no finality. Descartes extends this explanation even to the lives of plants and animals: so he looks upon animals as mere automatons without consciousness. But mechanism does not become *materialism until it explains conscious life in a mechanistic way and therefore denies that *soul and *spirit are essentially different from the body. — A special form of mechanism is the so-called *machine theory of* (organic) *life.* According to this view, an *organism is only a machine or ordered system of matter without a substantial carrier of the wholeness and the inner finality, i. e., without a substantial *life principle. But the machine theory does not necessarily reduce all life to purely mechanical powers and it does not necessarily deny all (external) finality; it usually considers the organized form of matter as something originally given that has always existed alongside of unorganized matter. — The machine theory of life was refuted by the proponents of *vitalism. In the realm of inorganic matter mechanism has been found wanting, at least with regard to the results of modern atomic physics. If, for example, a pair of electrons can be produced from a quantum of light, then in this case the mechanistic explanation is excluded, since a quantum of light cannot be thought of as composed of two electrons.

JdV

METAPHYSICS

The name "metaphysics" appears for the first time in the present-day meaning about the beginning of the 5th century A. D. in the work of the Neo-Platonic philosopher, Simplicius. The science designated by this term had already been systematically begun in the 4th century B. C. by Aristotle. It is concerned with the *metaphysical*, with that which is beyond the *physical*. However, "physical" did not at all mean the same thing to the Greeks as it does to the modern physicist; for, it meant the whole corporeal world of experience insofar as it is subject to *physics* or nature, i. e., subject to being born or simply to becoming in any way. Accordingly, that is called "meta-physical" which is essentially non-experienceable by the senses, unchangeable and in some way spiritual, but it is not, as Nicolai Hartmann affirms, the unknowable (*Intelligibility). — In the tradition of Aristotle we see metaphysics in a twofold way. Firstly, there is a non-experienceable something which resides in the world of experience as its innermost center: that undetermined or universal *existence which supports each and every existent. Secondly, there is a non-experienceable something which transcends the world of experience as its ultimate source: that infinite or divine existence which creates each and every finite existent. This distinction provides us with the two branches of metaphysics. The study of existence considers all existents under the aspect of universal existence and so it investigates the essence, properties and laws of existence as such; this science is commonly called *"ontology" (a term first used by Du Hamel in 1661). The science of God considers all existents in reference to absolute, divine existence and so it investigates the existence, essence and activity of the absolute; this science was called *theologike* by Aristotle; subsequently it was called "natural *theology" and also, though less properly, "theodicy." — Ontology and natural theology together make up *general metaphysics* because they consider every existent and also metaphysical existence itself. The philosophical study of the world (cosmology) and of man (rational psychology, anthropology, philosophy of man) are related to general metaphysics as the application of its principles

247

to particular areas of experience in order to understand their inner nature in terms of the more universal principles of existence as such.

The meaning of metaphysics can be grasped from what has been said above. It is the very heart of philosophy since it provides the ultimate foundation and principles for each of the particular areas of philosophical investigation. Therefore Aristotle called this science "First Philosophy" since it is concerned with that which is the first; for, in the order of reality existence and God are first: they are the source and support of everything else. When metaphysics begins to reflect upon itself it develops into the *theory of knowledge.* — The method of metaphysics (and especially of ontology) can be neither strictly analytical nor strictly inductive. The rationalists (e. g., Spinoza) proceeded analytically; this procedure is impossible because the many further determinations of existence cannot be arrived at through a mere dissection of the concept of being. Thinkers trained in the ways of modern, positive science (e. g., Kulpe and Becher) have attempted to establish an inductive metaphysics. By means of progressively inductive generalizations they hope to arrive at the most universal principles of being; it is to be objected against this method that every *induction presupposes the first principles of existence as already established and operative. Between these two one-sided views there is the metaphysics of a priori synthesis or synthetic necessity; this kind of metaphysical thinking adds somehow the further determinations to existence, but it grasps them at the same time in their intrinsic, essential and therefore a priori procession from existence itself.

At the present time materialists and positivists reject all metaphysics. In the language of *dialectical materialism, metaphysics is the name for every anti-dialectical consideration of nature or any view which excludes all intrinsic change and development; this is practically a mechanistic view of reality and it is certainly foreign to the concept of classical metaphysics which leaves plenty of room to nature. — At the same time, however, there is a limited return to metaphysical thinking. Indeed, in Kant there has been a certain rediscovery of the metaphysician, without however always overcoming his limitations. Thus, for example, Nicolai Hartmann does not get beyond *ontology, since he assigns to metaphysics only the task of defining the finally insoluble problems of each area of human knowledge. Kant is also the source of what may be termed an "irrational" metaphysics; according to this view metaphysics is often recognized only as a matter of *faith or of *Weltanschauung, but not as a *science. As far as method goes, inductive metaphysics is insufficient, since, if it were radically carried out, it would finally destroy itself. Heidegger (*Existential Philosophy) attempts to overcome the traditional metaphysics, insofar as this metaphysics as ontology investigates only the existent but, according to him, has not raised the fundamental-ontological question about existence itself. In so structuring his question, however, Heidegger has underestimated the clarification of existence which metaphysics has been engaged in for a long time.

JBL

METHOD

Method and *system make up the essence of *science; system concerns the content of the science while method has to do with the formal aspect. Put more exactly, "system" means the ordered totality of the knowledge or content of a science; "method," however, literally (Gk.: *methodos* = "after-road") designates the way in which this totality is acquired and built up. We approach an area of knowledge "methodically" when we study it according to a plan, work out its particular areas, organize the various bits of knowledge logically and bring out as many relationships as possible; finally, we seek to know about each and every thing not only "that" it is but also "why" it is the way it is, i. e., we desire to know not only facts but also the reason or basis of these facts.

The general method of "all" science described above must be applied according to the peculiarities and differences of the different objects or areas of knowledge. Thus it is the different objects of knowledge which prescribe the proper method to be employed in their investigation; accordingly, one thing that determines the method is the way in which man perceives the particular object (e. g., through sense perception or through deductive reasoning which transcends the sensible order); another determinative factor is the intrinsic structure or nature of the thing to be known; the method to be used must conform to this as best it can. The transference of the proper method of one science to a different area of investigation can result in great distortion and error; a good example of this procedure is the attempt to construct a whole metaphysics by using only the methods proper to the physical sciences. Thomas Aquinas prepared the way for the distinct clarification of different methods with his teaching on the three degrees of abstraction in human knowing; actually he developed this view out of some of the insights of Aristotle. According to his position, in addition to the *abstraction proper to the physical sciences and that proper to mathematics there is also metaphysical abstraction which considers the existent insofar as it is or has existence.

Among the many divisions of method reference should be made here to the distinction, very important for philosophy, between the **analytic and** synthetic methods. The former begins with the concrete existent and proceeds to its inner components (principles of being) and to its exterior causes. The latter puts the existent back together again out of its component parts. But there is more than this to the distinction between analytic and synthetic judgments. For the judgment: "The finite existent is composed of essence and existence" contains an analysis, but it is not an analytic but a synthetic essential judgment. Right here it is apparent that metaphysical analysis, even though it proceeds from things to their causes, i. e., from the more recent to the more remote, is not just *induction. Philosophy first has need of *analysis but through it prepares the way for *synthesis.

The scientific investigation of the problems concerned with method is called "methodology." A great help to the methodical development of science in any field is a clear *terminology* (Lat.: *terminus* = limit; or, the expression which clearly delimits one idea from another) or a technical language which should be neither too fluid nor too ossified.

JBL

MIDDLE, PRINCIPLE OF THE EXCLUDED

The principle of the excluded middle (*principium exclusi tertii*) means for the order of existence that there can be no middle between existence and non-existence — a middle ground that would be neither existence nor non-existence. It follows from this for the logical order that every statement is either true or false, and that therefore there is no third possibility (*tertium non datur*). The principle of the excluded middle follows from the principle of the excluded *contradiction: a middle or so-called third possibility would be different from existence, i. e., it would be non-existence (for that is the meaning of the word "different"); but it would also be different from non-existence, i. e., not non-existence; and therefore it would be a contradiction. The so-called *triple value or multiple value logic*, if correctly understood, does not contradict the principle of the excluded middle, since the truth values besides "true" and "false" (e. g., "undecidable" or "probable") are not exactly a third possibility over against "true" and "false"; rather, they are alternatives to "decidable as true" (or "certainly true") and to "decidable as false" (or "certainly false"). These concepts, however, are not contradictorily but contrarily opposed (*Opposition); and contrary oppositions can both be false, and therefore they allow of a third position.

JdV

MIRACLE

A miracle is a perceptible, extraordinary occurrence which surpasses merely natural powers and has God as its direct or indirect author. Only that aspect of the *supernatural that can be perceived by man is called a "miracle." The word "extraordinary" does not necessarily exclude frequency; it points rather to the fact that the occurrence is contrary to the established course of natural events. Metaphysical principles are not broken by a miracle and even natural laws are not actually suspended; instead, God prevents them from having their normal effect in a particular case. Moreover, in virtue of his *omnipotence which is not tied to any *natural law, God produces effects which exceed the capacities of the available natural causes. Therefore, natural science cannot give a complete explanation of a miracle, since this would mean that there was no miracle. — The possibility of miracles flows from the omnipotence of God, from the *contingency of things and from the purely physical *necessity of material things. Still, a miracle is not just a supplementary "repair job" on creation; when and where it occurs, it is taken up into the eternal plan of creation for the sake of some higher end. Accordingly, religious purposes are the first consideration, such as the confirmation of a divine *revelation as well as the propagation and strengthening of faith in it; only secondarily and subordinate to religious purposes do miracles affect earthly goods, such as an instantaneous cure, etc.

Because of the higher purposes served by a miracle, it must be knowable as such. Historical truth or the verification of the event itself (e. g., a cure) usually does not present any insuperable difficulties, especially with regard to events of the immediate past. But historical criticism must go to work on the accounts of miracles in the distant past. — It is much more difficult to prove conclusively the so-called philosophical truth of a miracle, i. e., to show that the alleged wonderful deed really does surpass all purely natural powers. Even though many areas of nature have not yet been adequately investigated, still, in order to verify the reality of a miracle, it is not necessary to know all the powers of nature; it is sufficient to know what nature absolutely cannot do in certain cases. The cure of a nervous or psychological ailment is always regarded with a certain reservation. Mere suggestion or other "artifices" are often excluded because of the physical and moral circumstances of the miracle and especially because of the moral, religious personality of the miracle-worker. — For the so-called theological truth of a miracle, i. e., that it can be traced back to God as the actual cause, the purpose and the moral circumstances are once again the guarantee. In any case, God does not work a miracle to satisfy man's curiosity or to confirm a religion that is fundamentally contrary to the moral order.

MR

MODALITY

Modality in the broadest sense means the way in which something exists or proceeds. However, modality is usually related to the *judgment and signifies the way in which the subject and the predicate are joined together.

This joining can be looked upon as a psychological happening. Then we have the psychological modalities of affirmation (e. g., timid, decisive, emphatic, etc.). If the judgment is taken in reference to the reality it is supposed to express, then one speaks of the valuating modalities of true and false (*Truth, *Falsity), which is also called the "quality"; in reference to the intellect's appropriation of the truth one speaks of *certitude and *probability. Immanuel Kant's view of modality is related to this. According to him, since the joining that occurs in the judgment is not the expression of an independent, objective reality, the modality concerns "only the value of the copula (*Judgment) in relation to thinking as such"; *problematic judgments* are those in which one accepts the affirmation or negation simply as possible (according to one's preference); *assertatory* are those in which it is considered as real (true); *apodictic* are those in which one sees the connection as necessary.

In traditional logic the modality of a judgment means the way in which the subject and predicate are joined, as this is made manifest simply from the nature of the content of the subject and the predicate. Its fundamental mode is *possibility from which the other modalities are derived through negation: the affirmation is possible (*Possibility) or not possible (*Impossibility); the negation is possible (*Contingency) or not possible (*Necessity). The corresponding modalities of *existence are the real foundation of these logical modalities of the judgment. The logical modality, however, does not have to be expressed in every judgment. A judgment in which the modality is expressed is called a *modal judgment* (e. g., Four is necessarily divisible by two). Here a distinction is to be made between the statement and the mode of the statement. — The modality of judgments, when the exact same content is involved, offers the basis for *modal conclusions* which proceeed from objective necessity to actual existence, from actual existence to possibility, and from impossibility to nonexistence.

WB

MOLINISM

Molinism is a theological system, named for its originator Luis de Molina (1535-1600), relating to the cooperation of free will with the grace of God. Here it will be treated only from a philosophical viewpoint. — According to Molinism, the freedom of the will consists in its ability, when all of the conditions for acting are present, to determine for itself the existence and the particular direction of its acts. This ability seems to be in direct contradiction both to the necessary influence of the first cause and to the divine foreknowledge. Molinism attempts to solve these difficulties and at the same time preserve human freedom. According to this view, the divine *concurrence does not consist in some sort of predetermination of the will-act; but God puts his intrinsically indifferent concurrence at the disposal of the will and then effects along with the will the will-act; and in spite of the duality of causes there is only one effect (e. g., two horses drawing one wagon). This is possible because God knows antecedently how the will would act in every possible situation; Molina calls this knowledge *"scientia media"* which is to be distinguished from the knowledge of necessary and actual things. — The teaching of this theory led to the famous dispute about divine grace between the Molinists and the Thomists, especially the group around Bánez.

WB

MONAD

Monad (Gr.: = *monás*) means "unity." Since the dawn of philosophy great thinkers have seen here an essential determination of existence. Therefore, ontology was also a study of unity or a *monadology* but this side of reality was not given primary interest until the advent of G. W. Leibniz (1646-1716). For, after many hesitations, he raised the monad to the central position in his finished philosophy; consequently, the name "monadology" best describes his characteristic position which stands in contrast to the positions of Descartes and Spinoza. In Descartes the duality of the thinking substance and the extended substance departs from the one basic principle of the monad; the teleology inherent in the monad overcomes the mechanism of Descartes. The monad also abandons the monism of Spinoza insofar as it makes a multiplicity of substances possible.

Essentially the monad is the simple, fully self-contained, first supporter of substantial existence; it is thought of as something soul-like which is also the source of everything corporeal. Finite monads are created by God, the infinite monad. He is unlimited with regard to the fullness of existence and the vision of the All. The created monads also contain the fullness of existence and reflect the All, but only according to the measure of their point of view — and this explains their finiteness and multiplicity. — Concerning the activity of the monads, it is to be noted that they are closed within themselves without a window. Only the uncreated monad can work on the created ones. There is no mutual causality between the created monads themselves, still an immanent activity develops in each one of them that fulfills the possibilities residing in each one. Thus, the monads are dynamic-teleological centers of power. Their stages of development correspond with each other (e. g., the death of a man and the shot of a gun) because God has constituted them in a predetermined harmony (*harmonia praestabilita*) something like the synchronization of many watches.

According to this theory, there are various levels of monads. That all monads are something soul-like is shown by their kind of immanent activity; for, this unfolds in perceptions (imaginations) and appetites (strivings). In the case of corporeal or naked monads these immanent activities remain unconscious because such monads are submerged in the individual moment. The monads on the sensible level raise themselves by the power of memory above the particular moment and incorporate it into a larger whole; in this way they attain a dull level of consciousness. Full consciousness belongs only to the spiritual monads insofar as they rise to the Eternal through the grasp of the first principles of existence and measure the moment in that light. Living things are ruled by just one soul-monad or spirit-monad, while their bodies are composed of innumerable naked monads.

The primacy of spirit that appears here shows up in some way in every true philosophy. Nevertheless, Leibniz gave too little attention to the transient activity of the monad and to the reality of bodies.

JBL

MONISM

Monism literally means the doctrine of unity (first used by Christian Wolff). It can be understood in such a way that the multiplicity of things can be traced back to one source that is different from them (in the sense of *Theism or *Deism). Usually, however, monism is understood in such a way that it does not express the unity of the source, but the unity of substance and being. This can happen either with regard to all reality or with regard to a limited number of objects. Universal monism affirms the essential oneness of God and the world (*Pantheism, *Atheism); thus, it denies every essential difference between the different realms of objects: matter and spirit, living and non-living substances, individual and community, etc. Depending upon which of the various opposites is elevated to the first place, there results a different kind of monism. The principal forms are *materialistic* and *spiritualistic* monism (*Materialism, *Spiritualism, *German Idealism). The consequences of monism are the denial of *free will and the advocacy of psycho-physical parallelism (*Body-Soul Relation).

Monism begins with the true principle that existence as existence is one. But it does not follow from this that there can be only one existent or that all things have one and the same essence. The monism of substance errs when it sees in the possibility of finite existence alongside of infinite existence a necessary *dualism or pluralism (*Multiplicity); for, this possibility itself is based upon one infinite existence and so a real dualism is excluded. Only if the finite existent were existence in the same sense as infinite existence, would there be a unicity of substance (*Analogy). Against materialistic monism the objection can be made that it is unreasonable to look for the principle of unity in matter, which is the principle of multiplicity. It is quite clear that all forms of monism run contrary to experience. The multiplicity of beings, especially of human persons, is just as much a fact as the understandable reduction of all things to one principle is a necessary requirement of spirit.

WB

MORAL EVIL

Moral evil is located in the free decision of the will that is opposed to the morally *good and the *moral law; it thereby differentiates itself not only from metaphysical evil (= creaturely finiteness) but also from the other non-ethical evils such as sickness, pain, death, ugliness, etc. (physical evil). Considered as a rejection of the divine law, moral evil is called *sin*; as an imputable, responsible act it is called *guilt. Moral evil, like all evil, is not something positive that is opposed to the good, as parsism, gnosticism and *manicheanism affirm; for, they assert a basic dualism involving two universal principles of all reality: a principle of good and a principle of evil. Just as the morally good is not identical with the important and the powerful, likewise in its origin it is not the same thing as the weak, the common and the ignoble, as Nietzsche would have it. Rather, moral goodness is on a higher, spiritual plane, above the level of the strictly biological. Moral evil is first of all the internal, free, spiritual decision and intention, then the external act, then the evil habit which arises from repeated evil acts; such habits are called *vices*. The desires that man finds within himself which frequently persist contrary to reason and will are given the general name of *concupiscence*; this does not mean that they are evil in themselves or independently of any free choice, but only in the sense that they incline the will towards moral evil. The source of moral evil is not to be found in an evil principle opposed to the goodness of the world nor in some divine "push" towards moral evil, but in the spirit's free rejection of the good. Of course, in the case of human beings evil desires or an external temptation of some kind are usually involved. The question about the meaning of moral evil comes to this: Why does the all holy God, who can never desire, cause or approve moral evil, permit it? or why does he not prevent the free spiritual beings that he has created from misusing their freedom and falling into moral evil? This permission, which does not include any approval of or responsibility for the moral evil in question, is motivated by the desire for other higher values. For, the morally good choice as a free glorification of God presupposes free choice and thereby the possibility of moral evil (*Free Will). The merciful goodness of God always forgives the fallen sinner who learns through his fall humility and his need of redemption. The injustice done to the neighbor offers the opportunity to practice patience and to persevere in love. Finally, the unrepentant sinner will receive a just punishment and so the violated moral order will be reestablished.

JoS

MORALITY

Morality (*ethos*) is the attitude of man with regard to the moral law which is based on his free decision. "Ethos" is sometimes taken to mean the definite character, based on the predominance of one particular value, of the moral attitude of one particular value, or the moral attitude of a whole people or a social group. A morally (ethically) *good* act is a free act of man which affirms an objective ethical value and which affirms the *moral law; morally *evil* is that which is opposed to ethical value and the moral law. A free act is morally *indifferent* if it is neither good nor bad with reference to its object. However, a man's free action in the concrete, particular case is always either good or evil, since at least the man's intention in performing the act is not morally indifferent — it is either good or evil. The source of all moral worth and worthlessness is first of all the free decision of the will, then the virtuous attitude flowing from it, and finally the person or the *moral subject*.

The moral life (*good will*) consists in the basic affirmation of the moral law. The individual act is morally good, not merely because it happens to conform to this law, but also insofar as it flows from moral conviction. The subjective value of the moral conviction finds its source in the moral value of the object; for the moral act is directed towards the object and receives its ethical character from it. Man becomes morally good by accepting the world of values as he finds them and by striving for the *good. The problem of the basic principle of morality (*Ethics) is a search for the foundation of all objective value. This cannot be found in the *autonomy and rational structure of the categorical imperative (Kant), for the latter position already presupposes the objective value of the moral act. On the other hand the good is clearly to be distinguished from the pleasureable (*Hedonism) or the useful (Utilitarianism). For it has the quality of perfecting the human person as a whole and so of protecting *human dignity*. The Greek ideal of striving for the Beautiful and the Good tends towards a somewhat exaggerated aesthetical harmony; but when man's spiritual and bodily harmony is intended, then the ideal is both correct and meaningful. — That which is objectively moral possesses a value which, in a certain sense, is unconditioned and absolute, even though it is not infinite; this value together with man's ultimate goal (*Happiness: which will be realized in the next world by the possession of God) and the divine law are the foundations of the unconditional binding force of the natural moral law. Moral *evil is characterized by an absolute worthlessness which cannot be compensated for by any other value no matter how high it may be. The absolute value of the moral order calls for the submission of the human will in spite of all selfish inclinations; it does not follow from this that the meaning of morally well-ordered inclinations is diminished in any way.

Customary norms approximate the laws of morality. These norms either apply the laws of morality to a definite, concrete situation and then possess the same degree of obligation as the requirements of the moral law or, more often, they prescribe certain actions for a social group or a people without at the same time imposing a strict obligation in conscience. The moral goodness or badness of particular actions has different sources. The most important of these is the immediate object which determines the will in its own way; to this should be added the *circumstances*, which are very important in moral questions, and the *purpose or intention. — Personal knowledge of moral values (= moral consciousness) is not produced by a special, irrational *moral sense*; however, it is greatly furthered by a highly developed sense of moral feelings such as respect, honesty and fidelity.

JoS

MORAL LAW

Moral law commands that good be done and *evil be avoided. It is also called the norm of morality; however, by the "norm of morality" one often means the moral principle which determines the nature of that which is morally good, without explaining the source of the obligation to do it. Strictly speaking, the moral law is not a human (civil or ecclesiastical) positive law; nor is it based on an implicit agreement between men. Rather, it flows necessarily from the natural order or the order of being. Therefore it is a natural moral law in contrast to the natural law which governs the physical world. With regard to content it coincides with the decalogue (the ten commandments of the Bible), with the exception of the special form of the third commandment. That part of the natural moral law which concerns rights and duties is the basis of all *natural rights. The natural moral law can also be inculcated by positive law or, so long as it allows different ways of compliance, it can be determined more precisely by customs (*Morality).

The basis of the moral law is the *ought* which, though not behind all moral *values, still is at the root of all those values which are necessary for the moral goodness of man. On the other hand, *evil is something which essentially ought not to be. Just as *moral positivism denies the existence of moral goodness, so also it denies all true moral obligation which is independent of human caprice. The more recent forms of *positivism hold that the moral law is only the expression of feelings. In contrast to the usual interpretation of Kant's *categorical imperative, *value ethics bases the "ought" of morality in a value, but it separates this value from the order of existence. In direct opposition to these views the phrase "natural law" refers to the fact that "value" and "ought" are rooted in nature (especially man's) and thereby also in the order of existence. Goodness and obligation are founded on existence, at least insofar as goodness as the natural perfection of the human person is ordered to man's true needs.

By the very fact that man recognizes the good as something which ought to be, he knows that he is obligated to seek it. Many ethicians hold that the moral law is sufficiently explained in this way. But if that were so then it would not be a *law in the strict sense; for a law is an order, a command of a higher lawgiver equipped with full *authority. It is clear that this lawgiver can only be God since all men are subject to him. Insofar as God in his eternal decree enjoins the observance of the natural moral order, one speaks of the *eternal law.* Insofar as man participates in this law through the use of his natural reason and thus knows that he is bound by an absolute command, one speaks of the natural law.

The natural moral law is unchangeable to the extent that moral demands are required with absolute necessity by the very structure of being itself. So long as the relevant structures of being are maintained the corresponding moral demands will remain. Therefore the moral norms which flow from the unchanging nature of man retain their validity and binding force at all times; they are also independent of the constant ebb and flow of human history. However, norms which are established on the basis of historically changeable circumstances lose their binding power with the disappearance of those circumstances (e. g., the prohibition against interest-taking in the Middle Ages). With regard to whether or not concrete circumstances in particular situations can suspend the binding power of the moral law, see *situation ethics.

Every man has some knowledge of the natural moral law, at least with regard to its basic requirements. However, social, historical and individual presuppositions surely enter into the process of acquiring this knowledge; they can either aid it or impede it. The more fundamental the requirements are the easier it is to know them. Thus the moral consciousness of men the world over manifests an amazing agreement in the basic demands of the moral law (respect for God, family, life, property). Where there is question of the more difficult applications of the basic principles to particular situations there is always the possibility of erring in good faith. The differences in the moral outlook of different peoples are to be explained in this way (e. g., with regard to divorce, monogamy, killing the innocent in extreme cases, suicide, dueling, lying). Frequently such errors are overcome only by the light of *revelation. On the question of whether or not man grasps the nature of moral value and the fact that it should be pursued, but does not grasp that it is commanded by a divine law; in other words, on whether or not the so-called "philosophical sin" is at all possible, see *guilt. If man cannot understand moral value itself without perceiving at least a vague relationship in it to the Absolute (*good), then it is easier to understand that normally the command of an absolute authority makes itself known at least obscurely within the context of the moral "ought."

JdV

MORAL POSITIVISM

Moral positivism claims that moral values are founded in culture and its development according to the variations of time and place. Therefore the moral goodness or value of human activity is not necessarily and unchangeably tied to the essence of the human person, but fundamentally is subject to all possible variations. Consequently the moral law is also not unchangeable; the same must be said of the value judgments which are reflected in the spirit of different men and cultures (*moral relativism*). The main proof for moral positivism is the testimony of history. Each people and each culture develops its own moral values and these values are frequently found to conflict. What was formerly allowed seems to a later generation to be less worthy of man or even atrocious. Moreover the basic principle of evolution is operative here: There is no such thing as a complete moral theory which, as it were, dropped down from heaven. The moral principles which can be established on the basis of experience (*moral empiricism*) evolved out of primitive, animal forms as, for example, language and the other aspects of human culture (*moral evolutionism*). The theonomous moral positivism of Ockham and others derives moral value not from an unchangeable essence of man, but from the free will of God who, therefore, in another conceivable order of things, could allow actions that in this present order are immoral, for example, lying; later Ockham excluded the love of God from his moral positivism.

Criticism of the above positions is in order. The clear discernment of good and evil can never be achieved by mere external experience, since sense experience tells man only what is and not what should be. A transempirical, metaphysical knowledge is already operative in a person when, as a youth, he begins to make moral value judgments and recognizes the moral law. This knowledge is the conception of the human personality as a finite spirit in matter who is basically open to all being. Ethnology shows that there is a certain basic agreement among all the peoples of the earth regarding the fundamental requirements of the moral law. Errors in this matter, sometimes quite fundamental ones, are due to a false application in concrete cases of the first principles of morality. There are also justified variations in more particular moral requirements, for example, in the differing attitudes towards modesty in dress, in the rules of etiquette or good behavior, etc. — In refutation of Ockham one must say that God's will is not a fickle whim, for it is identified with the wisdom of his immutably holy will.

JoS

MORAL STATISTICS

Moral statistics is the statistical presentation of regularity in free human acts which are posited under the influence of certain psychic, social, cosmic and other conditions (e. g., statistics on marriages, suicides, crimes, births, automobile accidents). The philosophical meaning of such statistics lies in the fact that they impressively point up the intimate relationship between man's motives for acting and the psychological-physiological conditions he finds himself in. They also demonstrate the impossibility of unmotivated willing or of a will-action not influenced by motives. On the other hand, moral statistics do not prove whether or not, in any particular case, a man acted without freedom (in the sense of a moderate indeterminism) or with freedom. For the metaphysical question about the freedom of the will cannot be decided one way or the other by the use of statistical methods.

AW

MOTION

Motion taken in its broadest possible sense (1) is every *change; the concept was used in this way in Aristotelian-scholastic philosophy. — In modern terminology motion (2) means the constant change in place of a body; this is also the preferred meaning of the term in Aristotle and in the scholastics. These schools distinguished between *natural* and *violent* motion (2). A given motion is considered natural if it goes to its natural place as the result of an inner tendency that belongs to the nature of the thing in question; thus according to Aristotle heavy bodies fall and light bodies rise. A violent motion is one that is communicated to a body from the outside contrary to its own natural tendency so that the constantly operating cause of the motion is located outside of the thing moving. — According to the present view, which is put forth by the physical sciences, every motion presupposes an *impetus* in the object moved — an impetus which is communicated to the object by the mover. The meaning of the *principle of inertia* is that every material thing resists a change in the state of its motion and this resistance can be overcome only by the application of *force. Accordingly, without the use of some external force a body remains in its present state of rest or uniform, rectilinear motion; and with every application of force it experiences an acceleration. A body at rest which receives an impetus from an external power is moved or is in a state of motion. As a result it changes its place in space constantly and uniformly. Therefore, a distinction must be made between these two aspects of motion (2): the internal state of motion (= absolute motion) and the external change in place (= relative motion). This internal state is a determination that belongs to a body absolutely and so independently of the state of other things; the change in place is a result of this state and consists in the constant change of its relative bearing to other bodies (*Relativity, Theory of). — From this point of view of *finality, motion (3) signifies the transition from a stationary initial state to the desired final state. *Rest* as the goal of purposeful motion is a state that is secured through activity. According to the laws of physics, rest is merely the absence of motion (2); therefore it is a state in which no power is operative and which is itself not the operation of a power. Relative rest is the absence of motion within the framework of a system of reference. — *Rhythm* is the alternating return of the same state in some given motion according to a definite measure of time. — In a transferred sense philosophers also speak of motion (4) within the area of spiritual activity.

NJ

MOTIVE

A motive in the broad sense (1) is anything that influences (feelings, drives, imaginations etc.) the beginning and direction of an act of the will (except the power of willing itself). In a narrower sense (2) a motive is thought to be some represented *value that as a final cause gives a foundation and meaning to willing. A motive (2), therefore, does not come under efficient causality, but under final causality (*Cause). Even in the rejection of or escape from an *evil the opposing good is sought. For, evil as such cannot be directly willed. The choice of an evil always takes place with reference to a real or apparent good. Thus value is the formal object of the will; in fact it is its essential law in which the intelligibility of the soul expresses itself. It follows from this, on the one hand, that the will strives necessarily (but without *Force) for an object which presents itself to it as both a value and a non-value. Therefore, even though a motive is necessary for an act of the will, it still does not follow that a motive renders the desire of limited values necessary or unfree. This also holds for a motive that is in fact *predominant*. For, it is predominant neither as an overwhelming efficient cause nor as the representation of a greater value, but as the result of a *free value judgment* that prefers the one value and thereby makes it be "overwhelming," although it may be clearly recognized as the lesser value. Therefore, motives always explain only why a particular choice could be made, but never why a particular choice was actually made. A motive makes a choice intelligible, but it does not remove its *contingency. — For a value to become a motive, it must be known or experienced in the most impressive way possible not just as a value in itself, but also as capable of attainment for the one willing.

For the moral grounding of an action it is not only necessary that the motive (2) itself be moral so that the *intention* is directed to a moral value, but also that the means used and the other circumstances of the action be morally acceptable. Any true value can be a moral motive, which can be derived from the immediate object or from the circumstances or from other purposes; but it is only actually moral insofar as it is subordinate to the moral law or necessarily connected with it. Therefore it cannot be just an abstract obligation (Kant), but must be something like the love of God, obedience and respect for his law, hope of happiness in the next life, etc.

With regard to the other faculties of the soul beside the will, one can speak of motives insofar as the will exercises some influence over those faculties. Thus, for example, concerning the so-called free *certitude, a distinction should be made between the logical foundation of it or the reasons for it which offer the intellect a guarantee for the truth of a proposition (and so induce it to assent), and the motives for assent which the will can have in addition, insofar as these motives offer a good to the will.

JoS

MULTIPLICITY

Multiplicity stands in opposition to *unity and affirms the division of being, but in such a way that the different elements as unities remove themselves from each other. Since the existent — insofar as it possesses existence — is one, multiplicity must be rooted in non-being. Just as there cannot be such a thing as pure non-being, but only a kind of non-being that is supported by existence, so also is pure multiplicity an impossibility. For, multiplicity must always be supported by some unity, i. e., multiplicity always actualizes itself only as a unity that is broken by multiplicity. Accordingly, where existence, raised above all non-being, exists in infinite fullness, there we find absolute unity without any multiplicity. Only where existence is limited by non-being, and is therefore finite, does multiplicity find its place. Finiteness and multiplicity belong together essentially, just as there is no multiplicity without finiteness, so also is there no finiteness without multiplicity. Two forms of multiplicity are characteristics of the finite realty: the multiplicity of existent things and the multiplicity of parts or elements at the heart of each individual existent. In both cases, greater finiteness is accompanied by greater multiplicity.

With regard to the multiplicity of individuals: God is only one, because he exhausts the infinite fullness of existence. Since every finite spirit possesses only a segment of this fullness, it is possible to have many finite spirits. Yet, according to Thomas Aquinas, in the case of pure spirits (angels) just one individual realizes the total perfection of his species. Thus there are many species, but in each species there is only one individual. In the case of men, the species develops into a multiplicity of individuals, since no one of them can express in itself the full perfection of its species. However, since the species cannot be exhausted all at once, it gradually displays itself in the three broad physical species of animals, plants and minerals; it also reveals itself in a vast quantity of empirical species, in ever new variations of them and in innumerable individuals. That is the philosophical reason for *diversity* in the world, which at the same time offers a multiplicity of the same. Therefore, this multiplicity can be grasped mathematically and this is especially true of that which has the most sameness, namely, inorganic things. The unity which supports the multiplicity of these separate individuals is revealed in the real physical unity of the cosmos; in man's world it shows itself in the real spiritual unity of his communities.

With regard to the multiplicity of parts in one individual: here is a question of a multiplicity of parts which are united together in one composite whole; and by the separation of these parts the whole is destroyed. Even in a pure spirit the duality of essence and existence, of substance and activity is opposed to the absolute simplicity of God. In corporeal things there is also the multiplicity of the essential parts (e. g., body and soul) and the extended parts (e. g., the limbs of the body). — On the question of a purely conceptual multiplicity, but one that is based on reality, see *Distinction*.

Although multiplicity is rooted in non-being, it is still not something in itself evil or something that ought not to be (as *Buddhism teaches); it is not mere appearance (as perhaps Parmenides and Brahmanism say), nor is it only a multiplicity of appearances within the same existent thing (as Spinoza and all forms of pantheism say). Multiplicity receives its full reality from the transcendent creator alone; for, in a rich multiplicity of separate things he wishes to portray and communicate to men the unity of his infinite fullness.

JBL

MUTUAL CAUSALITY

Mutual causality in the narrower sense is the mutual dependence of things upon each other on the basis of efficient causality. This is affirmed in the mechanical principle of the equality of action and re-action: Every activity of one body upon another elicits an equal and opposite re-action from that other. — In a wider sense one speaks of mutual causality when there is a question of reciprocal orientation and completion of dissimilar *causes, for example, the relation between matter and form, between the efficient and the final cause; in this situation, the one cause is sometimes the condition for the operation of the other cause. — A special kind of mutual causality is operative between the material and the spiritual aspects of man. Experience shows definitely that they mutually influence each other. However, it cannot be simply concluded from this fact that a mere relationship of mutual causality exists between the body and the soul (*Body-Soul Relation). — Also, we should not think of the mutual causality between the intellect and the will in the sense of efficient causality, but as an inner union of both kinds of activity rooted in the nature of one and the same soul. — Since mutual causality exists both between all the bodies of the universe and also between the body and the soul and since *free will does not exclude the influence of various motives, the influence of the stars on human character and conduct is probable; however, there is nothing about the stars that can substantiate predictions about the future, as astrology would have it.

VN

MYSTERY

A mystery is something in the order of existence or truth that is hidden from us or is very difficult to reach; examples would be the unknown meaning of a symbol or the difficult problems that confront man in the world. Frequently the idea "mystery" is associated with religion in some way. — Catholic theology distinguishes between mysteries in the broad and in the narrow sense. In the broad sense, mysteries are truths that are hidden from the finite intelligence either with regard to their existence or with regard to their essence. For example, in the order of existence it remains hidden what God has determined for the future. In the order of essence the intrinsic compatibility of God's attributes remains hidden; for, human intelligence can see that they must be compatible. However, mysteries in the narrow sense or *absolute mysteries* are truths that are hidden from every finite intelligence both as to their existence and their essence, so that their inner possibility cannot be understood even after their existence has been revealed by God. In this category are the fundamental truths of Christian revelation such as the inner tri-personal life of God and the Incarnation of the Son of God. For a truth to be a mystery does not mean that it is totally unintelligible either in itself or as far as we are concerned. Mysteries are intelligible in themselves and to God. Their existence is communicable through *revelation and man, through faith, can grasp something of their meaning even though such knowledge is analogous and imperfect. — In the ancient religions of Greece and Rome the "mysteries" were secret religious cults in which only the initiated were allowed to take part; and the devotees were held to a strict secrecy about their cult and teachings. See also *Supernatural, Supra-rational.*

WB

MYSTICISM

Mysticism (Gr.: mýein = to close one's eyes) literally means an interior, unfathomable experience, especially of a religious nature. In a very broad sense it is understood as any kind of inner union with God and in a narrower sense it means an extraordinary union with God. Mysticism as experience should be distinguished from mysticism as a *science* of mystical experience. — Catholic theology defines (Christian, supernatural) mysticism as man's experiential interiorization of divine grace. A common element in all mysticism seems to be that God is known in the depths of the soul in some experiential way. This experience is not a universal phenomenon; but down through the centuries it has been witnessed to unanimously by so many eminent men that a doubt about the fact itself is just impossible. Philosophy is particularly interested in the mystical phenomena attested to by non-Christians (cf. Plotinus' ecstacies, Buddha's visions). Whether or not there is such a thing as *natural mysticism*, and in what sense (*Supernatural), is disputed, but on the basis of the facts uncovered by comparative religion it seems probable. This is not to be thought of as an immediate vision of God, but as a purely spiritual mode of knowing that is in some way independent of the senses (contemplation); here the spiritual soul either recognizes a special influence of God (e. g., an infused idea) or knows itself intuitively in its immediate relationship to God (e. g., in its total dependence on God or in the openness of the spirit to the absolute). To be sure, such a mode of knowing would not be in accordance with the soul's actual dependence on the body (and to that extent it needs special divine help for it), but it would not totally surpass the nature of the spiritual soul (and so to that extent it would be "natural"). One can speak here of a *divinization* only in the sense of a transformation by the divine being, but not in the sense of a substantial union with God. If the natural activity of the senses ceases because of a mystical experience, then this is said to be an ecstacy.

WB

MYTH

Myth (Gr.: *mythéomai* = tell, relate) has the original meaning of (1) a narration, a saga from ancient times (myths of heroes and the gods), then (2) an image or parable to explain human life and the world (such as Plato's myths). Of great influence on the life and culture of peoples is the myth (3) as an intuitive, imaginary, usually personified *Weltanschauung or view of life; here the imaginary is not just an external allegory for the conceptual order, but it forms a primary, undivided unity with it, which is experienced especially by primitives as reality itself. — *Mythology* is concerned with myths — their origin, content and influence; it is related both to cultural anthropology and to the history of religions.

According to some modern views on the matter, myth (3) is an accumulation of parallel images — an accumulation that grows in the subconsciousness of generations — in which definite aspects of human existence find their symbolic expression. Myth is of less help for the explanation of reality than it is for the spiritual mastery of it and for establishing a viable relationship with it. The *natural myth* was a result of the naive view of nature and the *cultural myth* arose only from a later reflection on the evolution of a culture up to that time. Myth is not necessarily religious, but it can be tied to religious representations.

Scientific, abstract thinking is not a favorable climate for the birth and effectiveness of myths. In opposition to the rationalism of the Enlightenment, the romantics and later the advocates of life philosophy (e. g., Nietzsche, Rosenberg) effected a revival of the myth as an irrational, unscientific interpretation of the world. Although philosophy on occasion has made use of the myth as a concrete mode of representation, and although it recognizes the cultural value of many myths, still it must rise above the picturesque concreteness of the myth in order to arrive at the sharp and clear self-consciousness of thinking.

WB

N

NATURAL CAUSALITY

Natural causality is the special kind of causation found in external, sub-spiritual *nature in contrast to the type of activity of psychic or spiritual causes (*Causality). The relationship between natural events is not merely that of a mathematical *function, for it fulfills the notion of a true *cause; this is evident since according to the *principle of *causality* every effect requires an adequate efficient cause in order to explain the new reality. Since in the realm of sub-human nature there is no such thing as free self-determination, natural causes produce their effects with necessity. Therefore there is a clear relationship between cause and effect so that the same causes always have the same effects. A cause in the sub-human world can produce no other, no greater and no lesser effect than it actually produces (*Causality, Law of). In the organic world not only the external attractions but also the particular situation of the reacting organism itself must be numbered among the causes which directly bring about the effect. With regard to apparent exceptions to the law of causal relationships, see *quantum mechanics. Sub-human nature, however, is not closed off against spirit (*Body-Soul Relation) and the creator (*Miracle). There is no such thing as *closed nature*.

In contrast to the view of *occasionalism, the producing of the effect is to be looked at as the proper activity of a body. However, this activity in the inorganic world is not a self-determination of the body, but in every activity of nature on this level the respective bodies are involved in *mutual causality. Through the operation of its power one body evokes a change in another body. These changes of state are for the most part in the nature of energy. *Energy* means the ability to do *work and it takes on very different forms (mechanical, electrical, thermal energy). Since energy, which does not remain identically the same *accident, can pass over from one body to another, by reason of the effectiveness of the cause new energy is produced, while in the process other energy is used up. Thereby the principle of the conservation of energy is affirmed: according to this principle, the amount of new energy produced is equal to the amount used up. — A great part of the effectiveness of natural causality rests upon the powers of *attraction* and *repulsion*. Because of these two powers bodies stand in a mutual relationship to each other so that they seek either to approach each other or to separate from each other. In this case there is never such a thing as an unmediated effect at a distance (*actio in distans*), i. e., a material cause cannot produce an effect at a far distant place witout connecting bodies lying in between. Whether such a telekinesis is also absolutely impossible cannot be proved with certainty, but it is probable. In order to explain the influence of one body on another some philosophers have assumed the existence of what they call ether which is defined as an unweighable elastic medium that fills the empty space around weighable bodies.

NJ

NATURALISM

Naturalism is the name given to the philosophical view which gives a decisive or even an exclusive role to *nature (according to any one of its many meanings). Of special interest in this system is its opposition to *spirit and the supernatural order. Thus naturalism (1) as a general philosophical theory directs itself onesidedly to sub-human nature, especially to its biological dimension (*Biologism), and considers that which is specifically human (spiritual knowing-willing, history) as a mere extension of the biological order according to the principles of physical science. In the thinking of Giordano Bruno and F. W. J. Schelling this view takes on a pantheistic coloring; according to the analogy of an organism, they look upon the totality of nature as one living organism animated by the absolute. In the field of ethics this kind of naturalism (1) often leads to recommending that one's natural drives be satisfied without the direction of a norm independent of these drives. Also, according to naturalism (1) art has only the task of imitating nature in the most perfect way possible without developing higher ideas. — In opposition to the *supernatural order there is a type of theological naturalism (2) according to which no other communication of God to man is possible except that which belongs to man's nature and in this sense is owed to him. This kind of naturalism (2) is also ultimately founded on a misunderstanding of *spirit and of its openness to the infinite.

WB

...sophical sense is a tendency, residing in all ...ite kind of activity. We speak here of a *law ...on natural things possess a necessity to act. ...is different according to the nature of the thing ...the same in the inorganic, organic and human-...e area of human activity the natural law is the same ...moral law; and its necessity consists in the obligation ...-human world the natural inclination is the reason for ...nings; however, organic life does enjoy a certain latitude ...tractions which work on living things get a different ...ng upon present need. Only in the realm of inorganic ...natural law mean constant uniformity of action. Such ...is called natural law by some scientists; it is expressed ...general laws and with regard to the inorganic world receives its exac. quantitative formulation in mathematical equations. These natural laws of the physical sciences are of two kinds: (1) *dynamic natural laws* are the direct expression of a particular, causally determined event; (2) *statistical natural laws* concern events which appear to be governed by some law and which are arrived at by taking the average of a large number of individual experiments as, for example, in the case of the laws of gases. Not all laws can be of a statistical nature; there must be some dynamic laws at least in the world of the micro-elements (*Causality, Law of). — The necessity of the natural laws governing sub-human events, since they control the real events of the order of contingent existence, is not an absolute but only a contingent necessity (*Contingency). Moreover, these laws are dependent upon the general conditions, which cannot be perfectly formulated, of the whole natural order accessible to us; as a result, the extension of the natural laws known to us to situations in which very different conditions are operative (extrapolation) is not legitimate. An exception to events covered by natural laws cannot be effected by nature itself, since the tendency to act is necessarily connected with things themselves and their activities; exceptions, however, can be produced by a preternatural cause (*Miracle). — The knowledge and formulation of the natural laws is a primary task of the sciences; in order to accomplish this they make extensive use of *induction.

NJ

NATURAL PHILOSOPHY

Natural philosophy (*cosmology*) is that part of *philosophy which has as its object living and non-living *nature (4). Its purpose is to explain the phenomena of nature from the aspect of their existence and to trace them back to the conditions of their possibility. This involves three things: a theory of the knowledge of nature, a metaphysics of nature and a natural philosophy in the more restricted sense. The theory of the knowledge of nature, which can also be considered a part of the philosophy of science, is a critical evaluation of the type, value and meaning of man's knowledge of nature. Just as the theory of knowledge investigates the general problems of human knowing, so also the theory of the knowledge of nature investigates the special problems involved in man's knowledge of nature. This study must take into consideration both the pre-scientific knowledge of nature and also the principles, methods and presuppositions of the scientific knowledge of nature. The metaphysics of nature attempts to understand natural phenomena and the basic concepts of physical science, such as space, time, motion, power, energy, matter, organic life, etc., it tries to understand them as best it can by reducing them to the ontological conditions of their possibility which are implicit in the concrete world of nature and by grasping the metaphysical essence of corporeal existence. The method to be employed in this search cannot be aprioristic, as it was among the disciples of Schelling. For natural reality is only one of many possible worlds which was called into existence by a free act of the creator. Therefore, the metaphysics of nature must be completed by a natural philosophy in the more restricted sense which takes into account both the demands of the metaphysics of nature and man's actual knowledge of concrete nature, as is clear from the results of scientific investigation when one reflects critically on its methods. However, it is not sufficient simply to fit all of these facts together into one closed total picture of reality, since such knowledge does not surpass the scientific knowledge of the physical world. For the limited purposes of *physical science those concepts are sufficient which give a working knowledge of some kind of characteristic property of natural things. But the purpose of natural philosophy as a branch of applied metaphysics is to arrive at concepts which give an answer to the question about the natures of things and which show the proper relationship between natural reality, man and the whole of reality, including the Absolute.

NJ

NATURAL RIGHTS

A *right is a moral claim on another; every right is ultimately based in the *nature of things and so when all is said and done in God, in God's essence and in his holy will which is in perfect agreement with his essence. Just as the holy will of God manifests itself in the whole created order as the natural *moral law (nature-law) so also it manifests itself as a natural right in those essential modes of human behavior in which man's social life and the legal system supporting that life is rooted. Consequently, natural rights are a part of the natural moral law and the whole legal order is only a part of the entire moral order. Every human explicitation of law (positive law) must conform to the God-given principles; and the only thing human positive law can do is either to further develop the legal principles of the natural order (*per modum conclusionis*) or, in those areas where the natural order of duties and rights leaves open a broad area of choice, by means of concrete determinations to fill in this broad area of choice according to the practical needs of the particular time and place (*per modum specificationis*). This is principally, but not exclusively, the job of the State which establishes laws for the common good of all; but every social group has the right to establish laws governing those things which pertain to its own particular good (*Subsidiarity).

This traditional view of natural law was superseded for a time by what has been called the "right of reason"; the latter opinion was proposed under the misleading name of "natural right." At the peak of *rationalism and of the *enlightenment many intellectuals were convinced that they could deduce from the universal principles of reason the rules, even the most minute, that would govern every aspect of human life, including also the ordering of all social life. The attempt ended up in absurdity. Ever since that time those who have not been able to see the difference between traditional natural right and the rationalistic version of natural right have tended to consider the traditional natural right position as something that simply cannot be taken seriously. As a result, legal positivism has held almost complete sway over the legal world. It was only the calamities of recent decades, the complete abandon with which the dictatorships and totalitarian states have trodden human dignity into the dirt, which have brought about a re-consideration of rights which *precede* and *transcend* the positive legal order; in actual fact, if not in name, this signals a return to the classical theory of natural rights. Thus the declaration of human rights included in the United Nations Charter does not say that these rights are granted by those who drew up the charter, but they are presented as rights which are simply given and unalienable. The atheist bases them on nature and the freedom of man. The Christian, however, and all who believe in God are able to give them an essentially deeper and stronger foundation in the order of creation: just as their ultimate source is to be found in God, so also do they have their inviolability from God.

OvNB

NATURE

Nature is etymologically derived from the Latin *natura* which in turn is an exact rendition of the Greek *physis*. Both words point to the connection with the act of being born or birth; first of all they mean (1) that characteristic of a living being which is natural, pertaining to birth, growing or proceeding from birth. Then, in a broader sense nature (2) means the essence of every existent which comes to it from its very origin. Although frequently a distinction is not made between nature and essence, nevertheless strictly speaking nature adds a dynamic element to the notion of essence; in this sense "nature" is the principle of the development of a thing, the inner foundation of its action and passion. From this point of view every existent has its own nature, including man and even God himself (but in God excluding all imperfection). This nature (3) is the building plan residing in every existent and thereby also the determining norm of its activity; i. e., the *natural law is rooted in nature. Subhuman things obey the natural laws without insight and therefore necessarily; the natural law, however, which is operative in the spiritual life of man has a moral character because man knows it as an ethical "ought" which challenges his freedom. Consequently whatever conflicts with natural laws, especially with the moral natural law, is *unnatural*. — Against this background, nature (4) as an all-embracing whole means the totality of those things which have a developing nature. According to *pantheism that is the totality of absolutely all existents (e. g., in Spinoza: "*Deus sive natura*"); in other systems it means the totality of all spatio-temporal existents insofar as they, by reason of their own special nature (3), perfect, develop and unite themselves into some kind of order — the natural order (1). Seen in this light nature (4) as the all-protecting order is often personified (e. g., "mother" nature); of her it is said that she does nothing in vain and that she makes no leaps (*non facit saltus*). This order, to which man is also subject, is ultimately based in God and in his creating and conserving rule of the world.

In order to make our position clearer, further distinctions are necessary. In the first place, a distinction must be made between nature and *spirit. Nature (5) in this sense includes all those beings which lead an unconscious, instinctive existence — primarily the world of biological life. Even though man participates in this nature (5) with many levels of his being, still he as it were encounters it as a possessor of spirit, i. e., of a conscious life that is freely realized. That type of *naturalism which would like to make man into a piece of nature (5) (Neitzsche, Klages) basically misunderstands what man is; still it does contain within it a legitimate concern, namely, the desire to overcome the unhealthy overconsciousness and caprice of a degenerate spirit. Actually, this can be accomplished by tying man more closely to nature (5).

Secondly, a distinction should be made between nature and *culture. Nature (6) also means the state of man and of all visible things as this state develops by itself out of the laws of nature and as it renews itself ahistorically in the eternal cycle of generation and corruption. Culture, on the other hand, is that which man makes out of himself and out of his environment by means of intellectual planning and shaping and it is that wherein he actualizes himself as a historical existent in order to achieve an even more perfect development. Since man necessarily produces culture there is no such thing as a purely *natural-state* (1) of man; the primitive races are simply nearer to it than civilized nations are. Of course, if culture gets too far removed from nature, then Rousseau's solution of "Back to nature" has a certain justification.

Thirdly, a distinction should be made between nature and the *super-natural. Nature (7) or the natural includes everything that belongs to a created thing, either as an integral part (soul, body, intact limbs), or as a property, inclination or power flowing from it (intellect, will), or as a necessary means so that an existent can maintain itself and arrive at its goal (food, education). From this point of view the natural order (2) means the totality of all created things (even created spirits) with every-thing that belongs to their nature (3) as creatures of God. In contrast to this, *supernatural* means the participation of the created spirit in the divine nature (3) or in the divine life through the grace of adoption; according to Christian revelation, this participation was granted to man from the very beginning so that he never existed in the purely natural-state (2) (here understood in a sense essentially different from (1) above). — A perfection which indeed surpasses the powers of one being but not the powers of all created nature is called *preternatural*. In this category belongs the *miracle which in certain cases can be worked by the almighty power of God in order to testify to *revelation.

JBL

NECESSITY

The necessary is that which cannot be otherwise, or that whose contradic-tory opposite is impossible. Necessity includes *possibility. It stands in contradictory opposition to *contingency in the broad sense (= the pos-sibility of non-existence), and in contrary opposition to *impossibility. — *Absolute, metaphysical* or *unconditional* necessity is founded on the rela-tions of essences that are mutually inclusive or complementary. The ab-solute necessity of existing certainly belongs to God, but it cannot be concluded to by us from the concept of God prior to some kind of *demons-tration of *God's existence*. The absolute necessity open to us on the basis of concepts is a necessity of essential relationship or of inner pos-sibility. *Relative* or *conditioned necessity* is a necessity that is dependent on a presupposition. If this dependence is related to a definite natural cause, then we speak of physical necessity (*Natural Law). All necessity dependent on free causes is called *moral* necessity. It is subjective if a certain way of acting is expected because of innate or acquired habits (*Certitude), but objective with regard to a means that is absolutely necessary for the attainment of a predetermined goal. — *Logical* necessity is the necessity of a conclusion that flows from its premises; therefore, it is not a necessity of the conclusion as such, but merely of the consequence or sequence. — From an epistemological point of view, a distinction is made between *subjective* and *objective* necessity. The necessity to connect certain experiences together as the result of associations and complexes, is subjective; the necessity to connect certain experiences, concepts or principles together because of insight into the concrete reality or into abstract essential relationships, is objective and universally valid. See also *Modality, Determinism, Force.*

WB

NEGATIVE THEOLOGY

Under the influence of Proclus the neo-Platonist, the Christian thinker Dennis, the pseudo-Areopagite, distinguished between an affirmative and a negative *theology. While affirmative theology starts from God's effects in the order of creation, makes statements about him that are based on creation, and so attributes many names to him, negative theology rises by way of negation to the infinite and nameless One who is above all positive and negative determinations. At the conclusion of this ascent it unites itself with him in the ineffable obscurity of mystical experience. — The teachings of the negative theology exercised a great influence on the theology and *mysticism of the Middle Ages. Thus, even Thomas Aquinas claimed that we know more about what God is not, than we do about what he is. Meister Eckhart made extensive use of this idea in order to give an expression, often paradoxical, to supra-conceptual, mystical experiences; so also did Nicholas of Cusa. The pattern of thought of negative theology (although under different names) is more noticeable in oriental philosophy than it is in western. Thus, we find that the Indian sages preface every statement about the Absolute with a solemn cry of "Not so!", that the Buddhists (*Nagarjuna*) or the Chinese philosophers speak of the great "emptiness," and the *Nishida* in Japan proclaims a philosophy of "nothingness." — Negative theology is well adapted to sharpen our sense for the infinity and incomprehensibility of God. It cannot, however, deny the possibility of making positive statements about God without slipping into *agnosticism.

WB

NEO-PLATONISM

Neo-Platonism is not just a revival of Plato's philosophy, as the name might imply; it is a philosophical system of great speculative power which combined the Platonic philosophy with the other main trends of ancient thought, with the exception of *Epicureanism, and even included religious and mystical elements, some of them taken from oriental philosophy. — Although founded by Ammonius Saccas (ca. 175-242), Neo-Platonism was first expounded by Plotinus (203-269). At the beginning of his system Plotinus places the One which stands above all opposition. Since each existent is only through its oneness, the One is before the existent. It is unknowable and unnameable. Even the designation "the One" should be understood in a negative sense. In opposition to all multiplicity it is the first reality, the highest perfection which neither loses of its fullness nor suffers any change in the production of multiplicity. The procession of multiplicity out of the First is mediated by a gradation of beings. These are: the Spirit or the Intelligible world, the World-Soul and Matter. Since this succession is timeless the world as a whole is eternal. The descending movement of the world from the higher to the imperfect is purposeless, while the striving directed back to the First is ruled by higher and higher ends depending on the level it is on.

The essence of spirit (*nous*) is the unity of thought and existence. Spirit is turned toward the One from which it was produced. Spirit receives its content, its ideas, from the One; the ideas form a multiplicity, however, or a system in the spirit. The formation of the system leads to the categories and the numbers, and also to *intelligible matter* as the substratum of all the ideas (forms). — Just as the One brings forth the spirit (nous) so also does spirit bring forth soul as its imperfect image. Though in itself indivisible, the soul can still enter into and animate the spatial-sensible world which it created; but it does not communicate itself to the world, just its activity. It is part of the soul's nature to bring forth *sensible matter*. Matter does not partake of the nature of the One and the Good and thus is not capable of any further generation. Without order and form it is darkness and the principle of evil. This soul is the soul of the world or of nature. Particular souls are contained in the world-soul and identical with the ideas which the world-soul receives from spirit.

It is an inner determination of soul that it turn itself away from the sensible world and direct itself to spirit; through the spirit it is able to return to the One. Such an experience, however, in this life is possible only rarely and for brief moments. Yet each soul must strive for this return during this life, otherwise it will not be capable of it in death and so will be joined to a body once again. — Since the goal of man's life is to become like God, it is not enough to cultivate just the social virtues. Rather, he must strive to free his soul from the contaminating influence of the body through purification (catharsis) and through a life immersed in spirit to prepare it for final union with the One in ecstasy.

Plotinus' teaching is a form of pantheism. But he also leaves room for polytheism in his system. Porphyry (ca. 233-300) and Jamblichus (ca. 330) tend even more towards polytheism. For Jamblichus developed Plotinus' thought regarding the triple succession by introducing more triads. Proclus (410-485), the last systematic neo-platonic thinker, followed in the direction of Jamblichus. According to him, as the foundation for the ecstatic union, man possesses another spiritual power over and above reason, which power he calls the "One". In addition to the material body he also ascribes an aetherial or "light body" to the soul; and this body is incorruptible. — Neo-Platonism was the last great philosophical system worked out by the ancients. It had profound influence on *patristic philosophy, Christian *mysticism and *scholasticism.

WB

NEO-SCHOLASTICISM

Neo-scholasticism occasionally means the renewal of scholastic philosophy and theology which began in the 16th century, but it usually means the scholastic movement of the 19th and 20th centuries. The name neo-scholasticism is rejected by some scholars because it too easily gives the impression that the movement is merely a revival of old ideas, whereas in fact its goal is much broader. First of all the scholastic tradition, which was almost lost in the Enlightenment, had to be taken up again. This was accomplished in Italy by V. Buzzetti († 1824) and his pupil S. Sardi († 1865) in the sense of a pure Thomism which gradually prevailed over the eclectic approach of S. Tongiorgi († 1865) and others.

In Germany in the first half of the 19th century thinkers such as Fr. V. Baader, A. Günther and M. Deutinger attempted to construct a new foundation for a Christian philosophy, profiting from the wealth of ideas they found in *German idealism. Yet these attempts were doomed to failure because they neglected to go back to the rich tradition of the Christian Middle Ages. It was first of all necessary to do the painstaking historical study of the tradition and thus bring it into focus: this was accomplished by J. Kleutgen in his *Philosophie der Vorzeit* (1860). But neo-scholasticism received its strongest impetus from Leo XIII's encyclical *Aeterni Patris* (1870) which advocated the study of the philosophy of St. Thomas Aquinas. Alongside the Thomistic approach the Suarezian view was also cultivated, especially in Spain, Germany and France. It should also be remembered that ideas derived from 18th century scholasticism, which was influenced by philosophical rationalism, were still at work in this neo-scholasticism.

The historical research into the scholasticism of the Middle Ages, which was cultivated especially in Germany (H. Denifle, Fr. Ehrle, Cl. Baeumker, M. Grabmann) and France (P. Mandonnet, É. Gilson), has gone beyond the requirements of the college classroom. Thus the Franciscans have initiated a serious study of the Franciscan school (Bonaventure, Scotus);

the center of this research is located at Bonaventure College in Quaracchi near Florence, Italy. Thus the lively questioning of the medieval thinkers and their wealth of ideas plus their solution to problems have received more and more attention. These studies have aroused a new respect for medieval philosophy. They also facilitate the distinction between the permanently valid elements in scholasticism and those which are temporally conditioned.

Further systematic development resulted from the encounter with modern science and empirical psychology. The insertion of the new knowledge into the older natural philosophy and rational psychology required a more or less thorough revision of certain doctrines. Also the development of epistemology was furthered by a better knowledge of both the physiology and the psychology of the senses ("Critical Realism"). In this regard the "Institut Supérieur de Philosophie," founded by Cardinal D. Mercier at Louvain, deserves special mention.

In the 19th century philosophy was greatly influenced by positivism, so much so in fact that it was little more than a theory of knowledge. But since the turn of the century there has been a renewed interest in real philosophical content; in this situation Christian thinkers now feel that a creative exchange with modern philosophy is their chief task, an exchange not just with contemporary philosophy but also with the best modern philosophers of the past 300 years; for present-day philosophy can only be understood in the light of the work since Descartes. The real failure of neo-scholasticism, especially since the 17th century, has been that it was too removed from the intellectual life of the time. Thus "modern" philosophy went its own way while the perennial philosophy became more and more a purely internal affair of seminaries and religious schools. What Aquinas did in his day with regard to Aristotle, Avicenna and Averroes, was not done by his followers with regard to the modern philosophers. And yet, if scholastic philosophy is to be a living reality, then it must take up contemporary problems and apply its fundamental principles to them in a creative way.

It follows from this that even though the basic principles of scholasticism are eternally true they will still have a somewhat different character in different cultures. For if this is truly Catholic philosophy then it cannot be forced on Anglo-Saxons in a Latin form or on orientals in a Western European form. The special recommendation of the philosophy of St. Thomas by the Church is not opposed to the realization of this goal especially since the Popes have stressed repeatedly the need for a "suitable freedom" in this matter.

Actually there are many important studies of contemporary problems by scholastic philosophers and thinkers. Mention should be made of the philosophical-historical studies done at the Catholic University of Milan

(Fr. Olgiati and others), of the analyses of *phenomenology and *existential philosophy, of J. Marechal's daring but controversial attempt to relate the Thomistic metaphysics of knowledge with Kant's transcendental method, of the Catholic encyclopedias for Japan and China which explain for the oriental peoples the heritage of Christian philosophy in a way that they can understand.

JdV

NOMINALISM

Nominalism is the teaching that denies the existence of universals both in the world of thought and in the world of things. The most radical form of nominalism appeared in the 11th century in the person of Roscellin of Compiegne who attributed universality to names only. This view is in direct contradiction to the clear testimony of consciousness which manifests an awareness of universal meanings as the basis of all universal names. Modern forms of nominalism, also called sensism, should be distinguished from the medieval versions. The English philosophers Berkeley, Locke, Hume, Stuart Mill, Spencer, and the German philosophers Wundt, Ziehen, Mach, because of their deficient theory of knowledge have recourse to sensible schemas as a substitute for valid *universal concepts. Their reason for this position lies in their misunderstanding of intellectual *abstraction, which alone can explain how a man, in the formation of concepts, is totally dependent on his experience and still transcends that *experience so that he can form universal concepts. Frequently the *conceptualism of the late Middle Ages, especially that of Ockham, is called nominalism or terminism; there is some justification for this, since universal concepts as the conceptualists understand them are hardly more suited to the demands of science than the sensible schemas of the nominalists.

JS

NOTHING

Nothing (*nihilum*) is not something particular alongside of existence, but rather the absence of all existence; therefore, even the concept itself is formed through a denial of existence. A distinction is made between *absolute* or *negative* nothing and *relative* or *positive* nothing. The former denies both the reality and the possibility of existence, while the latter denies only the reality but not the possibility of some existent. The expression, "God created the world out of nothing," uses the word "nothing" in the second sense. Existence and nothing constitute the most fundamental opposition there is; this opposition is expressed in the *principle of *contradiction*. But Hegel seems to deny the absolute incompatibility of existence

NUMBER

and nothing that is expressed in this principle (*German Idealism, *Dialectic).

In various ways *nihilism* reduces existence to nothingness. In its metaphysical-ethical form (1) it looks upon metaphysical reality and absolutely binding values as empty fictions of the mind. Nietzsche thought that the growth of this kind of nihilism is unavoidable and so he tried to overcome it by positing a wholly new set of values. At present Jean Paul Sartre advocates the same nihilism insofar as he accepts no God and no order of essence or value, and says that fundamentally everything is absurd anyway. In its political-social form (2) nihilism rejects the existing order and frequently also rejects all social and political order. Developed in opposition to a brutally despotic government in Russia in the middle of the 19th century and formed into complete anarchism, it finally grew into the Bolshevistic workers' movement. — When the mystics (e.g., Meister Eckart) say that God is "nothing," then that means only: God does not exist in the same way as all the existents of our experience, which are finite and nameable; since his existence surpasses all finite names, it must be expressed as nothing finite. — The nothing that is the center of Heidegger's philosophy has often been explained in the sense of absolute nothingness, but according to Heidegger's later writings it is actually the veil of existence (*Existential Philosophy).

JBL

NUMBER

From ancient times until the development of algebra in modern mathematics this word was limited to so-called positive whole numbers (also called "natural numbers"): 1, 2, 3, ... (/, //, ///, ...). Aristotle defines this number as "a multiplicity measured by unity" (Metaph. X, 6: 1057a 3f.). — Alongside this so-called *predicamental number* which belongs in the category of *quantity, the scholastic philosophers also spoke of a *transcendental number* which can be applied to immaterial beings. (This concept is to be distinguished from that of non-algebraic numbers, also called *transcendental numbers*). — The modern set-theoretical foundation of natural numbers (Frege, Russell) begins with a correspondence (also called a "mapping") between the elements of sets. Then if there is a one-to-one correspondence between the elements of two sets, we say that the two sets are *equivalent* or that the same *cardinal number* belongs to both. The theory of sets has extended this concept to infinite sets. The cardinal number of a denumerable set (i.e., one in correspondence with the sequence of natural numbers) is designated by χ_0. The so-called higher *transfinite* cardinal numbers: $\chi_1, \chi_2, \chi_3, \ldots$ ("Cantor's Paradise") from a constructive standpoint lack a definite sense (*Mathematics, Philosophy of). — The series of natural numbers can be given by an inductive definition: (1) / is a number;

(2) if x is a number, then x / is also a number (x/ designates the successor of x). In the axiomatic foundation of arithmetic the two indicated parts of the definition occur as two of Giuseppe Peano's five axioms. Also, by means of inductive definitions different operations with numbers (addition, substraction, multiplication, etc.) can be introduced. For example, for addition the schematic definition runs: (1) $x + / = x/$; (2) $x + y/ = = (x + y)/$.

By means of abstraction (also called "definition by abstraction") one can extend the concept of number and introduce other kinds of numbers: positive-rational, negative, imaginary numbers. The introduction of *positive-rational* numbers by means of abstraction occurs thus: One proceeds from the pairs of natural numbers (m_1, n_1), (m_2, n_2), ... and defines an equality between them in the following way: Two pairs (m_1, n_1) and (m_2, n_2) are equal if this equation is valid: $m_1 . n_2 = m_2 . n_1$. The abstraction consists in this, that one restricts oneself only to such statements about these pairs ("fractions") whose validity is not changed by the replacement of one pair by an equal pair. Thus, one then speaks of new "abstract objects" — the positive-rational numbers.

The introduction of *real numbers* offers an essentially more difficult problem. Even in the ancient world the discovery of the *irrational numbers* (incommensurable occurrences of quantity) by the Pythagoreans brought Greek mathematics into a state of crisis. This discovery is supposed to have occurred in connection with the pentagon — the symbol of the Pythagoreans. For, the sides and the diagonals of the pentagon are incommensurable quantities. The solution of this problem gave rise to the *Eudoxian theory of proportions*, which was also included in the fifth book of Euclid's *Elements*. It makes possible talk about incommensurable occurrences, since it compares the latter with proportions (today we say: with rational numbers). Two occurrences are called equal if they lie between the same proportions. Thus the Greeks considered only those occurrences that allow themselves to be constructed. From the standpoint of current basic research the level of this proportional theory is an ideal model. The Aristotelian notion of the continuum and of the potentially infinite was in accordance with this proportional theory. — On the other hand, in the modern theory of real numbers (Dedekind, Cantor) one speaks of the set of all real numbers, which are defined by Dedekind as "cuts" of rational numbers. Thus, the indefinite character of this concept was overlooked; i. e., its potential infinity was not seen. This resulted in the modern crisis of mathematics. Taking this indefiniteness (as Lorenzen showed in 1965) into consideration allows a satisfying interpretation of the essential elements in classical analysis (differential, integral) from a constructive point of view. Work is now proceeding on a constructive theory of real numbers and analysis. See also *Mathematics, Philosophy of.*

VR

O

OBJECT

Literally an object is that which is "thrown against" someone and so it essentially signifies a relation to someone whom it confronts. Strict philosophical terminology holds fast to this relative meaning of the word; therefore it does not use the word, as sometimes happens in ordinary life, simply as a synonym for "thing." In a wider sense, an object (1) is everything to which a conscious act of a *subject is directed; or it is that to which a power of the soul or a habit or even a particular science is directed and it is the end or goal of the act (power, habit, science) as such. Therefore, the existent taken purely as such is not an object but only insofar as it is knowable, desireable, etc.; and it becomes an object in a new way when it is actually known and desired. Scholastic philosophy distinguishes the *material object* which is the whole concrete existent at which the subject aims, from the *formal object* which is the special characteristic or aspect ("form") which is singled out for consideration in this whole. The formal object of a power, a science or a virtue is the aspect that is common to all of their objects, as in the study of man from the point of view of his anatomy. — In a more limited sense, object (2) does not mean any and every known or willed, but only that which independently "opposes" the subject so that the subject must attend to it. In this sense God's creative mind and will do not have an object, but his knowledge can more aptly be called projecting and originating. — From another point of view the concept "object" (3) is restricted to the material existent directly aimed at in the perception, while everything subjective and personal, i.e., one's own ego that is experienced only in the performance of its acts, as well as the person of the other, that is grasped in a kind of co-performance of his intentional acts, is called *non-objective.* The confinement of the concept "object" (4) to the object of a pure drive for knowledge should also be connected with this meaning.

Where knowledge occurs through the mediation of a conscious intelligible species, the object itself must be distinguished from the "content" of the knowledge. Thus, for example, the thought-content is the representation contained in the *concept or the judgment, but the object is the existent which is independent of the thought. If the thought-content itself is thought of as the real object, then that leads to epistemological *idealism which affirms that the object is the product of thinking. This idealistic meaning of "object" (5) is sometimes what is really meant when someone says that God could never be the object of our thinking. — Closely connected with the distinction between the thought-content and the object is the fact that *the given* does not always coincide with the object. Everything that immediately manifests itself without the conscious assistance of the subject is called the (immediately) "given." Thus, that which becomes immediately conscious in the perception of the external is the "given"; but, according to the view of moderate *realism, that "given" is not the external object in its own proper, real existence, but the inner, representative (intentional) existence in which the object is seen. — In a broader sense, sometimes every object (2) that independently encounters the knowing subject is called a "given"; for example, as in the case where one would say that our knowledge is a representation of a pre-given object.

JdV

OBJECTIVE

Objective literally means that which is related to an *object. In almost all of its meanings it stands in opposition to subjective. Since "object" does not at all mean the same thing as "really existing," the use of the word "objective" in the sense of "actual" or "real" in contrast to the word "subjective" in the sense of "unreal" or "mere thought" (in spite of the frequency of this usage) should be avoided in a philosophical language that strives for clear distinctions; in fact, all should be on their guard against an extreme and thoughtless use of the expressions "objective" and "subjective." In a legitimate sense, that which is proper to the object (as such), that which is in the object, can be called "objective" (1), in contrast to the "subjective" as that which is proper to the *subject or in the subject (cf. the opposition between objective and subjective *evidence). In its most important philosophical sense, "objective" (2) means: determined by the object, based on the object, in contrast to "subjective," which means, not based on the object, but determined only by feeling or the haphazard positing of the subject (cf. the opposition between objective and purely subjective *certitude). In this sense, *objectivity* is required by *science. Of course, this requirement must not be misunderstood in the sense that science must disregard all *value inherent in the object and look upon it as if it has almost nothing to do with us; such a conclusion follows only from the false presupposition that value is something unreal, something attributed to the object on the basis of feeling alone. Objectivity, therefore, also does not mean thought and research devoid of all personal involvement.

Another meaning of objective (3) is present when *intentional acts are called "objective" insofar as they are related to the object; and "subjective" insofar as they are acts (accidents) of the subject. Thus, the objective concept (better: the concept considered objectively) is the concept insofar as by means of the thought-content present in it, it is a representation of the object; and the subjective concept (better: the concept subjectively considered) is the concept as a real thought-act of the subject. If even here the subjective is the real in contrast to the objective (as the representation that is related to an object), that is especially true of the older understanding in scholastic philosophy of the expressions "objective" (4) and "subjective"; this meaning is based on the idea that not just the bearer of intentional acts, but every substantial existent is called a subject. In this sense, to exist subjectively means: to really exist in oneself; and to exist (only) objectively means: to exist (only) as an object of thought (but not in itself); thus, for example, a being of the mind is defined as that which exists objectively only in the mind. This meaning is directly opposed to the improper use of the term mentioned above. — Since in epistemological *idealism (e. g., Kant's *Critical Philosophy) the object cannot confront the thought-content, a distinction between objective and subjective can be defended only on the basis that the objective (5), as that which is formed by the categories of the transcendental subject, is equated with that which is universally valid (= valid for all thinking beings) in contrast to the subjective, as that which exists only for the individual. In connection with the impossibility in physics of thinking of the objects of microphysics as similar to the objects of our sense experience or, in other words, of "objectifying" them, that is also thought of as objective (6) which is "objectifiable" in the sense above.

JdV

OBJECTIVE REALITY

By "objective reality" we mean an object that corresponds to a *judgment and is expressed in that judgment, not primarily insofar as it is thought in the judgment but much rather insofar as it exists independently of judgmental thought. Objective reality, therefore, consists in the fact that some sort of a determination (attribute, activity, relation — whatever is expressed by the predicate) belongs to some existent (which is expressed by the subject of the judgment). However, the structure of objective reality is not necessarily the same in every respect as the logical structure of the judgment; the situation of identity between subject and predicate is present only in our thinking, and not, as *logical transcendentalism* maintains, "in itself."

Of course, often a more or less analogous relation (e.g., the relation between substance and accident) in the objective reality corresponds to the logical relation; however, the objective reality does not necessarily have the structure of a real relation. (For example if we says: "God is a spirit," a real relation between God and his spirituality does not correspond to this proposition.) For, the logical form of the judgment is only *our* way of thinking, and the *truth of the judgment does not demand that our "mode" of thinking is literally present in the thing, but only that the objective content corresponds to the "content" of our thought. — A distinction is made between *necessary* and *contingent* objective realities. Absolutely necessary objective realities — if we prescind from the actual existence of God — are simply *essential contents* which in themselves still do not affirm actual existence; thus, the objective reality: $2 + 2 = 4$ does not mean that somewhere $2 + 2$ really exists, but only that the essence of $2 + 2$ necessarily implies the relation $= 4$, so that if at any time $2 + 2$ is actualized it necessarily $= 4$. Contingent objective realities exist only insofar as actual existence is given to them and to a particular time; they are also often called "facts." — This expression is misleading: that "a *negative objective reality* existing in itself" corresponds to a true, negative judgment. For, the negative judgment is true if the objective reality denied in it is *not* to be found in the order of existence; it is self-contradictory to attribute "existence in itself" to a negative, since the negative "exists" only in our thinking.

JdV

OBJECTIVISM

Objectivism, in contrast to *subjectivism, is the philosophical position according to which the value of knowledge is measured by the *object that is independent of the subject. One can likewise speak of objectivism in ethics and aesthetics, if the object or the objective order is recognized as normative for moral goodness or for beauty. According to Aristotelean-Thomistic *realism, the object, which is the measure of knowledge (moral goodness, beauty), ultimately is the existent and existence itself along with the essential orders rooted in existence. However, objectivism is a wider concept than that of realism. For, logical transcendentalism (e.g., some representatives of *Phenomenology) is a kind of objectivism, but it is not realism; for, it recognizes as the ultimate norm an objective world completely independent of the subject, but this world has not real existence — only *value.

JdV

OCCASIONALISM

Occasionalism is the philosophical position that denies to finite beings their own proper efficient causality so that they are only *occasional causes* for the activity of God which is the only real activity. Universal occasionalism is based either on a mechanistic world view (*Mechanism) or on a false idea of the divine *concurrence. Particular forms of occasionalism grow out of the Cartesian difficulty with regard to the *body-soul relation which rejects any mutual causality between the two. While all occasionalists agree that God is the only principal cause of all activity, some consider creatures as mere conditions of divine activity (Malebranche) and others look upon them as passive instruments (Geulincx). Since existence without *activity is impossible, occasionalism logically leads to pantheism. See also *Causality, Cause*.

WB

OCCULTISM

Occultism (Lat: *occultum* - hidden) is the profane or non-religious concern with that which has not yet been made known by means of man's normal knowing powers or that is wholly closed off from those powers. The sensible-rational mode of knowing that is naturally given to each man is the normal thing; its end result is the empirical and scientific view of the world. Therefore, the *occult* is everything that is known in an abnormal but profane way; it is also this mode of knowing itself. In the realm of religion, *faith and *mysticism are concerned with the mysterious. Depending upon the degree of diversion from the normal, the occult can be categorized as follows: 1. There is the unusual or a-normal that occurs only in individual persons in unusual circumstances resembling sleep (*trance*); there is also sickness that can result in a disturbance to one's faculties so that they err in perception. In this category are found unusual activities of the subconscious mind in sleep and in dreams, under hypnosis and in a state of hysteria. — 2. There is the extraordinary which occurs either without one's normal faculties or even contrary to them (occult in the narrow sense), and this can be either in one's consciousness (*parapsychology*) or outside of it (*paraphysics*), for example, knowing things spatially and temporally not present ("sixth sense"), the communication of mental states without a sensible expression, effects of the will outside of one's own body without a recognizable mediation through space. In this category belong: *telepathy*, which is the transmission of images, emotions and will-acts to others by simply willing it internally; *telaesthesia* and *clairvoyance*, which is the direct vision of some reality unknown to anyone else, without the use of known senses, so that telepathy is excluded; *telephysics*, which is the production of movements (*telekinesis*), sounds, materializations, facial and hand impressions without physical contact and this is done without any known external activity. — 3. There is the preternatural; here the causality seems to proceed not from living men, but from bodiless beings (the souls of the dead or of other purely spiritual beings) such as "spirits" and "intelligences." To be included here are such things as the accounts of phantoms, ghosts, goblins, etc.

Evaluation of the first group: The explanation of these occurrences as mere deviations from the normal is now being handled and will finally be resolved. Evaluation of the second group: Distant effects certainly proceed from living men who have a special talent for it (*mediums*); but up till now there are not satisfactory theories about "how" this takes place. Some of the theories that have been advanced are: unknown radiations from the nervous system, direct activity from soul to soul by means of telepathy without corporeal cooperation, the conquering of time and space by means of clairvoyance; but we are still almost totally ignorant of these things. However, since effects produced at a distance are repeatable under certain conditions, in contrast to the *miracle they point to natural laws that are still wholly unknown to us. — For the evaluation of the third group see *Spiritism.

KF

OMEGA POINT

Omega point is the future focal point of evolutionary convergence in the theory of evolution developed by Pierre Teilhard de Chardin. Evolution proceeds in the direction of greater organization of matter (complexity) and of correspondingly higher degrees of *consciousness. The evolutionary process has passed through the critical point of the appearance of *life, has resulted in ever more complex forms of life with commensurately higher levels of consciousness, and has passed through a second critical point of qualitative change of state, the appearance of man. Evolution continues, now conscious of itself in mankind, through increasing *socialization, through tighter and more complex organization of human communities and correspondingly higher levels of culture and general human consciousness. The question is: is there some limit, some maximum point beyond which evolution cannot go? Teilhard de Chardin's answer is yes. He calls this limit the Omega point.

Evolution is a convergent process. This is because it is now taking place entirely or almost entirely in mankind in the form of human progress, in the form of increasing socialization. Socialization can advance only in the direction of greater unanimity. However, this increasing socialization and growing unification of mankind cannot continue into an infinite future. The *world is composed of finite elements. There must, then, be some future maximum point of socialization, of the centration of mankind upon itself. At this hypothetical future point of convergent evolution mankind will have reached a maximum of unification and, because true human union personalizes, a maximum of personalization of the individual. This is the Omega point, the hypothetical maximum limit of the human socialization process, and therefore convergent evolution's future terminal point.

Omega is the limit point of socialization and so of evolution itself. Since it is a limit, it is somehow a part of the evolutionary process as its terminal point, and yet it is outside that process since Omega is not itself subject to further evolution. Teilhard asks the question, "What are properties of Omega?" He finds that the Omega point must already exist somehow, even though it is in the future; further, Omega must somehow guarantee the irreversibility of the evolutionary process. For if there is no guarantee of an ultimately successful and irreversible outcome of evolution, then evolution — now conscious of itself in man — would slow down and stop. But that evolution would be eventually self-defeating makes less sense than that it would have an assured successful outcome. Teilhard therefore makes the existence of a future Omega point a part of his theory of evolution. He adds to his general hypothesis of evolution the notion of an already existing and irreversible focal point of convergent evolution; in so doing he passes from the idea of Omega as a future state of mankind to the idea of Omega as transcendent (because in the future but already existing) and autonomous (because evolution depends on Omega, not Omega on evolution). Omega can now be seen to be the prime mover "from up ahead" of the whole process of evolution. Since the appearance of man, however, evolution takes place in the thinking envelope of earth, in mankind, in the form of socialization. Since evolution takes place at the level of reflexive consciousness, at the level of persons, Omega — to be the prime mover of evolution, must be somehow personal.

One might imagine the total process of evolution in the form of a cone. Evolution is converging toward the apex of the cone, an Omega that is autonomous, transcendent, irreversible, personal, and creative (because the prime mover of evolution). Teilhard points out that these are the qualities that men usually attribute to God. He therefore makes God-Omega part of his theory of evolution. This does not, of course, mean that Teilhard de Chardin's theory of evolution is meta-physical proof for the existence of God; it remains a theory of evolution, and God-Omega is a hypothetical God, extrapolated and posited that the theory might make more sense.

Beyond this point, Teilhard de Chardin's theory of evolution becomes a presentation of reasons for accepting Christian *faith. He argues from the probable existence of God-Omega to the probable existence of a communication or special *revelation from Omega to men. He suggests that the place to look for this probable revelation is in one or more of the religions of the world. By a closely reasoned phenomenological treatment of *religion, he determines that the most likely religion in which such a revelation might be found is Christianity. Teilhard then passes explicitly into the realm of Christian *theology where, using the presuppositions of the Christian faith as well as his theory of evolution, he identifies the central axis of evolution with Christianity, the terminal point of evolution with the end and transformation of the world at the Parousia, and Omega with the risen Christ.

RLF

OMNIPOTENCE

Omnipotence is that attribute of God in virtue of which he can effect everything that does not imply an inner contradiction. From the side of God this attribute presupposes his creative power (*Creation). For only through independence of all pre-existing matter can his activity really be unlimited, while in our activity we are dependent on some pre-existent matter and limited by it. — From the side of the things to be produced what is required is that they do not involve an inner contradiction (objective *Possibility). For, God cannot make something that is intrinsically impossible (e.g., a square circle), because it is a nothing. Likewise God cannot sin because sin would imply a conceptual contradiction to his essential and absolute holiness. This means, therefore, that God cannot change the metaphysical and moral principles of being. Descartes' assertion that God could even produce things that are intrinsically contradictory rests on the erroneous assumption that the intrinsic possibility of things is based not on the essence of God, but on his free will. — Because of his omnipotence God is able to work *miracles and also to elevate a spiritual creature above the limits of his own nature to a higher order of existence (*Supernatural).

MR

OMNIPRESENCE

Omnipresence is the attribute of God in virtue of which he is present in all things. Bodies occupy space by reason of their extension and so exclude other bodies; pure spirits, however, since they are not subject to the laws governing material things, are present by reason of their influence on extended bodies. Thus, God is also present in things because he sustains them and works in them. Since he himself is non-spatial and simple (*Simplicity), spatial things cannot have a spatial relation to him. In this sense God is neither "inside of" nor "outside of" the world. He does not fill the world like some rarified ether nor does he work on it "from the outside"; rather, within the context of existence he is wholly intrinsic to the world (immanent) but still different from it (transcendent), since he is never fused together with it in the sense of forming a substantial unity. It follows from this that even infinite space cannot be an attribute or appearance of God (Spinoza). — Omnipresence presupposes the existence of created things; it is therefore a relative or "temporal" attribute of God, but one that implies a real relation only from things to God, not from God to things. Immensity or *immeasureability* is God himself insofar as he can, because of his infinity, create and sustain larger worlds and therefore be present in them.

MR

OMNISCIENCE

Omniscience means that God's knowledge is infinite and therefore embraces everything knowable in the most perfect way. — As a purely spiritual being without any potentiality whatsoever (*Act, *Potency) God is always knowing. In this divine knowledge the knowing subject, the known object and the act of knowing are all the same thing. Therefore God is always consciously present to himself and with infinite clarity he comprehends his whole existence in one, immutable act (= comprehensive knowledge). Since, however, his infinite essence is the existential foundation for the intrinsic *possibility of all finite essences, in his own essence he also knows all possible things and truths (= knowledge of simple intelligence). But he knows the reality of things as well as (as far as we are concerned) all past, present and future events in his resolve to create or effect them (= knowledge of vision) (*Concurrence). Nevertheless, according to *Molinism this resolve presupposes the so-called *mediate knowledge* of God with regard to the free acts of creatures; by reason of this knowledge God would know in his own essence from all eternity the conditionally future free acts of creatures.

Accordingly, then, God's knowledge is in no way passive. God is not determined to know, as we are, by the physical influence or activity of things; rather, he knows them in their total particularity and existence in the perfect knowledge of his own essence and of the resolve of his will.

MR

ONTOLOGICAL PROOF

This is the name Kant gave to Anselm of Canterbury's (1033-1109) famous proof for the existence of God. The proof attempts to demonstrate the existence of God from the mere concept of God without any other presuppositions. Anselm began with the concept of the absolutely greatest being which cannot be surpassed by any greater being; he then concluded that a being that is so constituted that it necessarily exists in reality, is greater than one that may exist only in our minds and therefore is not a necessary being. Anselm's contemporary, Gaunilon, objected that in this way one could just as easily conclude to the existence of the largest island, and Kant remarked that a hundred real gold pieces would be no more than a thought of a hundred gold pieces. However, both objectors missed the decisive point, namely, that the absolutely greatest being (the infinite) has an *essentially* different relationship to *existence than the finite being has. Anselm was correct in saying that God as the absolutely greatest being and as the most perfect in existence cannot be thought of at all without thinking of him as necessarily existing. But whether or not objective reality or only possibility belongs to the concept of the absolutely greatest being, is a point that is still not decided. And to establish this point the mere thought-possibility that involves no contradiction is not, as Leibniz held, enough. Therefore, the ontological proof was rejected by Thomas Aquinas and by many (not all) scholastics. But it found general acceptance in *rationalism (Descartes, Leibniz, Wolff) which recognized the order of concepts as an ontological order. Kant correctly attacked this position. However, his claim is not correct, that all proofs for the existence of God logically presuppose the validity of the ontological proof and therefore are to be rejected along with it. For, if the existence (or real possibility) of the absolutely greatest being is established in some other way, for example, by reason of a causal argument, then the conclusion to the inner necessity of its existence is justified.

WB

ONTOLOGISM

Ontologism, prepared for by Malebranche (17th century) and taken up again in the last century by some Catholic schools of thought, historically is a result of the Cartesian epistemology and of *occasionalism, according to which the "activity" of creatures is really caused by God alone. Creatures themselves are only apparently active. Therefore, we also are not active in our knowing, nor do things work upon our senses and intellect. Sensible things are only occasions to "pray," i.e., to direct our attention to God in whose essence we see everything or at least the ideas of spiritual things. Nevertheless, this vision of God is not the same as that of the blessed; it is just a vision of his essence insofar as it is the exemplar of all ideas (Malebranche), or the cause of all created things (Gioberti). This knowledge too, to the extent that it is related to the divine essence, is not clear — it is obscure; it is more a passive acceptance than a judging knowledge. Only the finite member of the relationship is known clearly and reflectively. God, the first existence (*primum ontologicum*; therefore the name "ontologism"), is also the first known in whom we know everything else. — The principal advocates of ontologism in the last century were Gioberti and Ubaghs (Louvain School); it seems that Bosmini was falsely accused of ontologism. — The chief error of ontologism resides in the confusion of abstract, indeterminate existence as such, that we grasp in every perception and in every act of thought, with the infinite, divine existence.

MR

ONTOLOGY

Ontology is a word that was coined about the middle of the 17th century; it was also at this time that the expression "philosophy of being" (*philosophia entis*) was used for the same thing. According to its Greek roots the word means: the theory about existent being. Accordingly, one could equate ontology with Aristotle's "first philosophy," which was later called (pure or general) *metaphysics. In actual fact, however, ontology is only the first part of metaphysics, namely, the theory about existent finite beings as such and that which belongs essentially and immediately to them; there remains the theory about the divine existence that stands over against them. As Aristotle and Thomas knew long ago, the study of existence and the study of God constitute *one* science only; for, the problem of God is only the fully developed problem of existence and the latter is nothing else but the undeveloped problem of God. However, since existence and God are removed from each other as two poles, it is possible to concentrate primarily on existence; and so we come to the science of ontology. But ontology should always retain a very close connection with the study of divine existence.

Since ontology, especially through the work of Christian Wolff, became a special branch of knowledge, the connection between existence and God has been much too flimsy in modern thought. Kant did away with both a knowledge of God and a knowledge of existence; because he thought that existence is unknowable, he saw in human consciousness the ultimate reality to which everything else must be traced back. In opposition to Kant, in the 20th century a new ontology has grown up out of neo-Kantianism and *existential philosophy — an ontology that once again takes existence as the ultimate. Still, Nicolai Hartmann closes his ontology off from the idea of God and the existence that Heidegger considers the foundation of the finite existent remains wholly unexplained. — An explanation and evaluation of these beginnings, the overcoming of all rationalistic and Kantian encumbrances, and a real understanding of the great metaphysical tradition — that is what is required of ontology today.

On a more profound level the name "ontology" indicates the relationship between the existent and spirit; for, spirit appears as the place where the existent as such or in its existence manifests itself. Thus spirit appears as the primordial type of existence where existence is most itself, where it is wholly present to itself. Therefore, the more an existent approaches spirit or is spirit, the higher it stands in the scale of existence. In recent years there has been a tendency more and more to separate existence from spirit and the absence of spirit has been advocated as the measure of the level of existence (Sartre). Thus, a fundamentally different ontology has been the goal which really no longer merits the name of onto-*logy*; for, it is equivalent to restricting existence to finiteness and thereby ultimately shows itself as impossible. — Along with existentialism a distinction should be made between the terms *ontic* and *ontological* — words which were usually understood by the scholastics to mean the same thing. So the term "ontic" means the existent in its own existence as not yet grasped by spirit (*intelligible in potentia*); but the term "ontological" means the existent as illumined in its existence and so become one with the perceiving spirit. — See also *Existence*.

JBL

OPPOSITION

An opposition exists between two realities when the positing of one in some way excludes the positing of the other. Different kinds of opposition result according to the mode of the exclusion. In *contradictory opposition* the exclusion between existence and non-existence is complete and therefore also between every reality (which in any way participates in existence) and its negation. Consequently, contradictory opposition does not admit of any middle ground. — *Contrary opposition* is present when two realities, both of which are something positive within the same area, exclude each other: for example, in the same species, in the same individual, in the same place or at the same time (as joy and sorrow, white and black). Moreover, the greatest possibile distance from each other within a common area is proper to contrary opposition in the strict sense. Therefore, contrary oppositions admit a middle ground. — A *privative opposition* (*Privation) exists between a perfection and its absence (like health and sickness) as well as between the subject of a perfection and a subject who lacks it (healthy person and sick person). The opposition between opposed relations and their subjects is *relative* (e.g., between father and son). A mere difference in the term of the relation is not enough for this kind of opposition. Opposed relations exclude each other only relationally, i.e., in the same subject and in the same direction, but at the same time they are required in different subjects and in the inverse direction. Relative oppositions as such admit of no middle ground. *Polar opposition* or *polarity* (cf. the poles of the earth; man and woman) in some sense participate in contrary and relative opposition, in which case however they fit into a whole. Polar oppositions demand each other and admit a middle ground, but not insofar as they participate in relative opposition.

According to the different contents, a distinction is made in the opposition of concepts, judgments, real existents and their intrinsic essential principles. Examples of conceptual opposition are given above. In simple categorical judgments contradictory opposition (contradiction) prevails between affirmative universal (or particular) judgments and negative particular (or universal) ones with the same subject and predicate (as: All trees have roots — Some trees have no roots). Taken together the two propositions cannot be simultaneously true or simultaneously false. If one is true, the other is false and vice versa. Contrary opposition prevails between universal affirmative and universal negative judgments with the same subject and predicate (as: All trees have roots — No trees have roots). Both together cannot be true, but they can both be false. If one is true, the other is false; but if one is false it does not follow that the other is true. In the real world of existence there can be contrary, privative, relative and polar oppositions, but not contradictory. However, a contradictory opposition occurs in mental acts if something is denied in such a way that the denial as an act presupposes that which is denied (e.g., if someone affirms his own non-existence). A *dynamic opposition* is present in efforts and activities that are going in opposite directions, whether in different existents or in the same one. In a state of equilibrium this opposition can remain hidden. A polarity obtains among the intrinsic principles of *existence which bring forth the particular existent. If this polarity is not complete because of the *transcendence of one of the partial principles (as in man), then the result is the possibility of a dynamic conflict in the same subject (sensuality and spirit). Dialectical opposition also belongs to dynamic opposition. — See also *Dialectical Materialsm, Identity, Distinction, Relative, Dynamic, Mutual Causality.*

WB

OPTIMISM

Optimism in the psychological sense (1) is that attitude of mind that tends to see everything in a good light (world-affirmation, openness to the world). In the metaphysical sense, optimism is the view that the present world, as the necessary expression of the wisdom and goodness of God, is the best of all possible worlds (2) Leibniz, *Enlightenment), or that basically everything in the world is good and *evil resides only in the finiteness of creatures (3) (Stoics, Spinoza). The scholastic position can be characterized as moderate optimism (4); for, according to it the existent in itself has a *value, but evil, which is not just a decrease in something good but the non-existence of something that should be, by the wisdom and goodness of God is used to further the good, although we cannot always see how in individual cases (*God, Philosophy of). — What is known as "cultural optimism" (Lessing, Herder, Fichte, Hegel, Marxism) reckons with an alleged higher development of the human race and *culture; all evil (physical as well as moral) is only a necessary stage that will be elevated into a higher good. — Optimism (2) in its most radical form fails to see that the infinite can never find its absolutely necessary expression in the finite. To be sure, the world was created by infinite wisdom and goodness; still, it is not the best possible, because the finite by its very nature does not permit the best, since it can always be surpassed on every level of its realization. *Evil is not just finiteness — it is the absence of something that should be. Also, *moral evil cannot be justified by the one who does it by appealing to the good results that may flow from it.

WB

ORDER

Man encounters the world as a series of orders and for this reason it was called "cosmos" by the Greeks. Although sometimes disturbed, still order predominates, especially in the realm of nature (natural order). In the area of logic and morality the norms of order are only prescribed for man; he himself has the task of creating order in his own thinking and willing (logical and moral order). Also, he is the creator of order in the shaping of the world (cultural order). — We speak of order when a multiplicity of members, elements or parts is ruled by one law, one meaning or one principle of *unity; we speak of *harmony* when multiplicity is present at the same time in unity and the aesthetic sense is satisfied. The component parts can be either independent beings like soldiers in an army, or dependent members like the parts and functions of an organism. — Conceptually, order is very close to *wholeness. However, the concept of order is wider than that of wholeness, since we speak of wholeness only when the elements of an order form a unity as the result of being together (like the bricks in a house), while there are also orders in which the elements do not come together to form a whole (like the open series of numbers 1, 2, 3 . . .). For us the most convincing example of order is the *organism. But it is precisely the organism that shows that order is not the same as *uniformity*. The more that meaning and unity permeate a multiplicity, the more uniformity disappears; for, in uniformity multiplicity is overcome only externally and not from the inside. Nor should order be equated with something static. For, order can be either *static or *dynamic as, for example, in an organism or in the ethical order.

Since the existent exists to the extent that it is in itself one (*Unity) and enters into a certain *multiplicity only in its finite manifestations, the full reality of the existent reveals itself as very ordered interiorly (*Existence, Levels of); for, the pure unity of subsisting existence contains within itself on a higher level the whole multiplicity of finite perfections. But the order of the finite existent manifests itself not only in the union of all the principles of *existence that go to make up an existent and through the substantial act of existence, but also in the union of all finite existents through their manifold *relations; for, ultimately all of these point to the absolute unity of subsisting existence.

Prepared by Plato's thinking on the world of ideas, the idea of order (especially in neo-Platonist thought) became a prime consideration for the philosophers. Thus, Plotinus placed the "One" at the head of all existence and claimed that from the One all perfection descends in an orderly fashion to all other beings. It was this neo-Platonic, Augustinian idea of order along with Aristotelianism that was decisive for the metaphysical synthesis that was forged by Thomas Aquinas and then applied to the various realms of reality.

WB

ORGANISM

Material living beings appear in the form of organisms, which are determined by the following characteristics: they are natural, corporeal wholes (*Wholeness); they are composed of parts which vary according to position, chemical constitution and structure (the structure and order of these parts = *organization*); the different parts of an organism have their own special activities which they exercise in dependence on the whole and for its good, i.e., as *functions of the whole. According to their structural differences the parts of an organism are called its "members," and according to their functional differences they are called its "organs." The name *organic* (opposite: *inorganic*) is given to all bodies constructed on the pattern of organisms, to all materials produced in nature only by organs (e.g., the white of an egg), and finally to all functions performed by organs. The most important general functions of an organism are: development and growth, self-preservation and self-affirmation in the surrounding world (nutrition, etc.), *reproduction,* i.e., the formation of a part that is specifically the same as the whole from which it came and which can continue to exist as an independent organism after separation. The totality of these functions in the different organisms makes up what is known as *organic *life* (*biology* = the study of organic life). Insofar as this life (also in animals and men) is carried on unconsciously, it is called *vegetative life.* — Organisms in the above sense are not just many-celled living beings, but also one-cell beings, since they also are organized wholes both in structure and function. Decisive for the distinction between organic and inorganic is not the wholeness of the structure, which is also present in crystals, but the organic function. The concept of an organism does not take into consideration the question of whether or not its function is possible with or without a *life principle that is different from matter itself. — These biological expressions are also used in a transferred sense. Thus, "organism" is used for totalities that resemble biological organisms, for example, economy, society, army, a system, etc.) and as a result of this transfer unjustified conclusions are often drawn: *Biologism); "organic" is used for that which has different functions all of which relate to the whole; "organization" is used for a whole whose parts, hierarchically arranged, work together; and "organ" is used for a part of the whole that has a special function.

The communications- and command-systems that are present in the brain and in the nervous systems of higher organisms offer the opportunity for a comparative study of these systems with electronic computers (*Cybernetics). These investigations can do much to clarify the material bases of psychic happenings. Computers, however, are to be distinguished from living organisms first of all by the fact that they are given the program, according to which they operate, by a man, while the "program" of an organism belongs to it naturally; secondly, by the fact that the governing program of a machine constitutes a concrete part of it that can easily be changed, while in an organism the program is present in the whole organism in an inseparable and non-concrete way; thirdly, by the fact that the purpose of the machine is to work and produce for the programming man, while the constitutive and worthwhile goal of the activity of an organism is the organism itself.

WB

P

PAIN

Pain in current psychology usually means a certain kind of *sensation, whether in the skin or in the internal organs, which produces great discomfort even with minimal intensity. Special "pain points" have been discovered as the organs of this sensation; these pain points are spread irregularly over the whole skin in great numbers (2-4 milion) and have a specific reaction. That the most diverse sensations change into pain when they become too intense, comes from the fact that neighboring pain points also get stimulated. The internal organs often seem to be less sensitive to external influence, but they can be affected by many internal changes (e.g., inflammations). The purpose of pain is to protect the living being from harmful stimuli or to move it to care for already-incurred injuries. Pain, therefore, is in this sense an *evil, that it is the experience of an evil. Since pain unleashes great discomfort, in everyday language this discomfort itself, which is a person's resistance to the perceived evil, is also called "pain." In this expanded sense, pain can be found both in the sense powers and in the spiritual faculties; thus, it can be related to the knowledge of corporeal injuries. Then it is called *spiritual pain*.

WB

PANTHEISM

According to pantheism there is only one substance or nature, namely, absolute, eternal, infinite, impersonal existence. There are a number of different conceptions of this: it is said to be life (Bergson), immutable substance (Spinoza), abstract and undetermined existence (Hegel), absolute ego (Fichte), blind will (Schopenhauer), will and idea together (Eduard von Hartmann). — According to this position, things (and men) are not independent substances, but only determinations (*modi*) or reflections of the Absolute. Thus, when a man knows himself, then God truly knows himself. Looked at empirically, things are distinguished from each other; but in their inner metaphysical nature they are just one with each other and with God. As the generating principle of things God is the *natura naturans* and things are the *natura naturata*. Since all things are in God and since there is only necessity in inner divine life, all free choice is excluded, both in God and in creatures.

Here are the principal forms of pantheism: (a) With regard to the identity between God and empirical things, a distinction is made between: *immanentistic* pantheism (*Monism) which fully identifies God with things and so resembles crass materialistic *atheism (Ostwald, Haeckel, Taine); *transcendental* (mystical) pantheism which finds the divine only in the depth of things, especially in the soul, so that the creature becomes God only after stripping off the veil of the flesh (Indian pantheism of the *Vedanta philosophy, Plotinus, Scotus Erigena); and *immanent-transcendent* pantheism according to which God fulfills and reveals himself in things (Spinoza, *German Idealism, Goethe, Schleiermacher, Eucken). Here also belongs *panpsychism* according to which the All is animated by a world-soul or a world-intelligence. With the use of this idea *biological* pantheism attempts to explain the internal and external *finality of organism. — b) With regard to the origin of things, a distinction is made between: *emanationist* pantheism which sees things as coming forth from the unchanging Absolute (*Neo-Platonism); *evolutionist* pantheism, in which God realizes himself and comes to full self-consciousness by means of the development of the world (Fichte, Schelling, Hegel, Gentile, Croce); and finally, *static* pantheism which simply ignores the problem of the origin of things (Spinoza). — c) From the epistemological point of view a distinction is made between: *realistic* pantheism, which attributes to things an existence that is independent of divine thought (Spinoza, Eduard von Hartmann), and *idealistic* pantheism, which claims that all things are only thoughts of the Absolute. Then we have the *panlogicism* of a Hegel in which thoughts and existence are identical. — d) Depending upon whether the primacy is given to God or to the world, one speaks of pantheism in the narrow sense in which God is identified with the world, and of *panentheism* according to which the world is merely a mode of appearance of God. Related to this is the distinction between pantheism and *theopanism;* according to the former, God is subject to the All, but according to the latter, the All is subject to God.

A few observations that point to the rejection of pantheism. First of all, pantheism falls immediately into inner contradiction as soon as the immutable and simple *God is necessarily included in the change and multiplicity of the world; for, determinations and modes of appearance necessarily affect and flow from the ground of existence. — Through the destruction of freedom all responsibility is removed from man and the distinction between good and evil disappears. In this way, as well as through the denial of personal immortality, the foundations of morality are done away with, and by making God and man equal the essential bases of religion are destroyed. — Finally, pantheism contradicts our human consciousness: for, if we were not independent substances we could not have a personal awareness of ourselves.

MR

PARTICIPATION

Participation was originally one of the key concepts in the Platonic theory of ideas. Every supra-worldly *idea perfectly realizes some essential content according to the fullness of its possibilities; therefore it shines over the earthly realm as the *ideal. The things of this material world manifest only a participation in the ideas insofar as they are capable of expressing only a fraction of their possibilities. Therefore, it is only the ideas that are the truly existing things, while visible earthly things, caught up in non-being or matter, are just a shadow of that higher world, as Plato has so movingly described it in the famous cave-myth in his *Republic*. In addition to the static sense which maintains between the exemplar and the representation, the Platonic doctrine of participation also has its dynamic side. For, it is supposed to bridge the gap between the supra-wordly idea and the earthly thing. Since the idea itself does not enter into the composition of the thing, it still needs to be explained how the thing is shaped according to the idea. Plato says that it "participates" in the idea, but he is not able to give a clear explanation of this participation.

The notion of participation accompanies Platonism down through the centuries. It is developed further in *neo-Platonism, in Augustine himself and in the later *Augustinianism. Thomas Aquinas gave it a rather classic turn when he incorporated it into his Aristotelianism. The expression "*participatio*" was coined in Latin (from *partem capere* = "take a part"). — For Aquinas the ultimate foundation in which everything participates is the fullness of God who, as existence itself or absolute (infinite) existence, actually contains within himself all perfections in the highest degree or according to all their possibilities (*God, *Perfection). He possesses in himself in a unified and so in a higher way (*modo eminenti*) everything that appears dispersed in creation. As pure existence he is also subsisting existence, while the finite existent is essentially composed of form and a subject (*Act, *Subsistence). In sharp contrast to all pantheistic and emanationistic theories, participation takes place by means of creation which embraces inseparably God's efficient and exemplar causality. According to exemplar causality, creatures are fashioned after the exemplars in the mind of God, so each thing in its own way reflects an aspect of the divine fullness. The various levels of *existence of these things correspond to the stages of this assimilation. The proof for the existence of God that is based on these degrees of perfection is a key point in the theory of participation. — At the threshhold of the modern period Nicholas of Cusa placed the participation-idea at the heart of his endeavors. Contemporary philosophers have taken a new look at participation. From the inhabitation of the exemplar in its limited representation and from the essential relationship between the two, we have come to a deeper understanding of the ineffable union of God with his creation or of the *immanence of God in the world.

JBL

PASSION

Passion is the inclination of the sensible, emotional life towards strong reactions; sometimes it can erupt with sudden violence and overwhelm the soul (e. g., irascibility) and sometimes it can hold the soul on its normal course for a long time. Thomas Aquinas distinguishes eleven basic passions: the six more common concupiscible passions (*passiones concupiscibiles*) and the five irascible passions (*passiones irascibiles*) which are based on the first six and which are aroused by opposition to desire. Depending upon whether the object of desire is a present, past or future good or evil he distinguishes in the first group *love* and *hate* as the fundamental passions (the words "love" and "hate", however, are not to be understood in the modern, more complex sense, but only as a drive towards attraction or revulsion), and then adds joy and sorrow, desire and aversion; in the second group he lists hope and despair, courage and fear, and anger. Long ago Plato very incisively stressed the positive or negative power of the passions in a man's life when he compared them to fiery steeds which are either controlled and directed by the strong hand of the charioteer or run crazily out of control without a firm handling. Experience teaches that a life wholly without passion is a cripped life indeed, while a life wholly ruled by passion loses all true value.

AW

PATRISTIC PHILOSOPHY

Patristic philosophy includes the thought world of the Fathers of the Church and of Christian antiquity. Patristic philosophy was never a unified philosophical system, but it is important in the history of thought because it was a preparation for *scholasticism. The philosophical insights are imbedded in the vibrant Christian life of the time and in the considerations on the deposit of faith, for the latter was the norm for everything. Only in a few authors, and especially in Augustine, does philosophy reach a certain independent development.

PERFECTION

At first Christianity, secure in its faith in the divine revelation in Jesus Christ, had no need of philosophical activity. That situation did not change until it became necessary to explain the Christian faith to educated pagans formed in the Greek tradition (e. g., the Apologetes). In their polemics against polytheism the Christian thinkers used some of the basic ideas of the ancient philosophers, while rejecting their whole philosopical outlook as a sufficient basis for man's life. The conflict between the Church and the new religious speculations of gnosticism brought about another contact with philosophy. The gnostics were not satisfied with the traditional faith of the great religions (whether pagan, Jewish or Christian), but strove, in addition to that, to arrive at *gnosis*, a speculative, esoteric, redemptive knowledge. Clement of Alexandria (+ 215) opposed the fantastic syncretism and symbolism (*Symbol) of the "false" gnosis with the "true" gnosis, i.e., a combination of Greek philosophy and Christian tradition which attempts to develop speculative, systematic dogma through the adaptation and transformation of the best philosophical heritage. Origen (+ 254) was the first Christian actually to do this. Although in some points this movement was rejected by the Church, the principle of joining philosophy and theology remained in force and through Augustine was handed on to the scholastics.

Christianity always rejected *epicureanism and *stoicism. Even Aristotle, whose school devoted itself especially to literary activity, had very little influence on patristic philosophy. Actually, its sources are to be found primarily in *stoicism, *Platonism, Philo and especially *neo-Platonism whose teachings, however, were not adopted indiscriminately or without a profound transformation. From a historical point of view patristic philosophy had its greatest influence through the writings of Augustine. (*Augustinianism).

WB

PERFECTION

Perfection (Lat.: *perfectio*) literally means that which is thoroughly made. It also includes the notion of "completeness." It can be realized in different ways: either it is fully there right from the start, or it grows gradually.

Only God is perfect right from the start and without any becoming. *Absolute perfection* is ascribed to him as the infinite One, because he is perfect in every conceivable way; all the possibilities of existence are actualized in him unconditionally. — The finite existent always possesses only *relative perfection*; i.e., within the limit assigned to it through its essence— a limit that includes some definite possibilities of existence but excludes others. Moreover, it attains its own perfection only through becoming; it proceeds from the creator's hand in an unfinished state and is supposed to perfect itself. This development runs through many stages so that there are different meanings of perfection.

In the most proper sense we call the final stage of a thing its "perfection." It is here that all the possibilities of an existent are found realized; and therefore it is here that the existent attains the end or ideal laid out for it. Here "perfection" (1) means "fully completed"; in this sense we speak of a perfect master. This final state is composed of many elements among which each one represents an aspect of perfection or makes the thing in question perfect from a definite viewpoint. Just as we call the final stage perfection, so do we also call each particular element *a* perfection (e.g., health, virtue, knowledge). What has so far been described as "perfection" always involves development or growth of aptitudes and it is the result of an activity that further promotes the original given state of a thing. In a broader sense, the original, undeveloped state itself is also designated as a perfection (2), since in this case an existent fully possesses at least the basic structure of its being (the newly born child is also a man). Finally, in the broadest sense possible every participation in existence, even the smallest, is a "perfection," since in every case it means a step towards completeness (and is identified with *act). — On the distinction between pure and mixed perfections see *Act*).

Moral and religious perfection refers to the attainment of the moral virtues and of a personal relation to God. It also requires that a person not neglect his other talents, but develop them as much as he can.

JBL

PERSON

Person is the name given to the *individual in the spiritual order. Therefore, the person is an individual being, endowed with a spiritual nature that is also incommunicable. In the visible world only man exists as a person; the person is designated with his own proper name and appears as the subject of all statements and as the carrier of all attributes; Paul is a man, he is an artist, he is healthy, etc. (therefore, the Latin: *suppositum* = that which is placed under; Greek: *hypostase* = that which stands under). Only the capacity for spiritual self-consciousness and the corresponding self-determination belongs essentially to the notion of the person, not necessarily the actual realization of this capacity; thus, the unborn child is a person. To be sure, the spiritual nature of the individual must be realized in an incommunicable manner; therefore, the divine essence and the humanity of Christ, although individual realities, are not a person, because the former belongs to the three divine Persons, while the latter is given to the Son of God as his human nature.

PERSONALITY

Men have always been aware of the incomparable worth of the person. While sub-spiritual supposita are wholly lost in service to their own species, the person has his absolutely unique destiny and end over and above the good of the species or the good of society (*personalism*). This preeminence shows itself especially in the freedom of the person by which he determines his own way without being bound to the laws of the species with inescapable necessity; and it shows it in the immortality of the person by which he strives for a perfection open to him alone. Therefore, the person should never be used like a mere thing as a means to an end; still, presupposing the preservation of personal dignity, the individual person must also contribute to the community; he may be required to make great sacrifices, even to offer his life itself.

Historically, Christianity has made a permanent contribution to the inviolable dignity of the human person by its constant advocacy of man's spiritual nature with its freedom and immortality. By contrast, the person has often received very opposite evaluations. Having been influenced by *Buddhism, Schopenhauer saw in personal individualization a fundamental suffering that calls for salvation by being absorbed into the All. Continuing the development from Parmenides to Plato in an extreme fashion, Hegel tended to reduce the person to a mere passing moment in the development of the absolute idea; and it is here that the collectivistic tendencies of *dialectical materialism find their foundation. Therefore, while on the one hand the person is sacrificed to the group, on the other hand, under the influence of *conceptualism, the group itself is dissolved into nothingness. The person is placed alone and without outside help and so the way is cleared for the deterioration that results from an unbridled *individualism; to a serious degree this has been the fate of the modern period since the renaissance. In Nietzsche we find both collectivistic and individualistic traits, depending upon whether we consider the masses or the supermen. At present, the *existential philosophy, which derives from Kierkegaard and was prepared for by Scheler, has taken up the defense of the person. Still, it places too much emphasis on the act-side of the person, even though it remains true that a person rises to authenticity or to existence (i.e., to the full realization of personal existence) only by making decisions by means of which he takes over his own destiny. — Thus, we can see the task is imposed upon man as a person: He is to develop himself according to the law written in his own heart, but in freedom, and so he should grow from a person to a *personality.

JBL

PERSONALITY

Personality in the empirical-psychological sense is the *wholeness, the structural integrity of a man's spiritual *tendencies and permanent inclinations. Insofar as these are the foundation for the individual style of value judgments and convictions, very often the words "personality" and "character" are used in practically the same sense. Since the higher (e.g., the spiritual) functions are to a great extent conditioned by the lower ones, in analogy to geological levels one can speak graphically of the *levels of personality*. Nevertheless, it should be noted that not only are the higher levels (spiritual experience) as it were "carried" by the lower ones (sensibility, subconsciousness), but also the functions of the lower levels can be influenced by the higher, so that the various levels exercise a mutual influence on each other; further, it should also be noted that the higher levels of spiritual life, in spite of their being conditioned by the lower, in the order of existence are different from them and have their own special functions (*Spirit, *Thinking, *Will). While normally the I-relationship of the different functions are correctly experienced and the different levels of experience fit together into a structural whole, this "unity of personality" can be greatly upset in certain forms of mental derangement (e. g., split personality). — Even though a truly harmonious, all-embracing and perfect development of all aspects of the personality is hardly ever possible, it is still in accordance with the dignity of the *person to strive for a certain full development of the psychological personality and especially to strive for the person's orientation towards the absolute values of the morally good and the norms of an ethical personality.

AW

PESSIMISM

Pessimism psychologically (1) is a general attitude that inclines a person to look at the bad side of everything. Metaphysically, pessimism is the view that the essence of things is fundamentally evil (2) or that evil and suffering in the world outweigh the good (3) (Eduard von Hartmann). By "cultural pessimism" is meant the idea that each culture comes to full term only to disappear, that there is no way to prevent the disintegration of cultures (Troeltsch, Spengler). According to Schopenhauer, the classical representative of pessimism (2), the essence of reality is "will," i.e., the purposeless drive that pushes on to ever new forms. Man escapes the pain of it all only by destroying the will to live, by rejecting the world and by fleeing from it. Aesthetic pleasure is only a means of temporary rest. *Tragic pessimism* attempts to affirm the world and life in spite of the overpowering meaninglessness of everything (Nietzsche), or in spite of man's existence towards death with its grounding of all existence in nothingness (*Existential Philosophy); however, caution is recommended in the reading of Heidegger. — The victory over pessimism is essentially achieved by the insight into the value-character of existence. However, *evil, *moral evil, *suffering and *pain, which cannot be driven out of the world by any philosophical theory, also have a positive meaning for the totality of reality. See also *God, Philosophy of.*

WB

PHENOMENALISM

Phenomenalism is the epistemological theory according to which we can know only the *appearances (phenomena) of things, not the existent itself (*Thing In Itself). If the existence of things in themselves is denied, then the word "appearance" really loses all meaning, since there is no longer anything there that "appears"; in this case it is better to speak of (empirical) *idealism. Phenomenalism in the proper sense, in contrast to epistemological idealism, asserts the existence of things independently of the mind; but what these things are in themselves remains unknowable to us; and by reason of this difference a distinction is made between phenomenalism and *realism. The phenomenalists claim that things make impressions on us; in these impressions things appear to us according to the particular nature of the subject and these passively received appearances are the object of our knowledge; thus, phenomenalism is to be distinguished both from realism and from true (not purely empirical) idealism, which says that the object is actively produced by the mind. Since the appearance can be different according to the peculiarities of each subject and since in phenomenalism the "true" is what appears, phenomenalism is logically a form of *relativism. The most noted advocate of this position is David Hume. — Phenomenalism is often restricted to the knowledge of the external world, while a realistic view of knowledge is retained for the inner world of consciousness. — In any event, unlimited phenomenalism contradicts the fact of human *consciousness. The type of phenomenalism that restricts itself to the knowledge of the external world is refuted by the same evidence that manifests the knowability of the external world.

JdV

PHENOMENOLOGY

Phenomenology in a broad sense is the science of phenomena or *appearances. However, since objects reveal themselves to us in our consciousness, in a narrower sense phenomenology means the science of phenomena that manifest themselves in our consciousness. Phenomenology was founded by Edmund Husserl as a new direction in philosophy. In order to establish an unassailable foundation of all sciences, he made use of the *phenomenological method.* This begins with a double reduction (bracketing):

305

eidetic reduction suspends belief in the existence of the ego, of the perceiving acts and of the objects and it considers simply their essence (*eidos*), but in its full concretion. In the second or *phenomenological reduction* the independence of these things is also shut out. Phenomenology considers its objects merely "as" objects (theory of objects), as correlatives of consciousness. Thus, pure, but certainly not empty, *consciousness* still remains. It has two aspects: "being conscious of" (*noesis*) and the "consciously known" (*noema*). The consciously known is not contained in *noesis* as a real part, but it is constituted as an object by *noesis*. Therefore, the *noema* can be grasped and described in an immediate *ideation* or *intuition of essence.* Accordingly philosophy should be defined as a purely descriptive essence-doctrine of the immanent structures of consciousness. Since all objects of experience are regulated by their essences, an eidetic science or a *regional ontology* corresponds to every empirical science. But all the "regions" (= realms of objects) for their part are rooted in pure consciousness, and the science that is ordered to consciousness is the "first" science or philosophy.

While Husserl's philosophy concentrated primarily on the problem of truth, Max Scheler turned to the philosophy of value. For him, a "value feeling" (as a non-rational grasp of a value) takes the place of theoretical ideation. Against the formalism of the Kantian School Scheler proposed a material *value ethics. Finally, in Martin Heidegger phenomenology changed into *existential philosophy: now the essence of existence is not transcendental consciousness — it is historicity and time.

Even though phenomenology (especially Husserl) as a method has its positive value in the fight against empiricism and psychologism, still it fails to ask the much more radical question about existence as such and about the relationship of the existent (which it still presupposes by "bracketing existence") to the world of phenomena. — In Hegel the "phenomenology of the spirit" is the transformation of self-consciousness into absolute knowing.

Pierre Teilhard de Chardin calls his theory of evolution a scientific phenomenology of evolution. Theilhard's phenomenology has very little in common whith the phenomenology of such men as Heidegger, Husserl, or M. Merleau-Ponty. It can be called a phenomenology because it is a world view based on the development of the world seen as phenomenon. Teilhard de Chardin's phenomenological method is a generalized scientific method: collection of data through observation of phenomena, arrangement of the data to form a hypothesis, verification of the hypothesis, ordering hypotheses so as to form a general theory of evolution. Teilhard de Chardin's criterion for verification of his hypotheses and his general theory of evolution, his criterion for the truth of his conclusions, is the two-fold criterion for the truth of any scientific conclusions: coherence and productivity. A conclusion, hypothesis, or theory is true to the extent that it makes sense in the light of the available data and to the extent that it is fruitful for prediction and for further research. — See also *German Idealism.*

WB-RLF

PHILOSOPHY

Philosophy means literally the love of wisdom. The name itself indicates that man can never perfectly possess a comprehensive understanding of all that is meant by wisdom but continually and ardently strives for it. With regard to what it does, philosophy is that knowledge of human reason which penetrates to the ultimate foundations of things; and it is concerned with all reality, but especially with the existence and purpose of man. — A certain understanding of himself and of reality always characterizes the life of the mature human being. This spontaneous world-orientation is his pre-scientific philosophy. It is characterized to a great extent by instinct and feeling, but nevertheless it grows out of a type of thinking which, though anchored in the trivialities of everyday life, is not restricted to it. Such reflection has driven the men of all ages to discover a knowledge of the real that is methodical, organized and clearly expressed; the result is: scientific philosophy.

The object and goal of philosophy becomes clearer when it is compared with other sciences. Like them philosophy is a knowledge of the causes of things, but in a very special way. For all other sciences are particular sciences because they concern themselves with just a part of reality and look for the causes operative within that one restricted area of the real. Philosophy, however, is the universal science because it considers the totality of reality and investigates the basic causes of all things; it pushes on to the ultimate and absolute cause of all being. — The primary starting point of philosophy is human activity, especially man's acts of knowing and willing, which is the first immediately given reality for man, in which he becomes aware of existence — his own and that of the other. From this point of view all philosophy is an explanation of human activity that reaches down to its deepest roots. In a broader sense, the starting point of philosophy is any knowledge of the real that precedes philosophical investigation; this includes everyday common sense knowledge of the individual, the cultural heritage from the past and also the results of the other particular sciences. Such knowledges help philosophy, but she also helps them inasmuch as she establishes and clarifies their basic principles.

With regard to the *method of philosophy it can be said that she accomplishes a basic illumination of the world of which man is a part; she does this by means of human reason and is therefore a kind of worldly wisdom. The counterpart of philosophy is *theology or divine wisdom which treats of God and his activity in the world but on the basis of a supernatural revelation. Even though philosophy is a product of *reason it is still not the creature of a dangerous *rationalism; for reason itself is an integral part of man's make-up and fits in harmoniously with man's other characteristics. Therefore philosophy not only satisfies man's search for truth, but it also clarifies and directs the orientation of human life; on the other hand this relationship keeps philosophy related to life and helps to keep it free of useless speculations. — Philosophy in this sense can never be the product of one individual who can easily fall under the sway of the passing fancies of his own personal experiences or the fads of his age and thus present a distorted picture of reality. An honest and at the same time critical confrontation with the philosophical heritage of mankind is the surest and only way to arrive at the highest truth. For the eternal questions that plague all men have received answers which are spread through all ages and all systems and form a perennial philosophy (*philosophia perennis*). Still, the true philosopher cannot give blind faith to the authority of the great philosophers of the past and merely repeat their propositions and formulas; rather, each age is confronted with the task of asking the eternal questions anew and answering them anew.

Concerning the division of philosophy, one can distinguish with Thomas Aquinas between the various types of existents which reason encounters and the various types of acts which are the basis of reason itself. In the first group the *theory of knowledge is concerned with reason itself insofar as it reveals the existent. *Metaphysics penetrates to the very core of existing things. As general metaphysics it investigates the basic principles of being as such, either according to its inner structure (Ontology) or according to its first, absolute origin (*Theodicy or Philosophy of God). As special metaphysics it applies the general principles of being to particular areas: as cosmology it investigates nature and as psychology or philosophy of man it considers man in that which makes him specifically human. From both of these areas proceeds a philosophical view of man: *Anthropology. — The second group is formed according to the kind of act involved. *Logic studies the correctness of thinking; the goodness of internal and external acts, which brings about the fulfillment of man in this life, is considered by Ethics and the *philosophy of *religion;* the *philosophy of *culture* with its different branches deals with the questions of *art and the fashioning of material things. — The division of philosophy into theoretical and practical is not exactly the same as the division given here. "Theoretical" philosophy includes everything relating to knowleldge, therefore also logic; "practical" includes only making insofar as it is more than just knowledge.

JBL

PHYSICAL SCIENCE

PHYSICAL

Physical (Gr.: *physis* = *Nature) is generally related to the notion of *natural." In the widest sense "physical" (1) means the real, the actual, the effective in contrast to the merely imagined, the conceptual, the intentional, the abstract (e.g., physical bodies as opposed to mathematical bodies, which are merely imagined according to their dimensions). However, since reality is not exhausted by the world of sense experience, a distinction is made between the physical (2) in a narrower sense and the metaphysical (*Metaphysics) as that which is beyond sense experience. The "physical" (2), therefore, designates something insofar as it can be encountered in internal or external experience and is subject to the laws of experience. In a still narrower sense, the "physical" (3) can be understood in contrast to spirit (freedom, morality). Then it means the corporeal or the psychic insofar as it is determined by the body (e.g., physical pain). In the narrowest sense, the "physical" (4) is understood in contrast to everything mental as that which is purely material and pertains only to sense experience.

WB

PHYSICAL SCIENCE

Physical science has as its object the totality of nature (4) which it endeavors to understand scientifically. Thus physical science and *natural philosophy share a common object, but they appraoch the same object from different points of view and employ different methods. Physical science attempts to analyze all natural phenomena by means of *induction which relies on observation and experiment; it also attempts to discover the laws operative in nature (*Natural Law) and so to establish an orderly system (the scientific view of the world) that offers an intelligible explanation of nature. More profound problems, especially those which concern the essences of things, it leaves to the *speculation of philosophy. The exact physical sciences, i.e., those which express their results in mathematical formulas and thereby are capable of attaining significant precision, manifest a very special competence and perfection. — In the ancient world and in the Middle Ages the study "physics" meant every scientific investigation of nature, including that of the soul. In the early modern period a distinction was made between physical science and natural philosophy. Physics now in the broadest sense means the science of inorganic matter, just as biology in its broadest sense means the science of all living things. In a more restricted sense, physics, because of its exact method, is a specially distinguished part of the general study of inorganic nature; and it is primarily concerned with bodily changes (which do not affect the natures of things) and their composition. In modern physics a sharp distinction is made between physics as an experimental science which establishes the facts by means of experimentation, and physics as a theoretical science which formulates the laws of nature (4) mathematically and then proceeds to further conclusions by mathematical means. — The division of physical science into its various branches (physics, chemistry, astronomy, minerology, etc.) is for the most part determined by the practical necessity of a division of labor.

NJ

PLATONISM

Platonism is the philosophical teaching of Plato (427-347 B.C.) and the school founded by him which was known as the *Academy*; it had a revival in *neo-Platonism, Augustine, the Renaissance and has had at least some influence on most of the great philosophers of the Western tradition. After having been deeply influenced by Socrates, Plato originally intended to become the educator of Athenian youth after the example of the Pythagorean community. When this plan fell through he founded the Academy and incorporated his philosophical ideas into his justly famous *Dialogues*. He based his proposals for political reform on his view of the world which included his conviction that there are unchanging, universally valid values. The philosophical expression of this world view is contained in Plato's *Theory of Ideas*. While our senses reveal to us only the world of becoming and corruption, which is a kind of middle between true existence and nothingness, reason (*nous*) pushes on to discover the ideas, the forms, the eternal non-sensible objects which exist above and beyond the sensible things of this world and give true meaning to the changing world and the life of man. Corruptible things participate in the ideas, imitate them. The ascent to the world of ideas, especially to the Good and the Beautiful, takes place through the passion and *eros* which is the desiring and seeking (Platonic) love of the beautiful and the true. The ideas are anchored in God (= the Idea of the Good).

The world was not created: matter is eternal but it was shaped by the Demiurge into the cosmos and animated with a world-soul. The soul is the principle of movement and life; it comes from a higher world beyond this one. The ascent of man's spirit to the contemplation of the ideas occurs through the remembrance (*anamnesis*) of the ideas which were seen intuitively by the soul in its pre-existent state; this process is set in motion by material things which are faint shadows of the ideas. The goal of human life is to become like God, the perfect Idea of the Good. The condition of attaining this goal is a proper formation and education in and through the reasonably organized community; Plato describes this ideal community in detail in *The Republic* and again, though less radically, in *The Laws*, which was composed in his old age. Just as there must be

310

harmony in man's soul between its three parts, the concupiscible, the irascible and the rational, so also harmony and justice must reign in the larger community of the state whose purpose, for Plato, is one of education; for the state also has three parts: philosophers as rulers, military people as protectors and the ordinary people who engage in business; each one should fulfill the function allotted to him. A careful program of training should prepare the philosophers and the military for their position in the community. These two groups are to have possessions, wives and children in common, according to very strict regulations. Through the myth of the transmigration of souls and eternal punishment (*The Republic*, book 10) Plato attempts to take a position against the primitive beliefs of the common people and the skeptical attitudes of the younger sophists with regard to the universal problems of personal immortality, of the final end of man, and of responsibility in the next life for the deeds of this life.

JoS

PLEASURE

Pleasure is an agreeable *sensation (in contrast to *pain) or a feeling of satisfaction. Pleasure arises out of the fact that striving or desire finds its natural object; this can be either in the real order or in the world of a lively imagination. Spiritual satisfaction is called *joy*. The teleological meaning of pleasure, as Aristotle remarked, consists in this, that it is supposed to elicit the right kinds of activity on the part of living things (but always under the control of reason) and as satisfaction it is the echo of a certain perfection already achieved. It does not follow, however, that pleasure is the foundation and criterion of what is morally *good, as if an activity were morally worthwhile simply because it affords pleasure (*Epicureanism, *Hedonism and Eudaimonism); yet within definite limits and in harmony with man's ultimate end pleasure is indeed morally important and a legitimate motive provided that it truly furthers man's real good. The idea of legitimate recreation, involving play and relaxation, does not receive sufficient recognition in the rigoristic rejection and undervaluation of joy and pleasure.

JoS

PLURALISM

Pluralism, in opposition to *monism, indicates the view that (1) reality is not composed of one unique substance or one kind of substances (*Multiplicity); it also signifies the view that (2) reality can be broken up into a number of different spheres which can in no way be reduced to a *unity; this idea can be seen in the field of ontology when existence is deduced from two or more absolute principles (*Dualism) or in the field of ethics when value is completely separated from existence (for example in the neo-Kantian *Value philosophy).

One can also speak of pluralism (3) in the social realm, insofar as a particular society is composed of a multiplicity of relatively independent groups and organizations representing different areas and different occupations; the reason for this is that all truly human values can contribute towards building community (*Subsidiarity). Opposed to this would be a totalitarian monism which recognizes only the state as the source of all power to organize society. Modern society tends towards an extreme pluralism (4) according to which all social living should be organized purely according to the viewpoints of individualistic groups. In this situation the special pleading of particular groups threatens to destroy the unity of the state (*anarchy*) or to let civil authority become the plaything of these groups; this can easily lead to the oppression of minority groups (*dictatorship of the majority*).

Closely related to sociological pluralism is philosophical pluralism (5): men have basically different views with regard to first principles, especially with regard to religion and the ultimate meaning of human life. This situation can lead to deep conflicts, especially in those areas where a common value system must be presupposed in order to arrive at common social and political action in a particular society; such conflict can be overcome only by recognizing that we all have something in common through the possession of the same human dignity (*Tolerance). But that type of pluralism (6) is to be rejected which seeks to justify a multiplicity of philosophies by affirming that all truth is relative and which considers all philosophical and religious convictions in the sense of a pure *relativism as personal opinions which all have the same value. Apart from error, which is always possible, the multiplicity of philosophies of life is better explained by the fact that man does not enjoy an immediate, spiritual vision of reality as such and so different men look at the same thing from different points of view.

WaK

POSITIVISM

Positivism is now a general term for philosophical positions which stress the factual aspects of *knowledge, particularly scientific knowledge, and generally try to reduce factual statements to some foundation in *sensation. The term "positivism" was introduced by A. Comte (1798-1857), who explained the development of human thought in terms of three stages: the theological stage, where events in nature are explained in terms of the will or whim of gods; the metaphysical stage, where these events are explained through general laws of nature: and the positive stage, where science concentrates on collecting and ordering facts rather than on attempting to explain them. His later attempts to transform positivism into a new religion tended to discredit his views. But the emphasis on facts, the identification of facts with sense observations, and the attempt to explain general laws by induction from a factual basis was accepted and, in different ways, extended by J.S. Mill (1806-73). E. Mach (1838-1916), K. Pierson (1857-1936), and P. Bridgeman (1882-1961).

Logical positivism (also neo-positivism, Vienna Circle) represented a fusion of the empirical tradition stemming from Hume, Mill, and Mach, with *symbolic logic as interpreted by L. Wittgenstein. According to this theory all meaningful sentences must be either analytic or synthetic. Analytic sentences are either true (tautologies) or false (contradictions) solely by reason of their logical form and contain no factual information. Synthetic, or empirical, sentences are either reports of sense observations or generalization based on empirical observations. Synthetic sentences are meaningful to the extent that they can be verified. Metaphysical and theological statements fit neither category and were dismissed as meaningless pseudo-statements. This original formulation (of M. Schlick, R. Carnap, O. Neurath, and others) gradually underwent a series of modifications as its shortcomings became more apparent. Verification, as the criterion of meaningfulness, was successively modfied into verification in principle, confirmability, and finally the insistence that empirical evidence must play a significant role in the acceptance of a scientific statement. At the same time the factual basis was broadened from sensations to observation reports, to empirical language. Present positivism explains scientific knowledge in terms of three components: a theoretical language, an observational language, and correspondence rules linking the two. The positivistic emphasis perdures in the insistence that only the observation language expresses factual information while statements in the theoretical language have no factual meaning until they are translated into the observation language by means of the correspondence rules.

Though logical positivism was originally developed as an interpretative basis for the natural sciences it has been extended to the *human sciences. In psychology it found a natural ally in *behaviorism and operationalism. In ethics (Ayer, Stevenson) it attempted to explain the meaning of statements expressing moral obligation in terms of their emotive connotation. In jurisprudence, the prescriptions and prohibitions set by a *community were seen as the ultimate basis of law rather than *natural law or transempirical norms, e.g., Kant's categorical imperative.

The philosophical limitations of positivism and the intrinsic difficulties in its formulations have led to a gradually growing reaction against logical positivism, even among empirically oriented philosophers. Its logical inability to grant a realistic status to any entities whose names are not a proper part of the observation language necessitated explaining electrons, genes, etc. as fertile theoretical constructs rather than real entities. The idea that observation reports simply express the given of immediate experience rests on a naive realism which both linguistic and phenomenological analysis has gradually undermined. The sharp distinctions postulated between: analytic and factual statements, *a priori* and *a posteriori* propositions, necessary and contingent statements, and theoretical and observational terms do not fit the actual usage of either ordinary or scientific language. Yet these sharp dichotomies played an essential role in the repudiation of *theology and *metaphysics. However, positivism did make a contribution in stressing the role of logical structures in scientific *explanation and the decisive importance of empirical confirmation in the acceptance of scientific laws and theories. It also raised the questions and formulated the problems that more adequate accounts of scientific explanation must answer.

EM

POSSIBILITY

The possibility of an existent or its objective *potency can be considered either in itself (= inner possibility) or with reference to the active or passive power on which it depends (= external possibility). *Inner possibility* belongs to everything which is not contradictory and which affirms some positive, existential relation. *External possibility* belongs to that which can be effected by a cause. In this matter the non-philosophical sciences judge possibility and *impossibility only according to the proximate causes given in experience; philosophy must also consider the highest cause that is not given in immediate sense experience (*Omnipotence, *Miracle).

To the metaphysical order belong not only all the things that have ever existed but absolutely everything capable of existence, even if they never actually exist (the *pure possibles*; this is the opposite of Spinoza and the pantheists). The possibles are not in every sense nothing. For, absolute nothing can neither exist nor be defined nor can it be distinguished from another nothing by means of definite characteristics, while these statements can be made about the pure possibles. Also, the possibles are not mere beings of the mind, since according to their essence they can be real even outside of the realm of thought. However, there is no such thing as a kind of *diminished" existence that belongs to the possibles; for, between existence and non-existence there is no middle ground. Finally, they are founded on God who himself does not belong to the order of the merely possible, because in him possibility and actuality are identified.

314

POSTULATE

The extent of the possible depends neither on the order of actually realized existence nor on our intellect, but on God alone whose existence is the source of all finite existence and whose vision is the measure of all things. Accordingly, inner possibility is not just logical conceivability (against Kant), but also the metaphysical possibility of existence. Kant opposes the real possible and the intuitively evident to the logically possible or the thinkable. He does not acknowledge a non-intuitive but yet real possibility.

Although the external possibility of finite existence is based on the *omnipotence of God, this is still not the ultimate foundation of inner possibility. Likewise, inner possibility depends neither on the omnipotence of God nor on his will or good pleasure (against Descartes). On the contrary, the omnipotence and freedom of God presuppose the inner possibility of finite existence. The reason why the possible belongs to the ontological order is the immutable essence of God or the coupling of the possible with necessary existence. However, the expression of the possible in its manifold forms rests on the creative but necessary knowledge of God, who is able to manifest his perfection in the structure of the finite (*Idea) with infinite variety.

WB

POSTULATE

Aristotle and Thomas Aquinas understand by a postulate (*petitio*) a proposition that is not immediately seen to be true, but which is temporarily assumed to be true in a scientific discussion by dispensing with a proof of it; however, the proposition is presumed to be proved elsewhere. The postulate is distinguished from the*presupposition (*suppositio*) in this, that in a formal disputation the latter is accepted by both sides as true, while in the case of the postulate one side of the argument takes no position on the truth of the proposition. In modern philosophy a postulate is frequently understood as a proposition that is neither directly intuited nor even demonstrable, but which is nevertheless accepted as absolutely necessary. Thus, Kant speaks of the postulates of the practical reason; such a postulate is "a theoretical but as such non-demonstrable proposition insofar as it is inseparably attached to a practical law that is absolutely binding a priori"; i. e., it is a proposition that must be accepted if the moral law is not to appear meaningless. Postulates in this sense according to Kant are the freedom of the will, the immortality of the soul and the existence of God. — Actually, in order to attain true certitude the *evidence of objective reality is always required and this cannot be supplanted by blindly accepted postulates. See also *Critical Philosophy*.

JdV

POTENCY

Potency (Lat.: *posse* = to be able) constitutes the finite existent as a partial factor along with *act. The notion of potency was first developed by Aristotle (he called it *dynámei on*) and later expanded by the Scholastics; the idea also lived on in Leibniz's concept of power and Hegel's idea of "in-itself." In recent times biology (Driesch) and also physics have re-discovered this idea. With regard to the essence of potency, it can only be described through its relation to act as the real possibility or capability for act. There are two basic kinds.

Passive potency is the capability to receive an act. This is not the same thing as *objective potency*, i.e., pure or non-real *possibility, which is left behind by the finite existent when it begins to exist and so does not enter into the composition of the existent as a partial principle. This potency is called "objective" since the purely possible as such exists as an object only in the mind of the creator. Here, however, it is a question of *subjective potency* which helps to constitute any real thing as the real carrier (*sub-iectum*) of the act that is ordered to it. This is *pure (act-less) potency* if it is not accompanied by any act and does not presuppose any other act that supports it. It is in this way that Aristotle and many scholastics view the basic "stuff" of all corporeal things (*materia prima* = *prime matter) which receives its total actuality from the act (here: essential form) which is ordered to it and which it accepts. A *mixed potency* either posits an act itself or else is rooted in another act which is its foundation. An example of the former is the essential form which is potency only with regard to existence, but is at the same time act with regard to prime matter. An example of the latter are the accidental potencies which have as their support the substance as act (e. g., susceptibility for knowledge in man). Insofar as this passive potency signifies only susceptibility, in itself it is still not act, but also it is not completely nothing and so is something real; for example, a stone does not have the capacity for knowledge, so it lacks something proper to a man. The extent of this potency determines the kind and extent of the act that an existent can receive; thus it limits the act.

Obediential potency (*potentia obedientalis*) is usually classified with passive potency. This is the name for the capacity of a creature to be influenced by God's activity in a way that exceeds the limits of his nature, without however destroying it. This is the necessary presupposition of a *miracle and the *supernatural elevation of man.

Over against passive potency stands *active potency* as the ability or power to produce an act. Act in this instance is at least the activity proceeding from a power (e. g., an act of thinking or willing), and often it is a product (e. g., a child or a house). An active potency already includes within itself a certain act, since according to the principle of causality no one can produce something that he does not already possess in some way. While passive potency cannot exist in God, since it contradicts his very nature, he does have the active power to produce — not indeed his own activity, but some product or thing; moreover, God's active power lacks all passive receptivity which is an essential ingredient in all finite activity (e. g., before we can teach we must first learn).

JBL

POWER

Power is the ability to act, to bring something to completion; therefore, it is active *potency. It is an *accident of an effective substance and the proximate *cause of activity. Its nature is made known on the basis of the principle of causality. The clear occasion for the formation of the power-concept is the personal experience of the expression of power and the conflict of powers. There is power in all the areas of existence: in the spiritual, vital and material areas. The powers operative in inorganic nature between the various bodies are usually thought of in terms of human experience of spiritual and physical powers, although the former are not endowed with vitality. The necessarily operating powers situated in natural things are the foundations of the *natural laws. — According to the terminology of physics, power is the time rate of doing work (e.g., 550 foot pounds of work per second equals one horsepower). This definition is included in the law of inertia (*Motion). — According to Leibniz, teleologically directed power or force is constitutive of a substance. The *monads, according to him, are in themselves non-spatial centers of force which produce extended space for bodies only through their activity.

NJ

PRAGMATISM

Pragmatism originated in the informal meetings of a Harvard group called the "Metaphysical Club" which gathered in Cambridge about 1870. This group included Charles Sanders Peirce, William James, Oliver Wendell Holmes, Jr., and others. Their interests frequently centered on scientific questions, and Darwin's *Origin of Species* figured prominently. In the discussions Nicholas St. John Green frequently appealed to Alexander Bain's definition of belief as "that upon which a man is prepared to act." The beginning of the movement is generally dated by an article of Peirce's which appeared in 1878 entitled "How to Make Our Ideas Clear."

The article contains the statement: "Thus we come down to what is tangible and conceivably practical, as the root of every real distinction of thought, no matter how subtle it may be; and there is no distinction of meaning so fine as to consist in anything but a possible difference of practice." This article was not widely noticed until William James defended the pragmatic criterion in an address delivered at the University of California on August 26, 1898. *Studies in Logical Theory* which was published in 1903 brought to general attention that John Dewey and others at the University of Chicago were thinking along similar lines. Because of differences of emphasis, after 1905 Peirce called his position pragmaticism to distinguish it from the others.

Peirce traced the term pragmatism to a statement from Kant's first Critique: "Such contingent belief, which yet forms the ground for the actual employment of means to certains actions, I entitle *pragmatic belief.*" While Peirce's positions are complex, he was in general interested in the method of science, a theory of logic, and the determination of concepts. He called himself a scholastic realist, and used the pragmatic criterion of consequence to define concepts or meanings. James was interested in the concrete individual and used the pragmatic criterion to establish truth. He traced the term to the Greek word *pragma*, and emphasized action. Dewey was interested in social problems and used pragmatism as a leading principle for public planning. The movement and the pragmatic criterion tended to take on a different hue depending upon the interests of its many adherents. In 1908 Arthur O. Lovejoy published an article entitled "The Thirteen Pragmatisms" to indicate some of the many senses in which the term was being used. As a theory of truth Lovejoy has indicated that because of its emphasis upon consequences, propositions are not true, but become true. This method of veri-*fication* is not a theory of knowledge. All propositions are deferred payments; they are barren in regard to the present. He states that the only true proposition is a dead proposition. Among its many uses pragmatism may be a method, a tool of criticism, a theory of meaning, or a theory of truth, or some combination of these factors.

The movement was strong in the first quarter of the present century. It was represented in England by Ferdinand C. S. Schiller; in Italy there was a group referred to as "The Pragmatic Club" and for a while Giovanni Papini was an adherent. There were sympathizers everywhere. While pragmatism is no longer identifiable as a movement, it continues to have influence in some sectors of contemporary thinking.

TRG

PREDICABLES

Universal concepts can be considered both according to their content and according to the nature and way in which they can be applied to the objects that fall under them. Thus, for example, the concept "house" differs from the concept "machine" according to the content. But both are affirmed in the same way of the objects they refer to, i. e., as a genus which includes in it several species. While the arrangement of concepts according to their content leads ultimately to the *categories, the concepts according to their mode of expression constitute five classes which are called the "predicables": genus, species, specific difference, property and logical accident, which includes relations and special characteristics. Working within this framework, the concepts themselves are also called "predicables" insofar as they fall under one of these classes. Since our thinking first of all adverts to the content and only after some *reflection to the mode of expression, the categories are also called *first intentions*, while the predicables are called *second intentions* or *reflex universals*. The categories belong in *ontology, the predicables in *logic. — The five modes of expression give us five predicables: A concept is affirmed of objects either wholly or in part. The total concept means either the fully determined essence: the *species* (e. g., man), or the essence as open to further determination: the *genus* (e. g., living being); a genus always includes several species. But the partial concept means either the determination found in the specific concept, *specific difference* (e. g., "rational" with regard to man), or a determination that lies outside of the specific concept. This can be connected with the specific concept necessarily or *per se*: *property* (e. g., the ability to laugh), or merely accidentally (*per accidens*): logical *accident* (e. g., laughter). The list of predicables established by Aristotle, by reason of its deduction, is seen to be both necessary and complete.

JS

PRE-SOCRATICS

Members of this group include the Ionian philosophers of nature: Thales of Miletus (ca. 585 B. C.), Anaximander and Anaximenes who look for the basic elements of the world (water, the unlimited, air) and make no distinction between living and unliving things (thus the name Hylozoism). The celebrated Pythagoras (ca. 532 B. C.) was the founder of a special sect, with ascetical and political leanings, which believed in the transmigration of souls (cf. "the Pythagorean bean"). According to him number as the expression of the inner harmony of being is the foundation of the world. The first metaphysician was Heraclitus "the obscure" from Ephesus (ca. 500 B. C.) who held that each existent is in a state of constant becoming and therefore cannot be grasped by fixed, clear concepts. Only the law of the cosmos stands above all change. In contrast to this position, Xenophanes of Elea (Eleatic School: Parmenides, Zeno) recognized only one real existent as the Absolute and the basis of everything. Being is one, unchangeable, the only object of thought and one with it; therefore the sense world is mere appearance. From these metaphysical heights the so-called younger natural philosophers (Empedocles, Anaxagoras, Leucippus, Democritus) descend to the consideration of the sense world. The world is composed either of a few (four) elements or of an infinite number of elements, some similar and some different, which were set in motion by *nous* (reason), but, according to a mechanistic-materialistic atomism which sounds curiously modern, the world is made up of very small particles which come together by chance or strive to separate themselves (Democritus). Almost all of these philosophers were critical of the anthropomorphic concepts of God which characterized the popular religion of the time. In ethics they preached that the goal of life is happiness which is obtained by moderation in all things. Aristotle developed his metaphysical ideas with regard to matter and form as the basic principles of every material existent in the course of carefully examining the tenets of Heraclitus and the Eleatic School (Everything is in movement; there is no true movement).

JoS

PRESUPPOSITION

Presupposition in the narrow sense (*logical presupposition*) is literally a "position" that is taken "prior to" the thinking process that is going to be engaged in here and now; it is a proposition which is used in a demonstration as a premise, without being proved itself (at least for the moment). "Presupposition," however, is often understood in a wider sense; thus, it is applied to every conviction, mental attitude or even external situation that historically and phychologically influences the creation of new ideas, convictions and intellectual movements. For, the new never begins as it were in a vacuum or with absolutely no antecedents.

Correspondingly, the demand for a *presuppositionless beginning*, for a *presuppositionless science*, can have a double meaning. In the narrow sense this means that a science must establish each one of its principles and must not accept anything unexamined; of course, this does not mean that it must "prove" every principle (*Sufficient Reason, Principle of). But those who demand presuppositionlessness in the sense of the liberal ideal of science have a different understanding of the word "presupposition": They say that *science ought not to be influenced from any direction that is not of an intellectual nature; above all they want to remove science from any influence of relgious *faith. This view rests upon a one-sided evaluation of thought and research as something that exists for its own sake (rationalism); this view fails to see that science can be fruitful only if it preserves an awareness of the partial and serving role it plays in the totality of human life — a life that is ordered to eternal goals.

320

Today there is a much greater danger that, in the sense of an irrational *life philosophy or of *pragmatism, thinkers will overlook the just claim that is behind the demand for presuppositionlessness in science. Pressed to make decisions daily, certainly a man cannot wait until science offers him formal certitude about everything; he must base himself over and over again on pre-scientific, natural certitudes, but even these should not be completely blind. It is especially true that real science, if it is going to avoid the pitfall of *relativism, cannot be built up on a sentimental foundation of feeling, but must demand a grounding in the object itself. Of course, the particular science cannot get off the ground without some logical presuppositions. It is the task of philosophy, especially of *metaphysics and the theory of *knowledge, to examine the ultimate foundations of every science. Only metaphysics can proceed in this without presuppositions, and that only in the sense of logical presuppositionlessness. Yet, for methodological reasons it is often recommended (even in the case of particular investigations) to restrict the number of presuppositions as much as possible.

JdV

PRIME MATTER

Prime matter (Lat.: *materia prima*) according to the explanation of *hylemorphism is the first existential foundation which is common to all bodies; prime matter itself is not a body and it is not matter in the sense of the physical sciences (it is not *materia secunda* or "second *matter"), but it is the determinable essential part of every body which only becomes a definite body by receiving and being determined by the essential *form. Aristotle gives the following definition of this difficult concept: prime matter is "the primary substratum of each thing, from which it comes to be without qualification, and which persists in the result" (*Physics*, 1, 9; 192 a 31 f). According to Thomas Aquinas, by the words "in a way which is not merely accidental," prime matter is supposed to be distinguished from *privation which is only an accidental principle of becoming. Prime matter is adduced as the ultimate reason for the filling of space and for the passivity of bodies. According to the strict Thomistic viewpoint, it is pure *potency and therefore of itself wholly undetermined; others, however, attribute to it a minimal amount of actual determination. Another disputed point is the Thomistic view which says that "prime matter with quantity" (*materia quantitate signata*) is the principle of individuation or the principle of the "thisness" of bodies (*Individual).

JdV

321

PRINCIPLE

A principle is that from which something takes its origin in some way — according to the order of existence or of becoming or of knowledge. — *First principles* are those that in their own order do not proceed from another principle; but this does not exclude the possibility that they still have principles in another, higher order. — The concept of principle is broader than the concept of cause or of element. The concept of *cause* includes the difference of existence and the dependence of the caused on the cause; the concept of *element* includes the notion that it enters into a whole as a basic part. The concept of principle neither includes nor excludes these determinations. See also *Ground, Cause, Knowledge, Principles of, Existence, Principles of.*

WB

PRIVATION

Privation in general means the lack of some circumstance or some attribute that a thing is capable of having and that it should have in order to be a complete member of its own kind (e. g., blindness in a man). Therefore, privation does not signify simply the denial of all existence, but it always presupposes a subject that does not have everything that it should have according to its nature. If this lack of perfection is viewed from the point of view of goodness, then it is called *evil. — Privation is not itself something real, but it does designate an objectively real state of affairs. — In Aristotelian natural philosophy (*Hylemorphism) privation is understood as the principle of *becoming: A body, whose principles are matter and form, is the starting point of a formal change when, under the influence of an efficient cause, it comes to a state of privation with regard to a form other than the one it actually has; in other words, when its accidents have been so changed by the efficient cause that its matter can no longer support the previous form and demands another, new essential form. See also *Opposition.*

VN

PROBABILISM

In order to lead a moral life it is important for a man to have certitude about the rectitude of his actions. This certitude, which is easily attainable in most daily affairs, in a number of complex cases where even experts in ethics are divided is difficult to achieve or not attainable at all. To be sure, a man must make an honest effort to form an objectively valid judgment and use whatever outside help he can get, but the press of daily life that demands practical decisions cannot wait for the theoretical solving of such problems. In such situations there must be a way, even without direct certitude, and a way that is based on the object itself, to arrive at an indirect certitude about the moral liceity of acting. The so-called *moral systems* attempt to give an answer to this problem. Their purpose is not to solve the theoretical problem of whether or not a questionable law actually exists, but to present a way to decide whether or not an obligation that binds in conscience actually binds in this concrete case. According to *tutiorism*, one may follow the opinion that favors freedom only when it is certain or most probable; according to *probabiliorism*, when it is more probable than the view favoring the law; according to *aequiprobabilism*, when it is equally or almost equally probable. Since the probability of a proposition, even when it is greater than that of the opposite, does not negate the probability of the latter and therefore never produces certitude (which is what one is looking for in judgment of conscience), the weighing of probabilities offers no solution to the problem. It is much more certain that an uncertain obligation is no obligation at all. Accordingly, as long as serious reasons can be adduced against some apparent obligation, it is certain that that obligation is not binding on this particular man, since obligations make themselves felt on the subject of the obligation only through knowledge. This is the position of probabilism. The following should also be noted: a doubt about a fact (*dubium facti*), by itself alone, is no basis for a doubt about an obligation (*dubium legis*); for example, a doubt about the presence of a person on a firing range does not give me the freedom to start shooting. See also *Rigorism, Laxism.*

WB

PROBABILITY

A judgment or statement is said to be "probable" when good reasons support its truth, but support it in such a way that they do not clearly exclude the opposite so that no real *certitude is given. In contrast to a certainly true judgment, a probable judgment is only an *opinion*. The same judgment can at the same time be probably true and probably false. And even the greater probability of one judgment does not in itself destroy the probability of the opposite opinion. However, a judgment that possesses only a slight, loosely grounded degree of probability, is usually said to be "improbable." In daily life one must often be satisfied with that high degree of probability that is well founded but does not exclude the possibility that the opposite might be true; this is called *"moral certitude"* in the broad sense. The theory of *probabilism teaches how it is possible, in spite of only a probable judgment about the liceity of a particular course of action, to move beyond it to moral certitude.

PROBLEM

Mathematical probability designates the relationship between cases favorable to an event and the other cases that are equally possible. It is called *a priori probability* if it is calculated on the basis of general considerations carried on independently of the experience of the actual cases that have occurred; it is called *a posteriori probability* if it is deduced according to statistical laws from the events that have actually occurred. The concept of mathematical probability is naturally different from that of the theory of knowledge and also from that of daily practical living and it should not be confused with these. And it should be noted that an unobjectionable theory of mathematical probability is still lacking. — Probability calculation achieved great importance in modern physics through the discovery of statistical *natural laws. The conclusion as to the invalidity of the *principle of *causality*, which was arrived at by applying statistical methods to modern quantum mechanics, is based on a positivitistic prejudice and is therefore unjustified.

NJ

PROBLEM

Not every question is called a problem, but only the one that is not easily answerable because of the difficulty involved in it. Correctly stating the problem is of decisive importance for the progress of science, especially for philosophy. The statement of the problem must be based on certain evidence or on that which is already known through careful investigation; from this vantage point it can then evolve questions which result from the continuing obscurities connected with the object. In addition to clearly posing the question, the methodical formulation of a problem requires that the reasons both for and against, the *aporien*, be sharply delineated. Long ago Aristotle emphasized (at the beginning of Book III of his *Metaphysics*) the great importance of this correct "doubting" (*Doubt) for every scientific investigation.

Just as a proper statement of the problem is most beneficial for scientific investigation, so also, in an opposite way, a false statement of the problem leads to confusion. The most harmless are the *apparent problems* which, under a facade of high-sounding words, conceal questions which can be easily solved once they are clearly recognized, because their answer is self-evident or because the questions themselves are meaningless. Much more serious are those faulty statements of a problem which tacitly proceed on the basis of a false presupposition and so direct the investigation down a false trail. There are problems which do indeed contain a possible statement of a question, but they are still unfruitful either because their solution fundamentally surpasses man's powers or because the necessary scientific preparation is still lacking or because the solution, even if it is possible, is not worth the effort because of its minor importance.

JdV

PROCESS PHILOSOPHY

Process philosophy is characterized by an attempt to escape the strictures of a mathematical or mechanistic model of intelligibility. Leucippus, the Greek founder of atomism, asserted that everything happens from necessity. The mathematician Laplace two millenia later reached the same conclusion. Among the Greeks Heraclitus emphasized change, but conceived of change as controlled by a *logos* or master plan. Leibniz insisted on spontaneity, life, and freedom, but subordinated every occurrence to the exigencies of a controlling pattern.

In the modern period Hegel (1770-1831) stressed life, *development, and history, and used process or *becoming as a primary source of explanation. In reaction to a stress upon intelligibility in terms of fixed principles and unchanging ideas, he denied the principle of non-contradiction, and rejected clear and static concepts. His dialectical process begins with the concept of being which is abstract and totally empty. Being posited as a thesis generates its own negation which is nothing. These two are one and the same in the identity of inseparable opposites. From the synthesis of being and nothing comes process or becoming. This synthesis in turn becomes a thesis which generates its own antithesis in the continuing development of the dialectical process. Because each step in the development is necessary, some interpreters of Hegel see the whole of the process as controlled by a fixed and finished master plan. In reaction to Hegel's systematic emphasis Soren Kierkegaard (1813-1855) posited the free individual as the central factor which demands explanation. He stresses *freedom, responsibility, and the anguish we feel in the face of major decisions, and implies that any attempt at system will have to confront these data as primary facts to be explained. Kierkegaard's influence upon the existentialists has had some effect upon the emphasis on freedom and development which is found within that movement. Darwin's (1809-1882) *Origin of Species* (1859) gave added impetus to the stress on growth and development. In France Henri Bergson (1859-1941) opened a sustained attack on the frozen ideas of rationalism, and insisted instead upon temporal development. He considered the positing of a fixed goal for the evolutionary process to be mechanism in reverse. With both teleology and mechanism time becomes ornamental. Time as it appears in science is measured by homogeneous units. While this is a useful tool, it is not adequate to reality. Real duration is ongoing, irreversible, and heterogeneous. Édouard Le Roy (1870-1954) was a student of Bergson's, and Pierre Teilhard de Chardin (1881-1955) had read both authors.

In the United States William James (1842-1910) was strongly influenced by Darwin, and the emphasis on process or development appears in his psychological description of the "stream of consciousness" or thought. He insisted that while the past influences the present, it does not determine it. As a result he rejected any completed pattern of history, or what he called a "block universe." John Dewey (1859-1952) in turn was influenced by James and Darwin. He holds for an endless temporal development, in which progress has no priority over catastrophe; both are natural events. Progress depends upon our use of reflective intelligence, which in turn has no guarantee of success. He states that in western thought the unchanging has generally been taken as the source of intelligibility. Plato posited eternal *ideas. Aristotle held *motion tends to a state of rest in a natural place, and he explained generation and growth by reference to an eternal species. Dewey sees process as replacing rest, fixed species, and unchanging ideas as the leading factor in explanation. Alfred North Whitehead (1861-1947) with his emphasis upon *organism, creativity, and process is a central figure in the movement. Whitehead had read both Bergson and James. His doctrine of the ingression of "eternal objects" into events makes his approach distinctive when compared with other authors we have mentioned.

Since all of these men have had wide influence, this is by no means an exhaustive account of the representatives of the movement. Freud's (1856-1939) explicit definition of science is deterministic, but his concern and that of other psychologists with the development of the *personality and the factors which inhibit development has tended to reinforce the process emphasis in contemporary thought. The mathematical or mechanical model of *intelligibility tends to a closed system in which every detail is fixed. In theology this model of intelligibility tends to subordinate all else to the problem of predestination. In every area this pattern in thinking produces what James and Dewey call a "block monism." Process philosophy rejects this conception of system. One free individual would destroy the entire Laplacean construct. Some of the process philosophies remain open to systematic statements, providing these statements concern the relations which are found between free and developing individuals. — See also *Becoming, Development, Evolutionism.*

TRG

PROPERTY

The ordered use of all non-rational things in this world by man, who possesses reason, presupposes a subordination of these things to individual men or groups of men; property establishes this subordination. The moral right of the rational creature to make use of irrational creation for his own purposes precedes the notion of property; property regulates the exercise of this right in man's relationships with his fellow men. I have the right and the authority to dispose of that which belongs to me according to my own discretion and for my own needs. This right is basically all-inclusive, but still it is limited in some sense by the higher rights of the *community and by the requirements of the *common good; the reason for this is that a *right can never be opposed to the community and something opposed to the good of the community can never be a right. — The institution of property as such is founded on nature and is therefore a natural right; its concrete shape in a given culture is variable and therefore subject to the positive law of the civil society in question. In actual fact, the laws governing property and its use are very different in different countries (e. g., Anglo-Saxon, German, Roman).

The unhealthy distribution as well as the misuse of property drove large numbers of the "dispossessed" to oppose the very institution of property as such (communism) or the possession of the means of production (*Socialism). What is required is a healthy ordering of the social structures and the economy with a regulation of property that guarantees both to the individual and to the group what they have a right to. The abolition of property would kill all cultural life. The more men there are who are property owners, the more secure is the institution of property and the more beneficial its results. — According to its very concept property is always of some special kind; thus, the property holder can be an individual person, or a group of persons (family, tribe, corporation: private property), or civil society (city, state, nation). — Property guarantees a certain yield or profit; therefore it is a source of income or at least it can be. The income from property can be limited for special reasons (e. g., common good); but to eliminate income as such would be to destroy property itself.

Property confers the "legal" right to dispose of a thing (*property right*), while *possession* consists in the "actual" power to control something ("custody"). Property and possession usually coincide, but they can be either legally or illegally separated. The limitation of the *power* connected with property and its possession is even more important than the limitation of the income from property. The most extreme way to achieve this limitation is through socialization. — See also *Economics*.

OvNB

PROVIDENCE

Providence (Lat.: *providentia* = "to see beforehand") is the name given to the activity of God whereby he directs creatures to their appointed ends. In the first place it embraces God's *eternal plan* to lead creatures in particular and as a totality to their supreme end — the glory of God. Through this plan both the end and the means (natural tendencies, existential situations, etc.) are determined in advance. In the second place providence includes the execution of the eternal plan or the *government* of the world which is not only a result of the wisdom and omnipotence of God, but also an effect of his love and goodness. For the attainment of the end for creatures means a participation (each according to its own nature) in the perfection of God. — In governing the world God utilizes the activity of created secondary causes, not because his own power is insufficient for the task, but in order to let creatures take part in the dignity of being a true cause. — Depending upon whether God has assigned a natural or a *supernatural end for his (rational) creatures, a distinction is made between a *natural* and a *supernatural end*. That the providence actually exercised by God is supernatural, is something that we know only from *revelation. — *General providence* extends to the totality of all creatures; *special providence* concerns rational beings to whom all other things are ordered. Providence, therefore, is all-embracing so that from God's viewpoint there is no such thing as *chance.

By *fate* is understood the sum total of all the events of a human life that do not depend upon man's free will. To conceive of this fate as a blind law to which God himself is subject (= *cosmic fatalism*) is to misunderstand the absolute omnipotence of God. With regard to the components of fate: To be surrounded by the laws of matter, of life and of history with the physical and moral evils connected with these areas is a situation that is known by God, willed by him or at least permitted. — To see fate as an unchangeable, capricious pre-determination willed by God — whether for eternal salvation or eternal damnation (= the *theological fatalism* of Mohammedanism and Calvinism) — means in effect the removal of human freedom. Certainly, nothing happens that is not willed by God or at least permitted by him, but in his omniscience God has included the free moral actions of man in the eternal plan. And therefore the *prayer of petition* is not meaningless: the praying man does not wish to struggle against an immutable plan fixed by God; rather, through his prayer he is trying to fill the place in this plan that God in his love and mercy has assigned to him.

VN

PSYCHOLOGISM

Psychologism gives absolute priority among all sciences to *psychology. In a special way it claims to take the place of *logic and the *theory of *knowledge*, since for psychologism spiritual causes that produce the judgment are at the same time the *norms of *truth*: that thinking is true that occurs normally, i. e., according to the laws of psychological causes. Depending upon how this norm is understood, a distinction is made between the different forms of psychologism. For *anthropologism* the norm consists in the specific nature of man so that there is one common norm of truth for all men and only for them. Other forms of psychologism restrict the norm even more: according to *typological* psychologism (Dilthey, Leisegang), different types of thinking necessarily lead to different world-views; according to *historicism, the current stage of cultural development exercises a decisive influence on the norm of truth. A certain generality of truth is claimed either because of a "culture-soul" (Otto Spengler) for the same level of culture, because of a "race-soul" (*Biologism) for the same race, or because of economic conditions (*Marxism). The *relativism of truth is a common element in all forms of psychologism.

Basically the rejection of psychologism flows logically from the refutation of relativism. With regard to the combination of psychology with logic and epistemology, it can be said of course that these sciences are really concerned with the same object: i.e., with knowledge, but from essentially different points of view. Psychology deals with a happening in a *subject, with the conditions of its origin and existence, and only with the content to the extent that it exercises some influence on the origin. Logic, however, abstracts from all of that; it is concerned only with concepts and their relationships to each other, with the correctness and validity of thinking. Epistemology studies the truth of knowledge, i.e., whether or not it is formed the way the object demands. Thereby a norm is established that is independent of the nature of the subject. Even logically incorrect conclusions and objectively false judgments conform to certain psychological laws in their production. Accordingly, the norm of truth, logical laws and psychological laws are all different realities.

JS

PSYCHOLOGY

The term "psychology" seems to have been coined by Philip Melanchthon in the 16th century. The history of psychology shows its long and close relationship with philosophy. From at least the 5th century B. C., philosophy has treated questions that concerned man's rational nature, his powers and acts. It has concerned itself moreover with sensation and cognition in both man and lower animals as well as with the intellectual and volitional operations of man. Philosophy has endeavored to answer the questions it raised in these areas by philosophical methodology rather than by scientific methodology. Accordingly, the philosophical approach to psychological problems has been labeled "pre-scientific psychology."

For centuries psychology was regarded as a branch of philosophy. Aristotle treated psychological issues in both his *De Anima* and *Parva Naturalia*, as did Augustine in his *Confessions*. Maimonides and, even more so, Aquinas dealt at considerable length with psychological problems. Descartes' dualism and Leibniz's parallelism both had clear psychological implications. Locke, Berkeley and Hume emphasized the importance of experience in psychological studies while Hartley and the Mills, father and son, stressed the role of association in psychological processes. A number of the existentialist philosophers have had considerable impact on psychological thinking. In view of this long historical relationship, it is hardly surprising that contemporary psychologists are quick to point out that psychology has finally achieved its complete separation from philosophy.

Physiology has also had a notable influence on psychology. It is the field of physiology which has provided psychology with exact information about the central and automatic nervous systems. The same discipline has contributed accurate knowledge on the functioning of the sensory receptors. Psychology's debt to physiology is a heavy one. It stems from the fact that all learning is mediated through the nervous system. Besides, more highly adaptive behavior in man and animal depends primarily on that area of the central nervous system known as the cerebral cortex. Highly correlated with variations in the central nervous system are changes in the various types of adaptive behavior. Motivational and emotional patterns of behavior and physiological functioning are notably interdependent. Consequently, physiological psychology is currently recognized as a branch of scientific psychology.

Contemporary psychology is regarded as one of the *behavioral sciences*, i. e., those sciences (psychiatry, sociology, anthropology, political science, biology and linguistics) which treat of the behavior of man. Psychology is often listed also as a *social science* and, at times, as a *life science*.

Psychology is currently defined as the scientific study of behavior. It spans the entire ambit of animal behavior with particular emphasis on that of Homo Sapiens. An enumeration of the areas studied in contemporary psychology covers the following: behavioral development, sensation, perception, motivation, learning, emotion, psychological measurement, personality, biological basis of behavior, experimental psychology, social psychology, intelligence, abnormal behavior and clinical psychology. Moreover, areas in which psychology has a recognized application would include education, advertising, industry, vocational guidance, crime, psychometrics, politics, religion and music.

Modern psychology frequently uses definitions that are operational. An "operational definition" indicates the procedures, or steps employed to produce that which needs to be defined. For example, an operational definition of anxiety would be an accurate description of both the behavior that is called anxiety and the means which produced that behavior. The basic methods of psychology include at least three: *observation, correlation* and *experiment*.

PSYCHOLOGY

In the *Method of Observation*, the psychologist carefully notes and records specific occurrences or events in his environment. This is termed *controlled observation* when the investigator arranges the situation, such as in a doll play situation for young children. It is called *uncontrolled* or *naturalistic observation* when the observing occurs in native natural situations, as for instance, in noting the play behavior of children in their own playground or neighborhood. It should be pointed out that the observations made by clinical psychologists and psychiatrists on their clients and patients belong to the *Clinical Method*. The closely related *Method of Case History* focuses on the analysis of biographical description of an individual's behavior. The *longitudinal developmental* approach studies the same children over a period of years, whereas the more freqeuntly employed *cross-sectional developmental* approach studies different groups of children at different age levels. Again, the observations made on the behavioral characteristics of a *sample* (small group) of individuals taken from a population (large group) are proper to what is called a *survey*.

The *Method of Correlation* determines the degree to which two or more events occur together. If when one event occurs the other is likely to occur, the two events are said to be *positively* correlated. If when one event occurs the other is likely not to occur they are held to be *negatively* correlated. An index of the extent of correlation is called a *correlation coefficient*. The discovery of a correlation, positive or negative, does not warrant a conclusion that either variable is the cause of the other. Though a correlation gives little explanation it does furnish grounds for prediction.

In the *Experimental Method* the experimenter holds control over the variables involved. He creates a situation in which he screens off the effects of specific variables from the effects of other variables. For example, in studying the impact of repetition on retention (memory), the experimenter would hold constant (control) all variables with the exception of the one he was studying. Here repetition would be the *independent* variable, the one he manipulated so as to observe its influence on the *dependent* variable — retention.

Statistical methodology is the mathematical tool used by psychologists to gather and describe data, from which inferences and conclusions are drawn. By means of this tool the experimenter is given a clearer picture of the data being investigated.

Finally, by 1970, psychologists were giving increasing attention to the work of B. F. Skinner. This behaviorist's main contribution to psychology is in the area of *operant conditioned responses* in learning. Such learning comprises changes in an animal's random responses which have been previously rewarded or punished.

JJE

331

PURPOSE

Purpose according to the older terminology means the same thing as the Latin *"finis"*: that for the sake of which something else is or takes place. In modern terminology, the word "purpose" for the most part is applied only to the end that is pursued through the use of certain *means*. Therefore, the means are ordered to and subordinate to the purpose, but the being itself that is striving for the purpose as its end is not subordinate; this is especially true for the person (*End). That arrangement of the means is useful which is suitable for the achieving of the purpose. On the other hand, an existent or an activity is *purposeful* if it directs itself to an end either consciously or unconsciously (=natural inclinations, instincts). The indication for us of a truly natural inclination is the observation that even in changed conditions an existent again and again so adapts itself that ultimately the same effect is always produced. A machine is only useful, while nature is purposeful. By the "usefulness" of nature both aspects are usually understood, according to the older terminology; still, in the case of "purposefulness" the emphasis is on the adaptation (for example) of bodily organs as means to their end. Usefulness is *self-serving* if the profit goes to the agent himself as an individual; it is *species-serving* if the preservation of the species is furthered; it is *other-serving* (altruistic) if the advantage goes to things of another order, as in the contribution of plant-life to the formation of swamps for insects which cannot exist without such fetid pools; the shaping of nature for man's purposes also belongs here. The grounding of usefulness is to be found in *finality (*Purposelessness). — Concerning the moral influence of a purpose: while means, which in themselves are neither good nor evil, by being used for a morally good purpose thereby participate in the goodness of that purpose, the use of means which by their nature are evil cannot be justified no matter how good and noble the purpose is; in this sense, therefore, the proposition "The end justifies the means" is untenable. — See also *End, Finality.*

KF

PURPOSELESSNESS

Purposelessness is the opposite of purposefulness (*Purpose). The use of the word varies according to the conception of the purpose that something is opposed to. In common parlance everything contrary to one's own comfort is said to be purposeless or meaningless. Philosophically speaking, purposelessness is a denial of *finality so that the purpose is faulty or else it is not attained. This denial reveals itself in the use of inadequate means (e. g., unnatural births, mental illnesses) or in the application of goal-striving to the wrong objects (e. g., when bacteria attack men and animals). Many consider the opposition between self-serving or altruistic purposefulness and certain concomitant phenomena, which make the attainment of the end very painful, to be purposeless or senseless (e. g., pain, the ferocity of beasts of prey).

This "purposelessness" can only be judged correctly if the contingency of being and the special nature of finality are taken into consideration. With contingency is given the changeableness (for living things this means deterioration and mortality), and the limitation of natural things and of their finality. The special character of finality consists in the incorporation of things and their purposes into the total order of reality. This total order is composed of partial orders so that the lower levels are subordinate to the higher, and all serve the unity of the whole cosmos. In addition to that, natural things also serve the higher purposes of God, the supra-worldly director of nature. The highest purpose immanent in this world is the spiritual, moral and religious perfection of man who is brought to the knowledge of the creator through God's self-manifestations in nature itself and who is supposed to direct the world to its final, transcendent end — the glorification of God. Only that which is meaningless under all of these aspects is really "purposeless." Looked at in this way, insufficiencies and disharmonies cease to be purposeless. Thus, for example, as a result of pain and epidemics man comes to the realization of his own contingency; they have also been the reason or occasion for many great cultural advances. That many things become meaningless when all ends that surpass nature have been excluded from this world, is merely an indication that these ends are necessary. Whoever fails to arrive at the ultimate purpose of the world can never hope to grasp the meaning of the world. See also *Evil, Finality, Suffering, Theodicy.*

KF

Q

QUALITY

Quality in general means every condition of a thing, whether it belongs to it necessarily or is just added to it. In a more limited sense, all accidental *forms are qualities. As a special *category, quality is an inner, absolute determination of substance which is distinct from *quantity (e. g., redness, roundness, elasticity). As an inner determination quality expands the existential richness of the *substance (in contrast to the external determination of place and time), without however changing its essence (in contrast to the substantial form). As an absolute *accident, quality determines the substance with regard to itself and not directly with regard to other existents (in contrast to *relation). Quality is to be distinguished from quantity, which confers extension and divisibility on its bearer, in that it, indivisible in itself, is divisible only by reason of its dependence on its extended bearer. Whether or not quality is really distinct from the substance and the quantity of a corporeal being, depends upon whether or not there are inner corporeal changes of bodies which are not reducible to mere spatial changes of the parts (*Mechanism). — Unity of quality in the midst of a difference in the bearers of the quality is called *similarity*. — In logic, the affirming or denying characteristic of a judgment is called its quality. — See also *Sense Qualities, Intensity*.

WB

QUANTITY

Quantity (Lat.: *quantum* = how large) is that characteristic which distinguishes a corporeal thing from all other forms of existence; as a result of quantity a *body can be divided into parts having the same nature as the whole and having the capacity to exist as independent, separate bodies (*Divisibility). The most important consequence of quantity is *extension* through which the parts of a corporeal being are in a spatial juxtaposition and correspond to the parts of *space. Although quantity is a characteristic springing from the essence of a corporeal substance, nevertheless it is not, as Descartes thought, simply to be identified with corporeal substance; therefore, a separation of quantity from substance

QUANTITY

(e. g., as is assumed in the theology of the Eucharist) does not involve a contradiction, even though there is no explanation which provides a positive understanding of such a state.

Extension is either *continuous* or *discontinuous*. An extension is discontinuous when its parts are separated from one another by borders or limits. If the limits come together so that the extensions of the parts touch each other at a common limit, then they are said to be *contiguous*; thus several houses built together can be considered contiguous. If the limits do not come together, so that one or more other bodies lie in between, then this is said to be a *discrete quantity* (*quantitas discreta*) as, for example, in the case of the extension of the heavens. Continous extension (= a continuum) does not have any inner limits, but stretches itself out in space without interruption. The *limit* of an extension consists in this, that an extension ceases at a certain dimension (= a mere *end*) and at the same time a new extension begins from that end (= a real *limit*). A limit itself has no extension in the dimension in which it is limit. The limit for body is surface, for the surface the line, for the line the point; a point has absolutely no extension in any kind of dimension. Therefore a line cannot be constructed out of points, nor a surface out of lines, nor a body out of surfaces. Every continuum is rather, as far as pure extension is concerned, at least conceptually divisible into parts endlessly — and these parts then have continuous extension. To this extent every continuum is potentially infinite. — The extension which is found in things as an accidental determination is called *physical extension*. In actual fact, however, things are not continuously extended in the way in which they appear to the senses; for continuity is realized at best in the ultimate structural elements of bodies. *Mathematical* extension, on the other hand, is the abstract concept of extension as such without regard for a possible realization in the objective world of things. Since qualitative differences also characterize physical extension, a distinction is to be made from this point of view between *homogeneous extension* whose parts are all the same, and *heterogeneous extension* whose parts are dissimilar. Formerly an *organism was considered to be a heterogeneous continuum.

From the spatial order the concept of quantity in the sense of size was transferred to the non-spatial order of reality. Thus it was applied especially to change of place (speed), which is closely connected with space, and to time; then it was transferred from the measureable effect of a force or power to the power itself (intensive size, *Intensity); finally, it was applied to non-corporeal objects (e. g., great virtue) so that quantity in the widest sense can signify anything to which the predicates large and small, much or little can be attributed. — In logic, the quantity of a *concept means its extension. The quantity of a judgment is determined by the extension of the subject; accordingly, a distinction is made between universal, particular and singular judgment.

QUANTUM MECHANICS

Quantity is without doubt an important basic determination of all corporeal existence and for this reason it is included in the categories of both Aristotle and Kant. According to Kant it is a class of *categories which embraces unity, multiplicity and totality. However, a *quantitative Weltanschauung*, which attempts to reduce all *qualities of things to quantitative determination, is an over-simplification of a complex reality (*Mechanism).

NJ

QUANTUM MECHANICS

The physics of molecules, atoms and elementary particles is called "quantum mechanics," because here the natural constant of Max Planck's *quantum of action* plays a decisive role. In the older quantum mechanics from 1900 to 1925 physicists assumed that in the molecular and atomic world, in addition to the already known laws of the so-called "classical" physics, additional "quantum conditions" are normative; from the perspective of natural philosophy these conditions were often thought of as the effects of a principle of totality inhering in atoms and molecules. However, since 1926 it has been known that these quantum conditions represent only special cases of the (generally valid) *double nature* of the elementary particles, atoms and molecules: Each one of these structures, depending on the experimental arrangement with which it is observed, must be described now as a spatially narrow, localized corpuscular *particle*, now as a widely extended *wave*. A more exact analysis of this situation leads to the conclusion that in a quantum mechanical structure there are always measurements whose result *fundamentally* is not open to a certain prediction, for example, the precise point in time of the breakdown of a radioactive atom. If we project a measurement of the position or the momentum (= product of the mass and velocity) of an elementary particle, and if we designate with Δq or Δp the limits of error which the prediction of the result of the position- or momentum-measurement is basically subject to, then Heisenberg's *uncertainty relation* is valid: $\Delta q \cdot \Delta p \geqslant h$ (h = *quantum of action*). However, this unpredictability can hardly be interpreted as the expression of a real, objective realm of indetermination in nature ("real" understood in the sense of an epistemological *realism); for, such a supposition could be reconciled with certain quantum mechanical evidence ("interlaced" systems) only by means of additional and otherwise unfounded hypotheses. Thus, the double nature of the elementary particles seems to indicate that, in the case of these objects, it is a matter of non-spatial and non-temporal structures which can be described only inadequately by means of the spatio-temporal images of a corpuscular particle or wave.

WoB

QUESTION

Man is constantly asking questions about everything. Philosophical reflection on the act of questioning shows that the question involves both knowledge and ignorance in a unique relationship. For, in order to ask a question I must have at least a rudimentary knowledge of the thing being questioned, but I cannot have total knowledge about it since, if I did, it would be completely known and so there would be no reason to question, to seek, to inquire. The questioner is always striving beyond what he already knows to what he does not know as yet; he knows that he does not know in a knowing not-knowing.

Every particular question such as "Where is my book?" presupposes a particular horizon or framework of previous knowledge within which it is posed. Every particular question is directed to being or existence — it wants to know what *is* — so it also presupposes some previous knowledge of being as such. But everything exists and everything can be questioned (e. g., I can ask, "What is the meaning of the universe?"). This question in turn implies that I have some preliminary knowledge of the totality of being, of being as such. Also, I can know and question the limits of my knowledge, but to know a limit as limit is already to be beyond it. Thus, implied in my act of questioning is my basic openness to the horizon of being as such.

Accordingly, a metaphysical analysis of actual questioning reveals that it presupposes in man the questioner a pure pre-knowledge of being, a transcending of the already known and an anticipation (= a knowing not-knowing) of that which is still unknown. This anticipatory knowledge of being is the condition of the possibility of every question.

Since man is striving for the fullness of being and since as a finite, historical being he actually finds only bits and pieces of it, it follows that man is *necessarily* a questioner. This innate drive in man for more knowledge is especially apparent at the present time. The sciences are progressing in knowledge each day, more sciences are founded as knowledge becomes more specialized; research in all areas is a must. Thus, the insatiable thirst for knowledge is made visible and concretized by man's incessant questioning of everything, even his own power of questioning.

In recent years two philosophers, Karl Rahner and Emerich Coreth, have made use of the question as the starting point of metaphysics. Coreth has developed a whole metaphysics, including a methodology, by reflecting on the act of questioning present in man and the conditions of its possibility. See also *Horizon, Lonerganism, Thematic, Transcendental Method.*

KB

R

RATIONAL

Rational (Lat.: *ratio* = reason) in general designates the specifically human mode of conceptual, discursive knowledge. Therefore, "rational" does not mean the same thing as *"intellectual."* Not all intellectual knowing takes place necessarily in *concepts. The grasp of *beauty is not discursive. The way of knowing proper to *mysticism is wholly non-conceptual, but it is still intellectual. Even the consciousness of one's own inner mental acts is intellectual, but not necessarily tied to concepts. — In particular, "rational" means: conclusive, logical, methodical. A *rational science* is a *deductive* or a *reductive science* (i.e., either proceeding from principles or reducing the given to principles). A *rational number* is one that can be expressed by the relationship between two whole numbers.

WB

RATIONALISM

Rationalism (Lat.: *ratio* = reason, intellect). Human knowledge is a concrete whole that grows out of the contributions of sense and intellect. The inner connection of both finds its expression in the doctrine of abstraction and the knowledge of the essential contained in sensible appearance. Also, in the totality of a man's life there is the influence of the powers of willing and feeling. If one of these elements is neglected in favor of the intellect or even wholly denied in its special nature, then we have rationalism. It does not always appear as an explicit doctrine, but sometimes merely as a psychological bent or frame of mind. This attitudinal rationalism is present in all periods of history and in the different philosophical tendencies. In a very narrow fashion it prizes knowledge exclusively for its own sake and therefore it strives for knowledge "unconditionally" (*Presupposition), without consideration for the full meaning of life or for the goals of the will. Men with this attitude forget that all knowledge about finite things is ultimately only a part of a full human life and that, if knowledge alone is pursued, it leads to a sterile and harmful science.

Epistemological rationalism was defended as a philosophical position especially by Descartes, Spinoza and the philosophy of the *enlightenment (Leibnitz, Wolff). The late medieval decay of the Aristotelian-scholastic synthesis of soul and body (*Body-Soul Relation) and the accompanying separation of sense knowledge from intellectual knowledge led Descartes to his theory of innate ideas. But if concepts do not have to be arrived at by abstraction and by induction from experience, but basically are similar to God's creative ideas, then with their help an aprioristic-deductive treatment of all sciences must be a possibility. Rationalism was strengthened in this conviction by the mathematical ideal of pure science that was common among the thinkers of the time; according to this ideal all certain knowledge is a result of necessary, a priori principles of the intellect. According to the rationalists, reason is the only source of human knowledge. The sensations involved in sense knowledge are just *confused concepts*. — The excesses of rationalism led to the opposition of the English empiricists. Kant tried to overcome this opposition, but he was not completely successful, since the subjective forms and the concepts of the mind remain foreign to the sensations they work on.

Epistemological rationalism does not do justice to the full breadth of human knowledge. It limits it unduly in two ways: firstly, it does not recognize the full reality of sense knowing and so it allows conceptual knowledge to deteriorate into empty formalism (the rationalists' lack of understanding of history is connected with this); secondly, in spite of the apparent approximation of human concepts to the divine ideas, it still tends to limit intellectual knowledge to the specifically human mode of conceptual-discursive thinking (*Rational) and so to make of it the first norm of all knowledge and all existence.

When this type of thinking is used in theology we end up with *theological* rationalism which judges everything, even *faith and *revelation, according to the standard of purely human reason, nor will it recognize the existence of anything beyond it (*Mystery). In the area of religion, it recognizes either only a rational religion or else it deprives positive *religion of its dimension of mystery and so explains it as a product of human history.

Just as epistemological rationalism encroaches upon sense knowledge for the sake of the intellect, so also does *ethical* rationalism greatly restrict the importance of the will and the emotions. For, according to ethical rationalism, knowledge alone of the good is normative for the moral conduct of man. Socrates is the typical representative of ethical rationalism (*Socratic Method). — Rationalism often means the same thing as intellectualism; on the distinction between the two see *Intellectualism*.

WB

REALISM

Realism literally means a standpoint of reality. In a general metaphysical-epistemological sense realism (1), in contrast to *idealism, is the position that a real existent subsists "in itself" independently of my thinking about it, that existence therefore is not just a positing of the thinking *subject, that the meaning of human knowledge is to conform oneself to the known existent — to grasp it as it is in itself, and that this goal is also attainable, at least within certain limits. This last conviction also distinguishes realism from *phenomenalism. But it would be an exaggeration to define the "real" exclusively as that which subsists independently of our thinking; rather, it is that which has *existence, even if this existence, such as that of our internal and external activities, depends upon our thinking, willing and acting. — If someone speaks of *ideal realism*, this can refer to the conviction common to all Christian Platonism and Aristotelianism — in contrast to a materialistic realism — that all being is ultimately shaped according to the divine ideas and therefore is not "irrational," but spiritually transparent. Of course, the name can also designate untenable attempts at a reconciliation between idealism and realism or refer to forms of realistic decorations on epistemological idealism; an example of this is offered when it is said that the ideal itself is the real.

Alongside of the general meaning of realism, explicit mention of realism is made in two partial areas of our knowledge, i. e., with regard to the knowledge of the external world and with regard to the validity of *universal concepts. As a realism (2) regarding the external world it stands in contrast to the so-called acosmic *idealism, which absolutely denies the existence of a corporeal world, and to *phenomenalism insofar as it denies the knowability of the world. It is called *naive realism* if, in the knowledge of the external world, no problem at all is recognized and the data of the senses are simply accepted as real; *critical realism* if it gives a justification of man's natural conviction of knowing the real. It is better not to equate this distinction with that of indirect and direct realism. For, *direct realism* (e. g., Rehmke, Gredt) assumes that in sense perception (at least the sense of touch) external reality is directly "given" (*Object) and that therefore the judgment about this reality is based on immediate *evidence. Consequently, an existence in bodies similar to that contained in the act of sensation is also ascribed to *sense qualities. The chief difficulty for direct realism is to explain the doubtless reality of sense deceptions. *Indirect realism* admits that the real existence of things is not given immediately; certainly an existent that is independent of consciousness announces itself in the data of the senses (especially because of the irresistibility with which they force themselves upon the person), and at a purely instinctive level it moves perception to external actions that correspond to the reality of things. Real existence is not immediately intuited in the data of the senses, but it is added to them (correctly) by an act of thought; even this "objectification" occurs instinctively, but it is constantly re-affirmed by the experienced relations between man and his surroundings. It is the task of philosophy to raise man's naturally given certitude to scientific knowledge by explicitly formulating the reasons behind it. Such a philosophical foundation of realism is sometimes called "realization" (e. g., Oswald Kuelpe). Indirect realism need not assume that all determinations given in the senses (including sense qualities) are present in things in exactly the same way (*Quantum Mechanics). — If all intellectual evidence for the actual existence of things is denied and their real existence is accepted only on the basis of will or feeling, then one speaks of *volitive, emotional* or *irrational realism* (represented by Max Scheler and Nicolai von Hartmann).

Realism (3) as applied to universal concepts stands in opposition to *nominalism, which denies the existence of such concepts, and to *conceptualism, which considers them to be mere mental forms. But realism says that the content of concepts — the conceptualized "essense" — is actualized in the existent itself. Exaggerated realism proposes that the mode of existence of real essences is the same as the thought-mode: thus just as the universal is thought of as abstracted from the particular, so also do universal essences exist, either in things themselves or apart from things (*Platonism). According to moderate realism, however, the content of the concept is in particular things "in another way," i. e., not abstracted from the determinations that constitute the individual as such, but actualized with them in the concrete unity of an existent.

In the area of practical philosophy, realism (4) demands that action be in accordance with existence and therefore that moral norms ultimately be based on the essential order of the existent. And just as the good is to be measured by this order, so also is the beautiful. This of course does not mean a justification of aesthetic realism (5) which says that art should only express reality in its essential characteristics without "idealizing" them (e. g., a photograph as contrasted to a painting).

JdV

REASON

Reason in the broad sense (1) is man's spiritual knowing-power in contrast to his sensibility; therefore it means the same thing as *intellect. But often within reason in this broad sense an opposition of two kinds of activity is manifest from this or that respect; then they must be distinguished as intellect and reason in the narrow sense (2). In general, "intellect" refers mainly to abstracting, comparing and analyzing thinking, while "reason" means the higher activities of the mind which strive for order and positive unity in thought and action. The scholastics make a distinction between *intellectus*, which approaches a type of spiritual vision in its immediate *essential knowledge and in its grasp of the first principles of *knowledge, and *ratio*, which is the power of discursive thinking and which is characteristic of the human, abstracting intellect; in English "*intellectus*" is usually translated as "intellect", "*ratio*" as "reason." In Kant (*Critical Philosophy) the intellect is the power of forming concepts and judgments, while reason in the narrow sense is the power of inferring and so of seeking the unconditioned in the conditioned. Thus reason is unavoidably entangled in fallacies and so it is inferior to the intellect in the value of its knowledge. *Practical reason* (in the broad sense) insofar as it determines the will by means of the moral law. In Hegel the intellect remains stuck in abstract, fixed concepts; on the other hand, speculative reason fully realizes the dialectical movement of the concept and in this way comes to "concrete" concepts. Therefore, it surpasses the intellect and is the true power of metaphysical thinking.

JdV

REFLECTION

Reflection in a very general sense (1) means a thoughtful, examining meditation in contrast to a simple perception or to immediate, involuntary judgments about an object. What is known as "ontological reflection" belongs here; many modern scholastic philosophers speak of this as a turning of oneself again to the known object. However, ontological reflection as the method of *metaphysics can also be understood in a more precise and more profound sense, insofar as the *abstraction of existence (as the proper object of metaphysics) from the concrete existent means at the same time a return of the spirit to its own innermost essence. — This return (reflexio = bending back) is the real meaning of reflection. Thus, reflection (2) especially means the directing back of one's attention *from* the external objects, which in the natural course of things are first noticed, *to* one's own spiritual activity and to the mode of existence that belongs to these objects only as the objects of this activity. Therefore, the concept of reflection is related to the concept of *consciousness. However, the mere awareness of one's own acts, "accompanying consciousness," is better not referred to as "reflection"; this name should be reserved for the explicit attention to these acts and their subject, the *ego. Some modern scholastics designate such reflection as a *second* intention in contrast to the direction of one's view to the external objects as a *first* intention. In the terminology of classical scholasticism these expressions do not designate the act of turning to the object or to one's own activity, but they refer to the concept which is formed on the basis of this "turning"; accordingly, then, first intentions are the concepts abstracted from the objects of intuition and second intentions are concepts formed on the basis of reflection; preferably, concepts formed on the basis of logical reflection are called second intentions. A distinction should be made between *psychological* reflection (i. e., reflection on one's own acts and ego) and *logical* reflection, which is concerned with the (abstract) mode of thinking and the logical relations given with it — which relations belong to objects only as thought-objects. These relations are the "second intentions" which are the object of logic and of mere beings of the mind (e. g., the subordination of concepts according to genus and species: *Predicables). The expression "reflective consciousness" is sometimes used as equivalent to reflection; in a more restricted sense it does not signify the mere attention to one's own acts, but their own mental expression in a concept (reflective concept) or a judgment (reflective judgment or judgment of consciousness). Reflection, especially in its perfect form as found in reflective consciousness, is characteristic of spirit alone, while the simple awareness of one's own acts is also proper to sense knowing.

JdV

RELATION

Relations have a decisive meaning for the structure of the world. From ancient times men have been aware of a profound unity at the heart of a multi-faceted universe. Some have been so captivated by the unity of all things that they have proclamed unity as the only reality, while rejecting multiplicity as mere appearance (e. g., Parmenides). In contrast to this view, however, it is necessary to preserve the reality of multiplicity without at the same time destroying unity. Both of these aspects of the real world were bound together by the Greeks in their idea of the vibrating "cosmos"; this notion was further developed in the Middle Ages into the idea of "order" which is based on God himself. In this way the world is established as a multiplicity of beings which are joined together into "one" whole by means of various relations; for without relations there would be no unity of *order. This order manifests that the manifold relations are ultimately rooted in the absolute unity of God which includes everything in a unified way which, because of *participation, is dispersed and so constitutes the world. Thus the relational unity of creation reflects the absolute unity of the primordial source of all things.

To be more exact, a relation is the habitude (Lat.: *habitudo*) or reference of one thing to another. It is also called a *proportion*, though in this sense for the most part only in mathematics or in areas connected with mathematics. A relation presupposes a *subject*, a *term* and a *foundation* (in the subject); in the relation of fatherhood, the father is the subject, the son is the term and the act of generation is the foundation. Depending upon the situation, a relation can be either unilateral or mutual; there are some that are the same on both sides (e. g., friendship between two adult men) and some that are different (e. g., father-son); again, some involve two different beings while others involve many (e. g., the relational complex between the parts of a clock). Moreover, relations diverge from each other according to depth and duration (e. g., the act of buying bread in a store in contrast to the marriage bond); they also arise sometimes out of necessity (as in the case of an infant) and sometimes out of abundant wealth (here we might think of Plato as the head of the Academy).

The most important distinction is that between the *transcendental* or *essential* relation and the predicamental (categorical) or *accidental* relation. The former exceeds the limits of just one category and applies to all of them; it also enters into the essential constitution of its bearer (cf. the relation between the principles of *existence, the relation of creatures to God). The latter is added as a further determination to a bearer which is already complete in its essential constitution and is itself one of the special *categories of *accident (cf. the relation of non-essential dependence or reference).

So far we have been considering *real* relations; there are also *logical* relations (relatio rationis). These are certain aspects of things which, although in themselves not relations, are grasped by our minds as relations because we cannot grasp them in any other way; such relations are beings of the mind, which however have a foundation in reality (cf. the relation between the concept of a species and the real individual existent; or the identity of a thing with itself which we think of as a relation). These logical relations are considered especially by *logic and *symbolic logic.

JBL

RELATIVE

Something is relative insofar as it is referred to another or is the bearer of a relation. Viewed conceptually, the relative is that which cannot be defined without reference to something else (e. g., father, son). — Considered from the angle of existence, the relative is: (1) what possesses existence ony with reference to another (e. g., *accidents*); (2) a being whose existence is the basis of a real relation to another (all finite existence). — According to its validity, the relative is that which has worth only conditionally. — Often "relative" means the same as "subjective" or "related to a subject"; or it can mean "conditioned," in which case the *condition i*s understood as that upon which something in any order depends. The "correlative" is that which stands in a mutual relationship to something else (e. g., larger, smaller). See also *Relation, Absolute, Relativism, Relativity, Theory of.*

WB

RELATIVISM

Relativism is characterized by a definite interpretation of the notion of truth. Finite *truth as a conformity of knowledge with its object essentially involves a relationship and so is relative. But one can only speak of relativism when, in place of the object being judged, something else is established as the norm of truth (e. g., the make-up of the subject, special cultural conditions). While the object is a norm of truth that is valid for all *subjects, no matter under what conditions knowledge takes place, the general norm of truth is lost as soon as it is placed anywhere but in the object itself. Then truth becomes relative in the special sense that it is valid for one subject but at the same time not valid for another. Thus, relativism abandons the principle of *contradiction and the universal validity of truth. — However, it is not relativism if one grants that our knowledge is able to grasp the object more or less depending on the knowing power and the other conditions of knowing, but that it can never grasp it comprehensively. It should also be granted that often influences other than the objective reality are operative in human knowing.

The changeability in sense knowledge resulting from variations of time and place is not a valid argument for relativism. For, intellectual knowledge can rise above these variations by indicating the circumstances of the observer. But we would have a type of *perspectivism* if the exact same object could be judged differently from the same point of view and still be true in both instances. — The relativity of truth has nothing to do with the theory of *relativity. It is likewise to be distinguished from *relationism* which reduces all existence to mere *relations. — Against universal relativism speaks the fact that we undoubtedly possess knowledge of absolute truth, i. e., truth that is valid for every intellect (e. g., judgments about the simple data of consciousness), and the fact that universal relativism entangles itself in a contradiction when it claims to have discovered the relativity of truth. For, if it knows the relativity of truth as it is, then it knows it in a way that is universally valid. But if relativism were correct, we could never know that it is absolutely correct. — See also *Psychologism, Pragmatism.*

JS

RELATIVITY, THEORY OF

The theory of relativity is the modern mathematical-physical theory of motion. The earlier, so-called classical physics was aware of a principle of relativity — that of mechanics. It says that in every frame of reference which is moved with respect to another in a uniform, rectilinear way, all mechanical laws are valid in the same way; or in other words: it cannot be established by means of mechanical events whether or not a body is in a state of absolute rest or of uniform, rectilinear motion. Only relative motions can be verified. — In 1905 this principle received a fundamental extension from Einstein in the field of the *special theory of relativity*. In order to remove the contradiction to which the experiments regarding light-ether had led, Einstein extended relativity also to electro-magnetic phenomena. According to this principle there is no occurrence in the world which would make it possible to establish absolute rest or uniform, rectilinear motion. The second fundamental principle of the special theory of relativity (which is also a consequence of the ether-experiments) is the principle of the constancy of the speed of light in all systems moving with respect to each other uniformly and rectilinearly. The mathematical calculations based on these two principles led to the relativity of space and time; i. e., space and time measurements show themselves as dependent on the state of motion of the measuring observer in contrast to the object being measured. For the moving observer, the lengths are shorter and the times are longer. — In 1916 the special theory of relativity was expanded into the *general theory of relativity* when accelerated motion was also included in it (which includes rotational-motion). According to this principle, it is absolutely impossible to establish any absolute state of motion. For the mathematical description of space a non-Euclidian geometry must be employed (*Mathematics). — In 1950 Einstein produced a still greater generalization of the theory, one which concerns primarily the field of pure mathematics. The meaning and validity of his later position is still not clear.

The experimentally verifiable consequences of the theory so far have shown themselves to be correct, and so the theory of relativity has become the common property of physicists. Their propositions, however, are less concerned with nature itself than with the observation and description of nature. — Viewed philosophically, the theory of relativity gave rise to a great deal of discussion in which basic misunderstandings came to light. First of all, the theory does not in any way teach the *relativism of truth. Further, it is not a question of the relativity of *space and *time in the philosophical sense; rather, it concerns the relativity of space and time measurement, even though the positivistic thought and expression patterns of many physicists often give the impression that space and time are wholly relative. Moreover, the theory does not assert that all *motion is essentially relative; what it says is that only relative motion is verifiable, which naturally presupposes absolute motion. The most important philosophical conclusion from the theory of relativity is the knowledge that many unstated presuppositions are involved in man's cognition of nature; and it is the task of the theory of man's knowledge of nature to uncover them.

NJ

RELIGION

Religion is derived more properly from the Latin *relegere* (= read again) than from *re-ligare* (= bind again or to). Accordingly the word "religion" means to turn oneself to something again and again, to consider something very carefully. The object of such concern must merit such attention and even require it because of its own lofty excellence. The other meaning of "religion" gives some indication of the nature of this being: to bind to — in this case to the first origin and the ultimate goal. Because a greater importance is attached to this First and Last than to all other things, it should be given special consideration in preference to all others.

All things receive their existence from *God and so proceed from him; they also strive back towards him. Still man is the only being who exercises religion since as spirit he is both aware of his relation to God and freely realizes it, i. e., he knows that God is his origin and goal and recognizes this situation. Since religion is concerned with what is most sublime, by embracing it man strives to fulfill his principal moral obligation and attain his loftiest perfection. Without religion man remains a cripple in his most noble part, no matter what other rich gifts he may have or admirable things he may accomplish; he is like a beautiful gold setting from which the precious jewel has been taken. — In religion the whole man turns to God; therefore it embraces all the higher powers of his soul: knowing, willing and feeling. But since lived religion is more a gift of self than it is knowledge, it appears especially as the product of a will inserted in feeling and sees in God absolute existence as the absolute value. If, as often happens nowadays, this value is called the *numinous* or the *holy*, there is no basic reason to object; however, many thinkers understand by this a separation of value from existence and thereby render the religious attitude fully irrational. In reality absolute existence is identified with absolute value just as religious devotedness is fully penetrated with knowing — a knowing, of course, that is not discursive, but wholly intuitive or experiential. Because of its spiritual-intellectual nature religion exerts a certain influence on the body and our sensitive life: thus it creates for itself visible expressions in the area of words, behavior and *symbols. For this reason a purely internal, spiritual religion is contrary to man's nature and cannot last; by the same token mere external show without the corresponding interior sentiments signals the death of true religion.

Finally, since man is by nature ordered to social living, religion cannot be just the private affair of the individual, in fact it should also be promoted by the community; for it is in the community that religious life achieves its full development. It follows from what has been said that religion of the subjective spirit (religion as a fact and a personal attitude) is intimately bound up with religion in the sense of the objective and the objectified spirit (religion as religious doctrine, community, institutions, custom) which is either the source and foundation of the former or its destruction.

Some kind of religion has existed among all peoples and at all times; neither history nor pre-history attests to a religionless state of mankind. Religion appears everywhere as a primary datum; and nowhere is it derived from non-religious manifestations like animism, animatism, totemism or magic. By *animism* is meant a belief in souls (*anima*) and spirits as well as their veneration; by *animatism* the belief in a kind of soul or power that is invisibly present in everything. *Totemism* believes in the relationship of an individual or a group with a *totem* which is usually an animal; in primitive cultures this totem is unknown. *Magic* and *witchcraft* try to control the divine powers by means of incantations, while the religious man subjects himself to them in prayer. Actions resembling sorcery which are not referred to a higher power are not magic, but the results of a primitive conception of the powers of nature and how they are related.

Religion is the same thing as the adoration of God., i. e., it views God as a person, as even paganism saw and the philosophy of religion has impressively shown (Scheler). However, many corruptions are included in the pagan idea of God. Alongside of the one God often the personified powers of nature are also given divine adoration; frequently little distinction is made between the Godhead itself and its material image: idolatry. In *fetishism* material things are venerated, not because they are images of gods but because of a higher power that has been charmed into them as if it were something personal. The pantheistic distortion of the idea of God comes close to *polytheism*. Indeed out and out *pantheism is the ruination of all authentic religion; for usually an impersonal primordial "ground" takes the place of God, and ultimately man himself becomes god. But this kind of pantheism as an actually lived religion is not found; at most, it manifests a pantheistic coloring, as in India, which stems from the basic philosophical-theological orientation. — When the absoluteness of God is transferred to earthly values and these are surrounded with religious fervor, one speaks of a *substitute-religion*.

The discussion so far has concerned natural religion which grows out of the created spiritual nature of man. Natural religion is to be contrasted with *positive* religion which is either established or determined in some way by a historical act of God (*Revelation) and the corresponding acts of man (unwritten and written laws). There is no such thing as a purely natural religion, but it does form the background of all historical religions. Still, *deism goes too far when it declares that the area of natural religion is wholly self-contained and impenetrable, since it excludes here and everywhere all divine intervention. — Since man can clearly recognize his creature-relation to God and the revelation of God which has occurred in time, he may not be indifferent either with regard to religion in general or with regard to the one true revelation-religion; thus he may not embrace *indifferentism.*

A revelation-religion, especially the Christian religion, shows clearly how the religious life grows and develops. Basic to this life are faith, hope and love. The corresponding attitudes in natural religion are an experience of God which is carefully nourished and constantly deepened, a striving for God as the ultimate goal with confidence in his assistance and the embrace of God in imperishable love. This is the stuff out of which personal familiarity with God in *prayer* grows. This is first manifested in *adoration,* i. e. a respectful submission of oneself before the infinite grandeur and absolute glory of God. Adoration finds its most festive, visible expression in *sacrifice*; for in sacrifice man offers to God something valuable of his own as an external sign of his self-surrender; and in order to make the offering irrevocable, it is often destroyed by fire. *Thanksgiving* to the giver of all good things and the *request* for future blessings are joined with adoration; a man is moved to these acts by the constant experience of his own limitations. The practical consequence of true religion is a life of dedication to fulfilling the divine will. — *Cult* is made up of interior acts and external actions whose exclusive or at least primary sense is directed towards the adoration of God.

JBL

RELIGION, PHILOSOPHY OF

This science is the philosophical investigation of what religion as such is or that by means of which the historical religions distinguish themselves precisely as religions from all other cultural manifestations. It first investigates the essence of religion and what it should be according to the full meaning of the concept. It then proceeds to determine a limited concept of religion — a concept that is broad enough to include within itself the accumulated historical experience of religion and definite enough to exclude all substitute or apparent religions (*Religion). In order to throw some light on the essence of religion the philosophy of religion makes use of natural *theology, which seeks after God by the use of reason and raises the question of the possibility of knowing him. However, in order to understand religion in its various historical manifestations, the philosophy of religion needs the assistance of comparative religion and the phenomenology of religion; for it is these latter sciences which attempt to describe the nature of religion and thus bring out what is characteristic of the fundamental religious acts. Since the philosophy of religion measures the various religions which have arisen in the past with its developed concept of religion, it is able to make a value judgment about them. Both the nature of God as a personal being and the fact that many religions, in order to prove their truth, appeal to divine revelations, make it imperative that the philosophy of religion take up the question of the possibility of *revelation. — Investigations about the actual conditions necessary for the origin and expression of religion in individual persons belong in the field of the *psychology of *religion*; questions relative to the social forms of religion and its attitude towards culture and the intellectual life belong in the field of the sociology of religion.

As a separate philosophical discipline the philosophy of religion was established by the neo-Kantians. They tried to trace religion back to a special religious a priori. They were correct insofar as they saw that man is by nature directed towards a religious attitude; but they were wrong in denying any real existence to the object of religion.

WB

RELIGION, PSYCHOLOGY OF

The psychology of religion is concerned with the special psychic manifestations and norms of the "religious experience," i. e., the subjective, psychic behavior of man with regard to God and generally with regard to the doctrines and demands of the religious life which objectively present themselves. This science is distinguished according to its object and method from the history of religions, from the *philosophy of *religion* as well as from the philosophy of God and dogmatic *theology. It questions neither the objective truth of particular religious convictions nor the *supernatural character of the activity of divine grace in the soul; thus it limits itself to the natural, psychic aspects of religious phenomena. Thus, on the one hand, the limits of its possibilities and competence are indicated; but on the other hand the supernatural aspects (known from theology) of the religious life of the soul (*Mysticism) do not make the psychology of religion a useless study; for even the supernatural experience as an activity of the mind and the soul has its own "aspect" which can be examined psychologically.

The main question asked by the psychology of religion is directed to the inner structure of religious experience: how is this experience to be distinguished from other forms of experience? to what "level" of the soul does it belong to principally — intellect and will, instincts or the emotions? Is it essentially rooted in repressed complexes, or in some kind of a "break through" of the personal subconscious, or in the arche-types of the collective *subconscious mind, or in the spiritual-intellectual soul of man? Penetrating into the inner chambers of man's spiritual life, it asks questions with broad implications, such as how to reconcile the tension between the individual and society, between the rational in man and the irrational in him; it questions a man's limitations because of his particular bodily type and stages of development, because of his mental health and his abnormalities.

The psychology of religion is not something specifically new or modern. An abundance of psychological observations, perhaps unsystematic but still very penetrating, can be found in the ascetical and mystical writings of former centuries. In order to counter the influence of the enlighten-ment and of critical philosophy about the year 1800, many thought that the values of the religious life could only be saved by placing religion essentially in the sphere of one's emotional life as a matter of mere feeling and by giving only secondary importance to intellectual and dogmatic questions (religion of feeling; Schleiermacher's teaching of the feeling of co-existence with the infinite; later, his teaching of the feeling of absolute dependence). So began a psychological interpretation of religious experience which was aprioristic, emotionalistic and one-sided; around the turn of the last century this view was the dominant one in the field of the psychology of religion — and this continued for a number of decades. At the same time the opinion spread that the real source of religious experience should be looked for in the subconscious only (Sabatier, W. James, Flournoy, Janet and others). Leuba developed a materialistic psychology of religion, while W. Wundt considered religion as essentially a socio-psychological phenomenon. Rudolf Otto in his phenomenological analyses saw the heart of religious experience in the feeling of the "*mysterium fascinosum et tremendum*" as the effect of an emotional, a priori category of feeling. The investiga-tions of Girgensohn and Gruehns brought about a change. They showed that an intellectual grasp of God, joined with an attraction towards him, is at the very center of religious experience.

Certainly the most varied psychical strata can be found in the religious attitude, some of which may either increase the religious experience or positively distort it (e.g., in pseudomysticism). But when researchers, who are opposed to religion and who do not have any real inner understanding for it (Janet, Freud), wanted to interpret all religious experience as either pathological or a manifestation of the sex drive, they showed a deplor-able ignorance of what healthy religious experience is. C. G. Jung looked for the psychological source of religious experience in the religious *archetypes* of the "collective subconscious." This teaching in comparison with Freud's psychoanalysis, shows a greater openness for the psychological value of religion, but even it pays much too little attention to the fundamental source of religious experience which is to be found in the spirit and consciousness of man. The religious archetype itself properly interpreted is the essential dynamism (*appetitus naturalis*) of the created spirit in its surge towards God — a surge which is prior to all conscious experience.

When fully developed the religious act is a complete turning of the human person towards *God as the most actual and elevated value operative in one's life; the soul stands before this transcendent value in attitudes, which complete and demand each other, of a distance that maintains respect and a love that seeks union. Respect and *love in this case are not meant as a kind of emotional agitation, but as complete mental attitudes by which the deliberate Yes to God which recognizes the divine majesty is rooted in the very center of human experience. Religious experience is not the actuation of a special *religious sense* ranged alongside our general spiritual powers; but it is the actuation of the religious inclination which is deeply imbedded in the soul of man and oriented towards the infinite. This inclination is not restricted to certain elite types of men, for it is rooted in the very nature of man. But it does need to be developed and cultivated by good training; when this is lacking it can wither up and die.

AW

RESPONSIBILITY

Responsibility is a necessary consequence of human *free will and the imputability based on it. Because of this imputability the moral person as the decisive cause of his good and evil deeds must answer for them before his own conscience, before the moral judgment of others and especially before the divine judge; he must also accept the inevitable consequences of his actions. The bearer of responsibility is the *person who is capable of a moral act. The object is the fully human act which proceeds from the spiritual part of man through his free will. The *spontaneous* reaction of sensual desires (anger, lust) as such is not immediately free, but it can be influenced by free will through a certain restraint. The fundamental orientation of the will to the *good in general and to the final end of happiness is indeed *voluntary* (since it proceeds from the will), but it is always there. Only the direction of this basic striving to particular, finite ends is free, so that the will could also omit them. But the person is responsible for his acts only when he has sufficient moral knowledge and when his free will is not impaired by an irresistible force or by the pressure to make a quick decision. Mental disturbances of many kinds also diminish imputability and responsibility — and at times completely exclude it. The dignity of the human person is clearly revealed in his personal responsibility.

JoS

REVELATION

Revelation literally means every manifestation of something hidden. In the religious sense, revelation is the manifestation of the hidden by a higher power, namely, by God. In daily language sometimes a sudden knowledge, which was prepared for in the subconscious mind and whose causes are not seen (e. g., artistic inspiration), is called a revelation. Related to revelation in this sense is the Modernistic conception of revelation according to which revelation is only a religious feeling that rises out of the subconscious spirit. However, for revelation in the true sense there must be someone who makes the hidden known, someone who receives the communication, and a truth that is made known. Mere awareness of one's inner relationship to God (*Mysticism) is not revelation. — The manifestation of the existence and certain attributes of God that is necessarily given with creation, is called *natural revelation.* According to Catholic theology, natural revelation is to be distinguished from revelation that occurs as a result of the personal word and witness of God himself. Such revelation is called *supernatural,* because there is no necessity for it either from the side of human nature or from the side of the laws of nature. By "word" is not meant a physiological event but an influence of God that works mediately (through signs) or immediately on the human spirit; by means of this influence God communicates to a man not just certain thoughts, but he also leads him to understand through certain signs (*Miracle) that it is He who is giving him these thoughts and Who guarantees their truthfulness. The object of this communication can be *mysteries which by their very nature are hidden from man, or natural truths which are not essentially unknowable by man but which, as a result of the divine testimony, are now known and held with an infallible certainty. The possibility of supernatural revelation is based on the fact that God is a personal, free being whose actions outside of himself are not limited by natural laws. The change brought about by revelation rests exclusively on the side of the receiving, finite spirit. — Religions are called *revealed religions,* if they appeal to a supernatural revelation for their essential doctrines and institutions. Different religions, insofar as they contradict each other in the area of doctrine, cannot be based simultaneously on true revelation. For the acceptance of revelation, which occurs in *faith, to be obligatory, the fact of revelation must be ascertained with at least practical *certitude. Neither on the side of God nor on the side of man is it necessary that revelation be directed immediately to each person; it can take place through the testimony of credible witnesses. That man has to reckon with the possibility of meeting God in revelation and so in history, is rooted in the nature of man as a historical being.

WB

RIGHT

Right and *justice occupy a very special place within the whole moral order. However, there is some ambiguity in the more common usage of these terms. For example, in the language of theology justice is sometimes taken to mean *holiness and "justification" is understood as the communication of sanctifying grace. That usage is quite widespread which joins rights so directly with personal worth that absolutely everything that belongs to a *person as such is characterized as his "right." In this way the unconditioned sovereignty of God over all creation is called his "right" of sovereignty; similarly, man's power to sustain and shape his life, his power to dominate irrational creatures and to use them for his own purposes, is spoken of as his "right" to life, to develop his own personality, to possess, etc. All these "rights" are based in the personal dignity of the one possessing them or, more precisely, in the essential superiority (Lat. *dominium*) of the free human person over the objects it is related to. On the basis of sound metaphysics these rights are simply inalienable.

In order to arrive at a precise concept of right which clearly brings out its special nature within the framework of the universal moral order, it is necessary to put narrower limits on the area of rights. Jurisprudence and the philosophy of law, therefore, see in the superiority of the person not the fact that he is endowed with rights, but that he is something prior to all rights and this is the foundation on which the whole structure of rights is established. According to the classical axiom: *ius est ad alios* (a right is a relationship to others; it is the arrangement of interpersonal relationships), only relations of one person to another person belong to the world of rights in the strict sense of the word (therefore it includes neither the relations of persons to things [*Property] nor the relations between a person and his own personal goods, e. g., his own life or his own conscience). But not all interpersonal relationships (e. g., love, gratitude, trust), and in fact not even all the norms governing social life, have a *legal* character. From the multitude of these normative relationships only those stand out as "rights" which protect a man from others in all that concerns his personal dignity and individuality, and which bind him as an essentially social being to larger social groups, both natural and freely organized. Since rights relate the two orders — the individual and the social — to each other, they determine the structure of social life and form the supporting frame around which the structure of society must be built. In this sense the *social order* and the *juridical order* are two names for the same thing. Now clearly since the regulation of the life of a community can never be in opposition to that community and its true needs, a right that militates against that community is no right at all. For the same reason, the law is never dead and inflexible, but it is always alive; it is not only capable of adaptation, but it is also always moving in the direction of progress (on justice and the common good see *Justice). What men in the past have established as the regulation of their community can age and die out; it can also be preserved only as a corpse for a long time. Law is either young and fresh as life, or it does not exist at all.

The one word "right" must serve to designate: 1. The *juridical order*, and also every particular juridical norm which forms a part of this order (*ius normativum*); 2. that which corresponds to the juridical order or to the particular juridical norms, whether it is a structure, a circumstance or human conduct; 3. the powers which belong to the members of a juridically ordered community.

Since rights concern the relations between persons in a community, only persons can be the subjects of rights and duties. From this notion comes the idea of a "juridical person" which is used for corporations and organizations which have rights and duties. — If man enters into a juridical relationship to God that can only come about because God lowers himself in some way to the level of man in order to associate man with himself in a kind of community.

Law as the regulation of the life of the community is by its very nature ordered to the building up of community; only a complete distortion of law can fragment society. Since there are those who break the law, for the sake of order and peace it is necessary that the law be enforceable, at least insofar as that which is covered by the law is able to be enforced. With the progress of law and society the tendency has been and is to reserve to the State the right to enforce the law.

In contrast to the above, *legal positivism*, misunderstanding that rights are based on the essential free personality of man and that man's fundamentally social nature is also rooted in the fact that he is a free person, asserts that it is up to the community exclusively to determine the nature and content of all rights. Therefore it recognizes only positively formulated propositions (also customs) as law and its does not grant that the formulation of new laws must be guided by pre-given or inalienable rights; thus it is prepared to affirm that even those laws are "just" which we would consider to be contrary to the essential nature of man and the moral order. In its most extreme form this theory maintains that the power to pass and enforce a law determines whether or not it is just. Sometimes, however, it seems that what is meant is that only organized society (especially the *State) can bring that technical perfection to the juridical order which is adequate for the complex needs of modern life. If this is so then it is just a dispute about words, i. e., whether the basic reason behind all formulated law is called *natural right or whether as a substitute for this rather ambiguous phrase a new, clearer expression is used.

Legal formalism agrees with legal positivism to the extent that it also does not admit the existence of legal principles which precede and transcend all positive formulations; rather, it will only admit certain "formal" principles such as freedom which can co-exist with the "similar" freedom of all others (Kant). Since everyday living requires definite norms, they must be positively expressed in a body of laws. Thus mere legality takes the place of innate rights.

The *philosophy of Law* is concerned with the essence of law as such and attempts to trace it back to its ultimate foundation.

The man who fulfills all his legal obligations and respects the rights of others exercises the virtue of *justice. The requirements of the law are fulfilled even when the motive for obeying is not out of respect for the law; the motive can be either of a lower (reasonable self-interest) or a higher order. Therefore justice does not exclude love: an obligation in justice can be and often is fulfilled also out of a motive of love.

OvNB

RIGORISM

Rigorism in general is that doctrine and attitude of mind which, in the conflict of opinions about the liceity of some act, on principle holds for the narrower and stricter view. In a more restricted sense rigorism is the same as *tutiorism*, which demands that a person in a state of doubt about the liceity of an act can never decide in favor of freedom and against a probable law as long as the opinion favoring freedom is not completely certain. Real tutiorism is no less objectionable than its opposite, *laxism. For, the danger of committing a moral fault by acting contrary to a doubtful law is valid only on the (unproved) presupposition that a truly doubtful law is binding in conscience. History shows that rigorism has led its stubborn advocates to violate a number of certain obligations. See also *Conscience, Probabilism.*

JoS

ROMANTICISM

Romanticism as a movement stretches from the end of the 18th century into the middle of the 19th. Its influence, however, is still felt in the modern world. Characteristic of romanticism is the fact that it embraces and affects man's spiritual life in all dimensions. With regard to philosophy in particular, there are philosophers who can justly be called romantics (Schleiermacher and especially Schelling), and at least one romantic who deserves to be listed among the philosophers (Friedrich Schlegel).

Considered historically, romanticism arose in opposition to the *enlightenment with its overemphasis on reason and the universal concept. Between it and *German idealism there is a great deal of mutual influence along with a number of contradictions. Just as the movement was influenced by the productivity of the ego and the imagination through the writings of Fichte and by the primacy of aesthetic stimuli found in Schelling, so also on the other hand was Schelling encouraged and formed by the impulses of the movement; likewise, Hegel's view of historical becoming was enriched by it (primarily through Schlegel).

With regard to its content, romanticism is a many-faceted, changing and sometimes confusing picture; but we can detect some common elements in it. First of all, in place of reason and conceptual knowing life in its totality moves to the center of interest and everything revolves around it; it was not in vain that Friedrich Schlegel wrote his "philosophy of life." A sense for the special nature of life is awakened; just as reality itself presents a comprehensive, organic unity in which the opposition between nature and spirit is rooted, so also the human grasp of it can be no less "organic." Thus, a new look is taken of the organic conditions in which man finds himself; for this reason there is strong interest in culture and language. Finally, related to this is a true evaluation of history in its uniqueness and of that which has come about historically; with this awareness men joyfully turned to the Middle Ages in the hope of making new discoveries. — Now man is viewed as a totality. Feeling and imagination are valued more than intellect and will, so that romanticism is more at home among artists and poets. Thus, the movement fosters an irrational feeling of at-oneness with all things — and at the same time it appears to be intellectual intuition. This intuition resists all clear conceptualization and accompanies life in its constant progress or infinite becoming. — With the repulsion of the universal concept the individual once again became the center of interest; at first of course, interest was focused on the extraordinary individual. Even though the pantheistic disappearance of the individual into the All is not completely overcome, still the individual grows greatly in importance. Of course the other danger of the evanescence of the objective order of being for the sake of the subject is a real threat here; there is a danger of a lack of seriousness which would reduce existence to mere poetry and express itself in romantic *irony*. Yet men like Schlegel have taken the objective order so seriously that they have ultimately arrived at a personal God. — The basis of all serious thought that can be directed against romanticism is the fact of its one-sided irrationalism (*Irrational) which, however, does not rob its guiding insights of their fruitfulness.

JBL

S

SCHOLASTICISM

The word itself is derived from the Latin *schola, scholasticus* (school, teacher) and means "the science of the school." More precisely, it refers to the theological-philosophical science that was developed in the great schools of Europe in the Middle Ages. Here only scholastic philosophy will be considered. — Its chief characteristic is that it is *Christian philosophy. It serves theology (*ancilla theologiae*), but at the same time strives to grapple with the basic human problems and becomes an independent science with its own principles, problems and methods. To this extent it is primarily a matter of the schools. This means respect for the tradition, hesitation regarding hasty innovations, organic growth, continuance of the basic matter according to content and method. Still, within this framework a creative development of the inherited past manifests itself which is incorporated into the authentic advance of the new thinkers; a lively exchange takes place between very gifted and intelligent personalities; in fact, a genius like Thomas Aquinas is able to introduce a radical revolution. That scholasticism is not lost in abstractions and empty constructs is clear from the fact of its close contact with the vibrant mysticism of the time and its keen observation regarding the world of natural phenomena.

Out of the above movement grew the "scholastic method" for teaching and writing. The *lectio* (lecture) opened up the ancient texts through a series of explanations which were then written up in commentaries. The *disputation was directed to a more profound grasp of particular questions; it was regulated according to set rules for speeches and rebuttals. The collections of scholastic *quaestiones* (questions) come from this source. The construction of a scholastic question includes the reasons for and against the proposed point of discussion which are usually based on authorities; then comes the development and establishment of the positive solution, followed by the answers to the objections. The commentaries also frequently use this schema so that the particular author can attach his own, independent ideas to the original text; thus the great theological *Summae* proceeded. A looser form was also used, usually in the philosophical *Summae* of Aquinas (*Summa Contra Gentiles*) and in the shorter investigations (*opscula*), which was applied to very particular problems. A precise formulation of the question, clear concepts, logical proof and unequivocal terminology are the characteristic marks of the scholastic method.

Three main sources contributed to the origin of scholasticism. From the patristic era Augustine had incalculable influence. Also, *neo-Platonism worked through Augustine, the pseudo-Areopogite, Proclus and the Islamic-Jewish philosophers. But Aristotle gave the movement its peculiár stamp; some of his works were handed down by Boethius and his complete writings were gradually translated into Latin from about the middle of the 12th century. The third influence came from the Greek and Arabian commentaries (esp. Avicenna and Averroes) and the other writings of the Islamic-Jewish philosophers. — In the development of scholasticism a distinction must be made between early, classical and late scholasticism. The way was prepared by the pre-scholastics who merely handed on what they had received; John Scotus Erigena (ca. 810-877) stands out in this period because of his idealistic system with its pantheistic coloring. Early scholasticism includes the end of the 11th and the whole of the 12th century; this period was opened by Anselm of Canterbury, often called "the father of scholasticism." The chief problem of the time was that of universal concepts; the greatest development came through Peter Abelard who developed a middle position between nominalism and ultrarealism. Among the outstanding schools of the time were those of St. Victor and Chartres.

Along with the new discoveries of sources, the flowering of the universities (esp. Paris) and the scientific activity of the religious orders ushered in the era of classical scholasticism. The Christian Aristotelianism of the new Dominican school eclipsed the *Augustinianism of the older Franciscan (Alexander of Hales and Bonaventure) and Dominican schools. Albert the Great inaugurated the herculean task of reconciling Aristotle with the inheritance from Augustine; it was brought to completion by Thomas Aquinas, the principal thinker and systematizer of the period. The Franciscan school of the time was influenced by Aristotle, even though it continued to develop the Augustinian approach; it took its start in the critical work of John Duns Scotus and is therefore called *Scotism. In opposition to these Christian currents there was a purely philosophical Aristotelianism, e. g., the unchristian Averroism of Siger of Brabant.

The late scholasticism of the 14th and 15th centuries developed in the religious-order schools; it made significant advances in the study of nature (in the tradition of Albert the Great and Roger Bacon). At this time German mysticism came to life again and Meister Eckhart turned to neo-

Platonism. Still, creative thinking became increasingly rarer and scholars got lost in formalistic subtleties; especially destructive was the *nominalism of William Ockham, even though he did contribute in a positive way to the development of logic. Thus, in a state of degeneration, scholasticism faced humanism and was severely criticized, though the severe criticism does not apply to the classical scholasticism. Still even the classical type has its limitations, for its theory of knowledge was not fully developed and it had little understanding of history and change. Yet this was an important movement which has left a permanent stamp on western thought because it was the first attempt to ground and systematize Christian philosophy. It did not violently distort the real, but strove to illumine it in its inner essential structure. For this reason Christian philosophy in each age can only be realized in an organic continuation of scholasticism. See also *Neo-Scholasticism.*

JBL

SCIENCE

While the word "knowing" signifies in general some certain *knowledge (*Certitude), in a narrower sense a confirmed knowledge and in contrast to *faith a knowledge based on one's own experience and insight, science never means a single piece of knowledge, one isolated judgment; rather, it signifies a whole body of ideas which refer to the same object (or realm of objects) and are logically interconnected. Therefore, systematic coherence is essential to science. The principles of the object and its basic relationships are reflected in the perceived logical connections. That the metaphysical principles of the object reveal themselves to us only in the slow procedures of science, is based on the peculiar nature of our intellect which is not characterized by a spiritual vision of reality but by *thinking. Complete certitude with regard to each individual proposition and reason is not necessary for true science, since it can also include within itself *hypotheses and *theories that are not yet fully established. On the other hand, frequently associated with the concept of science (scientific knowledge) is the subordinate idea that the successful methods and the proved results should be basically open to all researchers; however, it seems better not to include this requirement in the definition of science. Besides, because of the objectivity of science and the essential similarity of men's intellectual powers the fulfillment of this requirement is in general guaranteed. Objectivity is essential to science, because as (spiritual) knowledge it must necessarily strive for truth. Another essential characteristic of science is its methodology (*Method). For, the logical connections it is looking for are not arrived at by aimlessly joining together many disparate observations and ideas; rather, science demands organized, methodical observation and thinking.

SCOTISM

An important methodological aid is *scientific terminology* which tries to establish the clearest possible linguistic expressions for the concepts of science.

The unity of every science is rooted in the unity of its *object. The scholastic theory of science makes a distinction between the *material object*, i. e., the concrete object that the science considers, and the *formal object*, i. e., the particular aspect under which it considers the whole material object. What is distinctive of every science is its formal object, while the same material object can be studied by many different sciences. The division of the objects of study has led to an ever-increasing *specialization* of the sciences; this movement is accompanied by the danger of a narrow view of a limited area of investigation, while an expanded grasp of the inter-relatedness of all reality disappears from sight.

This reason and others have led many men to a low estimation of science, especially of "pure" science or science that cannot be used directly in technology, medicine, etc. It is certainly true that a one-sided intellectual training can distort one's view of life and that an exaggeration of strictly scientific form and method to the detriment of solid content can lead to a dry *rationalism. However, in the proper order of striving for full human perfection science undoubtedly has great formational value, since it expands a person's appreciation for the heights and depths of reality. Just as irrationalism is anti-scientific and is to be rejected, so also is that *scientism* to be rejected which, with the methods of the particular sciences (i. e., the physical sciences), attempts to solve the most basic problems of reality and by means of a "scientific *Weltanschauung*" tries to make *metaphysics and *religion superfluous.

JdV

SCOTISM

Scotism is a philosophical school of the Middle Ages based on the work of John Duns Scotus (1266-1308). This view was advocated by the so-called younger Franciscan school of the Middle Ages and produced some famous names into the 17th century; in recent times it has also experienced a certain renascence. Scotus' penetrating criticism was directed against Thomas Aquinas, Aristotle and the Arabians. Essentially he remained true to the Franciscan tradition (*Augustinianism), even though he did abandon its position on the divine *illumination of the intellect in the act of knowing. In opposition to moderate realism he taught, in the question of the objective validity of universals, a formal distinction between the universal nature and the individual (Formalism, Ultra-Realism). Since Thomas Aquinas' teaching on analogy, according to which our limited concepts of God are valid only in an analogous, imperfect way, in Scotus' view prevents man from knowing God, he maintained a certain logical univocity of the concept of being. A principal point of his teaching concerns the primacy of the will over the intellect. All things emanate from the infinite, free, selfless love of God. The divine will is the only cause of his willing, while the divine wisdom is the reasonable basis for the willing and is thus tied to metaphysical principles. The essence of human happiness consists in willing, not in knowing. The principle of individuation is not matter, but an ultimate distinction of the form (the scotistic *Haecceitas*). The soul is the essential form of the body, but it is not its only form. The extent of demonstrable knowledge is curtailed. Thus the existence of God can be demonstrated in a strictly philosophical way, he says, but not God's omnipotence and omnipresence.

JoS

SELF-DEFENSE

Self-defense is the repulsing of a present, unjust, violent attack on one's person or goods, which in some cases can result in injury and death. Self-defense is morally permissible (even as protection for others) and in some circumstances it can even be required. The use of force as such, i.e., without further determination as just or unjust, is morally indifferent and is morally justified by the need to protect the important goods both of the individual person and of the state, while the unjust aggressor must ascribe to himself the evil consequences of his attack. The defender does not appropriate to himself an immediate and direct right over the life of the unjust aggressor, since in a morally allowable self-defense the possible killing of the aggressor is not the means of defense, but the unintended, though foreseen, consequence. For this reason also the use of force is allowable only for the repulsion of an actually existing attack, but not in order to prevent a possible future attack. Further, a limitation on the use of self-defense is that one may not exceed the measure in a justified self-defense, i. e., the defender should use only as much force as is necessary to effectively repell the attack. And the defender must leave retribution to the public authorities.

JoS

SELF-LOVE

Self-love is self-estimation as well as the will resulting from it and the striving for one's own good. It is the drive for *self-preservation* that characterizes all living things, insofar as it is knowing and willing. Self-love turns an individual against everything which, in his opinion, threatens his own existence and it strives for whatever supports and furthers his existence. The self-love contained in the drive for self-preservation is immediately concerned with the individual, but mediately it also serves the preservation of the species. An ordered self-love is a moral obligation, since the real foundation of human self-estimation rests in man's likeness to God; and by his own activity man has the task of developing himself in every way possible. Self-love as the desire for one's own good is an ordered love if it strives for those goods that are suitable to man's nature (each in its proper place) and if it does not infringe on the just rights of others. — A justly ordered self-love can never stand in opposition to the true good of others — actually, it furthers it. With regard to moral and spiritual goods, the exclusion of one of them by another is absolutely impossible. In the case of material goods, if the laws of justice were really observed by all, then it would be possible for each person to acquire what he needs. If all strive for their essential perfection, then the order and welfare of the whole group is also secured. — Self-love is disordered if it prefers the inferior goods to the superior ones and if it violates the rights of others by excessively claiming everything for itself. When this happens it has deteriorated into sheer *egotism*. — Whoever injures his own body and life (e. g., through self-mutilation and *Suicide) or whoever acts against his own spiritual and moral good, has gone against the moral obligation of self-love; so also does the person who, because of sloth, fails to strive for his own development and perfection. — See also *Love*.

JK

SENSATION

Sensation in ordinary language means some kind of direct experience or feeling. Historically psychology has used the word to signify the final element in a sense perception, such as blue or sweet; this is sensation in the narrow sense. It always forms a part of a larger complex — here it would be a part of a perception (e. g., of a house that I see). — There are certain pre-given conditions of sensation. Thus, corporeal processes in the external world condition seeing, namely, electromagnetic waves which are reflected from objects in an irregular manner and which produce corresponding changes in the retina of the eye. As the result of this stimulus a corresponding stimulus is communicated to the optic nerve and finally to the brain. A truly living sensation and perception, along with shape, color, size, etc., is dependent on these corporeal changes. Such corporeal conditions are called "*stimuli.*" They are partially external, outside of the organism, and they are of various kinds: mechanical, acoustical, optical, etc.; some are also internal, in the sense organ and in the nerves. In the brain the different senses are located in different places: the sight-sphere, the sound-sphere, etc.; the activity of the nerves and the conscious act that accompanies it are called the *psychophysical activity*.

SENSE

From the psychological point of view, sensation manifests a number of different characteristics: quality (species), intensity (strength), spatial aspects (figure, size), and temporal aspects (a point in time, duration). These characteristics do not exist in the same way in the external world as they do in the one sensing; they are *intentional since they pertain only to the image of perception as such. For, it is not the conscious act as such that is green or square, but the object of knowledge; we have the sensation of a green thing or of something that is extended in some way, etc. — A characteristic of sensation that is proper to one sense cannot be taken away without at the same time taking away the corresponding sensation. There is no sound with an intensity of zero or with a duration of zero. But all of the above-mentioned characteristics do not belong to all of the senses; for example, extension pertains only to the senses of sight and touch. The *power of discrimination* is the ability to perceive differences in quality, intensity, etc. The lesser the differences that can be noticed, the greater the power. With regard to musical notes, perhaps a one-tenth variation in the quality of the note can be discerned by the human ear, but certainly not a one-thousandth variation. — The *intensity of sensation*: the weakest stimulus that can still produce a sensation is called the *stimulus threshold*; thus, the air waves must exceed a definite intensity before a sound can be heard. The absolute sensibility of a particular sense is inversely proportional to the stimulus threshold; the weaker the audible stimulus is, the more acute the sense of hearing. Weber's law regards the *threshold differential*: Within the average limits of the strength of the stimulus this differential is proportional. Consequently, for the middle ranges the relative threshold differential (= the differential divided by the stimulus) is constant though it deviates from the constant value at the extremes; thus, if a stimulus of strength 10 requires an addition of 1 so that the increase can be noticed, then a stimulus of 30 requires the addition of 3. — The *location of sensation* is the bodily process in the organism with which the conscious sensation is connected. Thus, sensation takes place in the brain. For, if the connection with the brain is cut off or if the corresponding sphere of a sense, which is located in the brain, is destroyed, the corresponding sensation stops even though the sense organ remains wholly intact.

JF

SENSE

Sense is used both with a subjective and an objective meaning. Taken subjectively, we find many senses as the knowing powers of men and animals which immediately or intuitively grasp the appearances of the corporeal world (1). Although essentially they are parts of the soul, still the sense powers are necessarily tied to bodily organs (*Sense Knowledge).

SENSE

A distinction is made between *external senses*, which produce the first sensations from received impressions, and *internal senses*, which further "interpret" the sensation material. The notion of *sensibility is derived from this source. "Sensibility" refers to the totality of all the sensible powers — not only in the order of knowing but also in the order of desire; the latter are called "sensible" because they are wholly dependent on the senses. If sensibility, understood in a narrow sense, refers only to the sense drives and ultimately only to the sexual powers, then from a philosophical point of view it is of lesser importance. — The meaning of "sense" given so far is applied also, in an expanded way, to the life of the spirit. Through his senses man is receptive of colors, sounds, etc. Therefore, when a person is open to or receptive of something, we can also say: He has a sense (2) for that (e. g., for music, for athletics, for religion). — These powers have for their common source man's sensibility as that spiritual medium through which he is open to everything and related to everything; moreover, his thinking and willing depend on this medium (e. g., "to sense something," with the meaning of "to know it") (3).

Objectively, sense (4) means that which in the object corresponds to man's sense power (3), that which is related to his *understanding and makes the existent intelligible. In this case, "sense" refers to that for which something else exists: *teleological sense* (5). The state of being ordered to some goal constitutes the sense of something, to the extent that it allows us to understand that "something" in its special nature or at least in its factual presence. Thus, we speak of the sense of life, of history, of evil, of an activity or event, of organizations (e. g., universities). A more static "formal sense" is to be associated with the predominantly dynamic character of the teleological sense. We call the structure of the part meaningful if it contributes to the whole: likewise, we call the structure of the whole meaningful if it is suited to its purpose (e. g., the structure of the eye). Equally dynamic and static are the sense-structures which have been uncovered in the activities and creations of spirit by the *human sciences and which are intelligible from the values that purposefully determine them. The teleological sense always requires that the goal be attainable and in itself intelligible; otherwise, goal-striving is senseless. — Here we discover the ultimate basis of all "sense" or meaning. Goals and values receive their intelligibility from existence that both in and from itself is meaningful, because it justifies itself by itself, not only for understanding but also for striving: *metaphysical sense* (6). Existence and sense coincide — they are identified absolutely in God. The finite existent participates in this identity according to the measure and the mode of its existence; if it does not have its meaning or "sense" in itself alone, then it finds its meaning in another to which it is ordered. Therefore, since existence itself is not senseless, meaning does not first come to it from an unreal world of "value" which is supposed to exist on its own independently of existence as such (e. g., forms of neo-Kantianism). Even when man builds sense into reality in the process of developing culture, all he does is creatively bring out the full meaning that already resides in the existent.

Related to the objective sense is the *semantic sense* (7), i. e., the reference of a *sign pointing to that which is signified or to its *meaning* (cf. the significance of a handshake). Of special importance is the sense that belongs to our words and sentences (*Language).

JBL

SENSE KNOWLEDGE

Sense knowledge is the kind of knowledge in whose production bodily organs (external sense organs, brain) are immediately involved; defined from the point of view of the object, it is an apprehension of mere *appearances in contrast to the essence and existence of things. Actually, both definitions agree, since knowledge tied to bodily organs always remains relative, and conversely spiritual knowledge, which is independent of organs, is necessarily related to the existent as such. The objects of sense knowledge are primarily the so-called secondary *sense qualities (colors, sounds, etc.) proper to the particular senses, but they must be present in their spatio-temporal order (the "primary sense qualities": size, shape, motion).

We distinguish between *external* and *internal* sense knowledge, depending upon whether it is caused by a sense impulse that affects the external organs (eyes, ears, etc.) or whether it is produced by a mental cause or stimulation of the brain without a concomitant influence on the external organs. With regard to external sense knowledge, the sense organs accept a very limited number of impressions from the great variety that is constantly bombarding them from the material world, so that the stimulation, transmitted by the nerves to the brain, leads to the determination of the sense power and to the actuation of sense knowledge itself by the production of a sense image (it leads to sensations of light, sound, pressure, temperature, taste, smell, pain, pleasure, to the apprehension of one's spatial position and the movement of one's body by means of the static and kinesthetic sense, to diffuse sensations of the bodily organs, such as hunger, thirst, fatigue). Thus, each sensory organ is so ordered to its own particular and adequate stimulus that it can respond to inadequate stimuli (e. g., pressure on the eye), if they result in any sensation at all, only with sense images that belong to its own class (e. g., sensation of light). The sense image itself is not to be understood as an unconscious representation of the attributes of things that immediately manifest their inner nature; rather, the sense image is a conscious experience in which the conditions of the external world are reflected according to the ability of each sense;

with regard to the epistemological problem of how true to reality such representations are, see *Realism.

The *internal senses* produce not only *representations (in contrast to the *sensations and perceptions caused by external stimuli), whether they are memories or newly produced imaginations, but they also have their irreplaceable importance for the formation of the perception image. Following Aristotle, scholastic philosophers point to five internal senses: the common sense, memory, *imagination, estimative sense (vis aestimativa), and in men only, the cogitative sense (*vis cogitativa*). The common sense, the common base of the external senses, unifies their data into one intuition: for example, it serves to localize a heard sound to a definite place within the field of vision. Memory and imagination complete the momentarily fragmented view of things on the basis of formerly received impressions (e.g., somehow they bring in the representation of the reverse side which is now invisible) and they build the order of time into the sensibly given. The estimative sense relates the presently given sensation to the whole life of the sense-endowed being and evaluates it as either helpful or harmful; this occurs primarily through feelings of pleasure and pain (instinct). In men the estimative sense is also guided by an influence from the intellect which is called the "cogitative sense"; this power unites the sense impressions into concrete images which, as the sense images that correspond to the concepts of corporeal things (e. g., dog, table, tree), are the immediate starting point for the activity of the intellect. — Whether or not there is such a thing as "extra sensory perception" (ESP) in addition to sense knowledge that is produced by the known senses, is a question that is treated elsewhere (*Occultism).

The meaning of sense knowledge for purely animal life is exhausted in the fact that it moves animals to activities that are essential for the maintenance of their lives. In man, however, sense knowledge, as the instrument of the intellect, achieves its highest significance in this, that first of all it supplies most of the material necessary for the formation of spiritual concepts and, secondly, that even the most abstract thinking must always retain some connection with sense images. Therefore, a care of and a healthy cultivation of sense knowledge is most important for the proper development of the human spirit.

JdV

SENSE QUALITIES

Sense qualities (1) are the various determinations or attributes of bodies which are grouped by the sensibility of the sensing and perceiving subject. They appear either (as *common sensibles*) within the range of several senses (e. g., shape for sight and touch) or they belong (as *proper* *sensibles*) exclusively to particular senses (e. g., color for sight). According to this last distinction the individual senses are defined by their psychologically experienced differences. — While exaggerated *realism wants to place the multiplicity of subjective sensations in the world of objects, extreme epistemological *idealism sees absolutely no connections between subjective sensations and the qualities of objects. In the sense of moderate realism the qualities of sensation should be understood as subjective states corresponding to the object; such sensations arise because the perceiving subject transposes data transcending himself in a way that is proportional to his own structure, in which case the kind of transposition is co-conditioned by the disposition of the object. Thereby the objectivity (*Objective) of knowledge is sufficiently preserved and can be understood in a way analogous to the recognition of a chemical substance after it reacts with something else. — Within the particular sense qualities there are varying degrees of objectivity and subjectivity: shape, size and motion are more objective; color, sound and smell are more subjective. The influence of the subject on the sense qualities is especially evident in the law of *specific sense energies*, which are often also called "the specific sense qualities" (2): i. e., the individual senses have a reaction potential proper to each one of them alone, so that in spite of objective differences in the stimuli a similarity of sensation, conditioned by the organ itself, manifests itself (e.g., both an electrical charge and physical pressure exerted on the optic nerve would produce the same kind of experience, namely, visual experience). The distinction into *primary* and *secondary* sense qualities sometimes means the difference between common sensibles and proper sensibles, but sometimes it also refers to the difference between objective and subjective sense qualities.

GT

SENSIBILITY

Sensibility (1) in the realm of *knowledge is the power or receptivity for *sensation as a function of the *senses; because of this power of receptivity the encounter between the corporeal and the corporeally perceptible world takes place. Sensibility grasps the *individual being and the *concrete being and so is essentially receptive, but not wholly passive; rather, it actually affects the thing received through the mode of the reception. According to *critical philosophy (Kant), sensibility (2) is pure receptivity which makes it possible for us to produce *intuitions when we encounter objects; *thinking is then built up on these intuitions. The determination of sensibility (2) as far as the subject is concerned is realized in the forms of *space and *time; the object as such is not presented by these forms alone, but only the way in which the object imposes itself upon sensibility (2). In a somewhat broader concept of sensibility (2) the power of imagination also belongs to it, because it can only represent objects as they appear in sensibility (2).

In the realm of striving, sensibility designates (in contradistinction to spiritual willing) the spontaneous function of one's drives insofar as these precede a conscious, willed direction of the spiritual person (3). Kant calls sensibility in this sense the natural obstacle to performing one's duty; man's recognized obligation to the moral law always confronts this obstacle. Thomas Aquinas understands sensibility in a more restricted sense (as *sensuality*) with the meaning of a *sensible striving power* = sensibility (3); he divides it into the *concupiscible* and the *irascible* appetite. The former is ordered to the sensibly pleasant, while the latter is ordered to that which is useful for the individual or the species; the useful here does not immediately appear as something sensibly pleasant and can be achieved only by overcoming opposition. Accordingly, the sub-spiritual impulses of *emotion, feelings and *passions, as the subjective states of the striving person, are associated with sensibility (3). Love and hate, desire and aversion, joy and sorrow are the emotional movements of the concupiscible appetite; hope and despair, fear and anger are the movements of the irascible appetite. According to Aquinas, however, sensibility (4) in a wider sense includes both the powers of the external and internal *senses as well as the appetitive faculties ordered to them. — If sensibility (5) or sensuality is used in an ethically derogatory sense, then it signifies sensible excitability or pleasure seeking, insofar as this seems to be contrary to the true good of the person. See also *Psychology*.

GT

SIGN

A sign is everything that, as a previously known, leads to the knowledge of something else. For a sign to be able to carry out its task, there must be a recognizable connection between it and the reality it is supposed to designate. If this connection is given by nature itself, then we have a *natural sign*, e. g., the crying of a baby as its expression of pain. However, if the connection is arbitrarily set by man, then we have a *conventional sign*. Language and writing in their developed form belong in this latter category. The *symbol stands more or less in the middle between the two classes of signs. According to the purpose in mind, signs can be either just communicative or also representative, depending upon whether the sign merely points to something (as a clock keeps time) or also in some way takes the place of the thing signified (e. g., the keys of the city which in former times were handed over to the conqueror as a sign of the transfer of power over the city). — In conjunction with *symbolic logic and with the efforts of constructing an exact language, in recent decades the general theory of signs and symbols has been developed greatly. Here one finds a number of areas of special investigation: the *theory of syntax* which studies the relations of signs to each other; *semantics* which is the study of the relations between the sign and the signified; *pragmatics* which is the study of the relations between the sign and its users. — Signs are of the utmost importance for all human social living; without signs there can be no communication, no language and therefore no culture. The necessity of using signs is a consequence of the body-soul structure of man.

JS-WB

SIMPLICITY

Simplicity is a species of *unity and it is opposed to *composition*. Composition means that the thing in question has parts which are either quantitative or essential; thus, man is composed of a head and a torso or of a body and a soul. If the parts are separated from each other, then the composite being loses its wholeness or is destroyed. Simplicity, however, means that a being has no parts into which it could be resolved; therefore it is *indivisible*. *Quantitative simplicity* is characteristic of the parts of a quantum and *essential simplicity* is characteristic of the parts of an essence; both are found in pure spirit, i.e., one that is not tied to a body, and (less perfectly) in the soul. — A major distinction should be made between the simplicity of indigence and the simplicity of abundance. Concerning indigence, after the removal of all abundance only a minimum remains which then indeed possesses simplicity because of its extreme poverty. In this category are to be found the mathematical point or in the realm of logic the concept of being which manifests only the one aspect of existence. When physics speaks of atoms or indivisible parts, this is not to be understood as a real simplicity, but only in the sense that the decomposition of the whole atom would destroy the particular chemical element. The simplicity of abundance belongs to beings that are not spread out in parts, but possess themselves wholly in an undivided and indivisible unity. They should not be thought of as mathematical points, but as essentially elevated above all spatial limitations. Nevertheless, they can enter into the spatial order; if they do, then they are not there in bits and pieces, for this requires parts so that they can be here with one part and there with another (as a body); rather, they can be present to the individual parts of space, which they fill, only in their totality.

We encounter this simplicity of abundance primarily in the *simplicity of the soul*. As the non-extended ground of life it is existentially bound, along with the extended body, to the one whole of the living being. This simplicity seems to be still imperfect in the *life principle of plants and in the soul of animals; for, in spite of their simplicity both of these principles are so dependent upon the body that they cannot exist without it. The simplicity of man's *soul is of a higher order. For, since it is spiritual, it is able to continue to exist after the death of the body, although at the same time it inclines to its essential union with the body. But the simplicity of all souls is surpassed by that of pure *spirit which constitutes a whole all by itself and is not just a part of some other composite whole. The *simplicity of God* is absolutely perfect. His simplicity excludes all those forms of composition that even every finite spirit is subject to; in particular, in God essence and existence, substance and life are absolutely identified.

JBL

SKEPTICISM

Skepticism is the fundamental doubting of the possibility of true knowledge. What is known as universal skepticism extends *doubt to absolutely everything, while ethical, religious and other forms of skepticism restrict it to definite areas. Skepticism consists either in an attitude of doubt with regard to all knowledge or in a more or less scientifically founded teaching about the doubtfulness of all human knowledge. From these two forms should be distinguished skepticism as a method whose goal is indeed certainty, but which selects a serious universal doubt concerning all knowledge as the starting point for a *theory of *knowledge*. A methodical *doubt which questions the legitimacy of human knowing, without actually doubting it, in its general application has nothing to do with real skepticism. — The usual reasons adduced in support of skepticism are: the apparently insoluble contradictions contained in human knowledge (e. g. Sophism), the relativity of *sense knowledge and the absence of an adequate norm of *truth (Sextus Empiricus). Pyrrho taught that a man must refuse assent to any and every proposition (= *epoche*), since the reasons for and against always have equal weight (Pyrrhonism). Later representatives of skepticism were Montaigne and Charron. — The best refutation of universal skepticism consists in showing that man really possesses certain, well-founded knowledge, as for example the fact of his own self-consciousness and the fact that he questions himself and everything else. As a basic position skepticism cannot be consistently maintained, since every human act includes within itself a judgment regarding its feasibleness. And even if this judgment is held to be only probable, then the agent must at least be certain of the presence of probability. Thus as soon as skepticism is proposed as a doctrine it involves itself in contradictions: it affirms that nothing is certain and at the same time that still something is certain. With regard to skepticism as a method see *Knowledge, Theory of*.

JS

SOCIALISM

Socialism appears as a complete view of human life, as a system of ordering society, and especially as a movement of social reform in the fields of politics, organized labor and cooperative groups. Constructed out of very different, even opposing intellectual currents, socialism today less than ever before is a unified force. Only from the middle of the 19th century until World War I was *Marxian socialism* the dominant force, so that there was a high degree of theoretical unity and one could equate socialism with *Marxism. Since the final split of Marxian socialism into communistic, revisionistic and free-democratic wings, and since the latter wing has removed itself more and more not only from *dialectical and *historical materialism but even from the economic theories of Marx, non-communistic socialism no longer has a common basis. The only remaining unifying factor is an explicit social criticism of *capitalistic* economy and society. Quite extensive, though not universal, is a practical and exclusive concern for this-worldly values.

Irreconciliable with the Christian vision of man is a socialism which bases human society and the social nature of man exclusively on man's physical needs and on the usefulness of the division of labor and thus looks upon society merely as a "practical organization" which, as such, cannot make any ethical demands on man. A type of socialism which would completely free itself of this limited view, is not necessarily opposed to Christian teaching.

For the "man on the street" socialism still means the same thing as the nationalization of private industry. However, in many countries the socialists have laid the emphasis on economic planning.

OvNB

SOCIALIZATION

Socialization (1) in sociology, anthropology, psychology, and psychiatry refers to the process by which children become adequate adult members of society and by which adults continue to adjust to changing social patterns. It can also signify (2) the development of an abundance of associations and organizations for promoting social cooperation and general progress; the term is used this way in the encyclical of Pope John XXIII, *Mater et Magistra*, and in the Second Vatican Council's *Pastoral Constitution on the Church in the Modern World (Gaudium et Spes)*. "Socialization" (3) is used in a similar although much more developed and precise sense, by Pierre Teilhard de Chardin in his theory of evolution.

For Teilhard de Chardin, socialization is the main evolutionary mechanism by which human evolution takes place. The process of evolution did not stop with man. Just as evolution, when it reached the critical point of the appearance of living things, did not stop but rather accelerated in the zone of living beings, in the "biosphere," so too, with the appearance of man, evolution has again accelerated and now takes place chiefly in human society, in the "thinking envelope" of the earth, in the "noosphere" (from the Greek *noos*, "mind"). Once the evolutionary process resulted in the appearance of man with his superior type of awareness, self-awareness in the form of reflexive consciousness, the process of evolution continued and still continues in mankind.

Evolution continues, but with the differences that come from the fact that it is now going on at the level of human consciousness; in man, evolution is conscious of itself. Evolution at prereflective levels proceeds by means of the mechanisms of heredity and adaptation. So, too, societal evolution takes place partly through analogous evolutionary mechanisms. Heredity is achieved at the conscious level through language, education, and communications media; culture is transmitted through increasingly improved systems of schools, libraries, and communications, through social heredity. Again, human evolution uses the mechanism of adaptation. Now, however, at the conscious level, evolutionary adaptation does not have to depend on a groping process that must wait to take advantage of the appropriate random mutations. Human evolution takes place through conscious invention, and to the extent that it is not so much that man adapts to his environment as that he adapts his environment to himself. Both social heredity and conscious adaptation are parts of a broader, more inclusive, and far more important process that is called "socialization."

Unlike the prereflexive living species, mankind does not split and branch into separate and diverse species. Every species of living things shows the tendency, over long periods of time, to split into varieties and subspecies, some of which become true species. But in the case of the human species, the tendency to branch has been overcome. No new human species has developed, nor will it develop in the future. The fundamental divergent tendency of any living species in its evolution is, in mankind, overcome by a stronger force, by the socializing force of reflexive consciousness. Men, because they are reflexively conscious, aware of themselves as knowing subjects, as persons, tend to unite with one another in societies. Human groups tend to merge and interpenetrate to a greater extent than they tend to diverge. Instead of branching out like the other living species, mankind tends to fold in upon itself. This process of "infolding" is socialization.

The socialization process has two phases: the phase of expansion and the phase of compression. The expansion phase extended from the beginning of mankind up until recent times; during this long period, man progressed in civilization and in culture, but much of mankind's evolutionary energy was spent in the gradual occupancy of the earth. Sometime near the end of the last century the phase of expansion ended and mankind entered into the compression phase of socialization. Once man was sufficiently spread out over the surface of the earth, once the main frontiers were gone, the phase of compression began. It has been accompanied by rapid population growth and by great progress in human intercommunication. The result' has been an almost incredible acceleration in socialization.

Mankind evolves through socialization, and this process follows the direction of all evolutionary process. Evolution always moves in the direction of producing, over long periods of time, progressively more highly organized entities that have correspondingly higher degrees of awareness or consciousness. Evolution, now in the "noosphere" or terrestrial sphere of reflexive consciousness, continues to follow an axis of increasing complexity (greater organization of more and more elements) and of correlatively higher levels of consciousness. Human society evolves according to a material component or "increase in complexity" that includes technology, rules or laws of organization, institutions of various kinds. Society evolves also according to a spiritual component or "increase in consciousness," a particular outlook that is ethical, religious, aesthetic, philosophical, and that gives meaning and direction to the community. In recent times this socialization process has sharply accelerated. There has been almost incredible progress in technology, in communications, in industry; there has been, too, great political change in the direction of collectivization and greater organization.

Does this rapidly increasing collectivization mean that mankind is inevitably headed for a kind of totalitarian superstate, a sort of ant-hill society in which the individual will be lost and crushed? No, because it is not through totalitarian organization that real socialization takes place, nor does true socialization lead to totalitarianism. All evolutionary progress takes place through increasing organization, but the organization that is necessary is always organization of elements by interior attraction, never organization imposed from without. When applied to human communities, this means that it is only through mutual interior attraction of persons, only through union of some form of love, that true socialization can occur. Socialization is the process of increasing human union, and a union is truly human only when it is voluntarily entered into or at least willingly accepted by the persons united.

At this point in his discussion of socialization, Teilhard de Chardin introduces the principle that union differentiates. True union never confuses the elements united; it further differentiates them within the unity. Whether we speak of a union of cells to form a body, the members of a team, or the elements of any synthesis, union always differentiates, and human union further personalizes the persons united. It is not union that is depersonalizing; it is egoism and selfish individualism that is retrogressive and depersonalizing. Self-seeking ends finally in the reduction of self. Man finds himself in the "other." Union differentiates, personalizes, develops the persons united.

Since socialization has entered its phase of compression, men are being forced into closer association with one another and are so being urged to union with one another. To the extent that men accept one another and become united, true socialization will go on, and the result will be increasing personalization. The notions of "person" and "community" are not opposed; they are correlative, as are the concepts of personalization and socialization. Person and community grow and deepen together.

RLF

SOCIAL PHILOSOPHY

Numerous social sciences (sociology, the science of social forms and conditions; social ethics, social psychology; political science, jurisprudence, economics) investigate, order and explain the various phenomena of social life according to their own particular viewpoints. Social philosophy seeks to understand *society itself and social living as such from its ultimate foundation, i. e., the naturally given social orientation of man. — Does this orientation consist merely in insufficiency and so in the need of outside help in order to reach certain goals, or does it consist rather in the possibility, through the abundance of its own abilities, to establish a community as a higher unity and in this community with others to arrive at its own full development? In actual fact everything that we call *culture is realizable only through spiritual communion with others. According to the first view, social living is only an accidental appendage or help of man; according to the second view it is something essential to man, so much so that only here is he able to fulfill his true humanity. This is not to deny that many social bodies (e. g., business groups) are only helps; but at the very least family and *state are necessary for the essential self-fulfillment of a man.

There are three possible positions to take in this matter: 1) One considers man to be perfect in himself, so that he associates with others only on the basis of usefulness (the advantage in the division of labor). The individual person is everything, society is simply a means with no proper worth: *Individualism. — 2) One considers man as basically incomplete in himself and as one who has meaning and purpose only as the member of a community. The community is everything, the individual as such lacks all proper worth, he lives and dies only for the sake of the community: *Collectivism. — 3) The individual person possesses the inalienable worth of his own moral *personality which prevents his ever being used as a mere means to an end or as a mere part of a larger whole. Nevertheless, he is not simply closed off from all others, for he is essentially related to the community. The community is not opposed to its members as something that is foreign to them; rather, it is nothing but the members themselves in their unity. Because of their personal independence the members cannot be either superior to or inferior to each other; instead, it is more like a binding relationship of each individual to the whole community and the reciprocal binding of the whole to each of its members. Since we are considering human society, every social philosophy must begin with *man; since it is a question of explaining society from its ultimate foundations, it must understand man in his first essential principles. Thus, social philosophy is *metaphysics (ontology), or more precisely *anthropology. If man comes from God and if God is his ultimate end, then the fundamental outline of social philosophy is already laid down. If God has elevated man to a supernatural order, this necessarily means that his social dimension has been vastly expanded; a social philosophy that deliberately attempted to close itself off from this truth would distort the facts instead of explain them. — See also *Pluralism*.

OvNB

SOCIAL PSYCHOLOGY

The drive towards spiritual community with other persons is rooted psychologically in the real fullness of the human person — a fullness going out to others, and at the same time in his lack of self-sufficiency. In this situation the individual person with his giving and receiving, with his rights and duties (with an eye on the perfection of the community) conducts himself like a "member" in an organism, while retaining his own inalienable independence, his personal dignity and rights. It is the task of social psychology to study the psychic foundation of human (and, in the widest sense, also animal) communal living — the psychological dimension in the basic forms of common living and how this influences the psychic life of the individual. The evident fact, which has been stressed for ages, that man is a social being, occasions the questions as to how the "other-ego" is known, what the medium is between two persons, and why man naturally strives for social contact.

The knowledge of the other spiritual person in his existence and individuality has received different explanations: some attribute it to instinct, others (Max Scheler) base it on a kind of immediate intuition of the soul of the other — an intuition rooted in an original existential unity. However, it cannot be adequately explained by any one-sided interpretation; rather, it requires a synthesis of different and complementary interpretations.

The mode of communication from person to person is *language, taken however in the broadest sense. If understood in this way, language embraces both the primal functions (common to men and animals) of the ordinary information derived from experience and the gaining of experience through the manifestations of others (pre-logical language) as well as the spiritual function (which is built upon the functions just mentioned and partially uses them), proper to man alone, of representing objective realities in a universal way. Language does this through a system of randomly selected signs and symbols — also called the psychology of language.

Just like human language, the human inclination for society embraces both instinctual and spiritual elements. The reservoir of *social instincts* includes, among other things, the drive to associate with those of one's own kind, to instinctual "mutual agreement" (pre-logical communication), to negative social conduct in attack and flight, to combine positive and negative reactions in sexual matters, and finally to play together. A spiritual-social attitude as such places the spiritual-personal existence of man in relation to the personal existence of the other as a value-carrier. This attitude reveals two aspects which complement each other and in a certain sense demand each other: *respect*, which lets the other person be free, and *love*, which is directed to the worth of the other person in a creative way that moves towards union. The different degrees and kinds of spiritual "social involvement," the typical differences in objectives, the greater or lesser completeness of one's social attitude or affinity, are determined by changing particular situations and by differences in personality.

With regard to general human structures, a distinction is made between structures based on generation, agreement and accumulation; in other words, there are *social organisms* like the *family*, the *organization*, and the mere *aggregate*. Depending upon whether the purely instinctual or the spiritual attitude predominates among the psychic factors contributing to a social structure, one can distinguish between a *mass and a true *community. The primordial forms of human association are friendship and *marriage, from these two comes the family, and from these three comes the more extensive community of a tribe, a people or a nation (*State).

The real foundation of the drive to community is not a mysterious "supra-individual soul" in which all share or a primordial unity of one consciousness that permeates each individual. Rather, it is on the one hand the involvement of spirit in the conditions of biological life, and on the other hand the transcendent consciousness of the personal spirit moving towards self-manifestation to other personal existents.

Social psychology is regarded by most of its adherents as a purely empirical science. As such it is less concerned with philosophical pre-suppositions and abstract theorizing than is indicated in the foregoing exposition. Man has always utilized a kind of "folk" social psychology and in man's social nature we find the ultimate roots of an independent discipline. In 1908, in the United States there appeared two books both entitled "Social Psychology." One was written by William McDougall, a psychologist, the other was written by a sociologist, Edward A. Ross. The different backgrounds of these two writers manifested itself in the approach to the subject and these two men set the course of social psychology for years to come. Within the past few years there has been a convergence of the two approaches and as a result there is now emerging an entirely new and independent science — social psychology.

Social psychology, as an empirical science, is defined as the scientific study of the experience and behavior of individuals or groups in relation to other individuals or groups in a social situation. It strives to understand human behavior in the social context. To do this it has built up its own apparatus using field studies, field experiments, natural experiments and laboratory experiments within an elaborate framework of scientific techniques to arrive at its conclusions which it describes as hypotheses or theories. As a science it is concerned with understanding, predicting and controlling human behavior. It analyzes the socialization processes, motivation, attitudes and their formation and modification, roles, the function of communication, group behavior, leadership, authority, the instruments, nature and use of social controls, etc. The findings of social psychology have been applied in every field of interpersonal relationships and a knowledge of it has become a valued asset in practically every human endeavor. — See also *Psychology, Socialization.*

AW-VFC

SOCIETY

Society (1) as synonymous with *community means: every permanent, effective association of men for the realization of a common goal or value. — Society (2) as distinguished from community: society is a man-made artifact, while community is a structure based on a natural bond. — Society (3) is the totality of all structures and relationships that flow from man's social nature; therefore, it is humanity as a unity: nations, cities, unions, families, tribes, peoples and the sum total of all free associations. — Society (4) as the most influential and richest level, i. e., those circles that "socially" associate with each other and in general tend to think that the marriage of one of their members to an individual from a lower social level is a big mistake. — Society (5) taken in contrast to the *state: in this sense the state is understood as a politically organized national community, while society is considered as the same national community (but in actual fact it is usually only the social circles in the sense of (4) as a supposedly independent sphere) without any inner connection with the framework of the state that surrounds it: this concept of society was the basis of the liberal-bourgeois view of the state in the 19th century. — Society (6) in the legal sense means especially property mergers, usually unions of ability and capital for the purpose of making money.

Some social activity is essential to every social structure. But since it is not the structure itself but only men that can think, will and act, in order to be able to act in the first place the social structure needs very definite organs and therefore also an *organization*. The leading organs need *authority, since the other members should follow them as free men. Moral (and legal) superiority and subordination, the power to command and the obligation to obey are essential to every social structure and therefore, since they are given with man's social nature, they are willed by God. Any social authority finds both its foundation as well as its limitation in the *common good.

OvNB

SOCRATIC METHOD

Socratic method is the teaching and method of Socrates (469-399 B. C.) who because of his powerful influence on Plato introduced the golden age of Greek philosophy. In his battle against the skepticism of the sophists, the new teachers of the Athenian youth, Socrates tried to be a true teacher. His teaching method consisted in the artful use of proper questions so that, with the help of clear inductive examples, he could induce those conversing with him to arrive at the proper conclusions on their own and thus think for themselves instead of accepting conclusions on the authority of others; he also tried to bring his listeners to the recognition of eternal, unchangeable essences (of virtues and things), performing in this way the function of a spiritual midwife. A characteristic of Socrates' questioning and teaching is the use of irony; thus he claimed to have a low opinion of his own knowledge and repeatedly asserted that he did not know anything. The chief concern of his philosophizing is ethics and the art of living; the goal of life is happiness. The good consists in that which is truly useful. Real virtue or excellence is so determined by a profound knowledge that the place and function of will and freedom are neglected. Nietzsche saw in the philosophy of Socrates the fateful turning point of Western philosophy from myth and instinct to a life-destroying "rationality"; and Kierkegaard made effective use of Socratic irony.

JoS

SOLIPSISM

Solipsism is a form of idealism which recognizes nothing but the act of thinking and one's own subjective person as certainly given realities.

379

Everything else is either unknowable or uncertain. There were some proponents of solipsism in the 18th century who raised the Cartesian proposition "I think therefore I am" (*cogito ergo sum*) to be the only object of knowledge. In the 19th century it appears in the thought of Max Stirner as a reaction against Hegel and his overemphasis on the universal. Now it is no longer just a theoretical point of view — it is practical egoism. Solipsism cannot claim to be a teachable doctrine without contradicting itself. For a more extensive refutation see also *Idealism*.

JS

SOUL

Soul (Gr.: *psychē*) in man refers to the immaterial substance that perdures amidst the changes of life, that produces and supports psychic activities, and that animates the organism. (Certain psychological theories, still under the influence of positivism, speak of the totality of mental processes as the soul, while others use it to refer to non-rational experience). According to the three levels of life, a distinction is made between the *vital soul* (entelechy, *Life Principle), the *sensible* or *animal soul* (the principle of sensible-animal life), and the *intellectual* or *spiritual soul* (the principle of the spiritual activities of thinking and willing). — With regard to the question of the existence and the philosophical demonstrability of the soul in man, evidence for it is supplied by simple everyday experience, by mankind's constant conviction — psychological, ethical, religious, as well as by the wholeness and unity of spiritual life which is so much stressed by modern empirical science. The existence of an immaterial soul is denied by the advocates of *materialism, for they admit only the existence of matter in motion. Philosophies of becoming tend to deny the existence of a soul as a substance. Thus, they reduce all perduring existence to mere becoming, to deeds without a doer, and consequently designate as "soul" only the constantly changing complex of mental activities and experiences (Heraclitus: *panta rhei* = everything is in flux; the psychologies of Wundt and Bergson: There are no things, just activities). — The positivists contest the philosophical knowability of a soul, in accordance with their postulate that truly scientific thinking should not take the step into metaphysics; it is also contested by the Kantian *critical philosophy for whom all theoretical knowledge of the soul is based on a fallacy.

In contrast, alongside almost all the great religions of the world stands the very ancient, constant conviction also of the philosophers with regard to the existence of the soul: It was affirmed by the classical ancient philosophers (Plato, Aristotle, Plotinus), by the Fathers of the Church, by the scholastics, by the rationalists, Descartes and Leibniz, and even by the first empiricists (Locke, Berkeley), by Kant in his *Ethics* (who at least "postulates" the soul), down to the return of some modern philosophy to a theory of the soul and the life principle (Driesch, Becher, Pfänder, etc.).

The existence of the soul manifests itself in man's immediate experience of his own self and in the experience of the other person. For, we do not experience a soul detached from its acts, but we do experience our own conscious states as the activities of our *ego — not an ego floating along unsupported in itself but a thinking, willing... I. We experience the fullness of all things at once and the changing flow of our conscious states, one after the other, as belonging to one and the same ego that remains identically the same amidst the change of intellectual acts. (The apparently contradictory, pathological phenomena of the "spirit personality," when examined more closely, turn out to be not "spirits" in the ego but false judgments or even bizarre images produced by a disruption of the normal sense-unity of experiences). We experience our ego not as a mere "reference point" of our activities, not as a mere "happening and becoming," but as an essence standing on its own — an essence that "posits" its own acts, "generates" and possesses psychic realities as its very own and is responsible for them (at least partially and under certain conditions: *Free Will); in short, we experience our ego as the abiding and supporting principle of all spiritual, conscious life. Therefore, it must be a substantial being which is not itself just "activity." The objections of *positivism and of *critical philosophy against the possibility of a metaphysics of the soul are refuted and overcome by the positive grounding of *metaphysics in a general *theory of *knowledge*.

The human soul as the principle of spiritual life is simple (*Simplicity) and spiritual (*Spirit). At the same time it is the principle of sensible-animal life (as the unity of sensible-spiritual consciousness shows) and as the life-form of the body it is also the principle of vegetative life in the organism (*Hylemorphism, *Body-Soul Relation). *Trichotomism*, which assumes the existence in man of a spirit, a soul and a vegetative principle as three really different principles, cannot be reconciled with the unity of human experience. Rather, the spiritual soul itself expresses itself in its sensible-vegetative life in order to make use of it and to incorporate it into a full human life. — As a spiritual reality the human soul could not have evolved out of a purely animal soul, no matter how the body of the first man came into being. Nor can the human soul stem from other human souls (traducianism), because a spiritual soul cannot shed off parts of itself which in turn develop into new souls. Every human soul owes its existence to an immediate creative act of God. Once it has been created, the simple, spiritual soul cannot be destroyed by any created power (i. e., dissolved into parts), but God will never annihilate it because he himself has made it immortal. — See also *Immortality*.

AW

SOUL, POWER OF

The powers of the soul are the *potencies or powers of soul-activities that pertain to the essence of the *soul and are dynamically ordered to their own actuation. They are distinguished according to their formal objects (e. g., truth, value, color, etc.) and also according to the experience of their acts. Thus, we speak of memory, emotions, will, sense desires, intellect, sense powers, etc. The powers of the soul are not the *parts* of the soul because the soul is simple and spiritual. Whether or not they are really distinct from the substance of the soul and so from each other, has been a disputed point between the Aristotelians and the Augustinians since the 12th century. But much more important than this question is the fact that the soul operates by means of her powers (which do not act independently like separate persons) and that thereby a delicate balance of "mutual cooperation" between the different powers is maintained (e.g., harmony between knowledge, desire and the emotions). The spiritual powers of the soul are on a higher level than the sense powers. But simply to give the primacy to the intellect or to the will is hardly appropriate, since it always depends upon the point from which the question of such primacy is asked (*intellectualism, *Voluntarism). — The contrapuntal interrelationship of the various powers of the soul is of course an expression of their limitation; however, it is also the foundation of the richness of human life when the powers of the soul are properly subordinate to each other. To speak of the spiritual element in man as simply an "enemy of life" and to place a value only on the irrational powers of the soul is to ignore the full reality of the soul. See also *Appetite, Knowledge, Will.*

AW

SPACE

By space is usually understood an extended vacuum in which bodies are located as it were in a receptacle. Thus space is related to the extension of real bodies, but at the same time it is not simply to be identified with extension. For it persists (at least for human imagination) even if it does not contain any actual bodies. Space occupied by no body is called empty space or a vacuum. Pure space, which is also called *absolute* or *imaginary* space, is thought of as having no boundaries or limits (infinite space) and as a motionless, always-existing container in which the universe is placed. *Finite* space is a definite part of infinite space. The spatial *finiteness of the world* signifies that the world could be larger than it actually is. In the vocabulary of the *theory of *relativity* some affirm today that the world is indeed finite, but still unlimited, similar to the way in which the curved surface of a sphere is also finite without having limits (*Quantity).

SPACE

What reality can be attributed to space? In order to answer this question a distinction must be made between space as a representation of our power of imagination, as a concept and as an object existing in itself. It is certain that our space-representation (at least up to the second dimension) is not arbitrary or a mere fiction, but it necessarily permeates and shapes all our sensible representations of the external world. In this sense Kant rightly names space an a priori form of our (external) sense knowledge. But this does not in any way say or prove that the objects of our senses lack real extension, that space, therefore, is purely subjective. Space as a concept arises in us from reflection on the relationship of a necessary space-representation to the extension of real bodies (extended vacuum as if it were the container of bodies). By means of this concept space can be thought of as an object existing in itself in addition to the extension of real bodies, without however attributing any real existence to it. Thus space as an existent in itself is a being of the mind, but there is a foundation for it in the reality of the extension of real bodies. As a consequence of this foundation in reality, with the help of the space-concept objectively valid statements can be made concerning existing spatial relationships, as the *position* of a thing (i. e., the relation of its place to other known places) or the *distance* of several objects (i.e., their spatial difference). If this distance is small, then one speaks of spatial closeness; if their spatial limits coincide, then one says that they are touching or that they are contiguous.

With the help of the space-concept the different kinds of spatial *presence* can also be expressed in words. A body is present in space if it actually exists with its own extension. Non-corporeal beings are present in space by means of an immediate effect produced in a real body. Extended bodies fill space with their extension in such a way that the individual parts of the body correspond to the individual parts of imaginary space (*circumscriptive presence*); simple substances like the spiritual soul are present in space in such a way that they are wholly in the occupied space and whole in every part of it (*definitive presence*). The fixed part of space that an object occupies is called its internal place; the spatial limits of those things surrounding it are called its external place. By means of *motion a body changes its place, but it does not leave space. In accordance with the laws of nature a simple presence in space belongs to every body, i. e., at one and the same time it can only be in one place. A multiple presence of a body in several places at the same time (bilocation) is not unthinkable, since it would mean only a duplication of the relation and not of the related object.

The measureability of space is based on its relation to extension; for, only extension is directly measured by comparison with an arbitrarily chosen unit of extension which is called a measure (e.g., yard, meter). Space stretches out in three directions which are perpendicular to each other: thus it has a triple dimension. By *mathematical* space is understood the abstract extension which is the object of geometry. Modern physics takes space (physical space) to mean the real extension of things; it also understands space as that in which beams of light are considered as "straight" lines, but in the field of gravity of the universe these lines are not straight in the Euclidian sense (= curved space). When mathematics and physics speak about a space of more than three dimensions, they mean only an arithmetical multiplicity which is an aid in describing space relationships mathematically; they are not actually ascribing more than three dimensions to space itself.

NJ

SPECIES

Species (*eidos, species*) is the whole substance of an existent insofar as it is common to many *individuals. Plato thought of the species as a supra-sensible idea, existing for itself, in which the sensible individual beings of daily expience participate (*Participation). According to Aristotle, however, the specifying essence is located in individual things, whereas species as such (as universal) is only a concept. The species-concept (e. g., Man) is to be distinguished from the genus-concept (e. g., sentient being) in that the latter, by omitting the specific difference (*differentia specifica*, e. g., rational) conveys the essence only in a conceptually undetermined way, while the species-concept which is composed of genus and difference offers the whole substance. — The perfect *definition attempts to precisely circumscribe the species-concept understood in this way. According to the classical theory, the differences among the individuals grouped under the same species concern only accidental characteristics, whereas different species are distinguished from each other by their different essential forms (*Form). As long as this strictly onotological species-concept is mantained only a few true species can be identified with certainty. Thus, for example, the *biological species*, as it has been understood since the work of Carolus Linnaeus (1707-1778), is not a species in the ontological sense. Biological species are the inferior groups of animals and plants, distinguished by characteristics which are significantly different in the various groups, which are not blurred by intermediate forms and which are hereditary. Ranged under these species are the varieties and races. Actually, however, the boundaries between a variety and a species are often hazy. Indeed, it depends to a great extent upon personal preference whether or not individual differences are thought of as "considerable" or essential. Consequently, it is possible to construct a purely *logical species-concept* which includes the characteristics that here and now are considered, by the one making the division, to be essential for his purpose. — See also *Evolutionism, Predicables, Essence.*

JS

SPECULATION

Speculation in Latin is related to the verb *"speculari"* which means "to spy out," "to investigate"; even here it is a matter of uncovering something hidden. Philosophical speculation is a creative type of *thinking which does not simply receive the data of *experience passively; rather, it actively penetrates them with the spiritual power (*A Priori) all the way to their ultimate roots. Such thinking essentially surpasses both sense experience and the phenomenological illumination of the given (*Transcendence) and constitutes the heart of philosophy. Still, speculation is rooted in experience, because only there can it find its starting point. Therefore, the results of its labor are also indirectly confirmed or refuted by experience, although they are never directly reachable by purely sensible experience. — Speculation probes more precisely into the inner meaning of the experienced reality — all the way to metaphysical existence; at the same time it uncovers the absolute essential and existential principles. Thus it grasps the constitutive principles (*Existence, Principles of) and the first *causes of everything that can be experienced, especially the ultimate source of unity: God. From this vantage point, speculative thought tries to understand all reality in a unified way and to bring it together into a *system.

Concerning the *method, speculation makes special use of *essential knowledge, *analysis, a priori *synthesis, and *deduction. What is decisive here is a lively, creative insight which usually precedes all formal concepts and reasoning and is articulated only afterwards. It grows out of a proper balance in the whole man and is not given to all men in the same degree. — Speculation degenerates if truly human insight becomes obscured and rigid concepts are used in haphazard combinations, which often happened in the period of late scholasticism. Through these corruptions and because of modern *rationalism, speculation received such a bad name that even today one often encounters it only in a caricature. Kant also contributed to this insofar as he restricted theoretical reason to the realm of possible experience and despaired of all efforts going beyond that as empty "speculation" which produce only transcendental appearance. In contrast, Hegel certainly worked with the *speculative proposition* which overcomes contradiction and expresses a synthesis, but even he brought speculation into discredit by his exaggerated use of it.

In Aristotle speculation is clearly identified with *"theoria."* It completes the intuitive-reasoning investigation of the existent and is set over against both moral actions and practical (and artistic) creativity. Today a distinction is made between speculation and theory. Thus, speculation is only a part of theory insofar as theory, in addition to its speculative grasp, also includes a phenomenological foundation. *Theory is used in modern science in a limited sense that is often far removed from speculation.

JBL

SPINOZISM

The Jewish philosopher Baruch Spinoza († 1677) expounded his system chiefly in his *Ethics*, which is supposed to be an introduction to a happy life through the control of one's passions . — According to Spinoza, there is only one, necessary, eternal, infinite *substance* — God, which is defined as "that which is from itself and is understood only from itself, and thus it is that which does not need another in order to be understood from it." Therefore, it is the cause of itself. An *attribute* is an aspect of the essential fullness of the divine substance. Of the infinite number of God's attributes only two are known to us — thinking and extension; of these two, both are identical with God and with each other, yet they express two different aspects of God. — The *modes* are the limited appearance-forms of God's two infinite attributes known to us, i.e., finite things in which the parallelism of the two attributes manifests itself as soul and body. — The human soul is only the idea of its body and it disappears with the dissolution of the body. Just as the attributes are identified in God, so also in man the modes of thinking and extension coincide. Thus it is understandable why the double-sided developmental moments correspond to each other. Yet, for our knowledge there is no bridge from the corporeal to the spiritual or vice versa, nor do we discover anywhere in the infinite succession of *"modi"* the substance that carries them; rather, we possess a purely immanent "causality" both in the realm of ideas and in the corporeal world.

Spinoza is clearly a pantheist. God is the *"natura naturans"* and the modes are the *"natura naturata,"* but basically everything is one. This one-sided rationalism also reduces "willing" to thinking and leaves no room for true freedom, either in God or in creatures. Consequently, even the distinction between good and evil is maintained only verbally. And in such a geometrically designed system there is no place for "purpose." — Although Spinoza's philosophy was vehemently attacked by some even during his own lifetime, it still exercised great influence after his death, especially because of his emphasis on the unity of the cosmos and also to some extent because of his position on human passions. Among those who were influenced by Spinoza, mention should be made of Schelling with his system of identity, Schleiermacher and Goethe. — Spinoza was never able to overcome the contradiction in his thought between the immutable God and his changing modes.

MR

SPIRIT

Spirit (Lat.: *spiritus*) is an immaterial, simple, substantial being that is capable of self-possession through self-consciousness and self-determination and is capable of grasping and realizing supra-sensible values (= subjective spirit). Its *immateriality* excludes not only total materiality, but it also rules out that "basic dependence on matter" by reason of which plant and animal souls, without the closest connection with the corporeal, cannot operate or exist (*Hylemorphism). The *simplicity of the spirit implies such a fullness of existence that it is composed neither of spatially separate parts nor of essential parts. On the one hand, the spirit's ability to possess itself through self-consciousness (*Consciousness) is rooted in her simplicity and immateriality, as is also, on the other hand, her ability to know all being in its truth, goodness and unity and to strive for supra-sensible values. Since spirit is not restricted in its activity to a small corner of reality (as animal and plant souls are) but is ordered to existence as such, it possesses an unlimited horizon of the knowing-power (*Understanding, *Reason) which seeks the truth as such; consequently, it also possesses an unlimited horizon of the *will which seeks value as such. The ability to choose freely between known partial goods is rooted in these extensive powers and in the "sovereignty" over all partial values that results from them; their chief result, therefore, is the power of self-determination (*Free Will). Finally, the nature of spirit along with its horizon, which can never be completely filled by the finite goods of a limited existence, demands an unlimited continuance in existence: spirit is destined for immortal life (*Immortality). Spirit, as the bearer of these perfections and possibilities of existence, is a substantial being and these perfections are the natural foundation of all personal existence (*Person).

There are different levels of spiritual perfection. In the infinite, *divine spirit* all potentiality, all purely accidental being and all dependence on another are totally excluded. In the created *pure spirit* (mentioned in the Bible, but philosophically problematic) all dependence in existing and operating is also excluded. The spiritual *soul* of man, however, even though its actual connection with the body is not the condition of its existence, as the essential form of the body has a necessary and essential relation to the body (*Body-Soul Relation, *Hylemorphism). As such a "form" the human soul constitutes, in its sense-knowing and striving, an effective unity with the body; in its spiritual activity also, as long as the connection with the body lasts, it is dependent at least indirectly on the material pre-conditions of its spiritual activity; for, the understanding produces its concepts for the most part from sense impressions, but willing and the experience of values are involved in the totality of the spiritual-sensible soul (*Thinking, *Understanding, *Emotion, *Will). That there are, besides the human soul, earthly spirits like ghosts is a common belief among children, primitives and those with a lively imagination, but it has never been proved by incontrovertible facts.

SPIRITISM

Under the influence of the neo-Platonic concept of *pneuma*, St. Augustine in his commentary on Genesis used "spirit" to designate the reproductive imagination. He distinguishes three kinds of vision: corporeal, spiritual, and intellectual. Spiritual vision is that vision by which the "spirit" sees the likenesses of bodies. This terminology is found in many medieval writers influenced by Augustine, including Alcuin, Walafrid Strabo, St. Aelred of Rievaulx, Peter Lombard, Alexander of Hales, St. Bonaventure and St. Thomas.

As the subject of a driving quest for values the subjective spirit expresses itself not only in its relatively permanent value judgments and attitudes, but also in the creations of spirit: science, art, technology, industry, social bodies, etc. (= objective spirit: *Spiritual Existence). When the human spirit in particular cultures forgets its close relation to everything human by falling into a kind of exaggerated *spiritualism, then such narrowmindedness will express itself in false forms of cultural life. A biased *life philosophy drew from this the right, amidst grossly distorted charges, simply to outlaw "spirit" (understood as the power of forming concepts) as a principle hostile to life itself. In actual fact, however, the spiritual human soul is also the principle of man's sense life (*Soul, *Body-Soul Relation). Thus man's spirit expresses itself in the biological realm; it posits its own non-spiritual antithesis — not just as something opposed to the spiritual, but as its own area of activity and expression that is intimately tied in with the totality of human existence. In those cases where the sense life removes itself from the unity of the whole man in order to pursue its own desires, then it has a destructive effect. Since spirit is the highest reality in man and the forming principle of all cultural values, and also since, because of its immortality, it surpasses the whole realm of earthly values, the proper development of spiritual life is the most elevated task of human formation.

AW

SPIRITISM

Spiritism (Lat.: *spiritus* = spirit) means: (1) a scientific theory about the causality of so-called preternatural happenings which are supposed to be produced not by living men, but by the bodiless souls of the dead or by other spiritual beings: ghostly activities and appearances; (2) a visionary-religious sect which tries to render spirits benevolent by oral incantations or symbolic ceremonies in order to gain information about the next life or just to satisfy curiosity. — The reality of strange happenings and apparitions, in which trickery and illusion are certainly not present, cannot be denied. *Spooks* are events, similar to effects produced at a distance (*Occultism), but they are not, like them, effected by living persons (mediums) in a knowable way (noises, movement of tables and chairs, words, sighs).

SPIRITUAL EXISTENCE

Apparitions are visible forms either of dead men whose bodiless souls somehow effect a bodily "appearance," or they are forms of other bodiless beings. — The identity of these forms allegedly has been proved by wax impressions, photographs and the communication of things known only to them. While the spiritists explain these happenings by bodiless spirits, the animists (from *anima* = soul of a living man) try to explain everything by the special psychic powers of men, either present or absent; they claim that the wax impressions are not clear and could have been produced by living mediums; they say that the photographs are all suspicious — most of them have been shown to be frauds; they say that the verbal communications reflect the knowledge and inclinations of those present (mental telepathy). In actual fact, such "proofs" are usually quite banal and they are often contradictory. The animistic theory suffices to explain the usual "seance." Events of this nature certified by credible witnesses, where a serious preternatural intent is manifested and where no incantation is present, must also be given a preternatural explanation.

KF

SPIRITUAL EXISTENCE

Spiritual existence is a way of describing both subjective and objective spirit. Concerning *subjective spirit* or spirit as an individual, active subject confer *Spirit, *Soul. *Objective spirit* is the special world of objects that the subjective spirit does not just find already there but produces in and from itself. This creative, subjective spirit is not each individual by himself, but the spiritual community or the collective spirit (e. g., of a family, of a nation). Thus, the objective spirit is the point of cohesion and the unity of the creative elements of a community; it is the very essence of the cultural world which is the object of the thinking and willing of individuals (*Culture, *Human Sciences): it is the world of language, morality, art, science, religion, etc. This internal object of spirit is to be distinguished from its external, material realizations. In order to distinguish them from objective spirit they are called the *objectifications of spirit* or *objectified spirit*. Close relations, however, are maintained between both spirits; this is especially clear in art where objectification is absolutely essential.

Objective spirit is not the timeless reality of possible essence and essential relationships; rather, it has an existence that presupposes the existence of subjective spirit and its psychic activity without being identified with it. Objective spirit lives in subjective spirit, but it has its own laws; and these laws cannot be reduced to a mere psychic function as *psychologism maintains. As a temporal reality it has a history; this is not the history of a particular spirit, but of the spiritual community as such (e. g., the history of Platonic philosophy). It is present in the individual spirits that participate in it, but it is not restricted just to them. What individuals contribute to its growth or change is small in comparison to what they get from the collective spirit. — While Dilthey sees only the destruction of general human nature in this objective spirit, according to Hegel it is an emanation of the Absolute, the appearance of an absolute idea. In this case Dilthey fails to see that human nature also must have a deeper foundation (perhaps in a divine idea) and Hegel fails to see that every realization and concretization of ideas takes place within the realm of *contingency and *freedom.

WB

SPIRITUALISM

Spiritualism (Lat.: *Spiritus* = spirit), in contrast to *materialism, is the name given to the doctrine of the reality of spirit or spiritual beings. — *Metaphysical* spiritualism tries to understand existence from *spirit. The monistic form of spiritualism assumes that all reality is spirit — just the one absolute spirit (e. g., in *German Idealism); according to the pluralistic form of spiritualism, reality is composed of a multiplicity of spiritual beings: in this view, the body does not have an existence of its own (e. g., in the *Idealism of Berkeley, in Leibniz' theory of the monads, etc.); according to the theistic form of spiritualism, the primary source of all reality is spirit and therefore all reality is related to spirit in some way. — *Psychological* spiritualism holds for the spirituality of the human *soul, either as the result of metaphysical spiritualism or as a contrast to the material body. The theory of Descartes represents a crude form of psychological spiritualism; he sets spirit (= thinking and freedom) over against matter (= extension and mechanical necessity) immediately and he does this without the in-between stages of vegetative-sensible life, which is not wholly material but still is dependent on matter. — *Ethical-sociological* spiritualism stresses the essential difference between animal and specifically human-spiritual interests. In an exaggerated fashion it looks upon the body only as a servant for the spirit, or simply considers it a non-value or even an evil. — A clear distinction is to be made between spiritualism and *spiritism.

WB

STATE

The family does not exhaust all the social possibilities of man; nor is it able to take care of all human needs. For both reasons the socialization of man cannot stop with the family. Freely willed societies are also not enough. We need an adequate degree of socialization which gives assurance that the social nature of man is fully provided for and which is capable of providing for all the necessities that the family cannot take care of. This definite form of socialization is the *natural society* (*societas naturalis*) because man's very nature demands it. It is a *perfect society* (*societas perfecta*) because it possesses all the means and powers, the lack of which is the reason for the insufficiency of the family. This human socialization and the social structures in which it expresses itself do not have as their immediate goal (as the family does) the welfare of the individuals who are the members of it; rather, the immediate goal is the common good (*bonum commune*): therefore it is called a commonwealth or republic (*res publica*).

In ancient Greece the city (*polis*, the root of "politics") was the body politic; for, there was no higher unity. Man's socialization would find its final perfection in an organized unity of the human race; this has been attempted by the League of Nations and the United Nations, but there is still much to be done. There are many middle stages between the smallest public bodies (towns, cities, etc.) and the whole of mankind. They are all public bodies but it is only their joining together that produces the perfect society. In the course of time, however, local political bodies of a higher kind came into being, to which the new name "state" was applied; they reached such a level of importance that we have become accustomed to look upon them simply as *the* political body.

These "states" claimed unlimited authority with regard to internal affairs and concerining external affairs they disclaimed any connection with their equals, not even to mention some higher community. One war after another resulted from this view so that leaders began to take a second look at the situation. The concept of the state that was tailored for the national states of the period before 1914 is gradually disappearing. "Stateness" is now being shared on many levels: from the local township, to a province, to a nation, to a whole alliance (European, Atlantic, Russian), to the United Nations; and it fans out to international structures like the World Bank, the European Common Market, etc.

Thus, what we, who are caught up in 19th century ideas, were wont to say about the state, we must now apply to a large number of structures. The state is a "community of persons" and an "institution"; as a community of persons it is also a society of authority and fellowship. The more the institutional element is stressed (bureaucracy), the more it must be said: "*We* are the state." — States can come into existence in many different ways. The necessity rooted in man's nature of founding the state — but not of founding "this" state — must always be carefully distinguished from the creation of the particular state, a creation which can always be traced back to a free human choice (either for particular strong men or of all the members). Ultimately, there are always "common concerns" around which a *community builds itself. If it is a question of concerns that are essential to *man, i. e., concerns that are indispensable for a truly human life, then a man is not free either to belong or not to belong to such a community; in this sense the community is an obligation for him. Thus, a "social contract" in the sense of Rousseau is superfluous, as is also the "submission contract" of Hobbes. The same common concerns direct man to conduct himself conformable to the community, i. e., he should order his actions and omissions to the requirements of the community and of its *common good. Therein lies the foundation for the *authority of the community over its members. Insofar as this authority is derived from no higher earthly society, it is based on factual necessity that is outlined by the order of creation; in this sense therefore it is "immediately from God." According to the way in which authority is exercised in the state, a distinction is made between the different forms of the state (monarchy, aristocracy, *democracy, dictatorship of one or of a group, theocracy, etc.).

Essential for every state is the presence of the people, i. e., the totality of those who compose the state. The state as a local political body presupposes a particular territory as the spatial basis of it. For the complete organization of the state there must be an establishment of the different state organs as the legitimate bearers of state authority. However, it is not state authority or those who exercise it that constitute the state; rather, the state constitutes its organs, including the highest office in the state. In what sense the highest state organs are holders of state authority, is a disputed point; accordingly, there is a difference of opinion as to how and under what conditions it is permissable to take their authority away from them. In any event, state authority is not authority over the state, but authority of the state over its affairs and over its citizens; and it is authority over the citizens insofar as this authority promotes the common good, but not beyond that. State authority is indivisible. The so-called division of authority is only a distribution of different functions to the different organs of the state. In this way some assurance is given that each function will be carried out properly; at the same time the check and balance system is supposed to make it impossible for one organ of the state to become too powerful and so to be able to use its power in a way that runs contrary to the common good.

OvNB

STATIC

Static is a term that can be applied to everything that is related to a state of rest. That which is static is found only accidentally in the order of the changeable insofar as a thing is temporarily unmoved and unchanging;

however, in the order of unchangeable essential relationships that static element is essential. These essential relationships are the real object of the static mode of consideration. In order to know the full reality it must also be complemented by the *dynamic mode of consideration. Since activity as such does not involve any motion, the static is opposed to the dynamic only insofar as the dynamic element in question involves some *motion, but not insofar as it involves *activity. In the dimension of pure activity the opposition between the dynamic and the static is not present.

WB

STOICISM

Stoicism was the philosophy of a Greek and Roman school which was influential from about 300 B. C. until 200 A. D.; it received its name from the column-lined hall (*Stoa*) in Athens where the philosophers regularly congregated. Usually a distinction is made between the early Stoics (Zeno, Cleanthes, Chrysippus), the middle Stoics (Panaitios, Posidonius) and the late Stoics (Seneca, Epictetus, Marcus Aurelius). The Stoics combined the doctrines of the ancient philosophers with the thoughts of Plato and Aristotle; with great conviction they taught a new ethos and a new attitude which had a profound effect on ethics. Among the three parts of philosophy — logic, physics, ethics — the last has the first place of honor. The Stoic ideal is *the wise man* who lives in accordance with nature, controls his affections, endures suffering calmly and as the goal of his life is content with virtue as the only source of happiness (*Eudaimonia*). God is a species of world soul; he possesses the germs or seminal powers (*logoi spermatikoi*) of every development within himself so that every event seems to be planned and to be the result of providence; in each case, however, personal freedom is excluded (Fatalism). Instead of being a highly speculative, systematic philosophy Stoicism is rather a view of life deeply concerned with man's emotions; as a substitute for religion it attempts to show a man how to possess his soul in peace. This attitude influences its treatment of the virtues; and Stoic writings tend to be moralizing in tone. The advocacy of the equality of all men is characteristic as is also a certain cosmopolitanism. Many Stoic concepts and distinctions were adopted by the Christian Church Fathers, but only after they had purified them of a moralistic pride in virtue and of a too negative regard for human affections.

JoS

SUAREZIANISM

Suarezianism, named after Franz Suárez (1548-1617), is a branch of *scholasticism related to *Thomism; however, it also contains many ideas borrowed from *Scotism. The principal difference between Suarezianism and Thomism is in the concept of existence. While Thomism sees in existence as *act the "inner ground" of the existence of the existent, according to Suarezianism existence is only the "state" of existing. Of course, these two views do not necessarily exclude each other, but rather complement each other; yet they are often advocated in an exclusive sense and so lead to two different schools of thought. The Thomistic view is based on formal abstraction — the Suarezian on total *abstraction. In the Thomistic view existence is logically thought of as really distinct from the essence, while in Suarezianism it is thought of as really identical with the essence. Accordingly, Thomism stresses the analogy of proportionality with regard to existence, and Suarezianism emphasizes the analogy of attribution (*Analogy).

Similarly, the two views differ on the principle of individuation. According to Suarezianism, the *individual is this particular individual wholly through itself; according to Thomism, there must be a principle in material individual things by means of which they belong to this specific level of existence (the essential form) and another principle through which, within their own species, they are distinguished from others of the same species (prime matter which makes possible spatio-temporal multiplicity) (*Hylemorphism). With regard to the theory of knowledge, the result is that for the Thomists the object which is grasped by the intellect in the concept is only an abstract and universal essence which is concretized only by its relationship to the sense impression; for the Suarezians, however, the intellect forms concepts of concrete particular things as such and then from these, by abstracting from the particular characteristics, it progresses to universal concepts.

In general, Thomism considers existence more from a purely metaphysical point of view, while Suarezianism looks at it insofar as it is actualized in the world of appearance. — Suarezianism exercised a great deal of influence not only on Catholic scholasticism, but also on Protestant scholasticism; its influence was also felt in more modern times (Leibniz, Schopenhauer). And it was very important for the whole development of thought on natural rights and political philosophy.

WB

SUBJECT

Subject literally means that which is "thrown under" or "lies under"; therefore it has a meaning similar to substratum (*spread under*) and substance (standing under). The *ontological* meaning of "subject" corresponds to this literal sense for the most part. Accordingly, the subject (1) is the basic or "carrying" reality, the "carrier"; therefore it essentially asserts a relationship to a reality that "rests" on it, that it is "carrying." The latter reality is somehow dependent on the carrier, since it is the existential determination of the carrier and in the widest sense it is called its *form. The dependence of the form on the subject as such is not a dependence of effect on its cause; thus the form is not necessarily produced by the subject. What is meant by the figurative expressions of "carrying" and "receiving," is originally given to us immediately only in the relationship of our *ego to its own acts and mental states. The experienced fact that the ego "possesses" the acts as its own acts, that the acts are "in" the ego is expressed philosophically by saying that the ego is the subject of the acts. Although that subject is preferably called a subject which (like the ego) for its part is not also a determination of another, but is itself an independent reality, still the relationship of subject to form is not simply the same as that between *substance and *accident. For, apart from the fact that a substance is not necessarily a subject of accidents (God is a substance but he is not a bearer of accidents), even an accident itself can be a subject of further accidental determinations (e. g., the proximate subject of speed is motion which is itself an accident of a body); morever, the "form" which is received by the subject is not necessarily an accidental form — it can also be a substantial form (e. g., the body as the subject of the soul; and in general, *matter as the subject of the form: *Hylemorphism).

A special case of the ontological subject is the *psychological* subject, the ego, insofar as it is the carrier of its own acts. Insofar as these acts as *intentional acts are related to an *object, by means of them the ego in a conscious way is set over against another, namely the object. Now the ego is called a subject insofar as it is opposed to the object; thus the word "subject" also carries a second meaning. In this sense, the subject (2) is the ego insofar as it is related to an object knowingly, willingly or emotionally. Here we have the concept of the subject in contrast to the object. In this case, either the "*psycho-physical subject*" (= the whole man composed of body and soul) or only the "*psychological subject*" (= the Ego conscious of itself, which is actually the soul) is thought of as the subject. — Especially in the *theory of *knowledge* the opposition between the (knowing) subject and the (known) object stands right in the middle of the debate. In this context sometimes the "*epistemological subject*" is set over against the individual, psychological subject as something essentially different (found explicitly in neo-Kantianism). All the individual aspects of the psychological subject are placed on the side of the object, so that the only thing remaining is an indefinite, supra-individual "absolute *consciousness" as the epistemological subject. Now it is certainly possible to abstract the universal concept of a knowing subject from the individual Ego; also, the conditions in the individual subject for universally valid knowledge can be considered by themselves, but the actually thinking and knowing subject in the last analysis is always an individual ego. And if someone says that the ultimate subject can no longer be an object, then that contradicts the essence of *spirit which has the special quality of being able to bend back upon itself.

A further meaning of "subject," which is also connected with the ontological meaning (1), is that of the *logical* subject (3) in contrast to the predicate. In the judgment, when one is speaking of an existent or an actual subject, a determination (form) is affirmed as belonging to the subject. Therefore, even the concept, which designates the object that is to receive a further determination by means of the predicate, as such is also called a subject.

JdV

SUBJECTIVE

Subjective literally means that which is related to the *subject; in daily use it usually means that which is related to the subject in contrast to the *object; thus, the "subjective" almost always stands in opposition to the "objective." In non-philosophical language the precise meaning is very often vague and ambiguous; for the sake of clarity one should constantly be warned against an excessive, thoughtless use of the word. Philosophically, "subjective" (1) can mean first of all: pertaining to the subject, in contrast to that which is "objective" = pertaining to the object. The most important philosophical meaning of "subjective" (2) is: that which is not founded in the object, but is conditioned only by the feelings or arbitrary assertions of the subject (e. g., purely subjective *certitude). There is also another meaning when *intentional acts are called "subjective" (3), insofar as they are considered not in their relationship to the object, but only as real acts (accidents) of the subject (thus: a subjective concept; or better, the concept considered from a subjective point of view). In the older scholastic terminology the word "subjective" (4) was often used of the subject in the sense of "that which exists by itself"; from this point of view "to exist subjectively" means: to stand by itself as an actual existent (and not just as an object of thought). See also *Knowledge, Theory of, Objective, Ontology, Potency*.

JdV

SUBJECTIVISM

Subjectivism, in contrast to *objectivism, is the philosophical position according to which it is not the *object that is decisive for the validity of knowledge, but rather the dispositions and states of the *subject; this view corresponds to the well-known saying of Protagoras: Man is the measure of all things. It is understood as pertaining either to certain thought-forms which are common to all thinking beings, or to the peculiarities of certain races, psychological types or individuals; the view that stresses the priority of the individual is preferably called "subjectivism." If the forms of all thought or a common human nature are considered normative, then truth seems to be grounded in a *transcendental or psychological structure of the subject; otherwise, usually more or less fluid feelings and inclinations are considered to be decisive; then it becomes clear as day that subjectivism means *relativism. The feeling-theories find many supporters especially in the question about the nature of *values; these same supporters will reject subjectivism in the realm of metaphysical knowledge (subjectivism of values). Thus, for example, in the matter of moral value a special "moral feeling" is thought to be the ultimate norm, and the measure of beauty is said to be the "taste."

All subjectivism is ultimately based on this, that one fails to see that the essence of *spirit is to be open to the totality of existence; therefore, the subject seems to be handed over necessarily to his own inner thoughts and emotions. Thus, although at first sight subjectivism seems to elevate man, since is places him at the center of everything, yet, when seen in all of its implications, it really means the isolation and truncation of man. However, an exaggerated objectivism is not the answer either. Certainly there is a "subjective" side to all our knowledge, i. e., an aspect conditioned by the subject; true this can be an occasion for error. But man's mind is not subject to a blind necessity to confuse the object with its own subjective reactions; rather, it always retains the freedom to let itself be determined by the *evidence of the existent alone. See also *Idealism, Knowledge, Theory of, Psychologism, Relativism.*

JdV

SUBSIDIARITY

Subsidiarity (assistance, completion) is the fundamental relationship of *society to the human person. Society in every sense of the word always exists only *in* its members and therefore also *for* its members. The *common good, which comes before the good of the individual, as a functional value is properly fostered only when it helps the members of a community to fully actualize the powers given them by the Creator; this applies to those forms of human growth that either naturally or for other reasons cannot be attained without the help of society. Therefore, society perverts its own inner meaning when, in place of helping the members to grow in a human way, it actually impedes their progress, when it suffocates in the regimentation of the collective, or when it sacrifices its members for the greedy goals of the collective.

SUBSISTENCE

According to the principle "Every agent is perfected by its own activity," it follows that society should not take away from the individual, nor should the more extensive social body absorb from the smaller group, what they can do just as well or even better on their own initiative. Within the context of the family, excessive guardianship instead of education for independence, responsibility and self-reliance violates the principle of subsidiarity. In public life the *state violates this principle when it assumes total power at the expense of the self-help of the citizens and the self-government of the smaller communities or bodies, whether public or private. — The content and validity of this principle is as old as man; but explicitly proclaimed as the principle of subsidiarity it first appeared in the papal encyclical "Quadragesimo Anno" (May 15, 1931, No. 79) in opposition to the growing threat of *collectivism and totalitarianism.

OvNB

SUBSISTENCE

Subsistence of ontological independence belongs to that which possesses *existence not in another, but in itself. Therefore, subsistence belongs primarily to the complete *substance. Since "subsisting" means the same thing as "existing in itself," neither accidents nor the essential form of a body nor any part can properly be said to subsist; only the concrete whole subsists. The spiritual soul of man, however, presents a certain exception in this regard; for, the human soul possesses its existence originally in itself and independently of matter and then communicates existence to matter. Thus, the subsistence of the soul does not depend on the subsistence of the concrete whole; rather, the subsistence of the whole depends on the subsistence of the soul itself. — A pure *spirit is a subsisting essential form. Subsisting *existence is an existence that exists in itself; therefore, it exists absolutely and without any relation to an essence different from itself, so that it is beyond all categorical determinations (*Transcendence). The nature of finite things subsists in them themselves according to their finite mode of existence; according to their positive existential content, without the limitations proper to the finite, they are also in subsisting existence, which pre-contains in itself all finite existence in a higher way (*"eminenter"*) because of its infinity. The more an existent approaches subsisting existence, the more spiritual it is and the less bound it is to matter. For, the levels of subsistence are also the levels of *identity and spirituality. That which subsists absolutely or relatively different from another is called a supposite (*suppositum*); if a supposite subsists in a rational nature, then it is called a "*person" (in scholastic terminology).

WB

SUBSTANCE

Substance literally means that which stands under or that which remains under the appearances of a thing as the permanent element. However, that which is most characteristic of substance is not its special relation to the accidents, but its own independence (*Subsistence). For, substance is that which has its existence not in another, but in and for itself. Just like existence, substance also has its own meaning and value in itself; therefore, in contrast to the accidents, it can be defined philosophically without reference to a carrier or subject. But the independence of a substance, by reason of which it possesses its existence in itself, does not exclude the fact that it has received this existence through the activity of an efficient cause. In a very special way, substance is a kind of persistence in being; this persistence is absolute in the case of the divine substance and relative in the case of finite substances with reference to their accidents. Finite substances are always the supports of accidental determinations; also, every substance is an inner principle of activity or a *nature. — Following Aristotle, a distinction is to be made between *first* and *second substance*: first substance is the individual essence which is determined by real accidents and which can be affirmed of no other substance (e. g., Socrates = substance in the sense defined above); second substance is the universal essence which has been derived from individuals by means of abstraction and which can be affirmed of the first substance (e. g., man). — Hylemorphism makes a distinction between *complete* and *incomplete* or *partial substances*. Incomplete substances possess a natural ordination to another principle of essence with which they form a composed complete substance. Incomplete substances differ from accidents in that they constitute the whole being, while the accidents give only a further determination to something already constituted in its essence. Morever, incomplete substances have their existence more "with" the other than "in" it. — Substantial existence which is in and for itself allows for degrees of more and less. From this point of view, first substance is above second substance, complete above incomplete, living above non-living; and the highest form of substance is the *person.

Many philosophers have had a different idea of substance than the one presented here. The confusion of a limited autonomy with absolute independence made its first appearance in the thinking of Descartes: this line of thought was carried to its logical conclusion by Spinoza who arrived at the notion of the unicity of substance and so to pantheism. — Kant restricts the application of the substance-idea to the world of experience. In his view the decisive characteristic of substance is perdurance in time. — Materialists find the substance-idea realized only in corporeal things. — Since Leibniz the *dynamic aspect of substance has been emphasized one-sidedly especially by philosophers with a bent for physical science. Finally, modern theories of actuality, life philosophy and existential philosophy have completely given up the notion of substance: for them the only reality is activity, not the carrier which produces the activity.

Since we begin from the knowledge of our own egos, we are able to know the reality not only of one substance, but of many different substances. We discover within ourselves the acts of thinking, willing, etc., which we are the source of. But these acts are necessarily related to a center or subject from which they proceed. This subject experiences itself as one or as identical with itself in the midst of a multiplicity of acts. That this subject does not exist in another as in its subject, we know from our consciousness of personal responsibility for our free acts. We rightly conclude from the substantiality of our own Ego to the same quality in the Ego of the other. Animals and plants manifest certain activities which point to an intelligible unity as the basis of their *finality; this presupposes that they possess an existence in and for itself after the fashion of a substance. We also perceive an intelligible unity in the case of inorganic bodies that permits us to conclude to a certain substantiality there, although it is very difficult in each case to isolate the individual substance from a collection of substances. Finally, since the substance-idea excludes all imperfection in its characteristic note — i. e., existence in and for itself, but on the contrary belongs necessarily to the existent as such, it must therefore also be applied to God himself, keeping in mind of course that it is applied analogously and only after excluding all accidental determinations from him.

JS

SUFFERING

Suffering ordinarily means (1) the *privation of some good or a change for the worse: one suffers a loss. In a somewhat broader sense (2) suffering means undergoing a change, whether for better or for worse. In the widest and improper sense (3), every reception of a determination can be called a "suffering," even when no loss of another determination is in any way connected with it (as we find in the case of the determination of a knowing power to the act of knowing).

When suffering in its narrower meaning (1) is predicated of a being endowed with knowledge, then the intention is not merely to signify a change for the worse, but at the same time also to actual experience of the change. The magnitude and the depth of the suffering (1) depends then not only on the extent of the injury endured, but also on the kind and the extent of the knowledge that is involved. Since animals are capable of only an imperfect consciousness which does not include reflective self-consciousness, they are therefore also less sensitive to suffering and pain than man is. God is incapable of any suffering because he cannot undergo any injury or loss. The possibility of suffering (1) is not merely a necessary consequence of finiteness; as the experiences of innumerable men have shown, it is also very well suited to educating a man to full maturity. But this value is not brought home to man simply by the fact of suffering itself, but primarily by the way in which he meets and accepts it; and since failure is possible here, this particular value may be lost. Suffering teaches a man in a deeply personal way that he is a limited and dependent being; that we men must help one another; that we cannot find our final happiness in this earthly life, etc.

All suffering is related to some "doing" or activity. In a very special way suffering (2) or *passion* is the opposite of *action*. Action and passion in the world of bodies are only the two aspects of *change: the exact same occurrence is called "action" when it is referred to the efficient cause of the change, and it is called "passion" when it is referred to that which is changed. In this sense action and passion belong to the Aristotelian *categories. The physical law regarding the equality of action and re-action does not negate the contrast between action and passion. For, the re-action is only elicited as the result of the produced change — as the result, therefore, of the passion. — See also *Evil*.

WB

SUFFICIENT REASON, PRINCIPLE OF

The principle of sufficient reason as an *ontological* principle means that every existent (or better: every *Objective Reality) has a ground of existence; as a *logical* principle it means that every judgment (every proposition) must be able to be proved as valid before the court of reason by means of a ground of knowledge. For, an unfounded proposition could with the same justification (or lack of it) be just as well denied as affirmed. Insofar as the logical principle of sufficient reason is related to certain judgments, it is equivalent to the demand for *evidence. Therefore, it ultimately rests on the connection between our thinking and existence; certainly, the proximate ground of a proposition is often to be found in other propositions (e. g., in every proposition established by means of a *demonstration), but the ultimate ground is always the self-manifesting existence of the objective reality itself. Hence the demand for a grounding of every proposition is not the same as the impossible demand that every proposition be demonstrated, and so it does not lead to an *infinite regress* (*regressus in infinitum*). — The ontological principle of sufficient reason means that every objective reality has a ground of existence. In its application to essentially necessary objective realities, i. e., those that stand on the basis of the essence of a thing, it is given along with the principle of contradiction. Insofar as it includes a further, new statement of decisive importance, it is equivalent to the demand for a *cause for every *contingent reality, every contingent existent. The *principle of *causality* in the ordinary sense is to this extent a particular case of this universal principle of causality that it determines the cause more exactly as an "efficient" cause. The establishment of the validity of the ontological principle of sufficient reason, insofar as it concerns not only necessary but also contingent existence, is therefore the same as that of the principle of *causality, only with the omission of the last step which grounds the necessity of an "efficient" cause. — Due to the close connection between the principle of sufficient reason and the principle of causality one is also able to understand why neither Aristotle nor the scholastics of the Middle Ages formulated the principle of sufficient reason as such; Leibniz was the first philosopher to give formal expression to the principle.

JdV

SUICIDE

Suicide is the direct taking of one's own life by one's own authority (and so, for example, not as the carrying out of the death penalty). By reason of the natural moral law suicide is forbidden, even in so-called exceptional cases (e. g., painful, incurable disease; a threatening danger to one's honor and good name), because it is an unjustified attack on the right to life — a right that is reserved to the creator alone. God must retain for himself the right to terminate a man's life, because this *life carriers the character of a time of trial and the power is not given to the one being tested to determine the length of his trial. The one who commits suicide only appears to be courageous. A man manifests true courage (because exercised for a moral value) when, in the midst of the most difficult trials, he perseveres in the task assigned to him by God (Plato). The responsibility to ward off shame, scandal, etc., extends only to the use of licit means. — Suicide is also a serious violation of true *self-love because by a freely willed suicide a man renders impossible the attainment of his ultimate goal, eternal *happiness. The glorification of suicide by the Stoics and by not a few moderns does not contribute to true moral responsibility for human life and its goals. Like suicide, self-mutilation, castration and sterilization are also forbidden. A person may injure a part of his body or even cut it off only for the good of the whole body. *Indirect killing* or great danger, which is different from suicide and sometimes allowable for good reason, is an act or situation in which, from a morally permissible action, both a good effect and death or its hastening are the immediate result (i. e., without making death the means to the end). The causes of suicide and its frequency are physical and mental illness, social pressure, and especially the loss of faith in God which tends to suppress the proper view of human life.

JoS

SUPERNATURAL

Supernatural in the terminology of Catholic *theology means that which neither belongs to *nature, nor flows from nature, nor is demanded by nature. In this definition nature can be understood as the essence of a particular thing or as the totality of all finite things. Accordingly, a distinction is made between "supernatural" in reference to a particular nature (= the preternatural) or the *absolutely supernatural*, i. e., in reference to the totality of created nature. That which is preternatural for a particular nature (e. g., life for a stone) can be natural for another being (e. g., life for a plant). That which is supernatural pure and simple, is natural only for God and belongs to him in such a way that it cannot naturally pertain to any creature. However, if it is offered to the creature by God as a goal, then it is the result of grace (participation in the divine nature as a gift). The content of the absolutely supernatural is called *supernature*. Although supernature is never the completion of nature in its own right, still it does not contradict man's spiritual nature. Moreover, for *spirit with its openness for being and goodness as such there is also the possibility (*potentia obedientialis*; *Potency) in addition to its natural capacity for fulfillment, to be elevated by God's omnipotence to participation in his own inner life. Therefore, supernature does not destroy nature; rather, it presupposes it and perfects it beyond its own capacities. — By *supernaturalism* is understood either (1) the recognition of the supernatural order, or, in a derogatory sense, (2) every theory or praxis that downgrades nature in comparison with supernature. — For an understanding of Christian revelation the concept of supernature is fundamental. The *supernatural in substance* is distinguished from the *supernatural in mode* (e. g., an effect which is essentially natural, but which in the mode of its production transcends the natural powers of the creature, for example, a miraculous cure of cancer). In non-theological language "supernatural" sometimes refers to the supra-sensible or the spiritual when nature is contrasted with spirit; sometimes it also simply refers to the divine. Catholic theology, however, makes a sharp distinction between God as the creator (in the natural order) and God as the source of grace (in the supernatural order). —See also *Mystery*.

WB

SUPPOSITION

Supposition is a special way of using words. A word usually refers to something distinct from itself, to a concept, and by means of the concept

403

to an object: *formal, signifying supposition.* If a word is used as being identified with itself without referring to something else, then one speaks of *material supposition*, as in the sentence: Man is a one-syllable word. *Formal supposition* (use of a word for a signified object) is either *logical* (use of a word for a concept as a concept: for example, Man is a species-concept) or *real* (use of a word for the thing itself: All men are mortal); this latter type of supposition includes a number of variations. The kind of supposition in question can be deduced from the way a word is used in a proposition. In syllogistic thinking the same supposition of the words must be retained all the way through.

JdV

SUPRA-RATIONAL

Supra-rational literally means that which goes beyond *reason. However this cannot be understood with regard to reason as such. For, reason as such is ordered to being as such, so that beyond reason as such there would only be absolute *nothing. Therefore, the term "supra-rational" must be referred to finite reason in its finite mode of existence. For infinite reason there is no such thing as the supra-rational. Accordingly, the supra-rational is that which, in its full existential reality, lies beyond the intellectual power of a finite (especially human) reason. The positive mode of existence of pure spiritual beings and especially the realm of divine existence must also be termed "supra-rational"; for, we can think of these things only analogously and imperfectly through negation and through comparison with other finite, material existents. That which is *absolutely supra-rational*, i. e., not only for our human reason but for every finite reason, is the absolutely *supernatural. — Therefore, the "supra-rational" is not the same as the "self-contradictory" or the "irrational"; for, the *self-contradictory* is that which is repugnant to reason as such and so to every reason, while the *irrational* is that which (objectively or subjectively) possesses no reason at all.

WB

SYMBOL

Symbol (Gr.: *Symballein* = throw together, bring together) literally is a recognizable sign by which a piece that is broken off from something (e. g., a ring) can be fitted back to it. In current terminology sometimes every element of a system of signs is called a symbol; thus, one speaks of *symbolic logic. In the proper sense a symbol is the same thing as an image and signifies a sensible *sign of a supra-sensible reality; such signs naturally have a certain propensity to illustrate these realities and within a definite community they are immediately intelligible (e. g., a scepter as a symbol of supreme authority). If immediate intelligibility is lacking and the interpretation depends upon complicated mental processes, one speaks preferably of *allegory*. From man's point of view, the basis of symbolism is his need somehow to make clear to himself the spiritual realities that he naturally grasps only in abstract concepts. The things in the sensible world answer this need because of the analogy that runs through all levels of existence. All things have their exemplar ultimately in God; but visible things, because of their many differences and infinite variety, reflect the pure light of the spiritual world as it were in many different rays. Therefore, the intuition of sensible things is able to replace for us to some extent the deficient intuition of the spiritual world, if a meaningful idea is connected with the intuitively given image. If the symbol is not able to express analogously, as conceptual thinking can, the supra-sensible in its own proper existence (because the symbol has no specific similarity with the supra-sensible) still it has this advantage over conceptual thought, that it can, in a suggesting way, manifest a greater fullness of spiritual reality, and therefore it also makes a direct appeal to the emotions of man.

The use of symbols is sometimes called "symbolism" (1). As a philosophical position, symbolism (2) refers to certain views according to which our knowledge is based only on symbols. Thus, certain representatives of neo-positivism look upon the symbols of logic as the real objects of science. In *modernism*, conceptually grasped propositions about God (including dogmas of the Church) are understood as purely symbolic and therefore changing indications of an unknowable reality that reveals itself only in feeling. Both forms of symbolism basically destroy the concept of symbol itself, because they rob the symbol of its meaning. This also holds true for the modernistic view; for, if the idea itself is only a symbol, then there is no way to discover the meaning of this symbol; in addition, the symbol itself becomes something non-perceptual. — In art, symbolism (3) means the attempt to give an intimation of the supra-sensible through the use of the sensible symbol; in actual fact sometimes this symbolism reveals an inclination towards morbidity and eccentricity.

JdV

SYMBOLIC LOGIC

Symbolic logic (also, mathematical logic) admits of both a strict and a broad interpretation. In the strict sense it includes the propositional and predicate calculi. In the broad sense, sometimes called 'logistic' it includes a multiplicity of related systems. Each of these senses requires some explanation.

Superficially, the characteristic feature of symbolic logic is the use of a symbolic notation resembling algebra. On a deeper level its distinctive feature is its axiomatic structure whose validity is purely formal, i. e., independent of any content to which it may be applied. Logic, in this formal sense can not be considered rules of reasoning, though it may easily be employed as a tool in reasoning. Though such a logic was partially anticipated by Leibniz and others, the development of symbolic logic really began with the work of A. de Morgan (1806-71), who based logic on class inclusion; and G. Boole (1815-64), who tried to make logic a part of mathematics. The pivotal figures in the development of contemporary logic were: G. Frege (1848-1925), who introduced quantification and the formalization of logic; A. Whitehead and B. Russell, whose monumental *Principia Mathematica* (1910-13) attempted to derive all of mathematics from logic alone; and K. Gödel, who established the inherent limitations proper to any extended formal system. The formal logic that resulted from these efforts can best be understood in terms of levels.

The lowest level is the propositional (or sentential) calculus. Here propositions are treated as irreducible units. The relations that may obtain between propositions are systematized in terms of logical connectives, e. g., 'not', 'and', 'or', and 'implies', which depend only on the truth or falsity of the propositions and not on their meanings. A typical formalization of this logic postulates three axioms and one rule of inference from which one may derive *all* the logical truths proper to truth-functional combinations of propositions. These truths, viewed from within the system, are tautologies. They give no factual information but may serve as valid vehicles for inference. A slight extension of this system, based on the introduction of further axioms, reproduces the formal structure of Aristotelian logic.

Predicate calculus presupposes propositional calculus but adds the notion of quantification. That is, it can treat propositions as complex units which attribute a predicate to a subject and are qualified by 'some' or 'all'. This system can also be developed in a way that is complete and consistent. A further stage of development, one needed for the deduction of mathematics (i. e., the deduction of Peano's postulates for the natural numbers and techniques of extending this basis) requires higher order quantification. This involves predicates of predicates (or classes of classes) as well as first order predicates applied to subjects. This extended logic cannot be developed in a way that is both complete and consistent (Gödel's incompleteness theorem).

Logic in a broader sense, sometimes called 'logistic', includes both extension of the classical logic summarized above and non-classical logics. The most significant extension of logic (semiotics) treats formal logic as an object language which is discussed in various metalanguages. If the object language is considered a series of uninterpreted signs then one may introduce: a *syntactical* metalanguage, which states rules for concatenation (i. e., joining), formation and transformation of these signs; a *semantical* meta-language, which treats the meaning and interpretation of these signs; and a *pragmatic* metalanguage, which includes the subject using the logic and treats such questions as use and acceptance. It is often contended — and just as often disputed — that ordinary language serves as the ultimate metalanguage in interpreting formal logic.

Non-classical logics would include both those systems that disagree with some of the postulates of classical logic (e. g., Heyting's intuitive logic) and systems which attempt to extend the techniques of logic to new domains. Foremost among the latter are: *multi-valued logic*, which substitutes three or more values for the either 'true' or 'false' of classical logic; *modal logic*, which seeks to formulate a logic proper to propositions qualified by 'necessary' or 'possible'; and *deontic logic*, which seeks to formulate the logic of obligation, e. g., in ethics. The validity of each of these systems has been disputed. Though the role of logic in explanation has often been overstressed, e. g., by the logical positivists, there is no reasonable doubt about the facts that: contemporary logic represents a distinct advance over any logic preceding it; that it supplies a valuable, often indispensible, tool for the development of formal systems of thought; and that its technical formulations are of service in clarifying many philosophical problems.

EM

SYNTHESIS

Synthesis (Gr.: *synthesis*) literally means a "putting together." In philosophical terminology synthesis designates the unification of several ideas in order to make a complete conceptual structure; this is one of the most important functions of *consciousness. Accordingly, both the unifying activity and the whole produced by it can be called "*synthetic.*" — A synthesis, even though an activity for the most part unconscious, is already present in *intuition: The impressions received by the particular senses are joined together in the intuition of space by means of the *common sense* (*sensus communis*), complemented by imagination or memory on the basis of previous experiences and thus inserted into time; finally, they are combined into various "forms" or structures (*Sense Knowledge). — As a *method, synthesis is a conscious combination of conceptual structures into higher unities. In this sense it is the opposite of *analysis and its necessary completion. By means of synthesis the complex concept grows out of basic concepts; and by means of another kind of synthesis the *judgment grows out of concepts. Thus, if every concept can, with Aristotle, be called "a synthesis of concepts," still in a special way those concepts are termed "*synthetic judgments" in which the predicate adds something new to the notion of the subject; this new element is not something already contained in the notion of the subject, as is the case with the analytic judgment (*Analysis). A synthetic judgment is termed "synthetic *a posteriori" if the predicate is added on the basis of *experience; it is termed "synthetic *a priori" if it is added independently of experience and as a result of the insight that it necessarily follows from the content of the subject (*Knowledge, Principles of). With regard to the details of Kant's synthesis-doctrine: *Critical Philosophy. — Finally, by means of synthesis all particular knowledge is gathered together into the unity of one school or one point of view (*System), either as a *science or as a *Weltanschauung.

JdV

SYSTEM

A system is a multiplicity of ideas which are joined together according to one idea of *wholeness or according to one key idea. Neither one individual idea nor many unconnected ideas constitute a system. A system is established only through coherence and order according to a common principle of order by means of which a place and function is assigned to each part of the whole. Every science tries to systematize the results of its investigation. The principle according to which a body of knowledge is to be ordered is found either in the objects themselves or results from the way in which they are known or is imposed on the body of knowledge from the outside. The latter procedure produces a system only in an improper sense (= systematics). Mere systematics does not illumine the object itself, but it often helps to establish some order in the midst of a large body of knowledge. And it allows for much variation (cf. the systematization of plants according to non-essential characteristics).

If the ideas are arrived at not independently of each other through experience or direct insight — but rather by *deduction, then there is a fundamental relationship between them. Thus, all the propositions connected with this body of knowledge are either deduced or not deduced (basic systems, such as mathematics, logistics). The underived (self-evident or presupposed) propositions are called principles (axioms: *Knowledge, Principles of) and derived propositions are called theorems or theses. A demand is put on every thesis that it can be arrived at in a finite number of steps from a principle (= the impossibility of a regressus ad infinitum), since otherwise the thesis would be unfounded; for, every mediate proposition has validity only insofar as it is based on a principle. — The organization of ideas which the essential order, rooted in the objects themselves, gives expression to, results in a natural system (e. g., the Periodic Table of the elements). Some kind of system is a demand of reason itself which seeks unity and order in all multiplicity; and on the presupposition of metaphysical *idealism, it is also a demand of existence and reality. Striving for the natural system of all reality is the basic task of *philosophy. However, as Kurt Gödel has shown, a comprehensive system of all conceptual statements is impossible without including all the presuppositions outside of itself.

WB

T

TAUTOLOGY

Tautology is the term used for a judgment whose subject and predicate are identical not just in reality, but also conceptually. Tautology expresses the necessary and formal *identity between the subject and the predicate. Therefore, it is not meaningless. Every tautology is an analytic judgment, but the converse is not true. — In *symbolic logic the term "tautological" is given to logical structures which always give a "true" answer by reason of their form, no matter what variables are used. — In a derogatory sense, the use of different words in order to simulate another meaning or reason is said to be *tautological* (i. e., saying the same thing).

WB

TECHNOLOGY

Technology (Gr.: *téchnē*) in the ancient world and in the Middle Ages (*ars* = "art") meant (1) shaping of sensibly perceptible things in the service of some need or idea; therefore, it meant the ability to produce both the necessary (manufacture of things) and the beautiful (giving visibility to an idea). Taking that idea as basic, technology (2) also refers to the formal aspect of such shaping and to the laws governing it (e. g., the technology or technique of playing the piano). Technology (3) as opposed to *art is the exploitation of nature in order to satisfy man's needs. While handicraft (or manual technology) for a long time was limited to the use of hand-tools (= the means of bodily effectiveness; in the more restricted sense: without an increase of work-power) and so-called *work-machines* (= hand driven tools with an increase of work-power: for example, pulley, wedge), modern technology (4) (*machine technology*) has advanced to the use of *power tools* and machines (= tools driven by natural forces: for example, steam engines, electric motors, etc.). This progress was made possible only by greater knowledge of the laws of nature. Therefore, technology (4)

410

can be defined as the methodical utilization of natural resources and forces on the basis of the knowledge of nature, in order to take care of man's needs.

A *philosophy of technology* as a part of the philosophy of *culture should investigate the origin and conditions of technology in human nature; it should also look into the multiple influences technology itself has on man and on the concrete structuring of human life for the individual and for society in general. Even though technology offers many blessings we all enjoy and without it man's life and culture would no longer be possible at their present level of development, still we cannot fail to recognize a host of undesireable results; all of these, however, do not flow from the essence of technology, but often from a defective incorporation of it into the totality of human life. Partially necessary and partially avoidable or, through proper means, partially compromiseable results of technology were: the development of family economy into a factory economy, the separation of the laborer from his family, the accumulation of massive capital, the unequal opportunities for gain, the growth of the great cities, the multiplication of human needs, the preoccupation with machines and the resulting dangers to body and mind. The total independence or even domination of technology over the economy and over the other areas of human life (*technocracy*) necessarily leads to overproduction, to the enslavement of man to machines and to social disorganization. Technology is supposed to serve man, not dominate him.

WB

THEISM

Theism is the doctrine of God as a personal, transcendent being who called the world into existence out of nothingness by means of his creative act (*Creation). While *polytheism* assumes a multiplicity of divine beings, though often this is under the hegemony of one supreme god, and while *henotheism* in spite of the assumed variety of gods relates to one god in prayer or cult as if it were the only god, theism as monotheism in theory and cult adheres to one God only, beside whom there is no other nor can there be another. Consequently, it also rejects all forms of a contrary absolute principle that would seem to be the source of evil or matter (*Dualism). In contrast to *deism, it defends both God's conservation of all creatures and his constant cooperation with them as well as God's providence and the possibility of his extraordinary intervention in this world by means of revelation and miracles. Theism is clearly distinguished from *pantheism because of its strong emphasis on the substantial difference between God and the world and because of his personal nature. See also *God, Theology, Transcendence*.

MR

411

THEMATIC

The term "thematic" (or its negative "unthematic"), found principally in the works of German philosophers, signifies a special characteristic of human knowing and human *knowledge. A theme (Gr. *thema*) is that which is "put" or proposed; it is the stated subject of a discourse. In reference to knowledge "thematic" signifies that which is explicit, reflex, conceptually precise — it is the directly known content of an act of knowledge. "Unthematic" knowledge is just the opposite; it means that which is implicitly present in an express act of knowledge, that which accompanies a definite concept, that which is unreflexively present in any direct knowledge. Thus, when I know that "the book on the table is red," I know thematically that redness is a characteristic of the book on the table. There is also a great amount of unthematic or implicit knowledge contained in this affirmative judgment such as, for example, what a book is, that red is a color and (especially) that every object of knowledge and every act of knowledge is something that "is" or has being. Accordingly, because of the *transcendence of the human *spirit, a *metaphysics and a knowledge of Absolute Being is implied in a man's every act of knowing, willing and questioning. See also *Horizon, Question, Transcendental Method, Transcendence.*

KB

THEODICY

Theodicy (1) literally means the "justification of God," i. e., with regard to the objections that the unbeliever raises against God because of the many *evils in this world; the word itself was coined by Leibniz, and introduced into philosophy through the title of his work *Essais de Théodicée* (1710). Of course, it could seem presumptuous for man to try to "justify" God; however, not just because of the rash talk of atheists, but also because of the personal distress that even the best of men often suffer as a result of the apparent senselessness of evil, it cannot be a waste of time honestly to search for a solution to the tormenting question: How can evil be reconciled with the wisdom and goodness of God? However, a person should not make his belief in God depend on the solution to the problem of evil, since God's existence is attested to in many other ways independent of that (*God's Existence, Proofs for); moreover, man cannot, as it were, demand an accounting from God with regard to the Why and Wherefore of what he does and permits in particular cases. A solution, especially a purely philosophical one, can, only under the presupposition of faith in God, show in very general terms that God (no matter how obscure his ways may remain to us in particular) in his power, wisdom and goodness directs all suffering and evil finally to good.

THEOLOGY

The dualistic solutions of the problem, however, are impossible; for they attempt to trace evil back to a second basic principle of evil that is wholly independent of the good God (*Dualism, *Manicheanism). In this way God's infinity and omnipotence are in effect denied. The metaphysical *optimism of Leibniz is also untenable; he claims that the present world is the best possible world and that all of the evil found in this world is the smallest amount possible. But against Leibniz' position is the fact that God without doubt, through the use of his omnipotence, could eliminate each particular evil in this world without having to permit even greater evil somewhere else, as Leibniz maintains. Therefore, God remains free in his choice of possible worlds; he is under no necessity to create the best possible world and in fact there cannot be such a world, since God in his omnipotence could always create a better world. His infinite goodness demands just this: that the world which actually comes into being through his will as a whole is predominantly good and that therefore every evil in this world ultimately finds its justification in a higher good to which it is ordered.

God cannot wish any evil as an end in itself. Moreover, the ordination to good is different in the case of physical evil from what it is in *moral evil. God cannot only permit physical evil, but he can also directly will it as a means of achieving higher pruposes; on the other hand, he can never directly will moral evil because it contradicts the basic meaning of creation: the glory of God. But it is not impossible for God to *permit* moral evil, i. e., not to hinder it, although he knows that it will occur and has the power to prevent it. Even this permission of moral evil is always justified by a greater good which also pertains to the moral order. If it were absolutely necessary for God to prevent all evil, then his freedom would be unduly restricted and many positive values would be wholly excluded (e. g., courage, patience, mercy, repentance, redemption). Right here we find the greatest victory of good, namely, that God is able to direct the worst evil to good. A firm faith in the final victory of good — a victory guaranteed by our turning towards God, should give us the strength, in spite of the apparent senselessness and cruelty of life, to persevere in patience, in the struggle against moral evil and in the *hope* of final salvation.

In the 19th century the word "theodicy" (2) was used to refer to the philosophical study of God or natural *theology. However, at present this use of the word is less and less common.

JdV

THEOLOGY

Theology is the science about *God. If it begins with the natural knowledge of man, then it is called natural theology, *theodicy or sometimes the philosophy of God. Actually, it is that part of *metaphysics which investigates the existent under the aspect of its ultimate principle — a principle which escapes simple sense perception. Its object is God: his existence, his essence and his activity. The possibility of natural theology as a science rests in the fact that we can know with certainty the existence of God (*God's Existence, Demonstration of), that we can make conceptual statements about him (*God, Idea of) and then judge their validity. It is clear to every intelligent person that the study of God does not give us knowledge about God which is in every respect the same as the knowledge we derive from the study of the objects of our daily sense experience. Our conceptual statements about God do not give us an adequate knowledge of him, but only analogical knowledge (*Analogy). Two basic principles are operative in every judgment of natural theology: that which belongs to an existent as such belongs also to God, though in his own way; and: that which belongs to a contingent existent as contingent, must necessarily be denied of God (*Negative Theology).

Supernatural or *revelational theology* (this is what is meant when one speaks simply of "theology") bases its statements ultimately on supernatural *revelation which has come from God. Its task is, on the one hand, to show that revelation is a historical fact (fundamental theology) and, on the other hand, to expound the content of revelation from the theological sources (positive theology) and to develop its conceptual and scientific presentation (speculative theology or dogma). The object of supernatural theology is God, not so much as the ultimate source of nature but especially as the God of eternal salvation and as the founder of the visible means of salvation: the Church. — Theology as such is as little opposed to philosophy as *faith is to reason. However, theology uses philosophy for its own purposes without hindering it in the pursuit of its own end. It also judges philosophy, as it does all human knowledge, according to the measure of its own higher knowledge. This does not at all imply a disparagement of reason, since in this case reason is not judged according to a standard that is totally foreign to it but according to the measure of the infinite mind of God.

WB

THEORY

Theory (1) is generally used in opposition to praxis; accordingly, theory (1) is just knowledge or mere consideration of something, while *praxis* means every kind of activity outside of knowledge itself, especially activity directed to the outside world. However, there is no praxis (either in the ethical or technical sense) without theory. For, all praxis is bound by antecedent conditions and placed in an antecedent order with which it must reckon if it is to be successful. In the thought of Aristotle (and similarly also in Kant) the expressions "praxis" and "practical" were used to refer to the moral acts of the will, and the words "*techne*" and "technical" were used for the activity directed to external objects (*Technology). Closely related to theory (1) are *meditation* (heightened attention of the mind directed to one object) and *speculation. — In modern philosophy of science, theory (2) stands in opposition both to the finding of *facts and to the *hypothesis. In the realm of physical science, a unified, non-contradictory, mathematical (if possible) description of the facts as well as an explanation of them based on necessary laws and causes follows the confirmation of the facts by means of experience and experiment. However, as long as such an explanation is possible but does not really exclude another explanation, it remains a more or less probable hypothesis. Only when the proof is adduced that the given explanation is the only one that corresponds to the facts, does that explanation reach the level of a theory (2). A theory is thought to be confirmed when it leads to the discovery of new facts. It should be noted that often it is not the particular propositions of a theory but only the theory as a whole that can be verified in experience. When a theory is improved and further developed, the former understanding of the theory does not become false; rather, it becomes apparent that it was not wholly adequate. Those parts of a theory which are co-affirmed with it (either because unseen or because of philosophical prejudices) but which are not necessary for drawing valid conclusions from that which is observed, are themselves not confirmed by a theory that is otherwise true and certain.

WB

THEOSOPHY

Theosophy seeks to cultivate tendencies which, say its advocates, are naturally given in every man, in order to arrive at a vision of God and in this vision to find a mysterious knowledge of all things. We must distinguish between theosophy in general as a current that runs through the entire history of philosophy, and modern theosophy which has been influenced chiefly by *Buddhism and Hinduism. After leaving the society of theosophy, R. Steiner founded his own version called "anthroposophy" which depended more on the Egyptian and Greek mystery cults. — Modern theosophy is a form of *pantheism. It claims that the world is composed of a series of *emanations* which are various stages between spirit and matter, but there is no essential difference between these levels. The emanations are presented in a fantastic cosmogony, which is accompanied by a no less fantastic view of history. Man is an unstable composition of seven different substances of which four belong to the material level and three to the spiritual. The unifying bond is the "manas" (according to Steiner the "ego") which is essentially one in all men and is united with matter only temporarily — during earthly life. After death good and bad deeds work themselves out in new reincarnations, either in lower or higher forms of existence, which can finally lead to the liberation of the "divine seed" in each man and to its entrance into *nirvana* (*Transmigration of Souls). — In morality the theosophists follow the modernized forms of Buddhism. The law of brotherly love (in the Buddhistic sense) as well as bizarre forms of asceticism are primary concerns. Personal prayer is rejected and the salvation of one's soul depends completely on man. Theosophy and anthroposophy stand in direct contradiction to the basic doctrines of Christianity. Ideas and symbols borrowed from Christianity have been emptied of their original Christian meaning. Theosophy and anthroposophy cannot lay claim to any scientific validity. See also *Occultism, Mysticism.*

WB

THING

Thing is related philologically to "think" and thus means: that which is thought. The Latin word for this is *res* which comes from the same root as *reor* and thus means: that which is spoken. We can distinguish three basic meanings to the word "thing." First of all, it designates the concrete, spatio-temporal individual being that we ecounter through our sense experience; thus we speak of "the world of things." Indeed, even man can be called a thing; usually, however, we oppose man to the thing-world because as a spiritual person we do not consider him to be a mere thing. In a wider sense, the *object we are speaking or thinking about, or the object we make a judgment about, is also called a thing. Understood in this way, "thing" is equivalent to *something*; it includes both the abstract (e. g., number, justice) and the supra-sensible (God). Here the epistemological question can be raised: Is the *thing-in-itself accessible to us? In the deepest metaphysical sense, *res* belongs to the transcendental basic determinations of existence (*Transcendentals) and so of absolutely every existent. Being very closely related to the "existent," "something" looks to the static essence of the existent, while "existent" stresses the dynamic aspect of existence.

JBL

THING-IN-ITSELF

Thing-in-itself is a philosophical expression introduced by Kant; it signifies the thing, the existent, as it exists independently of our knowledge; therefore it signifies the actual existent, in contrast to all *appearance which does not exist "in-itself" but only "for-us." Kant also calls the thing-in-itself a *noumenon* in contrast to a phenomenon, i. e., an object of the mind in contrast to an object of the senses; he calls it a noumenon because it can be presented only to intellectual intuition, not to sense intuition. According to Kant, we can indeed think of the thing-in-itself, but we cannot "know" it or grasp it in any essential way. Thus, Kant's *critical philosophy is really a *phenomenalism opposed to *realism.

JdV

THINKING

Thinking is the non-intuitive mode of knowing that is ordered to the existent as such and to its essential relationships. It takes place in the human spirit in different acts of comprehension (seeing relationships, forming concepts, drawing conclusions) and of position-taking (questions, doubts, certitudes, etc.) in order to arrive at a final (or at least intended final) grasp of some reality in an assent of the judgment. In a rhythmic pattern human thinking moves from the peaceful contemplation of a known reality to the search for ever-new insights (*discursive thinking*) and from the merely imitative understanding of a common truth through a grasp of its logical connections to ideas developed by others (*reproductive thinking*) to more independent, *creative thinking* (inspiration; *Intuition).

There is an essential difference between thinking and *sense knowledge. For, thinking is ordered not only to the sensible but also to the non-sensible, and in the sensible it grasps the whatness of the thing that escapes the senses. It follows not only the laws of blindly working associations and complexes (= *subjective necessity of thought*), but it orientates itself ultimately by the necessary inner relationships of the objects themselves (= *logical or objective necessity of thought*). Yet, in spite of its manifold dependence on matter, it is not, as sense knowledge is, an activity that is directly produced by matter; rather, it is spiritual (*Spirit). Aiming for the real *existence of its objects and finding therein its formal object, it is somehow able, even though frequently only in an analogous way, to reach everything that in any way possesses existence. Therefore it has an unlimited horizon within which it operates. — Nevertheless, in many ways human thinking remains bound by the body-soul unity of sense knowledge (and so to matter and to the realm of the subconscious) in all of its acts. The contents of almost all of our concepts are derived from sense experience. Every act of understanding that is in any way complex and all creative thinking are subject to the influence of complexes and associations; and often this is so much the case that new "intuitions" or "inspiration" seem to be hardly more than a product of man's subconscious life. Yet these subconscious processes

417

are not real thinking; productive mental labor occurs in the conscious insight into spiritual and intelligible relationships.

Further, human thinking is conditioned by a "psychological *a priori," insofar as the typical or the accidentally individual peculiarities of the "mental temperament," the peculiarity of the acquired and habitual objects of thought (into which anything new will be logically incorporated), have a definite influence (which often goes unnoticed, but for that very reason is even more significant); this applies both to the process of the discursive search for insights and to their intelligent formation. Here also belongs the special character of a formal mode of thinking which tends to be more concrete or more abstract, the more synthetic or the more critical mind, the more tenacious or the more pliable person, the more integrated or the more disintegrated personality, and finally the absolute dedication to truth. Therefore, the more human thinking is concerned with the basic facts of life and the more it is searching for ultimate values, it is by that very fact more a "personal activity" that is supported by the whole human personality. Just as the type of personality influences one's thinking, so also, on the other hand, is a formal training to live by the truth, to be reasonably critical of oneself, to strive for clarity and logical order, to be open and docile, of utmost importance both for the balanced development of the whole personality and as a guide in finding objective truth. — According to Kant, thinking (in contrast to knowledge) means every use of concepts whether an object is thereby determined or not; in contrast to intuition it means the activity of determining through concepts the given multiplicity of things and of thereby establishing the unity of an object — all of which is equivalent to knowledge.

AW

THOMISM

Thomism is the philosophical-theological system of Thomas Aquinas and his school which has continued since the 14th century and includes important representatives right down to the present. If one understands by Thomism (in the broad sense) the most basic philosophical-theological positions of Aquinas, then in this sense many contemporary Catholic philosophers and theologians can be called "Thomists" (e. g., J. Maritain, E. Gilson, E. Coreth, K. Rahner, etc.). However, Thomism (in the narrow sense) often means Thomism as opposed to *Suarezianism; in the most limited sense it means the doctrine of *praedeterminatio physica* (= Bánēz) (*Concurrence).

In sharp contrast to the *Augustinianism of the 13th century, Thomas Aquinas boldly adopted the basic insights of Aristotle in the areas of epistemology and metaphysics. He reinterpreted the Augustinian view of knowledge as a kind of contact with the divine ideas. Man himself produces his first concepts not out of his own mind alone, but out of his mind and his sense experiences by means of the spontaneous power of the agent intellect; thus he achieves certitude regarding the first principles of existence without any special divine assistance. Metaphysics is founded on the analogy of being. Thomas applies the notion of act and potency not just to form and matter, where the latter (considered by itself) is thought of as pure potency, but also to the relationship between existence and essence in finite things: here the limitation of these things is grounded in the potentiality of the essence. The principle of individuation is spatio-temporally determined matter. The immortal soul is also the form and, in fact, the only essential form of the body, so that man results from that form and matter as his two essential principles. The real distinction between essence and existence, the positions on individuation and the soul as the only essential form — these ideas are characteristic of *Thomism in the narrow sense.* — With certain demonstrable knowledge man proceeeds from creatures to God himself — the first mover, the first cause, the absolutely necessary being (*esse subsistens, actus purus*), the principle of all order and purpose who at the same time is the final end of all creation and especially of man. Still, these characteristics of our God-idea are only analogous, i. e., they are determinable by a similarity with creatures that also includes an essential dissimilarity. Human knowledge does not contradict belief in supernatural revelation but is really its presupposition, just as it is also perfected by revelation. The end of man is eternal happiness which consists of the vision of God in the next life (primacy of the intellect over the will).

In his ethics and social philosophy Thomas Aquinas combines the rich insights of the Aristotelian doctrine on virtues with the Christian-Augustinian attitude: he also employs, but not without criticism, some Stoic and neo-Platonic ideas. Virtue is a matter of moderation and compromise between irrational opposites. It consists in maintaining the rational order which, as the expression of created being and its goal-orientation, corresponds to the divine will. In contrast to the Stoics, Thomas places a positive value on human sense desires. Marriage and private property in their essential aspects do not depend on the caprice of state laws. Civil society with its goal of the common good is an expression of the natural moral law; its authority does not come from the Church, but rather is rooted in the natural law.

JoS

TIME

Time is one kind of duration. Duration means continuance in existence. That which has no existence also has no duration. The duration of unchangeable being is called *eternity; the duration of changeable being is called "time." Scholastic philosophers make a further distinction between time and *aevum* according to which *time* signifies the kind of duration of corporeal creatures and *aevum* signifies the kind of duration of spiritual creatures. Just as *space exhibits a certain juxtaposition in extension, so time manifests a certain *succession* in duration; this succession signifies a constant movement of time from the past through the present into the future. The *past* is that which is no more; but the past is often preserved objectively in the effects it has left or subjectively in one's *memory. The *present* is that which lies between the past and the future — or what is existing right now. In the strict sense, only an indivisible part of time — the present moment, is actually present. Things and events which do not yet exist but will exist are said to be *future*; these things are often anticipated by our expectation. A *moment* of time is an indivisible element or part of time. Since the movement of time is constant, it cannot be constituted out of moments or points of time. The succession of time, which is conditioned by the changes of temporal things, is directed from the past into the future and is irreversible; and its course is firmly fixed by the relationship between cause and effect. Just as each thing and each event has its own duration, so also does it have its own concrete time or *physical* time. In addition to the time proper to each thing there is also such a thing as *imaginary* time; this is a representation of an empty, general schema in which all temporal events can be arranged in order — an empty scheme of possible happenings. It is an abstracted, temporal duration which is imagined as existing for itself and it is thought of as a smoothly flowing, one-dimensional continuum without beginning or end which is analogous to absolute space. The *simultaneousness* or coexistence of events means that the events are coordinated with the same point or part of imaginary time.

A worked-out position on the origin and validity of the time-concept is called a *theory of time*. Physical time and duration are real determinations of temporal things. Imaginary time is the result of a protracted conceptual process and as such it has no reality. It is a *being of the mind. But since this idea includes duration as an objective element, with its help it is possible to make objectively valid judgments about temporal situations and relationships. — The *measurement of time* means the comparison of one time with an arbitrarily chosen unit of time as the measure (e. g., second, minute, hour). Every periodic occurrence can be used as a unit of time, as the alteration of day and night, the swing of a pendulum, etc. — A distinction should be made between chronological time and experienced time which is a correlate of our perception. The temporal duration of inner experiences of *psychic time* is immediately perceived by us. Because of special psychological circumstances we may misjudge the length of various time-units.

420

TOLERANCE

The primary concern of Aristotle is *physical* time which he considers to be a succession in the field of motion; he defines it as the measure of motion according to a before and an after. — Kant takes as the basis of his considerations Newton's concept of imaginary time and sees in this concept an a priori form of *intuition which makes our ordered experience of the world possible. This form, according to him, has "empirical reality" and "transcendental ideality" (*Critical Philosophy). — For Heidegger time is "the present laying itself bare, i. e., the exposed expressed in the 'now'." It is "before all subjectivity and objectivity, because it is the condition of the possibility of this 'before'." (*Existential Philosophy). — The *theory of *relativity* is concerned with observable time. Many of its statements about time are really about the measurement of time.

NJ

TOLERANCE

Tolerance (Lt.: *tolerare* = to put up with) is the attitude of a person who will bear with the philosophical and moral convictions of others which he considers to be false or even objectionable; nor will he try to suppress their legitimate expressions. Such a position means neither the approval of such convictions nor indifference with regard to truth and goodness, nor is it founded necessarily on *agnosticism.

The necessity of tolerance in modern society is based on the *freedom of the person, to whom it belongs from personal insight, to judge for himself in the questions of truth and falsity, and about what is morally good or evil; it is also based on the incontrovertible fact of man's almost universal capacity to err. Therefore tolerance is demanded by justice which requires that each one receive what is his due. This right is not the right of error (for rights inhere in persons), but of the erring person or of the person whom many others think is in the wrong. The individual has no right to embrace error as error, but he does have a right to his own convictions which flow from his experience; in this situation error must sometimes be respected, since there is no other way to protect this particular right.

This personal right is not contradicted by the faith-conviction, based on *authority, which is required by Christianity (and by other religions), as long as the faith in religious authority itself remains a free, unforced act; it is important that this act be posited on the basis of a personal judgment or — as in the case of all primitive peoples — on the basis of an unopposed, commonly accepted world view of the people in question. — Tolerance recognizes a limitation where the principle of tolerance itself, i. e., the right of the person to act according to his own rights, is directly attacked. Since personal rights are not unlimited but are actually limited by the rights of other persons, activities must be opposed which are undertaken with an appeal to freedom of *conscience, but which are clearly opposed to the right of others or of society. On the other hand, no one is to be forced to act in a way which is contrary to the judgment of his own conscience; exceptions to this principle should be rare and only when the rights of others or of society have been flagrantly violated (e. g., the murderer who is imprisoned "against his will").

WB

TRADITIONALISM

According to the strict traditionists (De Bonald) the individual mind by itself is not capable of arriving at the knowledge of any truth. For this, it needs divine *revelation which is handed on to it by the tradition of the human race. In particular, man comes to conceptual thinking only by means of divinely given speech. Bautain, Bonnetty, Ventura and others restricted traditionalism to moral and religious truths. De Lamennais appeals not to divine authority, but to the universal reason of mankind. — Traditionalism is based on the false presupposition that a *metaphysics growing out of the use of human reason is impossible. In order to establish itself it must argue in a circle.

JS

TRANSCENDENCE

Transcendence (Lat.: *transcendere*) literally means: surmounting, surpassing. This basic meaning varies considerably depending upon how it is used. — From the point of view of the metaphysics of knowledge, transcendence (1) means independence from consciousness. The object surpasses the act of knowledge and stands over against it as something autonomous which was not posited by that act. This relationship is also true within the realm of self-consciousness; for, an act of knowledge which grasps an act of the will merely discovers it as something independent of itself. And it is particularly true that the external world surpasses our consciousness which encounters it as something already given in reality. — When referred to our human experience, transcendence means the supra-sensible and the sensibly non-experienceable. The essential nature of all visible things and everything spiritual surpasses our sensible-intuitive experience. Therefore, these things are *supra-sensible* and so transcendent (2), but they are not absolutely non-experienceable. For, through reflection we experience our own thinking and willing in their existential reality. And even with regard to the essences of things we can speak of experiences insofar as they are given in man's intuitive grasp of the real. Nevertheless, the essences derived from intuition, the principles involved and the spiritual as such surpass all experience, because these things can be grasped only by means of a new intellectual act added to experience (e. g., abstraction, essential insight, inference). Transcendence (3) in the sense of imperceptibility also belongs here. Thinking directed to non-experienceable reality is called *speculation.

In the order of existence transcendence (4) means supra-worldliness or above and beyond this world. Man's soul participates in this other-worldliness insofar as it surpasses the visible world by reason of its spirituality, although it is inserted into the world as the essential form of the body. The pure spirit which is neither a member nor a part of the world is a perfect expression of other-worldliness. The transcendence (5) or supra-worldliness of God is incomparable, for his infinity ineffably surpasses the world and everything finite, but at the same time his equally incomparable *immanence to the world must be affirmed by reason of his same infinity. Transcendence (4 and 5) points to transcendence (2 and 3) because supra-worldliness brings with itself also the strictest kind of supra-sensibility and imperceptibility. — From the point of view of formal logic, transcendence (6) belongs to those most universal concepts which rise above all the categories and all the particular orders of existence and so include in their extension absolutely everything. These are being and the so-called *transcendentals. — We will just mention briefly mathematical transcendence (7) which is attributed to a quantity that exceeds algebraic quantities (e.g., the number π).

At the present time *existential philosophy has rediscovered transcendence. Karl Jaspers speaks of existence as the all-embracing and he sees human existence constituted by transcendence, i. e., by opening oneself up to the absolute. Heidegger considers transcendence as the act of the individual existent going beyond itself to the world as such, to the totality of existent things, and even to existence itself, although it still remains undetermined what this existence is.

JBL

TRANSCENDENTAL

Transcendental means literally (1) that which is related to the transcendent and, according to the way it is used, to the transcendent that is opposed to the material world (*Transcendence). In this sense "transcendental philosophy" is the same thing as metaphysics. Even Kant uses the word in this meaning, as when he calls the application of the basic principles of pure understanding beyond the limits of experience "transcendental." — In neo-scholastic philosophy the word "transcendental" — as distinguished from "transcendent" — is usually used in a logical sense. While the transcendent is that existent which lies beyond the act of knowledge or consciousness or the world, the word "transcendental" signifies the concepts which, because of their universality, surpass the *categories or at least cannot be restricted to one category alone. Thus, the concept of the existent itself and the concepts of those essential attributes that belong to all existents are called above all "transcendental" (*Transcentals); Aquinas, Scotus and Suarez for the most part, however, in this case use *transcendens* instead of *transcendentalis*. A relation is called transcendental if it cannot be included in the category of *relation because of its necessary connection with the absolute determinations of existence. Since it is precisely the transcendental concepts that have decisive importance for the determination of supra-sensible reality and that alone are of any use in expressing the reality of God, it follows that transcendental in the logical sense has an essential relationship to the transcendent or metaphysical reality.

The word "transcendental" suffered an important change in meaning at the hands of Kant, even though a minimal connection with the original meaning is retained. Kant's whole investigation begins with the question: Is metaphysics as a science possible? According to him, in order to solve this problem it is unavoidably necessary to investigate the actual ways in which our knowing powers operate and how they are constituted in the essential make-up of the subject before all contingent experience (* A Priori). Thus, the transcendental question about the possibility of metaphysics takes on a new meaning of transcendental (3) in the sense of Kant's definition: "I call all knowledge transcendental which is concerned not just with objects, but with our way of knowing objects, insofar as this way of knowing is possible a priori" (*Critique of Pure Reason*, B 25). In this sense Kant speaks of Transcendental Aesthetics, Transcendental Logic, or simply of Transcendental Philosophy. In a similar vein, Marechal applies the term "transcendental" to the scholastic investigations into the formal object and the purposefulness of the knowing powers. Then the term "transcendental" is taken from the reflection on the a priori conditions of knowledge and is applied to the conditions themselves. In this sense the conditions of knowledge as such (i. e., those that make objective knowledge possible) which are rooted in the subject before all experience and all actual knowledge are called "transcendental" (4). Thus, Kant himself speaks of *transcendental imagination* and in the same way the a priori forms of sense and understanding and finally the subject himself as the ultimate point of unity of all knowledge are called "transcendental" (Kant: "the transcendental union of apperception," i. e., of consciousness). Since for Kant the transcendental investigation leads to the conclusion that only objects of experience can be known by means of the a priori forms, the transcendental takes on for him a certain opposition to the transcendent. Still we should not overlook the fact that it retains relations to the transcendent: By using the categories the transcendent can at least be thought about, even though, because of a lack of the proper intuition, it cannot be known; and the transcendental ideas are essentially related to the unconditioned, the metaphysical; and even if the metaphysical cannot be given and therefore cannot be known, still it is rightly assumed as a *postulate of practical reason.

JdV

TRANSCENDENTAL METHOD

Transcendental method is a phrase that refers to a way of doing *metaphysics. Metaphysics is the science of being *as being* (or: the science of all existing things under the aspect of their existence). Until the time of Immanuel Kant most Western metaphysics was object-oriented: it studied motion, change, substance, accident, the finite, the infinite, etc. Kant looked inward to the human act of knowing and correctly saw that before the act occurs there are certain conditions of the possibility of the act (a priori) and the object, without which the particular act of knowing cannot be adequately explained. A philosophy that proceeds in this way he called "*transcendental" and so this approach to metaphysics is called "the transcendental method."

Seeing a connection between Kant and the philosophy of Thomas Aquinas, Joseph Maréchal in the 20th century developed the transcendental method within the context of a modern scholastic philosophy that attempted both to be a true metaphysics and at the same time to come to grips with the contemporary problematic of a subject-oriented philosophy. His efforts have been continued and further developed by such thinkers as A. Marc, A. Brunner, K. Rahner, B. J. F. Lonergan and E. Coreth.

The transcendental method begins with the critical examination of an act of knowledge (e. g., affirmation — Maréchal; personal encounter — Brunner; judgment — Lonergan; question — Rahner and Coreth). By means of *reduction* one shows the conditions of the possibility of the act (e. g., openness to being); then, through the application of *deduction* a certain necessity is found to be present in human knowing and willing. Thus an on-going dialectic between *conceptual knowledge* and the *act of knowing* is found to be operative in man's grasp of and for the real. It soon becomes apparent that a certain pre-grasp of the *absolute is implied in every act of human, spiritual knowing and willing. Accordingly, the transcendental method facilitates the grounding of metaphysics in existence and in the absolute.

Coreth, in an advance over Rahner, begins his metaphysics with the *question which, when reflecting upon itself, becomes the question of the question. Thus the starting point — the question — mediates the method of metaphysics in such a way that nothing is presupposed, neither the object nor the method nor even logic itself. — See also *Metaphysics, Transcendental*.

KB

TRANSCENDENTALS

Transcendentals is the name given to those attributes which flow immediately and necessarily from the nature of existence and therefore accompany it inseparably in all of its manifestations. Just like *existence itself, they are not limited to a particular area of existents; rather, they surpass or transcend all the limited orders of existence. They show forth the inner self-revelation of existence which develops and manifests its nature in them. In the course of history it has become increasingly clear which attributes or determinations belong in this class. Since Thomas Aquinas three have been generally accepted: unity, truth, goodness. In recent decades more and more philosophers have been inclined to add a fourth transcendental: *beauty. There is a certain proportion here which can be stated as follows: to the degree that an existent possesses existence it also possesses these four characteristics; and conversely, to the degree that an existent possesses these four characteristics it also possesses existence.

We will now try to elucidate each of the transcendentals. Because of its *unity the existent is self-contained and set off from everything else. As is apparent from the comparison between inorganic matter and a man, when there is an increase in the level of existence there is also an increase in unity; for, while the truly individual thing is very difficult to recognize in physical matter, man as a person manifests a clearly defined individuality. A complete lack of unity or absolute fragmentation is equivalent to *nothing. — *Truth and goodness (*Value) mean that the existent being because of its existence is ordered to the knowing and willing of spirit, and that it can be grasped by spirit because of the essential relationship between them. The same principle holds here: the greater fullness of existence a particular existent thing possesses, the more closely it is related to spirit; the more it participates in the intelligibility of spirit, the more it offers goals to spirit for its own fulfillment. Nothingness or a complete lack of all existence is totally foreign to spirit. — *Beauty is not to be arranged alongside the other transcendentals, for it grows out of them as their fulfillment. It consists in the accord of unity, truth and goodness to which the harmonious mutual penetration of intuitive knowing and satisfied willing corresponds. Existence and spirit achieve rest in beauty because there they have completely found themselves. Some degree of this must everywhere be realized, since otherwise the existent would be completely alienated from itself and would fall into nothingness. — Along with this picture of existence a very definite image of God is given. For, since God is that existent who subsists in his own infinite fullness, from this point of view he manifests himself as the absolute perfection of unity, truth, goodness and beauty itself. — Those modes and differences of existence can be characterized as transcendentals in the wider sense which surpass the *categories and which belong to *existence necessarily, but only disjunctively, as finite and infinite, contingent and necessary, etc.

JBL

TRANSMIGRATION OF SOULS

The belief in the transmigration of souls (metempsychosis) has appeared under different forms among the primitive peoples, in the view of the Pythagoreans, in Plato and others. Since the Upanishads this idea has been fundamental for the Indian religions (*Vedanta, Philosophy of.) According to it, after the death of a man his soul must animate another body, whether it be the body of a man, an animal, or a plant; all depends on the fate the soul has merited for itself during its former life. The law according to which merit and guilt necessarily lead to a corresponding reincarnation (Palingenesis) is called Karma. Accordingly, even the present life is not viewed as the first life for this individual, but the pre-existence of the soul is assumed. The teaching on the transmigration of souls is based on the alleged recollections of certain seers of a former life. However, the basic reason, which even Plato brought forth, is the impossibility of reconciling in any other way the unequal fate of different men with the demands of justice. In the pantheistic systems the necessity and transcendence of creation are also appealed to; for, they seem to demand a beginningless and endless rhythm of procession from and return to the Absolute and so to require a circle of sequence of births (= Samsara). — *Buddhism also teaches rebirth as the way of continuing one's existence, but this is done without personal identity. — In a theistic metaphysics the supposition of metempsychosis is not necessary, since the dissimilarity of destiny flows from the loving free will of the creator who places his creatures in different life-situations independently of their merits or demerits; it is their own task to live morally in these circumstances in order to come to another, final state which statisfies the requirements of justice. — See also Soul, Immorality.

WB

TRUTH

Truth in the broadest sense is a similarity or agreement between spirit (spiritual knowing) and existence (adaequatio intellectus et rei); in the most perfect sense it is a fully mutual permeation of spirit and existence. — Our first encounter with truth is in the truth of our own knowledge; this *truth of knowledge (logical truth)* belongs properly to the *judgment and consists in this, that thinking assimilates itself to existence insofar as thinking expresses the *objective reality as it is. Our human truth, therefore, is not normative for existence; in fact, it is rather measured by existence itself (at least in theoretical knowledge). It affirms that thinking is determined by existence. This correspondence does not require that thinking present the object from every possible aspect nor in this sense must it be an *adequate knowledge*; rather, an *inadequate knowledge* is sufficient, if only the aspects and characteristics of the object (which are grasped in the judgment) are actually present in the object. In other words, truth demands only an assimilation (*adaequatio*) to the here-and-now grasped formal *object. — Real truth is *"universally valid,"* i. e., it holds good for every knowing mind; what is true for one mind cannot be false for another. In this sense every truth is *"absolute"* and so there is no such thing as *"relative truth,"* i. e., there is no truth that varies intrinsically according to the differences of knowing subjects (*Relativism). — Analogously to the truth of the judgment, a concept can also be said to be true insofar as it presupposes a true judgment; moreover, even a sense perception can be termed true insofar as it leads to a true judgment because of its correspondence to reality.

To be distinguished from the truth of knowledge is the *truth of existence (ontological* and, according to some, *ontic truth)* which belongs to the existent itself; such truth affirms a conformity of existence to spiritual knowledge. Truth in the sense of actual correspondence with the human mind is not essential to the finite existent. In this sense, we speak, for example, of "true gold" and mean that the designated metal really is what it is thought to be, while "false gold" is something that shines like gold but is not actually gold. When the truth of existence along with oneness and goodness are reckoned among the *transcendentals (i. e., pertaining to every existent without exception), what is meant first of all is the conformity of every existent to thinking; for, by reason of this conformity it can become an object of thought. In this the truth of existence is established for us as a transcendental determination of being in such a way that we find our human minds ordered to existing things without any limitation. In the order of existence this intelligibility of all being is conditioned in such wise that all non-divine being is fashioned after the ideas in God. Thus, the truth of existence ultimately means that every existent is measured by a divine idea and in this sense is spiritualized. This valid *idealism signals the decisive rejection of all *materialism. — Creaturely truth of knowledge and truth of existence have their ultimate existential foundation in *divine truth* where existence and spiritual knowing are perfectly one; the expression "God is light" emphasizes this in a figurative way.

Truth *in the moral sense* means the agreement of speach with one's inner conviction, and so the *truthfulness* of speech (*Lie). "Truth in itself," in the sense of *logical transcendentalism*, does not mean the truth of existence, but a truth that is supposed to be independent of both all knowledge and all real existence. For example, one conceives of a mathematical proposition as being independent of all thinking. Some philosophers arrived at this erroneous concept because they assumed that the logical form of the judgement (*subject-copula-predicate*) is transcendent to the act of thinking (therefore the name "logical transcendentalism"). — According to the truth-concept of the existentialists (Kierkegaard, Jaspers: *Existential Philosophy) real truth is the only truth that is achieved in the free search of the individual person who is seized with the passion of interiority. This truth alone is absolutely valid, but for this very reason it is not accessible to everyone and it is not universally valid; accordingly, universally valid truth, which remains in the realm of the universal, is not unconditionally valid. The oversight here is that the universal is not just a categorical projection of an absolute *consciousness; rather, it reproduces the essential order of the existent — an order that also permeates the existence of the individual man. But it should be remembered that the subjective performance alone is no absolute guarantee of truth; for, truth has absolute validity only inasmuch as it is a knowledge of existence.

JdV

TRUTH, DOUBLE

The doctrine of a double truth, first proposed in Latin Averroism and then later by Pietro Pomponazzi (1462-1525), says that the opposite to what is held theologically as a truth of faith can be true philosophically. In more recent times the Modernists taught something very similar; thus, they claimed that the denial of certain truths (e. g., the resurrection of Christ) on the basis of historical research can be reconciled with the acceptance of them in the act of faith. But genuine *truth cannot contradict truth. The theory of double truth really means, in the last analysis, that the character of genuine truth is removed from the teaching of faith and that they merely retain the value of a symbolic representation.

JdV

TRUTH, NORM OF

The norm of truth is the measure or criterion that makes it possible to distinguish a true judgment from a false one. The question as to whether a judgment is true or false is decided by whether or not it is based on an *objective reality . The nature of this grounding differs according to the objects being dealt with. It is the task of the particular science and its methodology to establish the conditions of this grounding. But in a universal theory of knowledge, while presupposing these particular norms of truth, the question regarding the universal and ultimate norms of truth must be raised. Here it is no longer a question of which objective realities a judgment is based on, but rather how any objective reality must be presented to a knower so that he can distinguish a true judgment from a false one and thus judge with *certitude. Therefore, the universal norm of truth leads to certitude only by concretizing a particular norm of truth. Since a judgment is true only if it agrees with the objective reality to which it is related, and since certitude about it is possible only if the objective reality manifests itself to the one judging, it follows that the universal norm of truth is *evidence. The other norms of truth that have been proposed all break down because they are either not universal or, as subjective attitudes, they offer no guarantee of the truth.

JS

U

UNDERSTANDING

Understanding is the mode of intellectual grasping that corresponds to the objective *sense (according to all of its nuances). Accordingly it is a question of the illumination of the external, that of itself is not intelligible, from its inner ground of reality. Three steps gradually lead down to a deeper level. *Semantic understanding* is concerned with sensible signs whose meaning it either grasps immediately or only after an explanation. A special importance pertains to the understanding of words as *signs of our thoughts. It is often possible to grasp the meaning of some objective reality that is made known by means of a sign. *Theological understanding* (*Finality) sheds light on the dynamism, the form or the mere givenness of something from its respective ends and principal values (2). That in turn is supported by a *metaphysical understanding* that is ordered to the meaning of *existence as such, insofar as existence justifies itself by itself or by reason of its own proper nature and so also the foundation of all values and ends (3). That "understanding" includes precisely the foundation of end and essence is clear from the intrinsic connection of the two; for, the *essence points to the *end, and the end is the anticipation of the perfection of the essence.

Just as the three ways of understanding are united already in *sympathetic understanding* as a sensitive appreciation of the reality and activity of another person, so also are they united in the method of the *human sciences. Today one usually thinks of this method when mention is made of understanding; in this context one immediately thinks of understanding in contrast to *explanation. The *physical sciences offer causal explanations, i. e., they reduce natural events back to the efficient causes, basic elements and universal laws that clearly determine them. This procedure is not adequate for a proper grasp of the spiritual life and what it produces. For, the free creativity of spirit is not subject just to purely causal determinations; also, the totalities proper to spirit cannot be explained just from elemental parts; finally, universal laws can never exhaust the full reality contained in the concrete unique event of history. "Understanding" is more than explanation, since it grasps the spiritual reality as the actualization of meaning and value. Thus it is subject to a supra-causal or value-carrying determination; thus its totalities as "structures of meaning" receive their special character from a value or a hierarchy of values. More accurately, understanding begins with signs (the remains of an epoch; the utterances of a personality) and moves through structures of meaning to ultimate values. Thus it is possible not only to understand, but also to judge historical appearances from these values.

By means of "understanding" as a method the human sciences do justice to the special character of spiritual reality; Wilhelm Dilthey especially was a pioneer in this matter. Still, the dangers of relativism and irrationalism that are noticeable in his work and in that of his followers should be avoided. Relativism: Values are not distinguished from cultural changes, since no one notices that "understanding" as the method of an experiential science can never give an ultimate justification for values and therefore must be grounded in a philosophical system of values. Irrationalism: There is a very strong tendency to place "understanding" in an area apart from rational concepts, although in its complete depth and fullness it is not just a conceptual event but requires a sympathetic immersion of the whole man into reality.

In Martin Heidegger's existential analysis "understanding" is located among the components of "being-in-the-world" between being and speech. Here it means not just knowing, but especially "capacity." In this understanding, human existence projects itself as the capacity for existence or according to its possibilities.

JBL

UNIQUENESS

Uniqueness signifies more than just singleness. Thus every unique thing is also an iindividual, but not vice versa. Singleness characterizes the concrete bearer of an essence in its non-communicable particularity: for example, this pine tree, this man Peter. Uniqueness adds to this that the individual in question has no equal, and therefore that beside this one there either are no other bearers of this particular essence (actual uniqueness) or indeed essentially cannot be (metaphysical uniqueness). This latter type is actually not found in the material world, but actual uniqueness is found. And it is found less in the non-human domains of nature, where the individual exists only for the sake of the species; therefore they exhibit only very limited individual characteristics, closely resemble each other and can replace each other. (Of course, we also commonly speak of a uniquely beautiful sunset or a uniquely faithful animal.) The individual man, however, as a *person is not consumed in the service of his species; for, he has his own very personal eternal goal by reason of which he achieves a certain "onceness" and irreplaceability. This develops into a profound, individual formation of men and it can increase into a magnificent level of uniqueness. Thus, for example, Plato, Augustine, Francis of Assisi and Shakespeare are unique, incomparable figures. While no individual (not even the great man) in this world is able to exhaust the existential fullness of his species, the angel (according to Thomas Aquinas) does exactly that and therefore each individual angel is necessarily the only one of that species. But since one species is never able completely to realize all the richness of pure spirit, even on this level there are many species, all of which belong to the same genus. The *uniqueness of God* alone is absolute; since he, as this individual, exhaustively possesses the infinite fullness of existence, a second individual alongside him is impossible.

JBL

UNITY

Unity is the most basic of the essential characteristics or *transcendentals of existence. This means that *existence essentially posits unity. Every realization of existence has unity within itself and every form of unity is rooted in existence. Just as there is no existence without unity, so also there is no unity without existence. The degree and kind of existence determine the degree and kind of unity; conversely, the degree and kind of unity manifest clearly the degree and kind of existence. As the most basic transcendental, unity is closest to the essence of existence: existence is above all unity. As the primary transcendental, unity presents itself as the foundation of the other transcendentals: upon the degree and kind of unity depend the degree and kind of *truth, goodness (*Value) and *beauty; unity permeates all of them. — The *logical* unity of the concept is opposed to the *real* unity of existence. The latter means that an existent is un-divided in itself, closed off and so divided off from every other. The former gathers together, in one universal concept, a real multiplicity into a unity. The unity of certain concepts, such as the concept of man, animal, existence, etc., is logical or mental. Still, this unity is founded on the real world, insofar as the individual things included in the concept are essentially like each other. — This real and metaphysical unity just described is metaphysical in character; therefore it is also found in God. But it is not to be identified with *quantitative unity* which is limited to corporeal things. Quantitative unity presupposes numerable things, i. e., things that are put on a par with each other; thus it does not apply to God, nor can it, strictly speaking, be applied to pure spirits.

Levels of unity are given right along with the levels of existence. Before all, a distinction is to be made between the unity of a thing that is composed of parts and the simple unity of a thing that is not composed of parts; each of these types also manifests further levels. In the case of the ascent from the inorganic world, through plant and animal life to man himself, one can see clearly how inner concentration and external separation (therefore unity) increase. — The *henological principle* expresses the primacy of unity over multiplicity. The principle is: Multiplicity necessarily presupposes unity; or, multiplicity cannot exist without being based on unity. When related to actual existence, this principle is identical with the principle of *causality. For, every multiplicity means contingency insofar as the same essence enters here in this individual thing and there in that one and so does not necessarily belong to any. The ultimate reason for this must be one being that cannot be multiplied and exists as one absolutely necessary being: this is the *unity of God*. Inasmuch as all creatures are related to this one source they are one in the real unity of the source. However, extreme *monism exaggerates this when it sees the whole universe as one unique individual (thus, with some reservations, Parmenides and Spinoza). *Pantheism says about the same thing. In this regard the logical unity of the concept of existence and the real unity of absolute existence are frequently equated. — See also *Simplicity*.

JBL

UNIVERSAL CONCEPT

A universal concept is a *concept whose content can be affirmed of many individuals, taken separately, by the repetition of itself in each case. By being predicable of many, the universal concept distinguishes itself from the *particular concept*; because its content can be attributed to each one "taken separately," it is opposed to the *collective concept*, which is also predicable of many but only of the totality taken together and not of each one individually (e.g., the concept "herd" designates a multiplicity of animals, but not each individual animal of the herd). By the determination "a repetition of the same content" the universal is distinguished from that type of communion with which the concept "God" (according to Christian revelation) is affirmed by the three divine persons and indeed completely of each one, without, however, assuming a multiplication of the divine nature. On the other hand, in the universal the designated form (nature) is multiplied: Peter is a man, Paul is a man, Peter and Paul are two men. — Depending upon whether the unity of the conceptual content is perfect or imperfect, a distinction is made between *univocal* and *analogous* universals; in the strict sense the former are universals, still even the latter are, unthinkingly, very often termed "universals" (*Analogy).

Universal concepts are not innate to man nor are they poured into us from some kind of "universal" objects; rather, their source is to be found in *abstraction from the concrete *individual given in *experience (*Concepts, Formation of); this implies that decisive importance must be given to inner experience (*Consciousness). Our *derived concepts* stand over against our *original concepts* that are taken directly from experience; we form these derived concepts by putting together, often also by partially denying our original concepts. — The universal, as it is predicated of things, is called a *direct universal*. Its content is generally at the same time the being-content of real things (*Realism), even though it is actualized in the thing "in a different way" than it is in thought. For, in the thing it is not *abstract, detached from the other characteristics of the thing, but it is "bound together" in a real unity in a *concrete wholeness with the other traits (especially individuation). The abstractness of the universal is the basis for its predicability of many, i.e., its universality. In logical *reflection on the direct universal we become explicitly conscious of this predicability; thus, we can form a second universal concept in which we mentally grasp the abstracted "whatness" or essence as predicable of many (e. g., we grasp the conceptual content "man" as a *species); this second universal is called a *logical* or *reflex universal*. Since universality belongs to the nature of the reflex universal, it is not to be found as such in the physical order outside of the mind; it is a *being-of-the-mind that has its existential foundation in external reality. The logical universal is divided into the five *predicables. — The direct universal is an *essential concept* insofar as it presents the *essence of things (*Essential Knowledge); it is an *empirical universal* insofar as it represents only the appearance that is common to many and that is not grasped in any essential way. Examples of the latter kind are the popular notions of the different species of animals, plants and minerals.

With regard to the validity of universal concepts: *Realism. Their importance follows from the fact that without them no *judgment is possible, since in every judgment at least the predicate is a universal; without universals there are no universal judgments and therefore — since every *inference demands at least one universal judgment as a premise — no progressive thinking, no going beyond immediately given experience, no *science, and especially no *metaphysics. Consequently, the devaluation of the universal logically leads to the positivistic splintering of the whole intellectual life, in the realm of practical philosophy and of social living to the dissolution of every moral and legal essential order and so to the rejection of the *natural law; finally, it leads to total subjective *individualism, since, on this hypothesis, the only reality is the individual, his personal experience and his arbitrariness.

JdV

V

VALIDITY

Validity (*Geltung*) in philosophical language means that something is as it ought to be, in contrast to that which just is or is thought; actually, the notion of "validity" is applied not so much to things as it is to mental structures such as concepts, judgments, conclusions, sciences, or in the practical order to norms and laws. Since the mere fact that something is thought is no guarantee of its validity, the validity of mental structures or constructs demands a foundation that transcends these structures themselves. According to *psychologism this foundation is the subjective necessity of thinking which is given with man's spiritual nature; but if that were so, then the validity of such things as mathematical principles would hold good only for us men, while perhaps another mathematics is valid for other spiritual beings (*Relativism). In order to avoid this conclusion Kant's *critical philosophy bases all validity in *consciousness as such; this solution, however, is not without its difficulties. In the *neo-Kantianism of the Baden school even consciousness as such appears still determined by transcendent *values which as "truths in themselves" do not have any real existence but just "have value"; therefore, validity is thought of as something completely independent — as subsisting "in itself" but without any reference to existence; something similar is found in other forms of "logical transcendentalism" (*Truth). However, this view is in contradiction to the transcendence of *existence and so to the principle of the excluded middle: That which in no way shares in existence is absolutely nothing. Ultimately, therefore, validity can be rooted only in existence; ultimately it is the validity of existence (real or ontological validity) which coincides in the judgment with its *truth; but in the concept it says that its content is not only a conceptual content, but also that it is or at least can be an existential content.

"Universal vilidity" can be taken in two senses: either as validity for all thinking subjects in contrast to just "relative validity," or as validity of all objects (of a definite class) in contrast to the validity only of particular objects of the class.

JdV

436

VALUE

The science of economics, which deals with the use and the exchange value of material things, first made general use of the word "value." Before the time of Rudolf H. Lotze (1817-1881) philosophers spoke only occasionally about values; and it was through his efforts that the problem of value became a prime concern of philosophy. With regard to the thing in question, actually philosophy always had dealt with the problem, but under the aspect of the good and its goodness (*bonum et bonitas*).

Modern value philosophy (Max Scheler) which began with Lotze makes a sharp distinction between value and *good. According to this view various goods belong to the existential order, while values are opposed to this order in "ultimate independence" and constitute their own domain. Here we meet a type of Platonic value-idea which stands out most strongly in the works of a man like Nicolai Hartmann. Since values in this sense are thought of as other-worldly ideas which can be introduced into the real world only through the instrumentality of men, it is legitimate to name this theory "value-idealism." Its opposite is value-realism or better, the metaphysics of value, which overcomes the separation of value from being. — Emphasizing the metaphysical side of value is necessary because some thinkers tend to consider existence in the sense of *positivism, i. e., only as a presently experienced reality without a trace of inner essential necessity; and of course, to base values on positivism means to completely relativize them. On the other hand, if one can grasp the metaphysics of existence with its absolute necessity (and this necessity is even present in material things in the form of essential principles), then it is precisely the grounding of value in *existence that guarantees its absolute character. In fact, it becomes clear that value belongs in the area of the *transcendentals; thus existence from its innermost nature is valuable and value from its innermost nature is existential; a separation would destroy both. A distinction between goods and values can have meaning only in the sense that by "good" particular things are meant insofar as values are realized in them, and by "values" are meant the value-ideas which are abstracted by the intellect from the concrete good things. After this long preface, we can now describe value as existence itself insolar as it means a perfection by reason of its objective content and so attracts the appetites or any kind of desire. The normative character of value is rooted in the essential laws of being which are given with the actual existence of each existent, and ultimately in the fact that absolute precedence goes to existence rather than to non-existence or nothingness.

The special character of our value-perceptions depends upon the essential nature of value itself. If value is separated from existence, then it is just not accessible to human reason which is directed towards existence; since it manifests itself to emotional feeling alone, the result is a kind of value-irrationalism. The exact opposite of this would be a kind of value-rationalism which reduces the special character of value to existence alone. Between these two extremes there is such a thing as an intellectual perception of value; in this view, value is perceived by the intellect because the object of intellect is being and being by its very nature is valuable. However, this cannot be the total explanation of value, because value perfects being and so only finds the answer that is completely in accord with being when it is also related to the emotions and to the will. Therefore intellectual value-perception is always conditioned by emotion and appetite.

The opposition between value and non-value as well as the priority of one value over another are aspects of the whole value question. Value is based on the order of being and the human activity which is measured by it; deviation from the order of being means non-value and it leads ultimately to moral *guilt. With regard to the priority of one value over another, the degrees of value correspond to the degrees of being. On a more formal plane a distinction is made between personal value, pleasure value and utility value. Personal value is sought for its own sake; pleasure value is dependent on personal value inasmuch as it is ordered to the latter and when possesed produces happiness; utility value aids personal value as the means to the end. Personal value shows the following steps in ascending order: economic, physical, spiritual (the true, the beautiful, the morally good), religious values (the holy). This order of priority is based on the order of being in which religious values take the highest place because they are immediately concerned with the infinte good (God).

JBL

VALUE ETHICS

Value ethics is the branch of ethical theory which sees in the question of *value the essential problem of ethics. A distinction should be made between the neo-Kantian view (Windelband, Rickert) and the phenomenological view (Scheler, Nicolai Hartmann). The former group understands by value only the universal, formal element which is approximately equal to the "ought" and is to be distinguished from *existence (grasped only empirically) as a transcendental determination (strictly formal ethics). Phenomenological value ethics claims to see in value a multifaceted, objective "something" which is distinct from existence and a priori; it makes the act of striving meaningful and is not at all to be identified with "ought" or obligation, for it is this value that is the very foundation of all obligation (material value). Of course, this phenomenological value ethics does not assume that there is any moral value which, as the object of the will, can make its act into a morally good act. Rather, moral value in this system is considered to be exclusively the value of the particular act; this is brought about by the fact that a man prefers that value, from among several that in themselves are not moral values, which here and now merits preference because of its loftiness or for other reasons (e.g., greater urgency).

When compared to *moral positivism, value ethics at least has the distinction of having explicitly defended the objectivity of moral values. Likewise, phenomenological value ethics is superior to formal ethics because it clearly develops the priority of value-content in contrast to the purely formal "ought" of the latter system. — Still, phenomenological value ethics also has its deficiencies. This is especially seen in the fact that it does not overcome the separation of existence from value (*Value Philosophy) because it also is excessively entangled in the positivistic concept of existence as a purely empirical reality. Therefore it misses the important fact that value as the essential perfection of any existent is rooted in existence and through an insight into the essence of a thing can be perceived as such. Consequently, an intentional value-feeling is not, as Scheler supposes, an ultimate simple principle, but a complex structure that unites both knowledge and emotions. Moreover, the moral value of an act cannot be reduced to objective values which in themselves are non-moral and from which a person chooses out the more lofty or the more urgent (*good). Finally, the question about moral value is indeed the basic question in ethics, but it is by no means the only question; it is especially questionable whether or not the *moral law can be explained on the basis of value alone.

JoS-JdV

VALUE PHILOSOPHY

Value philosophy developed as a recognizable philosophical position as a result of the work of R. H. Lotze. When one speaks of the "theory of value," the phrase is intended to include, along with the philosophical investigation of values, also other types of research in this direction, especially the psychological. Less often the name "axiology" is employed. — Right from the beginning, in the works of Lotze, the father of value philosophy, value appears as something separated from existence. Since, in this system, existence is limited exclusively to the mathematical-scientific laws which underlie our experience of reality, it is not related to values. Thus, values in which the meaning of human existence is rooted, constitute their own realm of influence. This doubleness corresponds to a duality of powers in man: just as the intellect knows being, so reason experiences values. — Lotze's suggestions led to two further developments: neo-Kantian value philosophy and phenomenological value philosophy.

The former takes up the aspect of *validity; this view was pushed by the Baden school (Windelband, Richert). It proceeds from the distinction between nature which can be explained by scientific laws, and historical culture which must be understood from the main values operative in it. Thus next to the value-free real world there is an independent world of values which have absolute validity but do not exist; consequently they can be described as unreal or non-existing. Both spheres meet in the "interstices of the world," i. e., in the actions of men which are based on values and which thus impress values on the real world and so create culture. — A similar position was held by Edward Spranger and Alexius Meinong in his later work.

Phenomenological value philosophy strongly emphasizes what it calls "value-feeling"; in opposition to the formalism of Kant which he worked out onesidedly, Scheler developed his material *value ethics. A reduction of values to existence understood merely in the sense of the present, given reality, would be the same thing as relativizing them. Therefore, their absolute character is assured only through their "ultimate independence" from existence; it is for this reason that they constitute their own realm of "material qualities" (i. e., meaningful determinations). Because of their separation from existence, values cannot be known by the intellect, but can only be grasped in an emotional-intuitive way by *intentional feeling*; directed towards values as to its proper object, this intentional feeling is distinguished from all merely subjective feeling. — Closely related to this theory of intentional feeling are the positions of Brentano on the proper characterization of love and of Meinong on emotional presentation; also there are a number of psychological theories which tend to reduce all values to purely subjective feelings. Nicolai Hartmann developed *value ethics in his own peculiar way. All of these systems have been characterized as "dualistically complementary theories"; for they complete only the value-free existence by placing alongside of it non-existent values, instead of developing the final unity of both. Actually, however, only scholastic philosophy has penetrated to the heart of this unity (Value).

JBL

VALUES, RELATIVISM OF

This view ascribes only relative validity to all values and accordingly maintains that they are binding only for a particular person or for a particular people or for a particular time. Thus there are no values which can be said to prevail absolutely or independently of these particular conditions. Consequently, all values without exception are subject to change; eternal, unchanging values binding on all men, peoples and times are denied. Insofar as such views grow out of a general *relativism which relativizes every truth, they are already judged in our evaluation of this philosophy. However, if relativism is advanced only with regard to values, then it separates value from existence. This frequently results in a kind of "psychologism of value" which falsely equates objective values with the personal evaluations of the subject, especially with his feelings. Or it falls into value-subjectivism, a theory according to which each individual (the subject) determines his own values. According to Nietzsche, the "masters of the world" establish the values for mankind in general and for various peoples in particular. — Obviously there are changeable values operative in human society — values which were first instituted by men themselves. However, the fundamental values of human existence are necessarily given with the essential structure of man and of being; for this reason they are invested with absolute, unchangeable validity.

JBL

VEDANTA, PHILOSOPHY OF

"Vedānta" designates first of all the end of the Veda, which is the sacred literature or knowledge of India; but then it also means the doctrine which sees the high point of true knowledge in the end of the Veda. On the basis of the contradictory traditions contained in the literature of the Upanishads, the Vedānta philosophy attempted to create a well-rounded system. There are different schools in the Vēdanta philosophy, but out of them all the school of Śankara (788 to ca. 820) attained such great importance that by "Vedanta" one usually thinks of his system. Śankara distinguishes between a higher and a lower knowledge. The highest truth is "non-twoness" = *advaita or strict monism*. Twoness or difference is only a veiling of truth, or appearance = *māyā*. The absolute, spiritual, first principle of the world = *Brahman*, or the divine self = *ātman*, is pure unity, but by means of its "māyā" it is able to project itself as multiplicity without being affected in itself by this appearance. Since an effect is only a change in the cause, it is not different from the cause and like the cause itself it is uncaused. True causality and becoming are meaningless. Universal-ātman and particular-ātman are related as all space and the space in individual jars. The difference between them consists only in limitation. Opposed to this higher knowledge of the Absolute is the lower knowledge of the relative which accords with the changing world. From this point of view, the Brahman is both the efficient and the material cause; he is the source of the world and the supreme lord who creates, rules and destroys the world. At the same time it is the "stuff" of the material world which in an endless repetition takes its rise from Brahman and returns to it.

According to Śankara, the world as we perceive it is not only a construction of the mind or nothing, but it is also real, at least from our relative

441

standpoint. This standpoint is common to all of us and it is decisive for our actions, but the absolute standpoint can be attained only by the individual for himself. The māyā is neither existing (since in the absolute sense it is deception) nor non-existing (since it is actually experienced). According to its true essence the soul is pure spirituality and Brahman. The division of the One into the multiplicity of individual souls comes from a not-knowing that subjects the soul to different conditions. In these belong the coarse body, the subtle body which serves as a support for the soul in its transition from one life to another and which is the carrier of Karman, and the different inner organs and powers. *Karman* are the effects of the works that determine reincarnation (*Transmigration of Souls). Good works help towards a good re-birth; they remove the obstacles to deliverance, but are not able to effect it. True *deliverance* (not from sin and guilt, but from the suffering involved in continual re-birth) belongs only to the person who possesses the higher knowledge. In that knowledge he knows himself as beyond the limits of good and evil, as absolute being, spirit and ecstasy. — Among the philosophers who shaped the Vedānta philosophy in a theistic sense, Rāmānuja (12th century) is the most important.

WB

VIRTUE

Virtue means the capacity, facility and inclination to perform certain actions which are proper to man. Virtue is not innate; only the tendency to virtue is pre-given; in fact, virtue can only be acquired through dedicated and constant exercise. A virtue is a perduring quality of the person; however, through neglect and contrary actions it can be diminished or totally lost. The opposite of virtue is *vice*, i. e., the propensity for improper acts. — There are virtues both of the intellect and of the will. The virtues of the intellect perfect man with regard to the knowledge of the truth. Concerning theoretical truth these virtues are: *insight* which is skill in judging; *science* which is facility in reasoning; *wisdom* which is the ability to penetrate to the ultimate foundations of truth; concerning practical truth these virtues are: *prudence* which is the capacity to make right decisions in particular cases; *art* which is the skill to make things correctly. The virtues of the intellect by themselves do not make a man morally good, with the exception of the moral virtue of prudence (*Cardinal Virtues).

The essence of the moral virtues consists in the constant readiness of the will to carry out what the intellect points out as right. They are virtues in the strict sense and make a man simply good or perfect. The immediate, proper subject of the moral virtues is the will because the will alone is free and because freedom is an essential component of all moral

442

acting. The virtues of the will are intimately related to each other and constitute a unity. In a state of perfection they must all be present at the same time, since prudence, when given in a truly perfect degree, must guide all of man's free actions.

Virtuous living embraces the essential perfection towards which each man is supposed to strive in accordance with the will of the creator. Therefore man has a moral obligation to strive for virtue. — Virtue is not an absence of passions, for the passions do not contradict virtue provided that they are kept within proper bounds through the guidance of prudence. Since virtue is acquired only by practice and is itself a tendency to act, virtue and a well-ordered *activism* are closely related and are opposed to a decisionless *passivity*. Since virtue is the true and essential perfection of man, without virtue there can be no true human *joy*, i. e., the satisfaction and rest of the will which results from the attainment of the good.

JK

VITALISM

Vitalism (Lat.: *vita* = life) is the scientific-philosophical theory about the inner constitution of the organic, living being. First of all, this theory sees an essential difference between living things and everything inorganic — a difference which does not allow reducing one to the other; and secondly, for the organic *life in the *organism it assumes the reality of its own substantial carrier. — The essential difference between the organic and the inorganic is manifest from the opposition between everything living and everything non-living — plants, animals, men. In the first instance the special forms of life (sense life and spiritual life) are not attended to. From a descriptive viewpoint this opposition consists of the following essential moments: 1. The organism is a material, internally individualized whole with a unified activity, i. e., the different chemical-physical parts and organs complement each other to form a unique individual and their partial functions combine into one total effect: nutrition, self-preservation, generation. On the other hand, all inorganic material systems (including crystals) always remain a multiplicity; such systems constitute a mechanically ordered collectivity, but not a complete whole. In the case of inorganic wholes formation and dissolution can be repeated indefinitely with the same system; the organic individual disintegrates in death and cannot be produced again out of the same or other material. Thus every organism is unique. — 2. Every organism (including the microbe) takes its rise by means of germination from already given organisms; multiplication through the so-called division of microbes is also a development. Germ or bud cells (sexual, non-sexual, vegetative, such as onions, runners, tubers) are already whole organisms, but in a potential, unfinished form. Through a developmental process their final state is produced; this process is unique for each individual. There is nothing in inorganic bodies that corresponds to this kind of growth; the so-called "germs" of crystals are already small, finished crystals produced by means of purely external accumulation.

Vitalism in the *proper sense* explains the autonomous activity of organic life — an activity that is not reducible to inorganic bodies and powers; it explains it by means of an equally autonomous natural power, a substantial and non-material bearer which is called the *life principle, entelechy (Hans Driesch), the essential form or soul (by the scholastics). Theories which assume, without the corresponding substantial bearers, the existence of special forces that belong exclusively to organisms, such as the "life power" of the older physiologists, "dominants," "organic system-conditions," etc., can be attributed to vitalism only in the *wide sense*. The irreducibility of organic life to inorganic forces is shown by the actual oppositions between the two: on the one hand there is the inner, individual wholeness and development from potential germinal beginnings; on the other hand there is a mechanically ordered collectivity (a machine) and no inner development. However, the experiment of Hans Driesch and others is really decisive for the autonomy of living activity and at the same time it supplies information about the peculiar nature of the *life principle.

KF

VOLUNTARISM

Voluntarism is the term applied to those philosophical currents which in any way give preference to the *will over the intellect (opposed to *Intellectualism). However, this can happen in many different ways. According to *metaphysical voluntarism*, reality in its most profound depths is will (Schopenhauer, Eduard von Hartman). *Psychological voluntarism* does not go that far, but it does give priority to the will over the intellect (Henry of Ghent: The intellect is purely passive and its object is subordinate to the object of the will; in a more moderate vein, Duns Scotus: The intellect is an ancillary cause of the will, but truth does not depend on the will). *Psychological voluntarism* is usually expanded to a *theological voluntarism* (the essence of beatitude is the love of God; the natural order and partially also the moral law depend on God's will). Martin Luther and (with a certain reservation) William of Ockham make the whole moral order depend on God's caprice; according to Luther, God is unknowable because he is absolute will. The *epistemological voluntarism* of Kant is different from the above-mentioned forms; according to him, the first place goes to the practical reason over the theoretical reason, because the former leads us to metaphysical convictions that the latter does not. It should be noted that *pragmatism is a form of epistemological

VOLUNTARISM

voluntarism. Nietzsche espoused an *ethical voluntarism* since he looked upon the will to power as the highest moral value. — Voluntarism usually confuses or identifies will with activity. Will (if it is not identified with blind impulse) and intellect naturally stand on the same level of existence. They complement each other inasmuch as the will moves the intellect and the intellect enlightens the will. In God they are really one.

WB

W

WAR

War is a violent, bloody battle between independent *states. Concerning the ethical permissibility of war, the following questions must be answered: 1) whether or not war is allowable at all, and 2) if it is, whether or not the necessary conditions have been fulfilled in a given case. 1) In general, war is not necessarily prohibited. If the creator, by reason of the natural moral law, wills the organization of peoples into states, then he must provide them with the necessary means. But this includes not only the right to impose the death penalty (*Capital Punishment) on criminals within its own borders, but also the right of *self-defense or protection against external enemies who unjustly attack one's country; some also extend this right to the recovery of something that has been taken away unjustly. To deny this right of self-defense which is commonly recognized in international law, is equivalent to strengthening the greedy and morally irresponsible aggressor and at the same time endangering true peace among nations. For, true peace among nations demands the right, and sometimes also the duty, of defending one's own autonomy. 2) Nevertheless, for the moral permissibility of a war a number of conditions must be filled: an actual, certain and serious injustice, the impossibility of defending one's just claims by peaceful means (International Court, United Nations, etc.), the possibility and hope of success, the avoidance of all unnecessary injury to innocent third parties, etc. If these conditions are present, then the other unavoidable evils must be laid at the feet of the unjust aggressor and not of the defender. The just defense of the public welfare takes precedence over the right of the unjust aggressor to his health and life, and also over the danger to the lives of one's own citizens. To be sure, unjust killing is not allowed. But since even a just war, especially with the advent of modern weapons of mass destruction, necessarily involves horrible suffering and moral damage, a healthy peace movement or even a *moderate pacifism* deserves the highest recognition. This form of pacifism works for peace by communicating to others a true desire for peace and the necessity that nations understand each other, without denying the basic liceity of war even in the present circumstances. *Extreme pacifism*, which advocates the absolute immorality of all war and encourages all young men to refuse to serve in the armed services, is to be rejected.

JoS

WELTANSCHAUUNG

Weltanschauung (world-view, philosophy of life) means a total view of the nature, origin, value, meaning and goal of the *world and of human life. "Weltanschauung" says essentially more than *"world image"*; for by "world image" is understood the synopsis and conceptual elaboration of the results of the physical sciences into a scientific view of the world. This view as such remains purely theoretical and does not ask the ultimate, metaphysical questions about the existence and meaning of the world as a whole. A *Weltanschauung* essentially surpasses the limits of the particular sciences; for, it involves a value judgment with regard to the whole world and therefore includes an answer to the basic questions about the origin, meaning and goal of the world. Thus, although the *"Welt"* in *Weltanschauung* refers primarily to the visible world, still its full import extends to absolute existence because of its questioning of origin and meaning; for, it is only from this question that the world as a whole can be given any final meaning.

A *Weltanschauung* is first of all a pre-scientific conviction that grows naturally in every man; an organized, scientific form is not essential to it. But if it is scientifically established and tied together, then it is fundamentally the same as a metaphysics of existence. The contrast between an irrational and a rational *Weltanschauung* is not to be confused with the opposition between a pre-scientific and a scientific *Weltanschauung*, since even a pre-scientific *Weltanschauung* can be based on very clear thinking in spite of the fact that it is not expressed in a scientific form. The opinion that a *Weltanschauung* in its innermost core can never have a rational foundation is based on false philosophical presuppositions (*Agnosticism or at least an irrational view of *Value). According to the source of the knowledge, a purely natural, philosophical *Weltanschauung* is to be distinguished from one that rests on supernatural revelation; thus we can find a theistic, a pantheistic, or an atheistic *Weltanschauung*.

The possibility of an atheistic (materialistic) or pantheistic (biological or idealistic) *Weltanschauung* shows that *Weltanschauung* and religion are not the same thing. But even a religious (e. g., Christian) *Weltanschauung* is not the same as religion (Christian religion). Of course, religion usually includes a religious *Weltanschauung*, but as a binding of

447

the whole man to God (through acts of worship, dedication, love, etc.) it means essentially more than a mere "view" of the world and its relationship to God. For the religious man there cannot be another *Weltanschauung* alongside of his religious world-view, since the ultimate meaning and evaluation of the world cannot disregard God. Therefore, the attempts to make a "peaceful" division in all reality are completely impossible; according to these ideas, a *Weltanschauung* free of all religion makes the ultimate judgment about the value of all earthly things, while religion is to be concerned only with the next life.

Concerning the origin of a *Weltanschauung*, as against the irrationalists we firmly hold that a *Weltanschauung* in its essential traits is the product of the knowing human spirit. In its particular forms (e. g., in the emphasis on this or that truth) it is of course conditioned by the ebb and flow of different historical influences (climate, race, character, tradition, culture, education, etc.); in fact, the errors in a *Weltanschauung* are usually due to an exaggerated effect of these influences. — See also *Pluralism*.

JdV

WHOLENESS

The concept of wholeness has played a significant role in the increasing rejection of the atomistic world-view that has been noticeable since the beginning of the 20th century. Thus, as a result of his biological investigations Hans Driesch came to assume a proper wholeness-factor or entelechy for all organisms (*Vitalism). Christian von Ehrenfels and others applied this idea of wholeness to psychological research and they concluded that neither particular experiences nor the complete life of the soul are intelligible from the simplest components (sensations, etc.), but rather represent primordial "wholes." At about the same time the idea of wholeness also won a victory over the individualism and liberalism of the 19th century in the area of sociology (but not without some exaggerations). Among scholastic philosophers the value of wholeness, an inheritance from the thought of Plato and Aristotle, was not lost or neglected.

Today "wholeness" is most frequently understood in the sense of the concrete *whole*. We speak of wholeness in cases where several parts are so ordered that together they constitute a unity (the whole). Wholeness is a subspecies of *order. The special character of "wholeness" consists of the fact that in it the components of the order (the parts) constitute a closed unity through their being together. If a part is lacking, then the whole is incomplete and itself only a part. Therefore, the *part* of a whole is that which, together with others, forms an ordered unity. By reason of the order of the parts (the structure) the whole is to be distinguished

WHOLENESS

from a *sum* or *aggregation* in which the situation and ordering of the parts are interchangeable in any way whatsoever.

The concept of wholeness, however, is not actualized in all wholes in exactly the same way, since *unity (which participates in the *analogy of existence) is of a different kind in different wholes. For us the prototype of wholeness is the organism. For, in it the parts receive their rationale to such an extent from the unity of the whole that without a relationship to it the individual parts (e. g., a hand) cannot even be defined. They have their essence and existence only as parts in a whole. (A severed "hand" is not a hand any more). Here the parts are joined to the whole through the community of the substantial existence. In a continuum (*Quantity) the parts disappear even more into the unity of the whole, for there the parts as proper unities are only potentially real. Elsewhere, as in the "elements" of mental experiences, the connecting factor is first of all the *finality of the function, but ultimately the substantial unity of a common ground of existence — the soul; for, without the soul it is impossible to understand the reality of mind. Of immense and also practical importance for the life of the individual and of peoples is the kind of wholeness present in communities (*Sociology). Even though a whole, for its part (from another point of view), can be part of a whole that is on a higher level, it should still be noted that there are wholes which by reason of their natures can never be mere parts of a whole just like the members of an organism: we refer here to the *person. All communities, however, are made up of persons with their inalienable personal dignity.

Here are a few axioms: The whole is more than the parts, i. e., the sum of the parts is still not a whole; for, a whole demands the order and organization of the parts and this presupposes a special *wholeness factor* (a *principle of unity and order). Further: The whole is before the parts (Aristotle); this does not mean that the whole exists temporally before the parts: there are some wholes in which the parts exist before they are incorporated into a whole (e. g., bricks before they become a house), while other parts come into existence only in a whole (as the organs in an organism). The full meaning of the second axiom is rather: What the parts are in themselves is not decisive for the reality of the whole, but rather what the whole makes out of them — the order and the unity (e. g., the blueprint actualized in the built house); parts, inasmuch as they are parts, are subordinate to the whole — they are there for the whole. This does not exclude, however, that from another point of view they may possess their own existence and worth.

"Wholeness" is the dominant idea of *Holism* which was begun by J. S. Haldane and given its name by J. C. Smuts (from the Gr. *hólon* = whole). According to Haldane, organisms are produced neither by their mechanical elements nor by primary organisms, but from the wholeness itself they develop their members which for their part can again become wholes. Matter, life and spirit are steps of one and the same vast process of evolution. Characteristic of Holism is its (questionable) derivation of the more simple from the more complex (physical from biological and biological from psychic) through mere *elimination* and *simplification*; to argue for this position it is necessary to mathematicize the higher realms. — See also *Collectivism*.

WB

WILL

Knowing and willing are the two fundamental modes of spiritual activity. Just as *activity does not necessarily mean change and spiritual knowing is not necessarily discursive thinking, so also "willing" does not necessarily mean a striving for a good to be attained or to be produced. The root act of will is the affirmation of a value or *love*. Therefore the spiritual fulfillment of infinite goodness, which lacks the note of striving for something, is also will (*Will of God). The characteristic object of absolute will is absolute *value or the good as such. Willing manifests itself as a *desire for something only where the good is neither identified with the will nor originally connected with it. Therefore the human will can be described as that spiritual power of man which either affirms or seeks values that are spiritually known. And its characteristic object is the same as that of absolute will, i. e., being as a value in itself, but mediated by the special nature of human knowing and *understanding. While sensual desire is restricted to the narrow realm of those things that offer sensual pleasure, the will has an unlimited field of objects. Of course, the will can move itself only to that which appears to it to be good in some way; but since all being is good in some way, the object of the will is the unlimited realm of all being.

The attracting goodness of the object works at the same time as a motive for the will; it takes on the aspect of a final cause which affects the will through the mediation of the spiritual knowledge. Thus willing is immediately rooted in the known motive; it is also mediately rooted in everything which contributes to the establishment of value judgments on the part of the different dispositions and "levels" of the soul. Actually, every aspect of man's mental and emotional life is involved in his grasp of values: frame of mind, temperament, health of body, character, personality type, unconscious complexes, etc. However, the ultimate orientation of the will, even in the midst of all conflicting motives, remains a free act of the will itself (*Free Will).

The object of a will-act which is desired because of its goodness must contribute in some way to the perfection of the one willing it. When there is a question of seriously desiring the attainment of some goal, then this goal should not appear as here and now unattainable for the one desiring it, since the will cannot seriously desire the impossible, just as it cannot directly will evil for its own sake. — On the basis of much experience a distinction is made between a strong and a weak will. Still, there is some question as to whether or not the "will" (as a special power) in its ontological structure can be called strong or weak and whether or not it can be strengthened by means of exercises. There are good reasons for maintaining that the meaning of so-called "will-exercises" does not consist in the actual increase of *will power*; rather, it seems that they produce a whole inner constellation of complexes by means of which certain objective values can now more easily be subjectively realized as the primary values; they also seem to reduce the number of inhibitions which hinder the will and under the aspect of good habits they facilitate the dominance of the will in the whole life of the soul (see Lindworsky's *theory of will*). — Will as a spiritual striving-power flows from spiritual knowing and embraces ends that are spiritually grasped. Therefore one cannot properly speak of unconscious willing as brute force (as is the case with all purely natural striving), unless one understands by will the same thing as *appetite. The view that the absolute source of all reality is to be found in unconscious willing (Schopenhauer, Eduard von Hartmann) contradicts the principle of sufficient reason, since the more perfect (the spiritual will) cannot have its foundation in the less perfect (unconscious appetite).

AW

WILL OF GOD

In God there is no blind natural necessity (Schopenhauer, Eduard von Hartmann) that gradually works itself up into full consciousness (idealistic *Pantheism); nor is God mere thinking or a mere idea. Rather, he possesses a conscious, spiritual will. In a way similar to the act of knowing (*Omniscience), the willing subject is not distinct from the act of willing and from its necessarily grasped principal object — the eternal, immutable and necessary existence of God. Therefore, one cannot call this will a "striving"; rather, it is a "self-affirmation," a "love of self," but not in a sense as if God would "posit" himself only through this act of willing (Fichte). Finite things as limited possible limitations of God are the object of his free will (*Freedom of God).

The most prominent characteristic of the divine will is its absolute *holiness.* God cannot sin because in him nature and moral norm are identical. He loves goodness and hates evil because he can love something only insofar as it is an image of his own existence. Still, we should be careful not to think of divine *loving* and *hating* after the fashion of human affections and passions. If, in the modern sense, we understand by "moral" the possibility of free choice between good and evil, then God would have to be placed outside the realm of morality.

MR

WISDOM

Wisdom is not just any knowledge, but a knowledge about what is essential in human life, about the ultimate principles and ends of finite existence. It is a contemplation and judgment of all earthly things in the light of eternity (*sub specie aeternitatis*); it is a knowledge that shows its worth by assigning each thing to the place that belongs to it in the context of the whole universe. Thomas Aquinas expresses this idea in the oft quoted phrase "*Sapientis est ordinare*" (It is the part of the wise man to order all things). A scientific form of expression is not essential to wisdom, but the agreement between thought and action is. Aquinas distinguished three levels of wisdom: The first level is the practical insight into life that grows out of philosophical considerations. The wisdom that comes from faith and theological knowledge is higher, for it orders all things in heaven and earth in the light of supernatural grace. The third level is the wisdom that is a gift of the Holy Spirit; in the power of this wisdom the man who loves God grasps the world properly no longer just through his own efforts; he now grasps it in the light of a divine movement, he feels himself ordered to the divine, and in a loving embrace he experiences the divinely willed order of all things.

JdV

WORK

A man works when he employs his spiritual or bodily powers in order to achieve an intended goal that can be reached or produced. Study and prayer are true work even though they do not bring forth material products; other spiritual and indeed all bodily forms of work lead to outwardly perceptible results which can be either a product of some kind or a qualitative change. The line between work and play may be clearly drawn on a conceptual level, but in actual fact it is quite fluid; that which according to its formality in other circumstances is *play* (= the non-utilitarian application of one's powers), for the persons involved can be serious, hard work. — Animals and even machines work, but only insofar as man directs them and uses their activity; animals share in the toil of human labor, while machines only share in the movement involved and in the triumph over the resistance of brute matter. In the full sense of the word, work is the privilege of man: it constitutes his dignity. — The steady pursuance of a goal and effort are both a part of work. The former contributes to the direction of the intellect and hence the moral responsibility and dignity of work; the latter increases the moral value of work insofar as it requires true human application and involvement.

Spiritual work has always been respected, but not manual labor. On the other hand, because of its obvious utility the work involved in the production of material goods was for a time overvalued in a one-sided way. The evaluation of work should first and foremost be "moral"; in order to achieve this value the economic utility of the fruits of work is the last norm. The "economic" evaluation of work abides by completely different standards; this evaluation is extremely important today because for millions of people the payment which they receive for their work is the basis of support for themselves and their families. — All cultural values can only be produced and sustained by means of work; and it is becoming increasingly more important to shape work itself and the living conditions of workingmen in a way that contributes to human culture, whether it is intellectual or manual, directing or executing. A culture organized for pleasure will break down; a *culture that respects and honors work will prosper. — Work itself is never a curse; rather, it is always a blessing. Nevertheless, it can become a curse when excessive and monotonous labors kill the spirit, when a great deal of dedicated work ends in failure, when the conditions of work are such that under them men deteriorate physically and morally instead of growing and finding satisfaction.

OvNB

WORLD

As contrasted with God, "world" means all reality outside of God; it is the whole of *creation. Yet while the concept of creation includes the relation of the world to God, the concept of world (1) disregards this relation and considers all other-Godly reality according to its own proper existence. In fact, the existence of the world is so independent that it can even turn against God in the free decision of the spiritual person. The religious (biblical) notion of the world (2) is related to the above, the world as a power hostile to God. By world (3) is often understood the totality of all visible things: the universe, the cosmos. The science of cosmology studies the cosmos both in the sense of a general philosophy of *nature and in the sense of cosmogony (theories of the origin of the world). Sometimes this concept of the world is applied to just a part of the universe (e. g., to the solar system or to the earth alone) as it is distinguished from other "worlds." World (4) also has a relative sense pertaining to one subject or a group of subjects, if we speak of the world of the animals or the world of man. This means the surrounding world, the totality of everything that concerns animals or man.

World (1) and God: Even *pantheism in most of its forms recognizes at least a relative difference between God and the world. The theistic notion of the difference in being between God and the world is unavoidable as soon as the real *contingency of the world is seen. God's absolute *transcendence certainly excludes the simple identity between him and the world, but it does not exclude his presence and activity in the world (*Immanence).

Unity of the world: The world (1) has the basis of its unity in its essential relation to God, its first begining and its last end (the opposite would be: a pluralism of *existence). A spatial or temporal multiplicity of world (3) (cosmic theory of many worlds) cannot be reconciled with this unity of the world (1). — The unity of the world (3) means that there is a spatio-temporal and causal connection between all corporeal beings. A consequence of this unity is that all of these bodies either in themselves or in their effects, can be perceived by a sense-endowed being that belongs to this world. At the same time it is likewise clear that a supposed multiplicity of worlds (3) can never be verified by using the methods of astronomy. — *Order and goal* of the world: the world (3) around us is an ordered world (*Finality); for this reason the Greeks called it the "cosmos" (= well-ordered, regular). Concerning the final goal of the world see *Creation*.

Beginning and end of the world: Abstracting from *revelation, which teaches a beginning of the world (1) in or with time and an end of the world (3) not by annihilation but as catastrophe and transformation (the new heaven and the new earth), just the fact of creation is still no reason to assume a temporal beginning of the world (1). For, continual dependence on an eternal, but free act of God's will does not rule out the possibility that we may never find a temporal beginning of the things of this world. The world is not thereby thought of as co-eternal with God, but only as beginningless (*Eternity), or always present in and with time. Also dependence on the creator is in itself no reason to assume that there will be an end of the world (1). — On the other hand, the constant development of the world that has been made known to us by the results of astronomy rules out an unlimited pre-history of the world (3) known to us; the physical law of entropy shows that "unlimited duration" is improbable. That the normal conditions of life on this earth will one day be destroyed by a cosmic catastrophe, is not only possible but also probable from the viewpoint of astronomy. — Pantheistic philosophical systems have always assumed either a beginningless and endless duration of the world or their periodic return (Heraclitus, the Pythagoreans, oriental philosophy). — More recently, Nietzsche spoke of the "eternal recurrence of the same events," by which he meant not only the periodic return of the world as a whole, but also all of its particular situations, including human experiences. — See also *Finite, Infinite, World Soul.*

VN

WORLD SOUL

The existence of a "world soul" is postulated by many advocates of biological *vitalism in order to explain the cooperation between living organisms and the different realms of nature. The relationship of the world soul to the visible world, according to them, is to be thought of as similar to that of the life principle (the soul) to individual organisms. Just as the soul, which belongs to a higher level of existence than the material components of the organism, guarantees the intelligible development of the organism and completely animates it, so also the world soul is supposed to constitute one massive organism out of the world. When examined more closely these views are found to vary; for, some look upon the world soul as also the world reason, identifying it with God (Schelling, Max Scheler in his late period) while others disregard the deeper metaphysical problems (E. Becher). *Stoicism assumes the existence of a world reason that is active in all things as a very fine, ethereal, fire-like matter. — The experienced fact of our own self-consciousness speaks against the existence of a world soul; such a world soul would reduce man to the level of a non-free cell caught up in a huge world-organism. The harmony, intelligibility and finality of the world can be explained by pointing out that the creator has implanted a life principle in each organism and has related all of them to each other in his wise plan for the world. See also *Finality.*

MR

455

Y

YOGA

Yoga (= restraining) in Indian philosophy (1) designates in general all systematic training of the body and the mind in order to arrive at mystical insight and to a redeeming, non-conceptual knowledge; the road to follow is that of inner recollection and meditation. In this sense yoga is not tied to any one system. The classical yoga (2) of Patanjali (5th century A.D.) for the most part borrows its philosophical principles from the dualistic Sānkhya philosophy. The goal of the *yogin* (= the practicer of yoga) is the suppression of the functions of the thinking substance in man in order to elevate them to another and higher substance. As a preparation for this "ascent" the following are especially helpful: the observance of a series of moral precepts, certain bodily postures and breath-control. The principal exercise, however, consists in restraining the senses from perceiving their objects, in recollection, in meditation and in total concentration.

WB

INDEX

460